MW00638775

THE PARADIGM

OF

THE KINGDOM OF GOD

GOD'S AMAZING PLAN

FOR

THE REDEMPTION OF HIS PEOPLE

DAN WESTERFIELD

ISBN 978-1-63885-963-5 (Paperback)
ISBN 978-1-63885-965-9 (Hardcover)
ISBN 978-1-63885-964-2 (Digital)

All biblical citations were taken from the New American
Standard Bible unless otherwise noted.

Covenant Books
11661 Hwy 707
Murrells Inlet, SC 29576
www.covenantbooks.com

CONTENTS

PREFACE

The seeds for this book were planted in a Sunday school class on Genesis taught by Ken Olles and Frank Seay in the late 1990s at Park Cities Presbyterian Church in Dallas, Texas. Although I could only attend occasionally, Ken and Frank introduced me to the themes, parallels, and paradigms in Genesis which are so foundational for understanding God's plan of redemption. I am making a general acknowledgment of my indebtedness to them because, after more than twenty years, I cannot cite particular discussions from those classes. Where I can attribute specific ideas or have access to a recording of a class, their contributions are acknowledged in footnotes. But this book includes sources and applications that go well beyond those classes to suggest a new way of viewing the whole of redemptive history. This understanding is based on the paradigm of the kingdom of God, and any related errors are my own.

I must also acknowledge the patient and thorough work of Marlea Evans, who read and reread the manuscript. She made many beneficial suggestions concerning composition and content, and her input was invaluable. In addition, my brother Gary offered encouragement and helpful comments.

In this work, I have summarized many accounts of Scripture and world history. Despite my efforts to be true to biblical and secular records, there is always the danger of misunderstanding a writer's intent. For this reason, I have included numerous references so the reader can access the associated writings. Unless otherwise noted, the biblical texts cited are from *The Hebrew-Greek Key Word Study Bible: New American Standard* (ed. Spiros Zodhiates [Chattanooga, TN: AMG Publishers, 1984]). Pages referenced in the *Key Study Bible* and other books are not preceded by *p.* or *pp.* These designations are used for cross references within this book itself. Also, a number of the internet references in this book have recently been removed from their sites, some apparently for political considerations.

It has been a blessing to study the unfolding of God's amazing plan of redemption. His mercy to us in Jesus Christ is beyond measure, and it is our only hope.

INTRODUCTION

I. Purpose

The purpose of this book is to show that God's plan of redemption, how He saves a people for Himself, is worked out through a historical paradigm[1]—the paradigm of the kingdom of God. The book is based on the following foundational concepts:

A. God's plan of redemption is the center of all history.
B. God reveals Himself and His plan through historical events, and then records and explains those events in the Bible.
C. Jesus Christ, the Son of God, is the central figure in all of redemptive history.
D. The plan of redemption progresses in a linear timeline through the paradigm of the kingdom of God.

Many theologians have noted the significance of the kingdom of God in Scripture. John Bright says although the words "the kingdom of God" do not occur in the Old Testament, the concept is "in one form or another, ubiquitous in both Old Testament and New."[2] He begins his book with Israel in the land of Canaan and then moves to New Testament discussions concerning the kingdom.[3]

George Eldon Ladd concludes that there are present and future aspects of the kingdom and focuses on the kingdom parables and the Sermon on the

---

[1] A paradigm is a pattern or model that is repeated or reoccurs.
[2] John Bright, *The Kingdom of God* (Nashville: Abingdon, 1978), 18.
[3] Ibid., 19.

Mount.[4] Herman Ridderbos agrees there are dual aspects of the kingdom and emphasizes Jesus's teaching in the Synoptic Gospels.[5]

These writers believe the kingdom is an important aspect of God's plan of salvation. But the kingdom is more than part of the plan; the kingdom is the plan, the historical framework through which God works out redemptive history. The goal of this book is to trace the kingdom from the past to the future, from the Garden of Eden to the new heaven and earth, to show that the entire plan of redemption progresses through the paradigm of the kingdom of God.

Someone might protest that this approach makes the kingdom the focal point of Scripture rather than Jesus Christ and His ministry. But this is not the case. Christ's sacrificial work as our Great High Priest is the supreme event in all of history, but it takes place within the context of the kingdom. The ultimate goal is for Christ's redeemed people to glorify Him in His everlasting dominion. This has always been God's plan, not just the saving of individual sinners from damnation (Dan. 7:13–14; Lk. 1:30–33; Rev. 1:4–6). After the last prophecy has been fulfilled, there remains for eternity the kingly reign of Christ with His people in the new heaven and earth, the consummation of the kingdom. Repetitions of the kingdom paradigm, beginning in the Garden of Eden, are the way God's plan of redemption advances to its glorious conclusion.

II. Background

For the last two centuries, there have been two primary conflicting views that attempt to explain and summarize God's plan of redemption. Covenantal theologians believe that God works out redemptive history through three theological covenants: (1) a covenant to redeem (made within the Triune Godhead in eternity past); (2) a covenant of works (Adam's probation in Eden); and (3) a covenant of grace (God's saving work after the fall). Dispensational theologians, however, see God completing his purposes through a series of dispensations, successive periods of history during which God deals with human beings in different ways. These theologians typically see seven dispensations: (1) innocence (pre-fall); (2) conscience (Adam); (3) human government (Noah); (4)

---

[4]   George Eldon Ladd, *The Gospel of the Kingdom; Scriptural Studies in the Kingdom of God* (Grand Rapids: Eerdmans, 1959).

[5]   Herman Ridderbos, *The Coming of the Kingdom*, trans. H. de Jongste (Philadelphia: Presbyterian & Reformed, 1962).

promise (Abraham); (5) law (Moses); (6) grace (Christ's First Coming); and (7) kingdom (Christ's Second Coming).

These opposing views parallel other disagreements between these two groups. Covenantalists trace their thinking back to St. Augustine (354–430) and emphasize doctrines refined during the Reformation in the sixteenth century and taught by men like Luther, Calvin, and Zwingli. They stress the sovereignty of God and the election of believers, and they believe that the Church is an extension of believing Israel and that the two share a common destiny.

Dispensationalism appears among the Brethren churches in Ireland and England in the nineteenth century and is promoted in the writings of John Nelson Darby (1800–1882)[6] and Cyrus Scofield's Reference Bible.[7] Dispensationalists often stress the necessity of an individual's free will choice in accepting Christ as Savior. They insist that national Israel must be seen as distinct from the Church, and they believe that Israel has a destiny that is apart from the Church. Dispensationalists also emphasize a literal hermeneutic and a complex eschatology that foresees a rapture of believers and a thousand-year reign of Christ on the earth prior to the final judgment.[8]

The differences between these two theological divisions are far-reaching, and their interactions are often contentious. But schisms exist not only between the two groups but within the groups themselves. Some Covenantalists question the concept of an inter-Trinitarian covenant before creation.[9] Others disagree over the covenant of works and end-time views. Dispensationalists differ

---

[6] John Nelson Darby, *Synopsis of the Books of the Bible, 5 vols.* (Sunbury, PA: Believers Bookshelf, 1992); also see, "John Nelson Darby—Father of Dispensationalism," *Christianity Today*, accessed January 27, 2020, https://www.christianitytoday.com/history/people/pastorsandpreachers/john-nelson-darby.html.

[7] First published by Oxford University Press, 1909, Protestant King James Version.

[8] For an in-depth description of the end-time views of Covenantalism and Dispensationalism, see Millard J. Erickson, *Christian Theology, 2nd ed.* (Grand Rapids: Baker Books, 1983), 1211–1231; or Wayne Grudem, *Systematic Theology* (Grand Rapids: Zondervan, 1994), 1109–1139.

[9] O. Palmer Robertson, *The Christ of the Covenants*, (Philipsburg, NJ: Presbyterian and Reformed, 1980), 54. Robertson says that to propose such a covenant "extends the bounds of Scriptural evidence beyond propriety." In addition to Robertson's objection, the use of the word *covenant* suggests the forming of an agreement, something unnecessary within the eternally harmonious and omniscient Trinity. It would be better to speak of an "eternal decree" to redeem.

over the number of dispensations as well as over aspects of their own involved eschatology.

A partial history of recent publications reveals the wide-ranging disagreements involving these issues. In 1991, John Gerstner wrote an effective and perhaps harsh critique of Dispensationalism.[10] Daniel P. Fuller soon published a volume challenging Covenantal views,[11] and Meredith Kline responded strongly.[12] In *Kingdom through Covenant*,[13] Gentry and Wellum seek to establish a middle ground. J. Dwight Pentecost has written a book that tries to make the concept of God's kingdom fit within the confines of his Dispensational framework.[14] Jon Zens has done a study comparing Dispensationalism and Covenantalism and has declared both of them to be unbiblical.[15]

These extensive differences suggest that neither view has compelling scriptural support and that it is time to consider an alternative to these two entrenched understandings. Redemptive history is a living story, and theological concepts should arise from the narrative itself, not be imposed on it.

Caution is necessary when proposing something new in such a longstanding dispute. But the lack of consensus and the significance of the issues justify the consideration of a new approach. It is important to understand the overall plan of redemption so that we can better apprehend our own roles and responsibilities in the era in which we live. We need to know our *Sitz im Leben* (location in life) to be faithful servants. Without a common view of the progress of redemption, congregations can become isolated religious communities without a sense of the larger purpose of the Church.

In addition, our perception of God's overall plan of salvation affects our interpretation of every theological issue. A mutual understanding of redemptive history could resolve many of the disagreements separating Covenantalists and Dispensationalists and help promote Church unity. And finally, a biblically

---

[10] John H. Gerstner, *Wrongly Dividing the Word of Truth: A Critique of Dispensationalism* (Brentwood, TN: Wolgemuth & Hyatt, 1991).

[11] Daniel P. Fuller, *The Unity of the Bible: Unfolding God's Plan for Humanity* (Grand Rapids: Zondervan, 1992).

[12] Meredith G. Kline, "Covenant Theology Under Attack," in *New Horizons*, Feb. 1994, Orthodox Presbyterian Church.

[13] Peter J. Gentry and Stephen J. Wellum, *Kingdom Through Covenant* (Wheaton, IL: Crossway, 2012).

[14] J. Dwight Pentecost, *Thy Kingdom Come* (Wheaton, IL: Victor Books, 1990).

[15] Jon Zens, "An Examination of the Presuppositions of Covenant and Dispensational Theology," *Studies in Theology and Ethics* (Malin, OR: Brem, 1981) 17, 28.

consistent view of God's program of redemption can inform and strengthen our faith.

This book will comment on problems with both established systems,[16] but its central purpose is to demonstrate that God is working out His plan of redemption through an ongoing historical paradigm. All the other paradigms, types, parallels, and repetitive themes in Scripture fall within and help construct this fundamental paradigm, the paradigm of the kingdom of God.

The paradigm of the kingdom goes through three complete stages in each era of biblical history. God first gives human beings a mandate to establish His kingdom, then they sin and rebel, and eventually, He sends judgment. God is holy, and His kingdom people must be holy; they must be righteous or He will judge them (Lev. 11:44, 19:2, 20:7; 1 Pet. 1:16).

This paradigm is repeated four times beginning with Adam and Eve in the Garden. It reoccurs with Noah's family and then again with the nation of Israel with the same end-result—God's righteous judgment instead of God's righteous kingdom. In each case, sin and rebellion prevent the kingdom from being established. But in the fourth and final repetition of the paradigm, God, in the fullness of time, sends His own Son to earth (Gal. 4:4–5). Jesus proclaims "the gospel of God," saying, "The time is fulfilled, and the kingdom of God is at hand; repent and believe in the gospel" (Mark 1:14–15).

Jesus establishes the kingdom, but it is not a political empire; it is the community made up of His faithful followers. But they are still sinners, and their sins must be punished. This time, God's judgment is poured out on His Son instead of His kingdom people. Jesus bears the punishment for their sins on the cross, and His own righteousness is imputed to them. They are justified, righteous in God's eyes. Through the work of the Son, God secures a people suitable for his kingdom, a kingdom which will not end because Jesus has dealt with the problem of sin. As Paul says in Colossians 1:13–14, "He has delivered us from the domain of darkness, and transferred us to the kingdom of His beloved Son, in whom we have redemption, the forgiveness of sins."

---

[16] The critical problems with both systems are summarized on pp. 407–409.

III. Overview—The Kingdom Paradigm as Revealed Through Adam, Noah, Israel, and Jesus[17]

1. Adam—The paradigm of the kingdom begins in Genesis immediately after God creates Adam and Eve. In Genesis 1:28, God tells Adam and Eve to "be fruitful and multiply, and fill the earth, and subdue it; and rule over the fish of the sea and over the birds of the sky, and over every living thing that moves on the earth." This is sometimes called the cultural or creation mandate,[18] but it is actually a kingdom mandate. Adam and Eve are, in effect, told to establish God's earthly kingdom, and they are placed in an ideal setting for accomplishing that purpose.

    Created upright and sinless, they are set within a beautiful paradise that provides all their needs. They are made in God's image and perfectly suited for each other. God communicates directly with them, and He tells Adam and Eve about their roles in the new creation. First, they are to be fruitful and multiply, fill the earth with upright children with whom God can fellowship. He is holy, and His kingdom people must be righteous and holy. Secondly, Adam and Eve are to rule; they are given dominion over the Garden and over every living creature.

    Adam and Eve are to establish the kingdom by filling the earth with sinless children and by ruling over it along with their offspring as God's faithful and righteous image-bearers. In this paradise, Adam and Eve have only one restriction, one test of their faithfulness: they are not to eat of the tree of the knowledge of good and evil that is in the midst of the Garden. If they eat of this tree, they will die (Gen. 2:16–17).

    It is important to note that this first negative command comes after God's positive command to begin His kingdom. This is not a random test of the first couple's obedience. God is forbidding Adam and Eve from creating a kingdom based on their own knowledge, their own autonomous concepts of good and evil. God's kingdom can only be established according to His wisdom and authority. But before Adam and Eve can begin fulfilling the kingdom mandate, Satan confronts them in the Garden.

---

[17] There is a single kingdom paradigm which is repeated, but for simplicity, the repetitions will at times be referred to as the paradigms.

[18] John Murray, *Principles of Conduct* (Grand Rapids: Eerdmans, 1957), 45.

Satan, who has already rebelled against God, tempts them with the suggestion that they can be like God by eating of the forbidden tree (Gen. 3:5). Adam and Eve are in a perfect paradise, but Satan draws them in with the possibility of being something greater than a creature—they can be like God and decide for themselves what is good and what is evil. Satan is telling them that they can initiate their own kingdom and rule according to their own concepts of morality.

Our first parents listen to this temptation and eat the fruit of the forbidden tree. They rebel against God and commit a disastrous sin which affects them and all their posterity. They are no longer righteous and no longer able or willing to establish God's righteous kingdom. They have died spiritually, and they will die physically as will all their descendants.[19] It is Satan who begins to build *his* kingdom and rule the earth (Gen. 3:1–19).[20] But there is a future hope for human beings. Even as God pronounces His judgments on Adam and Eve, He declares that there will be a future Seed of the woman who will destroy Satan and his dominion (Gen. 3:15).

There may be hope for the future, but Adam and Eve face immediate consequences. They are cast out of the Garden, and Adam must now earn food by the sweat of his brow from an earth that resists him. Childbearing will now be painful, and instead of raising up godly children, Adam and Eve beget sons who will kill each other, citizens fit for Satan's kingdom. Adam is the representative head of the human race, and his sin and rebellion are passed on to his descendants.[21]

Eventually, as the population increases, wickedness rises to such a level that God sends His judgment in the form of a flood that covers the earth. All human life is extinguished except for Noah and his family. The kingdom paradigm has progressed through its first two stages to the final stage of judgment, its first disastrous ending (Gen. 4:1–7:24).

---

[19] With the exception of Enoch and Elijah who will eventually be taken up to heaven without experiencing death (Heb. 11:5; 2 Kgs. 2:11).

[20] John 12:31, 14:30, 16:11; 2 Cor. 4:4; Eph. 2:2; 1 John 5:19.

[21] Adam's sin will be passed on in two ways. Human beings will now be innately sinful (Ps. 51:5); you do not have to teach a baby to grab, hit, or say "mine." And because Adam was the representative head for the entire human race, each person is seen as guilty of his sin, sometimes called imputed sin (Rom. 5:12–21).

2. Noah—Noah is a righteous man who finds "favor" with God (Gen. 6:8–9);[22] he and his family are chosen by God to be spared from the flood to continue the human race. To save Noah from the coming judgment, God instructs him to build the Ark. Just before the flood begins, Noah and his family enter the Ark along with two of each kind of animal (Gen. 6:8, 14). When God sends the worldwide deluge, only the sea creatures and those on the Ark survive.

    After the flood ends and the waters subside, God puts Noah and his family in a garden setting, a vineyard. They are not sinless like Adam and Eve, but they are redeemed—redeemed in the sense that they are rescued from a sinful world and spared from its judgment. God gives them a cleansed earth and a new start with the same mandate as Adam and Eve. They, too, are told to be fruitful and multiply and fill the earth (Gen. 9:1). They, too, are given dominion and told to rule over all the animals, but their rule is different from the reign of Adam and Eve in the Garden. Now the animals are given to them for food, and they rule them through fear (Gen. 9:2). But the responsibility for establishing God's righteous kingdom remains.

    The paradigm begins anew, but transgressions arise again. Noah eventually becomes drunk from the wine of the vineyard. His son, Ham, sins against him, and Noah pronounces a curse on Ham's son, Canaan. Ham and his two brothers have other children, but they are not descendants who will build a righteous kingdom. Instead of filling the earth, they conspire to stay together and build a city with a proud tower stretching up to heaven, saying, "Let us make for ourselves a name; lest we be scattered abroad over the face of the whole earth" (Gen. 11:4). Noah's descendants want to create their own self-sufficient kingdom based on their own desires. Like Adam and Eve, they are not satisfied to be human beings who follow God's directions. And once again, God's judgment falls. He does not destroy the earth with a flood again, but He confuses the language of the people so that they cannot understand each other. Their arrogant endeavor is halted, and they are scattered.

---

[22] Noah is called a "righteous" man, but he is not sinless. He may be more upright than those around him, but no one is without sin after the fall. He is spared from the flood because he finds "favor," mercy from God.

They do begin to fill the earth, but they cannot and will not establish a righteous kingdom. For the second time, human beings fail to inaugurate God's kingdom because they choose to disregard His word and again fall into sin and rebellion (Gen. 9:18–11:9).

3. Israel—Many generations pass, and in time, God calls Abram out of Ur of the Chaldeans. God tells Abram to "go forth…to the land which I will show you" (Gen. 12:1). With this mandate, the paradigm begins again, but this time, God commits Himself to multiplying Abram and giving him the kingdom. He tells Abram, "And I will make you a great nation, And I will bless you, And make your name great" (Gen.12:2). A righteous kingdom is now a certainty because God Himself is going to accomplish it. The kingdom is going to be a blessing bestowed through His grace.[23] And it is not only Abram that is going to be blessed. God says, "In you, all the families of the earth shall be blessed" (Gen. 12:3). Eventually, the kingdom will extend beyond Abram and his physical descendants to include people from all the nations.

Abram and his wife, Sarai, travel to Canaan with his nephew, Lot. God changes Abram's name to Abraham and Sarai's to Sarah. In due course, He gives them a son, Isaac, even though Sarah is past childbearing age. Isaac becomes the father of Jacob, and Jacob fathers twelve sons. God changes Jacob's name to Israel, and his sons become the twelve tribes of Israel.

The twelve tribes increase, but they are forced to leave Canaan because of a famine; they travel to Egypt where they are fruitful and multiply. Centuries pass, and the children of Israel become enslaved by the Egyptians. God sees the suffering of His people and uses Moses and great miracles to bring them out of captivity. Moses organizes the tribes and establishes a theocratic government; Abraham's descendants have become the nation of Israel. The kingdom paradigm has progressed from a sinless couple to a redeemed family and now to a chosen nation.

God has redeemed Israel from slavery. At Mt. Sinai, He tells them how they must live in His kingdom, and He writes it on stone. He dwells with them, first in the Tabernacle and later in the Temple. He leads them to Canaan, the promised land, a garden setting on a large scale. Israel is

---

[23] Suggested in a discussion with Ken Olles.

told to destroy the wicked inhabitants of Canaan and rule over the land (Deut. 20:16–18; Num. 33:51–53; Josh. 1:2–6).

In due course, King David and his son, Solomon, make Israel a mighty nation. But even in a land of milk and honey, with God's law imparted to them and God's presence in their midst, Israel falls into idolatry and great sin, and judgment follows. In 587 BC, Nebuchadnezzar, king of Babylon, begins a final siege against Jerusalem. He captures the city, burns the houses and the Temple, kills the nobles, and exiles the people to Babylon. Once again, sin prevails, and judgment falls after Israel, a chosen nation, fails to establish a righteous kingdom for God (Gen. 12:1–Malachi 4:6).

But God has made promises to Abraham, and despite Israel's failure, those promises will be fulfilled. Abraham and his descendants, his spiritual offspring, are going to be blessed; they will have an everlasting kingdom.

4. Jesus—A sinless couple, a redeemed family, and a chosen nation have all failed to establish God's kingdom. Although there has been an ongoing line of God's elect people, they all fall into sin and rebellion and cannot establish His righteous rule on the earth. But then, in "the fullness of the time" (Gal. 4:4),[24] God sends His own Son to earth in the Person of Jesus. He is born the Son of Mary and is a descendant of Abraham. When Jesus matures, He begins preaching, saying, "The time is fulfilled and the kingdom of God is at hand, repent and believe in the gospel" (Mark 1:15). The paradigm is beginning once more, but now Jesus is going to establish a kingdom that will endure. The promises to Abraham will be fulfilled because Jesus is going to do something about sin.

Jesus's earthly ministry begins with His baptism by John the Baptist when the Holy Spirit descends on Him and God the Father pronounces His divine affirmation. By accepting John's baptism, Jesus, the divine Son, identifies himself with His people; He is truly human but without sin (Matt. 3:13–16; Heb. 4:15).

Immediately after his baptism, Jesus is driven by the Spirit into the wilderness for a confrontation with Satan (Mark 1:12). This is an urgent

---

[24] This "fullness of the time" includes the universal use of the Greek language after Alexander the Great's conquests, a language especially suitable for the New Testament. This was also the period of *Pax Romana*, a time of relative peace under Roman rule lasting from approximately 27 BC to AD 180, which, along with Roman roads and ships, allowed a great increase in communication and travel; the gospel can go out to the known world.

conflict; it must take place. Jesus, as a sinless man, has a right to rule on the earth, but Satan does not intend to give up his domain. This is a clash of kingdoms. Jesus spends forty days in the wilderness being tempted by Satan, but He does not fall like Adam. After Satan leaves him, Jesus returns to Galilee, full of the Spirit, and begins teaching in the synagogues, "proclaiming the gospel of the kingdom" (Matt. 4:23). He preaches to the people, saying, "Repent for the kingdom of heaven is at hand" (Matt. 4:17).[25]

Through His preaching, Jesus begins to be fruitful and multiply. He does not beget physical children, but He raises up spiritual children. He calls disciples, and people from all types of backgrounds respond and trust in Him. Jesus is establishing the kingdom, and He begins to rule; He teaches, casts out demons, heals the sick, raises the dead, calms storms, and feeds the hungry. But God's judgment must still fall in this final repetition of the paradigm. Jesus's spiritual children may believe in Him,[26] but they are still sinful. God's righteousness is absolute; their sins must be punished.

Jesus is without sin, but He is identified with His people; He has been baptized with them and He calls them His family (John 3:13–17; Matt. 12:46–50). Jesus is one of them; He is their representative Head. The sins of His people are seen as His own; they are imputed to Him.

God's judgment falls on Jesus; His wrath is poured out on His Son instead of the sinners who deserve it. As a substitute for His people, Jesus pays the price for their transgressions by His suffering on the cross. He dies and is buried but is raised on the third day (Hallelujah!) showing that He is truly the Son of God and that His sacrifice for sinful human beings has been accepted by the Father.

In the previous paradigms, God's judgment ended those attempts to establish a kingdom. But Jesus's kingdom is going to endure. He has not only paid for the sins of His people; in a great exchange, His righteousness is imputed to them (2 Cor. 5:21). As Paul emphasizes, God is "just and the

---

25 The phrase "kingdom of heaven" is used by Matthew where ten other New Testament books use the phrase "kingdom of God." Jesus uses the phrases interchangeably (Matt. 19:23–24), and they correspond in parallel passages (Matt. 13:31 and Mark 4:30; Matt. 13:33 and Luke 13:20; etc.); the terms refer to the same kingdom.
26 Jesus's spiritual children include the Old Testament saints who looked forward to His coming and those who will believe in Him in the future.

justifier of the one who has faith in Jesus" (Rom. 3:26).[27] "There is therefore now no condemnation for those who are in Christ Jesus" (Rom: 8:1).

Those who have faith in Jesus stand justified before God.[28] Although they are still sinners, He sees them as righteous. God's wrath for their sins has been poured out. There is no further impending judgment; Jesus's infinite sacrifice has paid for even future sins.[29] Through the sacrificial work of the Son, God has a people suitable for His kingdom, a kingdom that will have no end.

The previous paradigms have demonstrated that the only way for God to have a righteous people is for that righteousness to be reckoned to them. It is a foreign righteousness, purchased at a great price, which allows sinners to be God's people and makes it possible for His kingdom to be established. Jesus's resurrection and the Church's initiation, the pouring out of the Holy Spirit at Pentecost (Acts 2:1–4; 2 Cor. 1:21–22), are the guarantees that this kingdom will endure.

*****

The kingdom begins to advance throughout the nations; the promises to Abraham are being fulfilled. Through the work of his seed, Jesus, Abraham is becoming a blessing to all the world. God's program of redemption is no longer being worked out through Israel, a single theocratic nation, but through a subculture in all the nations, the Church.[30] The Church, the congregation of true believers, is not the kingdom, but the two overlap, and membership in both is established by simply repenting and trusting in the one who has made the kingdom possible.

---

[27] God is just; He punishes every sin. Jesus bears the punishment for those who believe in Him. Those who do not believe will bear their own punishment in hell.

[28] This includes Old Testament Saints who understood their need for a Savior and looked forward to the Messiah.

[29] This raises the question, then, why not continue to sin? (Rom. 6:1) But true obedience, the desire not to sin, arises from love and gratitude for what God has done. It arises from "newness of life" (Rom. 6:4), the Law written on hearts, not on tablets of stone (Jer. 31:31–34). Complete sanctification, having no sin, come when believers receive their resurrection bodies at Jesus's Second Advent.

[30] Jesus builds His Church. It is made up of everyone who has true faith in Him (Matt. 16:16–18).

The kingdom is not a political entity, but it exists everywhere that God's righteous people acknowledge His authority and live according to His principles; it is the present reign of Jesus Christ on the earth. The kingdom is advancing and it cannot be stopped.[31] Satan, the strong man, has been bound, and his house is being plundered (Matt. 12:28–29).

The influence of Christians, and therefore the reach of the kingdom, extends into the secular world beyond the boundaries of the believing Church.[32] Christ's rule begins in the hearts of believers and the kingdom becomes most apparent through their loving actions and is part of the ongoing work of the Holy Spirit who convicts "the world concerning sin, and righteousness, and judgment" (John 16:8; also see John 13:35; 1 John 3:23; 1 John 4:7–16; Rom. 13:8–10). The consummation of the kingdom in the new heaven and earth awaits Jesus's Second Coming, but the kingdom is present now wherever believers order their lives according to God's will. It is present now as God's people look back on the finished work of Jesus and look forward to His return.[33]

IV. Further Considerations

This brief overview of the kingdom paradigm cannot answer all the questions about the unfolding of God's plan of redemption. There are still many issues to consider. How do Old Testament saints relate to the kingdom that Jesus establishes? How do the covenants found in Scripture fit within the individual paradigms? What is specific to one paradigm and what extends to other paradigms? What is the relationship of the Church to the kingdom? What does this mean for end-time views?

---

[31] The eventual extent of the earthly kingdom is unknown to us, but all of God's people will be called in before Christ's Second Coming.

[32] There is a believing or true Church within the larger outwardly visible Church.

[33] This understanding of the kingdom disagrees with the Dispensational view which says that the kingdom of God is not established until Christ's Second Advent when He reigns over the nation of Israel for a thousand years. There are two primary Covenantal views associated with the kingdom. The first says that we are in the time of the Church and there is no future millennial kingdom; instead, Christ reigns in heaven with the saints who have died until His Second Advent. The second Covenantal view claims that the kingdom began with Christ's First Advent and that it is going to overcome the world and usher in His Second Coming. This book agrees with the starting point of this last view but does not agree that we know the extent of the kingdom before Christ returns.

We could explore such questions individually, but it seems more effective to further expand the study of the paradigms and let history itself reveal the theology of the kingdom that Scripture imparts to us. All of redemptive history occurs within the framework of the kingdom paradigm, but the limits of time mean our study must focus on the central narrative of God's salvation plan beginning with the most essential revelations recorded in the books of the Old and New Testaments.

God establishes His program of salvation through historical events and records and explains those events in the Bible. We are to know and understand these revelations, but there are things we cannot know. We cannot know the secret things of God. We do not know why He created the universe and decided to establish a people for Himself when He was eternally complete and perfectly fulfilled within the relationships of the Trinity.[34] We can suggest that it involved to some extent His overflowing love, and an appropriate desire to reveal His glory. But we are not told, and our finite minds cannot grasp all the motivations behind God's grand design.

Similarly, we cannot know why God chose to work out His plan of redemption through thousands of years and many agonizing human experiences. But we know that Scripture records these things for our benefit (Rom. 15:4; 1 Cor. 10:11), and we can take note of certain realities. Although Adam and Eve were created sinless and placed in a perfect paradise, they were necessarily finite[35] and in continual jeopardy of falling into sin.

After the final judgment at the end of the age, when believers dwell with God in the new heaven and earth, His people will have a position superior to that of Adam and Eve at the beginning of creation. They will be in union with Christ with no potential for sin because their old sinful natures will have died and been buried with Him. In their resurrected bodies, they will have perfect righteousness and perfect security with no possibility of falling. As God's righteous people, they will rule with Christ in the fulfillment of the final and everlasting kingdom. The plan of redemption is the bridge between the jeopardy of Adam and Eve in the Garden and the total security of God's righteous people in the consummated kingdom.

---

[34] The God of Christianity exists as three distinct persons of the same essence—Father, Son, and Holy Spirit—present in the one Godhead. This is the one true God, the Triune God.

[35] God cannot create another eternal being. When God begins to create and says, "In the beginning" (Gen. 1:1), time has begun and every created thing is finite and subject to change.

SECTION 1

ADAM AND EVE AND THE KINGDOM

CHAPTER 1

THE BEGINNING OF THE PARADIGM

(1) Adam and Eve

God's plan to have a kingdom of righteous people for Himself begins with the Garden of Eden. God spends five days preparing a beautiful setting in Eden and then creates the first human beings: Adam, initially, and then his perfect helpmate, Eve.

Adam is formed on the sixth and final day of creation. The separation of the dry ground from the waters is complete, the heavenly lights are shining, and the garden is abundant with plants and animals. And now it is clear from God's special contemplation that He has come to the apex of his creative work. It is only with Adam that God announces His intentions; "Let Us make man in Our image, according to Our likeness" (Gen. 1:26).[36]

God makes Adam from the dust of the ground, something God has already created. Adam is finite. He is of the earth, but he is brought to life in a very special way. Not only does God make Adam in His own image, He breathes the breath of life directly into Adam's nostrils (Gen. 2:7). Adam begins life by breathing the very breath of God.

I once saw my father blow his breath into the nostrils of a newborn lamb that was not breathing. After the lamb started breathing and walking, and even after he nursed, he would follow my father, thinking he belonged with him. From Adam's first breath, he has a personal and internal connection with his heavenly Father (Acts 17:28, John 1:9; Rom. 1:19). He is made in the image of

---

[36] The plural pronouns *Us* and *Our* in this verse are an early indication of a plurality of Persons within the one Godhead. The Divine Trinity of Father, Son, and Holy Spirit is most fully revealed in the New Testament.

God and has intellectual, moral, and emotional attributes. Adam is made to be in fellowship with his Creator.

Eve is created out of Adam's own body, out of his rib, after God determines that Adam needs an appropriate companion. She is Adam's ideal counterpart and Adam's appreciation for her and their intimate relationship is evident when he says, "This is now bone of my bones and flesh of my flesh" (Gen. 2:23). They are perfectly suited for each other and wonderfully shaped and formed for their relationship and their roles in the new creation. They are to cleave to each other and become one flesh. In their sinless state, they can be completely transparent with God and each other. "And the man and his wife were both naked and were not ashamed" (Gen. 2:25).

God then blesses Adam and Eve and tells them their purpose. He gives them a mandate to establish His kingdom on the earth, "Be fruitful and multiply, and fill the earth, and subdue it; and rule over the fish of the sea and over the birds of the sky and over every living thing that moves on the earth" (Gen. 1:28). Adam and Eve are given the perfect setting and the wonderful purpose of populating the earth and ruling over it with their righteous children. They are to fulfill the kingdom mandate.

After forming Adam and Eve on the sixth day, God's creative work is complete, and He rests on the seventh day. There is shalom in the Garden. Adam and Eve are at peace with God and each other. There is complete harmony in the creation, including Adam and Eve's relationship with the Garden and its creatures. "And God saw all that He had made, and behold, it was very good" (Gen. 1:31).

(2) The Garden

Adam has a special connection with the Garden. He is made from the very dirt which sustains the plants that give him and Eve their food. God freely gives them permission to eat of the abundance of the trees, with the exception of the tree of the knowledge of good and evil (Gen. 2:16–17). We can only imagine the delicious perfection of the pre-fall fruit that the Garden provides for Adam and Eve and all the animals.

Genesis 2:15 says that God placed Adam in the Garden to "cultivate" and "keep" it. Some theologians believe that cultivating the Garden is the beginning of work.[37] To "cultivate" the ground today does involve what we would call "work," sometimes very hard work. But this direction is given to Adam before the fall. The earth is not resisting him. He does not earn his food by cultivating the Garden. Its fruit is given to him freely (Gen. 1:29–30). Adam's cultivation is creative activity emulating the Great Creator on a human level. It is an aspect of Adam's rule and is appropriate for one made in the image of God.

Adam is to be "active and productive"[38] in managing the earth and its plants, "subduing" his realm in the most positive sense of the word (Gen. 1:28). Cultivating the garden is a consummate joy to Adam, not work in the same sense that we see after the fall. Work, sweat-of-the-brow toil to earn bread is a result of sin and will be discussed further when we look at the consequences of the fall for Adam and Eve.[39]

Adam is also told to "keep" the Garden. This speaks to Adam's headship and his responsibility to protect and oversee the creation, including the well-being of his wife, Eve. Adam and Eve are equal before God in their humanity (Gen. 1:27; Gal. 3:28), in their essence, but they have different roles in the created order (Gen. 2:18; 1 Cor.11:3, 11:8–11; 1 Tim. 2:11–14). Adam was created first and was given the responsibility of headship and overseeing the Garden, but Eve's role as helpmate does not negate nor diminish her equal value before God (Gal. 3:28).[40] In Eden, both Adam and Eve are satisfied and complete within the roles for which they were created.

Satan has not yet appeared in the Garden,[41] but the command to "keep" has the sense of "guard" and has an element of forewarning about things to come. Adam and Eve and all of the created things are finite and subject to change. Part of Adam's headship, his rule, is to see that no harmful transformation comes about in the paradise of Eden.

---

[37] John Murray, *Principles*, 35–39; O. Palmer Robertson, *The Christ*, 79–81.
[38] This is R.C. Sproul's description of Adam's activity in cultivating the Garden.
[39] pp. 14–17.
[40] The secular world and many within the Church believe that equality in essence requires equality in roles and demand that women should be equal in leadership with men. But this concept is refuted within the Trinity where the Father, the Son, and the Holy Spirit are equal in essence and Godhood but have different roles with the Son submitting to the Father and the Spirit submitting to the Father and the Son (John 6:38, 14:26, 16:7).
[41] On the sixth day, "God saw everything that he had made, and indeed it was very good" (Gen. 1:31). Satan's rebellion must occur sometime after this pronouncement and before the temptation of Adam and Eve in the Garden.

(3) The animals

Adam is told not only to cultivate and keep the garden, but he and Eve are also to rule over every living thing (Gen. 1:28). We see that Adam, before Eve's creation, has dominion over the animals when God brings them to him so that he can name them.[42] It is a demonstration of Adam's authority as a sinless man. God wants to see what Adam will call the animals. This is an undertaking that involves Adam's understanding of the creatures and his relationship to them. God is apparently pleased with Adam's choices because "whatever the man called a living creature, that was its name" (Gen. 2:19).[43]

Adam has dominion over the creatures, but it is a reign without fear. In the paradise of Eden, both humans and the animals eat only from the plants, and no creature is a threat to another (Gen. 1:29–30). It is easy to imagine Adam calling to a bird flying overhead to come and sit on his hand so he could marvel at the beauty and wonder of God's creative work.

Later in the New Testament, we see that Jesus has a pre-fall relationship with the wild animals when He is tempted by Satan. Mark sums up the forty days of temptation in the wilderness by simply saying, "and He was with the wild beasts and the angels were ministering to Him" (Mark 1:13). Lions, leopards, wolves, and bears were numerous in the Judean wilderness. But these animals did not fear Jesus, and they did not harm Him, even though He was weak from hunger. It is Mark's way of telling us that Jesus did not fall like Adam. He is still a righteous man who has dominion over the animals. The wild beasts are present when the angels minister to Him. In Mark's brief summation, we see both aspects of Jesus's character after the temptation. He is a sinless man who has a right to rule, and He is a divine being whom the angels reverence.[44]

Isaiah describes the animals under the future reign of the Messiah in the consummation of the kingdom, "And the wolf will dwell with the lamb, And the leopard will lie down with the kid, and the calf and the young lion and the fatling together; and a little boy will lead them" (Isa. 11:6).

---

[42] The naming of a person, a city, or an animal indicates one's authority over that entity.

[43] Those who object to a literal six-day creation say that Adam could not have named all the animals in one day. We do not know if Adam named each subspecies of insect or if he gave a more general classification of the creatures. But an unfallen intelligent man could name many creatures in a short time, especially if they were all "brought" to him (Gen. 2:19).

[44] Jesus is different from and superior to the angels (Heb. 1:1–14).

The animals were a delight in the garden, and they will be a never-ending delight in the new earth.

(4) Summary

The first two chapters of Genesis tell us how God created the earth and give us a picture of the beauty and tranquility of life in the Garden. Adam and Eve are ideally placed to fulfill the kingdom mandate to populate the earth and rule over it. God has given them a paradise, but it becomes a paradise at risk when Satan rebels. After his rebellion, Satan has his own intentions for the world.

CHAPTER 2

THE TEMPTATION OF ADAM AND EVE

After the sixth day of creation, the world is at Sabbath rest. There is complete peace and harmony, and there is no sin in the world. We do not know how long this idyllic state lasts, but it ends before Adam and Eve begin to have children. It ends with the rebellion of Satan and the angels who follow him. Why Satan chose to rebel against God is not completely revealed, but as an angel, he had great beauty and power. Paul indicates that he became puffed up and was condemned because of his pride (1 Tim. 3:6).

The descriptions of the King of Babylon and the King of Tyre, who were destroyed because of their extreme arrogance, seem to point beyond the men themselves to the supernatural conceit and evil of Satan (Isa. 14:12–14; Ezek. 28:12–18). "I will make myself like the Most High," says the Babylonian king (Isa. 14:14). Long before these kings live, Satan uses this same illicit desire, the aspiration to be like God, to tempt Adam and Eve. Satan wants to take the place of God and rule the earth. After he and the angels who follow him are cast out of heaven, Satan intends to establish his own kingdom, and he approaches Eve in the garden.

Satan appears before Eve in the form of the serpent. Scripture tells us that the serpent was the most cunning of all the animals (Gen. 3:1), and Satan's plan is well thought out. He does not directly approach Adam, who has been given the role of headship and the ultimate responsibility for keeping the Garden. Instead, Satan approaches Eve, but it is clear from Genesis 3:6 that Adam was "with her." Adam is aware of Satan's conversation with Eve.[45]

Eve does not seem surprised that the serpent is speaking to her. Perhaps it is her innocence or perhaps interactions with animals were different before the

---

[45] For further discussion on the presence of Adam, see Larry Crabb, *The Silence of Adam* (Grand Rapids: Zondervan, 1995), 87–99.

fall. Regardless, Satan is aware that God has prohibited Adam and Eve from eating of the tree of the knowledge of good and evil. His strategy is to first raise doubt about God's word. He begins by asking Eve a question, "Indeed, has God said, 'You shall not eat from any tree of the garden?'" (Gen. 3:1).

Eve responds and says they can eat the fruit of every tree, except the tree "which is in the middle of the garden." But then she adds that they also cannot "touch it, lest you die" (Gen. 3:3). God had told Adam that if he ate of the forbidden tree, he would "surely die" (Gen. 2:17), but touching the tree was not mentioned in God's command (Gen. 3:3). Satan has questioned what God has said, and now Eve is adding to it. The authority of God's word is rapidly being eroded.

Satan next directly contradicts God and tells Eve, "You surely shall not die! For God knows that in the day you eat from it your eyes will be opened, and you will be like God, knowing good and evil" (Gen. 3:4). Satan has just said that God has lied and is withholding something good from Adam and Eve: the ability to be like God.

Eve listens to the serpent and so does Adam, and Adam does nothing to protect Eve and "keep" the Garden. He abdicates his headship. Eve assumes Adam's abandoned role, eats the fruit, and gives it to Adam, there "with her" (Gen. 3:6). Adam also eats, and the world changes.

Adam and Eve's eyes are opened,[46] but they are not like God. Their eyes are opened to the fact that they have sinned against the good God who had given them every good thing. They not only have a knowledge of good and evil, they have participated in evil. And they are consumed with guilt. No longer can they be open and transparent; "they knew that they were naked; and they sewed fig leaves together and made themselves loin coverings" (Gen. 3:7). Adam and Eve make a flimsy attempt to cover themselves and their guilt—a feeble attempt at self-righteousness. For the first time, they are ashamed, and they hide from God.

When God walks in the Garden in the cool of the day, they cower behind the trees from which they had freely eaten. When God calls out, "Where are you?" to Adam (Gen. 3:9), Adam expresses a new emotion: fear. He is now afraid of God who had provided a paradise for him; Adam knows that his dis-

---

[46] Their eyes are not opened until Adam eats (pointed out in a class on Genesis by S. Lewis Johnson). Adam is the representative head of the human race, and although he has already sinned in his heart, God waits until Adam transgresses His specific command before He enforces the consequences, which will now apply to all his descendants.

obedience has made it impossible for him to face a holy and just God. He and his sin stand exposed, and he replies, "I was afraid because I was naked; so I hid myself" (Gen. 3:10). Adam understands that he now faces the judgment of God and the consequences of his actions. Guilt, fear, and ultimately death are now the realities of his life.

God asks Adam if he has eaten from the forbidden tree, and Adam tries to shift the blame to Eve and ultimately to God himself; "The woman whom Thou gavest to be with me, she gave me from the tree and I ate."

Eve then passes the blame on to the serpent, "The serpent deceived me, and I ate" (Gen. 3:12–13).

Eve has generally been seen as the person who committed the first sin since she ate before Adam. First Timothy 2:14 tells us that "it was not Adam who was deceived, but the woman being quite deceived, fell into transgression." Some see this text as excusing Adam, but it does not; instead, it places a greater blame on him. This text does not say that Adam did not sin. It says he was not deceived. He understood the consequences of the serpent's temptation in a way that Eve did not.

Eve reacted to the conversation with the serpent out of her nature, according to the way God had created her. The tree was a delight to the eyes and good for food and could make one wise (Gen. 3:6). Eve responded intuitively to what seemed good about the tree and its fruit. She was not the one who had been told to keep the Garden, and she was not on guard against the serpent.

But Adam was not deceived. He had been created first and was given the responsibility of headship and protecting the Garden. While Eve focused on the fruit and its possibilities, Adam observed and understood the dilemma he was facing. He had to consider whether to obey God or try to become like God as Satan had suggested. And Adam had someone who could be a test case—his perfect companion. He decided to let Eve eat, and when she did not immediately die, Adam ate also. Adam sinned in his heart well before Eve ate the forbidden fruit.

Romans 5:12 tells us that "through one man, sin entered the world." This passage goes on to deal with imputation and headship, but it first makes clear that Adam brought sin into the world. It takes a moment for the sheer evil of Adam's sin to sink in. God had given Adam a paradise with every good thing, including his ideal helpmate. And yet he chose to listen to the serpent rather than God, wanting to become his own god and willing to risk Eve to do it.

The extent of Adam's sin is compounded when he tries to shift the blame not only to Eve but to God himself. "The woman whom Thou gavest" says Adam. Adam is saying it is God's fault that he was tempted and rebelled. He is trying to make God the author of sin. It is amazing that the God of creation does not vaporize Adam or send him immediately to hell.

But the God of creation is also the God of mercy and salvation, and He has a plan to save rebellious human beings like Adam. He has a plan for their redemption and still intends to have them populate a renewed paradise. The depth of God's mercy to Adam and his descendants who will now sin just like Adam is beyond finite comprehension.

We men cannot disparage Adam because we continue to do the same thing. Whether it is money, fame, political power, or sexual conquests, we also will sin and betray those around us for something that makes us feel like a god. And women instinctively know it. They are still "bone of our bones and flesh of our flesh" (Gen. 2:23). It is why wives need daily assurance that their husbands love them and why security is so important to women. They know that men, like Adam, will sell them out for the right price. And women will protect themselves, even if they must sin to do it.

Eve has been betrayed, but she also has rebelled against God and cannot be excused for her role in the fall. Even before she stepped outside her God-given role, Eve had added to God's word (saying that they could not even touch the tree) to imply that God was being overly strict about the forbidden fruit. Since He was not being fair, she could pursue something that was pleasing to her eyes and put her own intuition above what God had said.

The charge that women are treated unfairly has become a constant refrain, whether in reference to marriage, the Church, business, or politics. It is true that women have valid grievances in these areas, but this complaint has become a weapon for gaining control over men. When we look at the effects of the fall, we see that one of the consequences of Eve's sin is the desire of women to rule over men.[47] Women will use the failures of men to justify their own sinful behavior.

*****

---

[47] pp. 15–16.

Before we move on to look at the consequences of Adam and Eve's fall into sin, we need to look at one more aspect of Adam's decision to disobey God. There is another tree mentioned in Genesis 2:9. It is the tree of life, and it is mentioned in the same verse as the tree of the knowledge of good and evil. It is also in the "midst of the Garden" (Gen. 2:9); if not side by side with the forbidden tree, at least in close proximity. This verse tells us that "the Lord God caused to grow every tree that is pleasing to the sight and good for food;" and then immediately mentions the tree of life as though this is the tree that Adam and Eve should partake of first.

Adam and Eve were sinless, but they were fallible, subject to falling into sin and receiving the punishment of death. Their lives were maintained as long as they did not sin, but they were always in jeopardy. The tree of life was the tree of eternal life (Gen. 3:22). If Adam and Eve had eaten of this tree, they would have been confirmed in their righteousness and would have lived forever in the paradise of the Garden. Their roles as creatures in submission to God would have been confirmed forever, and the tree of the knowledge of good and evil would have no longer been a temptation. The tree itself was not evil;[48] the desire to eat of it in order to become autonomous, like God, was evil.

The tree of life was not withheld from Adam and Eve; its fruit was available to them (Gen. 2:16–17). Covenantal theologians, however, in their concept of the covenant of works before the fall, say that God was withholding this tree until Adam and Eve completed a time of probation. But there is no implication in the text that God was reserving this tree as a reward after a period of testing. Rather, the tree was accessible to Adam and Eve, and they could have eaten of it at any time.[49] Apparently, though, Adam, as the family head, felt no urgency to eat of the tree of life.

But in the confrontation with Satan, he had to make a decision. Adam was an intelligent man who talked with God. His mind was not corrupted by centuries of sin, and he was not deceived. He was aware of both trees[50] and

---

[48] The tree of the knowledge of good and evil was part of the whole of creation which God deemed "very good" on the sixth day (Gen. 1:31).

[49] We have already noted that the covenantal understanding of a covenant of redemption prior to creation is problematic (see p. ix, n. 9). Now an important aspect of the covenant of works seems invalid.

[50] After the fall, God places an armed angel to guard the way to the tree of life to prevent Adam and Eve from eating of it and confirming themselves forever in their sinful state (Gen. 3:24). They knew about both trees.

understood the choice they set before him. He and Eve could be confirmed in their sinless state in paradise by eating of the tree of life or Adam could seize the opportunity to be like God and eat of the tree of the knowledge of good and evil. Adam chose to eat of the forbidden tree. He chose to be his own god, to be autonomous,[51] deciding for himself what was good and what was evil. And all of his descendants are now born with this same heart attitude.

From the smallest of moral decisions to major issues, such as abortion and homosexuality, human beings are determined to decide for themselves what is right and wrong, without regard for what God has said. Everyone is a law unto himself (knowing good and evil), and our fallen hearts will not and cannot change unless there is divine intervention.

---

[51] Cornelius Van Til says that the assumption of autonomy is the root of all forms of non-Christian thought. See Cornelius Van Til, *A Christian Theory of Knowledge* (Grand Rapids: Baker Book House, 1969), 41–71.

CHAPTER 3

THE CONSEQUENCES OF THE FALL—
GOD'S JUDGMENT AGAINST SIN

God, in his perfect righteousness, must deal with the sin and rebellion that have arisen in the Garden. God pronounces two curses. The first curse applies to the serpent. Satan had assumed the personality of the serpent, but the snake is still held responsible for his role in the temptation and is addressed first.

"Cursed are you more than all cattle, And more than every beast of the field; On your belly shall you go, And dust shall you eat All the days of your life" (Gen. 3:14).

It appears that the snake may have carried himself in a more upright posture prior to the curse. John Calvin, however, believes that God simply confirms that the snake will never escape from his lowly mode of transport.[52] Whichever the case, the snake will now forever slither on his belly, continually eating dust. A snake will never again have a conversation with a human being. From now on, serpents will have to continuously flick their tongues to receive information from dust particles, a constant reminder of the man who was made from dust and who will now return to dust as will the snake and all living things.

The curse applies to Satan also, "And I will put enmity Between you and the woman, And between your seed and her seed; He shall bruise[53] you on the head, And you shall bruise him on the heel" (Gen. 3:15).

This enmity, this warfare between these two seeds will encompass all of human history and will be carried out through the repetitions of the kingdom paradigm. The seed of Satan will wound one who is a particular Seed of the woman, but this Seed will deliver a fatal blow to the head of Satan. Even as God

---

[52] John Calvin, *Genesis* (Carlisle, PA: Banner of Truth Trust, 1992), 167.
[53] The Hebrew word translated bruise can also be translated crush, or batter, which seems more fitting here.

pronounces His judgments, He promises that there will be one who comes from the woman who will rescue her and her seed, her descendants, from Satan and the sin and rebellion that she and Adam have freely chosen (Col. 2:12; Matt. 28:18).

This prophecy of victory over Satan is often called the *proto-evangelium*, the first gospel, because this is God's first promise of salvation in the Bible.[54] The seed of the woman and the seed of the serpent represent two lines of human beings as well as two spiritual forces whose conflict will rage throughout history until the Seed vanquishes Satan (crushes the head of the serpent), and the consummation of the kingdom of God begins.

But that is far in the future. God now addresses the human beings, and His judgments for the man and the woman are specifically appropriate for the way in which they have sinned. He says to the woman, "I will greatly multiply your pain in childbirth, In pain shall you bring forth children; Yet your desire shall be for your husband, And he shall rule over you" (Gen. 3:16).

Before her sin, Eve was to have the joyful role of giving birth to sinless human beings. But now there will be pain, not only physical pain at the time of delivery but the pain of a mother who sees her children sin, the pain of a mother who sees her firstborn son, Cain, kill his brother—the pain of a mother who knows her sin helped bring this about.

"Yet your desire shall be for your husband." This phrase would be difficult to understand if we did not have the same wording in Genesis 4:7. In this verse, God tells Cain that "sin is crouching at the door; and *its desire is for you.*" It is the same phraseology, and this is not love or physical attraction. It is sin's desire for dominion and control over Cain. The woman, who had been completely satisfied and fulfilled in her role as helpmate for her husband, will now attempt to rule over him. We see this manifested very openly by certain women's organizations that attack male leadership in the areas of business and politics.[55] But it is also evident in homes and churches where seemingly submissive women rule their families and sometimes entire congregations with a steel hand inside

---

[54] See "The Proto-Evangelium," *Ligonier Ministries*, accessed November 14, 2018, https://ligonier.org/learn/devotionals/proto-evangelium/ for a discussion of this passage.

[55] Recently, two women senators have directed *all* men to "shut up." See Tasbeeh Herwees, "Senator Claire McCaskill Has a PSA for Men: 'Shut the Hell Up,'" *GOOD*, November 10, 2015, https://www.good.is/articles/senator-claire-mccaskill-has-a-message-for-all-men; also see Steve Byas, "Senator Hirono Tells Men to Shut Up; Ford Should be Believed," *NewAmerican*, September 19, 2018, https://www.thenewamerican.com/usnews/politics/item/30114-senator-hirono-tells-men-to-shut-up-ford-should-be-believed.

a velvet glove—sometimes by simply taking over but perhaps more often ruling through the soft tyranny of manipulation.

Eve had stepped outside of her husband's authority, and Adam had failed to protect her. As a consequence, women now find it difficult to trust and be subject to (supportive of) their husbands.[56] Since the fall, women not only have a desire to rule; they feel they have to take control to protect themselves and their children when their husbands fail. But men will not give up their headship easily. Instead of responding with understanding and tenderness to this difficult dilemma women face, they respond with oppression ("and he shall rule over you"), often through financial control, verbal intimidation, or even physical strength.

Some couples will say, "Our marriage is not like that." It is true that the relationship between a man and a woman can be redeemed if both admit their sinful tendencies and put God and His gospel at the center of their relationship. But a failure to understand what the fall has done to the bond between a wife and a husband leads to many difficulties, even in a Christian marriage.

Adam is the last to be confronted by God:

> Because you have listened to the voice of your wife, and have eaten from the tree... Cursed is the ground because of you; In toil you shall eat of it All the days of your life. Both thorns and thistles it shall grow for you; And you shall eat the plants of the field; By the sweat of your face you shall eat bread, Till you return to the ground, Because from it you were taken; For you are dust, and to dust you shall return. (Gen. 3:17–19)

Adam had "listened to the voice of his wife." He had remained silent and allowed Eve to take the lead in the confrontation with the serpent. He abdi-

---

[56] Secular society scoffs at Paul's instruction for wives to be subject to their husbands (Eph. 5:22). But even the *New York Times* admits that women have become less happy after decades of "liberation." See Ross Douthat, "Liberated and Unhappy," Opinion of the Editor, *New York Times*, May 25, 2009; also Betsey Stevenson and Justin Wolfers, "The Paradox of Declining Female Happiness," working paper, National Bureau of Economic Research (Cambridge, MA, May 2009). It seems that most women are happier when their husbands lead *if* the men follow Paul's teaching and are willing to lay down their lives for their wives, as Christ did for the Church (Eph. 5:22–25).

cated his headship, the first sin, and let Eve proceed with something that he knew was wrong. Adam had failed in his duty to guard Eve and the Garden because he listened to the serpent and decided to be his own god. Men will now have to contend with their wives for leadership within the family. Although husbands should give serious consideration to the views of their wives, they must not abandon their God-ordained responsibility of headship.[57]

God pronounces His second curse, and it is on the ground, the earth, from which Adam was made.[58] Adam's sin affects even the inanimate earth, which now resists his attempt to rule over it. Before he fell, Adam ate freely from the trees of the garden and his "work" was fulfilling activity as he exercised his "image of God" capabilities. Now Adam must labor and gain his food from the field, by the sweat of his brow, while the earth resists his efforts with thorns and thistles.

Despite this, men can still have some success in their lives. Although they are now fallen, they are still created in the image of God. They have God-given abilities, and they can find sustenance and temporary satisfaction in work. God grants common grace and sustains the human race so the gospel can go out. But every working man knows the difficulty of earning bread in a fallen world; there are always hindrances to accomplishing plans. Things break, accidents and illnesses occur, and people are often unreliable and adversarial. Work becomes a painful necessity rather than a joyful activity. And there is never enough time. The reality of coming death now hangs heavy over every man's efforts. God had begun Adam's life in a very personal and significant way, but now that he has rebelled and chosen autonomy, his finite insignificance is driven home in a crushing way: "For you are dust, And to dust you shall return" (Gen. 3:19).

---

[57] As a matter of general observation, when a wife assumes the leadership role in a marriage, neither she nor her husband seems happy.

[58] Satan and the ground are cursed; both will eventually be consumed by fire (2 Pet. 3:10; Rev. 20:10). Being cursed by God means there is going to be a final ending with no future. The lines of the cursed are cut off. Satan will be cast into the lake of fire, and there will be a new heaven and earth. Adam and Eve are not cursed, and we have indications that both will be redeemed. The enmity between Eve and Satan indicates that she will be saved. Then, after the certainty of death is pronounced, Adam names his wife Eve, which means the "mother of the living," when she appears to be the "mother of the dying" (Gen. 3:20). Adam believed in the promise of a Savior.

CHAPTER 4

LIFE AFTER THE GARDEN AND THE FLOOD

Adam and Eve are cast out of the Garden. God places cherubim and a flaming sword at the Garden's entrance so that the sinful couple cannot reenter their lost paradise. R. C. Sproul sees this as the initiation of civil government because it is the first time that the power of the sword is used to control human beings. Before their rebellion, Adam and Eve were not innately sinful, and there was no need to have a government to prevent unlawful activity. Now, every human being will be selfish and many will be violent. As the population increases, civil authority with the power of lethal force must be established to prevent a vicious anarchy that could eliminate the human race and the coming of the Seed of the woman.[59]

Being cast out of the Garden is a punishment, but it is also a protection. With the certainty of death confronting them, Adam and Eve would be tempted to eat of the tree of life to preserve their existence. But that would confirm them in their sinful state, separated from God forever. Barred from the tree of life, their death is now inevitable, but the hope of redemption and eternal life is still open to them.

God, in his mercy, illustrates the basis for their future reconciliation. He replaces their self-made self-righteous fig leaves with garments made from

---

[59] I once attended a church in the Washington D.C. area whose leaders taught that human government is the natural enlargement of family rule and therefore a pre-Fall, and naturally good, institution. But Saint Augustine's belief that government is a post-Fall necessity due to sin, better fits the reality we see as governments exercise authority. This is an important distinction. If civil government is a pre-Fall, natural good, there is no theological basis for limiting its role in the lives of citizens. If it is a post-Fall necessity, it will be corrupt from its inception just like all entities after the Fall, and its role should be restricted whenever and wherever possible. See Herbert A. Deane, *The Political and Social Ideas of Saint Augustine* (New York: Columbia University Press, 1963), 117–153.

animal skins (Gen. 3:21). To cover their nakedness and guilt, God slaughters innocent animals.[60] This is the first time Adam and Eve have seen an animal killed, surely a horrifying experience for them. It is the first demonstration of the necessity of blood sacrifice for the covering of sin and an introduction to the concepts of atonement and propitiation (see Exod. 12:1–13; Rom. 3:24–26). Adam and Eve have been told about the coming Savior, and now they have been given a graphic revelation of what will be required of Him to cover their sins, to rescue human beings from their fallen estate.

*****

Adam and Eve resettle outside the Garden of Eden and begin to have children. Cain is their firstborn, and Eve seems to think that this son is already the promised Seed (Gen. 4:1). But Cain is not the promised one, and after he has matured, he reveals that he is of the line of Satan, not of the seed of the woman. When God does not have regard for Cain's offering (the fruit of the ground),[61] but does have regard for his younger brother's offering (the first of his flock), Cain attacks and kills his brother, Abel (Gen. 4:8). Cain's crime reveals the magnitude and consequences of his father's sin. The fact that Adam's sinful nature has been passed on to his posterity is brutally evident when his firstborn son commits the first murder.

God questions Cain in much the same way that he questioned Adam and Eve, asking, "Where is Abel, your brother?" (Gen. 4:9). Cain's response, in accord with his fallen character, is evasive and defensive, expressing no remorse and no repentance, "I do not know. Am I my brother's keeper?" (Gen. 4:9). But God sees everything, and He says, "What have you done? The voice of your brother's blood is crying to Me from the ground" (Gen. 4:10). God's judgment is swift (Gen. 4:11–12): "And now you are cursed from the ground,[62] which has

---

[60] It has been suggested that God made Adam kill the animals, as the Levitical priests will do in offering sacrifices in the future. But this is not stated in the text.

[61] Some theologians believe that the fault with Cain's offering was that it did not involve the shedding of blood. But Abel brought the "firstborn of his flock and of their fat," the best he could offer. Nothing similar is said of Cain's offering—see ns. on Gen. 4:4 in *Nelson's NKJV Study Bible*, gen. ed., Earl D. Radmacher (Nashville: Thomas Nelson, 1997), 12. It is the attitude of Cain, not the type of offering that warrants God's displeasure (1 Sam. 15:22). God will later spell out for Israel in great detail specific sacrifices to inform them about the person and work of the coming Seed of the woman (See the book of Leviticus).

[62] Cain is also cursed. His line will be cut off from everlasting life with God.

opened its mouth to receive your brother's blood from your hand. When you cultivate the ground, it shall no longer yield its strength to you; you shall be a vagrant and a wanderer on the earth."

Cain protests that his punishment is greater than he can bear and that someone will eventually kill him. God puts a mark on Cain so that others will not execute him, and He promises to take vengeance on anyone that takes Cain's life. Then "Cain went out from the presence of the Lord and settled in the land of Nod, East of Eden" (Gen. 4:16). There is a finality to this physical and spiritual departure from God, a finality resulting not from the murder for even that sin can be forgiven but from Cain's determined lack of repentance (1 John 2:9, 3:12).

Cain takes a wife[63] and refuses to accept his destiny as a fugitive and a wanderer. He decides to build his own city and his own way of life (Gen. 4:17). He will be a law unto himself, revealing the spirit of autonomy which now infects the entire human race. After the fall, human beings refuse to acknowledge their sins and try to build individual lives, cities, and nations apart from God. Cain may not be a physical wanderer—he will build his own "garden"— but he and his offspring will always be spiritual wanderers.

Cain's descendants follow in his footsteps. Lamech is particularly mentioned because he takes two wives.[64] He kills a man and a boy and brags about it in a song. Wickedness characterizes Cain's offspring, but they are still made in the image of God, and they have great abilities. Some become herders of livestock, and others make implements of bronze and iron. Others become skillful in the arts and play the lyre and pipe. The beginnings of social and commercial interactions are established, and societies begin to grow[65] (Gen. 4:18–22).

*****

---

[63] Cain had to marry a daughter of Adam and Eve; apparently, negative genetic issues from such a union had not developed at this early period of human existence.

[64] There is a different Lamech in Genesis who becomes the father of Noah (Gen. 5:28–29).

[65] The Bible gives no indication of the gradual development of human beings from earlier life-forms, nor does the fossil record. The trillions times trillions of transitional forms necessary for human beings to develop according to Darwin's theory of natural selection, based on time and chance, are missing in the fossil record. As microbiology increasingly reveals the incredible complexity of even the simple cell, the necessity of intelligent design in the universe becomes more and more apparent. Albert Einstein seemed to reject Darwin's theory when he said, "God does not play dice." Antony Flew, the most influential atheist of the twentieth century, renounced his atheism because of the ever-increasing evidence for

Adam and Eve have another son, and she names him Seth ("appointed" or "placed"). It is Adam's role to name his son, but Eve seems to recognize that the descendants of this boy will form the line of "the seed of the woman," and she gives him an appropriate name. Scripture indicates the character of Seth's descendants as opposed to the line of Cain; "Then men began to call upon the name of the Lord" (Gen. 4:26).

*****

The lines of Cain and Seth begin to multiply and expand (Gen. 5:1–32). Men live long lives of almost a thousand years, and they have many children.[66] But as the population increases, so does evil throughout the entire human race. There are two distinct lines of human beings, but both lines become exceedingly wicked. A crisis point comes when "the sons of God saw that the daughters of men were beautiful; and they took wives for themselves, whomever they chose" (Gen. 6:2). It seems that "the sons of God" may refer to the descendants of Seth intermarrying with Cain's descendants, the line of Satan. But "sons of God" also refers to angels in the book of Job. Possibly, evil angels were somehow cohabiting with the daughters of men.[67] Whichever is the case, the evil of mankind reaches such a degree that the line through which the Savior will come is threatened, and God will no longer tolerate it. "Then the LORD saw that the wickedness of man was great on the earth, and that every intent of the thoughts of his heart was only evil continually" (Gen. 6:5).[68] So the LORD said,

---

intelligent design. But academia and the mainstream media remain committed to Darwin's theory and suppress and ridicule the only viable alternative. See pp. 376–378 for further discussion of Flew and Darwin's theory.

[66] Jared lived 962 years, Methuselah, 969 (Gen. 5:20, 27). The long lives seem to be the result of the ideal climate conditions before the flood and the lack of time for genetic deterioration to occur. God had told Adam that if he ate the forbidden fruit that he would die. Gen. 5:5 says that Adam lived 930 years, "and he died."

[67] Frank Seay makes a convincing case that evil angels were co-habiting with the daughters of men. See Frank Seay, "Foundations: Genesis & Jesus, Gen. 6—Sons of God/Daughters of Men" (audiotape of a Sunday school lesson, Park Cities Presbyterian Church, Dallas, TX, May 16, 1999). Also see Job 1:6, 2:1, 38:7; 2 Pet 2:4–5; and Jude 6.

[68] Sin follows a consistent pattern whether in an individual or a society. First there is unbelief, not trusting God and what He has said. Then comes rebellion followed by immorality, sometimes overwhelming immorality—explained by S. Lewis Johnson while teaching on Revelation 17:1–5.

"I will blot out man whom I have created from the face of the land, from man to animals to creeping things and to birds of the sky; for I am sorry that I have made them" (Gen. 6:7).[69]

The world is overrun with evil, and God, in his righteous judgment, is about to destroy the world with a flood of water. But God has not abandoned his plan to have a kingdom of righteous people. Noah, an upright man of the line of Seth, finds favor with God. God makes a covenant[70] with Noah and tells him to build an Ark to save himself and his family (his wife, his three sons, and their wives—seven more people). God gives very specific directions on how to build the Ark because Noah is to take two of every living creature, male and female, along with sufficient provisions to keep them alive. He is also told to take seven of each clean animal, which will be used for his family's food and eventually for sacrifice after the flood. Noah follows all of God's instructions. "Thus Noah did; according to all that God had commanded him, so he did" (Gen. 6:8–21, 22).

Scripture does not tell us precisely how long Noah worked on the ark. But Gen 5:32 says that "Noah was five hundred years old and Noah became the father of Shem, Ham, and Japheth." It is after this that Noah is told to build the Ark. The flood comes when Noah is six hundred years old (Gen. 7:6), so Noah worked on the Ark less than a hundred years.[71] It is likely that he had to have the help of his mature sons for such a gigantic project.

A period of fifty to seventy years seems reasonable for building the huge vessel which was approximately 450 feet long, 75 feet wide, and 45 feet high.[72] This made it one and a half times the length of a football field and one and a half times the width of a football field. In addition, it had "lower, second, and third decks" (Gen. 6:16). The dimensions of the Ark made it a stable vessel almost impossible to overturn in even the roughest seas. It has been calculated that the Ark could hold as many animals as 569 modern railroad stock cars,

---

[69] God's plans are perfect, and He has no reason to regret anything he has done. But He uses human terminology to indicate His emotions and the fact that consequences are coming due to the actions of men.

[70] This is the first time the word *covenant* is used in Scripture. The terms of the covenant will be expanded after the flood.

[71] The reference in Gen. 6:3 that says man's days "shall be one hundred and twenty years" cannot refer to how much time Noah had before the onset of the flood. It may mean that the long lives of men are going to decline to a maximum of 120 years after the flood.

[72] The dimensions in Genesis are given in cubits; a cubit is approximately eighteen inches.

enough room to carry all the species required to repopulate the earth and the food necessary to sustain them. Water may have been carried aboard or there may have been a cistern system devised to capture water from the pouring rain of the flood. Noah had many years to plan for the deluge, and he had the help of God.

Second Peter 2:5 says that Noah was "a preacher of righteousness," which seems to indicate that Noah was proclaiming God's truth while he built the Ark. But even if he was not verbally preaching, the long, long process of building the Ark on dry land with no way to move it to water was a daily warning of the coming flood and a proclamation of God's approaching judgment. Noah and his family were surely ridiculed by the wicked inhabitants of the earth surrounding them during the construction of the Ark, ridicule which became pleas for help when the rain came pouring down.

*****

Seven days before the torrent begins, God tells Noah to enter the Ark with his family and all the animals. The animals are supernaturally guided into the Ark. "So they went into the Ark to Noah, by twos of all flesh in which was the breath of life. And those that entered, male and female of all flesh, entered as God had commanded him" (Gen. 7:15–16).

After Noah has all the animals aboard, it is time to shut the door of the Ark, and God himself secures it; "and the LORD closed it behind him" (Gen. 7:16). Noah has completed the gigantic project God had given him. Noah, his family, and the animals are safely sealed in the Ark, and the wicked world is sealed to its coming destruction.

"Then the flood came upon the earth for 40 days; and the water increased and lifted up the Ark, so that it rose above the earth" (Gen. 7:17).

This seems to be the first time that human beings have seen rain. Genesis 2:5 says that the Lord God had not sent rain upon the earth. "But a mist used to rise from the earth and water the whole surface of the ground" (Gen. 2:6). This mist-watering took place in the Garden of Eden, but there is no indication that this changed after the fall; the people around Noah saw no use for his huge boat. But even if there had been previous rains, there had never been and will never be again such a torrential downpour. Water also bursts forth from the earth itself; "on the same day all the fountains of the great deep burst open, and the floodgates of the sky were opened" (Gen. 7:11).

Water is cascading upon the earth from above and below. The deluge continues until the mountains are covered in water. This is a worldwide flood. "And all flesh that moved on the earth perished, birds and cattle and beasts and every swarming thing that swarms upon the earth, and all mankind; of all that was on the dry land, all in whose nostrils was the breath of the spirit of life, died" (Gen. 7:21–22). Nothing is left alive on the earth, except for the water creatures and the inhabitants of the Ark floating securely above the flood.

Summary

Adam and Eve's opportunity to establish God's earthly kingdom has come to a disastrous end. Adam and Eve were in paradise, but they chose to listen to Satan and disobey God. They ate the forbidden fruit in an attempt to become like God, wanting to decide for themselves what was good and what was evil. Their relationships with God, with each other, and with the Garden were broken. Human dispositions changed from love and obedience to selfishness and sin. The first opportunity to establish the kingdom is gone; Satan and sin rule the earth and death is a certainty. God's promise that the seed of the woman will destroy Satan and his dominion is the only hope for mankind. But the descendants of Seth, the ancestors of the coming Savior, fall into the same kind of evil as Cain's descendants. The whole world becomes full of wickedness, and God, in His righteous judgment, sends a flood which destroys the earth.

But He still intends to have a righteous people for Himself in an earthly kingdom, so He saves Noah, his family, and two of every kind of animal on the Ark. There still exists a people of God moving forward through history who will be given the responsibility of initiating His kingdom.

Adam and Eve have failed to establish the kingdom, but they have established the pattern of the kingdom paradigm. They were given a mandate to begin the kingdom, but they sinned and rebelled, and God's judgment followed. Once the flood subsides, the paradigm begins again with Noah and his family.

SECTION 2

NOAH AND THE KINGDOM

CHAPTER 5

AFTER THE RAIN STOPS—THE KINGDOM PARADIGM REPEATED

The torrent of water pouring onto the earth lasts for forty days (Gen. 7:17), and then, "God remembered Noah and all the beasts and all the cattle that were with him on the ark...the fountains of the deep and the floodgates of the sky were closed" (Gen. 8:1–2). God stops the flood of water, but the time on the Ark is just beginning. The whole world is covered with water. It will be a long time before Noah and the animals can exit the Ark.

Scripture is precise about the number of days the flood lasted, although it does not give the century in which it occurred.[73] The flood began in "the six hundredth year of Noah's life, in the second month, on the seventeenth day of the month" (Gen. 7:11). After God stops the deluge, the water begins to abate, and "in the seventh month, on the seventeenth day of the month, the Ark rested on the mountains of Ararat" (Gen. 8:4). This means a period of five months pass from the beginning of the flood until the ark settles down on a high mountain. And then in the six hundredth and first year, "in the second month, on the twenty-seventh day of the month, the earth was dry," and God tells Noah to leave the Ark (Gen. 8:14, 13–16).

Once the ark comes to rest, another seven months and ten days pass before the land is dry enough for Noah to leave the Ark. Scripture likely uses the lunar calendar of thrity days per month, which would mean Noah was on

---

[73] Harold Camping (1921–2013) says the genealogy verses in the Old Testament are a calendar. In his book, *1994?*, he uses Scripture, secular sources, and cross-references to determine when a begat meant an immediate descendant in order to date the genealogies. His date for the flood is 4099 BC, which seems reasonable. Mr. Camping mistakenly projected his calendar forward to predict the return of Christ in 1994, which damaged his reputation and caused his credible work on the Old Testament calendar to be ignored. See Harold Camping, *1994?* (New York: Vantage, 1992), 267–310.

the Ark 360 days plus ten days, plus the seven days it took for the animals to come aboard for a total of 377 days.

This a long time for animals and human beings to be confined together, but the Ark was large enough to contain compartments not only for food but also for waste. With a length of 450 feet and three decks, there is room to roam for both animals and human beings and space enough for Noah and his family, at least at times to separate themselves from the care, noise, and odors of the animals.

Forty days after the mountains become visible, Noah sends out a raven which continues to fly "here and there" as the waters dry up. He also sends out a dove until she returns with a freshly picked olive leaf. Seven days after this, Noah sends the dove out again, and she does not return. Noah knows that it is dry enough to exit the Ark, and God instructs him to leave with his family and the animals. They all depart in the same manner by which they came aboard, by families, for the dry ground (Gen. 8:5–19).

The first thing Noah does after leaving the Ark is to build an altar and offer burnt offerings of every clean animal and bird. Noah and his family are grateful for the miraculous deliverance that God has provided. The sacrifices are a soothing aroma to God, and He swears to never again destroy every living thing as long as the earth and its seasons exist (Gen. 8:20–22).

*****

Noah and his family are given a fresh start on a cleansed earth (1 Pet. 3:20–21). The emergence of the dry land from the water mirrors the history of creation. It is a new beginning for mankind, and God gives Noah and his sons the same kingdom mandate that He had given Adam and Eve, "Be fruitful and multiply, and fill the earth (Gen. 9:1)." He also restates their dominion, but after the fall and the flood, man's authority is different. Noah and his family are not sinless and they will now rule the animals through fear. And for the first time, the animals are given to them for food.

> And the fear of you and the terror of you shall be on
> every beast of the earth and on every bird of the sky; with
> everything that creeps on the ground, and all the fish of the
> sea, into your hand they are given. Every moving thing that

is alive shall be food for you; I give all to you, as I gave the green plant. (Gen. 9:2–3).

These are significant changes, but the responsibility for establishing God's kingdom remains. It has passed from a sinless couple to the redeemed family of Noah.

God had initiated a covenant with Noah before the flood and had told him to enter the Ark with two of every kind of animal so that they could repopulate the earth (Gen. 6:18–19). Now God adds to the covenant so that it includes all the living creatures. He promises that he will never again destroy the earth with a flood, and He sets his bow in the cloud as a sign of the covenant between himself and the entire earth (Gen. 9:9–12).

If the flood was the first time that it had rained (see p. 23), then the bow is a new sight for Noah and his family. It is a sign that from now on, the rain will stop before the entire earth is covered in water. God's signs always have redemptive significance. The bow that God set in the sky is a beautiful sight, and it is usually called a rainbow. But the word in the text is simply bow (as in bow and arrow), a weapon. To Noah and Moses, the writer of Genesis, it would have represented a decorated war bow, a drawn bow pointed at heaven where God dwells, not at the earth where sinful human beings live. God will eventually release the bow at Himself in the person of His Son—a Roman spear will pierce His side—but the human race, which deserves the arrow, will not be destroyed.

God says He will look on the bow and remember His covenant with every living creature not to destroy the earth with a flood. The rainbow is a sign of His grace, of His undeserved mercy (Gen. 9:16–17).

CHAPTER 6

THE CURSING OF CANAAN AND THE TOWER OF BABEL

Noah begins to farm, plants a vineyard, and makes wine. He eventually becomes drunk, and Genesis 9:21 says he "uncovered himself" in his tent. This is biblical language indicating that Noah was having sexual relations with his wife (see Lev. 18:6–18), but his intoxication leaves him in a vulnerable state, and he passes out (Gen. 9:24).

Genesis 9:22 says, "And Ham, the father of Canaan, saw the nakedness of his father, and told his two brothers outside."

From Leviticus 20:17, we see that "saw the nakedness of his father" does not mean that Ham was observing Noah. It means that Ham had an incestuous relation with Noah's wife, his own mother. He had taken advantage of Noah's drunken state and was brazen enough to tell his brothers about what he had done. His two brothers, Shem and Japheth, show respect for Noah and end this licentious episode by averting their eyes and covering their "father's nakedness," that is his wife (Lev. 18:8), with a garment (Gen. 9:23).

Genesis 9:24 says that, "When Noah awoke from his wine, he knew what his younger[74] son had done to him." Noah's curse follows in verse 25. But it appears that considerable time passes between Noah's realization about what Ham has done and the time of the curse because Noah pronounces the curse not on Ham but on Ham's son, Canaan. The question is why does Noah do this? Why is the curse directed at Canaan rather than his father, Ham, who had committed this shameful sin?

The first indication is in Genesis 9:18, just prior to the account of this sordid event. This verse says, "Now the sons of Noah who came out of the ark

---

[74] The NKJV says younger; the NAS says youngest. When Noah's sons are listed, it is always in the order of Shem, Ham, and Japheth, indicating that Ham is the second son, not the youngest. Since younger is the most frequent translation of the word and fits the order in which Noah's sons are listed, this appears to be the correct translation.

were Shem and Ham and Japheth; and Ham was the father of Canaan." That Ham was the father of Canaan is repeated in Genesis 9:22 in the same sentence that reveals Ham's incest with his mother. Ham had three other sons (Gen. 10:6), but they are not mentioned in this passage. Scripture is emphasizing that Canaan is Ham's son, not Noah's. And it is evident why in Noah's curse.

Noah reveals great anger in the curse, and it appears that he is speaking for God when he says, "Cursed be Canaan; A servant of servants he shall be to his brothers" (Gen. 9:25). Then verses 26–27 make it plain that the "brothers" to whom Canaan will be a servant are Shem and Japheth, but these are his father's brothers; they would normally be Canaan's uncles. Canaan can only be a brother to Shem and Japheth if they have the same mother. They are half-brothers. Canaan is the offspring of Ham's incest with his own mother, and Noah eventually realizes it and pronounces his curse on Canaan.[75]

The earth was supposed to be repopulated by Noah's three sons and their wives, not by the descendants of an illegitimate son of an incestuous relationship. In the curse, Canaan is condemned to be a "servant of servants" to his "brothers," Shem and Japheth (Gen. 9:26–27). He and his descendants will be the lowest stratum of society. And although his father committed the sin, Canaan is cursed just as the ground and Satan were cursed after the fall.[76] And just as they will be cut off—the earth burned and replaced by a new earth, and Satan cast into the lake of fire—so will Canaan be cut off and left without descendants.

Centuries later, when Israel has been rescued from Egyptian slavery and is entering the promised land, the descendants of Canaan, the Canaanites, occupy Palestine.[77] Israel is told to utterly destroy these inhabitants who were doing detestable things, which included child sacrifice and sexual perversions (Deut. 20:16–18; Lev. 18:21–27). Ham's sexual sinfulness was passed on through his son, Canaan, to his descendants, and God wanted it destroyed.[78] And Joshua

---

[75] For a concise discussion of this Genesis passage and Leviticus 18 and 20, see Nathan Bland, "Ham's Sin," *By Every Word* (blog), October 15, 2010, www.byeveryword.org./2010/10/hams-sin/.

[76] See p. 17, n. 58. The cursing of Canaan in no way means that every illegitimate child is cursed. Every child, however conceived, has a right to life and should be provided sustenance and education about God.

[77] Some of the Canaanites go by their tribal names (the Jebusites, the Amorites, the Hivites, etc.), but they are all descendants of Canaan (Gen. 10:15–20).

[78] It appears that the inhabitants of Sodom and Gomorrah were descendants of Canaan (Gen. 10:19).

begins to fulfill the curse. "Thus Joshua struck all the land… He left no survivor, but he utterly destroyed all who breathed, just as the Lord, the God of Israel, had commanded" (Josh. 10:40). Canaanites in other regions were not destroyed, and Israel will have conflicts with them throughout its history, even after the Babylonian captivity. But, eventually, their line is extinguished. Today, no one is known as a Canaanite.[79]

Ham is not cursed because that would mean he and his other sons would be cut off. Ham's family and their descendants must help resettle the earth. Genesis 9:18–19 holds true that from Noah's three sons, all of the earth was populated.

*****

Noah and his family are heroes in one of the most miraculous stories in the Bible. Yet Scripture does not hesitate to report their sins, even their most shameful sins. It is clear that the line of Satan continues after the flood. Cain had been cursed, but his spiritual rebellion survives the flood. Satan's offspring are now within Noah's own family. But the line of the seed of the woman continues also. After Noah curses Canaan, he says, "Blessed be the Lord, the God of Shem; and let Canaan be his servant" (Gen. 9:26).

"May God enlarge Japheth, and let him dwell in the tents of Shem, and let Canaan be his servant" (Gen. 9:27).

Shem is given preeminence over his brothers, and it is through his descendants that the Savior will come. God's plan of redemption will not be thwarted by the failures of sinful men.

*****

With sin reappearing in such a depraved way, it is not surprising when the descendants of Noah refuse to obey God's command to multiply and fill the earth. The tribes of Shem, Ham, and Japheth *do* multiply and begin to move toward the east. But when they eventually find a plain, a habitable region in

---

[79] Some Palestinians have tried to trace their lineage back to Canaan to establish a claim to the land of Palestine. But after Israel's occupation, the land was conquered and repopulated by Assyria, Babylon, Rome, and the Ottoman Empire. It does not seem possible to trace any Canaanite ancestry to the present time.

the land of Shinar,[80] they decide to settle there. They do not want to separate and fill the earth. Instead, the tribes plot to stay together to make a *name* for themselves (Gen. 11:4).

God had promised Shem precedence over his brothers in the progress of redemptive history (Gen. 9:26–27), and it appears that all the families know it. The word *Shem* means "name," a fitting designation for the one who will carry forward the godly line. Ham's and Japheth's descendants apparently resent the preference given to Shem's family. They rebel against Noah's prophecy and say, "Come, let us build for ourselves a city, and a tower whose top will reach into heaven, and let us make for ourselves a *name* (a different "Shem," their own approach to God as they try to establish their own kingdom), lest we be scattered abroad over the face of the whole earth" (Gen. 11:4). Satan's seed is trying to disrupt and replace God's plan to provide salvation through the line of Shem.[81] And apparently, some of the descendants of Shem are willing to help them.

It is becoming evident that God is working out his redemptive purposes through a chosen family of people, Shem's descendants, who are often just as sinful as the line of Satan. The building of a city with a tower stretching up to heaven is not just a show of arrogance and rebellion. This is a collective effort by the families of Ham, Japheth, and even Shem to construct their own approach to God, a different way of salvation. Like Adam and Eve, they want to be autonomous; they want to establish their own self-made kingdom.[82]

God sees the sin and rebellion of the people and once again sends judgment. He does not send a flood, but He confuses their language so that they cannot understand each other. This halts the construction of their city with its proud tower, and the families begin to disperse and settle in different areas of the Middle East, likely grouping together according to their now different languages (Gen. 10).[83] It is not what the tribes wanted, but they are going to fill the earth.

---

[80] Shinar was likely in what is present-day Iraq near the Tigris and Euphrates rivers.

[81] I am indebted to Ken Olles concerning the importance of the name *Shem*.

[82] When Jesus begins his ministry centuries later, both Satan and Peter will suggest alternative ways of establishing the kingdom, ways which do not require Jesus's suffering and death. Jesus rebukes them both (Matt. 4:8–10; Mark 8:31–33).

[83] This scattering of small family groups would have led to genetic isolation which seems to be the explanation for the development of different racial characteristics; see John D. Morris, PhD. 1989. "Where did all the races come from?" *Acts and Facts* 18/2, accessed May 17, 2020, https://www.icr.org/article/1062/.

The communication barriers and the dispersions, at least to some extent, separate Shem and his descendants from the line of the Serpent. It is a protection from the influence of Satan, to which Shem's family has shown it is susceptible. It is a protection for the lineage of the coming Savior.

Genesis 10 is sometimes called the Table of Nations because it is the genealogy of Noah's three sons and indicates where their tribes begin to settle and enlarge, even before the reason for their dispersion is given in chapter 11. After Scripture chronicles God's judgment on the Tower of Babel, only Shem's genealogy continues to be recorded because it is his line through which the Savior comes (Gen. 11:10–26). And this genealogy leads us to Abram, who becomes Abraham, one of the most important men in the Bible.

Summary

Noah and his family, like Adam and Eve, fail to establish God's righteous kingdom. For a second time, God's mandate is not fulfilled; sinful rebellion again leads to God's judgment. He does not send another flood, but He confuses the language of Noah's descendants, which halts their attempt to build a city and a tower to heaven, their own self-devised way of salvation through the creation of their own kingdom. Their arrogant tower becomes the Tower of Babel, a symbol of the incoherence of man-made religion. God scatters the families throughout the Middle East, and they do begin to fill the earth.

Although Shem and his descendants were willing to participate in apostasy, they are still the line of the promised Savior. Scripture traces Shem's genealogy to Abram, a crucial patriarch in the lineage through which the Savior and the kingdom will come. God is working out his plan of redemption, despite the sins of rebellious men. With Abram, the paradigm of the kingdom will begin again.

SECTION 3

ISRAEL AND THE KINGDOM[84]

---

[84] Stephen, a New Testament disciple, recounts the history of Israel from Abraham to Jesus, just before the Jewish leaders stone him to death (Acts 7:1–60).

CHAPTER 7

THE COVENANT WITH ABRAM—
THE PARADIGM BEGINS AGAIN

Shem's genealogy is traced down to Abram through Terah, his father.[85] Many generations have passed, and Noah's dispersed families are beginning to fill the earth. Abram is living with his father in Ur of the Chaldeans near the junction of the Euphrates and Tigris rivers in what is present-day Iraq. Terah decides to move to the land of Canaan, and he takes Abram, Abram's wife, Sarai, who is barren,[86] and his grandson, Lot, with him (Gen. 11:30–31).

Genesis does not tell us why Terah decided to move, but Acts 7:2 says that God had appeared to Abram in Mesopotamia and had told him to leave his country for "the land that I will show you." That event must have influenced Terah to begin the journey with his family, but Terah does not make it to Canaan. The family stops at Haran, far north of their destination, about half-way through their 1,500-mile trek. It may have been Terah's health that caused the pause because he dies in Haran before the rest of the family continues on to Canaan (Gen. 11: 27–30).

After recording Terah's death, Scripture reveals the full covenant that God had made with Abram while he was still living in Ur. Genesis 12:1–3 says:

> Now the Lord said to Abram: "Go forth from your
> country, And from your relatives And from your father's
> house, To the land which I will show you; And I will make
> you a great nation, And I will bless you, And make your

---

[85] Abram was born in 2166 BC (see p. 99, n. 159) about 2,000 years after the flood according to Camping's Old Testament calendar (see p. 27, n. 73).

[86] Being barren was a huge issue in Old Testament times. It not only meant that the husband would have no influence in the world after his death, but also that his wife would have no family to support her. A lack of children meant that God was withholding His blessing.

name great; And so you shall be a blessing; And I will bless those who bless you, And the one who curses you I will curse. And in you all the families of the earth shall be blessed."

With this poetic covenant, the kingdom paradigm begins again. This time, God goes beyond just saying be fruitful and multiply and rule. God commits Himself to making Abram a great nation. Abram will have a huge number of descendants,[87] and they will have a land, a kingdom; Abram will rule. God will bless Abram and bless those who bless him. And he will curse those who curse Abram; Abram's enemies will be God's enemies. They will be cut off without a future. This is an amazing statement of God's covenantal alignment with Abram for the purpose of establishing His kingdom.

God concludes his promises by saying that in Abram, all the families of the earth shall be blessed. The kingdom will eventually extend to all the families of Noah's three sons, despite their sinfulness and rebellion.

*****

God's covenant with Abram promised him great blessings, but it required him to do things that were unthinkable for an individual family in those days. Abram had to leave the safety of his country, leave his relatives, and leave his father's house for an unknown destination, a land that God would show him, a land that was 1,500 miles away. He had to make the journey with his father, his wife, and his nephew, using pack animals and carts while facing the problems of food, water, weather, and robbers.

Obviously, Abram's encounter with God had a great impact on him. Leaving the security of Ur required unusual faith and courage from him and his entire family. But Abram is also a direct descendant of Shem, who continued to live for 502 years after the flood (Gen. 11:10–11). Shem had centuries to pass on his experience of the flood[88] and the special blessings Noah had prophesied for him and his descendants. Although Abram was born centuries after Shem's

---

[87] Genesis 15:5 says that Abram's descendants will be as numerous as the stars of heaven.

[88] The religions which arose from the descendants of Ham and Japheth almost always have distsorted versions of the great flood in their mythological histories. See various articles listed at "Flood Myth," *Encyclopedia Britannica*, accessed November 16, 2018, https://www.britannica.com/topic/flood-myth.

death and had been worshipping idols (Josh. 24:2), he likely was aware of his family's history which helped him obey God's calling.

After Terah's death, Abram resumes the journey to Canaan with Sarai, Lot, and "all their possessions which they had accumulated and the persons they had acquired in Haran" (Gen. 12:5). Abram is seventy-five years old when he leaves Haran for Canaan. He is a wealthy man with herds, flocks, and servants, but he and Sarai still have no children (Gen. 12:4–5).

The family reaches Canaan and travels southward through the land until they come to the Oak of Moreh near Shechem. This is a place to stop and rest, and Abram needs time to consider his circumstances because Genesis 12:6 says, "Now the Canaanite was then in the land." It seems that Abram knows the story of Canaan and his descendants and realizes that their presence in the land is a problem for him. Instead of the Canaanites being his servants, as Noah had prophesied,[89] they possess the land God had promised Abram. But God appears to Abram and encourages him by saying, "To your descendants I will give this land." So Abram "built an altar there to the Lord who had appeared to him" (Gen. 12:6–7).

Abram moves his tents through Canaan, grazing his flocks and herds. He stops to build another altar near Bethel and Ai and calls on the name of the Lord. He then heads south toward the Negev, a semiarid region north of the Gulf of Aqaba. Apparently, the sparse rains for the region fail because a famine ensues. To save his family and his livestock, Abram heads west for the more fertile and more dangerous land of Egypt (Gen. 12:8–9).

*****

Sarai is a beautiful woman, and as Abram approaches Egypt, he begins to fear that the Egyptians will kill him to take his wife. He tells Sarai to tell the Egyptians that she is his sister, and it is true that she is his half-sister; they had the same father (Gen. 20:12). He wants Sarai to tell a half-truth to protect him. Pharaoh's officials see Sarai, and after hearing that she is Abram's sister, they take her to Pharaoh's house. Because of Sarai, Abram is treated well and given herds of livestock and male and female servants. But God protects the lineage of the Seed of the woman and strikes the Egyptians with plagues.

---

[89] See pp. 30–32.

Pharaoh soon realizes what has caused his afflictions, and he rightfully chastises Abram for what he has done. He returns Sarai to Abram and tells him to take his wife and go. Pharaoh's men escort Abram and all his livestock and possessions out of the country. Abram has failed to trust God and has acted deceitfully, and yet God has not only protected him, He has blessed and enriched him. Abram is the recipient of God's grace, His unmerited favor (Gen. 12:1–20).[90]

Abram leaves Egypt and again heads for the Negev. He moves north, stopping at the altar near Bethel and Ai to call on the name of the Lord. Abram has much for which to be thankful. He has completed the long and dangerous journey from Ur and has been rescued from the famine, then rescued again from Egypt without harm coming to Sarai. And he has become very rich in livestock, silver, and gold (Gen. 13:1–6).

Abram remains in Canaan, but he has accumulated so much livestock that his herdsmen, seeking sufficient grazing areas, clash with the herdsmen of his nephew, Lot, who also has acquired large herds and flocks. Scripture mentions at this point that the "Canaanite and the Perizzite were dwelling then in the land" (Gen. 13:7). With these potential enemies nearby, Abram and Lot must present a united front. Their men cannot be fighting each other.

Abram realizes that to avoid confrontations, he and Lot must separate so that each has sufficient room for his animals. In a magnanimous gesture, Abram gives his nephew the choice of which direction he wants to go. Lot looks toward the well-watered Jordan River valley and chooses to travel eastward toward this lush vegetation. He moves his tents as far as Sodom (Gen. 13:12). But his choice portends a potential problem because Genesis 13:13 adds, "Now the men of Sodom were wicked exceedingly and sinners against the Lord." As Lot journeys to Sodom, Abram moves westward and sojourns in the hills of Canaan (Gen. 13:5–13).

After the separation from Lot, God speaks to Abram again. He tells Abram to look in all four directions and that all the land that he can see will be given to him and his descendants forever. And he tells Abram that his descendants will be like the dust, so many that they cannot be numbered. This is the second time that God has said this, and it is hard to imagine the thoughts of Abram, a seventy-five-year-old man with no children, a barren wife, and the Canaanites

---

[90] God's mercy to Abram does not mean that God overlooks his sins. God will chastise His people for their disobedience and lack of faith.

and the Perizzites occupying the land he has been promised. He moves his tent south to Hebron and "there he built an altar to the LORD" (Gen. 13:18).

The pattern of Abram's life is established. He lives in tents, travels with his livestock, and builds altars. He is a sojourner in this world, and he calls on the name of the LORD.

CHAPTER 8

THE BATTLE OF THE KINGS AND MELCHIZEDEK

While Abram is grazing his flocks and herds in Canaan, a geopolitical event takes place that involves both Abram and Lot. Five kings of the Jordan Valley, including the kings of Sodom and Gomorrah, have been paying tribute to four stronger kings who rule in Mesopotamia far to the north. The four kings of the north include the king of Shinar where the sons of Noah had attempted to build their tower. This ruling alliance is led by Chedorlaomer, the king of Elam, from the area of Ur. The southern kings have been paying tribute for twelve years, but in the thirteenth year, they join together and rebel; they refuse to pay their tribute (Gen. 14:1–4).

The four kings from the north unite their powerful armies and move south to reimpose their reign over the Jordan Valley. As they advance toward Canaan, they attack and destroy the armies of six city-states, including the giant Rephaim, to insure their dominance over the entire region. After these conquests, the northern forces continue their march to the Jordan Valley. The five southern kings mass their armies and confront the invaders in the Valley of Siddim.

The northern kings defeat their rebellious vassals, killing some of their soldiers in the tar pits in the valley and sending others fleeing to the mountains. The kings of Sodom and Gomorrah die in the battle. The Mesopotamian kings have reasserted their rule, and they plunder Sodom and Gomorrah, taking captive many of the inhabitants. Lot and his family are captured along with their possessions. The victorious armies then begin their journey back to Mesopotamia with all their spoils and captives (Gen. 14:5–12).

A survivor of the battle finds Abram, the Hebrew,[91] and tells him about the defeat of the Jordan Valley kings. When Abram hears that Lot and his family have been captured by the Mesopotamian kings, he gathers 318 *servants* and starts after the four large armies moving north. Abram catches up to the invaders in northern Canaan. He divides his men, attacks at night, and routs the Mesopotamian forces. The victory is so decisive that Abram's men pursue fleeing soldiers beyond the city of Damascus. Lot, his family, and their possessions are rescued, along with the people and the goods seized in the Jordan Valley (Gen. 14:13–16).

*****

When Abram returns with his servants and the rescued captives, he is met by two kings, the new king of Sodom and Melchizedek, the king of Salem (Peace), whose name means King of Righteousness. Unlike Sodom, Salem (Jerusalem) does not appear to refer to an actual city at this time,[92] and there is no Canaanite king who can be called King of Righteousness. The reign of Melchizedek extends beyond a single city; it encompasses something larger, the realm of peace. Melchizedek is more than a local ruler in Canaan.

The king of Sodom meets Abram and says that he will take the people back, but Abram can keep the possessions he has recovered. But Abram refuses to take anything except the food his men have eaten. To accept the offer of the goods would allow the king of Sodom to say, "I have made Abram rich" (Gen. 14:23), thereby making him superior to Abram. Abram returns the people of Sodom and their possessions to their new king.

Abram's meeting with Melchizedek is much different. Genesis 14:18–20 says, "And Melchizedek king of Salem brought out bread and wine; now he was a priest of God Most High. And he blessed him and said, 'Blessed be Abram of God Most High, Possessor of heaven and earth; And blessed be God Most High, Who has delivered your enemies into your hand.' And he gave him a tenth of all.'"

---

[91] Abram is the first person to be called a Hebrew, derived from his ancestor, Eber (Gen. 10:24–25). The name will be used to distinguish the descendants of Abram from all the other races, the Gentiles.

[92] The first mention of Jerusalem in ancient history is in the nineteenth century BC Execration Texts found in Egypt, written approximately 200 years after Abram arrived in Canaan. The actual texts are now located in Berlin and Brussels. See, "The Execration Texts," *City of David—Ancient Jerusalem*, accessed November 16, 2018, www.cityofdavid.org.il/en/archeology/finds/execration-texts.

Abram has refused a reward from the king of Sodom, yet he gives a tithe of all he has to Melchizedek, king of Salem.

Theologians have long debated whether Melchizedek was an earthly king who is a type of the Savior to come or if this is actually a preincarnate appearance of the coming Savior. The context and events of this amazing story gives us the answer and reveal the reasons for Abram's different reactions to the two kings.

The armies of the four kings of Mesopotamia had marched south from the northern area of the Fertile Crescent. The Fertile Crescent, stretching from the Persian Gulf to Egypt, effectively comprised the developed world at that time. The four kings, en route to their victory over the Jordan valley kings, defeated every army that opposed them. Except for Egypt, the Mesopotamian alliance had conquered the civilized world.

This campaign was a huge military effort of four nations. Their well-organized armies marched over 800 miles while defeating every resisting force. The fighting soldiers and their logistical support would have involved thousands of men and a large arsenal of weapons. After sacking Sodom and Gomorrah and capturing Lot, the conquerors began their long march back to Mesopotamia. When Abram was informed, he led out his trained servants (Gen. 14:14–15). Although some of Abram's men were probably designated to provide security, he had no standing military force. Abram pursued and attacked the most powerful military force in the world with 318 shepherds and household workers.

In the initiation of his covenant with Abram, God had promised Abram that He would curse those who cursed him; Abram's enemies were going to be God's enemies. Although Abram employed military strategy, he divided his forces to appear more numerous and attacked at night, Abram knew the victory belonged to God.

When Abram returned to Canaan, he had just defeated the kings who had conquered the world, except for Egypt. But Abram had just plundered the Egyptians through the plagues God had sent on behalf of Sarai. As he looked out over Canaan, in an eschatological preview of the kingdom, Abram, a shepherd and a sojourner, was the ruler of the world. In this moment of triumph that God had given him, there was no earthly king above Abram. It was not fitting for the king of Sodom to try to reward Abram with worldly goods and thereby assume a status superior to him, so Abram returned the plunder to the king.[93]

---

[93] Elements of this section are discussed in a lesson taught by Ken Olles, "Foundations: Genesis and Jesus" (audiotape of a Sunday school class, Park Cities Presbyterian Church, Dallas, TX,

In contrast, Melchizedek, the king of righteousness and peace, who is also a priest of God Most High, offered Abram bread and wine, and Abram gave him a tithe. Tithes are only given to superiors, but at that time, there was no human ruler superior to Abram. The tithe was given to Melchizedek because Abram recognized his divinity.[94] Hebrews 7:8, in speaking of Melchizedek receiving tithes, says "but in that case one receives them, of whom it is witnessed that he lives on."

Two thousand years later, the writer of Hebrews says Melchizedek "lives on;" He is eternal, He is divine. He is the preincarnate Savior who is the King of Peace, who will bring about fellowship (bread and wine) with God Most High during His coming incarnation.[95] He will be a Seed of Abram, yet in this amazing moment in redemptive history, Abram gives his eventual Descendant a tithe of all he has.

When Jesus begins His earthly ministry, He infuriates the Pharisees by saying,

> Your father Abraham rejoiced to see My day, and he saw it and was glad. The Jews therefore said to Him, "You are not yet fifty years old, and have you seen Abraham?" Jesus said to them, "Truly, truly, I say to you, before Abraham was born, I am."[96] Therefore, they picked up stones to throw at Him; but Jesus hid Himself and went out of the Temple. (John 8:56–59)

The Pharisees will establish their own kingdom in Israel, and they will reject the kingdom that Jesus initiates, the kingdom of which Abram has had a foretaste. He has been blessed and has had fellowship (peace) with God Most High through Melchizedek, the King/Priest of God Most High.[97]

October 4, 1998).

[94] See Hebrews 7:1–10, especially noting verses 3 and 8.

[95] Communion with God using bread and wine is not mentioned again until Jesus institutes the New Covenant the night before His death on the cross.

[96] "I AM" was God's reply from the burning bush when Moses asked God for his name (Exod. 3:13). The Jews understood that Jesus was claiming to be the one who had spoken from the burning bush. For the Pharisees, there could be no higher form of blasphemy, so they immediately picked up stones to kill Jesus.

[97] The offices of priest and king were human roles that were not intermixed. The king rules and, when necessary, puts people to death. The priest intercedes and helps to save people

CHAPTER 9

THE COVENANT RATIFIED, A SON, AND SODOM AND GOMORRAH

Abram has seen God do great things for him, but he still does not have a son, an heir who will father his promised descendants. God appears to Abram again and tells him that his reward will be great. But Abram is getting desperate and suggests that Eliezer, a servant born in his household, should be his heir. God replies that his heir will come from his own body; it will not be Eliezer. God has Abram look at the stars and tells him, "So shall your descendants be" (Gen. 15:5).

Scripture then makes a significant statement about Abram and the means of salvation: "Then he believed in the Lord, and He reckoned it to him as righteousness" (Gen. 15:6). Abram is seen as being righteous, fit for God's kingdom, not because his behavior warrants it but because he believes in God and what He says (Gen. 15:1–6). And the God that Abram believes in has been further revealed through Melchizedek. Abram's faith now includes direct inter-action with the divine King/Priest who will bring about peace and fellowship with God Most High.

Abram then asks God how he can know that he will receive the land that God has promised. God replies by enacting a suzerainty treaty ratification rit-ual that was common for covenants of that day.[98] Such a treaty was between a suzerain, or overlord, and a vassal, with terms dictated by the suzerain. God

---

(explained by Ken Olles in a Sunday school class). King Saul will be rejected by God when he tries to act as a priest and offers a burnt offering (1 Sam. 13:11–14). But the coming Savior will be a King/Priest of the order of Melchizedek (Heb. 6:19–20). He is qualified to fulfill both roles. He will be rejected by the Pharisees but not by God.

[98] See "Suzerain Treaties & the Covenant Documents of the Bible," notes from lectures by Dr. Meredith Kline; presented at Westminster Theological Seminary, Philadelphia, PA, accessed November 16, 2018, at www.fivesolas.com/suzerain.htm.

tells Abram to divide three animals and kill two birds. The normal treaty formality was for the parties making the covenant to walk together between the animal halves and the dead birds, each person signifying that if he failed to keep the agreement that he should be killed like the animals.

But as the dark night comes upon him, Abram does not walk down between the split animals. Instead, a smoking oven and a flaming torch pass between the pieces, signifying God's ratification of the treaty without Abram. The fulfillment of Abram's covenant does not depend on Abram but on God. He will keep the covenant and see that it is accomplished (Gen. 15:7–21).

*****

But Sarai remains barren. In her distress, she devises her own plan for Abram to have an heir. God had said the heir would come from Abram, but he did not mention Sarai. So Sarai tells Abram to take her handmaid, Hagar, and have a child with her, which was not uncommon in that day. Hagar conceives but then becomes contemptuous of Sarai. Sarai responds so harshly that Hagar flees into the wilderness. The angel of the LORD appears to Hagar and tells her to return to her mistress; she will have a son and should name him Ishmael. He also tells her what this son will be like: "He will be a wild donkey of a man, his hand will be against everyone, and everyone's hand will be against him" (Gen. 16:12).

Hagar bears this son when Abram is eighty-six years old, and he names him Ishmael (Gen. 16:15–16). His descendants will be the Arabs, and Sarai's plan will result in terrible animosity within her family and far beyond.

*****

Thirteen years later, God appears to Abram again and once more confirms the covenant. He changes Abram's name from Abram (exalted father) to Abraham (father of a multitude) and tells him that kings will come from him (Gen. 17:5–6). God then inaugurates the rite of circumcision as a sign for His covenant. Every newborn male is to be circumcised on the eighth day, as well as male servants, whether born into the family or purchased. Any male that is not circumcised is to be "cut off from his people; he has broken My covenant" (Gen. 17:14). God also changes Sarai's name to Sarah and tells Abraham that he will have a son with her (Gen. 17:1–16).

Abraham laughs in his heart because he is now ninety-nine years old, and Sarah is ninety and still barren. He expresses his concern to God and says, "Oh that Ishmael might live before Thee" (Gen. 17:18). But God tells him that although Ishmael will become a great nation, Sarah will bear the son of the covenant. He is to be named Isaac, and God will establish His everlasting covenant with him. Then Abraham and all the males in his household are circumcised (Gen. 17:17–27).[99]

Despite his new name, Abraham still has only one son, Ishmael. Visiting nomads, because of his name, would have asked Abraham how many children he had. It must have been embarrassing for the "father of a multitude" to have to say "one." But then, near the terebinth trees of Mamre, the LORD and two angels in the form of three men appear to Abraham as he sits in his tent door. The LORD reassures him that he will have a son by Sarah and will be the father of many nations. Sarah overhears this and laughs because she knows she is well past the time of childbearing. The LORD rebukes her for her lack of faith; nothing is too hard for Him.

The two angels continue on their way to Sodom and Gomorrah, but the LORD remains to tell Abraham about the exceeding wickedness of the men in those two cities. Abraham realizes that the LORD is going to destroy the area where Lot lives, and he pleads for the people living there. The LORD finally says that if He finds ten righteous men in Sodom and Gomorrah, He will not destroy the two cities. Then the LORD departs, and Abraham returns to his place (Gen. 18:1–33).

*****

The two angels arrive at Sodom in the evening and see Lot sitting in the city gate. This is where official business is conducted, which means that Lot, likely due to his wealth, has become a man of influence in that city. The angels say they will spend the night in the city square, but Lot insists that they stay in his house; he is well-aware of the dangers of Sodom.

Lot prepares a meal for his guests, but the homosexuals who dominate the city demand that Lot turn the angels over to them. The physical appearance of

---

[99] It appears that God appoints the particular sign of circumcision to continually remind Abraham and his male descendants that the fulfillment of the covenant depends on God, not on the means of procreation that Sarah and Abraham have endeavored to employ with Hagar (suggested by Ken Olles in a Sunday school class).

the angels has resulted in an aggressive homosexual rage in the growing crowd. Lot tries to dissuade the men of the city and even offers his two virgin daughters to them, but they attempt to break down his door, and the angels must pull him to safety.[100] The angels then strike the mob with blindness to keep them from breaking into Lot's house. They tell Lot to gather his family and "bring them out of this place" (Gen. 19:12). But the men engaged to marry his daughters do not want to leave, and Lot hesitates to depart.

At dawn, the angels take Lot, his wife, and his two daughters and set them outside the city. One of the angels warns Lot and his family to head for the mountains and not look back, but Lot is afraid. He asks the angels if he can go to the nearby city of Zoar, and the angels give him permission. Just when Lot is entering that city, the Lord rains down fire and brimstone on Sodom and Gomorrah. Lot's wife looks back, her heart is still in Sodom, and she is turned into a pillar of salt.

Abraham looks from a distance in the hill country and sees smoke rising over Sodom and Gomorrah and the entire plain. The lush green land that Lot had chosen is now a smoking furnace. There had not been even ten righteous men in the two cities, but for Abraham's sake, God has spared Lot and his daughters.

Lot has escaped to Zoar, but he is afraid to remain there. He heads for the mountains with his daughters and finds a cave where they can stay. Lot's daughters have lost their mother and their future husbands. They see no hope of ever being married, and they will need children to take care of them in their old age. In a desperate attempt to continue their line, they make Lot drunk and lie with him. They each have a son, sons who will become the forefathers of the Moabites and the Ammonites. These tribes will be long-term enemies of Abraham's descendants. Sexual sin, whether the homosexuality of the Sodomites or the incest of Lot's daughters, always has its consequences (Gen. 19:1–38).

*****

---

[100] Lot knew the homosexuals would not be interested in his daughters and was trying to make the crowd relent. He is called a righteous man (2 Pet. 2:7), something that could not have been said of him if he had truly meant to offer up his daughters.

After the destruction of Sodom and Gomorrah, Abraham moves his tents south to the area of Gerar, and Abraham, once again for his own protection, has Sarah say that she is his sister. Abimelech, the King of Gerar, takes Sarah into his house, but before he can touch her, God tells him in a dream that he is a dead man for taking another man's wife. God also afflicts Abimelech, his wife, and his female servants so that they cannot conceive children.

Like the pharaoh in Egypt, Abimelech is very angry with Abraham, but he is also very afraid of Abraham's God. He restores Sarah to Abraham and gives him sheep, oxen, male and female servants, and a thousand pieces of silver to show that Sarah has not been violated. Abimelech also tells Abraham that he is free to dwell wherever he wishes in his kingdom. Abraham prays to God and Abimelech and the women in his court are healed. Once again, God blesses Abraham in spite of his fear and deceit (Gen. 20:1–18).

Abraham has faith in God, but it is an inconsistent faith. We saw in Genesis 15:6 that "he believed in the Lord, and He reckoned it to him as righteousness." Abraham believes the promises that God has made to him and has met face-to-face with Melchizedek, the preincarnate Intermediary who will bring about peace and fellowship with God Most High. He understands that it is his line through which the Savior will come. But in times of danger and in times of waiting, he turns to his own devices with his wife, Sarah, being not only a willing helper but an instigator. The covenant God has made with Abraham is going to be fulfilled, not because Abraham is faithful but because God is faithful. He is the one who passed between the split animals.

CHAPTER 10

THE BIRTH OF ISAAC AND ABRAHAM TESTED

The time finally arrives for Sarah to bear the promised heir. She gives birth to a son, and he is named Isaac, meaning "laughter" or "he laughs." Abraham's laughter of amazement and Sarah's laughter of disbelief have been changed into the laughter of joy and fulfillment. God is accomplishing His purposes—Abraham has an heir.

After eight days, in accordance with the covenant, Abraham circumcises Isaac. The boy grows, and when he is weaned (probably two to three years later), Abraham makes a great feast. But Ishmael, who is now about sixteen years old and apparently jealous, scoffs at the joy Sarah and Abraham have in Isaac. Hagar had despised Sarah, and now her son is mocking Isaac, the promised heir. Sarah's anger is fiercely reignited, and she demands that the slave woman and her son be cast out of the camp. This is very difficult for Abraham. He loves Ishmael, and this seems unfair and dangerous for Hagar and her son. But God tells Abraham to listen to his wife (Gen. 21:1–13).

Early the next morning, Abraham takes bread and a skin of water and sends Hagar and Ishmael into the wilderness of Beersheba. They wander in the desert until their waterskin is empty, and then Hagar puts her son under a bush and moves a distance away because she does not want to see him die. And she "lifted her voice and wept" (Gen. 21:16). But God hears the voice of the lad and tells Hagar not to fear; he is going to make Ishmael a great nation. He opens her eyes to a well of water, and she fills the water skin and gives her son a drink; Hagar and her son are saved. "And God was with the lad, and he grew; and he lived in the wilderness and became an archer. And he lived in the Wilderness of Paran; and his mother took a wife for him from the land of Egypt" (Gen. 21:20–21).

Ishmael is the first son of Abraham by Hagar, the slave woman, and he becomes the father of the Arabs. Isaac is the second son of Abraham by Sarah, his wife, and his descendants are the Jews. They are half-brothers, and their descendants rightfully claim Abraham as their father. The animosity between them begins early in their lives and continues through their descendants for more than 4,000 years up to the present time.

After Hagar and Ishmael are sent out of the camp, Abraham remains in the territory of Abimelech who has told Abraham that he may dwell wherever he wishes. Abimelech and Phicol, his military commander, recognize that Abraham's God is with him in all that he does, and they fear the God of Abraham. Abimelech asks Abraham to make a covenant with him and swear to not deal falsely with him or his posterity.[101]

Abraham agrees, but only after Abimelech acknowledges that a well dug by Abraham is Abraham's possession. Abraham is living in the territory of a pagan king, but Abraham is the one who is dictating terms; he is the one who is ruling. He plants a tamarisk tree to commemorate the covenant and then calls on the name of the Lord. Abraham stays in the area of Gerar, the land of the Philistines, for many days (Gen. 21:22–32).

*****

After a number of years, Scripture says that "God tested Abraham and said to him, 'Take now your son, your only son,[102] whom you love, Isaac, and go to the land of Moriah; and offer him there as a burnt offering on one of the mountains of which I will tell you'" (Gen. 22:1–2). This is a stunning and dismaying pronouncement, but Abraham knows that God has spoken to him and that he must obey.

Early the next morning, he saddles his donkey, takes Isaac, two of his men, and split wood and travels to Moriah.[103] Abraham sees the sacrificial site from afar and tells his two servants to stay with the donkey while "I and the lad will go yonder; and we will worship, and return to you" (Gen. 22:5). Even though Abraham knows he must sacrifice his son, he also knows that Isaac is

---

[101] This is the first covenant in Scripture recorded between men. God had initiated the previous covenants outlined in Genesis.

[102] Abraham has his other son, Ishmael, but he has been sent away and Isaac is the "only" son through whom the promises will come.

[103] Mt. Moriah is where Salem is located, where Abram met Melchizedek, where David will rule in Jerusalem, and where Solomon will eventually build the Temple.

the son of promise and that somehow he will live. So he says to the servants, "We will return to you" (Gen. 22:3–5).

Abraham takes the wood and lays it upon Isaac who is now old enough to carry such a burden. He takes fire and a knife, and he and Isaac start up the mountain. But Isaac questions his father, asking, "Behold, the fire and the wood, but where is the lamb for the burnt offering?" Abraham can only say, "God will provide for Himself the lamb for the burnt offering, my son" (Gen 22:7–8). Abraham's prophetic statement applies not just to his own son, Isaac, but eventually to God's own son, the Messiah.

The father and son continue their ascent until they come to the designated place; Abraham builds an altar and positions the wood on it. He then binds Isaac and lays him on the wood. Apparently, Isaac does not resist. He trusts his father, and his father is trusting God. Abraham stretches out his hand and raises the knife to slay his son. But before Abraham can strike the fatal blow, the angel of the LORD calls out to him, and Abraham says, "Here I am."

God says, "Do not stretch out your hand against the lad, and do nothing to him; for now I know that you fear God, since you have not withheld your son, your only son, from Me" (Gen. 22:9–12).

Abraham lifts his eyes and sees a ram caught in a thicket by its horns. He takes the ram and offers it as a burnt offering instead of his son. And he calls the place of his great testing, "The Lord Will Provide" (Gen. 22:13–14).

Then the Angel of the LORD calls to Abraham again and says in Genesis 22:16–18:

> "By Myself I have sworn," declares the LORD, "because you have done this thing, and have not withheld your son, your only son, indeed I will greatly bless you, and I will greatly multiply your seed as the stars of the heavens, and as the sand which is on the seashore; and your seed shall possess the gate of their enemies. And in your seed all the nations of the earth shall be blessed, because you have obeyed My voice."

Abraham's faith has become steadfast, and God repeats the promises to him. There could have been no greater test for Abraham. The necessity of sacrifice in the plan of redemption had been well established,[104] but now it has become an experiential as well as a prophetic reality for Abraham. He has known that the Savior, the Seed of the woman, is going to come through his line. He has believed God concerning the coming of this Son and the great blessings that he and his descendants will receive, and it has been counted to him as righteousness.

In the meeting with Melchizedek, Abraham encountered the divine Intermediary who will bring peace and righteousness for his people. But now he has been given an overwhelming preview of what the coming Savior will undergo and a glimpse of the emotions that his heavenly Father will experience when his own Son must be sacrificed. God had stayed Abraham's uplifted hand against his son, Isaac, but God will not stay His own hand against His own Son. He will let the blow fall in order to save sinners and have a righteous people for Himself.

Abraham's faith has not only become steadfast; it has been infused over the years with redemptive understanding. When Paul in New Testament times speaks of "the faith of Abraham" (Rom. 4:16), he is not speaking of a general belief in God but rather of a faith that has the content of Abraham's faith, hope in the Savior who provides fellowship with God Most High through blood sacrifice. Faith without such content is meaningless.

Scripture does not describe the emotions of Abraham and Isaac after their experience with God on the mountain. It simply says that they returned to their servants, went to Beersheba together, and "Abraham lived at Beersheba" (Gen. 22:19).

*****

Time passes, and Sarah, Abraham's beautiful wife, dies at the age of 127 years. It has been thirty-seven years since she bore Isaac. Abraham mourns and weeps for her (Gen. 23:1–2). She had lied to kings to protect Abraham. And although she had been willing to sacrifice herself for him, God had always protected her. She was with Abraham before he was called out of Ur of the Chaldeans and had shared all his hardships and experiences in Canaan. And, finally, she had borne him the promised heir when she was ninety years old.

---

[104] See Genesis 3:21, 4:3–4. Also, Abraham had been making sacrifices in the form of burnt offerings (Gen. 22:7).

After Abraham mourns for Sarah, he buys a field from the sons of Heth, a local family living near Hebron. The field has a cave and trees, and Abraham buries Sarah in the cave. He and his descendants have been promised all the land of Canaan, but so far, the only land Abraham owns is a burial plot for Sarah (Gen. 23:3–20).

*****

His wife has died, and Abraham is becoming advanced in age. He tells his oldest servant,[105] who rules over all of Abraham's possessions, that he must go back to Mesopotamia to Abraham's brother, Nahor, and find a wife for Isaac. He makes the servant swear that he will not choose a daughter of the Canaanites. Abraham apparently knows the ultimate fate of these immoral people, and he does not want the family line to be intermixed with them.

The servant takes ten camels and loads them with "a variety of good things" (Gen. 24:10), and he and his helpers begin the long 700-mile trek to Abraham's family living near the city of Haran (Gen. 24:1–10).[106]

The servant and his men complete the journey safely and stop outside the city of Abraham's brother. The servant has been concerned that he might not be able to persuade a suitable bride to leave Mesopotamia for the land of Canaan (Gen. 24:5)—convincing a young woman to leave her house and family in Mesopotamia for a tent and an unknown man in the wilderness of Canaan is a daunting assignment. He has the camels kneel down near the well outside the city where the women will come to draw water as evening approaches. The servant prays that the woman who offers him a drink, and then offers to water the camels also, will be the appointed bride for Isaac.

Before the servant finishes praying, Rebekah, the granddaughter of Nahor, approaches the well with her water jar. She is beautiful and unmarried. "No man had had relations with her" (Gen 24:16). After she fills her jar, the servant asks her for a drink. Rebekah is quick to comply and offers to draw water for the camels until "they have finished drinking" (Gen. 24:19); she is willing to do a great deal of work to take care of the thirsty animals.

---

[105] The servant is not named in this account, but it must have been his trusted helper, Eliezer. See p. 46 and Genesis 15:2.

[106] The camels could travel about twenty miles per day, so the journey will take approximately thirty-five days.

The servant watches her until she finishes watering the camels, and then he gives her a gold ring and two gold bracelets weighing a total of 10.5 shekels.[107] The servant is convinced that this is Isaac's bride. Rebekah tells him that her father is Bethuel, the son of Nahor, and that they have room for him to stay and also feed for the camels. The servant bows low and thanks God for bringing him to Abraham's family (Gen. 24:22–27).

Rebekah runs and tells her mother's household what has happened. When her brother, Laban, sees the ring and bracelets, he runs outside to see the servant. He invites him in and gives him and his men water to wash their feet. He feeds the camels and sets a meal before the servant. Rebekah's brother has seen not only the gold ring and gold bracelets but all the "good things" on the camels when he cared for them. This will incline Laban and his father toward a quick and affirmative answer when a possible marriage is proposed.

Before the servant eats, he tells Laban and Bethuel that the Lord has blessed Abraham and made him rich and that Abraham has sent him on this journey to find a wife for his son. He tells them about his prayer and his meeting with Rebekah. And then he asks them if they are going "to deal kindly and truly with my master" (Gen. 24:49). Without hesitation, and without consulting Rebekah, her brother and father agree that Rebekah should go with the servant and become the wife of Abraham's son. Then to demonstrate that it is not just about the gold and all the "good things" on the camels, they piously add "as the Lord has spoken" (Gen. 24:11–51).[108]

When the servant hears these words, he bows himself "to the ground before the Lord" (Gen. 24:52). He brings out "articles of silver and articles of gold and garments," and gives them to Rebekah; he also gives precious things to her brother and to her mother (Gen. 24:53). Then the servant and his men eat and drink and spend the night.

In the morning, the servant wants to start back to Canaan, but Rebekah's brother and mother ask if they can have ten days to spend with Rebekah. Once she leaves, they will never see her again. When the servant insists on departing,[109] they ask Rebekah what she wants to do. She says, "I will go" (Gen.

---

[107] Approximately 4.2 oz. At the Aug. 1, 2022, price of approximately $1,800/oz., a gift worth over $7,500.

[108] Rebekah's own future son, Jacob, will come to know how important riches are to her brother, Laban, pp. 64–66.

[109] The servant seems to understand that if he prolongs this painful time, the marriage agreement may become undone.

24:58). This is an amazing decision for a young woman who was likely no more than thirteen or fourteen years old. In those days, young girls were usually married as soon as they reached puberty. Rebekah will show herself to be a strong and determined woman in her dealings with Isaac and the twin sons she will eventually bear.

Rebekah, her nurse, and her maids mount the camels and follow the servant. They complete the long journey, and when they approach Abraham's tent in Canaan, they see Isaac walking in the field. Rebekah covers herself with her veil, a sign of modesty and respect, as she meets Isaac for the first time (Gen. 24:59–65).

"Then Isaac brought her into his mother Sarah's tent, and he took Rebekah, and she became his wife; and he loved her; thus Isaac was comforted after his mother's death" (Gen. 24:67).

*****

Abraham is getting old, but he obtains another wife and concubines and has more children.[110] As he approaches his last days, Abraham gives his riches to Isaac, except for some gifts to his new sons whom he sends away to the east, away from Isaac. Genesis 25:7–8 says that Abraham was 175 years old when he "breathed his last and died in a ripe old age, an old man and satisfied with life; and he was gathered to his people." Ishmael returns, apparently without incident, and he and Isaac bury Abraham in the cave near Hebron with his wife, Sarah. "And it came about after the death of Abraham that God blessed his son Isaac, and Isaac lived by Beer-lahai-roi" (Gen. 25:11).

*****

Ishmael lives another forty-eight years after the death of Abraham. He has a total of twelve sons who father twelve tribes, the ancestors of the Arabic people.[111] They settle from Havilah to Shur east of Egypt (Yemen today). Ishmael is 137 years old when he dies and is gathered to his people. The angel of the

---

[110] Abraham's second wife is named Keturah (Gen. 25:1–2). Jethro, a descendant of her son, Midian, will eventually be of benefit to Moses (Exod. 3:1, 18:5–27). Charles F. Pheiffer, Howard F. Vos, and John Rea, eds., *Wycliffe Bible Encyclopedia*, Vol. 1, (Chicago: Moody Press, 1976), 921.

[111] The Prophet Mohammed, who originates the religion of Islam, is a descendant of Ishmael.

Lord had told Hagar before Ishmael was born that he would be a wild donkey of a man and that his hand would be against every man and that every man's hand would be against him (Gen. 16:12). His descendants spread out through the Middle East and fulfill that prophecy throughout history, especially against Isaac's descendants who will become the nation of Israel (Gen. 25:17–18).

*****

We have gone into considerable detail in looking at Abraham's life for two reasons. The first is that he is the patriarch through whom the kingdom of God will come. God had told Adam and Noah to establish the kingdom, and they had failed. But God went much further with Abraham. He made a covenant with him and committed Himself to making Abraham a great nation. God is going to establish His kingdom through Abraham. He will be a great nation and a blessing to all the nations. But when he died, Abraham owned only his burial plot, yet he died "full" or "satisfied" with life (Gen. 25:8).

He had come to understand that the land which God had promised him and his descendants ultimately went far beyond Canaan. When the author of Hebrews reflects on Abraham's life, he says, "By faith he lived as an alien in the land of promise, as in a foreign land, dwelling in tents with Isaac and Jacob, fellow heirs of the same promise; for he was looking for the city which has foundations, whose architect and builder is God" (Heb. 11:9–10). "But as it is, they desire a better country, that is a heavenly one" (Heb. 11:16).[112] Abraham's kingdom is going to come, and it will endure, but it will not be the political kingdom that his descendants eventually desire and expect.

Secondly, it is important to see the human emotions and frailties associated with Abraham and his family. God's plan of redemption is worked out in the daily lives of ordinary sinful human beings (Acts 14:15; Jas. 5:7–8). Abraham's nature is the same as ours, even though God spoke directly to him in a way that He does not do with us today. Now that God has given us His

---

[112] Abraham was looking for a heavenly country. This disagrees with the Dispensational view that the promises to the nation of Israel, Abraham's descendants, are fulfilled in an earthly millennial kingdom. Also, as Paul makes clear, Jesus has broken down the dividing wall between Jews and Gentiles, making "both *groups into* one" (Eph. 2:14). He has reconciled "them both in one body to God through the cross" (Eph. 2:16). This seems to further negate the Dispensational concept of a separate destiny for the Jewish nation (Eph. 2:11–22). See pp. 247–251 for further discussion.

complete revelation in His Son and has recorded the Son's words and works in the Scriptures, it is no longer necessary for God to speak directly to individuals as He did with Abraham.

However, God continued to speak to Abraham's descendants, Isaac and Jacob, men with passions and failings just like Abraham. Scripture goes into great detail about their lives, but for our purposes, we have to briefly summarize their roles in the progress of the third repetition of the kingdom paradigm.

CHAPTER 11

Isaac's Sons—the Birthright and the Blessing

Isaac was forty years old when he married Rebekah (Gen. 25:20). He loves her, but like Sarah was for so long, Rebekah is barren. Isaac prays for his wife, and after twenty years, when he is sixty years old, Rebekah conceives (Gen. 25:26). But she is troubled because she can tell that there is a struggle going on within her. She inquires of the Lord, and He tells her, "Two nations are in your womb. And two peoples shall be separated from your body; And one people shall be stronger than the other; And the older shall serve the younger" (Gen. 25:23).

Rebekah gives birth to twin boys. The first son is "red all over like a hairy garment" (Gen. 25:25), so they call him Esau (hairy). When his brother is born, his hand grasps Esau's heel, so he is called Jacob (one who grabs the heel; supplanter or deceiver; Gen. 25:24–26). Isaac has been given two sons to carry on the line of Shem, but only one will inherit the promises made to Abraham.

The boys mature into very different young men. Esau becomes a skillful hunter, a man of the outdoors. But Jacob is a mild man, preferring to spend his time within the family tents. Isaac loves his strong son Esau who feeds him from his game; but Rebekah loves Jacob (Gen. 25:27–28), and the Lord has told her that the older shall serve the younger.

*****

Time passes, and a day comes when Esau returns from the field in a famished state to find that Jacob has cooked a stew. Esau is weary and impatient, and when he asks Jacob for some of his stew, Jacob sees an opportunity. He tells Esau that for his stew, he wants Esau to "first sell me your birthright" (Gen. 25:31). As the firstborn son, Esau's birthright gives him a double portion of the family's inheritance and makes him the presumptive heir of the covenant God had made with Abraham. But for Esau, his present need outweighs any future benefit, and he says, "Behold, I am about to die; so of what use then is the birthright to me?" (Gen. 25:32). He swears to Jacob and sells him his birthright for a bowl of lentil stew.

Scripture says that, "Thus Esau despised his birthright" (Gen. 25:34). The writer of Hebrews calls Esau a "godless person who sold his birthright for a single meal" (Heb. 12:16). He saw no value in the promises that God had made to Abraham, but his brother, Jacob, did. God works out his plan of redemption through the choices of human beings (Gen. 25:29–34).

*****

Isaac continues to live in Canaan, and his life mirrors the experiences of his father, Abraham. A famine comes, and Isaac moves his flocks to Gerar in the territory of King Abimelech, the same king who had taken Sarah when Abraham said she was his sister. God tells Isaac not to go to Egypt but to stay in the land of Gerar, the land of the Philistines. And He repeats the promises that He had made to Abraham; he will multiply Isaac's descendants like the stars of heaven, he will give them all this land, and his seed will be a blessing to all the nations because "Abraham obeyed My voice" (Gen. 26:5).

Isaac pitches his tents in Gerar, and Abimelech's men ask him about Rebekah because she is very beautiful. And like his father, to protect himself, Isaac says that she is his sister. But after a time, Abimelech looks out of his window and sees Isaac "caressing his wife, Rebekah" (Gen. 26:8). He summons Isaac and rebukes him for lying about his wife; he says one of his men might have taken Rebekah for himself and brought guilt upon Abimelech and his people. Abimelech is still very fearful of the God of Abraham. He tells all his people that if anyone touches Isaac or his wife, that person will be put to death (Gen. 26:6–11).

Isaac sows in the land and reaps a crop of a hundredfold. He prospers and becomes very rich with flocks and herds and a great number of servants. The Philistines become jealous, and they stop up the wells that Abraham had dug long ago. Abimelech then asks Isaac to move away from him, because "you are too powerful for us" (Gen. 26:16). So Isaac moves to the Valley of Gerar and finally is left alone; he digs his own wells and is able to prosper and flourish.[113]

---

[113] A well in that semiarid land was vital for supporting flocks and herds.

Abimelech sees Isaac's great prosperity, and as with Abraham, he wants Isaac to make a covenant to do him no harm. Isaac agrees. Like his father, Isaac is living in a land belonging to the descendants of Ham, but he is the one who is ruling (Gen.26:22–33).

God is blessing Isaac, but Esau causes another problem for him and Rebekah. After selling his birthright, he marries two Hittite women, descendants of Canaan living in the area. Esau is either unaware of or does not care about the curse that Noah had pronounced on Canaan. Genesis 26:35 says that these women "brought grief to Isaac and Rebekah."

*****

Isaac is getting old, and his eyes become "too dim to see" (Gen. 27:1). He believes his death is approaching, and he wants to give Esau his blessing. He asks Esau to make him a savory dish from his game so that he can bless him. But Rebekah overhears Isaac's request, and before Esau can return from his hunt, she prepares a meal, dresses Jacob in Esau's clothes, puts the skin of a young goat on Jacob's hands and neck, and has him take the food to Isaac. Isaac is suspicious but finally gives his blessing to Jacob, thinking he is Esau.[114]

Jacob had obtained his older brother's birthright for a bowl of stew and now has stolen his blessing. He is living up to his name. He is one who grasps the heel; he is a deceiver and a supplanter. Esau is dismayed when he returns from his hunt and learns what his brother has done. Isaac trembles at what has happened, but he cannot recall his blessing. Esau becomes so bitter that he decides to kill Jacob (Gen. 27:2–41).

When Rebekah hears about Esau's intentions, she moves to protect her favorite son. She asks Isaac to send Jacob to her brother, Laban, in Haran so that he might find a wife and not marry a Hittite woman like Esau's wives. Isaac agrees and sends Jacob away with the same promise that had been given to him and his father, Abraham; he asks God to bless Jacob, to multiply him, and give him and his descendants the land of Canaan (Gen. 27:42–28:5). Jacob is a deceiver, but he is the one through whom the kingdom will come.

When Esau learns that Jacob has been sent to Haran to find a wife, he realizes how much his own wives have displeased Isaac. He decides to go to Padan

---

[114] The blessing is a prayer and prophecy predicting prosperity and authority for the one blessed.

Aram, the area where Ishmael had settled, and he marries one of Ishmael's daughters (Gen. 28:6–9). Esau may have thought this would please his father, but marrying a granddaughter of the slave woman who was cast out of the camp just makes the division within the family more evident.

*****

Jacob begins the long trek to Haran and spends the first night in the open, sleeping with his head on a stone. He has a dream and sees a ladder reaching up to heaven with angels ascending and descending on it. The LORD stands above it and repeats the promises that he had made to Abraham and Isaac (Gen. 28:10–17).

The dream has a significant effect on Jacob. He vows that if he is able to complete his journey and successfully return to Canaan that the stone he has slept on and now sets up as a pillar will be Bethel (house of God) and that the LORD who had spoken to him would be his God. He pledges to give God a tenth of whatever God gives him (Gen. 28:10–22). Jacob is trying to bargain with God. If God blesses him, then Jacob will acknowledge him as his God. Jacob had been able to manipulate Esau and his father, but he will learn that he cannot bargain with the God of Abraham and Isaac. The LORD is Jacob's God whether or not He decides to bless him.

Jacob completes his journey to Haran, and as he approaches the city, he sees shepherds with their flocks around a well. They tell him that Laban's daughter, Rachel, will be bringing his sheep for water. Jacob waits for her, and when she arrives with the sheep, he rolls the stone from the well and waters the flock.[115] He then kisses Rachel, and while weeping, he tells her who he is. She runs and tells her father, and Laban comes and welcomes Jacob and brings him to his house (Gen. 29:1–14). Laban remembers when Abraham's servant had come for Rebekah many years earlier and had brought gold and many good things on camels.

Jacob stays with Laban for a month, but he has brought no camels with good things, so Laban asks Jacob what his wages should be (Gen. 29:14–15). Laban is still very concerned about money, and he is ready for Jacob to start working and earning his keep.

---

[115] Jacob sees not only a potential wife but also the sheep, a financial opportunity (Gen. 29:10).

Laban has two daughters, Rachel and her older sister, Leah. Leah is described as having weak eyes, but Rachel is "beautiful of form and face" (Gen. 29:17). Jacob has fallen in love with Rachel, and he says that he will work for Laban for seven years if he can then have Rachel for his wife. Laban agrees, so Jacob works with Laban's livestock, and the seven years pass quickly for Jacob because of his love for Rachel (Gen 29:18–20).

*****

When the seven years are completed, Jacob tells Laban that it is time for him to give him his wife. Laban gathers all the local men, and they have a wedding feast, which would have meant not only eating but drinking. Jacob perhaps drinks too much. He consummates the marriage, but when he wakes up in the morning, he is with Leah, not Rachel. He confronts Laban and demands answers, "Was it not for Rachel that I served you? Why then have you deceived me?" (Gen. 29:25).

Laban responds that it is not the practice in that place to give the younger daughter in marriage before the older. But he says that if Jacob will complete the week of celebration with Leah, he can also take Rachel as his wife—*if* he will then work another seven years for Laban. Jacob loves Rachel, so he agrees (Gen 29:21–27). Jacob, the deceiver, has been deceived. Laban has doubled the labor he will receive from Jacob from seven to fourteen years, he has gotten a husband for his older daughter with the weak eyes, and he has gotten Rachel married without having to pay for another wedding celebration. It is a good week for Laban.

In the space of seven days, Jacob has obtained two wives, but this does not make for a happy home life. Jacob loves Rachel, but like Sarah and Rebekah before her, she is barren. Jacob resents Leah, but she soon begins to have children. She gives birth to four sons in succession, and Rachel is very jealous. She tells Jacob, "Give me children, or else I die" (Gen. 30:1).

Jacob is helpless in this, and his anger burns toward Rachel. He says it is God "who has withheld from you the fruit of the womb" (Gen. 30:2). Jacob's household is filled with resentment and strife. Leah is unloved and Rachel is barren and no one is happy, including Jacob (Gen. 29:31–30:2).

Rachel decides to take things into her own hands, just as Sarah had done. She gives her maid, Bilhah, to Jacob as his wife. Bilhah has two sons, and Rachel feels vindicated. But when Leah sees that she is no longer having children, she gives her maid, Zilpah, to Jacob as his fourth wife. Leah is trying to win Jacob's affection by giving him sons. Zilpah delivers two sons, and Jacob has now fathered a total of eight sons. But then Leah begins to conceive again and has two more sons and a daughter, named Dinah. Jacob's family has grown to ten sons and a daughter, but he has no children with his beloved Rachel (Gen. 30:3–21).

More time passes, and finally, Genesis 30:22 says that, "God remembered Rachel, and God gave heed to her and opened her womb." She has a son and names him Joseph. Rachel says her reproach has been taken away, and she asks the Lord to give her another son.

*****

Jacob now has eleven sons and a daughter, and despite his complicated home life, he has made Laban very wealthy by the way he has managed his flocks and herds. When Jacob has completed his fourteen-year obligation to Laban, he decides that it is time to take his growing family back to Canaan, but Laban convinces him to stay in Haran by agreeing that Jacob can have all the spotted animals born to his sheep and goats. This would normally be only a small percentage of the animals, but Jacob manipulates the breeding cycles of the flocks, and whether it is his animal husbandry or the blessing of God, Jacob's animals increase far more than Laban's. As the years pass, he becomes exceedingly prosperous and accumulates large flocks as well as camels, donkeys, and male and female servants (Gen. 30:31–43).

Laban's sons become jealous, and Laban's attitude also changes. Jacob is outnumbered, and the greed in his father-in-law's family has become dangerous. He is concerned, and the Lord tells him to return to the land of his fathers. Rachel and Leah know that Laban has treated Jacob unfairly, and both women tell him to do what God has told him; their allegiance is with Jacob, not their father (Gen. 31:1–16).

*****

When Laban leaves for the countryside to shear his sheep, Jacob puts his wives and children on camels and, with his servants, begins driving all his livestock toward the land of Canaan. But before Rachel leaves, she steals her father's household idols.[116] With his combined families and all his animals, Jacob crosses the Euphrates River and sets his face toward the hill country of Gilead (Gen. 31:1–21).

Laban learns on the third day that Jacob has fled. Apparently, Laban's servants wanted Jacob and his family to escape safely and had delayed telling Laban about their departure. But Laban gathers his kinsmen and pursues Jacob. After seven days, Laban and his men catch up to him and his company in Gilead. Laban is very angry, but the previous night, God had spoken to him in a dream and had told him not to speak to Jacob "either good or bad" (Gen. 31:24). God has warned Laban not to harm Jacob.

Laban demands to know why Jacob has deceived him by leaving without giving him a chance to send Jacob away with joy and songs, without letting him "kiss my sons and my daughters?" (Gen. 31:27–28). And he wants to know why Jacob has stolen "my gods," the household idols.

Jacob responds that he was afraid Laban would take his daughters by force, and that if anyone is found with Laban's "gods," they "shall not live" (Gen. 31:30–32). Jacob does not know that Rachel has taken the household deities.

Laban searches Jacob's tent, the two maid's tents, and Leah's tent without finding the idols. He then enters Rachel's tent. She is sitting on the camel saddle in which she has hidden the idols. She asks her father to pardon her for not rising because "the manner of women is upon me" (Gen. 31:35). Laban searches her tent without finding his gods.

Jacob then angrily confronts Laban about his unfair treatment of him. He says that he has labored for Laban for twenty years, and his flocks have prospered, but Laban has not paid him fairly. Laban replies that the women are his daughters and the children are his children, and that all the flocks belong to him. But he realizes there is little he can do; his own daughters are against him, and he has been warned by God. He and Jacob make a covenant, and early the next morning, Laban rises, kisses his daughters and their sons, and returns to his home and possessions in Haran (Gen. 31:22–55).

*****

---

[116] The household idols would have been inherited by the family's primary heir. Rachel may have taken them to legitimize the ownership of all the possessions that Jacob was taking to Canaan, but it also seems that she was still involved in pagan practices (see Gen. 35:2).

Jacob continues his journey back to Canaan until he reaches the place where twenty years before, in a dream, he had seen angels on a ladder stretching up to heaven, the place he had called the house of God. The Lord does not speak to him as He had before, but the angels appear again. They are a needed reminder and an encouragement for Jacob because he now confronts a problem more serious than Laban. He will have to face his brother, Esau, who had planned long ago to kill him for taking his birthright and blessing.

Jacob sends messengers to Esau to let him know that he is coming with all his possessions and wishes to find favor in Esau's sight. The messengers return and say that Esau is coming to meet him with four hundred men. Jacob is afraid that he is going to be attacked, and he divides his family and livestock into two companies. If Esau strikes one group, the other may be able to escape.

Jacob then prays to the God of Abraham and Isaac. He is a humbler man than he was twenty years ago. He says he does not deserve the blessings God has given him; he had crossed the Jordan with only his staff, and now he has a large family and is rich with flocks and possessions. He asks God to deliver him from Esau, and he reminds God that He had told him to return to Canaan and had promised to bless him and make his descendants like the sand of the sea.

After his prayer, he prepares a gift for Esau, a gift that reveals just how wealthy Jacob has become. He tells his servants to take two hundred female goats and twenty male goats, two hundred ewes and twenty rams, thirty milk camels and their colts, forty cows and ten bulls, twenty female donkeys and ten foals, and to place them in separate droves to go ahead of him when he approaches Esau. Then he sends the women and children over the brook of Jabbok, and Jacob is left alone (Gen. 32:1–23).

That night, in a strange physical and spiritual encounter, Jacob wrestles with God. Luther has written about wrestling with God in the night watches, those spiritual struggles that every Christian experiences in dealing with sin and faith. But Jacob's encounter goes beyond this. He is fighting with God who is engaging him in the person of a man.

Jacob has prevailed in life by his own cunning. He had obtained Esau's birthright for a pot of stew and had deceived his father and stolen his brother's blessing. He manipulated the breeding cycles of Laban's flocks to increase his own share and, in his final confrontation with Laban, had credited his own efforts for the prosperity God had given him. Now he intends to pacify Esau with a huge gift. When he left Canaan twenty years earlier, he had bargained with God; if God would bless him and bring him back safely, then Jacob would acknowledge him as his God. Jacob has returned as a humbler man, but now God is going to deal with Jacob's self-sufficiency.

Jacob refuses to relent in this physical and spiritual wrestling match with God, so God touches his hip socket and puts it out of joint. With only one useful leg, Jacob has great pain and no leverage. Deprived of his natural strength, Jacob can only cling to his opponent. He cannot prevail, but he will not let God go. He says, "I will not let You go unless You bless me" (Gen. 32:26).

God asks Jacob his name. When he says Jacob, he is confessing that he is the deceiver, the one who grabs. God says that from now on, Jacob's name will be "Israel (*Prince with God*); for you have struggled with God and with men, and have prevailed" (Gen. 32:28).[117]

Jacob prevails not by overcoming God or by bargaining with Him but by clinging to Him and asking for His blessing.

In the morning, now limping after his struggle with God,[118] Jacob sees Esau coming with his four hundred men. Jacob's servants have already advanced with their droves of livestock. He next aligns his family, placing the two maids and their sons first, then Leah and her children, and finally Rachel with her son, Joseph. Then Jacob crosses the brook ahead of them and leads them to meet his brother, Esau (Gen. 32:24–33:3).

*****

Jacob bows down seven times as he approaches Esau and all his men; he does not know what his brother will do. But Esau runs to meet him, embraces him, falls on his neck, and kisses him, and they weep (Gen. 33:4).

Esau then turns to the women and children and says, "Who are these with you?" (Gen. 33:5). Jacob says they are the children that God has graciously given him. Each of the women then approaches with her children and bows down to Esau.

---

[117] Although Jacob has been renamed Israel, Scripture still uses the name Jacob most often. It is difficult to see any particular reason for which name is used. Eventually, his entire nation will be called Jacob as well as Israel. I have tried to be consistent with Scsripture in the use of the two names. For example, see Genesis 35:20–27; Psalm 78:5; Hosea 12:2.

[118] Genesis 32:32 says that God caused Jacob's hip muscle to shrink. This seems to be a permanent injury to remind Jacob with every step of his dependence on God's mercy (Gen. 32:31–32).

THE PARADIGM OF THE KINGDOM OF GOD

Esau asks about all the companies of animals that he has seen. When Jacob says that they are meant to find favor with him, Esau says that he has enough and that Jacob should keep them for himself. But Jacob insists until Esau accepts the extraordinary gift of livestock. Jacob is, in effect, admitting that he had stolen Esau's birthright and blessing and is offering recompense.

Esau wants Jacob to follow him back to his home in Seir. But Jacob says the children are weak and the flocks and herds are nursing, so he must move at a slow pace. Esau offers to leave some of his men with Jacob, but Jacob insists that it is not necessary. The reunion with his brother has gone better than he thought was possible, and he does not want to risk something happening that might revive old animosities.

Esau returns to Seir, and Jacob journeys to Succoth and builds himself a "house" and booths for his livestock (Gen. 33:17).[119] With the erection of these simple structures, Jacob is indicating his intention to remain in the land with his growing family. He has prevailed with Esau by the mercy of God (Gen. 33:3–17).

*****

After a time, Jacob returns to his tent and moves further into Canaan. He buys a parcel of land from the family of Hamor near the city of Shechem. This is where Abraham had built his first altar when he came to Canaan from Ur. Jacob erects an altar there and calls it "El Elohe Israel," literally *God, the God of Israel*. Jacob is acknowledging that the God of Abraham and Isaac is also his God, and he uses the name, Israel, that he had been given when he wrestled with God (Gen. 33:18–20).

*****

Jacob is back in the land of Canaan with his large family and all his live-stock. God has prospered him and brought him safely back to his homeland. Years pass, and his older sons become grown men; there has been some peace for the family, but it does not last.

Dinah, Jacob's only daughter by Leah, decides to visit the young women of Shechem. An unsupervised visit by a young woman is not safe or permitted

---

[119] These would have been very simple buildings, perhaps even "lean-to" type constructions.

in that society; that it occurs reveals the dysfunction remaining in Jacob's family. Shechem, the son of Hamor and the prince of Shechem, takes Dinah and lies with her. He has violated Dinah,[120] but he falls in love with her, and he and his father meet with Jacob to propose a marriage.

Jacob's sons are furious when they learn what has happened, but they listen to Hamor's plea for peaceful coexistence and a marriage between his son and Dinah. The brothers pretend to agree, but only if Hamor and all his men become circumcised. Hamor and his son accept this demand; they return to their city and convince all the men to undergo circumcision. Then, three days later, when they are in pain and somewhat disabled, Dinah's brothers by Leah, Simeon and Levi, attack the city with their swords, kill all the men, and take their women, children, livestock, and possessions.

Jacob is incensed with his violent sons; he is afraid that the Canaanites and Perizzites will join together to destroy him and his family. But the brothers say, "Should he treat our sister like a harlot?" (Gen. 34:1–31). Jacob's family is back in turmoil and danger.

*****

God directly intervenes again in Jacob's life. Jacob has not been able to control his family of four wives and four sets of children. God tells him to take his family back to Bethel (house of God). He is to return to the place where God first appeared to him in a dream when he fled from Esau, where the LORD had stood above the ladder from heaven and repeated to him the promises made to Abraham and Isaac. Jacob understands that changes must be made; he tells everyone to put away their foreign gods. The family idols that Rachel had stolen[121] have become influential in the family. Jacob had not dealt with this spiritual problem, perhaps due to his love for Rachel. He tells his family to purify themselves and change their garments. They are going to Bethel, and Jacob is going to build an altar there (Gen. 35:1–7).

The family gives all their idols to Jacob, and he hides them under a terebinth tree. Then they journey to Bethel where he builds the altar. God appears to Jacob again and reaffirms that his name is now "Israel." God also repeats the

---

[120] Dinah was only about fourteen or fifteen at this time. See *The Ryrie Study Bible*, ed. Charles Caldwell Ryrie, (Chicago: Moody Press, 1978), 62, n. on 34:3.

[121] Genesis 31:19; see pp. 65–66.

promises that He had made to Abraham and Isaac. And this time, He begins with the words He had said to Adam and Noah, "Be fruitful and multiply... And the land which I gave to Abraham and Isaac, I will give it to you, And I will give the land to your descendants after you" (Gen. 35:11–12).

Jacob then sets up a pillar to commemorate the place where God had spoken to him the first time, and now, again, many years later. Jacob has gone to the "house of God," and the promises have been repeated and confirmed.[122]

*****

Jacob journeys from Bethel toward Ephrath as he continues to pasture his flocks and herds. Rachel had prayed for another son, and she conceives again in her old age. She goes into hard labor near Ephrath (Bethlehem) and delivers a son, but she dies shortly after he is born. As her soul is departing, she names the boy Ben-Oni (son of my sorrow), but Jacob calls him Benjamin (son of the right hand). Jacob buries his beloved Rachel near Bethlehem (Gen. 35:16–20). She has given him two sons, Joseph and Benjamin, whom Jacob will love and favor above all his other sons.

Jacob now has twelve sons who will form the twelve tribes of Israel. The sons of Leah are Reuben (Jacob's firstborn), Simeon, Levi, Judah, Issachar, and Zebulun; the sons of Rachel are Joseph and Benjamin; the sons of Bilhah, Rachel's maidservant, are Dan and Naphtali; and the sons of Zilpah, Leah's maidservant, are Gad and Asher (Gen. 35:23–26).

Jacob has a large family that is difficult to manage. His spiritual leadership has been severely lacking as evidenced by the presence of foreign idols in the family, the violation of Dinah, and the deception and revenge of her violent brothers. After Jacob buries Rachel, another incident occurs which shows the depth of the family's problems. Reuben, the oldest son, the firstborn of Leah, lies with Bilhah, his father's concubine. Jacob hears about it but apparently does not confront Reuben (Gen. 35:21–22).

*****

---

[122] God again repeats His promises to Jacob, just as he repeats His promises to us in the Scriptures. God knows our weaknesses and lack of faith and gives us ongoing reminders and reassurances through His Word.

Jacob's father, Isaac, is growing very old, and Jacob goes to Hebron to visit him. Isaac has lived 180 years and has reached the end of his life. He breathes his last, "an old man of ripe age" (satisfied with life), like his father, Abraham (Gen. 25:8). The death of Isaac's wife, Rebekah, is not recorded, perhaps because of her deceit in helping Jacob obtain Esau's blessing.[123] Together, Esau and Jacob bury their father, Isaac, in the cave with Abraham and Sarah (Gen. 35:27–29). Many things have changed since Jacob fled to Haran many years ago, one of the most important being that Esau no longer intends to kill Jacob.

---

[123] Although Rebekah's death is not mentioned, Genesis 49:31 reveals that she was buried in the cave near Mamre with Abraham, Sarah, and Isaac.

CHAPTER 12

JOSEPH IN EGYPT

Joseph, Jacob's eleventh son and the firstborn of Rachel, reaches the age of seventeen and is helping tend the family's flocks with his half-brothers. When he returns to his father, he gives him a bad report about his brothers. Israel has already shown that he loves Joseph more than his other sons and has even made a special coat of many colors for him. The brothers are jealous of Joseph and have come to hate him intensely, and now after his critical account, they cannot speak peaceably to him (Gen. 37:1–4).

Joseph then has two dreams. In the first, he and his brothers are binding sheaves in the field. His sheaf stands upright, and his brother's sheaves bow down to his sheaf. Joseph reveals his dream to the brothers, and they say, "Are you actually going to reign over us?" (Gen. 37:8). They hate him even more for what he has told them (Gen. 37:5–8).

In the second dream, the sun, the moon, and eleven stars bow down to Joseph. He tells his father and also his brothers. His father says, "Shall I and your mother and your brothers actually come to bow ourselves down before you to the ground?" (Gen. 37:10). Joseph's brothers continue to envy and hate him, but Israel keeps in mind what his favorite son has dreamed (Gen. 37:9–11).

*****

After a time, Israel sends Joseph to check on his brothers and the animals they are pasturing near the trade route that runs from the northeast down to Egypt. The brothers see Joseph coming in the distance, and they decide to kill him. But Reuben, the oldest, convinces his brothers to not shed blood; instead, they throw Joseph into a dry well from which he cannot escape and then callously begin eating their noon meal. When a camel caravan carrying spices approaches, Judah tries to save Joseph by suggesting that they sell him into slavery. The brothers agree and get twenty pieces of silver from the spice traders who take their newly acquired slave and continue on to Egypt. The brothers cannot imagine how drastically this episode will affect their lives in the future.

They take Joseph's coat of many colors, kill a young goat, and dip the coat in its blood. Then they take the coat to Israel who recognizes it and concludes that a wild beast has killed and devoured his favorite son. Israel tears his clothes, mourns for many days, and cannot be comforted. Meanwhile, the spice traders reach Egypt and sell Joseph to an official named Potiphar, an officer of Pharaoh and captain of the guard (Gen. 37:12–36).

*****

After Joseph is sold, years pass, and another unusual episode occurs that reveals the ongoing problems in Jacob's family. Some of Jacob's sons have become old enough to have adult children. Judah, Leah's fourth son, has married a Canaanite woman and now has two grown sons. He takes a woman named Tamar to be the wife of his eldest son, Er. Scripture does not elaborate but simply says that Er was an evil man and that the Lord took his life (Gen. 38:7). In accordance with the practice of the time, Judah tells his second son, Onan, to marry Tamar and raise up an heir for his brother.[124] But Onan refuses to help Tamar conceive; this displeases the Lord, and He takes Onan's life also (Gen. 38:1–10).

Judah still has a younger son, Shelah, who is now obligated to raise up heirs with Tamar. But Judah, after the death of two sons, is reluctant to have Shelah marry this woman. He tells Tamar to wait until his son is older, and she returns to her father's house. But as time goes by, Tamar realizes that Judah does not intend to let Shelah marry her. Knowing that the deaths of her husbands were not her fault, she waits for a chance to vindicate herself.

More time passes, and Judah's wife dies. When the period for mourning has been completed, he decides to go to Timnah to visit his sheepshearers. Tamar knows his route and sits beside the road posing as a veiled prostitute. Judah does not realize who she is and wants to procure her services but has nothing to give her. Tamar accepts his signet, cord, and staff as a pledge for

---

[124] This is the first mention in the Bible of this custom that developed in clan societies because of a strong resistance to marriage outside the tribe. It becomes codified in Israel under Moses (Deut. 25:5) and is eventually called levirate marriage (from the Latin *levir*, meaning husband's brother).

future payment of his debt.[125] When Judah later sends a man with a young goat to redeem his belongings, the "prostitute" is nowhere to be found.

Tamar becomes pregnant by Judah. When he learns that she is with child, he calls for her to be burned. But when she is brought out, she has Judah's possessions and says, "I am with child by the man to whom these things belong" (Gen. 38:25).

Judah acknowledges what has happened and says that Tamar is more righteous than he because he did not let her marry his third son. He does not have relations with her again, and she gives birth to twin boys, Perez, the firstborn, and Zerah, the second.

Jacob on his deathbed will prophesy that it is through Judah's line that the Messiah will come. And that lineage will pass through Perez, Tamar's firstborn son (Ruth 4:18–22; Matt. 1:3; Luke 3:33). As we have seen before, God works out His plan of redemption through sinful human beings,[126] and Judah is one of them. He should not have married a Canaanite woman nor had relations with Tamar. But he has saved Joseph from the pit and acknowledged his guilt concerning his daughter-in-law. As we will eventually see with King David, repentance is an essential step in having a right relationship with a holy God. Judah will begin to play a leading role among his brothers.

*****

Joseph becomes a faithful and diligent worker for Potiphar, the official who has purchased him in Egypt. He finds favor in the man's eyes, becomes his attendant, and begins to manage Potiphar's affairs both in his house and in the field. The Lord blesses Potiphar because of Joseph, and Potiphar, recognizing that God is with Joseph, eventually puts him in charge of all that he has. His wife takes notice of the gifted young slave and tries to seduce him when her husband is away. Joseph flees, but she holds on to his coat and then accuses him of sexual advances when Potiphar returns.

Potiphar burns with anger, and he puts Joseph in the king's prison. The fact that he does not have Joseph executed may be due to his previous affection

---

[125] These articles identified Judah, like leaving a credit card and driver's license today.

[126] Ultimately, the plan of Redemption culminates with Jesus Christ, the God-Man, who has no sin.

for him, but Potiphar also likely knows that his wife is not completely innocent in this matter (Gen. 39:1–20).

*****

Although Joseph is in prison, God is still with him, and he again finds favor, this time with the prison warden. The warden puts him in charge of the prisoners and their affairs; he trusts Joseph because God gives him success in whatever he does.

As time passes, the reigning pharaoh becomes angry with his chief cup-bearer and chief baker. These are critical positions because these royal servants must not only provide the ruler with excellent food and drink, they must also protect him from enemies who would poison him. The two men are turned over to the captain of the guard for imprisonment, and he assigns them to Joseph's care.

Eventually, both these men have dreams and are dejected by what they have seen. Joseph interprets their dreams and tells the cupbearer that he will be restored to his position within three days and asks him to remember him and mention his unfair imprisonment to Pharaoh. But Joseph tells the baker that within three days, Pharaoh will execute him. On the third day, on Pharaoh's birthday, both dreams come true. The baker is hanged, and the cupbearer returns to his former position. But the cupbearer forgets about Joseph (Gen. 39:21–40:1–23).

*****

Two years pass, and Pharaoh has two dreams. He sees seven sleek fat cows come out of the Nile, which are eaten by seven gaunt and ugly cows. He then has a second dream in which seven healthy heads of grain on a single stalk are swallowed by seven thin and scorched heads. Pharaoh is troubled and sends for the magicians and wise men of Egypt. When they cannot interpret the dreams, the cupbearer remembers Joseph and tells Pharaoh about the "young Hebrew" in prison who could interpret dreams.

Pharaoh sends for him and God gives Joseph the interpretation. The two dreams mean the same thing: seven years of great abundance followed by seven years of famine. Joseph tells Pharaoh that he should put a man in charge of storing grain in storehouses during the good years so that there will be food in the famine years.

Pharaoh also sees that the spirit of God is with Joseph and puts him in charge of carrying out this plan, giving him authority over Egypt second only to himself. He puts his signet ring on Joseph, dresses him in royal clothes, and has him ride in a chariot as his second-in-command. He assigns Joseph the name Zaphenath-Paneah[127] and gives him Asenath, the daughter of the priest of On, to be his wife.

Joseph is thirty years old when he enters the service of the king of Egypt. He has amazing power and travels throughout the land, implementing his plan for storing the harvest of grain. As Pharaoh's dreams have foretold, the land produces abundantly for seven years, and Joseph stores grain beyond measure. During this time, two sons are born to him, first Manasseh and then Ephraim[128] (Gen. 41:1–40). Joseph is adapting to his new life.

The seven abundant years end, and the seven years of famine begin. There is hunger in all the nations, except in Egypt. But as the drought continues, the Egyptians also begin to starve, and they cry out to Pharaoh. He tells them, "Go to Joseph; whatever he says to you, you shall do" (Gen. 41:55). Joseph opens the storehouses and sells grain to the Egyptians. And then, all the countries "came to Egypt to buy grain from Joseph, because the famine was severe in all the earth" (Gen. 41:41–57). Joseph is feeding the Egyptians and the other nations, and he is making Pharaoh very rich.

---

[127] Probably meaning "The God Speaks and Lives;" see n. on Genesis 41:45, in *Nelson's NKJV*, 80.
[128] *Manasseh* means "making forgetful," and *Ephraim* means "fruitfulness," names reflecting Joseph's changing circumstances; see ns. on Genesis 41:51–52 in *Ryrie Study*, 74–75.

CHAPTER 13

ISRAEL AND THE MOVE TO EGYPT

Israel and his family are not spared from the famine in Canaan. He sends ten of his sons to Egypt to buy grain, but he keeps Benjamin with him. He is afraid that he will lose Benjamin as he lost Joseph, and he cannot bear losing Rachel's last son.

When the brothers reach Egypt, they must appear before Joseph to buy grain. They do not recognize him,[129] but Joseph recognizes them, and he remembers the dreams he had about them. He does not tell them who he is but instead accuses them of being spies (Gen. 42:1–12). Joseph intends to see if they have had a change of heart since they threw him in the pit and sold him to the spice caravan.

Joseph goes through a long process of testing his brothers. They want to convince him that they are not spies and mention their father and youngest brother left behind in Canaan. Joseph tells them that they can buy grain, but to prove they are not spying, they must leave one brother in Egypt and bring the youngest brother with them when they return for more grain. The brothers have no choice except to agree, but they discuss their dilemma and conclude they are being punished for the way they treated Joseph long ago.

They do not know that Joseph can understand their language, and when he hears what they are saying, he is overcome with emotion and turns away and weeps. But then he takes Simeon as a prisoner and binds him before their eyes (Gen. 42:13–24).

---

[129] Joseph was seventeen when his brothers sold him to the spice traders (Gen. 37:2). He became a ruler under Pharaoh when he was thirty (Gen. 41:46) at the beginning of the seven good years. Those seven years and two years of the famine time have passed when Joseph's brothers come to buy food (Gen. 45:6). Joseph's brothers have not seen him for twenty-two years.

The brothers begin the journey back to Canaan, but Joseph has had his steward put the money they paid for grain back in their sacks. When they discover the money, they are very afraid, but they continue to Canaan and tell their father all that has happened. Jacob is dismayed that Simeon has been kept a prisoner, but he does not want to send Benjamin with his brothers when they make their next trip to Egypt. Nonetheless, when the Egyptian grain is consumed, he has to change his mind. He sends Benjamin along with his brothers when they return to Egypt for more grain. They take double the money and gifts[130] for the Egyptian "man."

When the brothers arrive in Egypt, and Joseph sees that the brothers have brought Benjamin with them, he tells his steward to prepare them a noon meal. They are still very concerned about the money, but the steward tells them that he put the money in their sacks of grain. He brings Simeon out to them, and the brothers eat in Joseph's presence. They are amazed when he seats them in order of their ages. When the food is served, Benjamin is given five times as much as the other brothers. They eat and drink freely before Joseph, but he still does not tell them who he is (Gen. 42:25–43:34).

The next morning, all the brothers are sent away with their donkeys and more grain, but once again, Joseph has his steward place the grain money back in their sacks. He also has the steward place his silver drinking cup inside Benjamin's sack of grain. Before the brothers get very far, Joseph sends his steward after them, and when he overtakes them, he demands to know why they have taken his master's silver cup. They deny stealing anything and say that if the cup is found in anyone's possession, that person will die, and all of them will become Joseph's slaves. The cup is found in Benjamin's sack, and the brothers return to Joseph's house where he is waiting for them.

Judah speaks for the brothers, even though three of them are his elders. He says that he and his brothers cannot clear themselves, that "God has found out the iniquity of your servants" (Gen. 44:16). They are ready to become Joseph's slaves. They had not stolen the money nor the silver cup, but the brothers have come to realize that they are guilty of an even greater crime and deserve punishment from God. Without realizing it, Judah is confessing their sin against Joseph to Joseph himself.

---

[130] "[a] little balm and a little honey, aromatic gum and myrrh, pistachio nuts and almonds" (Gen. 43:11).

Joseph says that he will keep only one slave, the one with whom his cup was found. Judah knows that Jacob cannot bear to lose Benjamin, so he approaches Joseph and asks Joseph to let him take his brother's place.

It is through Judah's line that the Messiah will come. Rueben, the oldest son, had disqualified himself by lying with his father's concubine. The next two sons, Simeon and Levi, had deceitfully killed the men of Shechem. Judah is next in line, and he reveals the heart of the coming Messiah when he is willing to bear his brother's punishment.

Joseph can no longer restrain himself. He sends everyone away except for his brothers, weeps so loudly that the Egyptians hear it, and cries out, "I am Joseph! Is my father still alive?" (Gen. 45:3). His brothers are too dumbfounded to answer him; they are dismayed in his presence.

Joseph has seen his brothers acknowledge their sin against him, especially in the case of Judah. He asks them to come near to him and tells them not to grieve over selling him into slavery. He says that God has sent him before them to preserve their lives because the famine will continue for another five years. Joseph explains that Pharaoh has made him ruler over all of Egypt. They should hurry and go get his father and their families with their flocks and herds and possessions and come to Goshen in Egypt so they can survive the years of famine. He falls on Benjamin's neck, and they weep; then he kisses his other brothers, and they also weep and talk.

Pharaoh hears that Joseph's brothers have come, and he directs him to send for his entire family in Canaan. He says to send carts to carry all of their women, children, and possessions. They will live in the best land of Egypt. Joseph gives his brothers provisions and changes of clothes for their journey, but to Benjamin, he gives three hundred pieces of silver and five changes of clothes.

When Jacob's sons arrive back in Canaan and tell him about Joseph, he is stunned because he cannot believe what they are saying (Gen. 45:26). But when he hears the words of Joseph and sees the carts he has sent, Jacob's spirit revives, and he says, "I will go and see him before I die" (Gen. 45:28, 44:1–45:28).

Although the famine is widespread, it has a specific purpose for Jacob. Dinah's violation, the brutal revenge taken by her brothers, the influence of foreign gods, Rueben's incest, and the fact that Joseph's brothers were willing to commit murder show that he has failed to raise a godly family. Judah's marriage to a Canaanite woman means that Jacob's children are beginning to assimilate with idolatrous people. Jacob has been unable to establish a righteous family in

Canaan, and he is being removed from the land. He is being chastised, but his lineage is also being preserved. The Egyptians will isolate the family in the land of Pharaoh, and they will be able to be fruitful and multiply.

*****

Israel takes all that he has and begins the journey to Egypt. He stops at Beersheba to offer sacrifices where God speaks to him again in the visions of the night. God tells Israel not to be afraid to go to Egypt because He will make him a great nation there and bring him up again. God says that "Joseph will close your eyes" (Gen. 46:4); his favorite son, the firstborn of his beloved Rachel, will be with him at his death.

After his sacrifices, Israel sends Judah ahead to Egypt so Joseph can direct the family into the area of Goshen.[131] Israel and his large clan (seventy males plus wives and daughters, a total of at least a hundred people) make their way to Egypt. When they arrive in Goshen, Joseph comes in his chariot to meet his father. He falls on Israel's neck and weeps a long time (Gen. 46:1–28).

*****

Joseph gathers five of his brothers to appear before Pharaoh, who grants their request to dwell in the land of Goshen. He also tells Joseph to put his brothers in charge of his own livestock. The land of Goshen is a double blessing for Israel's family since it provides rich grazing for their flocks and separation from the Egyptians who consider every shepherd to be "loathsome" (Gen. 46:34).[132] Israel and his family have room to grow and prosper away from the physical and spiritual dangers of Egyptian society.

Joseph then presents his father to Pharaoh, and the monarch asks Jacob his age. Jacob replies that he is 130 years old, and his years have been evil and few when compared to those of his father's.[133] He blesses Pharaoh, an act only appropriate for one who is a superior. Jacob is living in Pharaoh's nation, but

---

[131] Goshen was a fertile region in the Nile Delta that provided good grazing for livestock.

[132] Since the Egyptians kept animals, this is likely the opinion of refined Egyptians and the royal court. These feelings would be more pronounced toward foreign shepherds.

[133] Abraham died when he was 175, Isaac when he was 180. Jacob seems to be feeling the weight of God's judgment in removing him from Canaan.

through his son, Joseph, he is the one who is ruling in the land of Egypt (Gen. 47:1–12).

*****

Joseph settles his father and brothers in the best land of Egypt and provides them food, but the famine remains severe in the rest of the nation as well as Canaan. The Egyptians buy grain from Joseph until their money is gone; then they must trade their livestock, lands, and labor for food. Joseph takes their possessions, but the Egyptian people are grateful that he has kept them alive. Joseph has both saved and plundered them. He has given Pharaoh control over everything in Egypt, except for Israel, his family, and their possessions (Gen. 47:13–26).

*****

Israel and his family dwell in Egypt, in Goshen, and Genesis 47:27 says, "and they acquired property in it and were fruitful and became very numerous." Jacob is seeing God fulfill the first of the promises. But as he grows old, he realizes, as did Abraham and Isaac, that the other promises are not going to be fulfilled in his lifetime. Yet he knows that his family will eventually inherit Canaan, and he wants to be there when they enter the promised land. Seventeen years pass, and as Israel approaches his last days, he makes Joseph swear that he will take his body back to Canaan after his death (Gen. 47:28–31).

Jacob soon becomes seriously ill, and Joseph, with his two sons, goes to see him. Jacob repeats for Joseph the promises that God had made to him, and then he blesses Joseph's sons. He tells them the younger will become greater than the older, and they will be given an equal portion with his other sons. Joseph has saved the entire family, and his descendants will have an extra share of the inheritance when the nation arrives in the promised land (Gen. 48:21–22).

Jacob then calls all twelve of his sons to him to tell them what will befall them in the "last days"[134] (Gen 49:1–28). He gives a prophecy for each son beginning with Rueben, the firstborn. Rueben is told that he is as unstable as water and will not excel because he went up to his father's bed. The cruelty of

---

[134] Jacob's prophecy goes far beyond the immediate lives of his twelve sons.

Simeon and Levi in killing the men of Shechem is recalled, and they are told they will be scattered in Israel.

Judah is next, and it is through his line that the Messiah will come. In Genesis 49:8–10, Jacob tells Judah that:

> Your brothers shall praise you; Your hand shall be on the neck of your enemies; Your father's sons shall bow down to you. Judah is a lion's welp; From the prey, my son, you have gone up. He couches, he lies down as a lion: And as a lion, who dares rouse him up? The scepter shall not depart from Judah, Nor the ruler's staff from between his feet, Until Shiloh comes,[135] And to Him shall be the obedience of the people.

This prophecy will find a temporary fulfillment in Judah's descendants, King David, and his son, Solomon, but its ultimate fulfillment will be with the Messiah's reign in the final kingdom, the new heaven and earth.

The other eight brothers are given prophecies fitting their characters and the roles their families will play when they finally enter the land promised to their fathers (Gen. 49:13–28). Israel then charges his sons to bury him in Canaan in the burial plot with Abraham and Sarah, Isaac and Rebekah, and Leah, his first wife. After Jacob finishes commanding his sons, he breathes his last and is gathered to his people (Gen. 49:33).

Joseph falls on his father's face and weeps over him. He directs the physicians to embalm Jacob, and the Egyptians mourn seventy days for him.

After the days of mourning, Joseph asks Pharaoh to let him go to Canaan to bury his father. Pharaoh not only permits Joseph and his family to go, he sends his servants and all the elders of Egypt with chariots and horsemen. It is an amazing funeral procession back to Canaan, and the Canaanites take note of the mourning for Israel. His sons obey their father's command and bury him in the cave with Abraham and Isaac in the cave that Abraham had bought for Sarah's burial. The three patriarchs had each been promised the land of Canaan, a kingdom, but so far, they only possess the cave in which they are

---

[135] Interpreters have difficulty with the word *Shiloh*, but it seems to mean "the sent" or "seed," and most agree that it indicates the Messiah.

buried. If God's promises are true, there must be a resurrection.[136] After Israel is buried, Joseph, his brothers, and everyone who had accompanied them return to Egypt (Gen. 50:1–14).

*****

When Joseph's brothers arrive back in Goshen, they begin to fear that Joseph will take revenge on them now that their father is gone. They send messengers to Joseph, asking him to forgive their trespass and sin against him. Joseph weeps when he hears their words confessing their guilt (Gen. 50:15–17).

The brothers come in person, bow down to Joseph, and declare they are his servants. Joseph's dreams of long ago have become reality. He tells his brothers to not be afraid; he is not in the place of God and will not take revenge on them. He says, "You meant evil against me, but God meant it for good, in order to bring about this present result, to preserve many people alive" (Gen. 50:20). God is going to preserve the line of the Messiah. Joseph's entire life is a testimony to the kind purpose and providence of God. He tells his brothers that he will provide for them and their little ones.

Joseph lives in Egypt and keeps his brothers and their families safe in the fertile land of Goshen. He reaches the age of 110 and sees his grandchildren and great-grandchildren on his knees. As he is approaching death, he tells his brothers that "God will surely take care of you, and bring you up from this land to the land which he promised on oath to Abraham, to Isaac, and to Jacob" (Gen. 50:24). Joseph then has the sons of Israel swear an oath, saying, "God will surely take care of you, and you shall carry up my bones from here" (Gen. 50:25).

Like his father, Jacob, Joseph wants to be in the covenant land when it is possessed by his family; he wants to be in the coming kingdom. Joseph dies, and they embalm him and put him in a coffin in Egypt (Gen. 50:22–26).

*****

---

[136] Jesus will debate the Sadducees who did not believe in a resurrection, and say, "Have you not read what was spoken to you by God, saying, '*I am the God of Abraham, the God of Isaac, and the God of Jacob*'? God is not the God of the dead, but of the living" (Matt. 22:31–32; Exod. 3:6).

Genesis ends with Joseph's family promising to take his bones with them when they journey to the land promised to their fathers.[137] It has taken many years and three generations of patriarchs, but Abraham's descendants have begun to fulfill the first of the promises given to him, the first directive of the kingdom mandate. They are being fruitful and they are multiplying. But as time passes, the descendants of Israel become so numerous that the Egyptians begin to consider them a threat. And that is where the book of Exodus begins.

---

[137] The first eleven chapters of Genesis describe creation and the primeval history of human beings. The rest of the book is focused on the choosing of Abraham and his descendants as the line through which the Savior comes. God's sovereignty over the universe and his providence and election in human history are clearly manifested in the first book of the Bible.

CHAPTER 14

ISRAEL'S ENSLAVEMENT AND THE CALL OF MOSES

Centuries pass after Joseph's death, and the Israelites become numerous and strong; they are in effect their own nation within the nation of Egypt. A new Egyptian dynasty arises with a king "who did not know Joseph" (Exod. 1:8). The great things Joseph had accomplished for Egypt no longer have any impact on this emperor and his officials. The new Pharaoh sees the children of Israel as a growing threat and directs his taskmasters to assign them the hard labor of building storage cities.[138] The Egyptians oppress the Israelites with harsh treatment and make their lives very bitter. But the more Jacob's descendants are afflicted, the more they multiply so that the Egyptians "were in dread of the sons of Israel" (Exod. 1:12). The earlier Egyptians had been Joseph's benefactors, but now their descendants have become Israel's slave masters (Exod. 1:1–14).

The Egyptian ruler decides he has to do even more to restrict this nation which is expanding within his own country, and he tells the midwives of Israel to kill all the newborn boys. But the midwives fear God and tell Pharaoh that the Hebrew women are so healthy that they give birth before they arrive to assist in their deliveries. God rewards the midwives for not obeying the king by giving them households of their own, and Israel continues to grow rapidly.

Pharaoh then commands the Egyptians to throw every newborn son of Israel into the river but to spare their daughters. Satan wants to destroy the seed of the woman to prevent the coming of the Messiah.

A couple from the house of Levi has a son, and his mother sees that he is a beautiful child. She hides him for three months, but when she can no longer conceal him, she puts him in a small ark of bulrushes and lays it in the reeds

---

[138] The memory of Joseph has faded, but the memory of famine and Joseph's preparations apparently remain.

growing in the Nile. The mother has the boy's sister watch the ark to see what will happen.

Pharaoh's daughter comes to the river with her maids to bathe. She sees the tiny ark, and when she opens it, the baby cries. She knows it is a Hebrew infant, but she has compassion on him. The baby's sister approaches Pharaoh's daughter and asks if she wants a nurse for the child. She replies, "Go." The sister hurries to get her mother who is paid wages to nurse her own son. After the little boy has had time to grow, his mother returns him to Pharaoh's daughter; he becomes her son, and she names him Moses, saying, "Because I drew him out of the water" (Exod. 2:10).[139] Moses is saved, but the other baby boys are not. With the severe labor, harsh treatment, and forced infanticide, life is becoming unbearable for the children of Israel (Exod. 2:1–10).

*****

Scripture does not say how long the infanticide continued, but Moses matures and is educated in the court of the Egyptians. He becomes a man mighty in words[140] and deeds (Acts 7:21–22). Exodus 2:11 tells us that after Moses was grown, he went out to see his "brethren" and watched as they struggled under their heavy burdens. Evidently, at some point, he had learned that he was a Hebrew, possibly from his birth mother, his sister, or Pharaoh's daughter. As he is observing his own relatives at their forced labor, he sees an Egyptian beating a Hebrew slave. When he realizes that no one else is watching, Moses kills the Egyptian and hides him in the sand. His wrath was triggered by the cruelty he had observed, but he also surely knew about the drowning of the baby boys.

He goes out a second day and tries to stop two Hebrew men from fighting, but one of them asks him who made him their judge and if he plans to kill him as he killed the Egyptian. Moses realizes that his crime is known. Pharaoh hears about what has happened and decides to kill Moses, but Moses escapes

---

[139] In Hebrew, the name Moses means "He who draws out," foreshadowing Moses's role in rescuing Israel through the Red Sea; see n. on Exod. 2:10 in *Nelson's NKJV*, 101.

[140] What Moses wrote (the Pentateuch) was powerful, but he was not an orator. God will eventually consent to have Aaron, his brother, speak to Pharaoh for him (Exod. 4:10–16).

and flees to the east across the wilderness of Paran. He comes to the land of Midian[141] and dwells there.

After some time passes, Moses is sitting by one of the wells in the region when the seven daughters of the priest of Midian bring their father's sheep to the well and begin to draw water for them. Some male shepherds soon arrive and start to drive the young women away so they can water their own animals, but Moses defends the women and then draws water for their flock. The daughters return to their father, Jethro,[142] and tell him about the Egyptian who delivered them from the hands of the shepherds.

Jethro says, "Where is he then? Invite him to have something to eat" (Exod. 2:20). Jethro is a man with seven daughters who need husbands, and here is an available man who has already protected his daughters and his sheep.

Moses is summoned, and he agrees to live with Jethro who gives him his daughter, Zipporah, as his wife. Moses works for his father-in-law and tends his flock. Once a prince of Egypt, he is now a shepherd like his forefathers, Abraham, Isaac, and Jacob. Moses has a son with Zipporah and names him "Gershom" (*stranger there*); Moses is a sojourner in a foreign land.

The king of Egypt who had intended to kill Moses eventually dies, but the children of Israel continue groaning in their bondage. God hears their cries and remembers his covenant with their forefathers. He is going to use Moses to rescue their descendants from slavery (Exod. 2:1–2:23).

*****

Moses continues to live in Midian and one day is grazing Jethro's flock in the wilderness of Paran near Horeb, the mountain of God,[143] when the Angel of the LORD appears to him in a flame of fire from the midst of a bush (Exod. 3:2). The bush is burning with fire but is not consumed. When Moses turns

---

[141] To reach Midian, Moses would have had to cross the wilderness of Paran (the Sinai Peninsula today) and the Arabah Valley, a distance of over 200 miles.

[142] Jethro is a descendant of one of Abraham's six sons by Keturah, who became Abraham's wife after Sarah's death. Abraham had sent these six sons, one named Midian, away to the east, away from Isaac, before he died. But he gave them gifts, and it seems that one of the gifts was the knowledge of the God of Abraham (Gen. 25:1–6). Jethro had become the priest of the land of Midian and now the future deliverer of Israel has come to him in the wilderness.

[143] This is Mt. Sinai where God will give Moses the Ten Commandments after he leads Israel out of Egypt.

aside to see this astounding sight, God calls to him from the burning bush and says, "Moses, Moses!" Moses replies, "Here I am" (Exod. 3:4).

God directs him to "remove your sandals from your feet, for the place on which you are standing is holy ground" (Exod. 3:5). He tells Moses, "I am the God of your father, the God of Abraham, the God of Isaac, and the God of Jacob" (Exod. 3:6).

Moses hides his face because he is afraid to look upon God.[144]

God says that He is going to send Moses to deliver His people from the hand of the Egyptians and that He will bring Israel to a good and large land flowing with milk and honey.

But Moses asks, "Who am I that I should go to Pharaoh, and that I should bring the sons of Israel out of Egypt?" (Exod. 3:11).

God tells him that He will be with him and that as a sign, when He brings the children of Israel out of Egypt, Moses will worship Him on this mountain.

Moses then asks God what he should say when the children of Israel ask for the name of the God of their fathers, the God who has sent him. God says, "I AM WHO I AM," and that Moses should tell the children of Israel that "I AM has sent me to you" (Exod. 3:14).[145] "Thus you shall say to the sons of Israel, the LORD (YHWH in Hebrew),[146] the God of your fathers, the God of Abraham, the God of Isaac, and the God of Jacob has sent me to you. This is My name forever, and this is My memorial-name to all generations" (Exod. 3:15).

The LORD directs Moses to gather the elders of Israel when he reaches Egypt and tell them that the God of Abraham, Isaac, and Jacob has seen what has been done to them and that He is going to lead them out of their afflictions to a land flowing with milk and honey. But the LORD knows the king of Egypt will not permit them to leave except under compulsion. He tells Moses that He will stretch out his hand and strike Egypt with wonders and then the king will

---

[144] Throughout Scripture, the reaction of human beings to an encounter with God is always great fear. Sinful human beings cannot face God in His Holy Essence.

[145] God says that He is "I AM WHO I AM" or "I Am the One Who is." God is the self-existent "I AM." He is not defined or determined by anyone or anything other than Himself.

[146] The LORD, literally YHWH, probably pronounced "Yahweh," is the most significant name for God in the Old Testament. The usual translation is "LORD" and is the designation used by God to emphasize His covenantal relationship with Israel. God uses different titles for Himself throughout Scripture to emphasize different aspects of his character. See Ryrie, *Ryrie Study*, 9, ns. on Gen. 2:4, and 96, ns. on Exod. 3:14–15.

let them go. God also says that the children of Israel will find favor with the Egyptian people and that they will give them silver, gold, and clothing when they depart. They will plunder the Egyptians as Abraham had done centuries before.

But Moses is afraid that the children of Israel will not listen to him or believe that God has appeared to him. God commands him to throw his rod to the ground, and it becomes a serpent. He then directs Moses to grasp it by the tail, and it becomes a rod again. God next instructs Moses to put his hand in his bosom, and when he takes it out, his hand is leprous. He puts his hand back in his bosom, and when he takes it out again, his hand is restored. God says that if the people of Israel do not believe him after these signs, he is to take water from the river and pour it on the dry land, and it will become blood (Exod. 3:15–4:9).

Moses is still reluctant; he protests that he is not eloquent and asks God to send someone else. God becomes angry with Moses but tells him his brother, Aaron, will come to meet him on his return and he will be Moses's mouth, his spokesman to the people. God ends the conversation with Moses by telling him to take his rod with him for performing the signs in Egypt (Exod. 4:10–17).

*****

Moses returns to Jethro and asks him to let him return to Egypt to see if his brethren are still alive. Jethro gives his blessing, so Moses takes his wife and sons,[147] sets them on a donkey, and begins the journey to Egypt with the rod of God in his hand. God tells Moses that the men who sought his life are dead. He also says that He will harden Pharaoh's heart and that Moses is to tell Pharaoh that Israel is the LORD's firstborn son and that the LORD will take the life of Pharaoh's firstborn son if he refuses to let His people go. God is signifying beforehand the ultimate threat in the coming confrontation with Pharaoh (Exod. 4:18–23).

Years before, Moses, as a prince of Egypt, had fled the power of Pharaoh and his court. Now he is a shepherd with his family, on a donkey, heading back

---

[147] Moses has a second son by this time, but his name, Eliezer, is not mentioned until Exod. 18:4.

across the Sinai desert on his way to challenge the ruler of the most powerful nation in the world.

*****

The fact that the Pharaoh who wanted to kill Moses has died does not mean that everyone has forgotten that Moses had killed an Egyptian slave master. In Egypt, when the reigning monarch died, the authorities dropped all pending charges, even capital murder cases.[148] Moses can return to the royal court without being arrested and executed, but the animosity toward him from court officials will remain.

Scripture does not describe it, but as Moses is making his journey to Egypt, the new Pharaoh is establishing himself politically and religiously in his inherited kingdom. When he ascended the throne, he became not only the supreme ruler but also a god—a god with a critical role among the hundreds of gods in polytheistic Egypt.[149] Each new pharaoh had to establish and maintain "Ma'at." Ma'at was the goddess of justice and order, but she represented a much larger concept. In the Egyptian world, Ma'at was the universal coherence involving everything—deities, human beings, and the physical universe.[150] For Egyptians, it was the essence of creation and the way reality functioned.

The role of the pharaoh was to see that all the disparate entities of the world functioned in one accord from relations among the gods and human beings to physical phenomena like the flooding of the Nile, which fed the nation. If the pharaoh was a successful god, the universe functioned in harmony, and Egypt prospered in all areas of its national life because he was maintaining Ma'at. The coming struggle between Pharaoh and Moses will be an encounter between the gods of Ma'at and the God of Israel, YHWH.

*****

Moses has begun the journey to Egypt, but he does not get very far before God confronts him. Moses has not circumcised his youngest son, and God

---

[148] N. on Exod. 2:22–25, *Nelson's NKJV*, 102.

[149] The Egyptians worshipped over 1,400 various deities ranging from dung beetles and frogs to the pharaoh and the sun.

[150] John D. Currid, *Ancient Egypt and the Old Testament* (Grand Rapids: Baker Books, 1997), 118–120.

intends to take his life for this serious covenantal lapse (Gen. 17: 10–14). But Zipporah takes a piece of flint and performs the circumcision herself, saving her husband. Moses is eventually going to receive the Law on behalf of Israel, and he must understand that he cannot ignore any of God's commands (Exod. 4:24–27).

After this dramatic incident, Zipporah and her two sons apparently return to Jethro in Midian. They are not mentioned again until months later when Jethro takes them to join Moses after Israel has crossed the Red Sea (Exod. 18:1–7).

God directs Aaron to go meet Moses, and they both continue their journeys until they connect at Mt. Sinai. Moses tells his brother what has happened and what God has said.

They then travel to Egypt where they assemble the elders of Israel. Aaron, speaking for Moses, recounts God's words for them and then shows the people the signs that Moses has received from God. They believe the signs, and when they hear that the LORD has remembered them and seen their affliction, they bow low and worship (Exod. 27–31).

*****

Aaron and Moses then speak to Pharaoh. It is not revealed how they gained an audience with the monarch, but the fact that he meets with them shows that the new pharaoh is very concerned about the children of Israel. Moses and Aaron tell Pharaoh that YHWH, the God of Israel, says, "Let my people go that they may celebrate a feast to Me in the wilderness" (Exod. 5:1). Pharaoh replies that he does not know YHWH and that he will not let Israel go. There are hundreds of gods in Egypt, and Pharaoh does not take the God of a slave people seriously. In the common theological understanding of the time, a conflict between nationalities was a conflict between their respective gods. The nation that gained the upper hand had the superior god or gods. The fact that Israel is a slave to Egypt proves that their God is an inferior God. For the God of an enslaved people to make demands is ludicrous to Pharaoh.

He is offended and directs his taskmasters to make Israel gather their own straw for making bricks but to keep their quotas the same. It is impossible for the children of Israel to make the same number of bricks, so the slave masters beat the leaders of Israel. When these men go to Pharaoh and question what is being done to them, he replies that since they have requested to go into the wilderness, they must have idle time. They will gather their own straw and still produce the same quota of bricks.

When the elders come out from their meeting, Moses and Aaron are waiting. The elders blame them for enraging Pharaoh and his court, saying, "You have put a sword in their hand to kill us" (Exod. 4:27–5:21).

Moses goes to the LORD and asks Him why He has sent him if this is to be the result. God tells him that Pharaoh will let His people go and that He will keep His covenant and bring them to the land He has promised. Moses relays this message to the people, but they do not listen to him because of their "despondency and cruel bondage" (Exod. 5:22–6:9).

The LORD speaks to Moses and Aaron to prepare them for their next meeting with Pharaoh. He is going to use Pharaoh to demonstrate his sovereign control.[151] They go before Pharaoh, and he demands to see a miracle, wanting to see if their God has endowed them with special powers. Aaron casts down his rod, and it becomes a serpent. Pharaoh calls for his magicians who cast down their rods, and they also become serpents. But then Aaron's serpent swallows up the serpents of the magicians. This is a crucial event that begins the confrontation between Moses and Pharaoh.

Serpents were very important in Egypt; they were feared and revered. The enraged female Cobra on Pharaoh's crown represented his power and divinity. To have his serpents swallowed by Aaron's serpent was a dramatic and public demonstration of YHWH's power over Pharaoh.[152]

The confrontation between Moses and Pharaoh is personal and religious, but it is also national and political. Pharaoh needs the forced labor of Israel to continue the construction of his storage cities and other building projects. To let this slave nation leave would be a total and unimaginable defeat for him. The conflict has begun with Aaron's serpent swallowing Pharaoh's serpents. It will end with the Red Sea swallowing Pharaoh and his army.[153] But for now, Pharaoh's heart grows hard, and he will not listen to Moses and Aaron.

---

[151] Proverbs 21:1 says "The king's heart is like the channels of water in the hand of the LORD; He turns it wherever He wishes."

[152] See Currid, *Ancient Egypt*, 92–94 for a discussion of this event.

[153] Ibid., see 85–86 for more on this parallel.

CHAPTER 15

THE TEN PLAGUES AND THE EXODUS

With Pharaoh unwilling to free the children of Israel from their captivity, God directs Moses and Aaron to begin what will be a series of ten plagues to convince the Egyptian ruler to let His people go. The plagues occur in the context of the confrontation between YHWH and the gods of Egypt. They will demonstrate at least three things: first, that YHWH is the sovereign LORD who reigns over everything, including the gods of Egypt; secondly, that Ma'at is a false conception of reality—it is a humanly contrived view of how the world functions; and finally, that Pharaoh is a false god who cannot maintain Ma'at against the power of YHWH. The ten plagues[154] begin with the LORD turning the Nile into blood:

1. The LORD tells Moses to meet Pharaoh when he goes to the Nile in the morning. When Pharaoh refuses his request to let the children of Israel go, Moses has Aaron strike the Nile with his rod, and the water in the river turns to blood. The LORD is showing his mastery over the Nile, the heart of the Egyptian economy, and a god that the Egyptians worship. YHWH can kill it, make it flow blood. Hapi and Khnum, the gods associated with the Nile, cannot protect it. But the magicians of Egypt do something similar and make water turn to blood. Pharaoh hardens his heart and will not let Israel go. The fish in the river die, and the Egyptians must dig wells to have water to drink (Exod. 7:14–25).

2. After seven days, God sends Moses to Pharaoh to tell him that if he does not let his people go, He will smite Egypt with frogs. The

---

[154] Ibid., see pages 104–120 for a summary of different views and theological understandings of the plagues.

Egyptians worship frogs and do not kill them.[155] Pharaoh refuses to let Israel go, so Aaron extends his rod toward the waterways of Egypt; frogs come forth exceedingly from the Nile, the streams, and the ponds. Frogs are a sign of fertility to the Egyptians, and now they infest their bedrooms and beds. They fill their ovens and kneading bowls. The Egyptians are overrun with frogs, and yet they must be careful not to kill one. The Egyptian magicians are also able to produce some frogs, but Pharaoh does not need more frogs. He asks Moses to entreat the LORD, and the LORD makes the frogs die. Then the Egyptians have to gather their dead gods and pile them up in stinking heaps. Egypt's gods have been ridiculed and slain, but when Pharaoh sees there is relief from the frogs, he refuses to let Israel go (Exod. 8:1–15).

3. The third plague is an infestation of small insects, perhaps gnats or lice. Aaron stretches out his rod toward the dust of the land, and the infestation covers Egypt. Pharaoh's magicians cannot reproduce this plague. They tell him that, "This is the finger of God," but he still refuses to let Israel go (Exod. 8:16–19).

4. The fourth plague is similar with swarms of stinging flies or perhaps mosquitos. In this plague, the LORD demonstrates his control over even the tiniest aspect of creation by keeping the flies from invading Goshen where the children of Israel dwell. Pharaoh again refuses to let the people go (Exod. 8:20–32).

5. The fifth plague is a disease on the Egyptians' livestock. Bull cults were common in Egypt,[156] and female deities were also represented as livestock animals. These cults represented fertility, and the actual animals provided food, clothing, and transportation for the Egyptians. Now they are dying, and the Egyptian gods and Pharaoh cannot save them. None of the livestock of the children of Israel dies, but Pharaoh still refuses to let YHWH's people go (Exod. 9:1–7).

6. The next plague is very personal. The LORD tells Moses and Aaron to take handfuls of ashes from a furnace and scatter it toward the heavens in the sight of Pharaoh. The ashes become fine dust that causes

---

[155] Ibid., 110. The goddess Heqet has the body of a woman and the head of a frog and is believed to be the wife of Khnum, the god of the Nile.

[156] Ibid., 111. Apis was the most important sacred bull-god, although Ra, the Egyptian sun god, was also represented as a bull.

boils on the Egyptians and their animals. The magicians are pain-fully infected and cannot stand before Moses. But the LORD hardens Pharaoh's heart, and he will not let Israel go (Exod. 9:8–12).

7. The LORD next demonstrates his control over the weather by sending an immense storm of rain and hail combined with fire (apparently lightning) over all of Egypt, except for Goshen. Everyone caught in the open is destroyed by the hail. Animals die and plants and trees are shredded. Only the children of Israel and their area of Goshen are spared. Pharaoh sends for Moses and says that he has sinned and that the LORD is righteous, an amazing admission for a man who considers himself a god. He says that he will let Israel go. Moses spreads out his hands to the LORD, and the thunder, rain, and hail stop. But when Pharaoh sees that the storm has ceased, he hardens his heart and will not let the children of Israel go (Exod. 9:13–35).

8. YHWH tells Moses that He has hardened Pharaoh's heart so that He can do these mighty works and show Moses's descendants that He is the LORD. Moses and Aaron go to Pharaoh again and ask him how long he will refuse to humble himself and not let the children of Israel go. They tell him that if he still refuses, the LORD God will send locusts to cover the ground, fill their houses, and consume the trees not destroyed by the hail. Pharaoh's servants have seen enough, and they tell him to let these men go serve the LORD their God. The royal court is no longer completely subservient to their pharaoh god, asking, "Do you not realize that Egypt is destroyed?" (Exod. 10:7).

Pharaoh agrees to let only the men go hold a feast to the LORD. He knows that the men will not abandon their women and children and will return to Egypt. But this is not acceptable, so once again, the LORD tells Moses to stretch out his hand over the land of Egypt, and the LORD sends an east wind that brings in the locusts. They cover the ground and eat every herb and all the fruit of the trees that have survived the hail. The locusts eat until there are no green plants left in Pharaoh's territory. He calls for Moses and Aaron in haste and once again admits that he has sinned. He asks them to entreat the LORD "that He would only remove this death from me" (Exod. 10:17). So the LORD sends a west wind that blows all the locusts into the Red Sea. But the LORD again hardens Pharaoh's heart, and he will not let the children of Israel go (Exod. 10:1–20).

9. The LORD then tells Moses to, "Stretch out your hand toward the sky, that there may be darkness over the land of Egypt, even a darkness which may be felt" (Exod. 10:21). Moses stretches out his hand, and a thick darkness covers all of Egypt for three days. Only the children of Israel have light in their dwellings. The text does not explain how this light occurred,[157] but the Egyptians are in complete physical and spiritual darkness; they cannot see each other, and they do not rise from their places for three days.

This is the most serious attack yet on the religion of Egypt. Ra, the sun god, is one of the most important, if not the most important, god to the Egyptians. He is seen as the creator god, and without his light, life is impossible. And now YHWH has extinguished him for three days; YHWH is in control of the universe, from the smallest gnat to the sun. Pharaoh calls Moses and tells him to go and that he can take everyone with him, except for Israel's flocks and herds. Moses replies that they must take their livestock and that not one hoof will be left behind. The LORD hardens Pharaoh's heart, and he will not let the children of Israel go (Exod. 10:21–27).

Pharaoh furiously commands Moses to, "Get away from me! Beware, do not see my face again, for in the day you see my face you shall die!" (Exod. 10:28).

Moses replies, "You are right. I shall never see your face again" (Exod. 10:29). But before he leaves Pharaoh, Moses tells him about the final plague that is coming.

10. Moses tells Pharaoh that at midnight, the LORD will go out into the midst of Egypt, and all the firstborn of Egypt will die from the firstborn of Pharaoh to the firstborn of the servant behind the hand-mill to the firstborn of all the animals. But not even a dog will bark against the children of Israel so that it may be known that the LORD makes a distinction between Egypt and Israel. Moses declares that Pharaoh's servants will come and bow down to him and tell him to leave and take all of his people with him. He concludes by saying, "After that, I will go out" (Exod. 11: 8), and he leaves Pharaoh in great anger. But

---

[157] In the final kingdom, the New Jerusalem, there is no need of the sun or the moon, "for the glory of God illuminated it" (Rev. 21:23).

the LORD hardens Pharaoh's heart, and for a final time, he will not let the children of Israel go (Exod. 11:1–10).

The LORD then inaugurates a ritual that is a protection for Israel during the final plague, a protection that will also be a continual remembrance of this final judgment against Egypt. He tells Moses and Aaron that in the first month on the fourteenth day, each household in Israel is to take an unblemished male lamb in its first year and kill it at twilight. They are to take the blood of the lamb and put it on the lintel and doorposts of the house where the lamb is slain. The lamb is to be roasted and eaten with unleavened bread and bitter herbs.[158] The people are to be clothed for departure and are to eat the lamb in haste. It is the LORD's Passover and an everlasting observance for Israel.

After explaining this ordinance, Moses tells the elders of Israel to pick out and kill the Passover lambs according to their families. The children of Israel do as they have been told, initiating the first Passover. They kill the lambs, put the blood on their lintels and doorposts, and eat the lambs quickly while dressed for departure.

At midnight, the LORD strikes all the firstborn in Egypt from the firstborn of Pharaoh to the firstborn of the captive in the dungeon to the firstborn of the Egyptian livestock. "And Pharaoh arose in the night, he and all his servants and all the Egyptians; and there was a great cry in Egypt, for there was no home where there was not someone dead" (Exod. 12:30). But in the houses of Israel, no one dies. The Angel of Death "passes over" those who have the blood of the Passover Lamb on their doorposts (Exod. 12:1–30).

While it is still night, Pharaoh calls for Moses and Aaron. His court officials tell them to leave (Exod. 10:29), to take the sons of Israel and their animals and go. And Pharaoh adds a request, "Bless me also" (Exod. 12:31–32). Pharaoh is admitting, at least for the moment, that YHWH is God.

The Egyptians urge the people of Israel to go quickly, saying, "We shall all be dead" (Exod. 12:33). YHWH has humiliated Egypt's gods and destroyed the Egyptian concept of the universe and how it operates. Pharaoh cannot protect his firstborn son, his successor god. Pharaoh's son and the concept of Ma'at are dead at the hand of YHWH.

The children of Israel gather their unleavened dough in cloths, place it on their shoulders, and depart. And as God had told Moses, the Egyptians give

---

[158] The unleavened bread signifies their sudden departure and the herbs their bitter enslavement.

them silver, gold, and clothing. They are willing to pay to stop the destruction of their land. The sons of Israel have gained their freedom, and like their father, Abraham, centuries before them, they have plundered the Egyptians.[159]

*****

The tenth plague is the culmination of the confrontation between Moses and Pharaoh and between YHWH and the gods of Egypt. It results in the freedom of the children of Israel and the vindication of YHWH as the one true God. It also inaugurates one of the most important religious rituals in Israel's history, the Passover. The Passover commemorates Israel's departure from Egypt, but it also illustrates the ministry of the coming Messiah, the ultimate Passover Lamb. His shed blood will save his kingdom people from the Angel of Death.

---

[159] First Kings 6:1 dates the Exodus as 480 years prior to the fourth year of Solomon's reign (966 BC from secular sources), which would give a date of 1446 BC for the Exodus. Some scholars say the 480 years are symbolic and prefer a later date, but the archaeological data is inconclusive, and there seems to be no definitive reason to reject 1446 BC as the correct date. Exodus 12:40 says Israel was in Egypt for 430 years, which means Israel arrived there in 1876 BC. Calculating back from 1876 BC, using the Old Testament genealogies, gives 2166 BC as the year of Abraham's birth. Paul in Galatians 3:17 says there were 430 years from the promises to the Law, apparently referencing the last affirmation of the promises to Jacob as he and his family were en route to Egypt (see Gen. 46:1–4).

CHAPTER 16

ISRAEL IN THE WILDERNESS

Israel sets forth from Egypt; their God has delivered them with a strong hand (Exod. 13:9). The nation has seen the initial fulfillment of the first promise to Abraham. His descendants have been fruitful and have multiplied exceedingly.[160] Now they are beginning their journey to the promised land where they are to rule and establish a righteous kingdom for the LORD.

Exodus 12:51 says that the LORD brought out the sons of Israel by their divisions. The Egyptians had not allowed Israel to establish a military structure, but the people had believed God and prepared for an organized departure. They are likely assembled by their tribal families according to the genealogical accounts of the nation. Men and women, strengthened by years of hard labor, lead the way with their smaller children and possessions on pack animals and carts. Shepherds drive their flocks and herds in a victorious procession (Exod. 12:32, 38). Israel is departing their captivity with boldness (Exod. 14:8), a high hand, while the nation that had enslaved them prepares to bury their firstborn.

As they are leaving, the LORD institutes another rite to commemorate Israel's rescue from Egypt. Since the LORD had spared Israel's firstborn, they are now to be dedicated to Him. This means that the firstborn son of each family is to enter full-time service to the LORD. Eventually, they will be redeemed and replaced by a Levite when the Levites become the family designated to serve in the Tabernacle (Num. 3:40–51).[161]

The firstborn of a clean animal is to be sacrificed to God, and the firstborn of an unclean animal is to be redeemed by offering a lamb in its place. The Lord will now refer to Israel as His firstborn, and He wants His people to

---

[160] The final fulfillment of this promise will be when all of God's people, from every nation and tribe, inhabit the new heaven and earth.

[161] Eventually, when there are not enough Levites to redeem all the firstborn males, they are redeemed by a five-shekel offering to the Levites (Num. 18:15–16).

continually remember how they were spared when all the firstborn of Egypt were slain (Exod. 13:1–2,11–16).

*****

The shortest route to Canaan is through the land of the Philistines (along the international trade route), but the Lord does not lead them that way because it would mean war with that well-armed nation.[162] He leads them in a pillar of cloud by day and in a pillar of fire by night; they travel by the way of the wilderness until they camp before the Red Sea. The LORD places them in a vulnerable position to tempt Pharaoh (Exod. 14:1–4).

Pharaoh realizes that Israel is trapped against the sea, and his heart is again hardened. He summons his chariots and army and pursues the slaves he has freed. The children of Israel see this large force in the distance rushing after them, and they are terrified; they cry out to the LORD and they rail against Moses. Moses tells them not to fear but to stand still and see the salvation of the LORD. He will fight for them, and they should hold their peace (Exod. 14:5–14).

The pillar of cloud moves between Israel and the approaching Egyptian army. It gives light to Israel but darkness to the Egyptians, and they cannot move forward to attack. God tells Moses to lift up his rod and stretch out his hand over the sea, and the LORD sends a strong east wind that blows all night and divides the waters so that Israel is able to pass through on dry ground. When the pillar of cloud moves, Pharaoh's army pursues the Israelites into the midst of the sea, but the people reach the far shore before the soldiers overtake them.

Early the next morning, when all the people have crossed over, the LORD directs Moses to stretch out his hand over the sea again, and the water rushes back to its place. Pharaoh and his entire army are drowned in the sea; not one of them is left alive. The people of Israel see the Egyptians dead on the seashore, and they fear the LORD and believe in Him and His servant Moses. Pharaoh and his army have been destroyed. They have been swallowed by the sea, and

---

[162] The Philistines and other Canaanite nations had developed chariots and weapons made of iron, which was plentiful and a significant step up from bronze metallurgy. The Philistines were on the leading edge of military armament (Josh. 17:16; Judg. 1:19).

the defeat of Egypt is complete. Moses and the people sing a song, praising the LORD for his triumph (Exod. 14:15–15:21).

*****

Egypt is no longer a threat to Israel, but the people need provisions in the wilderness. God sweetens the bitter water at Marah and sends manna, food from heaven, that the people gather from the ground. Each day, they collect enough for that day, but on the day before the Sabbath, they gather enough for two days so that the Sabbath can be a day of rest.[163] The manna is like white coriander seed and tastes like wafers made with honey. God tells Moses to keep an omer[164] of manna so that future generations will know how God fed Israel in the wilderness. The nation will eat manna for forty years until they enter the land of Canaan (Exod. 15:22–16:36).

*****

Israel continues their march into the wilderness of what today is the Sinai Desert. There is a lack of water, and the people complain against Moses. God has him strike the rock at Horeb with his rod; water comes out, and the people drink.[165] Then a local tribe, the Amalekites, attacks Israel. Joshua, a new military leader,[166] defeats them as Moses keeps his staff upraised overlooking the battle; it is the LORD's victory (Exod. 17:1–16).

Jethro, Moses's father-in-law, learns what God has done for Israel. He comes from Midian, with Zipporah and her two sons (see n. 147, p. 90 and p. 92) to greet Moses. He sees the heavy burden that Moses bears in dealing with all the people. Jethro tells Moses that he must set up men to help him

---

[163] This is the first command in Scripture that God's people should observe a weekly Sabbath rest. There is no indication that the patriarchs kept a weekly Sabbath before the manna was sent from heaven. Keeping the seventh day, Saturday, as a day of rest will be the Fourth Commandment given to Israel in the Decalogue at Mt. Sinai. But most Christians today keep the first day of the week, Sunday, as a day of rest because that is the day Jesus rose from the dead, and it seems to have been the pattern of the early Church (Acts 20:7; 1 Cor. 16:2; Rev. 1:10).

[164] An omer was a dry measure of two quarts.

[165] Paul draws a parallel between this rock and Christ, who will also be struck, and from whom will flow spiritual water (1 Cor. 10:4; also see John 7:37–38).

[166] This is the first mention of Joshua who will become Moses's successor as the leader of Israel.

administer order, and Moses establishes rulers of thousands, hundreds, fifties, and tens. With this chain of command, only the most difficult problems are to be brought to him. After helping with the organization of the nation, Jethro returns to his own land. The priest of Midian, a descendant of Abraham,[167] had given Moses refuge and a wife, and now he has provided wise counsel (Exod. 18:1–27).

*****

In the third month after their departure from Egypt, Israel arrives at the foot of Mt. Sinai. Moses goes up from the camp, and the LORD calls to him from the mountain. God reminds Moses of what He has done to the Egyptians and then says that if Israel will obey His voice and keep His covenant, He will make them His own possession among the nations. They will be a kingdom of priests and a holy nation. Moses relays God's message to the elders and the people, and they all answer together and say, "All that the LORD has spoken we will do" (Exod. 19:8).

The people of Israel have seen the mighty works of the LORD, and they are making a covenant to be a righteous people for His kingdom (Exod. 19:1–8). But the covenant that the LORD makes with Moses is different from the covenant made with Abraham.

God had chosen Abraham and had promised to give him many descendants and a kingdom. The fulfillment of the Abrahamic covenant does not depend on Abraham. God is going to accomplish His promises; it is a matter of His power and His electing grace (undeserved favor).[168] The first part of that covenant has seen its initial fulfillment; Israel has multiplied exceedingly, and now they are on the way to Canaan. The covenant that Moses is going to receive will tell the people how they are to live in the promised land. Adam and Eve had to obey one commandment to remain in the Garden of Eden. The Israelites will have many laws that they must observe if they are to remain in their Eden. The Mosaic Covenant does not save Israel; it tells them how they are to live as a redeemed people. They are to be a witness to the holy character of the one true God and thereby be a blessing to all the nations.

---

[167] See p. 88, n. 142.
[168] See pp. 46–47.

On the third day, after arriving at Mt. Sinai, thunder and lightning and a thick cloud of smoke enshrouds the mountain. The LORD is descending upon it in fire, and the entire mountain quakes violently; God tells Moses to warn the people not to approach it. Then Moses goes up Mt. Sinai and receives the Ten Commandments, all the other laws, and the instructions for building the Tabernacle, a tent of meeting where Israel can assemble and meet with God.[169] The LORD gives Moses two stone tablets of the Testimony inscribed by His own finger—Israel has written directions for kingdom life[170] (Exod. 19:9–31:18).

Moses is on the mountain for so long that the people become alarmed. Their anxiety escalates until they demand that Aaron make them "a god who will go before us" (Exod. 32:1). As is the tendency of all fearful people, the Israelites want something tangible to worship. They have seen the mighty works of the LORD, but now they want a god they can see and touch.[171] They give Aaron their ornaments of gold; he makes a golden calf and declares a feast for the next day. The people eat and drink and begin sexual play.[172]

When Moses comes down the mountain, he hears the noise and sees the golden calf and the people dancing. His anger burns, and he throws the tablets and shatters them at the base of the mountain (Exod. 32:1–19).

Moses takes the golden idol, burns it, and then grinds it into powder. He spreads the powder over water and makes the people drink it. He confronts Aaron, and Aaron says that the people gave him gold, and "I threw it into the fire, and out came this calf" (Exod. 32:24). Even after Moses confronts them and makes them drink the golden calf, some of the people remain out of control; Moses calls for help, and the Levites respond.[173] He directs them to start killing the rioting people, and about 3,000 people die before order is restored.

---

[169] Until the Tabernacle is constructed, Moses sets up another tent of meeting outside the camp where God speaks to Moses and the people. When Moses enters the tent, the pillar of cloud descends and stands at the entrance of the tent, and all the people stand and worship at the doors of their tents (Exod. 33:7–10).

[170] The book of Leviticus will go into great detail as to how Israel is to worship God in the Tabernacle.

[171] John 4:24 says, "God is spirit, and those who worship Him must worship in spirit and truth."

[172] The worship of bull cults involved sexual fertility rites.

[173] The Levites were the descendants of Jacob and Leah's third son, Levi. After coming to Moses's aid, they will become the tribe that oversees the Tabernacle and performs the duties of worship in the nation of Israel.

Moses goes before the LORD and tells Him that "this people has committed a great sin, and they have made a god of gold for themselves" (Exod. 32:31). Moses pleads for the people because he is afraid that the LORD will destroy them. Despite their gross idolatry, God is not going to eradicate the nation, and He tells Moses that he should lead the Israelites to the promised land. But God is not going to forget their sin. He is going to punish the people for the golden calf; those who have sinned against Him will be blotted out of His book (Exod. 32:20–35).

God has told Moses to guide Israel to Canaan, but He then says that He will not go with this "obstinate people" lest He destroy them on the way (Exod. 33:3). When the people hear this, they repent and strip themselves of their ornaments. Moses again beseeches God, and He relents and says that His presence will go with Israel on their journey to the promised land (Exod. 33:1–23).

God directs Moses to make two new tablets of stone, and he again goes up Mt. Sinai and receives the laws of God. He stays on the mountain forty days and forty nights, and God gives him a glimpse of His glory. When he comes down from the mountain, Moses's face is shining because he has seen the glory of God. The people have not fallen into idolatry this time, but when they see Moses's face, they are afraid to come near him. He calls Aaron and all the rulers, and eventually, the people approach Moses. He tells them everything that the Lord has told him on the mountain (Exod. 34:1–32).

It appears that Moses completes Leviticus during the remaining time at Mt. Sinai. The book outlines the duties of the priestly line, but it applies to all the people. Everyone in Israel is to keep the Law; the people must be holy to approach their Holy God (Lev. 19:2). But they cannot be holy in and of themselves; all of the rituals and sacrifices performed in the Tabernacle point to the character and sacrificial work of the coming Messiah.

*****

Israel had arrived at Mt. Sinai three months after leaving Egypt. They remain another nine months[174] while the nation's finest artisans complete the intricate and beautiful work of constructing the Tabernacle. The tent and its surrounding enclosure are made from rams' skins, finely woven cloth, and rich wood. The sacred fixtures are fashioned from gold, silver, and brass and dec-

---

[174] See Exod. 12:2, 19:1, and 40:17 for the timeline of this first year of freedom from Egypt.

orated with images of flowers and plants. It is fashioned exactly as God has specified with an outer court where the Altar of Burnt Offering and the Bronze Laver for ceremonial washings are located.

Inside the Tabernacle, a heavy woven curtain separates the area of the Holy Place from the smaller area called the Most Holy Place. The Golden Lampstand, the Table of Showbread, and the Altar of Incense are set in the Holy Place while the Ark of the Covenant is positioned in the Most Holy Place. The stone tablets of the Law are kept inside the Ark of the Covenant, which is plated with gold.[175]

Aaron becomes the first high priest, and his sons serve as priests (Num.3:3). They are to perform the rituals appointed for the worship of God in the Tabernacle. Holy garments are created for them to wear when they are executing their official duties as representatives of the people of Israel (Exod. 39).

The Tabernacle is a beautiful place, decorated like a garden, for meeting with God. It is a reminder of Eden before the fall where Adam and Eve could directly communicate with their Creator. It also points forward to the Temple, the New Jerusalem, and the new heaven and earth. But it also has an altar for the sacrifice of animals. Now that human beings are universally sinful, they can only approach God through atonement, the shedding of blood.

After all the work is completed, the cloud that has been leading Israel covers the new tent of meeting, and the glory of the LORD fills the Tabernacle (Exod. 40:35–38).

*****

It has been one year since Israel left Egypt, and now they are going to resume their journey to Canaan. But before they leave Mt. Sinai, they remember their rescue from Egypt and celebrate the Passover as the LORD has commanded; they eat their Passover lambs with bitter herbs and unleavened bread (Num. 9:4–5).

Israel is now an organized nation, and they travel with the twelve tribes and their armies arranged as a fighting force (Num. 10:14–28). The Tabernacle

---

[175] The Ark of the Covenant was the richest and most sacred of all the fixtures. It was a rectangular box (approximately 45" x 27" x 27") covered in gold with two golden angels on its cover, which was called the mercy seat (Exod. 37:1–9).

is disassembled and travels in the center of their national formation.[176] The cloud of the LORD is on the Tabernacle during the day, and His fire is in the Tabernacle at night. When the cloud moves, the people pack up their belongings and follow.[177] They carry with them the Tablets of the Law in the Ark of the Covenant. They are to spiritually follow God's law as they physically follow the sign of his presence to the promised land.

Their experiences in the wilderness on the way to Canaan are described by Moses in the book of Numbers, which takes its name from the two censuses of the nation, the first done at Mt. Sinai (Num. 1:1–54) before they begin their journey, and the second on the plains of Moab before Israel enters Canaan (Num. 26:1–51).[178]

---

[176] The Levites have been designated to serve in the Tabernacle. Only they are to take it down, carry it, and set it up. Any outsider who comes near is to be put to death (Num. 1:50–53).

[177] There must have been some interesting times when the cloud moved unexpectedly and parents shouted at each other and scrambled to gather their children and possessions to get in line before the nation moved out (Num. 9:21–23).

[178] The total number of Israelites that left Egypt is disputed. The Hebrew word *eleph* is usually translated thousand which in the first census seems to give a total of 603,550 men of fighting age (Num. 1:46). This would have been an exceptionally large military force for an era when the largest armies numbered in the tens of thousands (the Battle of Kadesh in 1304 BC, the first large battle where recorded numbers exist, involved 35,000 Egyptian soldiers and 27,500 Hittite fighters, including the men in chariots. See "Battle of Kadesh," HistoryNet, World History group, July 31, 2005, www.historynet.com/battle-of-kadesh.htm. 603,550 fighting men would be an enormous military force for that day, and the estimated total population of Israel would be over two million people, a number that would seem too large to pass through the Red Sea in one night. At fifty people abreast and counting two yards for each row of people, and not including the many carts and large herds of animals, the column would have been over forty-five miles long. It is possible that God made a very wide path through the water, but the general sense of the movement and governance of Israel does not indicate such a large group of people (see Exod. 23:29–30; Deut. 7:1, 7). Also, almost all the numbers for the individual tribes end in two zeros (Num. 1:21–43). This may have been a matter of rounding off to the nearest hundred, but it seems unusual when Israel was so precise with their genealogical records. Dan Bruce notes that God's instructions to Moses for the first numbering included an atonement offering. Each man over twenty was to give a ransom of ten gerahs (Exod. 30:11–13) for each member of his family (Exod. 30:14–16). Bruce suggests that this factor of ten is included in the census number for 603,550, which would be the ransom amount for the entire population, not just the men of fighting age, giving a total population of 60,355 Israelites leaving Egypt. This is a number that could pass through the Red Sea in one night and seems to correlate with Israel's experiences in route to the promised land. See "How Many Israelites Left Egypt in the Exodus? Hint: It wasn't Two Million!" Selected Controversial Topics, The Prophecy Society, accessed November

The direct route to Canaan from Mt. Sinai is to the north through the wilderness of Paran (the Sinai Desert) to Kadesh, a distance of about 170 miles. The nation could travel this route in a few weeks, but it will be thirty-nine years before they enter the promised land. The difficult terrain, hostile tribes, and the need for food and water make the journey difficult, but the main reason for the delay is the nation's lack of faith. Despite the great works God has done on their behalf and the covenant He has made with them, this generation will not trust God enough to move forward and occupy the Land He has promised them.

*****

With the cloud leading them, Israel moves north into the wilderness. As they journey deeper into the wasteland, the people begin to complain about having only manna to eat. God sends great numbers of quail into their camp, and they have an excess of meat, but this brings on a plague, and many of them die. Then Miriam, Moses's sister,[179] and Aaron complain about Moses's leadership and criticize Moses for having an Egyptian (Cushite) wife.[180] God strikes Miriam with leprosy for instigating this dissension. When she and Aaron repent, God heals her, but she has to remain outside the camp for seven days, and the nation halts its travel until she can return (Num. 10:11–12:16).

The nation reaches the southern border of Canaan and camps at Kadesh Barnea. Moses sends twelve men, one from each tribe, to spy out the land, and they return with samples of the rich bounty from Canaan. Ten of them say that the land is rich, a land of milk and honey, but the Canaanites have well-for-tified cities, and the men are giants; "and we became like grasshoppers in our own sight" (Num. 13:33).

This discourages the nation, and the people begin to weep and complain against Moses and Aaron. They collaborate together and say, "Let us appoint a leader and return to Egypt" (Num. 14:4). Only Caleb and Joshua, who were

---

16, 2018, http://www.prophecysociety.org/?p=8983. Some scholars say *eleph* can also be translated as *clans* which could lead to an even smaller number. The original numbers in the Bible are inerrant, but we may not yet know for certain how they should be translated.

[179] This would be Moses's sister that was watching the ark of bulrushes when the Egyptian princess rescued him from the Nile. She does not see her little brother as a great leader.

[180] Zipporah may have died or Moses may have taken a second wife since polygamy was permitted in ancient Israel. The complaint seems to arise from her ethnic background.

two of the twelve spies, urge the people to enter Canaan. They say the LORD is with them and will give them the land; they should not fear. The people rebel and decide to stone Caleb and Joshua. But before they can kill them, the glory of the LORD appears in the Tabernacle where everyone can see the light of His presence (Num. 13:1–14:16).

God is very angry and speaks to Moses and asks, "How long will this people spurn Me?" (Num. 14:11). He says He will destroy them with a pestilence and make an even greater nation from Moses. Moses once again pleads for the people, and God does not destroy them, but He declares they "shall by no means see the land of which I swore to their fathers" (Num. 14:23). The corpses of those who have grumbled against God shall fall in the wilderness, except for Caleb and Joshua (Num. 14:29).

The ten spies who feared the Canaanites and discouraged the nation are struck down by a plague before the LORD. The people mourn, and the fighting men who were afraid now decide to enter Canaan despite Moses's warning not to do so. These men have seen and heard God's judgment, and they do not want to die in the wilderness. But when they enter the land, they are attacked and defeated by the Canaanites and have to return to Kadesh (Num. 14:36–45).

God's judgment stands. With the exception for Caleb and Joshua, the people of the first wilderness generation, those who are at least twenty years of age (Num. 14:29), will not enter the promised land because of their lack of faith. With God's pronouncement against the adults in the congregation, it will be even more difficult for Moses to control the people.

*****

After the defeat by the Canaanites, Moses soon faces another challenge to his leadership from Korah, Dathan, Abiram, and 250 of their supporters. These three agitators are descendants of Levi, and they believe that their priesthood in the Tabernacle has made them equal to Moses. Moses tells them to bring their censers[181] with fire and incense to the door of the Tabernacle the next morning. The following day, Aaron also brings his censer, and he and Moses stand before the Tabernacle with the entire congregation watching. The three rebellious leaders refuse to meet with Moses; they instead stand in the door-

---

[181] Censers were vessels, usually covered, which were used by the priests to burn incense during religious ceremonies.

ways of their tents with their wives and children. God tells Moses to make the people stay away from these families. Moses speaks and says the people will see whether God has sent him or if he is acting on his own will. As soon as he finishes speaking, God opens up the ground, and it swallows up Korah, Dathan, Abiram, and their families with their tents and all their goods. God then sends a fire that consumes the 250 men who have brought their own fire and incense before the LORD. The rest of the people flee in terror (Num. 16:1–25).

God is to be worshipped and served as He directs. He has no mercy on those who devise their own approaches to Him. No one gets to bring strange fire; they will be consumed.[182]

But, amazingly, the congregation is still rebellious; they confront Moses and Aaron the next day and say, "You are the ones who have caused the death of the LORD's people" (Num. 16:41). The cloud suddenly appears over the Tabernacle, and immediately, a plague breaks out among the protestors. Moses tells Aaron to make atonement for them with fire and incense, and the plague is stopped, but not before many people die.

Moses realizes that he must reestablish control and unify the people. He tells each tribe to bring their leader's rod and place it in the Tabernacle before the Testimony. These rods are the means by which the leaders direct and control their flocks; they are symbols of authority. Aaron also brings his rod, and they are all left overnight.

The next day, Aaron's rod has budded with blossoms and ripe almonds (Num. 17:1–12). This miracle confirms Moses's leadership and Aaron's priesthood. Eventually, Aaron's rod will be placed in the Ark of the Covenant along with the tablets of the Law and the omer of manna (Heb. 9:4). Moses's authority has been confirmed by God, and order has been restored in the camp.

*****

After Israel's failure to enter Canaan and possess the land, the nation remains at Kadesh Barnea for "many days" (Deut. 1:46). Miriam dies at Kadesh and is buried there. She had known Moses since his birth and had seen his remarkable life, but she had opposed him at a critical time and had been severely chastised by God before she was brought back into the company of the nation.

---

[182] "It is a fearful thing to fall into the hands of the Living God" (Heb. 10:31).

The people run out of water at Kadesh and voice their usual complaint against Moses that they would have been better off in Egypt or dead. God tells Moses and Aaron that they should go to a certain rock and speak to it, and the rock will give forth water. They assemble the congregation, and Moses, perhaps out of exasperation with the people, does not speak to the rock but strikes it with his rod as he had done before. Water gushes out and the people and their animals drink. But God tells Moses and Aaron that because they did not honor Him by speaking to the rock as He had directed, they, too, will not enter the promised land[183] (Num. 20:1–13). God makes no exception for leaders who disregard his authority.

*****

The LORD tells Moses to leave Kadesh. After the long sojourn at Kadesh Barnea, Moses is apparently given some warning before the pillar of cloud and pillar of fire resume leading the nation. The children of Israel will journey in the wilderness for another thirty-eight years before they cross the brook, Zered, southeast of the Dead Sea and begin the last stage of their journey to the promised land (Deut. 2:14). The first wilderness generation is going to die in the wasteland for failing to believe God and take possession of Canaan.

*****

Moses leads the nation from Kadesh with the intent of entering Canaan farther to the north. The knowledge that he and Aaron will not be permitted to enter the promised land must have weighed heavily on his heart, but he has to deal with trouble immediately ahead. Moses wants to travel northeast along the King's Highway, but the King of Edom, the nation of the descendants of Esau, refuses to let the people of Israel pass through his country and threatens

---

[183] As noted previously, Paul draws a parallel between the rock which gives water to Christ who gives spiritual drink (see p. 102, n. 165). Christ, the Rock, will be struck on behalf of his people, but that will be done according to God's plan (Acts 4:27), not according to the anger of a mortal man. After Christ has been struck, He can be spoken to but never struck again.

to attack them (Num. 20:14–21). Moses tells the people to turn back, and the nation begins to retrace the way it came from Mt. Sinai.[184]

When they reach Mt. Hor, Aaron dies, and the people mourn thirty days for the older brother of Moses who spoke for him against Pharaoh. Aaron had sinned greatly with the golden calf, but he stood with Moses when the people rebelled against him, and he eventually became the first high priest of Israel.

After Aaron's death, the Canaanite King of Arad attacks Israel, but they defeat him and utterly destroy all his cities. The nation then resumes backtracking over its previous route. When the people become impatient and complain again, God sends fiery serpents to punish them. They bite the Israelites, and many die. The LORD tells Moses to make a bronze serpent and set it on a pole; when the people look at the serpent, they live[185] (Num. 20:23–21:9).

*****

Decades pass as the tribes travel and continue to graze their animals. After moving south as far as the Red Sea, they turn northward and continue their journey on the east side of the Arabah Valley. They spend a long time circling the area of Mt. Seir; apparently, the area has good forage for their flocks and herds (Deut. 2:1). The Lord tells the Israelites not to attack the local inhabitants because they are brethren, another group of Esau's descendants. Israel is also forbidden to make war against the nearby Moabites because they are the children of Lot. Eventually, thirty-eight years after leaving Kadesh Barnea, the LORD directs the nation to cross the brook, Zered, and the people camp east of the Dead Sea. All the fighting men of the first wilderness generation have perished from the nation as "the LORD had sworn to them" (Deut. 2:2–2:16).

God then instructs Israel to resume their journey (Deut. 2:24), and they move north and cross the River Arnon. Sihon, king of the Amorites, refuses to let them pass through his land, and Israel's second generation army defeats him and destroys his people. The nation occupies the cities of the Amorites for a

---

[184] There is an old song by Amy Grant about Israel in the wilderness. One line says, "Take another lap around Mt. Sinai till you learn your lesson, till you stop your whining and you quit your rebelling." This applies not only to Israel but to us.

[185] In John 3:14–15, Jesus draws a parallel between Himself and the bronze serpent and says, "And as Moses lifted up the serpent in the wilderness, even so must the Son of Man be lifted up, that whoever believes in Him should not perish but have eternal life." Those who looked to the serpent were healed physically; those who look to Christ are healed spiritually.

time (Num. 21:21–31; Deut. 2:26–36), but this is not Canaan. Israel has not reached its destination. After this brief respite, the nation again moves north into the land of Bashan where the King of Og attacks them. But the new fighting forces also defeat him, and the Israelites continue their journey. They reach the plains of Moab and camp beside the Jordan River across from Jericho, the first fortified city they will encounter in the promised land.

*****

The nearby Moabites, descendants of the incest between Lot and his oldest daughter (p. 49), fear Israel, even though they have not been attacked. Their king employs the diviner, Balaam, to curse the nation, but Balaam can only say what God tells him; he has to pronounce God's blessings on Israel instead of the king's desired curse (Num. 21:10–24:25).

Israel remains encamped, and some of the men begin to commit harlotry with the women of Moab[186] and Midian. They are soon drawn into the worship of their gods. These two nations cannot defeat Israel militarily, so they are trying to neutralize them through sexual and religious assimilation.[187] God directs Moses to execute the men who worshiped Baal, and the transgressions with Moab are halted. He also tells Moses that he will have to attack Midian and eliminate the nation because their immorality is a serious threat to Israel (Num. 25:1–16).

*****

Thirty-nine years have passed since the departure from Mt. Sinai, and except for Moses, Joshua, and Caleb, the last survivors of the initial Exodus generation have died in the wilderness. They had failed to trust the LORD and take possession of the promised land. God tells Moses and Eleazar the priest, Aaron's son, to conduct a second census. Like the first census, this one is for military purposes and is based on the number of fighting men in each tribe.

---

[186] As with the Canaanites, sexual sinfulness seems to be passed down through the generations of the Moabites.

[187] This is a tactic that Satan continues to use very successfully against the Church in the United States and the Western World.

The numbers vary for each tribe, but the total for the entire nation is virtually the same as the first census.[188]

The first wilderness generation has been replaced by the following generation with no loss of numbers (Num. 26:1–31). The LORD also tells Moses how to divide the territory of Canaan among the tribes. The amount of land is determined by the number in each tribal family, and the location is determined by casting lots (Num. 26:52–56).

It is time for Israel to enter the promised land, but Moses will not cross the Jordan River because he disobeyed God when he struck the rock to bring forth water. God reaffirms that Moses is going to die, and He directs him to take Joshua before all the people and lay his hands on him and inaugurate him as his successor (Num. 27:12–23). Moses follows God's instructions, and after confirming Joshua's leadership role, he orders the fighting men to take vengeance on Midian as God had directed; they destroy that decadent nation and divide the plunder (Num. 31:1–54).

Israel has been occupying the territory east of the Jordan River. It is an area of rich pastures that are good for livestock. The tribes of Rueben, Gad, and half the tribe of Manasseh have large flocks and herds and request permission to settle in this area.[189] Moses agrees but says their men must first join the other tribes in the conquest of Canaan (Num. 32:1–39).

*****

God tells Moses to make another covenant with this new generation before they enter Canaan (Deut. 29:1). After he reiterates the Sinaitic Covenant (Deut. 27:1–28:63), Moses adds, in what is sometimes called the Land or Palestinian Covenant, God's warnings that plagues and sicknesses will befall the people if they begin to worship false gods after they enter the land (Deut. 29:1–28). But

---

[188] See p. 107, n. 178, for a discussion of the census numbers.

[189] Gad and the half-tribe of Manasseh will occupy the area known as Bashan. David and the Prophet Amos will refer to the strong bulls and cows of Bashan in their writings (Ps. 22:12; Amos 4:1). Today, this area is called the Golan Heights and has been controlled by Israel since the Six-Day War with Syria in 1967. It is an important military location because its high northern plateau overlooks Israel's eastern border along the Sea of Galilee. I traveled through this area in 1994, and as someone who has owned cattle, looked with envy at the rich and empty pastures. Today, there are dozens of Israeli settlements in this territory once settled by the trans-Jordan tribes.

God also adds a prophecy; He tells Israel that they will not be obedient and that they will be uprooted and driven into other nations. Eventually, though, they will return to the LORD, and He will return them to Canaan. He is going to circumcise their hearts, and they will live and prosper in the promised land (Deut. 29:1–30:7). With this prophecy, the LORD is foreshadowing the time of the new covenant, a final covenant, when the Law is written on the hearts of His covenant people (Jer. 31:31–34).

Moses finishes writing the book of Deuteronomy, a summary of his previous addresses to the nation, focusing on the history of Israel and the Law the LORD God has given them. The second Exodus generation was either very young or not yet born when God parted the Red Sea and gave Israel the Law at Mt. Sinai. Moses wants this new generation to understand God's power and their obligations to Him.[190] The book is to be an enduring witness to the nation (Deut. 31:9–13).

The LORD then gives Moses His last instructions for the conquest of Canaan, emphasizing that Israel must drive out all the inhabitants of the land and destroy all their religious idols. If they do not completely rid the land of the Canaanites, they will become thorns in the sides of the Israelites and lead them into idolatry. If this happens, the LORD will do to the children of Israel what He has directed Israel to do to the Canaanites (Num. 33:50–56).

After his concluding admonitions to the people, Moses ascends to the top of Pisgah, a promontory on Mt. Nebo, where the LORD gives him a final view of the land of Canaan, the land promised to Abraham, Isaac, and Jacob. Despite all the hardships and obstacles, Moses has completed the calling that God gave him from the burning bush many years before. He has led the children of Israel out of Egypt and guided them to the promised land. His eyes are not dim, and his vigor is undiminished, but he dies on the mountain as God had said. Deuteronomy 34:6 says that God buried Moses in a valley in Moab and that no one knows where his grave is to this day.[191] The people know that Moses is gone, and they weep and mourn for thirty days. Joshua is now the leader of Israel, and he is going to guide the nation across the Jordan River into the land of Canaan (Deut. 32:48–52, 34:1–12).

---

[190] The last chapter of Deuteronomy records Moses's death, an addendum added to Moses's writing.

[191] Being buried by God is a singular honor given only to Moses. Moses and Elijah (who was transported to heaven in a whirlwind) will appear with Jesus at His transfiguration (2 Kings 2:11; Matt. 17:1–3), pp. 186–187.

CHAPTER 17

Joshua and the Conquest of Canaan

More than seven centuries have passed since God called Abraham out of Ur of the Chaldeans and made a covenant with him.[192] Now God's promises to Abraham are being fulfilled. His descendants have become a nation, and they are on the verge of obtaining the second promise, the land of Canaan. The third promise that Abraham would be a blessing to all the nations is still in the future. For the perverse and idolatrous nations occupying Canaan, Israel is not going to be a blessing, but instead, God's instrument of judgment.

God tells Joshua that He will be with him. He should "be strong and courageous" and meditate on the book of the Law day and night (Josh. 1:9, 1–9). The leaders of the tribal armies pledge their allegiance to Joshua, and he sends two spies across the Jordan to survey the walled city of Jericho, the first obstacle the Israelites will encounter when they enter Canaan. The spies make their way inside Jericho and go undetected by staying in the house of a harlot named Rahab. She hides them and tells them that the Canaanites are very afraid of the nation of Israel. They have heard how the LORD dried up the Red Sea and how Israel had utterly destroyed the kings east of the Jordan. Rahab asks that she and her family be spared. The spies agree and bring their report back to Joshua (Josh. 1:10–2:24).

Joshua prepares the nation to cross the Jordan, but the river is in flood stage. The LORD tells him to have the priests carry the Ark of the Covenant into the river ahead of the people. The waters of the Jordan are cut off upstream, and in a scene reminiscent of the Red Sea, the nation crosses into Canaan on dry land. They camp at Gilgal, just southeast of Jericho (Josh. 3:1–4:24).

---

[192] Abraham was born in 2166 BC, and Israel began the conquest of Canaan in 1406 BC. See p. 99, n. 159.

Israel is safely across the Jordan, but Joshua delays the beginning of his military campaign. The men that grew up in the wilderness have not been circumcised, and the LORD directs Joshua to have the nation complete this rite before moving on. It is also time for the Passover, and Israel celebrates this sacred day for the first time while in the promised land (Josh. 5:1–10).

On the day following the celebration of the Passover, the people for the first time eat of the produce of Canaan, unleavened cakes and parched grain. The next day, the manna from the LORD ceases. The children of Israel are in the promised land, and now they are to eat from its bounty (Josh. 5:11–12).

After the fighting men have healed, the Lord tells Joshua how to overcome the fortified city of Jericho. Joshua follows His instructions, and the men of war march around the city with seven priests carrying trumpets of ram's horns followed by other priests carrying the Ark of the Covenant. They march around the city once a day for six days. On the seventh day, they march around the city seven times, and when the priests blow the trumpets, the people shout with a great shout, and the wall of Jericho falls down flat. Israel rushes into the city and destroys all the people and animals in Jericho as the Lord had directed (Josh. 6:17–27).[193] No one is left alive, except for the harlot, Rahab, and her family.[194] The fame of Joshua and the fear of Israel spread rapidly throughout Canaan (Josh. 6:1–27).

Joshua then sends a company of men to destroy the nearby city of Ai, which is not as large as Jericho. But the men of Israel are driven back, and thirty-six of them are killed. There is fear and great concern until it is discovered

---

[193] God's command to kill all the inhabitants of Jericho and other Canaanite cities is troubling for many people. But we know that the religion and culture of the Canaanites involved many idols and gross sexual perversions including bestiality and child sacrifice (Lev. 18:19–24). God says the land is defiled, and He is going to visit His punishment on the evildoers. The land will vomit out its inhabitants (Lev. 18:25). Apparently, there reaches a point where a culture is so corrupt that God destroys it and everything associated with it, even its children and animals. Also, as previously discussed, the Canaanite tribes were all descendants of Canaan, the illegitimate son of Ham. Canaan was cursed because of his father's sin, meaning that his line would be cut off; he would be left without descendants. Israel is beginning to fulfill that curse (see pp. 30–32).

[194] Rahab is accepted into the nation of Israel. She becomes the wife of Salmon and has a descendant named Boaz, the same Boaz who marries Ruth as recorded in the Old Testament book bearing her name. Then, "Boaz begot Obed by Ruth, Obed begot Jesse, and Jesse begot David the king," the forefather of the Messiah (Matt. 1:1–6). Rahab is in the genealogical line of Jesus Christ and is included in the list of the heroes of the faith (Heb. 11:31).

that a man named Achan has stolen a Babylonian garment (a forbidden object), two hundred shekels of silver, and a wedge of gold weighing fifty shekels from the spoils of Jericho. The silver and gold were supposed to be turned over to the treasury. Achan and his entire family are stoned, and then Israel is able to destroy the city of Ai (Josh. 7:1–8:29).

Israel is learning that their success depends on God's favor, not their own might; when they are disobedient, they lose God's favor. Following the victory over Ai, Joshua erects an altar where the people offer burnt offerings and peace offerings. Then he reads all the words of the Law to the entire nation, including the women, the little ones, and the strangers among them. After the experience with Ai, Joshua wants everyone to know what God expects of them. He is reminding the people that they had vowed to keep the Mosaic Covenant. They are entering the promised land and they have to be a righteous people for the LORD (Josh. 8:30–35).

*****

Joshua, with his victories at Jericho and Ai, has militarily cut the land of Canaan in two. It will be difficult for the northern and southern kings to reinforce each other. But then Israel mistakenly makes a peace agreement with the Gibeonites in the south because they pretend to be from a far country. Israel had been given the option of making peace with other nations but not with the Canaanites.[195] Five kings from the south, including the king of Jerusalem, learn of this treaty, and they attack Gibeon. Gibeon is a large and strategic city (Josh. 10:2), and the kings of the south cannot allow this tribe to become allied with Israel. Despite the deception of the Gibeonites, Joshua honors the treaty and comes to their aid. He makes a night march, surprises the five kings arrayed against Gibeon, and destroys them and their armies.

Joshua then continues his campaign through southern Canaan, destroying the kings, the armies, and the people of the cities of Makkedah, Libnah, Lachish, Gezer, Eglon, Hebron, and Debir. Israel conquers all the land of southern Canaan, the mountain country, the wilderness slopes, and the lowlands, "because the LORD, the God of Israel, fought for Israel" (Josh. 10:42).

---

[195] The Canaanites had to be destroyed, "lest they teach you to do according to all their abominations which they have done for their gods, and you sin against the LORD your God" (Deut. 20:10–18).

With the conquest of southern Canaan complete, Joshua, the fighting men, and the rest of the nation return in triumph to Gilgal where they had crossed the Jordan River (Josh. 9:1–10:43).

*****

The king of Hazor in northern Canaan is very alarmed about the conquest of the south; he unites the kings of the north to stand against Israel. They mass all their armies, including many horses and chariots, at the waters of Merom northwest of the sea of Chinneroth (the Sea of Galilee). Their soldiers are like the sands of the seashore. But God tells Joshua not to fear because tomorrow, He is going to "deliver all of them slain before Israel" (Josh. 11:6).

The next day, Joshua and the men of war come quickly upon the massed northern forces. They defeat them and pursue them to Greater Sidon until none of them are left alive. They hamstring their horses and burn their chariots. Joshua then attacks the city of Hazor, destroys the inhabitants, and burns the city. The conquest of Canaan is finished; in five years,[196] Israel has destroyed thirty-one Canaanite kings and their populations. The land now rests from war. Of all that God had commanded Moses, Joshua has left nothing undone (Josh. 11:1–12:24).

*****

Israel has gained overall control of Canaan, but there are still individual fortified cities in the allotted tribal areas that have not been conquered. Military strategy had dictated that some of these walled cities be bypassed to rapidly secure dominance of the entire region. Now it is the responsibility of each individual tribe to possess their land and defeat the remaining enemies in their territory. The fighting with large forces is over, but there is still hard and dangerous work to do. These challenges are the result of Joshua's military strategy, but God is also testing the individual tribes to see if they will be faithful in possessing the land[197] (Judg. 3:1–4).

---

[196] This time is calculated from Caleb being eighty-five years old when the land rested from war. He was forty when Moses sent him and the other men to initially spy out the land from Kadesh-Barnea (Josh. 14:10).

[197] Like the Israelites, we all have areas in our lives that have not been possessed for the kingdom. God will test us, and we, too, must overcome our "fortified cities."

The nation assembles at Shiloh and after the Levites have set up the Tabernacle, Joshua addresses the important issues still facing the people. First, he urges the vacillating tribes to finish taking possession of the lands given to them. He also sets up cities of refuge to protect anyone accused of unpremeditated murder until the matter can be resolved by the elders. The Levites, the priestly line, have not been given a territory of their own, but Joshua assigns them individual cities where they can dwell and have livestock. The priests will be located throughout the land where they can minister to all the tribes.

The warriors of the tribes of Rueben, Gad, and the half-tribe of Manasseh have faithfully fulfilled their promise to help conquer Canaan. After five years of fighting, they want to return to their families and their lands east of the Jordan. Joshua blesses them and sends them on their way with their share of the spoils of war (livestock, silver, and gold), exhorting them to remain faithful to the Lord their God (Josh. 18:1–22:9).

*****

Time passes, and God gives the children of Israel rest from their enemies. The tribes are settled in their territories, although some of them have not yet destroyed the remaining fortified cities. Joshua has become advanced in age, and he summons the tribal leaders to meet with him at Shechem, where God had promised Abram that his descendants would be given the land of Canaan over seven centuries before.[198] Abram (*exalted father*) had been renamed Abraham (*father of a multitude*), and now his descendants have become that multitude, a strong nation which possesses the land of Canaan.

Joshua recounts for the people the history of Israel all the way back to Terah, the father of Abraham. God has kept his promises, and Joshua urges the nation to put away all other gods and serve the Lord in sincerity and truth. He says, "Choose for yourselves today whom you will serve...but as for me and my house, we will serve the Lord" (Josh. 24:14–15).

The people all say that they will only serve the Lord, but Joshua expresses concern that they will turn to idolatry. They once more swear to be faithful, so Joshua sets up a stone at Shechem to remind the people of the covenant they have made with the Lord. The children of Israel have reaffirmed their promise to be a righteous people in the promised land.

---

[198] See pp. 37–39 and Genesis 12:6–7.

Joshua has completed the work that God had given him. He is 110 years old when he dies and is buried in the mountains of Ephraim, the land assigned to his family in Canaan. After the burial of Joshua, the children of Israel also bury the bones of Joseph, carried with them from Egypt for more than forty-five years. As he had wanted, Joseph is buried in the promised land in the territory apportioned to his family (Josh. 24:29–32).

*****

This should be a happy ending for Israel. The tribes possess the land of Canaan, and they have promised to be faithful to the LORD. But, as Joshua feared, Israel does not remain true to the covenant they have made. It does not take Israel long to forget the LORD, who has kept His promises and brought them to the promised land, who gave them His Law so they could be a righteous people, and who manifested His presence with them in the Tabernacle. The book of Judges covers the next 350 years of Israel's history from approximately 1400 BC to 1050 BC, and it chronicles the recurring apostasy of the children of Israel.

CHAPTER 18

THE JUDGES AND THE KINGS IN THE PROMISED LAND

At the time of Joshua's death, most of the tribes still have remnants of Canaanites living within their regions. There is no central leader to assume Joshua's role and some of the individual tribes are still reluctant to fight the smaller battles necessary to take complete possession of their lands (Judg. 1:21–35). They have their houses and enough territory to prosper, and it is easier to coexist with the evil inhabitants and their gods than it is to remove them as the LORD had commanded (Judg. 3:5–7).

Israel had served the LORD during the days of Joshua, and the people remain faithful during the days of the elders who served with him. But then the next generation arises "who did not know the LORD nor yet the work which He had done for Israel" (Judg. 2:10). It takes the passing of only one generation for Israel to begin to abandon the LORD Who had delivered Canaan into their hands.[199]

The book of Judges records this period in Israel's history. It is a series of accounts with the same repetitive theme. Israel becomes unfaithful and turns to idolatry, the LORD sends oppressors to punish them, they cry out, and the LORD raises up a judge to deliver them.[200] Then the same pattern occurs again.

The writer of the book is unknown, but it was likely written after the period of the Judges during the reign of King Saul, the first king of Israel. It recounts the exploits of six major judges and six minor judges before the monarchy begins. These are the years of renowned warriors like Gideon with

---

[199] The men who witnessed what God had done on Israel's behalf were not faithful in instructing their children. The decline of the Church in the United States and the resulting moral corruption are for much the same reason.

[200] A judge in the book of Judges is a political or military leader, not the presiding official of a court. See *New Geneva Study Bible*, ed. R. C. Sproul (Nashville: Thomas Nelson, 1995), 331–332 for a condensed summary of the book of Judges.

his fleece (Judg. 6–8) and Samson with his hair (Judg. 13–16). The LORD uses the judges to rescue Israel, but they are not kings over the nation. Israel is a confederation of tribes, not a united monarchy; the LORD, through His Law, is supposed to be the King of His people.

When Gideon, the fifth of the judges, rescues the people from the Midianites,[201] the men of Israel want Gideon, his son, and grandson to reign, but Gideon says, "I will not rule over you, nor shall my son rule over you; the LORD shall rule over you" (Judg. 8:23). Under Gideon's leadership, Israel has peace for forty years, but when he dies of old age, the people again play the harlot with the Baals and make a Canaanite deity their god. There are other judges before and after Gideon, but their stories all come to a similar conclusion. The children of Israel do not want to submit to their heavenly King, and they turn to idols.

Israel has been fruitful and multiplied. The LORD has placed them in a Garden setting, and now they are to rule the land and be his people. But they have to be a righteous people; they have to keep the covenant, the Law of Moses. But the tribes never completely banish the Canaanites and their gods; they continually revert to idolatry and unfaithfulness as Joshua had feared.

The time of the judges is summed up in the last verse of the book, "In those days there was no king in Israel; everyone did what was right in his own eyes" (Judg. 21:25). Even though they are now in the beautiful "Garden" of Canaan, like Adam and Eve and Noah's family, the children of Israel are not content to be people who follow God's commands. They want to be like God and decide for themselves what is right and what is wrong—"everyone did what was right in his own eyes."

*****

At this point, we might expect the judgment of God to fall again in the final stage of this kingdom paradigm, but God is longsuffering with his chosen nation. After the Philistines defeat Israel in battle and capture the Ark of the Covenant, He raises up a final judge named Samuel.

The Philistines are unable to keep the Ark because wherever they send it, the Lord smites the Philistine men with deadly tumors. They send the Ark back

---

[201] The Midianites were hordes of raiders who rode camels and lived in the desert east of the Gulf of Aqaba. Moses's father-in-law, Jethro, was an early Midianite (p. 88, n. 142).

to Israel on a cart pulled by two unaccompanied milk cows. When the cart comes near Beth-shemesh, the local men lift the Ark from the cart, but some of them look inside it. The LORD strikes them down along with many other Beth-shemesh men because of their lack of reverence for Him. The survivors ask the men of Kiriath-jearim to take possession of the Ark. These men move it to the house of Abinadad where his son, Eleazar, is consecrated to watch over it. The Ark will remain in Abinadad's house until David becomes king and has it transferred to Jerusalem (1 Sam. 5:1–7:1).

With the Ark back in Israel, Samuel directs the nation to a military victory over the Philistines. He becomes a prophet and a revered man who leads Israel until he is old. He then appoints his sons as judges, but they are dishonest, take bribes, and pervert justice. The elders of the tribes confront Samuel about his sons and ask him to appoint a king to rule over them. They want to be rid of the sons, but they also want an earthly ruler to help unify and coordinate the tribes so they can deal with the internal and external challenges facing them. They want to be like the nations surrounding them (1 Sam. 1:1–8:5).

Samuel is displeased by this request, but the LORD tells him that "they have not rejected you, but they have rejected Me from being king over them" (1 Sam. 8:7). The LORD instructs Samuel to heed the voice of the people but to forewarn them that a king will take their sons for the army, use others to work his lands and make weapons of war, take their daughters to be perfumers, cooks, and bakers, confiscate the best of their fields and groves, conscript their servants and animals, and tax them. The LORD says that in that day, when the people cry out, He will not hear them (1 Sam. 8:6–18).

*****

The LORD sends Saul, a tall handsome man of the tribe of Benjamin, to Samuel and directs him to anoint Saul as the first king of Israel. Despite his stature and anointing, Saul is a reluctant leader and is not recognized as king until he assembles a large force to rescue Jabesh Gilead when it is besieged by the Ammonites. After the Ammonites are defeated, Samuel gathers the nation at Gilgal, and the people rejoice and coronate Saul as king. Samuel warns the people to serve the LORD with all their hearts because if they do not, they will be swept away along with their new ruler (1 Sam. 9:1–12:25). Israel had wanted a king, and now they have one, but the requirement to be a righteous people for God remains. They still have to keep the covenant they have made with the LORD; their ultimate allegiance is still to Him.

Saul has established himself as the first king of Israel, but the Philistines remain a serious threat. His son, Jonathan, is an able fighter and assists Saul, but one of the problems for Israel is that there are no blacksmiths in the nation. When there is peace, the Israelites must go to the Philistines to get their farming tools sharpened. When there are battles, the Philistines have swords, spears, and iron chariots. Saul and Jonathan have weapons, but their troops fight with their farm tools—mattocks, forks, and axes (1 Sam. 13:19–22). To be successful, Israel needs weapons, and they need to fight in the hills, not in the open valleys and flat lands where chariots are effective.[202]

After Saul has reigned for two years, Jonathan attacks the Philistine garrison at Geba. When the Philistines hear this, they mass thousands of soldiers, chariots, and horsemen at Michmash. The people of Israel are so afraid that they hide in caves, thickets, and holes; some of them flee across the Jordan River. Saul is at Gilgal with his army, waiting for Samuel to arrive to give his counsel and offer sacrifices. But when Samuel does not arrive in seven days, and the people begin to abandon Saul, he presents the burnt offering himself.

This is a serious mistake. Saul has disobeyed Samuel's command to wait for his arrival. Saul is not a priest, and it is not his place to offer sacrifices.[203] His unstable character and lack of faith are being revealed. Samuel arrives shortly after Saul has offered the burnt offering, and he is dismayed. He tells Saul that the kingdom will be taken from him[204] because God seeks a man who will keep His commandment, a man after His own heart. Samuel departs for Gibeah, and Saul is left alone with six hundred men to face the Philistine army.

Jonathan decides to take action and attacks a small advance company of the Philistines. With only his armor-bearer accompanying him, he kills about twenty men. This mighty deed sows fear and confusion among the Philistines, and some of them begin to abandon their positions. Saul, his men, and the men who had gone into hiding join the battle, and they rout the Philistines.

---

[202] As long as Israel stayed poor and in the hills, the major powers like Egypt and Assyria left the nation alone; these nations were mainly concerned about controlling the international trade route running through the flat land near the Mediterranean Sea.

[203] See p. 45, n. 97, concerning the separate roles of priest and king.

[204] Samuel has just pronounced a death sentence on Saul. There is no peaceful transfer of power from one king to the next unless it is passed on within the king's family. The kingdom can only be "taken" if the reigning king is dead.

The LORD has saved Israel again, but Samuel's declaration of Saul's demise remains certain (1 Sam. 13:1–14:1–23).

*****

Saul continues to rule and has ongoing battles with the Philistines and other hostile nations surrounding Israel. He collects valiant men to fight with him, and although he has victories, he disobeys God again when he defeats King Agag but does not kill him and keeps the best of the captured livestock for himself and his men. God had told Israel to destroy the people and animals associated with gross idolatry; they were defiled (Deut. 13:12–18). Samuel confronts Saul once more and tells him that he has rejected the word of the LORD and that the LORD has rejected him from being king over Israel. Samuel then kills Agag with his own hand and returns to Ramah. He will not see Saul again, but he mourns for him. First Samuel 15:35 says, "The LORD regretted that He had made Saul king over Israel" (1 Sam. 14:47–15:35).

The LORD then sends Samuel to Jesse the Bethlehemite[205] to anoint one of his sons as king to replace Saul. This has to be done in secret because if Saul finds out, he will kill Samuel. Samuel meets seven of Jesse's sons, but he recognizes that the next king is not among them. Jesse finally sends for his youngest son, David, who is tending the family's sheep. David is a musician and has been a faithful young shepherd; he has demonstrated his courage by killing a lion and a bear while defending Jesse's flock (1 Sam. 17:36). Samuel anoints him as the new king of Israel. But this is not made known, and Saul does not know that his successor has been appointed (1 Sam. 16:1–13).

*****

First Samuel 16:14 says the Spirit of the LORD departed from Saul, and a distressing spirit from the LORD troubled him.[206] Saul's servants notice the change in him and suggest that music would benefit the king. One of his attendants says that a son of Jesse the Bethlehemite is skillful at playing the harp, and

---

[205] David's family comes from the area of Bethlehem where the Messiah will be born.

[206] It appears that the bestowing of the Spirit of the Lord on leaders in the Old Testament was selective, temporary, and meant for a special role or purpose. After the coming of the Spirit at Pentecost in the New Testament, there is a permanent indwelling of the Spirit in all believers. Saul's distressing spirit was some type of influence sent by the LORD.

David, the future king, is invited into the royal court. His playing relieves the spirit of distress afflicting Saul, and Saul comes to love David—but he has no idea that this young man is his anointed successor (1 Sam. 16:14–23).

This begins a long and complicated narrative involving David, King Saul, and King Saul's family. The first important crisis occurs when David kills the giant Goliath with his slingshot during a standoff between Saul's army and the Philistines. This leads to a rout of the Philistine army; the women of Israel dance and sing songs about the victory and give young David more credit than Saul, saying, "Saul has slain his thousands, and David his ten thousands" (1 Sam. 18:7). Saul is extremely jealous, but before the battle he had promised to give his daughter and riches to the man who killed Goliath (1 Sam.17:25–27); Saul is obligated to David.

The next time David plays music for him, Saul hurls his spear at David in an effort to kill him, but David escapes. Despite Saul's attempt to murder him, David remains faithful to the king. Saul sees that the LORD is with David, and he comes to fear him because David is very popular with the people. Saul removes him from his house and makes him captain of a thousand in his army.

Saul eventually agrees to give his youngest daughter, Michal, to David as his wife, but since David is poor and without a dowry, Saul requests the foreskins of one hundred Philistines. Apparently, Saul had not only withheld his daughter but also the riches he had promised for killing Goliath. Saul is hoping the Philistines will kill David for him, but David brings back the foreskins of two hundred Philistines, and he marries Michal, the king's daughter. David is now not only a renowned military leader, he is the king's son-in-law and highly esteemed by the people (1 Sam. 17:1–18:30).

Saul then tells his son, Jonathan, and all his servants to kill David, but Jonathan is David's friend and tells him about Saul's plans (1 Sam. 19:1–2). When Saul sends his men to David's house, Michal saves him by letting him down through a window. Saul is furious with her, but she says that David threatened her life. David flees to Samuel in Ramah. Saul sends men to capture David, but they are overcome by the Spirit of God and can only prophesy before Samuel. Saul then goes to Ramah himself, but he too falls down and prophesies, and David escapes (1 Sam. 19:11–18).

Jonathan's allegiance to David is surprising because Jonathan is the presumed heir to Saul's throne, but Jonathan has come to love David as he loves his own soul. When Saul tells Jonathan that he will never be king as long as David is alive, Jonathan defends David. Saul is so incensed that he throws his spear at Jonathan as he had done with David; he tries to kill his own son. Jonathan leaves Saul's house and meets with David in the country. They weep and vow that there will always be peace between them and their descendants (1 Sam. 20:30–42).

*****

David is well known, and he has to change locations to avoid Saul's soldiers. Before long, various men, some who are discontented with the king and others who are just discontented, join with David until he is the captain of 400 fighters. He takes his parents to the ruler of Moab where they can be safe from Saul. Then David and his men move about in Canaan, staying in strongholds in the hill country and the wilderness of En Gedi, where it is difficult for Saul's troops to reach them. Twice, once when Saul enters a cave and once when Saul and his men are sleeping, David has the opportunity to kill the king, but he refuses to touch the Lord's anointed. In both instances, when Saul realizes that David has spared his life, he repents of his animosity toward David, but David knows he cannot trust the unstable ruler (1 Sam. 24:1–22, 26:1–25).

*****

Eventually, Samuel dies, and the people lament for the prophet and bury him in Ramah, his own city. Samuel had been a prophet and a revered leader as the last judge of Israel. He had led the transition to the monarchy when the people had demanded a king. At the Lord's direction, Samuel had anointed Saul as the first king of Israel, but Saul had proven to be a volatile and disobedient ruler. Long before his death, Samuel had stopped giving Saul counsel or even meeting with him.

Lacking Samuel's advice, Saul had turned to dreams, Urim,[207] and prophets for guidance, but he had received no directions from the LORD. Becoming desperate when facing another confrontation with the Philistines, he goes to the witch of Endor to try to contact Samuel and gain insight about the approaching battle. It is strictly forbidden to try to call up the spirits of the dead,[208] but

---

[207] Urim were objects on the High Priest's breastplate which were used to gain guidance from the LORD.

[208] Saul had driven most of the mediums out of the land (Deut. 18:10–11; 1 Sam. 28:3).

Samuel, or perhaps a demon impersonating Samuel, appears and tells Saul that he and his sons will die in the coming battle.

The next day, the Philistines defeat the army of Israel, and they kill Saul and three of his sons, including Jonathan, on Mount Gilboa (1 Sam. 22:1–31:13). When David learns what has happened, he and his men mourn and weep for Saul and Jonathan.

*****

The death of Saul opens the door for David to establish himself as king of Israel, but it is not an easy task to go from being a hunted enemy of the king to being king. The second book of Samuel records the ascendancy of David as he becomes ruler of all Israel. The author of the book is unknown. Samuel had died by the time of the book's writing, but he was the judge who transitioned to the era of the kings, and his name is attached to the book.

*****

After Saul's death, David goes to Hebron, a city located in the heart of the territory of his own tribe, the tribe of Judah. David had established a good reputation among his kinsmen while he and his men were on the run from Saul. He had protected the people from the Philistines and the Amalekites (1 Sam. 23:1–5, 30:1–30), and now they anoint him king of Judah. But Abner, the commander of Israel's army, proclaims Saul's remaining son, Ishbosheth, king over the remaining tribes of Israel. A war develops between the two kingdoms. Over time, David's forces grow stronger while Israel's grow weaker (2 Sam. 2:1–3:1).

A serious dispute arises between Ishbosheth and Abner when Abner sleeps with one of Saul's former concubines. This is tantamount to treason, a claim to the throne. When Ishbosheth confronts him, Abner angrily swears he will turn the kingdom of Israel over to David. Abner is the real power in Israel, and he tells the elders to support David as king. He assembles twenty men and goes to Hebron to meet with David. David provides a feast for Abner and his men, and Abner informs him that the leaders of Israel will support his reign over them.

Abner departs in peace, but David's commanding general, Joab, without David's knowledge, sends messengers to Abner asking him to come back to Hebron. When Abner returns, Joab takes him aside as though to speak to him privately but instead stabs him in the stomach and kills him. David is distraught over this treacherous murder by Joab. He weeps, tells the people to mourn for Abner, and then gives the general an honorable public burial in Hebron. All the people know that David was not the cause of Abner's death, but David does not punish Joab.[209]

When Ishbosheth hears about Abner's death, he loses heart and all the people of Israel are troubled. Two brothers, minor commanders in Israel's army, decide to kill the king. They slip into his bedroom while he is sleeping and stab him, then cut off his head and take it to David. The brothers expect to be rewarded, but David has them both executed and displays their bodies in Hebron. He buries Ishbosheth's head in the tomb with Abner. David has shown respect for both Abner and Ishbosheth and has made it clear that he was not involved in their murders.

Both the king and the commander of the army of Israel are dead, but the people do not blame David for the deaths of their leaders. The elders of Israel convene a meeting and go to David at Hebron. They anoint him king of Israel, and the nation is reunited. David has reigned seven years and six months in Hebron as king of Judah, and he will reign another thirty-three years as king over all Judah and Israel (2 Sam. 3:2–5:5).

*****

The first thing David does as king is to lead the army against Jerusalem. Jerusalem is located near the border that separates the two tribes of Judah and Benjamin, and apparently, both tribes had claimed the city (Judg. 1:21; Josh. 15:63). But because the city is a strong fortress and has valleys on three sides, neither tribe had been able to drive out the Jebusites that still occupy the city. The Jebusites feel safe and taunt David, but he manages to get men into the fortress through a water tunnel. Joab goes up first and apparently opens the city gates (1 Chron. 11:6). David's army is able to enter the city, and his soldiers destroy the Jebusites (2 Sam. 5:7–8).

---

[209] Abner had killed Joab's younger brother in the first battle of the war between Judah and Israel (2 Sam. 2:18–32), so Joab was taking revenge, but he also saw Abner as a threat to his position as head of David's army. David's reluctance to confront Joab indicates the power Joab has as the leader of the army, but he also is the son of David's sister; he is David's nephew.

David's purpose in taking Jerusalem is partly military—it gives him a city that is strong defensively—and partly political. Jerusalem had not been possessed by any tribe, and it is on the dividing line between the north and the south. Its choice as the center of David's power will raise little resentment from the tribes in the north or from Judah in the south. But the most significant reason for David to immediately take possession of Jerusalem is religious in nature.[210] Melchizedek, the King/Priest of God Most High, was called the king of Salem (Jerusalem) when he met with Abram and offered him bread and wine, fellowship with God Most High. And Mount Moriah, where Abraham was willing to sacrifice his son, is the same mountain on which Jerusalem is located.[211] This site is associated with Abraham's most significant encounters with God, and David wants to be in that place. He recognizes the historical nature of his faith—his connection with Israel's founding patriarch and the covenant that God had made with him. He is a man after God's own heart (1 Sam. 13:14).

David makes Jerusalem the capital of Israel; it will be his stronghold against all enemies. David builds his house in Jerusalem, and God is with him. He takes more wives and concubines; he will have many sons and daughters (2 Sam. 5:6–15).[212]

*****

---

[210] Suggested by Ken Olles in a Sunday School class.

[211] This "mountain" is just a high hill with deep valleys on three sides. The area is called Zion for the first time in 2 Sam. 5:7 when David captures the stronghold. The word *Zion*, or Mount Zion, is used over 150 times in the Bible and is synonymous with Jerusalem. The area referred to will expand when Solomon builds the Temple area to the north of "David's City." Mount Zion will come to have a spiritual aspect in the New Testament. Peter, quoting Isaiah 28:16, refers to Christ as the Cornerstone of Zion. See "What is Zion?," *Got Questions*, accessed November 16, 2018, https://www.gotquestions.org/Zion.html for a fuller discussion of the term Zion.

[212] The question of polygamy in the Old Testament is a difficult problem. The Torah does not condemn polygamy, but Jesus's teaching on marriage makes it clear that a man should have only one wife (Matt. 5:31–32, 19:3–12). Perhaps polygamy was permitted in the Old Testament because the continual warfare resulted in a shortage of husbands. Kings, such as David and Solomon, had the resources to support many wives and concubines. Kings also obtained royal wives from other nations to validate peace treaties and agreements. But for both David and Solomon, their many wives and extended families will have disastrous results.

When the Philistines hear that David has become king of all Israel, they understand that the reunited nation will be a powerful threat to them. They marshal their armies to deliver a preemptive strike against David's forces. But he defeats them at Baal Perzim and again in the Valley of Rephaim. The Philistines are driven back all the way to Gezer (2 Sam. 5:17–25).

After this initial military success, David has the Ark of the Covenant brought from the house of Abinadad to Jerusalem. He plans to make the worship of the LORD the center of the religious and political life of the nation. This is an act of devotion for David, but it will also help unite all the tribes. He dances for joy before the Ark as it is brought into the city and placed in the Tabernacle. He celebrates by giving everyone bread, meat, and raisin cakes. But Michal, Saul's daughter and David's first wife, despises him for his dancing and accuses him of trying to impress the women of the city.[213] David says that he was dancing for the LORD and he apparently ends his relationship with Michal; he has no children with her (2 Sam. 5:17–6:23).

*****

After the Ark is brought into Jerusalem, David, out of gratitude for his blessings, wants to build a house for the LORD. God tells David that he will not build a house for Him but that his son will, and He makes a covenant with David. Speaking through Nathan the prophet, the LORD says:

> When your days are complete and you lie down with your fathers, I will raise up your descendant after you, who will come forth from you, and I will establish his kingdom. He shall build a house for My name, and I will establish the throne of his kingdom forever. I will be a father to him, and he will be a son to me. (2 Sam. 7:12–14)

Abraham had been promised that kings would come from his offspring (Gen. 17:6). God now establishes that it will be through the line of David that the ultimate king will be born. There are dual aspects to the implementation of

---

[213] By this time, David has taken several other wives and has a number of sons. Michal was likely resentful and perhaps angry since David had taken her away from her recent husband, Paltiel, when David became king of all Israel (2 Sam. 3:13–16).

this covenant. Solomon, David's son, will provide a near-term fulfillment when he builds the Temple in Jerusalem and enlarges David's kingdom. But the permanent establishment of David's throne, the everlasting kingdom (v. 13), will be fulfilled by David's future descendant, the Messiah, God's only begotten Son who will build a living Temple—the congregation of believers who are indwelt by the Spirit of God (Eph. 2:19–22; 1 Pet. 2:4–5).

David praises God for his kindness to him and his future descendants who will dwell forever in the house of David, the final kingdom (2 Sam. 7:18–29).

This is the fifth covenant that God has specifically stated and instituted with men.[214] There will be one more covenant revealed in the Old Testament, the New Covenant, which will be foretold by the Prophet Jeremiah and instituted by the Messiah, Jesus, the night before He is crucified.[215] All of the covenants point to Him and His kingdom.

*****

David's reign is one of great political and military success; it appears that he can fulfill the last promise to Abraham by establishing a righteous kingdom that is a blessing for all the nations. David thoroughly defeats Israel's foremost enemy, the Philistines, and occupies their chief city. He conquers Moab, Zobah, Syria, and Edom, and controls the territory on both sides of the Jordan River from the Gulf of Aqaba in the south to Riblah in the north, far beyond Damascus. David enlarges his army with captured chariots and horses and acquires huge quantities of gold, silver, and bronze from the defeated nations. He puts military garrisons in the captured nations and forces them to serve him (2 Sam. 8:1–18). But then, at the peak of his success, he falls into terrible personal sins.

Israel has become a major power under David, but after defeating a powerful Aramean army, he seems to grow lax in his leadership. The next spring, when kings go out to battle, he sends Joab and the army out to attack the Ammonites and to besiege their capital city, but he remains in Jerusalem. One evening, he rises late and, from the elevated site of his house, sees a beautiful woman bathing in her courtyard. David sends for the woman and has rela-

---

[214] The four previous covenants are the Noahic, pp. 22–23, 29; Abrahamic, pp. 37–38; Mosaic, pp. 103–104; and Land or Palestinian Covenant, pp. 114–115.

[215] Jereniah 31:31–34; Luke 22:20.

tions with her. This woman, whose name is Bathsheba, is the wife of Uriah the Hittite, one of David's thirty chief men (1 Chron. 11:15, 41), a faithful soldier engaged in the battle against the Ammonites. Bathsheba becomes pregnant and informs David, who tries to cover his sin by calling Uriah back from the battlefield and telling him to rest at his house. But Uriah is a principled warrior and, in strong contrast to David, will not indulge himself while his fellow soldiers are fighting in the field. He sleeps at the door of the king's house and does not enter his own home. David then plies Uriah with food and drink, hoping that while intoxicated, he will sleep with his wife, but Uriah spends the night with David's servants.

When David sees that Uriah is not going to enter his house, he writes Joab a letter, instructing him to put Uriah in the heat of the battle and then withdraw from him so that he will be killed. David sends the letter by Uriah who delivers the orders to Joab—the orders for his own execution. Joab does not question David's directives. Uriah is left exposed near the besieged city and dies at the hands of the Ammonite archers. David has moved quickly from being negligent in his duties to committing adultery and now murder.

Bathsheba grieves for her husband. When the time for mourning has passed, David sends for her and takes her as his wife (2 Sam. 11:1–27).

The LORD sees what David has done and sends the Prophet Nathan to confront him (2 Sam. 12:1–7). Nathan begins by telling David a story about a rich man who had large flocks of sheep and cattle. But to feed a guest, the rich man took a poor man's only beloved lamb. David is furious at the rich man and declares that he should not live. Nathan, at the risk of his own life, says to David, "You are the man!" (2 Sam. 12:7).

When Saul was rejected as king of Israel, Samuel had referred to David as a man after God's own heart (1 Sam. 13:14). After his great sins, it is hard to see how David can be called such a man, but the answer is found in David's response to Nathan's indictment. He no longer tries to cover up his sin, and his grief and repentance are revealed in Psalm 51. Even for sins as terrible as adultery and murder, there is forgiveness for someone who truly repents.

Despite the severity of his sins, David is spared; God does not take his life. Instead of justice, David receives mercy. He has been pardoned through God's grace, but there will be consequences for his sins. Nathan tells David that the sword will never depart from his house. God will raise up evil against David from within his own family; a son will rebel against David and lie with his wives openly where David had committed adultery in secret. And the child born of his adultery with Bathsheba will not live.

As we have seen before, sexual immorality has terrible consequences. David will not be the man who establishes God's righteous kingdom (2 Sam. 12:1–23).

David will have four more sons with Bathsheba, including Solomon who will inherit David's throne. In all, David has fifteen sons and one daughter with his eight wives as well as additional sons and daughters with his concubines (2 Sam. 5:13; 1 Chron. 3:1–9). We have seen the great difficulties that Abraham and Jacob had with their polygamous families. But David, with more wives and concubines and the question of succession, will have even greater problems.

*****

David's first royal marriage for political reasons was with Maacha, his third wife and the daughter of Talmai, King of Geshur. After Saul's death, King Talmai apparently foresaw that David would ultimately rule all Israel, and he had made an early pact with David while he was the king of Judah. As was common in those days, Maacha was given to David as a seal of their treaty (2 Sam. 3:3). Maacha must have been beautiful because both of her children, her son, Absalom, and her daughter, Tamar, were noted for their attractive appearances (2 Sam. 13:1, 14:25).

When Tamar begins to mature, Amnon, David's first son by his wife, Ahinoam, develops an obsessive passion for his young half-sister who is still a virgin. He feigns illness and asks David to send Tamar to him so that she can make him some food. When she arrives, Amnon forces himself on her. He then despises her and locks her out of his house. Tamar is desolate and goes to stay with her brother, Absalom, in his home. He counsels her to remain silent, but Absalom has a bitter hatred for Amnon.

When King David learns of these things, he is angry but takes no action. Perhaps David felt guilty because he had told Tamar to go and prepare food for Amnon. He may have known or should have known about Amnon's obsession for Tamar. We have seen the failure of family leadership with all the patriarchs, and it is no different with David. Not to punish his firstborn son for the rape of his young sister seems inexcusable, and it eventually becomes clear that her brother, Absalom, sees it that way (2 Sam. 13:1–22).

Two years pass, and Absalom has a celebration during the sheep-shearing season. He convinces all of David's sons to attend, including Amnon. Absalom has his servants wait until Amnon becomes "merry with wine" (2 Sam. 13:28), and then they kill him. All the king's sons mount their mules and flee. Absalom flees also, for protection, to his grandfather, Talmai, who is still king of Geshur.

Absalom remains in Geshur for three years until David has completed mourning for his son, Amnon. Absalom must have been one of David's favorite sons because Joab sees that the king is still concerned for him. Joab intercedes and convinces David to bring Absalom back to Jerusalem, but he is relegated to a separate house and is not allowed to see David's face.

Absalom dwells in his house for two years and then tells Joab that it would have been better for him to have stayed in Geshur. He has not seen his father for five years. Joab again intervenes for Absalom, and David relents and welcomes him back into his presence with a kiss (2 Sam. 13:23–14:33).

*****

Once Absalom has reestablished himself in the royal court, he begins to expand his influence. He has his own chariots and horses, along with fifty men who follow him. He rises early and sits in the gate and ingratiates himself with the people by sympathizing with those who have complaints about David and the judgments he renders. After a time, he asks David to let him go to Hebron to fulfill a vow, and David gives his permission. Absalom positions himself in David's former city and sends his followers to all the tribes to encourage a rebellion against David. The conspiracy grows strong, and the people siding with Absalom rapidly increase in number.

David learns of Absalom's treachery and soon recognizes the magnitude and immediate danger of the insurrection. If he stays in Jerusalem, Absalom and his forces are going to kill him and his household. He leaves the city with his family and the people who are still faithful to him. Joab and the soldiers who remain loyal to David form an escort as the procession leaves the city. They cross the Brook Kidron and ascend the Mount of Olives, weeping as they go. David's head is covered, and he is walking barefoot in his sorrow.

The Levites have brought the Ark of the Covenant, but David tells them to return it to Jerusalem.

Absalom learns of David's departure, and he and his forces leave Hebron and immediately occupy Jerusalem. David and his demoralized company are very vulnerable, but Hushai, the priest who is secretly faithful to David, advises Absalom to wait and not pursue David until Absalom has assembled more men. Absalom accepts this counsel, giving David and his people enough time to cross the Jordan River where they can eat, rest, and organize.

David had left ten of his concubines in Jerusalem to care for his house (2 Sam. 15:16). Absalom erects a tent on top of David's residence and lies with these women in the sight of all Jerusalem. Nathan's prophecy has been fulfilled, and Absalom's break with his father is complete; now there is no turning back (2 Sam. 15:1–18:2).

*****

Once across the Jordan, David has time to coordinate his fighters into three companies; they are prepared when Absalom and Amasa, Absalom's cousin, soon lead their insurgent forces against them. David's supporters urge him stay out of the battle, and he heeds their pleas, but he orders Joab and the commanders to "deal gently" with his son, Absalom, words which all the people hear (2 Sam. 18:5). David's faithful men overwhelm Absalom's troops and kill thousands of them. During the battle, Absalom tries to ride under a terebinth tree, and his abundant hair is caught up in its boughs, jerking him from his mule and leaving him suspended helplessly in the air. When Joab is informed, he and his armor-bearers surround Absalom and kill him as he hangs from the tree. Joab blows the trumpet, and his troops stop pursuing Absalom's fleeing army. The insurrection is over.

Joab's soldiers throw Absalom's body into a pit and cover it with a large heap of stones. Then the men of Israel who had rebelled against David begin fleeing to their own tents (2 Sam. 18:1–17).

*****

Absalom's rebellion has been defeated, but now the nation is in confusion; David must reestablish his rule and reunite the tribes of Israel. But he remains across the Jordan, despondent in sorrow over the death of Absalom. The people realize that David's heart is more with his fallen rebellious son than it is with the allies who remained loyal and saved him and his family. There is a real possibility that David has won the battle but is now going to lose the kingdom.

Joab confronts David and tells him that he loves his enemies and hates his faithful servants and that he must reach out to the people or he will have worse trouble than what he has endured in all his previous conflicts.[216]

David listens to Joab and meets with the people who had remained loyal to him. He then reaches out to the priests, Zadok and Abiathar, and directs them to tell Amasa that he will replace Joab who had killed Absalom against his orders. This helps David win over Absalom's supporters, and they send word that he should return with all his servants. David's kinsmen from the tribe of Judah transport him and his household back across the Jordan River.

It appears the nation is going to be reconciled, but a quarrel arises between the tribe of Judah and the other tribes over who should have the most access to the king. Sheba, a Benjamite, tries to lead a second rebellion of the northern tribes. David tells Amasa to present himself and his men so that they can deal with this new uprising. But when Amasa delays, David sends Joab and his soldiers after Sheba. As Joab is pursuing Sheba, he meets Amasa and his men. Joab pretends to greet Amasa but then stabs him in the stomach and leaves him dying in the road. This is the second time that Joab has killed a rival for his position, and he has killed them both in the same treacherous way.

Amasa's men have to make a choice, and they join with Joab against Sheba. These combined forces corner Sheba and his supporters in the city of Abel and begin erecting a siege ramp to overcome the city's defensive wall. To save themselves, the people of Abel kill Sheba and throw his head over the wall to Joab. The second rebellion has ended. Sheba's followers and Joab's men return to their tents, but Joab returns to Jerusalem.

David reestablishes his throne in Jerusalem and reorganizes his government. He designates the official priests and appoints new leaders over forced labor and records, showing that he is responding to the complaints of the people. Joab remains in command of the army, despite the deaths of Absalom and Amasa. He is a powerful general who has saved David more than once. And he had carried out David's orders leading to the death of Uriah the Hittite; he has leverage that keeps him in his position.

---

[216] Joab is a ruthless and formidable military man who has been vital to David's success. He is also the son of David's sister, Zeruiah (1 Chron. 2:16), and he had carried out David's orders against Uriah. Joab feels free to confront David in a way that no one else can.

David has gone through a desperate struggle, but the kingdom has been stabilized, and he and his family have been saved. David composes a song of praise to God for his deliverance (2 Sam. 18:33–22:51).

*****

David has survived the strongest challenge to his leadership, but as he grows older and weaker, the question of who will succeed him becomes the central issue of his last days. David had promised Bathsheba that their son, Solomon, would inherit the throne (1 Kings 1:17), but David's fourth son, Adonijah, the son of Haggith, gains the support of Joab and Abiathar the priest. Adonijah prepares a feast, intending to declare himself king. Solomon, Nathan, and David's closest protectors, his mighty men, are not invited. If Adonijah becomes king, David and all these men, along with Bathsheba, will be killed.

Nathan informs Bathsheba, and she tells David that Adonijah is going to declare himself king. Even though he is physically weak, David takes decisive action. He tells Nathan, Zadok the priest, and his mighty men to put Solomon on his own mule. They lead him to the spring at Gihon where the people gather to fill their water jars. Zadok publicly anoints Solomon as king of Israel, and they blow the ram's horn. The people are pleased, and they rejoice and shout, "Long live King Solomon!" (1 Kings 1:39). When Adonijah and his supporters hear the roar of the people and find out what has happened, they become frightened and scatter. Solomon will be king after David's death (1 Kings 1:1–49).

*****

After assuring that Solomon will succeed him, David, knowing his death is near, gives Solomon his last instructions. He tells him to "keep the charge of the LORD your God, to walk in His ways, to keep His statutes, His command- ments, His ordinances, and His testimonies, according to what is written in the Law of Moses, that you may succeed in all that you do and wherever you turn" (1 Kings 2:3). David is urging Solomon to keep the Mosaic Covenant so that one of David's descendants will always sit on the throne of Israel as God has promised him. David does not tell Solomon how to deal with his half-brother, Adonijah, who had tried to take the throne, but he does tell him that Joab must not be allowed to live (1 Kings 2:5–6).

David has been king for over forty years—seven years and six months in Hebron as king of Judah, and thirty-three years as king of all Israel. He has been a great warrior and ruler with military and political triumphs that have made Israel into a strong and prosperous nation. He has been a musician and has written many Psalms inspired by the Holy Spirit. His wives and concubines have given him many children. He is an extraordinary man, blessed with great spiritual qualities, who has also committed great sins. But because he confessed his sins and turned to God for forgiveness, he is still a man after God's own heart. After giving his final instructions to Solomon, David rests with his fathers and is buried in the City of David.

David's reign was a time of military conflict, and he was not allowed to build a house for God.[217] Despite his accomplishments, he was not able to establish God's kingdom. Solomon will be the one who completes the Temple, and he will have an even greater opportunity in a time of peace to inaugurate a righteous kingdom for God.

*****

Solomon becomes established as king, but he soon faces a challenge when Adonijah tries to claim King David's last concubine, a clear sign of his half-brother's ongoing ambitions. Solomon orders him executed and has Abiathar, the priest who had supported Adonijah, exiled from Jerusalem. When Joab hears this, he flees to the Tabernacle and clings to the horns of the altar for protection. But because Joab is a murderer, the Tabernacle is no refuge for him, and Solomon has him struck down and killed in the sanctuary.[218]

Solomon next makes a treaty with the Egyptian Pharaoh, marries his daughter, and brings her to the city of David. Solomon has solidified his control within the nation and, with his Egyptian alliance, has assured that he will

---

[217] God had not permitted David to build the Temple because he had shed much blood (1 Chron. 22:8). His reign was involved with continual military and political battles as he made Israel into a great nation. He had also ordered the murder of Uriah to cover up his adultery with Bathsheba. His son, Solomon, will reign in a time of peace, a setting more suitable for the establishment of God's house in Jerusalem.

[218] The horns of the altar could be a place of refuge for someone who had caused a death without malice (Exod. 21:12–14), but this was not true of Joab. This nephew of David had been essential to David's success, but he was also a treacherous murderer, and his tumultuous life has come to its violent end.

have external peace. Solomon has acted shrewdly, and God appears to him in a dream and asks him what he wants to be given. Solomon asks for an understanding heart so that he might discern between good and evil when judging his people.[219]

This pleases God, and He says He will grant him not only wisdom but riches and honor beyond the kings of other nations (1 Kings 3:1–14). Solomon is positioned to complete the final promise made to Abraham. The first two promises have been fulfilled: Abraham's descendants have been fruitful and have multiplied into a strong nation, and they now rule the land promised to them. Beyond any previous son of Abraham, Solomon has the position and power to fulfill the third promise: to make Abraham a blessing to all the nations by establishing a righteous kingdom that will be God's witness to the world.

*****

Solomon begins by appointing priests, scribes, a recorder, a general for his army, and governors over the tribal territories of Israel. "Judah and Israel were as numerous as the sand that is on the seashore in abundance, they were eating and drinking and rejoicing" (1 Kings 4:20). It is a time of peace and great prosperity, and Solomon prepares to build the Temple, the House of the LORD, who has blessed his people and established them in the land He promised them.

Although David was not permitted to build the Temple, the Spirit of God had given David the plans for its construction, and he had begun to make preparations. He had formed work crews from foreign nations to cut and transport stones and prepare iron, bronze, and cedar for the building. David had dedicated 100,000 talents of gold and 1,000,000 talents of silver for use in the sanctuary.[220] He had given the plans for the Temple to Solomon, and he had commanded the leaders of Israel to help Solomon do the work (1 Chron. 22:1–9, 28:11–12, 19).

---

[219] In contrast to Adam and Eve, who decided to determine good and evil for themselves, Solomon looks to God for righteousness and objective truth. It will not endure, but it is a moment of spiritual clarity for Solomon.

[220] This is about 120 million ounces of gold and about 1.2 billion ounces of silver. At July 2022 prices, a total of at least 80 billion dollars. See n. on 1 Chron. 22:14, in Ryrie, *Ryrie Study*, 631. This is an astounding amount and means that the Temple, with its furnishings, will be the most expensive building ever constructed.

In the fourth year of Solomon's reign, 480 years after Israel's exodus from Egypt, he begins construction of the Temple. It takes seven years for thousands of the finest artisans from Israel and the surrounding nations to complete the magnificent building (1 Kings 5:1–6:38). It has the same basic arrangement as the Tabernacle and sits within an enclosure surrounded by an outer court, but the stone building itself is twice the size of the tent which was its predecessor.[221] The Tabernacle had been a portable sanctuary as Israel journeyed to Canaan. But now that Israel is established in the promised land, Solomon has constructed a permanent dwelling place for the God of Abraham, Isaac, and Jacob.

When all the work is completed, King Solomon assembles the elders and all the people of Israel to dedicate the Temple. The priests transport the Ark of the Covenant and the holy utensils from the Tabernacle to the Temple Mount. Solomon and the people sacrifice so many sheep and oxen that they cannot be counted. After the sacrifices, the priests carry the Ark of the Covenant into the Temple and place it in the Most Holy Place. When the priests exit this most sacred area, the glory of the LORD fills the Temple. The sign of His presence is so intense that the priests have to halt their acts of ministry (1 Kings 8:1–11).

Solomon speaks to the LORD and says that he has built Him a lofty house, "A place for Thy dwelling forever" (1 Kings 8:13). He then turns and blesses the people and praises God for keeping his covenant and "showing loving kindness to Thy servants who walk before Thee with all their heart" (1 Kings 8:23).

The LORD speaks to Solomon and tells him that if he keeps His statutes and judgments that He will establish Solomon's throne forever, but if he does not keep His commandments, He will cut Israel off from the land which He has given them (1 Kings 9:4–9).

*****

The Temple has been inaugurated as the center of Israel's religious life, and Solomon has internal and external peace for his kingdom. He has the favor and backing of the people. He has a strong military, a fleet of ships for trade, and immense wealth. Solomon writes proverbs and songs[222] and investigates and speaks on the nature of plants and animals; God has given him wisdom

---

[221] The Temple was ninety feet long, thirty feet wide, and forty-five feet high while the Tabernacle was forty-five feet by fifteen feet by fifteen feet high (1 Kings 6:2; Ex. 26:15–30).

[222] Solomon wrote 3,000 proverbs and 1,005 songs (1 Kings 5:32). Many of these proverbs are inspired by the Holy Spirit and are included in the book of Proverbs. Solomon is also

beyond all the wise men. The kings of other nations send men to Israel so they can profit from Solomon's knowledge (1 Kings 4:29–34). The Queen of Sheba visits Solomon with treasures and a grand entourage and is overwhelmed by his wisdom and his royal court. She gives him a hundred and twenty talents of gold[223] plus large amounts of spices and precious stones before she returns to her land with gifts from Solomon (1 Kings 10:1–13).

The LORD is with Solomon and has confirmed His favor by displaying His glory in the Temple. Solomon has every advantage needed to establish God's righteous kingdom. But from what we have seen with Adam and Noah, who also had great advantages, we are not surprised when he fails, just as they did.

Solomon's downfall begins with his love for foreign women. He eventually has a total of 700 wives and 300 concubines, many from nations with whom Israel is forbidden to associate. As he grows older, these women turn his heart away from the one true God to go after false gods; he goes so far as to establish high places for the idols of Moab and Ammon[224] (1 Kings 11:1–8). He also disobeys God when he multiplies horses for himself beyond what is necessary for Israel's military and transportation needs (Deut. 17:16–17). He sells horses and chariots to nations who could eventually use them against Israel.

Solomon is beginning to trust in his riches and military might (1 Kings 10:26–29), and he taxes the people heavily. But his own tribe of Judah has been excluded from being under a regional governor and the taxations that follow[225] (1 Kings 4:7–19). This injustice will be a factor in the future rebellion against his son, Rehoboam.

God becomes very angry with Solomon and tells him that He is going to tear the kingdom away from him, but for David's sake, he will leave him one tribe and will delay the judgment until the days of Solomon's son (1 Kings 11:9–13). Solomon is allowed to continue his rule, and he completes his own house and many other large construction projects (1 Kings 9:15–19). Israel

---

credited with writing the Old Testament wisdom books of Ecclesiastes and the Song of Solomon.

223 One hundred forty-four thousand ounces worth over 260 million dollars at July 2022 prices.

224 These two nations, descendants from the incest of Lot's daughters, continue to bedevil Israel a thousand years after the births of their patriarchs. See pp. 49 and 113, n. 186.

225 The split between Judah and the other tribes was already apparent in King David's day and was an ongoing source of friction. The animosity will reach a breaking point under Solomon's successor.

reaches the pinnacle of its political and military power during his reign, but God begins to raise up adversaries against him, men who have resentments going back to the time of King David. The Prophet Ahijah tells Jeroboam, a mighty man of valor who is over Solomon's labor force, that he is going to rule over ten tribes of Israel. Solomon learns of this and tries to kill Jeroboam, but he escapes to Egypt (1 Kings 11:26–40).

The seeds for the destruction of Solomon's legacy have been sown. He has not obeyed God, and he will not establish God's righteous kingdom. But the promises to Abraham have seen a brief near-term fulfillment. His descendants have become a nation, they have possessed the land of Canaan, and for a short period of time, they have been a witness and a blessing to the nations. But Solomon's kingdom is only a type of the final kingdom; because of Solomon's sins, the deterioration of his glorious reign has begun. God had told Solomon when the Temple was dedicated that if he did not keep His commandments, the land, and the Temple would be taken from Israel (1 Kings 9:6–9; p. 142).

The third step in the kingdom paradigm, God's judgment, is now going to come upon His chosen nation. The ultimate fulfillment of the promises to Abraham, as he and Isaac and Jacob had come to understand, will be found in another country, a heavenly one (Heb. 11:8–16).[226]

---

[226] The Dispensational view expects the fulfillment of the promises to Abraham to be an earthly thousand-year reign of Christ over Israel after his second coming and before the final judgment, with an unusual nation made up of some believers, some unbelievers, and some resurrected believers. This is difficult to envision and also difficult to justify from Scripture. See pp. 247–251 for a discussion of Paul's proclamation of the ultimate unity of Jews and Gentiles in Jesus Christ.

CHAPTER 19

A Divided Nation, the Prophets, and Jerusalem Destroyed

The judgment on the children of Israel is approaching; it will last for many centuries,[227] and it will be devastating. Solomon dies after reigning forty years and is buried in the City of David. His son, Rehoboam, ascends to the throne. Jeroboam, who had fled to Egypt, returns to Jerusalem, and with the leaders of the tribes of Israel, goes to the new king and says that if he will lighten Solomon's heavy burdens on the people,[228] they will serve him. But Rehoboam, influenced by his young allies rather than by Solomon's older advisors, tells Jeroboam that he is going to make their yoke even heavier.

The ten northern tribes rebel and make Jeroboam their king. Rehoboam assembles his army to attack this insurgent confederation, but he receives a message from the Prophet Shemaiah that he is not to fight against his brothers. The time of the divided kingdom has begun. The ten northern tribes have broken away from the tribes of Judah and Benjamin, which remain loyal to Rehoboam. The northern kingdom is now called Israel, and the southern kingdom is known as Judah.[229] (1 Kings 12:1-24)

---

[227] This judgment will end when the Jews become reconciled with Jesus the Messiah and are grafted back into their own natural olive tree (Rom. 11:1–36). Jesus has broken down the dividing wall between Jews and Gentiles and has made them into one new man, establishing peace that He might reconcile them both in one body to God through the cross (Eph. 2:13–22). The redeemed of God, Jews and Gentiles alike, are all part of the same olive tree. This rules out a separate destiny for the children of Israel and makes the very basis for Dispensationalism untenable. See pp. 247–251.

[228] The Prophet Samuel had warned the tribes about the heavy duties a king would impose. God had said that when the people complained, He would not hear them. See p. 124.

[229] The tribe of Benjamin is so small and insignificant that it is not treated like a tribe. The other tribes had attacked and almost annihilated the men of Benjamin when some Benjamites

Jeroboam rules from Shechem in the North and becomes concerned that many in his nation will want to return to Jerusalem to worship in the Temple. This could lead to reconciliation with Judah, which would lead to the collapse of his kingdom and to the death of himself and his family. He decides to make two golden calves and proclaims, "Behold your gods O Israel, that brought you up from the land of Egypt" (1 Kings 12:28). This is the same declaration the people made when Aaron molded the golden calf at Mt. Sinai (Exod. 32:4). Like Aaron, Jeroboam claims to be worshipping the God of Israel,[230] but he is just creating idols to protect himself.[231]

Jeroboam places one calf in Bethel and one in Dan so the northern tribes will have convenient places to worship and will not have to return to Jerusalem (1 Kings 12:25–30). The people, still influenced by their anger at Rehoboam, accept this arrangement. But Jeroboam is afraid the priests will not participate in such gross idolatry (2 Chron. 11:13–17). They know their history and remember what happened when Aaron made the golden calf at Mt. Sinai.[232] Jeroboam appoints his own priests, and the Levites abandon their cities and their possessions in the North and flee to Judah and Jerusalem. Jeroboam is compounding the sin of the golden calves, but the people of the northern tribes accept this further erosion of their historical faith. God, in His judgment on Solomon, has divided the nation of Israel physically; Jeroboam has now divided the nation spiritually.

Like David and Solomon, Jeroboam takes many wives and has many children, but he continues to do evil in the sight of the LORD. His son, Nadab, succeeds Jeroboam and reigns for two years. But then Baasha, a military commander, kills Nadab; he assumes the throne and kills all of Jeroboam's descen-

---

had raped and killed a priest's concubine (Judg. 19–21). But the remaining Benjamites see Jerusalem as part of their tribal territory and elect to stay with Judah.

[230] Churches today that have abandoned the gospel of Jesus Christ are doing the same thing, claiming to be Christian without the spiritual reality.

[231] This is what all human beings tend to do. As Calvin said, our minds beget idols. John Calvin, *Institutes of the Christian Religion*, ed. John T. McNeill, trans. Ford Lewis Battles (Philadelphia: Westminster Press, 1960), Vol. I, 108.

[232] Moses had called on the Levites to help restore order, and 3,000 people were killed. He also ground up the golden calf and made the Israelites drink it. See pp. 104–105.

dants. Although he destroys Jereboam's line, Baasha continues the worship of the golden calves as will every future king of Israel (1 Kings 15:27–34).

*****

The northern kingdom had broken away from Rehoboam in 931 BC. The nation exists until 722 BC when the Assyrians capture Samaria, the capital city, and carry away most of the population for resettlement. During its 209 years as the northern kingdom, Israel has nineteen kings. Scripture speaks of them as following the sin of Jeroboam, the sin of idolatry with the golden calves, and says that each of the northern kings did evil.[233] None of these kings were a descendant of David; they were not part of the everlasting covenant God had made with him.

Israel had managed to survive for over two centuries, but after the northern tribes were conquered, the deported people were gradually assimilated by other nations, and they have disappeared from history. They are often referred to as the Ten Lost Tribes of Israel.

After Assyria deported the majority of the Israelites, they imported foreigners to resettle their captured territory. These foreigners intermarried with the remaining Jews, and their descendants are called Samaritans after the capital city. These mixed race people are despised by the people of Judah because they are no longer fully Jewish, and they had worshipped the golden calves. In Jesus's day, the Jews will have nothing to do with the Samaritasns.[234] The third step in this kingdom paradigm, judgment, comes first upon the northern kingdom.

*****

Rehoboam reigns over the southern kingdom, and with the influx of the priests fleeing from the north, strengthens his nation for three years (2 Chron. 11:17). But then Rehoboam forsakes the Law of the Lord and all Judah follows

---

[233] One of the most evil kings was Ahab. His wife, Jezebel, was so depraved that her name has become a synonym for an evil woman. When King Jehu assumes power in the Northern Kingdom, he has her thrown to her death from an upper window of the royal palace in Jezreel, and the dogs devour her (2 Kings 9:30–37).

[234] See John 4:9.

him. They build high places for idol worship and commit gross abominations. Like the northern kingdom, Judah abandons the LORD and turns to idolatry.

In the fifth year of Rehoboam's reign, King Shishak of Egypt, who had given Jeroboam refuge from Solomon, attacks Jerusalem. Rehoboam, weakened militarily by the departure of the northern tribes, surrenders, and Shishak takes the precious treasures from the Temple and the king's house back to Egypt.[235] The Prophet Shemaiah tells Rehoboam and the leaders of Judah that this tremendous loss of treasure and prestige is due to their idolatry, and they humble themselves. The LORD has severely chastised Rehoboam, but He does not destroy him. He reigns for seventeen years before he dies and is buried with his fathers in the City of David (1 Kings 14:21–31; 2 Chron. 12:1–16). Josephus, in his history of the Jews, says that Rehoboam was a "proud and foolish man and lost dominions by not hearkening to his father's friends."[236]

*****

The consequences that the LORD had warned Solomon about have come to pass. The kingdom has been torn away from his son because Solomon did not keep the covenant and its statutes.[237] Rehoboam's arrogance triggered the rebellion that led to the division of the kingdom into two nations. The northern nation became completely apostate and was destroyed while Judah continued to lapse in and out of idolatry. Twelve of Judah's twenty kings are said to have done good while eight are condemned for doing evil.

*****

---

[235] Apparently, the Ark of the Covenant had been hidden. Three hundred years later during the reign of King Josiah (640–609 BC), he directs the Levites to return the Ark to the Temple (2 Chron. 35:1–6). The assumption of the Spielberg film, *Raiders of the Lost Ark*, that Shishak had taken the Ark to Egypt is incorrect. The final fate of the Ark, whether it is eventually hidden, destroyed, or perhaps taken to Babylon by Nebuchadnezzar, is not known.

[236] Flavius Josephus, "Antiquities of the Jews," in *The Works of Josephus*, trans. William Whiston (Peabody, MA: Hendrickson, 1987), 8.11.4. Josephus (AD 37–100) was a Jewish military leader who fought and then defected to the Romans. His writings are a helpful historical resource.

[237] Solomon had not kept the covenant given to Moses at Sinai and renewed by Joshua at Shechem (Josh. 24:14–26; 1 Kings 2:3).

The time of the divided kingdom is the era of the Old Testament prophets. The prophets preach, prophesy future events, and act as prosecuting attorneys for the LORD in holding Judah and Israel accountable for breaking the Mosaic Covenant. They lay out the case for God's judgment against both nations.

Some of the earlier prophets such as Nathan, Elijah, and Elisha did not leave their own written texts, so they are known by their deeds and proclamations recorded in the historical books. During the time of the divided kingdom, the prophets and their writings cluster around two major events, the fall of the northern kingdom in 722 BC and the fall of the southern kingdom in 587 BC.[238]

Amos and Hosea prophesy to the northern kingdom in the years prior to its demise (approx. 765–737 BC). Amos declares the disasters that are to come on both Israel and Judah (Amos 2:4–16). Hosea is given a particularly difficult ministry; God tells him to marry a harlot, who will be unfaithful to him, to demonstrate what Israel has become as a nation (Hosea 1:2–8). Both men prophesy coming destruction while also foreseeing a time of repentance and restoration for both nations. But the people of Israel and their rulers do not heed the warnings of Amos and Hosea and continue on their way to judgment.

During this time, Isaiah and Micah begin prophesying in Judah. Isaiah also preaches the judgment coming upon Judah and her eventual restoration (Isa. 1–3, 11:1–16). His rich and lengthy book is best known for his description of the coming Deliverer who will be a son of Jesse but also a Suffering Servant (Isa. 52:13–53:12). Isaiah is further defining the character and work of the Messiah first prophesied in Genesis 3:15. His prophecy of the Suffering Servant builds on the revelation given to Abraham when he was told to sacrifice his son Isaac on Mt. Moriah (see pp. 52–54). But the people of Judah do not want to hear about a Suffering Savior; they want a Messiah who will restore the glory of David's kingdom.

*****

After the destruction of the northern kingdom in 722 BC, Nahum, Zephaniah, Jeremiah, and Habakkuk prophesy to Judah (approximately 650 –575 BC). Nahum foretells the destruction of Nineveh, the capital city of

---

[238] Sproul, *New Geneva*, 1,018.

Assyria, which had destroyed the northern kingdom.[239] The destruction of this great city in 612 BC, a century after it had repented and been spared under the preaching of Jonah, should have been an object lesson for the people of Jerusalem. Nineveh had returned to its evil ways and had been destroyed; Judah's people should not presume that they are immune from God's judgment.

Zephaniah and Habakkuk both foretell judgment on Jerusalem at the hand of an invading army. Habakkuk specifically says it will be the Chaldeans (Babylonians), who, as Nahum had prophesied, help destroy Nineveh in 612 BC (Hab. 1:6). Habakkuk, viewing Judah's sins and foreseeing the coming destruction, also advances the understanding that "the just shall live by his faith" (Hab. 2:4), a concept introduced with Abraham (Gen. 15:6) which will be a focus for Paul in the New Testament, especially in Romans and Galatians. People and nations cannot save themselves through keeping the Law; they always fail. Salvation can only come by God's grace through faith.

*****

Jeremiah prophesies under the last five kings of Judah. He is known as the weeping prophet as he observes the sinfulness of God's people, especially the leaders in Jerusalem. In overwhelming grief, he foretells the devastating judgment and the seventy years of captivity that are coming for Judah at the hands of the Babylonians (Jer. 9:1, 25:8–11). Although the coming destruction is going to be catastrophic, the LORD also tells Jeremiah that there will be a renewal for Judah and Israel (Jer. 31:1–14). And He reveals to Jeremiah how this restoration will come about; the Lord is going to make a new covenant with His people.

In a prophecy that is crucial for understanding redemptive history and the fulfillment of the promises to Abraham, God says that He is going to make a new covenant with Israel and Judah, but it will not be like the covenant that the nation has broken. In the new covenant, God will not write His Law on tablets of stone but on the hearts of His covenant people. He is going to forgive their sins and remember them no more (Jer. 31:31–34; Heb. 8:6–13). And this is an everlasting covenant; it will never be broken (Jer. 32:38–41).

---

[239] Nineveh was thought to be an invincible city. Its conquest by an unusual coalition of Babylonians, Medes, and Scythians shook the entire Middle East.

Six centuries later, Jesus will inaugurate this Covenant with bread and wine as he shares the Passover meal with his disciples the night before He is crucified.[240] As Melchizedek, Jesus had offered Abram bread and wine, fellowship with God Most High.[241] At the Passover meal, He will offer Abram's descendants bread and wine, fellowship with God Most High through His shed blood (Luke 22:20; Matt. 26:28; Mark 14:24; 1 Cor. 11:25).

The inauguration of the new covenant will be a critical transition in redemptive history. God will no longer work out His plan of salvation through Israel, a single theocratic nation, but rather through a subculture in all the nations, the Church, those who have the Law written on their hearts, the true Israel (Rom. 2:28–29, 9:6–8; Eph. 2:11–18). The new covenant will be the means by which the promises to Abraham are ultimately fulfilled.

*****

Jeremiah is seen as a traitor as he warns Judah of the coming destruction and urges the national leaders to surrender to the king of Babylon in order to save lives (Jer. 21:1–10, 38:17–18). King Jehoiakim cuts up his writings and casts them into the fire, but Jeremiah has his scribe complete another scroll (Jer. 36:20–32). Eventually, King Zedekiah, the last king of Judah, has Jeremiah committed to the court of the guardhouse (Jer. 38:5–28).

Jeremiah remains confined until 587 BC when King Nebuchadnezzar and the Babylonian army lay siege to Jerusalem and overwhelm it. Nebuchadnezzar had previously attacked Jerusalem in 605 BC and again in 597 BC. He had taken captives to Babylon after these first assaults (including Daniel and his young companions in 605 BC) but had spared the city. Now, with the Jews continuing to resist, he has no mercy. The destruction is as great as Jeremiah had predicted. King Zedekiah and all the nobles flee, but they are captured and brought before Nebuchadnezzar. The Babylonian king kills all of Zedekiah's sons in front of him, puts out his eyes, and sends him in fetters to Babylon. Nebuchadnezzar then kills all the nobles, burns the Temple and the houses of Jerusalem, and deports the people to Babylon. He leaves some of the poorest people to care for the fields and vineyards (Jer. 39:1–10; 2 Kings 25:1–21).

---

[240] This meal will be referred to as the Last Supper.
[241] See pp. 43–45.

CHAPTER 19—A DIVIDED NATION, THE PROPHETS, AND JERUSALEM DESTROYED

The era of the kings of Judah has come to an end. The children of Abraham had been fruitful and multiplied and they had occupied the promised land, but they were not able to establish a lasting kingdom for God. Solomon had a glorious reign during which Israel reached the apex of its power, but like Adam and Noah, Solomon and the people of Israel fell into sin and rebellion, and judgment followed. The rule of the chosen nation, the third kingdom paradigm, has come to its own disastrous end, but the consequences for the Jewish people will continue far into the future.

*****

Nebuchadnezzar had learned during the siege of Jerusalem that Jeremiah was urging Zedekiah to surrender. After the fall of the city, he releases Jeremiah from confinement and treats him kindly (Jer. 39:11–14). Eventually, Jeremiah is taken against his will to Egypt by a company of Jewish survivors who think they will be killed if they remain in Judah. He continues to prophesy and apparently lives out his remaining years in this foreign land (Jer. 43:1–7). Jeremiah had shed many tears over the destruction of Judah, but he dies with the assurance that there will be a restoration of the nation through the new covenant; there will be a new covenant kingdom.

CHAPTER 20

THE BABYLONIAN EXILE AND THE RETURN

The people of Judah spend seventy years in captivity.[242] After the first two deportations by Nebuchadnezzar, Jeremiah had written a letter to the captives, telling them to build houses, plant gardens, and have families so that the nation would not completely perish in Babylon (Jer. 29:1–7). Those exiles followed Jeremiah's instructions, as do the thousands and thousands more that arrive after the destruction of Jerusalem. The Jews are settled along the Chebar River (Ezek. 1:1) where they receive fair and reasonable treatment from the Babylonians. Some of the families prosper and eventually become wealthy.[243] And amazingly, through God's providence, Daniel and several of his young companions become influential within the royal court.

*****

Daniel becomes prominent in Babylon after King Nebuchadnezzar has a troubling dream in which he sees a great figure with a head of gold, chest and arms of silver, belly and thighs of bronze, legs of iron, and feet of iron and clay. A stone cut without hands[244] strikes the feet of this image, and the entire figure

---

[242] The first captives were taken in 605 BC, and Cyrus freed the Jews in 537 BC, a period of sixty-eight years, but the end point of the captivity seems to be the exiles celebration of the Feast of Tabernacles back in Canaan. This, and the fact that the Jews counted a part of a year as a full year with the new year beginning in the fall means that, for the Jewish calendar, the captivity was from 606 BC to 536 BC, seventy years. See John Pratt, "When was Judah's 70-year Babylonian Captivity?", The Ensign 28, no. 10 (October, 1998), 64–65, http://www.johnpratt.com/items/docs/captivity.html.

[243] Many of the Jews are content to stay in Babylon after Cyrus frees them. See Berel Wein adapted by Yaakov Astor, "Babylon and Beyond," *Jewish History.org*, accessed February 14, 2019, https://www.jewishhistory.org/babylon-and-beyond/.

[244] A stone cut without hands means that the stone is not fashioned by men but by God.

is crushed, becoming chaff which is blown away without leaving a trace. The stone then becomes a mountain that fills the entire earth.

Nebuchadnezzar demands that his wise men reveal his secret dream and its interpretation. His oracles cannot know what he has dreamed, and Nebuchadnezzar becomes so angry that he orders all the soothsayers to be killed. Daniel, who is seen as one of them, is able to save his own life and stop further executions when God reveals the dream and its meaning to him in a vision. Daniel tells the king that the sections of the great figure represent four kingdoms which will be destroyed.[245] The stone represents a kingdom that God will establish. It will destroy all the other kingdoms, but God's kingdom will never be destroyed; it will be an everlasting kingdom, a mountain that fills the earth.[246] Nebuchadnezzar says that Daniel's God is the God of gods because He was able to reveal his dream to Daniel (Dan. 2:1–47).

Daniel and three of his Jewish friends are promoted to positions of authority in Babylon. His companions work apart from Daniel, but they remain faithful to the LORD, and this puts their lives in danger. When these young men, Shadrach, Meshach, and Abednego,[247] refuse to bow down to the king's golden image, they are thrown into a fiery furnace.[248] But a Man who looks like the Son of God walks with them in the flames, and they are not harmed. When they come out of the fire without even a hair being singed, Nebuchadnezzar returns the young men to their positions and decrees that no one may speak against their God (Dan. 2:48–3:30).

*****

---

[245] Biblical scholars generally see these four kingdoms as Babylon, Medo-Persia, Greece, and Rome.

[246] John the Baptist seems to have this kingdom, this mountain in mind when he begins his ministry by saying, "Repent, for the kingdom of heaven is at hand!" (Matt. 3:2). Jesus will begin his ministry with the same words (Matt. 4:17; Mark 1:15) and will go on to call Himself the stone that the builders rejected and the chief cornerstone. He says that if this stone falls on someone, they will be ground to powder (Matt. 21:42–44). Jesus comes to save, but the stone also means judgment, so both He and John the Baptist call for repentance (suggested by Ken Olles in a Sunday school class).

[247] These are Babylonian names given to them during their captivity.

[248] When the young men were threatened with the fiery furnace, they told the king, "Our God whom we serve is able to deliver us from the furnace of blazing fire....but even if He does not...we are not going to worship your gods or the golden image" (Dan. 3:17–18). May God give us such strength in our times of testing.

King Nabonidus succeeds Nebuchadnezzar as the next Babylonian king, and he is an unusual ruler. He soon begins making distant archaeological explorations accompanied by some of his military forces and turns the rule of Babylon over to his firstborn son, Belshazzar.[249] In 539 BC, with the combined forces of the Medes and the Persians threatening his fortified city, Belshazzar decides to use the gold and silver vessels taken from the Jerusalem Temple to have a decadent drunken feast. The Babylonians are praising their gods when the fingers of a man's hand writes on the plaster wall of the king's palace. The king is so frightened that his knees begin to knock, and he sends for his wise men. When they cannot decipher the writing, Daniel is called, and he interprets the inscription. He tells Belshazzar that he has been found wanting and that his kingdom will be given to the Medes and Persians.

Despite this ominous warning, Belshazzar clothes Daniel in royal robes and makes him the third ruler in the kingdom, perhaps hoping to delay the fulfillment of the prophecy. But that very night, with his father and his father's military escort absent, Belshazzar is slain (Dan. 5:1–30). It is unknown if he was killed by his countrymen or by infiltrators, but the army of Cyrus the Persian enters the city without any significant resistance and takes over Babylon.[250] Scripture says Darius the Mede received the kingdom (Dan. 5:31). This may have been a throne name for Cyrus or a general that he placed over the city (see note on Dan. 6:1, *New Geneva Study Bible*, 1341) but Cyrus is the ultimate ruler.

Cyrus, whom Isaiah had foretold by name 200 years earlier (Isa. 44:28–45:1), was known for respecting the cultures and religions of the nations he conquered. It was beneficial for him to keep the subjugated societies intact so they could pay taxes, but he also seemed to have a genuine concern for human rights. Daniel apparently maintains his good standing with the new king. In 537 BC, Cyrus decrees that the Jews can return to Canaan (Ezra 1:1–11).

---

[249] Nabonidus is not mentioned in Scripture, but he and his son, Belshazzar, are mentioned in the ancient Nabonidus Cylinder. This cylinder says that Nabonidus visited old ruins at the edge of his empire. He was more interested in archaeology than ruling. See "Daniel, Nebuchadnezzar, and Cyrus," *Articles, APXAIOC*, submitted November 28, 2014, http://apxaioc.com/article/daniel-nebuchadnezzar-belshazzar-and-cyrus.

[250] When Nabonidus returned to Babylon from his archaeological expedition, he was arrested but not killed. The Editors of Encyclopaedia Britannica, "Nabonidas," *Encyclopaedia Britannica*, accessed November 19, 2018, https://www.britannica.com/biography/Nabonidus.

During the exile, Daniel and Ezekiel had proclaimed the sovereignty of God over all the nations and had foretold the restoration of Judah.[251] Now their revelations are coming true; the people of Israel can return to their own land. Some of them are longing to go, but many others have become comfortable and even wealthy over the years and are reluctant to make the long difficult journey back to a destroyed country. After almost seventy years of captivity, a majority of the nation is made up of people born in Babylon who have never seen Jerusalem, and many of them decide to stay in this foreign land.

Zerubbabel organizes those who want to return and leads the national caravan on the dangerous trek back to Canaan.[252] With the help of Cyrus and his official decrees, the people reach Jerusalem. They begin to construct a new Temple, and when the foundation is laid, the people weep with joy because they are back in their land. But the older people, who remembered the first Temple and the former glory of Jerusalem, mix tears of sorrow with their tears of joy. Beginning this diminished Temple in a destroyed city demonstrates just how far the nation of Israel has fallen (Ezra 1:1–3:13).[253] They are few in number, they are not an independent nation, and they have no king.

*****

While the exiles are reestablishing themselves in Canaan, the reign of Cyrus, the benevolent Persian king, comes to an end. The circumstances of his death are uncertain, but his first son, Cambyses, assumes the throne. He reigns

---

[251] In the book of Daniel, his prophecies are explained by the only two angels known by name in the Bible, Gabriel and Michael (Dan. 8:16, 10:13). Centuries later, Gabriel will announce the coming of John the Baptist and tell the Virgin Mary that she will bear the Messiah (Luke 1:19, 26).

[252] Ezra 2:64–65 indicates 42,360 Jews returned initially. There are two smaller returns in the next century, one under Ezra, and one under Nehemiah. The books of Ezra and Nehemiah describe this period in Judah's history.

[253] The exiles have resources for rebuilding the Temple. Cyrus returned the gold and silver articles taken from the Temple when Nebuchadnezzar destroyed Jerusalem (Ezra 1:7–11). The Jewish people also donated 61,000 gold drachmas and 5,000 silver minas, a value of about $500 million dollars today. But King David had dedicated 80 billion dollars in gold and silver for the first Temple. In that sense, the first Temple was 160 times more magnificent. There is no golden Ark of the Covenant in the Holy of Holies in the Second Temple. See p. 148, n. 235.

for eight years before he also dies, and then his brother, Darius, becomes ruler over Babylon in 522 BC.

Daniel is about ninety years old at this time, but he continues to work and so distinguishes himself that the new king decides to promote him to second-in-command over Babylon. Daniel's enemies want to take his place, and they convince Darius to decree that no one may pray to anyone except the king himself. When Daniel continues to pray to the LORD, with his windows open, his adversaries are listening, and they report it to the king. He has no choice except to have Daniel thrown into the lion's den, but God shuts the mouths of the lions, and Daniel is not harmed.

The next morning, Darius rushes to the lions' enclosure, sees that Daniel is alive, and directs that he be brought up out of the den. The king then orders Daniel's accusers and their families to be thrown to the lions, but this time, God does not close their mouths (Dan. 6:1–24).

Daniel returns to his position, and God gives him several visions concerning the nations and the last days. He has a dream of four beasts that represent the same four kingdoms symbolized in Nebuchadnezzar's dream of the great metal figure (p. 153–154). In a night vision, he next sees one like a "Son of Man,"[254] who comes with the clouds to the Ancient of Days[254] and receives a kingdom which will not be destroyed (Dan. 7:1–14). The designation Son of Man will be the title that Jesus most often uses for Himself during His earthly ministry.[255] The national empires will have great power, but it is the kingdom of the Son of Man that endures forever.

God gives Daniel more information about future history with a vision of a ram with two horns which is trampled by a male goat. The male goat's large horn is broken and replaced by four notable horns. Then a little horn grows from one of the four horns and becomes exceedingly great; the little horn opposes the daily sacrifices and casts truth down to the ground (Dan. 8:1–12).

The Angel Gabriel then explains to Daniel that the ram with two horns represents a coalition of the nations of Media and Persia, which is trampled by the male goat, the nation of Greece. The four notable horns are the four kingdoms which arise from the division of Greece's realm (Dan. 8:15–22). Gabriel

---

[254] The Ancient of Days is God Almighty seated on His throne with thousands and thousands attending him (Dan. 7:9–10).

[255] Jesus will apply Daniel's vision of the Son of Man to Himself when He is tried before the Sanhedrin. They will immediately charge him with blasphemy and sentence Him to death (Mark 14:61–64).

then describes a king, apparently the little horn, who becomes a mighty and a fearful destroyer but who is eventually destroyed without human means (Dan. 8:23–25). The little horn seems to represent Antiochus IV who will desecrate the Temple in AD 167 and who appears to be a type of the antichrist mentioned by the Apostle John in the New Testament.

Daniel's visions have caused much debate and disagreement among scholars, and they also troubled Daniel (Dan. 7:28, 8:27). But he lives out his life in peace in Babylon, and as he approaches his death, an angel assures him of his future resurrection at the end of the age, the time he has foreseen in his visions (Dan. 12:7–13).

*****

The Jews in Canaan complete the second Temple in 515 BC. The people celebrate the dedication of the Temple with joy and sacrifice hundreds of bulls, rams, and lambs. They appoint priests according to the Law of Moses, and on the fourteenth day of the first month, they celebrate the Passover (Ezra 6:13–22).

The children of Israel, at least in part, are back in Canaan, and they have reestablished Temple worship, but they face opposition from the neighboring populations (Ezra 3:4–5). The returning exiles struggle and do not prosper. This does not agree with their understanding of the restoration foretold by the prophets. The people, along with the priests, become lax in their spiritual duties, and some of them begin to assimilate and intermarry with the local inhabitants (Ezra 9:1–4).

In the next century, Ezra and Nehemiah each lead smaller groups of returning exiles that join and reinforce the people in Canaan.[256] Ezra emphasizes the Law and stops intermarriages with foreigners (Ezra 9:1–15; Neh. 8:1–8). Nehemiah, despite the local opposition, leads the rebuilding of the wall around Jerusalem so that the Jews have more security (Neh. 2:11–3:32). The people have made progress but become negligent in their spiritual duties while complaining that the LORD has not blessed them (Mal. 1:2, 6–7, 3:7–9).

---

[256] The Reverend J. Stafford Wright's detailed study places Ezra's arrival in 458 BC and Nehemiah's in 445 BC. See John Stafford Wright, "The Date of Ezra's Coming to Jerusalem," *Biblical Studies/.org.uk*, accessed November 21, 2018, https://biblicalstudies.org.uk/article_ezra_wright.html.

Malachi prophesies during this time and holds the discouraged inhabitants accountable for their unfaithfulness (Mal. 1:1–2:17).

Israel has become more established in the land, but the people have not flourished. They have restored their historical worship but have fallen into a political and spiritual lethargy. They are not an independent nation, and in the eyes of the world, they are an insignificant people. Israel is far removed from the glory days of David and Solomon. God's judgment has been severe, but it has not yet run its course.

Malachi writes the last book of the Old Testament, and he ends his text with the prophecy of the coming of Elijah before the "great and terrible day of the LORD" (Mal. 4:5). Malachi is foreseeing the appearance of John the Baptist, who will have "the spirit and power of Elijah," and who will prepare the way for the advent of the LORD (Luke 1:13–17). Israel is back in the land of Canaan, but the people are uncertain about their future and what the coming of the LORD means for them.

CHAPTER 21

THE INTERTESTAMENTAL PERIOD[257]

God has been speaking to Israel through prophets for almost 450 years, but as the fourth century BC approaches, the prophetical pronouncements cease. Israel is a diminished and divided nation with most of its people in Canaan or Babylon with smaller groups in Egypt or other countries in the Middle East. It is the time of the "Diaspora" (dispersion). But some of the people cling to the covenant promises made to Abraham and look for the Messiah who will accomplish God's purposes for them.

Before the end of the fourth century BC, the nation is affected by drastic changes taking place in the world. In 336 BC, Alexander the Great succeeds his father and two years later leads the Greeks to victory over Persia and a rapid conquest of the Middle East, including Palestine. The spread of Greek (Hellenistic) culture to Israel causes conflicts within the nation between those who want to adapt to the new culture and those who intend to maintain the purity of their national heritage. These tensions will exist for centuries between the different divisions in the nation.

Alexander dies in 323 BC in Babylon at the age of thirty-three. His four generals divide his vast empire—Daniel's visions are coming to pass—and one of them, Ptolemy, becomes the ruler of Egypt and Palestine. The Jews are allowed to practice their religion under the new regime and, without their own king, the high priest becomes not only their chief religious figure but also their main political leader. Historical information is limited, but it seems the Ptolemies were primarily interested in collecting taxes.

---

[257] The following section describes the time between the Old Testament and the New Testament when God was not speaking to Israel. It relies primarily on the summary of this period in Sproul, *New Geneva*, 1497–1498.

These rulers face continual pressure from another Alexandrian general, Seleucus, who had taken over Damascus and the land extending to Babylon and beyond. In 200 BC, after more than a century of conflict, the Seleucids attack and defeat the Ptolemies near Mt. Herman. They occupy Palestine, and their conquest soon leads to radical changes.

In 175 BC, the Seleucid King, Antiochus IV, ascends to the throne and expedites the process of Hellenizing Palestine. When some of the Jews resist, he unleashes severe religious persecution. The Hebrew Scriptures are burned, and Sabbath observance and circumcision are outlawed. Violators are put to death. In 167 BC, Antiochus sets up an idol of Zeus in the Temple and sacrifices pigs on the altar. Some scholars see Antiochus as the "little horn" and his desecration of the Temple as "the abomination of desolation" prophesied by Daniel (Dan. 8:9, 9:27, 11:31, 12:11). Others see Antiochus as a very evil ruler but only a type of the coming Antichrist.

Antiochus's defilement of the Temple inflames a revolt led by Judas Maccabeus, known as Judas the "Hammer." He commands guerilla bands which defeat large Seleucid armies. The Jews manage to take control of Jerusalem, and they cleanse and rededicate the Temple in 164 BC, an event which is still celebrated today by the Jewish holiday of Hanukkah.

After the death of Judas, his sons continue the war against the Seleucids, and the Jews win their political independence in 142 BC. The Maccabeans take over the office of high priest, but despite leading the revolt for independence, they begin to adopt Hellenistic culture. This leads to further divisions within the nation. It is during these years that the sects of the Sadducees and the Pharisees are first mentioned by the historian, Josephus.[258] Since they oversee the Temple, the aristocratic Sadducees are mainly concerned with political stability and tend to support the ruling authorities. The Pharisees resist the influence of Hellenization and focus on the Law, but they develop an extensive oral tradition which alters many biblical requirements. This leads to a legalistic approach to God still very apparent in the first century when Pharisees confront and challenge Jesus (Mark 7:1–13; Luke 18:9–14). It is also during this time that the Essenes split away from Jewish society and form an isolated community near the Dead Sea, a community that has received additional scru-

---

[258] Josephus, "Antiquities," 13.5.9.

tiny since 1946 when the Dead Sea Scrolls were discovered in caves near their ancient dwelling site.[259]

The nation enjoys some years of prosperity under the Maccabeans, but the people are not unified, and they cannot halt the Roman invasion in 63 BC. The wars between the Seleucids and the Ptolemies had weakened both and made it easier for Rome to expand to the east. General Pompey conquers Jerusalem, but he soon returns to Rome, and sporadic unrest and rebellion continue. In 37 BC, the Romans appoint Herod as king of Judea, and he reigns until AD 4. Herod is Idumean by birth,[260] but he is also a Jewish proselyte. He rules with ruthless efficiency and accomplishes some amazing building projects, including a complete renovation of the Second Temple, which gains him the title of Herod the Great. But he also is an egotistical distrustful madman, going so far as to kill some of his own children.

As the Intertestamental Period ends and the New Testament era begins, Israel is ruled by Rome and an appointed despotic king. The nation is influenced by Hellenism and Romanism and is divided on how to respond to these cultural pressures. The people are still waiting for God to fulfill the promises He made to Abraham. They know about the covenant with King David and are looking for one of his descendants, the Messiah, to assume the throne and restore the glory of Israel.

---

[259] See Millar Burrows, *The Dead Sea Scrolls* (New York: Gramercy, 1986) for the translation and significance of the most noteworthy scrolls. The scrolls, especially the two Isaiah scrolls, further verify the accurate translations of the Old Testament books. I visited this Essene archaeological site in 1994 and looked in some of the small caves on the surrounding hills.

[260] This means that Herod was a descendant of Esau from the area of Edom. He was not a descendant of Jacob and therefore not in the kingly line of the Messiah.

SECTION 4

JESUS AND THE KINGDOM

CHAPTER 22

THE COMING OF THE LORD—THE FINAL PARADIGM

God has been silent for over 400 years; no prophet has spoken to the children of Israel since Malachi. But his prophecy about the coming of "Elijah," who will prepare the way of the LORD, is about to be fulfilled.

The Angel Gabriel appears to an elderly priest named Zacharias as he is ministering in the Temple in Jerusalem. Gabriel tells Zacharias that his wife, Elizabeth, will bear him a son and that he should name him John. The angel says many will rejoice at his birth, "For he will be great in the sight of the Lord...and he will be filled with the Holy Spirit, while yet in his mother's womb" (Luke 1:15).[261] Zacharias is very afraid and expresses doubt about the prophecy because he and his wife are old and have had no children. The angel tells him that because of his lack of faith, he will be mute until the birth of his son (Luke 1:5–25).

Elizabeth conceives. and when she is in her sixth month, the same angel appears to a relative of hers (Luke 1:36),[262] a young woman named Mary, in the village of Nazareth in Galilee. Mary is betrothed to a man named Joseph who is of the House of David. Gabriel tells her not to be afraid, that she has found favor with God. And then he pronounces an amazing message, "And behold, you will conceive in your womb, and bear a Son, and you shall name Him Jesus. He will be great, and will be called the Son of the Most High; and the Lord God will give Him the throne of His father David. And He will reign

---

[261] This is a conclusive argument against abortion. Not only is John considered a person in the womb, he is able to receive the Holy Spirit. God knows us even before we are conceived (Jer. 1:5).

[262] Mary and Elizabeth were apparently distant cousins. Mary was of the tribe of Judah while Elizabeth was a descendant of Levi. It appears that they knew or at least knew about each other.

over the house of Jacob forever; and His kingdom will have no end" (Luke 1:31–33).

This proclamation by the angel reveals the ultimate fulfillment of the covenants with Abraham and David. Mary's Son, Jesus, a descendant of David, is the one who will rule the house of Abraham's descendants forever. He will establish the final kingdom which shall have no end, the heavenly country which was the hope of Abraham, Isaac, and Jacob (Heb. 11:9–10, 16, 12:22–24).

Mary, who is probably thirteen or fourteen years old, asks how this can be since she is a virgin. The angel gives her an answer that goes beyond her immediate concern of how she will conceive. He tells her that, "The Holy Spirit will come upon you, and the power of the Most High will overshadow you; and for that reason the holy offspring shall be called the Son of God" (Luke 1:35).

Mary will conceive by the miraculous work of the Holy Spirit, and her son will be able to fulfill the promises of God because He is the Son of God.

This must be overwhelming for Mary. She is very young and in a small town far to the north of Jerusalem, far removed from the Temple and its priests, the center of the nation's religious life. As a Jewish girl, she would have known about the coming Messiah, but now she is being told that she is going to be His mother. And not only that, He is going to be the Son of God.

Gabriel goes on to tell Mary that Elizabeth, who had been barren, is now with child and is in her sixth month. He sums up his message to Mary by adding, "For nothing will be impossible with God" (Luke 1:37). Despite her youth and the stunning nature of the angel's revelation, Mary says, "Behold the bondslave of the Lord; be it done to me according to your word" (Luke 1:38).

Gabriel departs from Mary; with his angelic declaration, the final kingdom paradigm has begun. Mary had awakened to an ordinary day in the small Galilean town of Nazareth. Now, the Angel Gabriel has told her that she is going to give birth to the Son of God who will be given the throne of David, and His kingdom will be forever.

*****

Mary becomes pregnant by the power of the Holy Spirit and hurries to see Elizabeth. When Elizabeth hears Mary's greeting, the babe within Elizabeth leaps for joy. At six months in the womb, the baby John, filled with the Holy Spirit, is responding to the Messiah who is within Mary. Both women burst forth with praise to God for his everlasting mercy to Abraham and his descendants. Mary remains with Elizabeth for three months and then returns to her own house (Luke 1:39–56).

*****

When the time comes for Elizabeth to give birth, she delivers a son. When it is time to name and circumcise the boy, everyone except Elizabeth wants to name him after his father, who is still mute. Zacharias finally ends the dispute by writing on a tablet, "His name is John" (Luke 1:63). As soon as he does this, Zacharias's tongue is loosed, and he begins to praise God and prophecy, telling his son that he "will be called the prophet of the Most High. For you will go on before the LORD to prepare His ways" (Luke 1:76).

*****

After Mary returns to Nazareth, it becomes evident that she is with child. Apparently, Joseph does not believe her account of the Angel Gabriel's visit and her miraculous conception by the Holy Spirit. Nevertheless, he is a just man, and to spare Mary from disgrace, and possibly stoning, he intends to seclude her away from the eyes of the people. But before he can do this, an angel of the Lord appears to him in a dream and tells him what has happened to Mary and that he should not be afraid to take her as his wife.[263] He also tells Joseph to give Mary's Son the name Jesus, "for it is He who will save His people from their sins"[264] (Matt. 1:20–21).

Joseph listens to the angel and does not have relations with Mary until she has given birth to her firstborn son. This fulfills the prophecy of Isaiah 7:14, "Behold the virgin shall be with child, and shall bear a son, and they shall call His name Immanuel," which translated means, "God with us" (Matt. 1:23, 18–24).

Before the time comes for Mary to give birth, she travels with Joseph to Bethlehem because Caesar Augustus, the Roman Emperor, has decreed that all the world should be registered. This census is for administrative control and tax purposes; everyone must return to their place of birth to be enrolled. Although

---

[263] Mary's pregnancy would have been evident to the community of Nazareth and would have been a problem for the reputations of Mary and Joseph. The Pharisees eventually learn about this and insult Jesus by saying, "We were not born of fornication" (John 8:19, 41).

[264] Jesus is *Yeshua* in Hebrew meaning *YHWH saves*.

she is near her time of delivery, Mary makes the trek of almost ninety miles over the rough and winding roads, likely sitting on a donkey. When they reach Bethlehem after several days of travel, the small town is crowded, and Mary and Joseph can only find rest for the night in an animal shelter. Mary's time arrives, and she gives birth to Jesus, the Son of God, in a stable. She wraps him in swaddling clothes and lays him in a manger (Luke 2:1–7).

God announces that His Son has been born, but not to the religious leaders in Jerusalem. An angel of the Lord appears at night to shepherds tending their flocks in the fields near Bethlehem. The shepherds are terrified, but the angel tells them to not be afraid, "for behold I bring you good news of a great joy which shall be for all the people;[265] for today in the city of David there has been born for you a Savior, who is Christ the Lord" (Luke 2:10–11). The angel tells the shepherds that they will find the "baby wrapped in cloths, and lying in a manger" (Luke 2:12).[266] Then a multitude of angels arrive, praising God and saying, "Glory to God in the highest, And on earth peace among men with whom He is pleased" (Luke 2:14).[267]

When the angels leave and return to heaven, the shepherds decide to hurry to Bethlehem to "see this thing that has happened which the Lord has made known to us" (Luke 2:15). They find Mary and Joseph with the babe lying in a manger. After they have seen the child, they depart and spread the word about what they have been told concerning Him. Everyone marvels at the things the shepherds are saying. Mary ponders these things in her heart, and the shepherds return to their flocks praising and glorifying God (Luke 2:8–20).

God has made his announcement of the Messiah's birth to the most common of the common people.[268] The shepherds work in the fields with their flocks and accrue the dirt and odors associated with such work. They are relegated to the lowest rung of Jewish society and would not have been welcome in the most refined homes in Bethlehem and Jerusalem. But the choir of heavenly

---

[265] This proclamation goes beyond the nation of Israel to "all the people." Abraham had been told that he would be a blessing to all the nations.

[266] Bethlehem is a small town, and the shepherds would have known the places that sheltered animals.

[267] Since the fall of Adam and Eve, there has been enmity between sinful human beings and God. The Christ child is going to bring peace to those with whom God is pleased.

[268] In the Patriarch's day, shepherding had been a noble calling, but as Israel developed into a settled society much of the basic work of animal husbandry had been relegated to poorer people working for wages (John 10:12–13).

angels sang the good news to them while the Temple priests, with their incense and elegant robes, remained unaware that the Son of God has appeared in the physical world.[269]

*****

The details of Jesus's childhood are few, but Luke tells us that after eight days, he is circumcised and given the name Jesus just as the angel had instructed Joseph. When the days of Mary's purification have passed according to the Law, Jesus is presented to the Lord in the Temple. Since He is Mary's firstborn and therefore holy to the Lord, Mary and Joseph offer a sacrifice of two turtledoves to redeem their Son. They are too poor to offer the customary lamb[270] (Luke 2:21–24).

While they are presenting Jesus at the Temple, they encounter a devout man named Simeon, who had been told by the Holy Spirit that he would not die until he had seen the Lord's Christ (Messiah). He takes the baby Jesus up in his arms and says, "Now Lord, Thou dost let Thy bond-servant depart In peace, according to Thy word; For my eyes have seen Thy salvation, Which Thou hast prepared in the presence of all peoples, A light of revelation to the Gentiles, And the glory of Thy people Israel" (Luke 2:29–32).

Simeon is declaring that Jesus will not only bring salvation to Israel but will also be a revelation to the Gentiles, people with whom the Jews do not associate. But Simeon also has some knowledge of what the Messiah will face in the future. He tells Mary that "this child is appointed for the fall and rise of many in Israel" and that "a sword will pierce even your own soul." She will see the suffering and death of her Son (Luke 2:34–35).

There is also a prophetess in the Temple named Anna, who is eighty-four years old. She comes and gives thanks for the child and speaks about Him to everyone who looks for the redemption of Israel (Luke 2:36–38).

*****

---

[269] Recent studies indicate that the year of Jesus's birth was either 5 or 4 BC. See Ed Rickard, "The Birth Date of Jesus Christ, Lesson 1: Summary of the Evidence," *Bible Studies at the Moorings*, accessed November 21, 2018, www.themoorings.org/Jesus/birth/date.html.

[270] Each firstborn son in Israel is dedicated to the service of the LORD or they must be redeemed with an offering. The LORD had instituted this rite on the day He had brought His firstborn, Israel, out of Egypt, see p. 100.

After they leave the Temple, Mary and Joseph apparently stay for some time in a house in or near Bethlehem.[271] Almost two years pass,[272] and wise men from the east arrive in Jerusalem. They are following a star that is leading them to the one who is born King of the Jews, and they want to worship Him. King Herod meets secretly with the wise men and asks them when the star first appeared. Then he tells them to let him know when they locate the child so he can worship Him too (Matt. 2:1–8).

The star leads them to the house where they find Jesus with Mary. They kneel before Him and present Him with precious gifts of gold, frankincense, and myrrh.[273] After their adoration of the child, the wise men depart for their homeland by a different way; they know they cannot trust King Herod (Matt. 2:9–12). An angel of the Lord then appears to Joseph in a dream and tells him to take the young child and His mother and flee to Egypt because Herod will try to destroy Him. Joseph is to stay in Egypt until he receives further word from the angel (Matt. 2:13–15). The gifts from the wise men can help Joseph finance the journey.

When Herod realizes that the wise men have deceived him, he is enraged and orders his soldiers to kill all the baby boys two years old and under in Bethlehem and its surrounding districts (Matt. 2:16). He is going to destroy any potential rival. It is a horrible crime and similar to the infanticide ordered in Egypt during the time of Moses. Satan is determined to stop the coming of the Messiah. Jeremiah had foreseen this terrible act over five hundred years earlier and had said, "A voice was heard in Ramah, Weeping, and great mourning, Rachel weeping for her children,[274] And she refused to be comforted, Because they were no more" (Jer. 31:15; Matt. 2:18).

*****

---

[271] Possibly Elizabeth's house since she lived in a city of Judah (Luke 1:39), but Scripture does not tell us (Matt. 2:11).

[272] This time can be assumed from the fact that Herod orders the death of the male children of less than two years.

[273] Scripture does not say how many wise men there were. It is sometimes assumed there were three because three different gifts were given.

[274] Rachel, Jacob's beloved wife, had died giving birth to Benjamin near Bethlehem (Gen. 35:16–20). She had wept because she was not going to be able to nurture her new son, and now these women, her relatives, weep because they will never again nurture their sons.

Joseph, Mary, and the child are still in Egypt when Herod dies in AD 4. The angel of the Lord tells Joseph to return to Israel. He obeys, but when he learns that Herod's ruthless son, Archelaus, is ruling in Judea, he decides to return to Nazareth in Galilee.[275] This small town will be the home of the Christ child as He grows into maturity.

Scripture records only one other incident concerning Jesus's boyhood. When He is twelve years old, He goes with His parents to Jerusalem to observe the yearly Passover. When the celebration is completed, Mary and Joseph start for home with other Nazarene families, assuming that Jesus is somewhere within the company of people. After a day's travel, they realize that He is missing and return to Jerusalem.

After searching for three days, they finally find Him sitting among the teachers in the Temple, astonishing everyone with His knowledge. Mary asks Jesus why He has caused them so much anxiety. He replies, "Why is it that you were looking for Me? Did you not know that I had to be in My Father's house?" (Luke 2:49).

His parents do not understand His response, but He returns to Nazareth with Mary and Joseph and remains subject to them (Luke 2:41–51). Mary treasures all these things in her heart; "And Jesus kept increasing in wisdom and stature, and in favor with God and men" (Luke 2:52).

---

[275] After King Herod dies, his three sons—Archelaus, Antipas, and Phillip II—rule over different parts of his kingdom. Archelaus rules Jerusalem and Judea in the south and has already killed many Jews and canceled the Passover so Joseph goes to Galilee, farther to the north where Antipas rules. There are Jewish communities in this area but also many Gentiles, hence the reference in Scripture to Galilee of the Gentiles. Jews from the south tended to look down on Jews from Galilee. Nathanael, who eventually becomes a disciple of Jesus, will initially ask, "Can anything good come out of Nazareth?" (John 1:46).

CHAPTER 23

JESUS'S MINISTRY—THE KINGDOM ESTABLISHED

Years pass, and John, the son of Zacharias, matures and begins to fulfill the words of his father. He lives in the wilderness, wears a coat of camel's hair, eats locusts and wild honey, and begins preaching, saying, "Repent, for the kingdom of heaven is at hand" (Matt. 3:2, 4).

God is speaking to Israel again. People from Jerusalem and Judah come to John to confess their sins and be baptized (Matt. 3:11).[276] Their nation is being ruled by the Romans, and the people understand it is due to their sins. They do not have their own kingdom because they are not right with God. John is preparing the way of the LORD as Malachi and Isaiah had prophesied, "Behold, I send My messenger before Your face, Who will prepare Your way;[277] The voice of one crying in the wilderness, Make ready the way of the LORD,[278] Make His paths straight" (Mark 1:2–3).[279]

The Jewish leaders, both Pharisees and Sadducees, come to John for baptism, but he calls them a "brood of vipers" and tells them to produce fruits worthy of repentance (Matt. 3:7–8). The people wonder about John, but he knows he is not the promised Messiah, and he says:

> As for me, I baptize you with water; but One is coming who is mightier than I, and I am not fit to untie the

---

[276] The Jews used baptism in ritual cleansing rites for Gentile proselytes. Now John is saying that it is the Jews themselves who need to be cleansed, they need to repent. Eventually, baptism associated with Jesus will signify repentance and faith in Him for salvation. See https://www.gotquestions.org/baptism-of-John.html.

[277] Malachi 3:1.

[278] The translation LORD here is derived from YHWH who spoke to Moses from the burning bush. The one coming is the covenant-keeping God. See pp. 88, 89, n. 145, n. 146.

[279] Isaiah 40:3.

thong of His sandals; He will baptize you with the Holy Spirit and fire. And His winnowing fork is in His hand, to thoroughly clear His threshing floor, and to gather the wheat into His barn; but He will burn up the chaff with unquenchable fire. (Luke 3:16–17)

*****

As John is baptizing in the wilderness, the time comes for Jesus to make Himself known to the nation. Luke 3:23 tells us that Jesus is about thirty years old when He begins His public ministry.[280] His first act is to go to the Jordan River where John is preaching, but John is reluctant to baptize Him and says, "I have need to be baptized by You, and do You come to me?" (Matt. 3:14). John understands that Jesus has no sins which need to be forgiven.

But Jesus says to permit it to fulfill all righteousness. His baptism is to identify Himself with His people; He is going to be the one who stands in their place. He will bear their punishment, and He will be their righteousness. When Jesus comes up out of the water, the heavens open, and the Spirit of God in the form of a dove descends upon Him. A sudden voice from heaven declares, "This is My Beloved Son, in whom I am well pleased" (Matt. 3:17; 13–17).[281]

God has openly proclaimed Jesus as His Son; He is the LORD come to earth. But He is also truly man, and as a sinless man, He has the right to reign on the earth. Jesus's public baptism brings Him into immediate conflict with the one who is ruling the world, Satan himself. Mark gives us a sense of the urgency of this confrontation when he says the Spirit "impelled" Jesus into the wilderness to meet Satan; this is an encounter that must take place (Mark 1:12). Satan does not intend to give up his domain, and he challenges Jesus for

---

[280] After Luke indicates Jesus's age, he gives his genealogy of Jesus (Luke 3:23–38). Matthew gives his genealogy at the beginning of his Gospel (Matt. 1:1–17), but the two lines differ after King David. Scholars debate this issue, but the simplest answer may be that Matthew's genealogy follows the lineage of Joseph's father while Luke's traces the line of Joseph's mother. Both show that Joseph is in the line of David and therefore his "presumed" Son has the right to be king of Israel. See R. P. Nettelhorst, "The Genealogy of Jesus," *Journal of the Evangelical Theological Society*, June 1988, 169–172.

[281] In Jesus's baptism, we see a manifestation of the three Persons of the Trinity—God the Father, God the Son, and God the Holy Spirit.

forty days. Matthew records three of the ways that Satan tempts Jesus during this universal clash of kingdoms.

First, Jesus, in his human nature, becomes seriously famished. Satan suggests that He turn the rocks into bread, but Jesus resists the temptation to use His divine power to satisfy His physical needs. Jesus is one Person with two indivisible yet different natures, one divine and one human. Satan is trying to get Jesus to mix or confuse these two aspects of His being which would destroy His true humanity and His earthly ministry. For Jesus to represent his people, He must remain truly a man, and at this time, a starving man not fed by His own divine powers.[282] Jesus responds with the words of Moses, saying, "Man shall not live on bread alone, but on every word that proceeds out of the mouth of God" (Matt. 4:4; Deut. 8:3).

Then Satan dares Jesus to cast Himself down from the pinnacle of the Temple to prove that God's angels would rescue Him and bear Him up, "Lest you strike your foot against a stone" (Matt. 4:6; Ps. 91:11–12).

Jesus refuses to test or make a vain display of His special relationship with God the Father, again responding from Deuteronomy, "You shall not put the Lord your God to the test" (Matt. 4:7; Deut. 6:16).

Finally, Satan shows Jesus the kingdoms of the world with all their glory and says he will give them all to Jesus if He will fall down and worship Him. This is an offer Satan can legitimately make because he rules the governments of the world. He is suggesting an alternative way of establishing God's kingdom, a way that avoids the immense sacrificial suffering that Isaiah had foretold for the Messiah (Isa. 52:13–53:12) and that Jesus knows is coming. His future physical and spiritual anguish is so great that Jesus would avoid it if He could (Luke 22:41–44). But there is only one way for the kingdom to come, and Jesus ends the time of temptation by quoting Moses yet a third time, "Be gone, Satan! For it is written, 'You shall worship the Lord your God, and serve Him only'" (Matt. 4:10; Deut. 6:13–14).

Jesus remains true to God's Word and does not fall like Adam, who decided to disregard what God had said and determine good and evil for himself. Mark reveals the outcome of the temptation when he tells us that Jesus "was with the wild beasts, and the angels were ministering to Him" (Mark 1:13). Jesus

---

[282] The Council of Chalcedon definition (AD 451) is perhaps the best summary of Christ's two natures, although still inadequate. See "Chalcedonian Creed," Creeds and Confessions, Church History, *Theopedia*, accessed November 21, 2018, www.theopedia.com/chalcedonian-creed for an English translation of the creed.

remains a sinless man who has dominion over the animals, and He is a divine being to whom the angels minister.[283]

*****

Jesus leaves the wilderness and begins his ministry to the people of Israel. Matthew says, "From that time Jesus began to preach and to say, 'Repent, for the kingdom of heaven is at hand'" (Matt. 4:17). Mark tells us that He returned to Galilee, "preaching the gospel of God, and saying, 'The time is fulfilled, and the kingdom of God is at hand; repent and believe in the gospel'" (Mark 1:14–15).[284]

What Jesus means by "the gospel" will become more defined when He begins to teach the disciples about His approaching death and resurrection (Matt. 16:21–23). Paul will eventually sum up the gospel (good news) by saying, "that Christ died for our sins according to the Scriptures, and that He was buried, and that He was raised on the third day according to the Scriptures" (1 Cor. 15:3–4). Jesus and the New Testament writers will expound on different aspects of the gospel through their teachings on sin, grace, election, propitiation, justification, repentance, forgiveness, sonship, etc. It is through the gospel that Jesus will build His Church and establish the kingdom of God.

*****

Jesus begins to be fruitful and multiply; he preaches and begins calling disciples. As He walks by the Sea of Galilee, He sees two brothers, Simon (Peter) and Andrew, fishermen with whom He had previously had contact (John 1:35–42). Jesus tells them to follow Him and He will make them "fishers of men" (Mark 1:17). They immediately leave their nets and follow Him. He continues along the sea and comes upon two more brothers, James and John,

---

[283] As discussed earlier (p. 6).

[284] John the Baptist began his preaching by saying the "kingdom of heaven is at hand" (Matt. 3:2; p. 172). Now Jesus says the same thing, but the Dispensational view says the kingdom is not established until Christ's Second Advent. But "at hand" cannot mean some indefinite time over 1,900 years in the future. There is an immediate sense in saying "at hand" as is evident by the response of the Jewish people. Amillennial Covenantalists have a similar problem in that they do not see an earthly kingdom as being established during Jesus's earthly ministry, only in the new heaven and earth.

who are working on a boat with their father, Zebedee. Jesus calls to them, and they too leave their work and become his disciples (Mark 1:16–20).

Jesus also begins to fulfill the second part of the kingdom mandate; He begins to rule. After calling the four fishermen, He casts a demon out of a man in the synagogue in Capernaum. The people ask, "What is this? A new teaching with authority! He commands even the unclean spirits, and they obey Him" (Mark 1:27). His fame begins to spread throughout Galilee (Mark 1:21–28).

Jesus demonstrates His power by many miraculous healings. He not only has authority over the demons, but He has authority over every kind of disease. He heals Peter's mother-in-law of a fever, and people begin to bring those who are sick or demon-possessed, and He heals them (Mark 1:29–34).

Jesus preaches in the synagogues throughout Galilee, casting out demons from those afflicted. When He heals a leper, the news spreads rapidly, and Jesus cannot enter the cities because of the growing crowds. He stays outside in deserted places, but the multitudes still come to Him from every direction (Mark 1:39–45).

Jesus walks by the sea again, and as He passes the tax office, He calls to Matthew, a tax collector, who leaves his office and follows Him. Jesus dines with Matthew and his friends, who are sinners and tax collectors.[285] The religious leaders, the Pharisees, condemn him for eating with such people. But Jesus says, "It is not those who are well who need a physician, but those who are sick. I have not come to call the righteous but sinners to repentance" (Luke 5:31–32). The Pharisees do not realize that they are sinners just like the tax collectors; they are terminally ill but do not recognize they need to be healed (Luke 5:27–32). Unless we acknowledge our sins, we see no need for a Savior. Self-righteousness is an eternally fatal disease.

Jesus withdraws to the sea with His disciples, and a great multitude of people from Galilee, Judea, Jerusalem, Idumea, Tyre, Sidon, and beyond the Jordan follow Him. His disciples keep a small boat ready for Him in case the multitude begins to crush Him. The people press in to touch Him, and He heals them of their afflictions. When the unclean spirits see Jesus, they fall down before Him and cry out, "You are the Son of God" (Mark 3:11). But Jesus rebukes them; they are not the witnesses He wants at this time and place. He does not want the people to rise up and try to make Him a political ruler

---

[285] The Jewish people hated the Jews who acted as tax collectors for the Romans. They were seen as traitors, and many of them were corrupt, attempting to get rich from their positions.

(Mark 3:7–12). His purpose is much greater than being the king of National Israel.

After a time, Jesus again withdraws from the crowds and leads His disciples to a mountain where He appoints twelve of them to be His apostles (Luke 6:12–16). Jesus directs them to not go to the Gentiles or Samaritans but to go to the lost sheep of the house of Israel and to preach, saying, "The kingdom of heaven is at hand. Heal the sick, raise the dead, cleanse the lepers, cast out demons;[286] freely you received, freely give" (Matt. 10:7–8).

Jesus's disciples also serve and rule in the kingdom.[287] Their message is the same as the message of John the Baptist and Jesus; "the kingdom of heaven is at hand," and their works are going to help reveal the one who is establishing it.

*****

Jesus continues to travel throughout Galilee, preaching in the synagogues and healing people. The number that Jesus will eventually heal is not given in Scripture, but it appears to be thousands and thousands of suffering people (Luke 6:17–19, 7:21; Mark 3:7–12). The people are like sheep without a shepherd; they have been left untended by the religious leaders of Israel, but now they are being taught and healed by the Good Shepherd (Matt. 9:36; John 10:11, 14; Ps. 23).

He teaches them about the Law, marriage, loving your enemies, wealth, and many other things (Matt. 5:1–7:12). The disciples ask Jesus to teach them to pray, and He gives them a model prayer, saying, "Pray, then, in this way, 'Our Father who art in Heaven, Hallowed be Thy name. Thy kingdom come. Thy will be done On earth as it is in Heaven'" (Matt. 6:9–10).[288]

---

[286] The extent of demonic activity during Jesus's ministry is surprising. His earthly presence impels the demons to reveal themselves.

[287] The special powers given to the twelve apostles are claimed by some today, but their present-day miracles seem to go unverified. Without the Canon of Scripture, the apostles needed a way to spread and authenticate their message. Today, we have the written Word authenticated by the enlightenment of the Holy Spirit.

[288] In the Dispensational view, Jesus is telling the disciples to pray for a millennial kingdom, an earthly kingdom that is more than 1,900 years in the future and is not yet mentioned in Scripture.

177

His disciples are to be concerned about the holiness of God's name and the establishment of His kingdom before their own personal requests; God knows their needs (Luke 12:6–7).

*****

As Jesus travels through Galilee, there is a great debate in Israel about His role and message. By His words and actions, He is confronting the nation with the question that He will eventually ask His disciples, "Who do you say that I am?" (Matt. 16:15). The people and the religious leaders are wondering if Jesus could be the promised Messiah, the Deliverer of Israel, but He is doing nothing to establish his political leadership. Even John the Baptist, who has been imprisoned by Herod Antipas,[289] begins to wonder about Jesus and sends two of his disciples to ask, "Are You the Expected One, or shall we look for someone else?" (Matt. 11:3).

John had been preaching the coming of the kingdom and judgment, calling the religious leaders a "Brood of vipers" and saying that He who is coming "will thoroughly clear His threshing floor, and He will gather His wheat into the barn; but He will burn up the chaff with unquenchable fire" (Matt. 3:7–12). John had called Jesus "the Lamb of God who takes away the sin of the world!" (John 1:29). He had baptized Him and had heard a voice from heaven calling Him My beloved Son (Matt. 3:16–17). But Jesus is not executing judgment, and the kingdom is not being established in the way John had expected. John had not been given God's timing and had not understood the two advents of the Messiah. Jesus is establishing His kingdom during His first advent, but it is a time of salvation before His second advent and the consummation of the kingdom when He will exercise the judgment that John knows is coming.

Jesus instructs John's disciples to tell him that "the blind receive sight and the lame walk, the lepers are cleansed and the deaf hear, and the dead are raised up, and the poor have the gospel preached to them. And blessed is he who keeps from stumbling over Me" (Matt. 11:5–6). Jesus is quoting Isaiah 35:4–6 to show that His present ministry has been foretold. He wants John to know

---

[289] Herod Antipas had put John in prison when he criticized Antipas for taking Herodias, who was married to his brother, Phillip, to be his wife (Matt. 14:1–5).

that the kingdom is being established as prophesied; it is not yet the end of the age when judgment and the consummation of the kingdom will come.

*****

The Jewish religious leaders are well aware of what is taking place in Galilee. A few of them seem to give some credence to Jesus and His teaching (John 8:31–32). When He goes to Jerusalem for the Passover celebration, a Pharisee named Nicodemus secretly visits Him at night, seeking answers for his questions. Nicodemus becomes confused when Jesus tells him that he must be born again to see the kingdom of God (John 3:1–16). Jesus is speaking of a spiritual rebirth, and He tells Nicodemus that it is the work of the Holy Spirit. The actions of the Spirit are like the wind; the results can be observed by men but not controlled by them (John 1:11–13; 3:8). This heart change or regeneration is the result of God's electing grace (John 6:43–45). But the Pharisees believe they can save themselves and establish the kingdom by keeping the Law; they reject any teaching that threatens their self-righteousness.

The Pharisees are especially upset that Jesus heals on the Sabbath, which they consider work and therefore a violation of the Fourth Commandment (John 5:1–18). They want to show that Jesus breaks the Law and therefore cannot have come from God. Jesus points out that they will rescue one of their own sheep if it falls into a pit on the Sabbath, but they criticize Him for rescuing a human being on the same day (Matt. 12:11). They misuse the Law and have no mercy; He tells them that "the Son of Man[290] is Lord even of the Sabbath" (Matt: 12:8). Then, although it is the Sabbath day, Jesus proceeds to heal a man with a withered hand. The Pharisees are filled with rage at this undeniable miracle (Luke 6:6–11). They assemble and begin to plan how they can destroy Him (Matt. 12:1–14; Luke 6:11).

It may seem difficult to understand this rage over a man being healed. Some theologians say that Judaism was a religion of grace, not works.[291] And that is true as evidenced by God's election of Israel and the sacrificial system

---

[290] Son of Man, Jesus's most often used reference for Himself, refers to His humanity but also to His divine ministry. Any male person can rightfully be called a son of man. But for Jesus to indicate His humanity in this way is a continual reminder that the divine has taken on human nature for a purpose. See Dan. 7:13–14.

[291] Rami Shapiro, *Amazing Chesed—Living a Grace-Filled Judaism* (Woodstock, VT: Jewish Lights, 2013); also see, "The New Perspective on Paul: Judaism as a Religion

summarized in Leviticus. But by the time of Jesus's first advent, the practice of that faith had degenerated into strict law keeping. Jewish religious leaders maintained their prominence, their sense of self-righteousness, and their control of the people through their legalistic system, symbolized by Sabbath keeping. Jesus is threatening the very basis of the kingdom they have created, and like Satan, they do not intend to give up their domain. With such leaders, the people are "like sheep without a shepherd" (Matt. 9:36).

The Pharisees and Sadducees demand that Jesus show them a sign from heaven. They know about the miracles that have been taking place, but they want something that satisfies their own definition of proof. Jesus calls them hypocrites and says they will only see the sign of Jonah, a reference to his future resurrection after three days in the grave, just as Jonah was in the belly of the great fish for three days. He warns His disciples to beware of the leaven, the teaching, of the Pharisees and Sadducees (Matt. 16:1–4).

Jesus knows that the religious leaders, the common people, and often his own disciples do not understand how God is working out His plan of redemption. He teaches the disciples in parables and says that it is given to them to understand "the mysteries of the kingdom of heaven," but to others, it is not given (Matt. 13:11).

He tells them the story of the man who sows seed in which the seed represents the word of the kingdom. Some of the seed falls by the wayside, and the birds eat it—the wicked one snatches away any understanding. Other seed falls on rocky ground and the plants spring up but have no root and wilt in the heat—when persecution comes, many will not endure. Some seed falls among the thorns—many are choked by the cares and temptations of this world. But some seed falls on good ground and produces fruit, some a hundredfold, some sixty, and some thirty (Matt. 13:1–23).

Jesus is explaining why people are responding to Him in different ways. Those who are good soil respond to the Word and bear fruit. But they do not make themselves good soil; that is what God has made them. Jesus goes on to further explain the present character of the kingdom by telling the disciples the "kingdom parables:"

---

of Grace," *Reading Acts*, August 30. 2013, https://readingacts.com/2013/08/30/the-new-perspective-on-paul-judaism-as-a-religion-of-grace/.

"The kingdom of heaven may be compared to a man who sowed good seed in his field... But...his enemy came and sowed tares also among the wheat" (Matt. 13:24–25).

The owner said, "Allow both to grow together until the harvest, and... I will say to the reapers, 'First gather up the tares and bind them in bundles to burn them up, but gather the wheat into my barn'" (Matt. 13:26–30).

"The kingdom of heaven is like a mustard seed...smaller than all other seeds; but when it is full grown, it is larger than the garden plants, and becomes a tree, so that the birds of the air come and nest in its branches" (Matt. 13:31–32).

"The kingdom of heaven is like leaven, which a woman took, and hid in three pecs of meal, until it was all leavened" (Matt. 13:33).

"The kingdom of heaven is like a treasure hidden in the field, which a man found and hid; and from joy over it he goes and sells all that he has, and buys that field" (Matt. 13:44).

"Again, the kingdom of heaven is like a merchant seeking fine pearls, and upon finding one pearl of great value, he went and sold all that he had and bought it" (Matt.13:45–46).

"Again, the kingdom of heaven is like a dragnet cast into the sea...and when it was filled...they sat down and gathered the good fish into containers, but the bad they threw away. So it will be at the end of the age; the angels shall come forth, and take out the wicked from among the righteous, and will cast them into the furnace of fire; there will be weeping and gnashing of teeth" (Matt. 13:47–50).

Jesus is speaking about a kingdom that is present in His day and that continues to the present time. He is not speaking about a millennial kingdom that is over nineteen hundred years in the future.

Jesus concludes His teaching on the kingdom parables by saying, "Therefore every scribe who has become a disciple of the kingdom of heaven is like a head of a household, who brings forth out of his treasure things new and old" (Matt. 13:52). A disciple of the kingdom will understand the parables, the new teaching, and what God has said in Scripture in the past, the old teaching. They do not contradict each other; they come from the same treasure.

*****

Jesus and His disciples receive word that John the Baptist has been beheaded. Herod Antipas has had John killed to reward Herodias's daughter for a lewd dance at one of his banquets. When Antipas eventually hears about the miracles Jesus is doing, he is afraid that John has come back from the dead (Mark 6:14–29). But John has not risen again; his work on earth is finished. He had preached the coming of the kingdom and had prepared the way for the Messiah. Jesus tells his disciples that of those born of women, there was none greater than John the Baptist (Matt. 11:11).

Jesus continues to preach, teach, and heal many people. Thousands follow Him everywhere, and twice, he works miracles to feed the huge crowds who gather about Him. He feeds five thousand and then four thousand by multiplying a few loaves of bread and a few fish (Matt. 14:13–21, 15:32–39). He sails across the Sea of Galilee with His disciples and calms the wind and the waves when a nighttime storm threatens to sink their boat (Mark 4:36–41).

In a later incident, Jesus is on shore and sees the disciples straining at their oars against a strong wind in the midst of the sea. He walks to them on the water and stops the wind (Mark 6:45–52). He raises a widow's son from the dead (Luke 7:13–15) and does the same for the daughter of Jairus, a ruler of a synagogue (Luke 8:49–56). Jesus is demonstrating His authority and ministering to the deepest spiritual and physical needs of the people as He establishes His kingdom.

*****

With His message to John the Baptist and the lessons of the parables, Jesus has begun to explain the nature of the kingdom during His first advent. A brief survey further reveals the extent of His kingdom teaching from the beginning to the end of His earthly ministry, teaching that adds to the concepts of the kingdom parables. Some of his pronouncements refer to the kingdom as it is now on the earth, and some refer to the consummation of the kingdom:

1. Jesus began His preaching by saying, "The time is fulfilled, and the kingdom of God is at hand; repent, and believe in the Gospel" (Mark 1:15).
2. In Matthew 5, Jesus says that the kingdom of heaven belongs to the poor in spirit (v. 3) and those persecuted for righteousness sake (v. 10).

3. He instructs the disciples to pray for the coming of the kingdom (Matt. 6:10). His teaching in Matthew 5, 6, and 7, called the Sermon on the Mount, describes life in His kingdom.

4. Early in his ministry, Jesus says, "I must preach the kingdom of God to the other cities also, for I was sent for this purpose" (Luke 4:43).

5. Luke tells us, "And it came about soon afterwards, that He began going about from one city and village to another, proclaiming and preaching the kingdom of God" (Luke 8:1).

6. Jesus said to His disciples, "To you it has been granted to know the mysteries of the kingdom of God, but to the rest it is in parables, 'in order that seeing they may not see, and hearing they may not understand'" (Luke 8:10). Jesus quotes Isaiah 6:9 to show that God's electing grace is revealed by a person's response to His teaching on the kingdom.

7. "Blessed are you who are poor, for yours is the kingdom of God" (Luke 6:20).

8. "Many shall come from east and west, and recline at the table with Abraham, Isaac, and Jacob, in the kingdom of heaven" (Matt. 8:11). The everlasting kingdom will be made up of people from all the nations.

9. "It is hard for a rich man to enter the kingdom of heaven" (Matt. 19:23).

10. "Truly, truly, I say to you, unless one is born again, he cannot see the kingdom of God" (John 3:3). A spiritual rebirth brought about by the sovereign work of the Holy Spirit is necessary for entering God's kingdom (John 3:3–8; Titus 3:4–7).

11. The kingdom of heaven is like a landowner who has a right to reward his workers as he chooses. A person's reward depends on God's mercy, not on his own good works (Matt. 20:1–16).

12. To the chief priests and elders Jesus said, "Truly, I say to you that the tax-gatherers and harlots will get into the kingdom of God before you" (Matt. 21:31).

13. He told Israel's leaders that, "the kingdom of God will be taken away from you, and given to a nation producing the fruit of it" (Matt. 21:43). The kingdom is no longer going to progress through, Israel, a single theocratic nation, but through a subculture in all the nations, the Church under the New Covenant (see pp. xviii and 151).

14. The kingdom of heaven is like a king who invited guests (Israel) to come to his son's wedding, but they refused to attend. So the king sent out his servants to gather all they found on the highways, and his wedding hall was filled with people (Matt. 22:1–10).

15. "But woe to you, scribes and Pharisees, hypocrites, because you shut off the kingdom of heaven from men; for you do not enter in yourselves, nor do you allow those who are entering to go in" (Matt. 23:13). Legalism brings no one into the kingdom of God.

16. "Permit the children to come to me; do not hinder them; for the kingdom of God belongs to such as these" (Mark 10:14). Those who enter the kingdom have a childlike faith in God.

17. "But seek first His kingdom and His righteousness; and all these things shall be added to you" (Matt. 6:33). We should be more concerned about our spiritual needs than material possessions. God will provide what we require.

18. In speaking of the end of the age, Jesus says, "And this gospel of the kingdom shall be preached in the whole world for a witness to all the nations, and then the end shall come" (Matt. 24:14).

19. When Jesus is initiating the New Covenant the night before His death, He tells His disciples, "I say to you, I will not drink of this fruit of the vine from now on until that day when I drink it new with you in My Father's kingdom" (Matt. 26:29). The consummation of the kingdom will be a time of fellowship and celebration.

20. When Jesus is arrested, Pilate asks Him if He is a king. Jesus answers, "My kingdom is not of this world. If my kingdom were of this world, then my servants would be fighting, that I might not be delivered up to the Jews; but as it is, My kingdom is not of this realm" (John 18:36). Jesus's present kingdom is not a political kingdom. It is in the world but not of the world—"of this realm." It does not depend on military power; but the consummation of His kingdom will come with overwhelming power and usher in the new heaven and earth.

21. One of the thieves crucified with Christ realizes who He is and says, "Jesus, remember me when You come in Your kingdom." Jesus replies, "Truly I say to you, today you shall be with Me in Paradise" (Luke 23:42–43).

22. At Jesus's Second coming, when He comes in judgment as the King, He will say, "Come, you who are blessed of my Father, inherit the

kingdom prepared for you from the foundation of the world" (Matt. 25:34).

23. The writer of Hebrews says in 12:28, "Therefore, since we receive a kingdom which cannot be shaken, let us show gratitude, by which we may offer to God an acceptable service with reverence and awe."

We could look at other references, but these make it clear that Jesus's work on earth is done within the context of the kingdom from the beginning to the end. The kingdom is established with Jesus's first advent; the consummation of the kingdom awaits His second coming. This is the "already but not yet" aspect of the kingdom and kingdom life.

*****

As Jesus continues His teaching, He begins to reveal to His disciples the ultimate end of His earthly ministry. They are traveling through the villages of Caesarea Philippi when He asks His disciples, "Who do people say that the Son of Man is?" (Matt. 16:13). They reply that some say He is John the Baptist or Elijah while others say Jeremiah or one of the prophets. Jesus then directly asks them the question that every human being will eventually face, "But who do you say that I am?

Simon Peter answers, "Thou art the Christ, the Son of the living God" (Matt. 16:13–16).

Jesus says that Peter is blessed because this was not revealed to him by flesh and blood but rather by "My Father who is in heaven" (Matt. 16:17).[292]

Jesus goes on to say, "And I also say to you that you are Peter, and upon this rock I will build My church; and the gates of Hades shall not overpower it" (Matt. 16:18). The Roman Catholic Church has misused this verse to claim that Jesus was establishing Peter as the first pope, and they assert that there has been an unbroken line of successors up to the present day. But Jesus does not say, "upon *thee* I will build My church"[293] but "upon this rock," referring to Peter's confession of Christ's divinity as the foundation of the church. Peter is

---

[292] No one comes to a true knowledge of Christ by his own efforts. It is the work of God through the Holy Spirit (John 3:3–8, 1:12–13, 6:44; Rom. 9:16–18; Eph. 1:5–6, etc.).

[293] This is Jesus's first mention of the church. He will cite the church again in reference to church discipline (Matt. 18:17), but these are the only times that the word *church* is used in the Gospels. It will be used many times in Acts, the Epistles, and Revelation.

not the first pope, and he soon shows that neither he nor any other man can be the "rock" upon which the Church is built.

After Peter's confession, Jesus begins to tell His disciples that "He must go to Jerusalem, and suffer many things from the elders and chief priests and scribes, and be killed, and be raised up on the third day" (Matt. 16:21).

Peter takes Him aside and rebukes Him, saying, "God forbid it, Lord! This shall never happen to You" (Matt. 16:22).

But Jesus turns to Peter and exclaims, "Get behind Me, Satan! You are a stumbling block to Me; for you are not setting your mind on God's interests, but man's" (Matt. 16:23).

There is only one way to fulfill God's plan for the kingdom, and Jesus will not be deterred by His enemy, Satan, or by His misguided disciple, Peter. Jesus then says that if anyone is to follow Him, he must "deny himself, and take up his cross, and follow Me" (Matt. 16:24). Those who follow Jesus also face death, a death to self. Jesus tells the disciples, "For whoever wishes to save his life shall lose it; but whoever loses his life for My sake shall find it" (Matt. 16:25).

*****

Jesus goes on to say that some of them standing with Him shall not taste death "until they see the Son of Man coming in His kingdom" (Matt. 16:28). This is hard for the disciples to understand since He has just been teaching them about His approaching death at the hands of the Jewish authorities. But six days later, Jesus takes Peter, James, and John up a high mountain where He is transfigured before them. His face shines like the sun, His garments become as white as light, and Moses and Elijah appear and talk with Him.[294] An overwhelmed Peter suggests building tabernacles for all three, but a bright cloud overshadows them, and a voice speaks from the cloud, saying, "This is My beloved Son, with Whom I am well-pleased; listen to Him" (Matt. 17:5). The terrified disciples fall on their faces. Jesus comes to them and touches them; He tells them to rise and not be afraid. They look up and see only Him.

As they make their way back down the mountain, Jesus tells them not to tell anyone about what they have seen until "the Son of Man has risen from

---

[294] Moses and Elijah represent the Law and the Prophets in the Old Testament, which point to Jesus.

the dead" (Matt. 17:9). The disciples have been given a brief preview of Jesus's Second Coming when He comes in glory for the consummation of the kingdom, but first, He must die and rise again (Matt. 17:1–9; Mark 9:2–8; Luke 9:28–36).

*****

As Jesus approaches the end of His earthly ministry, He continues to teach the disciples about His coming death. He makes it clear that He is laying down His life in accordance with God's plan. He says, "For this reason the Father loves Me, because I lay down My life that I may take it again. No one has taken it away from Me, but I lay it down on My own initiative. I have authority to lay it down, and I have authority to take it up again. This commandment I received from my Father" (John 10:17–18).

*****

Jesus's ministry lasts approximately three years.[295] As time passes, and His following grows, the Jewish leaders become increasingly antagonistic. The Pharisees and Sadducees disagree with each other, but they are intensely united in their animosity toward Him (Luke 11:53–54). With the scribes and chief priests, they spy on Jesus and try to trick Him with questions so that they can arrest Him (Luke 20:20). But Jesus not only refutes their hostile reasoning, He exposes their motivations. He tells parables which show they are murderers in their hearts (Matt. 12:9–13, 23:1–36; Luke 13:14–17, 20:1–18, etc.) and publicly calls them whitewashed tombs, blind guides, hypocrites, and serpents, a brood of vipers.[296] He exposes their duplicity and offends their sense of personal self-righteousness (Matt. 23:1–36).

His adversaries become afraid to further question Him (Mark 12:34), but their hatred and opposition only increase. The religious leaders have established their own kingdom in Israel, and they are not going to let Jesus threaten what they have built. They have been planning to kill him for a long time (John

---

[295] Scholars differ on the length of time, but John mentions three Passovers after Christ begins preaching (John 2:13, 6:4, 11:55).

[296] Jesus is deliberately linking them to the Serpent in the garden. They are of the line of Satan; they are little serpents.

5:18), but as the yearly Passover celebration approaches, three events occur which convince them they must move quickly to end His life:

1. Early in His ministry, Jesus had been invited into the home of Martha and Mary, sisters who live with their brother Lazarus in Bethany, a city on the eastern outskirts of Jerusalem. The family is wealthy enough to make extensive preparations for guests, and these activities had become a focus for Martha. Jesus had gently corrected her excessive concern about such things (Luke 10:38–42), and he came to love each member of the family (John 11:5).

   As people in Jerusalem are preparing for the Passover celebration, Lazarus becomes seriously ill, and his sisters send for Jesus. But He delays in going to their home and tells His disciples that Lazarus's sickness is for the glory of God. When He does arrive in Bethany, Lazarus has died and been in the grave four days. Jesus sees Mary and her friends weeping, and He also weeps (John 11:35). Jesus knows that He is going to raise Lazarus from the dead, but death, the awful wages of sin, is a horrible and crushing reality.

   They then show Him where they have buried Lazarus. Despite Martha's protest about the stench of death, Jesus has the stone removed from the door of the tomb, and He cries out, "Lazarus, come forth" (John 11:43).

   Lazarus emerges from the tomb, still bound in his grave cloths. They unbind him and let him go. Many people who have come to comfort the sisters believe in Jesus when they see Lazarus alive, but some of them go and tell the Pharisees (John 11:1–46).

   The chief priests and Pharisees convene a council. This incident has not occurred in far-off Galilee. A well-known man near Jerusalem has been raised from the dead, and many people have witnessed it. The religious leaders cannot deny it. They are afraid that everyone is going to believe in Jesus, and they will lose their status and positions in the nation. The religious leaders must either acknowledge Jesus's authority or kill Him. From that day on, they make plans to arrest Him and put Him to death. Jesus withdraws to Ephraim with His disciples while the people seek for Him and discuss among themselves whether He will attend the Passover in Jerusalem (John 11:47–57).

2. Six days before the Passover feast, Jesus returns to Bethany and dines with Lazarus. Jews are coming from all over the nation for the annual celebration, and they not only want to see Jesus, they want to see Lazarus. Many people believe in Jesus because of him, and the chief priests decide they must also kill Lazarus (John 12:9–11). The religious leaders plan to murder the man that Jesus has just raised from the dead.[297]

    The next day, Jesus sends two of His disciples to Jerusalem to get a donkey. The people, knowing that the chief priests intend to seize Jesus, are still questioning if He will enter the city for Passover. In what has come to be known as Palm Sunday, Jesus rides the donkey into Jerusalem. When the people hear that He is coming, they tear branches from the palm trees and spread them, along with their garments, before Him, crying out, "Hosanna! Blessed is He who comes in the name of the LORD, even the King of Israel" (John 12:13; Luke 35:38).

    Jesus's dramatic entry fulfills what Zechariah had prophesied, "Rejoice greatly, O daughter of Zion! Behold your king is coming to you… Humble, and mounted on a donkey" (Zech. 9:9). A King arriving on a donkey, instead of a war horse, means that He is coming in peace; it is a time for salvation, not fear. But there will come a time when Jesus returns in judgment, and that will be a time of great fear. In John's vision of Jesus's second advent, he sees Him arriving on a white horse as he judges and wages war (Rev. 19:11).

    The Pharisees in the crowd tell Jesus to rebuke His disciples for hailing Him as King of Israel. But Jesus replies, "I tell you, if these become silent, the stones will cry out" (Luke 19:39–40). Jesus is acknowledging that He is the King of Israel. The consummation of the kingdom is future, but His rule over His kingdom people, the true Israel (Rom. 9:6–8), has already begun. The Pharisees see that they cannot quiet the crowd, and that the "world" is going after Jesus (John 12:19). The religious leaders understand that if they are going

---

[297] Scripture does not give us the circumstances of how Lazarus dies a second time.

to kill Him, they must do it quickly before His following becomes even stronger.[298]

3. After His triumphal entry, Jesus returns to Bethany, and on the next day, Monday, He goes back to Jerusalem and enters the Temple mount. He drives out those who are buying and selling, overturns the tables of the moneychangers and the seats of those selling doves, and does not let anyone carry their goods into the Temple area (Mark 11:15–16). He begins to teach and say, "Is it not written, 'My house shall be called a house of prayer for all the nations?' But you have made it a robbers den" (Mark 11:17; Isa. 56:7; Jer. 7:11).

This is the second time that Jesus has cleansed the Temple. Early in His ministry, He had used a scourge of cords to drive out the moneychangers, along with the sacrificial sheep and oxen for sale (John 2:14–17). Now He is directly challenging the chief priests again. The High Priest controls the merchants and the moneychangers and gets a percentage from the exorbitant prices charged the worshippers. Some of the priests, notably the sons of Annas, the High Priest, set up their own booths.[299] Now Jesus is showing that He has authority over the Temple, not them. And He is threatening their revenue.

With the Jewish people assembling in Jerusalem for their most important religious celebration, Jesus, who already had a significant following, has raised a man from the dead and many people have witnessed it. He has made a triumphal entry into Jerusalem where large crowds have hailed Him as King of Israel. And He has taken authority over the Temple Mount, cleansing it and threatening the incomes of the chief priests. Jesus is jeopardizing the kingdom of the

---

[298] The Sadducees, who rule the Temple, especially fear that their authority and positions will be taken away if the Romans hear that Jesus is leading an uprising.

[299] Josephus says that Annas (or Ananias), the High Priest, "was a great hoarder up of money," Josephus, "Antiquities," 20:9.2. Also see, "Second Temple: Moneychangers," Bible History Online, accessed November 13, 2018, http://www.bible-history.com/subcat.php?id=52, and "Jesus Clears the Temple of Money Changers," *ThoughtCo.*, accessed November 17, 2018, https://www.thoughtco.com/jesus-clears-the-temple-bible-story-700066.

religious authorities, and for them, it is now just a matter of how they are going to kill Him. Once again, we see a clash of kingdoms.

*****

Jesus spends the night in Bethany (Matt. 21:17) and on Tuesday returns to the Temple. He is teaching there when the chief priests and elders confront Him and demand to know by whose authority He is doing these things. He does not give them an answer, but He tells a parable about wicked vine-growers who kill the owner's son so they can take possession of the vineyard for themselves (Luke 20:9–18).[300] The religious leaders realize He is talking about them and want to seize Him, but they are afraid of the people. The crowds are a protection for Jesus, and He continues teaching them many things, including a discourse on the end of the age (Luke 20:1–21:38).

The next day, the chief priests and elders gather in the court of Caiaphas, the high priest. They make plans to arrest Jesus but decide it will have to be by stealth. They are afraid the people will riot if they seize Him publicly (Matt. 26:3–5).

During this time, Jesus is in Bethany at the home of Simon the Leper[301] when a woman approaches him as He reclines at table. She has an alabaster vial of very costly perfume with which she anoints Jesus. Some of the disciples are indignant because they see this as a waste of money that could have been given to the poor. But Jesus says that she has done a good deed and is preparing Him for His burial (Matt. 26:6–12).

This incident provokes one of the twelve apostles, Judas Iscariot, into taking action (Matt. 26:14–16). Judas is in charge of the money box for the disciples and, unknown to the others, has been stealing from it (John 12:6). Luke says that Satan entered into Judas and that he went to the chief priests and officers and discussed with them how he might betray Jesus. They gladly offer

---

[300] In this parable, Jesus is clearly implying that the Jewish leaders know that He is the Son of God, and that is one of the reasons they want to kill Him. They want to keep the kingdom they have constructed based on their own legalistic self-righteousness.

[301] Scripture says nothing more about this man (Matt. 26:6). It is likely that Jesus had healed him.

him money, and from that time on, he begins to seek a way to deliver Jesus into their hands when He is away from the people (Luke 22:3–6).[302]

*****

On Thursday of the Passover week, Jesus directs Peter and John to go and prepare the Passover meal so they can eat it that night. He tells them to go into the city where they should follow a man carrying a pitcher of water into a house. They do as they are told, and the owner of the house directs them to a large upper room where they prepare the Passover (Luke 22:7–13).

That evening, Jesus reclines with the apostles at the table in the upper room and tells them, "I have earnestly desired to eat this Passover with you before I suffer; for I say to you I shall never again eat it until it is fulfilled in the kingdom of God" (Luke 22:15–16).[303] This is a night of intimate fellowship and intense emotion for Jesus and His apostles. Jesus knows that before morning, He will be betrayed and turned over to the Jewish authorities. As a man, he faces separation from those He loves, terrible mockery, horrendous physical suffering, and then a brutal death on the cross.

But as the Son of God, He also knows that He must endure separation from God the Father when the Father's wrath is poured out on Him for the sins of His people. He has to be infinite God to bear such punishment. Before He faces such an unimaginable ordeal, Jesus wants to be with His closest disciples to give them His final words.

He begins by initiating the new covenant that Jeremiah had foretold (Jer. 31:31–34).[304] He takes bread, and after giving thanks, breaks it and gives it to His disciples, saying, "This is My body which is given for you, do this in

---

[302] Scripture does not tell us why Judas decided to betray Jesus. We know that Judas was a thief and loved money, but it may have been Jesus's reference to His burial that made him act. Many militant Jews were hoping that Jesus would lead a revolt against the Romans. When Jesus again made it clear that He was going to die, not lead a rebellion, Judas may have wanted to force a conflict in which Jesus would use His supernatural powers. But Luke's and John's statements that Satan entered into him are all that we know for certain (Luke 22:3; John 13:27).

[303] It appears that Jesus deliberately celebrated the Passover one day earlier than the customary date (John 18:28). Jesus, the true Passover Lamb, will be dying on the cross the next day at the same time the Jewish people are slaying their Passover lambs, a powerful overlay of type and antitype.

[304] See p. 150–151.

remembrance of Me" (Luke 22:19). Jesus then offers the cup to the twelve and says, "Drink from it, all of you; for this is My blood of the covenant which is poured out for many for forgiveness of sins" (Matt. 26:27–28).

Jesus, in His preincarnate appearance as Melchizedek, the priest of God Most High, had offered Abraham bread and wine, fellowship with God Most High (Gen. 14:18–20; pp. 43–45). Now, Jesus offers Abraham's descendants bread and wine, which represent His body and shed blood that will make it possible for them to have fellowship with God Most High.[305] He goes on to say, "I will not drink of this fruit of the vine from now on until that day when I drink it new with you in My Father's kingdom" (Matt. 26:29).

The disciples do not seem to grasp the full significance of this critical night and even debate among themselves who is the greatest. They still have only a partial understanding of the kingdom that Jesus is establishing through His sacrificial life and death. He points out to them that He Himself had come to them as one who serves and then says, "And you are those who have stood by Me in my trials; and just as My Father has granted Me a kingdom, I grant you that you may eat and drink at My table in My kingdom, and you will sit on thrones judging the twelve tribes of Israel" (Luke 22:28–30). Those who rule in Jesus's kingdom are those who have a heart to serve. The disciples will learn this lesson, and they will also learn the cost of serving. Church tradition indicates that nearly all of them are martyred, but they will have a prominent place in the final kingdom.

After the meal, Jesus washes the feet of the disciples. If the Son of God can perform this humble service, the task of a slave, it is clear what the attitude of His disciples should be. Peter at first refuses to let Jesus wash his feet, but Jesus says, "If I do not wash you, you have no part with Me" (John 13:8), referring to the shedding of His blood which will wash away the sin and guilt of His people. Peter replies, "Lord, not my feet only, but also my hands and my head" (John 13:9).

Jesus tells Peter that He is clean, which means His sins have been forgiven. But Jesus goes on to say that not all the disciples are clean, referring to Judas who is going to betray Him. After giving Judas a sop of bread, Jesus tells him,

---

[305] Jesus has instituted the new covenant, therefore making the old covenant obsolete; it is ready to vanish away (Heb. 8:13). As Jeremiah had prophesied, the new covenant people will have the Law written on their hearts, not on tablets of stone, and their sins will be forgiven on the basis of the shed blood of Jesus.

"What you do, do quickly" (John 13:27). Judas departs into the night and into spiritual darkness. Jesus is left with the eleven who are truly His disciples.

After Judas departs, Jesus says, "Now is the Son of Man glorified, and God is glorified in Him;" (John 13:31). The forces have been set in motion for Jesus to lay down His life for His people for the glory of God.

Jesus tells the disciples that He is going away, and He gives them a new commandment. He says that they should "love one another, even as I have loved you… By this all men will know that you are My disciples, if you have love for one another" (John 13:34–35). Paul will later explain that love fulfills the law because if you love your neighbor, you will not commit adultery, theft, or murder against him or even covet what he has (Rom. 13:8). The love that Christians show for each other, and also for those outside the faith, is often their most effective witness to the truth of the gospel.

The disciples are concerned about Jesus leaving them, and Peter wants to know why he cannot go with Him. Peter says, "I will lay down my life for You."

But Jesus tells him, "Truly, truly, I say to you, a cock shall not crow, until you deny Me three times" (John 13:37–38). Before the sun comes up, Peter will thrice deny that he even knows Jesus.

Jesus tells the disciples to not be troubled but to believe in God and also in Him. He reassures them by saying, "In My Father's house are many dwelling places; if it were not so, I would have told you; for I go to prepare a place for you. And if I go and prepare a place for you, I will come again and receive you to Myself; That where I am, there you may be also" (John 14:2–3).

Jesus goes on to make a declaration that postmodern thinkers cannot tolerate, "I am the way, and the truth, and the life; no one comes to the Father but through Me" (John 14:6). The popular assumption that all religions are simply different ways of approaching the same God is a deadly falsehood. There is only one way of approaching the one true God, and that way is Jesus Christ.[306] Jesus says that God the Father is revealed through Him. Whoever has seen Jesus has seen the Father (John 14:7–11). He and the Father are one (John 10:30). The gods of other religions are idols, false gods.

---

[306] Postmodernism strongly denies the concept of absolute truth; everything is relative, and therefore, all religions are equally valid. But Jesus proclaims He is the truth, and there is no other way to God except through Him. No other religion has a concept of salvation by grace alone. In all other religions, ultimate goals are attained by self-effort and good works, and there is no solution for sin.

Jesus continues with some of the most personally comforting words of His ministry. He says that He is going to His Father and that He will ask the Father to give them another Helper that will abide with them forever, the Spirit of truth, whom the world cannot receive. The Spirit will dwell with Jesus's disciples and will be within them; they are not going to be left alone as orphans (John 14:16–18).

Jesus has already told His disciples that He is going to die, but now He assures them that He will live again, and that they will live also because of their special union with Him, "I am in My Father, and you in Me, and I in you… and he who loves Me shall be loved by My Father, and I will love him, and will disclose Myself to him" (John 14:20–21).

Jesus is explaining the fulfillment of Jeremiah's prophecy concerning the Law written on the hearts of new covenant disciples. He goes on to say, "If anyone loves Me, he will keep My word; and My Father will love him, and We will come to him and make Our abode with him" (John 14:23).[307]

Jesus then further describes the future role of the Holy Spirit in their lives. He says, "These things I have spoken to you, while abiding with you. But the Helper, the Holy Spirit, Whom the Father will send in My name, He will teach you all things, and bring to your remembrance all things that I said to you" (John 14:25–26).[308]

Jesus tells the disciples that He is leaving His peace with them, and He repeats that although He is going away, He will return to them. He is telling them all these things so that when they occur, the disciples will believe. He says, "I will not speak much more with you, for the ruler of the world is coming, and he has nothing in Me; but that the world may know that I love the Father, and as the Father gave Me Commandment, even so I do. Arise, let us go from here" (John 14:30–31).

The time at the table has ended. The Passover meal, the Last Supper, is finished, but Jesus continues to teach His disciples as they prepare to leave the upper room. He tells them that He is the Vine and they are the branches; He has chosen them and they must love one another (John 15:1–17). Jesus warns

---

[307] Jesus's harshest words were to the Pharisees who see God as a harsh taskmaster that they can satisfy by their own righteousness rather than as a loving Father who is merciful (Matt. 23:1–39). They have a high view of their own holiness and a low view of God's mercy.

[308] It was the Holy Spirit who inspired the books of the Old Testament, and He will enable the writers of the New Testament books to remember what Jesus had told them (2 Pet. 1:20–21; 2 Tim. 3:16).

them that the world will hate them as He has been hated and that He is telling them these things so that they will not stumble (John 15:18–16:3). He teaches them more about the Holy Spirit and again assures them that He will return. They are going to have sorrow, but it will turn to joy because He has overcome the world (John 16:7–33).

In one of the final acts of ministry in His earthly body,[309] Jesus prays for His disciples, and not only for them but also for those who will come to believe in Him through their witness. He asks the Father to "glorify Thy Son, that the Son may glorify Thee" (John 17:1), and He prays for the unity of the Father, Himself, and those whom the Father has given Him. Jesus then concludes the Passover celebration by expressing His great concern for His present and future disciples in a lengthy, emotional, and beautiful prayer for all His people (John 17:1–26).[310]

*****

Jesus leaves the upper room with His disciples and crosses the Kidron Valley to a garden called Gethsemane on the Mount of Olives. He is in great distress about the terrible suffering facing Him and asks the disciples to watch with Him. He goes a short distance from them to pray, but the disciples keep falling asleep. Jesus prays, saying, "My Father, if it is possible, let this cup pass from Me; yet not as I will, but as Thou wilt" (Matt. 26:39).

An angel from heaven appears, strengthening Him. Jesus is in such agony and praying so fervently that His sweat becomes "like drops of blood, falling down upon the ground" (Luke 22:43–44). He knows there is no other way; the Son of Man must drink this cup.

After His prayer, Jesus returns to the disciples, who are asleep. As He tells them to arise, Judas arrives with a Roman cohort and a crowd of men sent by the chief priests and elders.[311] This large force approaches Jesus's small group with torches, swords, and clubs (John 18:3; Mark 14:43). After Judas identi-

---

[309] Jesus will minister to His disciples after He is raised from the dead, but He will be in His resurrection body.
[310] Each individual should personally read and consider this amazing prayer.
[311] A Roman cohort usually consisted of 300–600 soldiers (see n. on Matt. 27:27, Ryrie, *Ryrie Study*, 1499). Along with the men sent by the chief priests, this is a huge force to arrest one man.

fies Him with a kiss (Matt. 26:47–49), Jesus faces the crowd and asks them, "Whom do you seek?"

They answer "Jesus the Nazarene."

When Jesus answers "I am *He*"[312] (John 18:4–6), the crowd draws back and falls to the ground. Jesus is submitting to His arrest of His own will, not because of the power of Rome or the schemes of the chief priests.

The soldiers and the Jewish leaders regain their feet and lay their hands on Jesus. Jesus tells them that they should let His disciples go, but Peter draws his sword and strikes the slave of the high priest, cutting off his ear. Jesus rebukes Peter and tells him to put his sword away. He says, "The cup which the Father has given Me, shall I not drink it?" (John 18:8–11). Jesus touches the ear of the slave and heals him; He then faces the multitude and says, "Have you come out with swords and clubs as against a robber? While I was with you daily in the Temple, you did not lay hands on Me; but this hour and the power of darkness are yours" (Luke 22:50–53).

The Roman cohort and the Jewish leaders bind Jesus and lead Him away to the house of Annas, the high priest. All the disciples flee, but Peter and John return and follow Jesus and the combined forces that have arrested Him (John 18:15).[313] Just a few hours before, Jesus had told the apostles that this was going to happen. He had quoted the LORD's prophecy in Zechariah, saying, "I will strike down the Shepherd, and the sheep of the flock shall be scattered" (Matt. 26:31; Zech. 13:7).

---

[312] Literally "I am;" the name for Himself that the LORD gave Moses from the burning bush (Exod. 3:14, also see pp. 88–89).

[313] The Gospel of Mark reports that a certain young man was following Jesus and the crowd. Some of them attempted to seize the young man, but he slipped out of his linen sheet and fled naked. This seems to have been Mark Himself, years before he wrote his gospel (Mark 14:50–52).

CHAPTER 24

TRIAL, CRUCIFIXION, AND BURIAL

With the help of Judas, the Jewish leaders have managed to arrest Jesus at night away from the people; they move swiftly to put Him to death. Nevertheless, they are under their own law as well as Roman law, so they have to go through the appearance of a legal process. Israel's law forbids a capital trial at night,[314] but Jesus is taken before Annas, the "acting" high priest, for a hearing about one in the morning. Annas decides to question Jesus, even though the Romans have officially deposed him and transferred his office to his son-in-law, Caiaphas.[315]

When Annas asks Jesus about his teaching, Jesus says that he should ask those who heard Him teach. Jesus is pointing out that there are no witnesses present to bring charges; there is nothing to justify His arrest. One of the soldiers strikes Him; the physical abuse of the Son of God has begun. After a brief interrogation, Annas sends Jesus to Caiaphas where the Jewish elders and scribes have already gathered, even though it is well before dawn (John 18:12–24).

Peter, with John's help,[316] follows the crowd into the courtyard of the High Priest as the soldiers prepare to take Jesus inside. Twice, bystanders, one of them a servant girl, accuse Peter of associating with Jesus, and both times, he denies knowing Him. About an hour later, another man insists that Peter was with Jesus, but Peter denies it with a curse, saying, "Man, I do not know what you are talking about." Before he can finish speaking, the rooster crows (Luke

---

[314] See Harry Fogle, "The Trial of Jesus," accessed November 22, 2018, www.1215.org/lawnotes/lawnotes/jesustrial.htm for a list of more than a dozen ways the Jewish leaders blatantly violated their civil, rabbinic, and Mosaic laws in the trial of Jesus. Also see n. on John 18:13, Sproul, *New Geneva*, 1699.

[315] Although the Romans have given the office of high priest to Caiaphas, many of the Jews still consider Annas the true high priest. See n. on Luke 3:2, Sproul, *New Geneva*, 1608.

[316] The high priest knew John and the doorkeeper admits Peter with him (John 18:15).

22:54–60; Mark 14:71). Jesus turns and looks at Peter, and Peter remembers what Jesus had told him. He goes out and weeps bitterly (Luke 22:61–62).

The soldiers take Jesus before Caiaphas and the council of the Sanhedrin,[317] seventy chief priests and elders who have gotten up hurriedly during the night to deal with Jesus. As soon as daybreak arrives, they question Him and produce witnesses to testify against Him, but their accounts do not agree. According to Jewish law, they need at least two consistent witnesses to move forward with the trial, and they do not have them (Deut. 19:15).

Jesus has remained silent during the court proceedings.[318] Finally, Caiaphas demands, "Are You the Christ, the Son of the Blessed One?" (Mark 14:61).

Jesus answers by using the name He gave from the burning bush and then quotes Daniel 7:13, "I am; and you shall see the Son of Man sitting at the right hand of the Power, and coming with the clouds of heaven" (Mark 14:62).

The high priest tears his clothes and exclaims, "He has blasphemed! What further need do we have of witnesses?" (Matt. 26:65). The council immediately condemns Jesus to death (Mark 14:53–64).

The members of the Sanhedrin have concluded their sham trial, and now these religious leaders finally have the opportunity to vent their rage at Jesus. They spit at Him, put a blindfold on Him (likely a cloth draped over His head) and, along with the soldiers, beat Him and hit Him in the face (Mark 14:65). He cannot see the blows coming and cannot brace Himself. The number of angry men who struck Jesus is unknown, but many did, and His face is bloodied and terribly disfigured. Isaiah had prophesied, "His appearance was marred more than any man" (Isa. 52:14).

As they strike him, they mock Him, saying, "Prophesy to us, You Christ; who is the one who hit You?" (Matt. 26:68). After they have severely beaten Him, the council sends Jesus to Pontius Pilate, the Roman governor of Judea, hoping that he will order Jesus's execution (Matt. 27:1–2).

---

[317] The Sanhedrin was the highest Jewish court and had jurisdiction in Jerusalem. They could order the death penalty, but the Romans did not permit them to carry out executions so the case must eventually go before the Roman governor. See n. on Luke 22:66, Ryrie, *Ryrie Study*, 1592; also, Josephus, "Antiquities" 14.9.3.

[318] Isaiah, in his prophecy of the Suffering Servant, had said, "He was oppressed and He was afflicted, Yet He did not open His mouth; Like a lamb that is led to slaughter, And like a sheep that is silent before its shearers, So He did not open his mouth. By oppression and judgment He was taken away; And as for His generation, who considered That He was cut off out of the land of the living, For the transgression of my people to whom the stroke was due?" (Isa. 53:7–8).

When Judas sees what has happened to Jesus, he goes to the chief priests and elders and tries to return the money they had given him, confessing, "I have sinned by betraying innocent blood."

But they say, "What is that to us? See to that yourself!" (Matt. 27:4).

Judas receives no absolution from these religious leaders; he throws the pieces of silver into the sanctuary and goes away and hangs himself. The chief priests decide they cannot put the silver in the treasury because it is blood money. Instead, they use it to buy the Potter's Field as a burial place for strangers (Matt. 27:3–7).

*****

The entire council follows Jesus as the soldiers escort Him to Pilate (Mark 15:1). The governor is in Jerusalem to see that order is maintained during Passover and is staying at the Praetorium, his official residence while he is in the city.[319] The Jews accuse Jesus of sedition, saying that He claimed to be a king, but after questioning Him, Pilate says, "I find no guilt in this man" (Luke 23:4). The Jewish leaders accuse Jesus of treason before Pilate, not blasphemy. For the Romans, who acknowledge many gods, a man claiming to be a god is not a serious matter; a man claiming to be a king is a concern, but for Pilate, this severely beaten man with no apparent followers is no threat to Rome.

But the Jews refuse to relent in their accusations, and when Pilate learns that Jesus is a Galilean, he tries to resolve his problem by sending Jesus to Herod Antipas, the ruler of Galilee who is in the city for the Passover (Luke 23:1–7).

Herod is pleased to see Jesus because he has heard of Him and is hoping that He will perform a sign. The chief priests and scribes, who have again followed Jesus, vehemently accuse him before the king. But Jesus does not respond to them nor answer Herod's questions. Like the governor, Herod does not see this as a serious matter. He and the soldiers mock Jesus, dress Him in a royal robe, and send Him back to Pilate (Luke 23:8–11).

*****

---

[319] *Praetorium* was originally the word for a military headquarters, and for Pilate, it is likely the fortress of Antonio where Roman troops were quartered. See n. on Mk. 15:16, Ryrie, *Ryrie Study*, 1536.

When the entire contingent arrives back before the governor, he addresses the Jewish leaders again and tells them that he and Herod find no guilt in this man. Pilate understands that the Jewish authorities want Jesus executed because of their personal envy and hatred (Matt. 27:18). He tells them that he is going to punish Jesus, scourge Him, and then release Him. Pilate hopes that the suggestion of this severe punishment will satisfy the wrath of Jesus's accusers (Luke 23:13–16).

The governor also offers to let the Jews decide which Roman prisoner is to be released that day, an event which had become an accepted custom for Passover (John 18:39). They can choose between Barabbas, who is a robber and murderer (John 18.40; Mark 15:7), and Jesus. Pilate is trying to find a way to free Jesus before scourging Him. But a large crowd has gathered, and the chief priests and elders urge the people to demand that Barabbas be released and that Jesus be crucified (Matt. 27:20).This crowd is very different from the multitude that, just five days before, had hailed Jesus as King of the Jews. Many of those people had traveled to Jerusalem for Passover and were from the villages and rural areas where Jesus had ministered. Today, it is still early in the morning (John 18:28), and this crowd is made up of people that the chief priests and elders had gathered from within Jerusalem. Some of them are probably zealots who are frustrated that Jesus has not led a revolt against the Romans, but all of them are susceptible to the incitement and demands of the established religious leaders. The seventy members of the Sanhedrin, a large company themselves, can incite the crowd and intimidate Pilate.

The Roman governor is facing a growing predicament. He knows that Jesus, already severely beaten and abused by the religious leaders, is innocent. In addition, his wife, troubled by a dream, had spoken to him about Jesus, saying, "Have nothing to do with that righteous Man" (Matt. 27:19).

When the crowd calls for the release of Barabbas, Pilate asks what he should do with Jesus. The people shout "Let Him be crucified!" Pilate asks, "Why, what evil has He done?"

The crowd's only response is to cry out with ever increasing intensity, "Let Him be crucified!" (Matt. 27:22–23).

Pilate decides to go ahead with the scourging of Jesus, apparently still hoping that this brutal punishment will satisfy the angry mob. We must not pass easily over the scourging of Jesus. The scourge whips were made of leather with metal and bone attachments designed for ripping flesh. By the time the savage lashing is over, the skin and muscles on Jesus's back are shredded. His body is in shock and agony, and He is losing more blood.[320]

The soldiers next take Jesus into the Praetorium and strip Him of His clothes. They place a purple robe on Him, force a crown of thorns on His head, and put a reed in His right hand. They kneel before Him, mocking Him, and say, "Hail, King of the Jews" (Matt. 27:29). Some of them begin to hit Him in the face again (John 19:3).

Pilate addresses the crowd once more and declares, "Behold, I am bringing Him out to you, that you may know that I find no guilt in Him" (John 19:4). Jesus is led before the inflamed mob, still wearing the crown of thorns and the purple robe. Pilate cries out, "Behold, the Man!" (John 19:5).

But when the chief priests and Jewish officials see Jesus, they scream, "Crucify, crucify!" (John 19:6).

Pilate sees that he is accomplishing nothing and that a riot is developing; his position as governor may be jeopardized if unrest develops in Jerusalem. He takes water, washes his hands before the crowd, and declares, "I am innocent of this Man's blood; see to that yourselves" (Matt. 27:24).

The crowd cries back, "His blood be on us and on our children!"[321] (Matt. 27:25).

Pilate releases Barabbas and turns Jesus over to the Roman soldiers to be crucified (Luke 23:25).

The soldiers strip the purple robe from Jesus and put His own clothes back on him. They place the horizontal beam of the cross on Jesus and lead Him away to be crucified (Matt. 27:31). But He is so weak from the beatings and scourging that He cannot carry the heavy burden all the way to Golgotha, the place of crucifixion. The soldiers force a man from Cyrene named Simon to carry it for Him; Simon follows Jesus, carrying the means of execution. Two other men, criminals, are also led away to be put to death with Jesus. And the crowd follows them all.

Once they reach Golgotha, the soldiers nail Jesus's hands and feet to the cross and then lift it upright. They crucify the two thieves, one to Jesus's right

---

[320] The Romans used scourging to inflict terrible pain, but it also did so much physical damage that it shortened the time a man could survive if he was crucified. See "The Roman Scourge," *Bible History Online*, Accessed November 30, 2018, https:www.bible-history. com/past/flagrum.html

[321] This fevered and rash declaration cannot help but bring to mind the many persecutions the Jews have suffered during the last two thousand years.

and one to His left. The soldiers have completed their work—Jesus Christ, the Son of God, the Second Person of the Trinity, the Creator of heaven and earth, has been crucified. Jesus prays, "Father, forgive them; for they do not know what they are doing" (Luke 23:34).

Mark tells us that it is still early, just nine o'clock in the morning.[322] The chief priests and elders have moved swiftly and illegally to slay Jesus; they have finished their business quickly. Their hands will be ceremonially clean as they kill their Passover lambs; the lambs that point to the one whom they have just nailed to the cross.

At this point, it is easy to feel anger and revulsion toward the Jewish mob and especially toward the chief priests and elders. But we must remember that Jesus has been telling His disciples that He is going to lay down His life; it is not taken from Him (John 10:14–18; p. 187). If He is to die for our sins in our place, He must do it as truly a man. He cannot interpose His supernatural powers or He will not be one of us. By His own will and the will of God the Father, He lays down His life. It is our sins, the sins of His kingdom people, that nail Him to the cross. If we despise the chief priests, we must also despise the sins in our own hearts.

Like Adam and Eve, Noah and his family, and the Jewish people epitomized by their leaders, we want our own personal kingdoms. And unless God changes us, we will, like the chief priests, do whatever is necessary to seize and maintain them.

*****

Pilate had succumbed to the demands of the Jewish leaders, but now he decides to insult them by having the soldiers place a sign over Jesus's head that

---

[322] Mark uses Jewish time and says it was the third hour (9:00 a.m.) when Jesus was crucified (Mark 15:25). But John 19:14 tells us that Jesus was before Pilate "about the sixth hour" (12:00 noon if John is using Jewish time). Scholars have suggested three ways to reconcile this apparent discrepancy in the order of events that day: 1. There was an early copying error in John's gospel. 2. John was giving a generalized time for the crucifixion events of that day. 3. John was using Roman time where a new day began at midnight rather than at six in the morning for Jewish time. This would then place Jesus's second appearance before Pilate at about 6:00 a.m., preceding Mark's time for the crucifixion at 9:00 a.m. John has already told us that it was early when Jesus appeared before Pilate the first time (John 18:28–29), so this third choice seems to be the most likely explanation since John was writing about the action of a Roman court and likely referenced Roman time.

says, "THIS IS JESUS THE KING OF THE JEWS" (Matt. 27:37). The chief priests demand that Pilate change it, but he says, "What I have written I have written" (John 19:22). God uses Pilate to publicly declare the truth that the Jewish leaders have rejected.

The two robbers who are being crucified for their crimes begin to hurl insults at Jesus while the soldiers who nailed Him to the cross cast lots and divide His clothing among themselves (Matt. 27:35–38).

The crowd continues to disparage Jesus as He hangs on the cross. They wag their heads and mock Him, saying, "If You are the Son of God, come down from the cross" (Matt. 27:40). The chief priests scorn and taunt Jesus, proclaiming, "He saved others, He cannot save Himself. He is the King of Israel; let Him now come down from the cross, and we shall believe in Him" (Matt. 27:42). Jesus has the power to come down from the cross, but the chief priests are correct in saying that He cannot save Himself; He cannot save Himself if He is to save His people. As He told Peter at His arrest, He must drink this cup (John 18:11; see p. 197).

Many of the women who had followed Jesus from Galilee are watching the crucifixion from a distance (Matt. 27:55). But Jesus's mother, her sister, and Mary Magdalene are standing by His cross along with "the disciple whom He loved," apparently the Apostle John (John 19:25–26).[323] When Jesus, as a firstborn son, was presented in the Temple, Simeon had prophesied about Jesus but had also told Mary that, "a sword will pierce even your own soul" (Luke 2:35; p. 169). Mary is now going through that excruciating experience.

Jesus sees His mother and His disciple and says to her, "Woman, behold your son" (John 19:26).[324] And then to John, He says, "Behold your mother." From that time forward, the disciple takes her into his household (John 19:27).[325]

---

[323] The reference to "the disciple whom Jesus loved" is used six times in the Gospel of John and is generally accepted as the way the Apostle John refers to himself. This is the only time that Mary's sister is mentioned in Scripture.

[324] Some have wondered why Jesus would address His mother as "Woman." But Mary's time as His mother has ended; He is now dying for her as a woman, as a sinful human being. But Jesus shows His love for her and commits her into the care of John.

[325] Apparently, Joseph is no longer living, and Mary's other children have not come to support her. Jesus's siblings had not believed in Him early in His ministry (Mark 3:21; John 7:5). At least two of His half-brsothers, James and Jude, will come to faith, and they will write New Testament epistles.

One of the robbers continues to rail at Jesus and says, "Are you not the Christ? Save Yourself and us!" (Luke 23:39). But something has happened to the other malefactor. He has been watching Jesus and God has changed his heart. He responds to the first thief, saying, "Do you not even fear God, since you are under the same sentence of condemnation? We are receiving what we deserve for our deeds; but this man has done nothing wrong." He then turns to Jesus and says to Him, "Jesus, remember me when you come in Your kingdom!"

Jesus replies, "Truly, I say to you, today you shall be with Me in Paradise" (Luke 23:40–43).[326]

*****

Beginning at the sixth hour (12:00 noon), darkness falls upon the whole land; for three hours, there is no light as God's wrath is poured out on His Son (Matt. 27:45). At the ninth hour, Jesus cries out, "My God, My God, why hast Thou forsaken Me?" (Matt. 27:46). Jesus is undergoing horrendous physical suffering, but worse than that is the spiritual agony of separation from God the Father as Jesus pays the full price for the sins of His people.

When Jesus knows that all things have been accomplished, when He has borne the full weight of God's judgment, He says, "I am thirsty" (John 19:28). The soldiers raise a sponge soaked with sour wine to Jesus. He drinks from it and says, "It is finished!" (John 19:29–30). Jesus has accomplished what He came to earth to do; He has paid for the sins of those who trust in Him. With a loud voice, He cries out and says, "Father, into Thy hands I commit My spirit" (Luke 23:46). Having said this, He breathes His last.

As soon as Jesus dies, the veil of the Temple, the heavy woven ornate curtain too strong for men to tear, is torn in two from top to bottom (Matt. 27:51). The veil that shielded transgressors from the Most Holy Place, the place of God's presence in the Temple, is ripped apart. God has done it, not men;

---

[326] We can note several things from this amazing picture of salvation: (1) It is never too late to turn to Jesus Christ for salvation; (2) even this criminal had some knowledge of Jesus's kingdom; (3) when a believer dies, he goes immediately into the presence of the LORD; there was no purgatory for even this very sinful man; (4) although we should baptize believers, it is not essential for salvation.

with the death of Jesus, the ultimate sacrificial Lamb, there is now access to the Holy of Holies for sinners who believe in Him.[327]

The earth shakes, rocks split, tombs are opened, and the bodies of saints are raised. The spiritual and physical worlds react to the completed work of the Son of God (Matt. 27:51–52).

The Roman centurion overseeing the executions was standing directly in front of Jesus when He gave up His spirit (Mark 15:39). This hardened soldier had seen many men die on a cross, but none like this. Men at the point of death on a cross expired when they were too weak to lift themselves up to take another breath.[328] But Jesus had the strength to cry out with a loud voice when He committed His spirit into the hands of the Father.

The centurion seems to realize that Jesus gave up His life of His own will. This Gentile soldier had observed Jesus during the crucifixion, experienced the noontime darkness, and felt the earth quake. Now he says, "Truly, this Man was the Son of God!" (Mark 15:39, Matt. 27:54).[329]

*****

The Jewish authorities do not want the crucified men left on their crosses during the Sabbath. To satisfy them, Pilate orders the soldiers to break the men's legs that are nailed to the upright timbers; they will not be able to lift themselves up to breathe and will quickly die. The soldiers break the legs of the two thieves, but when they come to Jesus, they see that He is already dead. To make certain, one of the soldiers plunges his spear into Jesus's side, and blood and water gush out (John 19:31–34). Psalm 34:19–20 had said that not one of the bones of the righteous would be broken, and Zechariah had recorded the prophetical words of the LORD, saying, "they will look on Me whom they pierced;" (Zech. 12:10). The prophecies concerning the suffering Savior will all be fulfilled.

Joseph of Arimathea, a member of the Council who did not agree with the verdict against Jesus, goes to Pilate and asks for His body. Luke tells us that

---

[327] For a discussion of the veil, see Pheiffer, Vos, and Rea, *Wycliffe Bible*, Vol. 2, 1767. The many priests who come to faith in Jesus are likely influenced by the torn curtain. See n. on Matt. 27:51, Ryrie, *Ryrie Study*, 1500; also Acts 6:7.

[328] Pheiffer, Vos, and Rea, *Wycliffe Bible,* Vol. 1, 405.

[329] We have no further record of this Roman soldier, but in effect, he speaks for every Gentile who comes to faith in Jesus Christ.

Joseph was a good and righteous man who was waiting for the kingdom of God (Luke 23:50–52). After determining from the centurion that Jesus is dead, Pilate grants His body to Joseph (Mark 15:45). He and Nicodemus, the Jewish leader who had secretly come to Jesus at night (John 3:1–2; p. 179), take Jesus's body, wrap it in strips of clean linen cloth with spices, and place it in a garden tomb in which no one had been buried (Matt. 27:59; John 19:38–42). These two men show great courage (Mark 15:43); they are probably persecuted by the Jewish authorities, but Scripture does not give us those details.

The women who had begun following Jesus in Galilee had followed Him to the cross, and now they follow Him to His grave. They see where He is laid and watch as Joseph rolls a stone against the entrance of the tomb. Jesus is dead and buried (Mark 15:46).[330]

The chief priests and Pharisees know that Jesus has said that He will rise three days after His death. They go to Pilate and ask him to secure the grave lest Jesus's disciples steal the body and claim that He has risen. Pilate grants their request for a guard and tells them to make the tomb "as secure as you know how" (Matt. 27:65).

The Jewish leaders follow the Roman soldiers to the tomb where they place a seal on the stone that has closed the opening to Jesus's grave. The soldiers set a guard to assure that no one disturbs the tomb (Matt. 27:66).

---

[330] The most likely date for Jesus's crucifixion is AD 33 when He was thirty-seven or perhaps thirty-eight years old. See "How Old was Jesus when He was Crucified?," *Bible.org.*, January 1, 2001, https://bible.org/question/how-old-was-jesus-when-he-was-crucified.

CHAPTER 25

THE RESURRECTION[331]

Early on Sunday morning, after the Jewish Sabbath has been observed, Mary Magdalene,[332] Joanna, Mary, the mother of James, and the other Galilean women start for the tomb with spices and perfumes to anoint Jesus's body (Luke 23:55–56, 24:1,10, Mark 16:1, John 20:1). They are wondering if there is anyone to remove the stone for them (Mark 15:3), not knowing that an angel with an appearance like lightning and a garment as white as snow has already rolled the stone away. The Roman soldiers guarding the tomb had been over-whelmed with fear and had become like "dead men" when the angel appeared (Matt. 28:2–4), but before the women arrive, they regain their faculties and flee.

When the women reach the gravesite, the area is deserted, and the tomb is open. Alarmed, some of them enter the tomb and discover that the body of the Lord Jesus is gone (Luke 24:2–3). Mary Magdalene immediately races to tell Simon Peter and the Apostle John that someone has stolen the body of Jesus (John 20:1–2).

The rest of the women wait anxiously outside the tomb, and suddenly, two men in dazzling apparel appear before them. The women are terrified and bow their faces to the ground (Luke 24:4–5). One of the angels speaks to them

---

[331] Each of the four Gospels reports some but not all of the events of the resurrection day, so it is difficult to determine a definite sequence for everything that happened. The time lines of Charles Pope ("A Chronological Sequence of the Resurrection Appearances," April 6, 2010, http://blog. adw.org/2010/04/resurrection-sequences/, and J. Gene White, "The Resurrection of Jesus Christ," accessed January 31, 2019, http://theologue.files.wordpress.com/2014/05/harmony-resurrectionofchrist-jgenewhite.pdf) are helpful but not identical to my own understanding.

[332] Mary Magdalene was one of the women Jesus had healed during His early Galilean ministry; Jesus had cast out seven demons from her (Luke 8:2; Mark 16:9–20). She and other women had aided Jesus and the disciples in Galilee and had continued to follow Him.

and says, "Do not be afraid; for I know that you are looking for Jesus who has been crucified. He is not here, for He has risen, just as He said. Come, see the place where He was lying" (Matt. 28:5–6).

The women enter the tomb and, as they look to the right, they are amazed to see a young man wearing a white robe where before there was no one. He says to them. "Do not be amazed; you are looking for Jesus the Nazarene who has been crucified. He has risen; He is not here; behold here is the place where they laid Him. But go, tell His disciples and Peter, 'He is going before you into Galilee; there you will see Him, just as He said to you'" (Mark 16:5–7).

When they exit the tomb, the angel who had first spoken to them emphasizes what they have just heard and encourages them to go quickly and inform the disciples. The women leave with fear and great joy (Matt. 28:7–8). They are so afraid that they say nothing to anyone as they hurry to tell the disciples what has happened (Mark 16:8).

*****

Mary Magdalene finds Peter and John and tells them that someone has stolen the Lord's body. The two disciples begin running to the tomb, leaving Mary to follow behind them. John runs faster than Peter and reaches the gravesite first. By now, the frightened women have departed, and the angels are not in sight. When Peter arrives, He enters the tomb followed by John. They see the linen grave clothes lying there and the face-cloth folded by itself (John 20:2–8). At this point, John tells us that he "saw and believed" (John 20:8).

Peter also marvels when he sees the grave clothes (Luke 24:12). The linen wrappings apparently appear undisturbed, amazing the apostles.[333] But both of them, frightened and confused, return to their homes without telling the other disciples about the empty tomb (John 20:3–10). This seems unusual, but we must remember that Peter had denied knowing Jesus three times the night before His death, and the other disciples are in hiding for fear of the Jews (John

---

[333] If someone had stolen Jesus's body, they would not have taken time to unwind the linen wrappings, and even if they did, the linen strips would have been strewn all over, not "lying there" in place. See n. on John 20:6, Ryrie, *Ryrie Study*, 1640.

20:19). The disciples still do not fully believe what Jesus has been teaching them about His resurrection.

*****

Mary arrives back at the gravesite and remains there after Peter and John leave. She is alone and weeping when she looks in the tomb and sees two angels sitting where the body of Jesus had been lying (John 20:11–12). They ask why she is weeping, and she replies, "Because they have taken away my Lord, and I do not know where they have laid Him" (John 20:13). Mary turns around and sees Jesus but does not recognize Him, perhaps because of her tears and the distance between them. He asks her why she is weeping and whom she is seeking.

Mistaking Him for the gardener, she replies, "Sir, if you have carried Him away, tell me where you have laid Him, and I will take Him away" (John 20:15).

But when Jesus says, "Mary," she immediately recognizes Him and says in Hebrew, "Rabboni! (which means, Teacher)" (John 20:16). She grasps Jesus, probably falling at His feet,[334] and He tells her to stop clinging to Him because, "I have not yet ascended to the Father" (John 20:17a). Jesus is going to return to heaven, and Mary cannot keep depending on His physical presence. Jesus has told the disciples that He is going away but that He will send the Comforter, the Holy Spirit, to be with them. This is something that all His followers will have to learn. He tells Mary to go to the disciples and give them the message that, "I ascend to My Father and your Father and My God and your God" (John 20:17).[335]

Mary had followed Jesus when He was traveling through Galilee, preaching the message of the kingdom of God (Luke 8:1–2). Now He sends her to tell the frightened disciples that He has risen from the dead (John 20:11–18). Jesus's first appearance after His resurrection is to a woman from whom He had cast out seven demons and whose testimony would not have been allowed in the Jewish courts. Yet Mary is given the privilege of being the first witness, the first person to see, touch, and speak to the resurrected LORD.

After leaving Mary, Jesus appears to the women who are on their way to tell the disciples about the empty tomb. After He greets them, they approach

---

[334] See Matt. 28:9.

[335] Jesus has brought believers into an amazing relationship with the Triune God—something too wonderful for our finite minds to fully grasp.

Him, fall down and hold His feet, and worship Him. He calms their fears and says, "Go and take word to My brethren to leave for Galilee, and there they shall see Me" (Matt. 28:8–10).

*****

Meanwhile, the Roman guards have returned to Jerusalem after fleeing from the site of the tomb. Fearful of reporting to Pilate, they seek out the chief priests and tell them what has happened. The Jewish authorities are alarmed and assemble all the elders. They decide to give the soldiers a large sum of money to say that Jesus's disciples stole His body while they slept. This is a dangerous falsehood for the Roman soldiers. Falling asleep while on guard duty could lead to severe punishment, even execution,[336] but the chief priests assure the guards that they will keep them out of trouble with Pilate. When Matthew writes his gospel some thirty years later,[337] he says the story about the theft of Jesus's body is still common among the Jews (Matt. 28:11–15).

*****

The Galilean women, followed by Mary Magdalene, return to the city and find the apostles. These women have seen the risen LORD, spoken to Him, and touched Him, but when they tell the apostles, they do not believe them. They think the women are telling them nonsense (Luke 24:8–11). Jesus had instructed the women to tell the apostles to go to Galilee, but the men do not leave their hiding place. They cannot believe that what Jesus had told them about His resurrection has actually occurred. They are living by sight, their own perceptions of reality, not by faith. They had seen Jesus raise others from the dead, but they cannot believe that He Himself has risen.

Jesus understands the weak faith of human beings and will appear in person to the disciples and many others over the next forty days, giving them many convincing proofs. And He will speak to His followers about "the things concerning the kingdom of God" (Acts 1:3). Jesus's earthly ministry began within the context of the kingdom. After His resurrection and ascension, redemptive

---

[336] See Acts 12:18–19.
[337] A good estimate for the date that Matthew wrote his gospel is AD 64–70. See the introduction to Matthew, Sproul, *New Geneva*, 1503.

history will continue to progress within the framework of the kingdom He has established.

*****

Jesus next appears to Peter (1 Cor. 15:5; Luke 24:34). The details of this meeting are not recorded in Scripture, but the encounter begins to change Peter from the man who denied Christ with a curse (Mark 14:71) into the witness who will preach fearlessly to the Jews on the day of Pentecost (Acts 2:14). Peter will become the man he claimed to be before the crucifixion.

After the meeting with Peter, Jesus approaches two of His disciples as they are walking to Emmaus, a village about seven miles from Jerusalem. They are discussing the things that have been happening, and Jesus begins to speak with them, but their "eyes are prevented from recognizing Him" (Luke 24:13–16). When Jesus questions them about their conversation, they are surprised that He does not seem to know about the recent events.

One of them, named Cleopas, tells Jesus about the Man they had hoped "was going to redeem Israel" (Luke 24:21).

Jesus sees their distress and begins to explain all the things that point to Him in the Scriptures. At the end of the day, they invite Jesus to spend the night with them. When He blesses the bread at their evening meal, they recognize Him, and He disappears from their sight. Then they say to each other, "Were not our hearts burning within us while He was…explaining the Scriptures to us?" (Luke 24:17–32).

They quickly return to Jerusalem, intending to tell the apostles that they have seen the risen Lord. But on the way, the disciples meet Peter who tells them that Jesus has also appeared to him (Luke 24:34). After talking to Peter, they find the "eleven"[338] who, with other followers,[339] are still in hiding. The two disciples tell their story and add that Jesus has also "appeared to Simon"

---

[338] Luke uses the term *eleven* to designate the apostles as a group, even though no more than nine are present; at least Peter and Thomas are missing (Luke 24:34; John 20:24). Paul appears to make a similar reference, likely referring to the same appearance when he says that Jesus appeared to Cephas and then to the "twelve," indicating the corporate identity of the apostles, not the exact number (1 Cor. 15:5). Matthias has not yet been appointed to replace Judas (Acts 1:26).

[339] The Galilean women and Mary Magdalene are likely still with the apostles (Luke 24:33).

(Luke 24:33–35). But just as the apostles did not believe the women, they do not believe these two disciples (Mark 16:12–13).

Then, suddenly, Jesus stands in their midst. Everyone is startled and frightened, believing they are seeing a spirit. But Jesus asks them, "Why are you troubled, and why do doubts arise in your hearts? See My hands and My feet, that it is I Myself; touch Me and see, for a spirit does not have flesh and bones as you see that I have" (Luke 24:38–39).

His disciples are so overwhelmed with joy that they cannot believe it is really Jesus. He asks if they have anything to eat; they give Him a piece of broiled fish and some honeycomb, and He eats it before them (Luke 24:36–43).[340] Jesus is giving His disciples proof that He has a resurrected body; they are not hallucinating or seeing a spirit.

Before Jesus leaves them, He explains how the Law, the Prophets, and the Psalms are fulfilled in Him, just as He had done with the disciples traveling to Emmaus. Jesus breathes on them and says "Receive the Holy Spirit" (John 20:22), foreshadowing the outpouring of the Spirit on the Church at Pentecost. Jesus opens their minds so that they can comprehend the Scriptures. They are to be His witnesses (Luke 24:44–48; John 20:19–23).

*****

The Apostle Thomas was not with the other apostles when Jesus appeared to them. When they tell him about seeing the risen Lord, Thomas says he will not believe unless he sees and touches the wounds in Jesus's hands and side (John 20:24–25).

The following Sunday, the apostles are still hiding behind closed doors when Jesus again appears among them. He says, "Peace to you," and then He turns to Thomas and tells him to "Reach your finger, and see My hands; and reach here your hand, and put it into My side; and be not unbelieving, but believing" (John 20:26–27).

Thomas replies, "My Lord and my God!" (John 20:28).

Jesus says, "Because you have seen Me, have you believed? Blessed are they who did not see, and yet believed" (John 20:29).

---

[340] We can draw some conclusions from this passage about our own resurrection bodies. We will have flesh and bones and be recognizable. We will eat and drink and, perhaps, pass through doors and walls like Jesus.

We would all like to meet Jesus in His resurrected body and see the wounds that He bore for us. But Jesus's disciples are going to become too numerous for each one of us to have a physical encounter with Jesus in the present age.[341] However, we can read about and be reassured by the experience of doubting Thomas.

*****

Paul tells us that Jesus next appeared to more than five hundred "breth-ren" at the same time (1 Cor. 15:6). This appearance likely took place in Galilee after the apostles finally follow Jesus's instructions to return to that region (Matt. 28:16). The number of disciples in Jerusalem was still small (Acts 1:15), and such a large group was more likely to gather in Galilee where Jesus had conducted most of his ministry. Although Paul does not give us details of this meeting, it is important because many of these people were still alive when Paul wrote 1 Corinthians and could have refuted his claims if his account was untrue. In addition, such a large group counters any claim that Jesus's followers were hallucinating when they saw Him.[342]

Paul also records that Jesus appeared to His half-brother James, who may have followed the apostles to Galilee. James will become a leader in the Jerusalem Church and write his own Epistle (1 Cor. 15:7).

*****

Scripture does not say if the apostles were present when Jesus appeared to the large crowd, but it is likely because they are back in Galilee. Seven of them are by the Sea of Galilee when Peter decides to go fishing. The other six, including James and John, quickly decide to go with him. These men have been through extremely stressful experiences and the chance to engage in famil-iar physical labor must have been a welcome relief for them. They fish through the night but catch nothing. As day is breaking, a man calls to them from the shore, telling them to cast their net on the right side of the boat.

---

[341] Jesus's resurrected body is now part of His eternal being. In the consummation of the kingdom, in the new heaven and earth, we will have forever to meet Him face-to-face.

[342] The rapid growth of the early church would seem to be due in part to this large crowd that had seen the resurrected Christ. For the rest of their lives, theirs was a story that did not go untold.

The apostles comply, and their net is so filled with fish that they cannot draw it into the boat. When John says, "It is the Lord!" (John 21:7), Peter jumps into the water and starts for shore; the other disciples follow in the boat, pulling the net full of fish. When they reach the shore, they see a fire with bread and fish cooking. Jesus tells them to bring some of their catch and invites them to have breakfast with Him (John 21:1–14).

After they have eaten, Jesus walks with Peter and asks him three times if he loves Him. Each time Peter answers that he loves Him, and each time, Jesus tells him to tend or feed His sheep. Peter is grieved that Jesus asks him three times, but Peter had boasted of his allegiance and then denied the Lord three times. Jesus is making sure that Peter no longer relies on his own proud self-sufficiency. He also tells Peter that at the end of his life, someone will take him where he does not want to go, signifying his eventual martyrdom (John 21:15–19).

The Apostle John has been following them, and when Peter notices, he turns to him and asks Jesus about John's future. Jesus tells Peter that he should not be concerned about John but should follow Him (John 21:20–22). The main concern for every believer has to be following Jesus.

*****

After this meeting, the eleven apostles proceed to a mountain in Galilee as Jesus has told them to do. There they see Him and worship Him, but even now, some remain doubtful (Matt. 28:17).[343] Jesus comes up to them and says, "All authority has been given to Me in heaven and on earth. Go therefore and make disciples of all the nations, baptizing them in the name of the Father and the Son and the Holy Spirit, teaching them to observe all that I commanded you; and lo, I am with you always, even to the end of the age" (Matt. 28:18–20).

*****

Up to this point, Scripture has documented ten appearances of the resurrected Savior over a period of forty days. But Luke and John indicate there were

---

[343] Because we are weak human beings, our faith is not consistent, even for the apostles who have personally seen Jesus after His resurrection. It is why we must be continually sustained by the Holy Spirit through the study of the Word and fellowship with other believers.

many other physical manifestations which are not recorded (Acts 1:3; John 21:25). Jesus's final earthly interaction with the apostles will be the occasion of His ascension into heaven.

*****

The apostles return to Jerusalem where Jesus appears to them and begins to give them His final words (Luke 24:44–49). He reminds them that the Law, the Prophets, and the Psalms are fulfilled in Him and tells them that they should proclaim repentance for the forgiveness of sins "in His name to all the nations, beginning from Jerusalem" (Luke 24:47). He instructs them to remain "in the city until you are clothed with power from on high" (Luke 24:49).

The apostles ask Him if He is going to restore the kingdom to Israel at this time (Acts 1:6). The disciples do not understand God's timing or the eventual extent of the kingdom; they want its consummation to begin immediately, but Jesus says, "It is not for you to know times or epochs which the Father has fixed by His own authority; but you shall receive power when the Holy Spirit has come upon you; and you shall be My witnesses both in Jerusalem, and in all Judea and Samaria, and even to the remotest part of the earth" (Acts 1:7–8).

Jesus then leads the apostles out of Jerusalem as far as Bethany. As He lifts up His hands and blesses them, He is lifted up, and a cloud receives Him out of their sight (Luke 24:51; Acts 1:9).

As the apostles gaze intently into the sky, two men in white clothing appear. They stand beside the apostles and say, "Men of Galilee, why do you stand looking into the sky? This Jesus, Who has been taken up from you into heaven, will come in just the same way as you have watched Him go into Heaven" (Acts 1:11).

After hearing this, the disciples return to Jerusalem with great joy. They remain in the city as they have been told where they are "continually in the temple, praising God" (Luke 24:52–53).

*****

Jesus has concluded His earthly ministry and has ascended to heaven. Colossians 3:1 tell us that Christ is "seated at the right hand of God," signifying that His sacrificial work for His people has been accomplished. Hebrews 7:25 says that Jesus ever lives to make intercession for those "who draw near to God though Him." It is an amazing encouragement for believers to know that the Son of God Himself is interceding with God the Father on our behalf. He is our Great High Priest "forever according to the order of Melchizedek" (Heb. 6:20).

While He was on the earth, Jesus had initiated His kingdom, but with His ascension into heaven, things will change. Now the kingdom will advance through the work of the Holy Spirit and the Church, rather than through the bodily ministry of the Lord Jesus.

Jesus had told the chief priests and Pharisees that "the kingdom of God will be taken away from you and be given to a nation producing the fruit of it" (Matt. 21:43). Israel, as a nation, has rejected the Messiah and has failed to establish a righteous kingdom for God. Redemptive history will no longer progress through this single theocratic nation but through a subculture in all the nations, the Church, which will soon be initiated by the Holy Spirit on the Day of Pentecost. Peter will tell the early Christians, "You are a chosen race, a royal priesthood, a holy nation, a people for God's own possession, that you may proclaim the excellencies of Him Who has called you out of darkness into His marvelous light" (1 Pet. 2:9).

The Church will soon begin proclaiming the work of Jesus Christ and calling in His kingdom people.

CHAPTER 26

THE APOSTOLIC AGE OF THE CHURCH

Jesus has completed His earthly ministry. The Son of God and Son of Man has come to earth and lived a sinless life as a human being. He was born as an infant, grew into adulthood, preached and established His kingdom, was crucified dead and was buried, rose again on the third day, and ascended into heaven where He is seated at the right hand of God the Father, making intercession for His people. He has told the disciples that He will build His Church (Matt. 16:18) and that He will send the Holy Spirit, who will be their Helper and Comforter (John 15:26, 16:7).[344]

Future believers, the "royal priesthood" (1 Pet. 2:9),[345] must now be called into the kingdom by the work of the Church. The Church's role will be to proclaim the gospel and convert sinners who will then extend Christ's kingdom by their sanctified lives in the different nations of the world.

The apostles have seen Jesus ascend into heaven and have returned to Jerusalem with great joy. They are continually in the Temple, praising God as they wait for power from on high as Jesus had instructed them. These men are still worshipping in the Temple, the religious center of national Israel. But when the Holy Spirit comes, that will begin to change; the religious rites of Israel and its Levitical priesthood will give way to the Church and its sacraments established by Jesus Christ. Under the new covenant, the Levitical types will be succeeded by the realities to which they pointed.

*****

---

[344] Luke records the beginning of the Church in the book of Acts, a continuation of his gospel. The Apostle Paul calls Luke "the beloved physician (Col. 4:14)," and he will become Paul's companion in his latter travels.

[345] God takes common, sinful, rebellious sinners and changes them into a "royal priesthood" through the work of Jesus Christ.

All eleven of the apostles are staying in an upper room in a house in Jerusalem. They are of one mind and are continually devoting themselves to prayer "along with the women, and Mary the mother of Jesus, and with His brothers" (Acts 1:14).[346] The apostles decide that they should replace Judas, who had "turned aside to go to his own place" (Acts 1:25). Matthias, who had been with them from the beginning and was a witness of the resurrection, is chosen to now be the twelfth Apostle (Acts 1:21–22, 26).

The disciples are filled with both joy and anxious anticipation. Just before His ascension, Jesus had told them that, "John baptized with water, but you shall be baptized with the Holy Spirit not many days from now" (Acts 1:5). These men know that something new and significant is about to occur.

*****

It has been ten days since Jesus ascended into heaven, and the day of Pentecost has arrived. Jews from many lands are crowding into Jerusalem for the festival that celebrates the wheat harvest. It is fitting that the beginning of the Church, God's instrument for the ingathering of His new covenant people, occurs on the day that Israel celebrates the harvest of the wheat. The twelve apostles are together on this early Sunday morning; the women and other disciples have not yet joined them (Acts 2:1, 14).

Suddenly, there comes from heaven the sound of a violent rushing wind; it fills the whole house where the apostles are sitting, and tongues of fire appear and rest on each one of the men. The apostles are all filled with the Holy Spirit and begin to speak in other languages as the Spirit gives them utterance (Acts 2:1–5).

The residents of Jerusalem and the visitors in the city hear the sound of the rushing wind, and a multitude begins to gather. The apostles go out and astonish all the people by speaking to the foreigners in their own dialects. "Parthians and Medes and Elamites, and residents of Mesopotamia, Judea and

---

[346] According to the Pew Research Center, this small number of believers grows to 2.18 billion by 2010. See "Global Christianity—A Report on the Size and Distribution of the World's Christian Population," *Pew Research Center*, December 19, 2011, www.pewforum. org/2011/12/19/global-christianity-exec/. Even if we concede that many of the 2.18 billion are not genuine believers, it is still an amazing growth and can only be explained by the historical realities of the faith—the resurrection of Jesus Christ, the work of the Holy Spirit, and disciples willing to proclaim the gospel.

Cappadocia, Pontus and Asia, Phrygia and Pamphylia, Egypt and the districts of Libya around Cyrene, and visitors from Rome, both Jews and proselytes, Cretans and Arabs" are hearing the apostles proclaim the mighty deeds of God in their own languages (Acts 2:9–11).[347] The people are amazed and perplexed; some ask, "What does this mean?" (Acts 2:12), but others mock and say, "They are full of sweet wine" (Acts 2:13).

Peter stands with the eleven, raises his voice, and tells the multitude that these men are not drunk but that, "this is what was spoken of through the prophet Joel: 'And it shall be in the last days, God says, That I will pour forth of My Spirit upon all mankind, And your sons and your daughters shall prophesy...I will in those days pour forth of My Spirit'"(Acts 2:16–18; Joel 2:28–29).

Peter goes on to preach a sermon directed to the men of Israel. This is a different Peter from the one who had denied even knowing Jesus when He was arrested—he has received power from on high. He continues his proclamation, saying:

> Jesus the Nazarene, a man attested to you by God
> with miracles and wonders and signs...this Man, delivered
> up by the predetermined plan and foreknowledge of God,
> you nailed to a cross by the hands of godless men and put
> Him to death. And God raised Him up again, putting an
> end to the agony of death, since it was impossible for Him
> to be held in its power. (Acts 2:22–24)

Peter proclaims, as the Jews already know, that David had written about the resurrection of the Christ, saying, "He was neither abandoned to Hades, nor did His flesh suffer decay" (Ps. 16:10; Acts 2:31). Peter concludes by saying, "Therefore let all the house of Israel know for certain that God has made Him both Lord and Christ—this Jesus Whom you crucified" (Acts 2:36).

The Jews have killed their long-awaited Messiah, but He has risen from the dead as David had foreseen. Those who have heard Peter's sermon are pierced to the heart and say to the apostles, "Brethren, what shall we do?" (Acts 2:37).

---

[347] God had confused the language of the tribes of Noah when they had refused to establish His kingdom. Now God reverses that process as the Church begins to fill the kingdom that Jesus has established.

Peter tells them, "Repent, and let each of you be baptized in the name of Jesus Christ for the forgiveness of your sins; and you shall receive the gift of the Holy Spirit" (Acts 2:38). He continues to exhort them, and about three thousand souls are baptized and numbered with the disciples (Acts 2:39–42). Jesus has sent the Holy Spirit into the world and has begun building His Church.

*****

In the new covenant that Jesus has inaugurated, the Holy Spirit is now working within believers in a new way. Under the old covenant, saints had to be regenerated and brought to faith by the Holy Spirit, just the same as new covenant believers. But now after Pentecost, the Spirit is empowering New Testament believers in a way that goes beyond His work in the lives of the Old Testament saints. Although there were people in the Old Testament to whom the Holy Spirit gave special powers, usually kings and prophets, under the new covenant, each true believer has the permanent indwelling of the Holy Spirit. This is the final step in the transition from the old covenant to the new, from redemptive history being worked out through a single theocratic nation to being worked out through a subculture in all the nations, the Church.

Now the Law is written on hearts instead of tablets of stone, and Abraham becomes a blessing to all the nations. Through the work of the Holy Spirit in believers, the kingdom will advance until Christ's Second Advent and the consummation of the kingdom. These new covenant realities will have important ramifications when we look at kingdom life in our present day.[348]

*****

The new believers continually devote themselves to "the apostles' teaching and to fellowship, to the breaking of bread and to prayer" (Acts 2:42). Signs and wonders are taking place through the apostles, and the community has a sense of awe. They want to share with each other and begin to sell their possessions to help those in need.[349] Breaking bread from house to house, they take their meals with gladness and sincerity of heart while praising God. The entire

---

[348] pp. 407–418.

[349] Some liberal writers have used this early community to justify socialistic government. But voluntarily giving your possessions to people you know is very different from government officials taking your money through taxes and giving it to people they know. See Art Lindsley,

fellowship finds favor with the people of Jerusalem, and the Lord adds to their number day by day (Acts 2:42–47). God's kingdom is expanding.

Peter heals a lame man in "the name of Jesus Christ," and the man, walking and leaping, follows Peter and John to the area on the east side of the Temple called the portico (porch) of Solomon. When the people see this man, who had been lame from birth, walking and praising God, they rush after him and the apostles. Peter takes this opportunity to again preach Jesus to the people, exhorting them to repentance. But while He and John are still speaking to the crowd, the priests, the captain of the Temple guard, and the Sadducees[350] approach them. These Temple officials are upset that the apostles are preaching about Jesus and His resurrection; the Roman soldiers had been paid a great deal of money to prevent this story from being told. The Jewish leaders take Peter and John to jail, but many of the people who had heard Peter's message become believers.[351] The community has grown quickly and now numbers about five thousand.

The next day, Peter, John, and the healed man are brought before Annas, Caiaphas, and the ruling elders. When the Jewish leaders begin to question them, Peter, filled with the Holy Spirit, preaches to them. He says the sick man has been made well by "the name of Jesus Christ the Nazarene, whom you crucified, whom God raised from the dead" (Acts 4:9–10). He goes on to declare that "there is salvation in no one else; for there is no other name under heaven that has been given among men, by which we must be saved" (Acts 4:12).

The Jewish leaders are surprised at the confidence of these untrained men, and they recognize that they have been with Jesus. The members of the Council see the healed man standing there and have no reply for Peter. They cannot deny that a miracle has taken place, but they command Peter and John not to speak or teach in the name of Jesus.

Peter and John answer them and say, "Whether it is right in the sight of God to give heed to you more than God, you judge. For we cannot stop speaking what we have seen and heard" (Acts 4:19–20). The Jewish leaders believed they had eliminated the threat to their kingdom by crucifying Jesus, but now they realize that may not be true. They threaten the two apostles but are afraid

---

"Does Acts 2–5 Teach Socialism?," *Institute for Faith, Work, & Economics*, September 12, 2012, https://tifwe.org/resource/does-acts-2-5-teach-socialism/.

[350] The Sadducees controlled the Temple and taught that there was no resurrection after death.

[351] The designation "Christians" has not yet been applied to these early disciples.

to take any further action because the people are glorifying God for what has happened.

The apostles return to their friends and report what the Jewish leaders have said. The believers praise God and pray, saying (Acts 4:27–29):

> Truly in this city there were gathered together against Thy holy servant Jesus, whom Thou didst anoint, both Herod and Pontius Pilate, along with the Gentiles and the peoples of Israel, to do whatever Thy hand and Thy purpose predestined to occur.[352] And now, Lord, take note of their threats, and grant that Thy bond-servants may speak Thy word with all confidence.

After their prayer, the place where they are assembled is shaken. They are all filled with the Holy Spirit, and they begin to speak the Word of God with boldness (Acts 3:1–4:31).

*****

The believing community continues to live in harmony, and those with property sell it and share the proceeds with those in need. A man named Joseph, a Levite of Cyprian birth who is also called Barnabas by the apostles (which means Son of Encouragement), sells a tract of land, and lays the money at the apostles' feet. Barnabas will become a prominent figure in the early Church, and eventually, a close associate of the Apostle Paul (Acts 4:32–37).

After seeing Barnabas give his generous gift, a married couple named Ananias and Sapphira decide to do something similar. They sell a piece of property and pretend to give the full value to the apostles but withhold some of the money for themselves. Peter becomes aware of this and confronts Ananias, not because he kept some of the money, but because he lied about it—not "to men but to God" (Acts 5:1–4).

Ananias falls down dead before Peter. Those who hear about his death are very fearful, and the young men remove Ananias's body for burial. His wife, Sapphira, unaware of what has happened, comes before Peter and continues

---

[352] These early disciples have the assurance that God's predetermined plan is being worked out through them. It should be no different for us today.

the deceit. Peter tells her what has happened to her husband and that the same thing is going to happen to her. She also dies at his feet, and the young men take her body and bury her beside her husband. Fear now comes upon the whole Church and all who hear about these events (Acts 5:1–11).

The penalty of death seems to be a severe punishment for this offense, but we must consider the circumstances. Harmony and trust among God's kingdom people are essential to the spread of the gospel. Pretense and deceit for personal recognition will destroy the community if not confronted. And as Peter had said, Ananias and Sapphira had lied to God. There is a lesson here for churches today about virtue, discipline, and God's holiness. The nation of Israel had come under judgment for failing to be a righteous people for God. Church members will also be held accountable for their behavior. We must not lie to God with our words or our deeds. It is still a terrifying thing to fall into the hands of the living God (Heb. 10:31, 12:29).

*****

The apostles continue doing many signs and wonders, and Solomon's portico becomes a primary gathering place for the members of the Church (Acts 5:12). The beginning of the separation from Judaism has begun, but many of the believers still attend Temple worship as well as the Sabbath meetings in the synagogues (Acts 2:46).

The synagogues had been established as places of worship during the Babylonian captivity after the Temple was destroyed by Nebuchadnezzar. These buildings were simple rectangular structures with pews or benches facing a raised area where Jewish rabbis read the Old Testament Scriptures and led in prayers and singing. The services also included teaching and discussions. Jesus had used the synagogue services to teach the people and challenge the Jewish leaders (John 6:59; Luke 4:14–15, 13:10–15) as will the disciples in the future, especially Paul on his missionary journeys (Acts 13:5, 17:10, etc.).

The early church follows the pattern of synagogue worship (Col. 3:16), but the people have to meet in houses (Acts 2:46). The meetings are held on the first day of the week, Sunday, the day Jesus had arisen. The worship includes the breaking of bread in remembrance of the Savior's death (Acts 2:42).[353]

*****

The people of Jerusalem think highly of the disciples, but many are afraid to associate with them because they fear the Jewish authorities. And, yet, believers are continually being added to the Church, "multitudes of both men and women" (Acts 5:14). The mention of women joining the Church is an early indication of the reality of the new covenant that Jesus had instituted at the Last Supper.[354] Women in the Old Testament were saved by faith in the coming Messiah, but they were included in the old covenant, regardless of what they believed, because they were physically part of the nation of Israel. Now women are members of the new covenant through their own personal faith, not national association. When they believe, they are included in the new covenant and they are baptized; they receive the sign of the covenant the same as men (Acts 8:12).

People are bringing sick and demon-possessed people to the apostles, and they are all being healed. But this only angers the high priest and the Temple officials. They arrest the apostles and put them in prison. But that night, an angel of the Lord opens the prison doors, brings the men out, and tells them to, "Go your way, stand and speak to the people in the temple the whole message of this Life" (Acts 5:15–20).

The next morning, the high priest and the council send officers to the prison to transfer the apostles to the court. When they reach the prison, the officers find the doors shut and the guards in place but no prisoners inside. The Jewish leaders are informed and are wondering what is going to happen next when they learn that their prisoners are now teaching in the Temple. The

---

[353] Although the early disciples at times met in the Temple (Acts 2:46), they apparently recognized that Jesus's death was the fulfillment of all the animal sacrifices and stopped participating in these rites; there is no mention of sacrifices in the meetings of the early Church. Paul's offering in Acts 21:26 to fulfill a vow does not seem to be an animal sacrifice. There have been no animal sacrifices in Israel since the destruction of the Temple by the Romans in AD 70. See Robert L. Faherty, "Sacrifice In The Religions Of The World," *Encyclopaedia*, accessed February 23, 2019, https://www.britannica.com/topic/sacrifice-religion/Sacrifice-in-the-religions-of-the-world.
[354] See pp. 192–193 for Jesus's initiation of the New Covenant.

officers take custody of the apostles again and take them before the council but without violence because they fear the people (Acts 5:21–27).

The high priest demands an answer, saying, "We gave you strict orders not to continue teaching in this name, and behold, you have filled Jerusalem with your teaching, and intend to bring this man's blood on us!" (Acts 5:28). But Peter and the other apostles answer and say:

> We must obey God rather than men. The God of our fathers raised up Jesus, whom you had put to death by hanging Him on a cross. He is the one whom God has exalted to His right hand as a Prince and Savior, to grant repentance to Israel and forgiveness of sins. And we are witnesses of these things; and so is the Holy Spirit whom God has given to those who obey Him. (Acts 5:29–32)

This enrages the Jewish rulers, and they decide to kill the apostles. But a Pharisee named Gamaliel, a respected teacher of the Law,[355] says that they should wait and see what happens with these men; if this work is not from God, it will come to nothing.[356] The council agrees; even though they are furious, they do not want to risk inciting the people. They beat the apostles, command them not to speak in the name of Jesus, and let them go. The apostles depart, rejoicing that they have been "considered worthy to suffer shame for His name" (Acts 5:41). Despite the council's order, they return to the Temple the next day and every day, teaching and preaching Jesus as the Christ (Acts 5:33–42).

*****

As the believers continue to multiply, those who are Hellenistic Jews[357] complain that their widows are being neglected when distributions are made to the poor and needy. Apparently, the native-born Jews are being unfair to the

---

[355] Saul, who eventually becomes the Apostle Paul, studied under Gamaliel (Acts 22:3).

[356] It would be unimaginable to these Jewish leaders that by the year 2010, 2.18 billion people would call themselves Christians.

[357] The Hellenistic Jews were Jews from other nations who did not speak Hebrew. They spoke Greek and perhaps the languages of their resident countries. After Nebuchadnezzar destroyed Jerusalem in 587 BC, Jews not only went into captivity in Babylon but were scattered to other nations.

foreign Jews. The twelve apostles assemble the church and direct them to find seven men of good reputation who can oversee the functions of the congregation. This pleases everyone, and a man named Stephen, who is full of faith and the Holy Spirit, is appointed along with six others.[358]

This allows the apostles to continue to devote themselves to prayer and the ministry of the Word. The church continues to grow, and even many temple priests become obedient to the faith (Acts 6:1–7).

*****

Stephen, full of faith and power, is doing great wonders among the people. Some of the synagogue leaders from foreign countries dispute with him, but they cannot counter the wisdom and Spirit with which he speaks. These leaders then convince others to accuse Stephen of blasphemy, and he is brought before the Jewish council. When the high priest questions him, he recounts the history of Israel from Abraham to the present day, telling the council members that just as their fathers murdered the prophets, they have become the betrayers and murderers of the "Righteous One" (Acts 7:52); they themselves do not keep the Law.

The Jewish officials are so angry they gnash their teeth at Stephen, but he gazes into heaven and says, "Behold, I see the heavens opened up and the Son of Man standing at the right hand of God." (Acts 7:56).

The enraged Jews cry out with a loud voice, refuse to listen any more, rush at Stephen, and force him out of the city. Laying their coats at the feet of a young man named Saul, they begin to stone Stephen. He calls on God and says, "Lord Jesus, receive my spirit." Kneeling down, he cries out with a loud voice, "Lord, do not hold this sin against them"[359] just before he falls "asleep" (Acts 7:60). Stephen has become the first martyr of the young Church with Saul looking on and giving his approval (Acts 6:8–8:1).

*****

---

[358] These men are the first church deacons. The apostles are acting as elders.

[359] These words are very similar to Jesus's prayer on behalf of those who were crucifying Him (Luke 23:34; p. 203).

After Stephen's death, several devout and brave men carry him to his burial and lament over him. His death emboldens the enemies of the church, and a great persecution breaks out against the believers in Jerusalem. Saul helps lead the assault, "entering house after house; and dragging off men and women, he would put them in prison" (Acts 8:3). Those who can escape begin fleeing to the different regions of Judea and Samaria.

The persecution focuses primarily on the Hellenistic disciples; the apostles are able to stay in Jerusalem, maintaining a central point of contact for the dispersed believers. The Jewish leaders want to destroy the Church, but the scattered disciples preach the Word wherever they go. These faithful witnesses become the seeds of the Church throughout Palestine (Acts 8:1–4). History will show that God uses persecution to purify assemblies and expand the kingdom.

*****

The Apostle Phillip travels to the city of Samaria and preaches Christ to this mixed-race people whom the Jews despise.[360] The Samaritans see the miracles Phillip is performing, and they heed the words he speaks. Many lame and demon-possessed people are healed, and the city greatly rejoices (Acts 8:5–8). When the apostles in Jerusalem hear that Samaria has received the Word, they send Peter and John to them; they pray for the Samaritans and they receive the Holy Spirit.[361] Peter and John preach the gospel in many Samaritan villages and then return to Jerusalem (Acts 8:14–25).

Phillip is then directed by an angel to the road between Jerusalem and Gaza for an encounter with an Ethiopian eunuch. This man is a very powerful official under Queen Candace and is in charge of her entire treasury. He is riding in his chariot and reading the book of Isaiah when Phillip approaches him. Phillip explains what he is reading, and the man believes, is baptized, and goes

---

[360] After the Assyrians defeated the northern kingdom in 722 BC, they deported most of the population. The poorer Jews left in Samaria intermarried with the Gentiles that were brought in to repopulate the area. See p. 147.

[361] The Samaritans had believed and been baptized but did not receive the Holy Spirit until Peter and John arrived. This seems to be God's way of maintaining Church unity. The Samaritans had to be identified with the Jerusalem Church so there would not be a separate Samaritan Church.

on his way, rejoicing; the gospel is making its first inroad into North Africa (Acts 8:26–39).

*****

Saul continues to breathe threats and murder against the disciples. He obtains letters from the high priest so that he and his allies can arrest believers in Damascus. As they are on their way to that city, a light from heaven suddenly shines on him, and a voice says, "Saul, Saul, why are you persecuting Me?"

Saul falls to the ground and asks, "Who are You, Lord?" (Acts 9:4–5).

The Lord answers, "I am Jesus, whom you are persecuting. It is hard for you to kick against the goads" (Acts 9:5).[362]

Saul is like a defiant draft animal that kicks against the prodding of its owner. He has heard the gospel but has rejected it and attacked those who believe. But now, the former persecutor is the one who is overwhelmed and afraid; he asks, "Lord, what do You want me to do?" (Acts 9:6).

The Lord tells him to go into the city where he will be told what to do.

The men with Saul hear the voice but see no one, and they are speechless. When Saul arises from the ground, he opens his eyes but cannot see anything; he is completely blind. His friends lead him to Damascus where he does not eat nor drink for three days.

The Lord tells a disciple in Damascus named Ananias to go to Saul and lay his hand on him that he may receive his sight. Ananias is reluctant because he knows Saul's reputation, and he is afraid. But he goes to the house where Saul is staying and lays his hands on him,[363] telling Saul that the Lord has sent him so that he might receive his sight "and be filled with the Holy Spirit" (Acts 9:10–17).

Saul is immediately able to see; he arises and is baptized.[364] He begins to eat again, is strengthened, and spends time with the disciples in Damascus.

---

[362] Acts 9:4–6 quotations are from Sproul. *New Geneva*, 1727. Goads are not mentioned in the New American Standard translation but appear to be in the original text in 26:14. The ox goad was a long pole with a sharp metal end used to prod oxen pulling loads. If they kicked against the goad, they injured themselves.

[363] The laying on of hands in the early Church at times imparted power and blessings but at other times was just a sign of solidarity and support.

[364] It appears that Saul was converted about AD 37, four years after Jesus's death and resurrection. There are various chronologies of Paul's ministry; two helpful ones are Matthew McGee,

He begins going to the synagogues where he preaches that Christ is the Son of God. The people are amazed at this change in Saul. He gains more strength and confounds the Jews in Damascus, proving in his teaching that Jesus is the Christ (Acts 9:18–22).

After preaching in Damascus, Saul travels to Arabia (Gal. 1:17). Paul himself is the only one to mention this visit, and he does not tell us the purpose of this brief journey—he does not mention any encounters with human beings. In Saul's day, Arabia would have included the Sinai Peninsula where Mt. Sinai is located. Perhaps Saul needed some time to contemplate and reconcile his pharisaical past with his apostolic future. After his short sojourn, Saul returns to Damascus where he will minister for the next three years (Gal. 1:17–18).

Saul resumes his witness in Damascus, and the Jewish leaders become more and more enraged at him as they see this Pharisee continually preach salvation through Jesus the Christ whom they crucified.[365] They finally decide that they must kill him and watch the city gates, hoping for an opportunity to seize him. But their plot becomes known, and the disciples go to Saul at night, put him in a large basket, and lower him outside the city walls. He makes it safely to Jerusalem and tries to join the disciples, but they are still afraid of him (Acts 9:23–26).

Barnabas (the son of encouragement) intercedes and takes Saul to the apostles, and he meets with Peter and James, the brother of the Lord (Gal. 1:18). Barnabas tells them what has happened with Saul and that he has preached boldly in the name of Jesus in Damascus. Saul stays with Peter for fifteen days and moves freely about Jerusalem. He speaks fearlessly in the name of the Lord Jesus and disputes against the Hellenistic Jews. They try to kill him, but the brethren take Saul to Caesarea and then send him north to his hometown of Tarsus (Acts 9:27–30).

With the dispersion of the church after Stephen's death and now with Saul's departure, the persecution begins to diminish, and the believers find some peace in Judea, Galilee, and Samaria. They walk in the fear of the Lord

---

"Chronology of Apostle Paul's Journeys and Epistles," *Bible Chronology, Wielding the Sword of the Spirit,* accessed December 1, 2018, http://matthewmcgee.org/paultime.html; and Dennis McCallum, "A Chronological Study of Paul's Ministry," *Xenos Christian Fellowship,* accessed July 6, 2020, http://www.xenos.org/essays/chronological-study-pauls-ministry.

[365] Jesus was crucified during Passover week, and these leaders would have been in Jerusalem and involved with what took place.

and the comfort of the Holy Spirit while their numbers continue to increase (Acts 9:1–31).

*****

Although Saul has had to leave Israel, Peter is able to travel throughout the region, and the Lord continues to work miracles through him. In Lydda, he heals a paralyzed man, and in Joppa, he brings a dead woman named Tabitha back to life. These miracles become well known, and many people come to believe in the Lord. Peter remains in Joppa for many days, staying with a tanner by the name of Simon whose house is beside the Mediterranean Sea (Acts 9:32–43).[366]

During this time, a Roman centurion named Cornelius, who lives in Caesarea, forty miles to the north, receives a vision from an angel of God, telling him to send for a man named Peter who is staying with Simon, the tanner at Joppa. Cornelius obeys the angel and sends three men to tell Peter about his vision (Acts 10:1–8).

Meanwhile, Peter is praying and falls into a trance during which he sees all kinds of birds and animals being let down to the earth in a great sheet. A voice tells him to, "Arise, Peter; kill and eat" (Acts 10:13). Peter protests that he has never eaten anything common or unclean, but three times, the voice says, "What God has cleansed, no longer consider unholy" (Acts 10:15). Then the sheet with all the creatures is taken up into the sky.

Peter is in deep thought about the vision when the men from Caesarea arrive and tell him about Cornelius and his vision. Peter invites the men to spend the night, and the next day, he and some brethren from Joppa accompany them back to Caesarea. Cornelius is waiting anxiously and has called together his relatives and close friends. He has been greatly affected by his angelic vision, and he falls down to worship Peter, but Peter tells him to stand up and tells him that he is only a man (Acts 10:17–26).

Cornelius, an important man in the Roman army, has been humbled by his vision. But Peter's pride in his Jewish heritage has also been challenged in his vision; he is not to consider Gentiles as unclean or lesser human beings

---

[366] Simon's house is not a seaside villa. Ancient leather tanning involved the hides of dead animals, bad odors, and salt water. Since touching dead animals makes one ritually unclean, Simon's house is located outside the city, isolated by the sea. Like shepherds, he is not in the upper echelon of Jewish society.

(Acts 10:28–29). Jews and Gentiles can have fellowship and common purpose if they do not look down on each other. Up until now, the evangelism of the Church has been focused on Jews and their Samaritan relatives, but with Peter's vision and his visit to Cornelius, that will begin to change.

Cornelius recounts his vision, and Peter says, "I most certainly understand now that God is not one to show partiality, but in every nation the man who fears Him and does what is right, is welcome to Him" (Acts 10:34–35). He begins to preach Jesus and His resurrection to Cornelius and his friends. While he is speaking, the Holy Spirit falls upon all those who are listening to his message, and they begin to speak with tongues and exalt God. The Jews who have come with Peter are amazed that this has happened to Gentiles. Peter orders them to be baptized, and the new converts ask Peter to stay with them for a few days (Acts 10:30–48).

The apostles and the brethren throughout Judea hear that the Gentiles have received the Word of God. When Peter returns to Jerusalem, the Jewish believers take issue with him for visiting uncircumcised men and eating with them. He tells them about Cornelius and his own vision (Acts 11:1–17). When the Jews hear that the Holy Spirit fell upon the Gentiles, they calm down and begin to glorify God, saying, "Well, then, God has granted to the Gentiles also the repentance that leads to life" (Acts 11:18).

God had told Abraham that he would be a blessing to all the nations. His Seed, Jesus, has initiated His kingdom, and the Gentiles are being called in through the ministry of the Church and the work of the Holy Spirit.

*****

The believers who fled the persecution in Jerusalem disperse to different areas, some to Phoenicia along the Mediterranean Sea, others to the Island of Cyprus, and some to Antioch, further up the Mediterranean coast. They speak to the Jews about Jesus wherever they go. But some of the men in Antioch begin preaching to the Greeks also, and a large number turn to the Lord. When the church in Jerusalem hears this, they send Barnabas to Antioch; he sees the grace of God at work and encourages the new believers. He continues north to Tarsus, finds Saul, and brings him back to Antioch.

The two of them meet with the new disciples and teach in the church for an entire year. It is during this time in Antioch that the believers begin to be called Christians (Acts 11:19–26).

*****

A widespread famine begins to affect the Middle East, and the church in Antioch sends Barnabas and Saul to Judea with a collection to aid the suffering brethren. Herod Agrippa I, who is the grandson of Herod the Great and ruling in Judea at this time,[367] wants to find favor with the Jews and begins to seize and persecute some of the disciples in Jerusalem. He has James, the brother of John, put to death by the sword. These two brothers were two of Jesus's earliest and most faithful disciples,[368] and now James has become the first apostle to be martyred. When Agrippa sees how this has pleased the Jews, he decides to arrest the Apostle Peter. He puts him in prison and orders four squads of soldiers to guard him (Acts 11:27–12:4).

The Church prays fervently for Peter. He is in his cell, bound by chains and sleeping between two soldiers, when an angel appears. The angel awakens Peter, and his chains fall off without disturbing the soldiers. Peter follows the angel past the other guards, not certain that what is happening is real. They reach Jerusalem's iron gate, it opens, they enter, and the angel departs.

Peter comes to himself and realizes that the Lord has actually rescued him. He goes to the house of Mary, the mother of John Mark,[369] where many disciples are praying, and knocks on the gate leading to the house. Mary's servant girl goes to the door, hears Peter's voice, and runs to tell everyone, leaving Peter locked outside. The disciples do not believe her, but Peter continues knocking until they open the door. He joins the amazed gathering, and after motioning for them to be quiet, tells them what has happened before he departs for another place.

---

[367] Herod Agrippa I ruled from AD 41–44 and was popular with the Jews for his mistreatment of the Christians. See
Pheiffer, Vos, and Rea, *Wycliffe Bible*, Vol. 1, 35–36.

[368] See Mark 1:19–20, also pp. 175–176.

[369] This is the Mark who will write the Gospel of Mark and who witnessed the arrest of Jesus (see p. 197, n. 313). Apparently, his mother, Mary, is a wealthy woman. Mark is also the cousin of Barnabas (Col. 4:10), so his mother is likely Barnabas's sister or aunt. There is no mention of Mark's father, but perhaps he was a Roman because Mark is a Roman name.

When daybreak comes, there is a great disturbance among the soldiers who had been guarding Peter. Agrippa orders a search for him, and when Peter is not found, he has the guards executed (Acts 12:5–19).

Agrippa soon leaves Jerusalem to go to Caesarea where he meets with the people of Tyre and Sidon with whom he is very angry.[370] He speaks to them from his throne, and the people, seeking favor, keep crying out, "The voice of a god and not of a man" (Acts 12:19–22). Agrippa accepts this praise as though it is due him; he is glorifying himself as though he is a god, and an angel of the Lord immediately strikes him down (Acts 12:23). Josephus says Agrippa was overcome by a violent stomach pain and died five days later.[371]

The most recent persecutor of the disciples has met his end. Peter has been freed, and the Church continues to grow. Barnabas and Saul complete their donation to the disciples in Jerusalem and return to Antioch, bringing John Mark back with them.

*****

The prophets and the teachers in Antioch, led by the Holy Spirit, understand that Saul and Barnabas have been set apart as evangelists to serve the Lord. The leaders fast and pray and lay hands on the two men before sending them on their way. Taking John Mark as their helper, they travel to Seleucia where they set sail for Cyprus (Acts 13:1–4). The island of Cyprus is a Roman province, and Saul is a Roman citizen, so he begins using his Gentile name, Paul (Acts 13:9).[372] The trip to Cyprus begins for him what will eventually be four different and very difficult missionary journeys. Paul, the Pharisee of Pharisees, a Jew of Jews (Acts 23:6), is going to be God's instrument for advancing the kingdom among the Gentiles.

After landing in Salamis in eastern Cyprus, the three disciples begin traveling west, speaking in the synagogues of the Jews. When they reach Paphos on the southwestern end of the island, they are summoned by the Roman governor, an intelligent man named Sergius Paulus, who wants to hear the word of

---

[370] Scripture does not reveal the reason for Agrippa's wrath, but both cities were wealthy trading ports, so the dispute almost certainly involved commerce—money.

[371] Josephus, "Antiquities," 19.8.2.

[372] Paul was from Tarsus, a Roman city in what is Turkey today. He was a Pharisee as was his father (Acts 23:6). He was also a Roman citizen by birth (Acts 22:28), but it is not certain if his citizenship was through his family or by place of birth.

God. But a false Jewish prophet named Elymas, who attends Paulus, opposes the meeting. Paul speaks to the prophet, and he becomes temporarily blind—a physical blindness to match his spiritual blindness. The governor is amazed when he hears the teaching of the Lord and becomes a believer when he sees what has happened to the Jewish prophet (Acts 13:1–12).

After their time with the governor, Paul and his two companions sail for Perga, a city in Pamphylia on the northern Mediterranean coast, about 300 miles west of Tarsus. When they reach Perga, Paul intends to preach to the cities in Galatia, but John Mark leaves and returns to Jerusalem. Scripture gives no reason for Mark's decision, but Paul sees his departure as a serious failure; it will affect not only his feelings toward Mark but eventually his relationship with Barnabas.[373]

Paul and Barnabas travel north to Pisidian Antioch,[374] and on the Sabbath day, they enter the synagogue and speak to the Jews. Paul recounts the history of Israel and then preaches Jesus and His resurrection for the forgiveness of sins. Many of the Jews respond, and the next Sabbath day, almost the entire city, including the Gentiles, gathers to hear the Word of God. The Jews who have rejected Paul's teaching become jealous when they see the large crowds, and they accuse Paul of blasphemy. But he and Barnabas speak boldly and tell them that they have rejected God's Word and proven themselves unworthy of eternal life. They declare that they are now going to preach to the Gentiles (Acts 13:46) and quote the prophecy in Isaiah where God says of the Messiah, "I have placed You as a light for the Gentiles, that You should bring salvation to the end of the earth" (Isa. 49:6; Acts 13:47).

When the Gentiles hear this, they begin "rejoicing and glorifying the word of the Lord; and as many as had been appointed to eternal life believed" (Acts 13:48). Jesus had told the chief priests and elders that the kingdom of God would be taken from them and given to a nation producing the fruit of it (Matt. 21:43; p. 137). His prophecy is beginning to be fulfilled.

The Word of the Lord spreads throughout the region, but the Jews instigate a persecution against the two disciples and drive them out of the district. Paul and Barnabas shake the dust off their feet in protest against them and leave

---

[373] Acts 15:37–39; p. 241.
[374] This is a different and smaller Antioch, "Pisidian" Antioch.

for Iconium.[375] But the new disciples they leave behind are continually filled with joy and the Holy Spirit (Acts 13:13–52).

*****

The two evangelists teach in the synagogue of Iconium, and many believe, both Jews and Greeks, but the Jews, hostile to Paul, stir up opposition, and the city is filled with strife and division. When their antagonists urge the city leaders to stone Paul and Barnabas, they flee to nearby cities where they continue to preach the gospel (Acts 14:1–7).

In Lystra, Paul heals a lame man. When he leaps up and begins walking the people proclaim, "The gods have become like men and have come down to us" (Acts 14:11). The Greek pagans, who worship many deities, want to offer sacrifices to the two Christians, and Paul and Barnabas have difficulty restraining them. But then the Jews who have followed them from Pisidian Antioch and Iconium take advantage of the confusion and so incite the people that they begin stoning Paul; they drag him out of the city and leave him for dead. But the people who have become believers remain with him.

He eventually regains consciousness and is able to get back on his feet and return to the city. The text does not say that Paul had actually died, but it is a miracle that he survives the brutal blows of the stones.[376] God must have aided his recovery because the next day, he and Barnabas leave Lystra for the city of Derbe (Acts 14:8–20).

After preaching the gospel and winning many converts in Derbe, they return to Lystra, Iconium, and Pisidian Antioch to strengthen and encourage the new disciples in these cities. They tell them that "through many tribulations we must enter the kingdom of God" (Acts 14:22), and they appoint elders for them in every church. After fasting and praying, Paul and Barnabas

---

[375] When the Jews returned to Israel from a foreign country, they stopped before entering the land and shook the dust from their feet so as not to bring anything unclean into the nation. When Paul and Barnabas shake the dust from their feet, they are indicating that it is now the unbelieving Jews who are unclean.

[376] The intense anger and hatred that leads to Paul's stoning may seem almost beyond reason. But Paul is challenging the religious kingdom the Jews have built for themselves. He is a threat to their concept of reality and their basis for self-worth. He is challenging their view of God in the way that Moses challenged Pharaoh. Paul knows their religion better than they do, and his confidence, derived from his direct experience with Jesus, just further enrages them.

236

commend them "to the Lord in whom they had believed" and then continue their journey (Acts 14:21–23).

They pass through Pisidia and into Pamphylia. After preaching in the city of Perga, they travel southeast to Attalia where they board a ship and sail for Antioch. Paul has completed his first missionary journey, and he and Barnabas have accomplished the work commended to them by the saints in Antioch. When they arrive back in the city, they gather the church together and report all the things that God has done with them and how He has opened a door of faith to the Gentiles.

After giving their account, it seems that Paul and Barnabas take time to rest and recover; they spend "a long time with the disciples" (Acts 14:24–28).

*****

Time passes, and Paul and Barnabas remain with the church in Antioch. It has been fourteen years since Paul's conversion[377] (Gal. 2:1), and the Church has grown throughout the region, but a crisis arises in Antioch which will affect the faith everywhere. Some Jews from Judea come to the city and begin teaching that unless the Gentiles are circumcised, they cannot be saved. These men are saying that faith in Christ alone is not sufficient for salvation. Paul and Barnabas strongly disagree, and when a great dispute arises with the Judeans, the Church decides to send Paul, Barnabas, and others to the apostles and elders in Jerusalem to discuss this crucial issue.

On their way to Jerusalem, they visit the churches in Phoenicia and Samaria and share in detail the conversions of the Gentiles, bringing great joy to the brethren.[378] When they reach Jerusalem, they are received by the apostles and the elders, and they report to the Church everything God has done in their ministry to the Gentiles. But some of the believing Pharisees make the same demand as the Jews in Antioch, saying, "It is necessary to circumcise them, and to direct them to observe the Law of Moses" (Acts 15:5). Everyone has accepted that Gentiles can be saved; now the question is, *how* are they saved? Do the

---

[377] The year is probably AD 51 since the likely date of his conversion is AD 37. See p. 229, n. 364.

[378] The Church had begun with Jews in Jerusalem, then Phillip had taken the gospel to the mixed-race Jews in Samaria, and now Gentiles have been converted. The kingdom will continue to grow, but Abraham is already a blessing to the nations, and they are rejoicing in their common salvation.

Gentiles have to, in effect, become Jews and keep the Law to receive salvation? This is the first council to debate what it means to be saved by faith alone.

After much discussion, Peter stands up and speaks of his experiences with the Gentiles, asking the Pharisees why they are placing on the disciples the yoke of the Law, "which neither our fathers nor we have been able to bear? But we believe that we are saved through the grace of the Lord Jesus, in the same way as they also are" (Acts 15:10–11). Peter is telling the Pharisees that neither the Jews nor the Gentiles can keep the Law, so it cannot be a requirement for salvation.

When Paul and Barnabas again recount the signs and wonders which God has done among the Gentiles, James, the brother of the Lord, declares that the Jews should not burden the believing Gentiles, except to "abstain from things contaminated by idols and from fornication[379] and from what is strangled and from blood" (Acts 15:20).

James is agreeing with Peter. His proposed restrictions do not address the issue of salvation but rather Church unity; he wants the Gentiles to refrain from practices that are so offensive to the Jews that they would hinder fellowship.[380]

James's and Peter's declarations are decisive: Gentiles do not have to become Jewish to be Christians. As Peter has said, salvation for both Jews and Gentiles is by God's grace. The apostles will further explain and emphasize this foundational understanding in the books of the New Testament, especially Paul in Galatians and Romans. Christ has instituted the new covenant—the Law is written on the hearts of God's people, and the old covenant is becoming obsolete and ready to disappear (Heb. 8:13).

Two men, Judas and Silas, are chosen to accompany Paul and Barnabas back to Antioch. They take a letter of greeting for their Gentile brethren describing the decision of the council. When it is read to the church in Antioch, the message reassures the congregation, and they rejoice. Judas and Silas[381] stay with the church in Antioch for some time, encouraging and strengthening the

---

[379] Fornication would have been forbidden for both Jews and Gentiles, so this could refer to marriage between close relatives.

[380] Paul addresses similar concerns in Romans 14.

[381] Paul apparently establishes a good relationship with Silas. He will accompany Paul on his next missionary journey.

disciples until they depart in peace and return to Jerusalem. Paul and Barnabas stay in Antioch, teaching and preaching the Word of the Lord (Acts 15:1–35).

*****

The first Church council has come to an agreeable ending. The understanding of salvation through God's grace has been advanced, and a procedure for settling disagreements within the expanding Church body has been established. These are crucial outcomes for the Church as it grows and moves beyond the direct influence of the apostles.

*****

After the success of the first council, the Church continues to increase in strength and numbers. The apostles, who hid in fear after the crucifixion, now boldly preach salvation through Jesus, despite death threats and beatings from the Jewish authorities. Such a change can only be explained by their encounters with the resurrected Son of God and the bestowing of the Holy Spirit on the day of Pentecost. Cowardly and fearful men do not suddenly become willing to risk their lives for a contrived story. They know what they have experienced is real, and they are compelled to proclaim salvation by grace through faith in the long-awaited Messiah.

*****

The early Church has the benefit of direct contact with the apostles, men who had seen, touched, and been taught by the resurrected Lord; men who understood, as demonstrated by Peter and James, that salvation is by grace through faith in Jesus. But as the church increases in numbers, many believers are converted through the testimony of someone who has not seen Jesus nor an apostle. Oral testimony has been effective in spreading the gospel, but the apostles recognize that an authoritative record of what Jesus has said and done must be made. This is necessary to prevent adulterations and errors that can easily develop though oral transmissions of the gospel message, especially in foreign lands.

Two apostles, Matthew and John, write historical books, as do the disciples Luke and Mark.[382] Paul, Peter, James, Jude, John, and the author of Hebrews write letters to the different churches explaining and establishing the doctrines of the faith set forth in the words and deeds of Jesus. These nine men[383] write the twenty-seven books and epistles (letters) which are recognized as inspired by the Holy Spirit and are eventually included in the New Testament.

But other men are writing also, and it takes time for the Church to distinguish and collect the books that are part of the inspired Canon. Most of the New Testament manuscripts are in circulation by AD 70, except for the works of the Apostle John, which are probably written from AD 90–95.[384] The epistle of James seems to be the earliest manuscript, dated about AD 48. It should be noted that the majority of these books are written within forty years of Jesus's death and resurrection. Many people are still alive who had been involved in the recorded events and can protest if a false narrative is being presented.

The manuscripts are at first distributed on an individual and limited basis. To be duplicated, they must be copied by hand on scrolls, which is costly, and the Church's resources are limited.[385] Although the early churches have only some of the individual books and letters, they are very important because as time goes on persecutions arise against the apostles wherever they go, and the Church will soon begin to lose these leaders and their teaching ministries. The twenty-seven New Testament books are listed, in order, in Athanasius's Easter letter of AD 367,[386] so the entire New Testament Canon had been recognized, collected, and organized before this date.

*****

---

[382] These are selective histories. The authors chose events to inform readers about Jesus and His ministry, but they are factually accurate accounts and affirm secular records.

[383] This is assuming that someone other than Paul wrote the book of Hebrews.

[384] For a discussion on the dating of each book, see D. A. Carson, Douglas J. Moo, and Leon Morris, *An Introduction to the New Testament*, (Grand Rapids: Zondervan, 1992).

[385] The church will begin to use the new "codex" or "book format" with a binding by AD 100. See Steve Rudd, "The New Testament First Popularized the Codex Form in 100 AD," *Canon of the New Testament, Canon of the Bible*, accessed December 1, 2018, http://bible.ca/b-canon-codex-printing-press.htm.

[386] The Bishops of Alexandria, because of the famous school of astronomy in their city, were authorized by the First Council of Nicaea to announce the date of Easter. See Glenn Davis, "Athanasius of Alexandria," *The Development of the Canon of the New Testament*, accessed December 1, 2018, www.ntcanon.org/Athanasius.shtml.

Paul is still in Antioch (about AD 52) when he tells Barnabas that they should visit the churches in the cities where they had proclaimed the Word of the Lord. Barnabas agrees, but he wants to take his cousin, John Mark, with them again; Paul objects because Mark had abandoned them on their first journey. Their dispute becomes intense, and they part ways. Barnabas takes Mark, and they sail for Cyprus to visit the disciples there (Acts 15:39). Scripture does not describe their journey, but eventually, Mark will be reconciled with Paul.

Paul chooses Silas to accompany him, and after the brethren have committed them to the grace of the Lord, they travel north and then west through Syria and Cilicia, and then on to the cities of Derbe and Lystra where Paul had been stoned and left for dead. In Lystra, they meet a young disciple named Timothy,[387] the son of a Greek father and a Jewish Christian mother. He is highly commended by the brethren, and he joins Paul and Silas as they continue their journey west. In each of the churches, Paul and Silas deliver the decree about salvation through grace alone which had been affirmed by the apostles and elders in Jerusalem. They encourage the disciples who are daily increasing in number; the churches that Paul and Barnabas had planted are flourishing (Acts 15:40–16:5).

When they reach Troas on the Aegean Sea, Paul has a vision of a man asking him to "Come over to Macedonia (northern Greece) and help us" (Acts 16:9). He and his two companions sail across the Northern Aegean and begin working their way west and then southward, through the cities, toward Athens. In Philippi, Paul meets a woman named Lydia who sells expensive fabric, and she and her household believe and are baptized. He heals a slave girl of a spirit of divination, enraging her owners who have been profiting from her. They bring charges against Paul and Silas, and the magistrates beat them and throw them into the city's inner prison.[388]

That night, an earthquake opens the prison doors; the jailer assumes that his prisoners have escaped, and he draws his sword to kill himself. But Paul stops him and tells him that the prisoners have not fled. The man falls down before Paul and Silas; they witness to him, and he and his household believe and are baptized. He brings the two disciples into his house, and the new

---

[387] Timothy remains involved with Paul and his ministry to the end of Paul's life. Paul will write his last letter to Timothy just before his death and addresses him as my beloved son (2 Tim. 1:2).

[388] Apparently, Timothy is not seen as a threat and is not put in jail.

believers treat their wounds and set food before them as the jailer rejoices over what has happened to him and his family.

After Paul and Silas are returned to the prison, the magistrates learn that both men are Roman citizens. They become afraid and beg the men to leave the city.[389] The two disciples exit the prison, and after visiting with Lydia and the brethren, they take Timothy and continue their journey (Acts 16:8–40).

The three evangelists pass through Amphipolis and Apollonia and arrive in Thessalonica where Paul reasons with the Jews in the synagogue for three Sabbaths. Many believe, both Jews and Greeks, but other Jews become jealous and form a mob that stirs up the people and the city authorities. The brethren send Paul and Silas to Berea, and when they arrive, they teach in the synagogue. The Bereans are noble-minded and receive the Word eagerly, studying the Scriptures to see if Paul's teaching is true. Many people believe, but then the Jews from Thessalonica arrive and incite more crowds against Paul. Some of the brethren manage to escort him safely to Athens; he sends them back to Berea with instructions for Silas and Timothy to join him as soon as possible (Acts 17:1–15).

While Paul is waiting in Athens, his spirit is provoked by all the idols in the city. He visits the Areopagus and preaches a sermon when he sees an altar devoted to an "unknown god." The Athenian philosophers listen to him until he begins to speak of Jesus's resurrection, and then some begin to sneer, but others believe (Acts 17:16–34).

*****

Before Silas and Timothy can join him, Paul travels to Corinth where he meets a Jewish couple named Aquila and Priscilla who are originally from the region of Pontus. They are tentmakers and had been expelled from Rome when the Emperor Claudius ordered all the Jews to leave the city (Acts 18:1–2).[390]

Paul knows how to make tents, likely a skill passed on from his father in Tarsus; he works with Aquila and Priscilla and reasons with the people in the synagogue every Sabbath. But when Silas and Timothy arrive in Corinth, he begins to devote himself entirely to the Word, testifying to the Jews that Jesus is

---

[389] The scourging of Roman citizens was prohibited.

[390] Claudius was Emperor from AD 41–54; the likely date of the edict is AD 49. See F. F. Bruce, "Christianity Under Claudius," *Bulletin of the John Rylands Library, 44,* no. 2 (March, 1962), 17.

the Christ. When they resist and blaspheme, Paul shakes out his garments and says, "Your blood be upon your own heads! I am clean. From now on I shall go to the Gentiles" (Acts 18:6).

But then the leader of the synagogue, Crispus, believes in the Lord with his whole household, and they are soon followed by other Corinthians who are converted and baptized. The Lord speaks to Paul and tells him to keep speaking because many residents of the city belong to Him (Acts 18:3–10).

Paul stays in Corinth for a year and six months, teaching the Word of God among the people. Eventually, the Jews again rise up and bring charges against him, but the governor refuses to get involved in what he sees as a Jewish affair (Acts 18:11–16). Paul continues his work and, during this time, writes his two epistles to the church at Thessalonica (1 Thess. 1:1; 2 Thess. 1:1), addressing some of their concerns about the return of Christ and commending them for remaining firm in the faith.

This has been a long stay for Paul, and he decides it is time for him to return to Antioch. He takes leave of the brethren and boards a ship bound for Syria; Priscilla and Aquila go with him. When they stop in Ephesus, Paul reasons with the Jews in the synagogue. Despite their requests for him to stay longer, Paul departs when the ship sails, but Priscilla and Aquila remain to work with the Ephesians (Acts 18:26). Upon landing in Caesarea, Paul makes the short trip to Jerusalem and greets the church before returning to Antioch (Acts 18:18–22).

Paul's second missionary journey has taken three years; the churches established on his first journey have been strengthened, and new ones have been planted. Paul has done a substantial work in Corinth where many people have been saved. The gospel is going out, and the kingdom of God is being established among both Jews and Gentiles.

*****

While Paul has been at Antioch and traveling on his missionary journeys, Peter and the other apostles have also been evangelizing and preaching the Word. We know that Peter's ministry was primarily to the Jews (Gal. 2:7–8), but he and John had also followed up Phillip's work in Samaria (Acts 8:14–25, p.

228), and Peter had traveled to Antioch after the Jerusalem council.[391] Church tradition speaks of the apostles traveling to distant lands, Peter to Britain and Gaul, Andrew to Scythia and Asia Minor, Matthew to Ethiopia, Thomas to India, and so on.[392] These travels are not recorded in Scripture, but they are the kind of ministries that would be expected, and they seem to be verified by the rapid spread of the faith to different countries.

*****

Paul spends some time in Antioch and then starts on his third missionary journey, likely in early AD 54.[393] He travels through Galatia and Phrygia, visiting and strengthening all the disciples (Acts 18:23). Paul's heart is with the churches that he has started.

When he reaches Ephesus, he meets some disciples and then speaks boldly in the synagogue for three months, "reasoning and persuading them about the kingdom of God" (Acts 19:1–8).[394] But when the Jews become belligerent, he withdraws to a location called the school of Tyrannus. Paul teaches from this building for two years; the Word of the Lord is going out to all those who live in Asia, both Jews and Greeks (Acts 19:9–10).

*****

During this time, God is granting Paul special powers to heal the sick and cast out demons. Some of the Jewish exorcists want to do the same; they enter a house and try to cast out a demon from a man by using Jesus's name. But the demon answers and says, "I recognize Jesus, and I know about Paul, but who

---

[391] In Antioch, Paul had confronted Peter for his reluctance to eat with the Gentiles, even though he had proclaimed in Jerusalem that Jews and Gentiles are saved in the same way (Acts 2:11–21). It was difficult for the Jews to transition from the old covenant to the new, and the same is true for some churches today (see pp. 414–418).

[392] Robert C. Walton, *Chronological and Background Charts of Church History* (Grand Rapids: Zondervan, 1986), Chart 1.

[393] McGee, *Chronology.*

[394] In the Dispensational view, Paul would have to be talking about the millennial kingdom, a kingdom concept that has not yet been mentioned because it is based on a verse in Revelation, which is not yet written. But Paul is teaching about a present kingdom, the kingdom that Jesus instituted and that the Church, through the Holy Spirit, is continuing to advance.

are you?" (Acts 19:15). The possessed man then attacks the entire group of exorcists and overpowers them. They flee from the house, naked and wounded.

This becomes known to everyone in Ephesus, and the name of the Lord Jesus is magnified. Many who have been practicing magic bring their sorcery scrolls and burn them in the sight of everyone. They add up the price of the writings and find it to be fifty thousand pieces of silver.[395] The word of the Lord is advancing and prevailing (Acts 19:11–20).

*****

Paul stays in Ephesus for three years (Acts 20:31), and it appears that it is during this time that he learns of trouble in the churches in Galatia (Gal. 1:6–7). Some Jewish agitators are again telling the Christians that they must be circumcised to be saved. Some of the Galatians are accepting this doctrine, even though Paul and Silas had delivered the Jerusalem declarations to them during their previous journey (Acts 16:4). This Jewish demand strikes at the heart of the gospel message that Paul has been preaching from the beginning. Disappointed and angry, he writes a severe letter to the Galatians, calling them foolish for abandoning the doctrine of salvation through grace for the bondage of the Law. They are putting themselves back under commandments which they cannot keep, commandments which will only condemn them, not save them (Gal. 3:1–14). Paul ends his letter with some encouragement and still calls the Galatians brethren; he has not abandoned hope for them (Gal. 6:15–18).

We are not told how the Galatians responded, but this letter is for all Christians. We all would like to be able to tell God that we have kept the Law—we have been good or good enough—and He must bless us and not condemn us. But we are sinful human beings; we cannot keep the Law, and we can never make a holy and infinite God obligated to us. He does not owe us anything, except judgment. We are saved by grace or not at all, and Paul makes this clear in his letter to the Galatians.

*****

---

[395] If the silver drachma is meant, the sum would be more than $10,000. See n. on Acts 19:19, Ryrie, *Ryrie Study*, 1682.

Paul also writes his first epistle to the Corinthians while in Ephesus. He has received a disturbing letter from the church that he had established while working with Aquila and Priscilla in Corinth (Acts 18:1–4). The congregation is having difficulties; there are divisions and immorality among the members. The people also need counsel concerning marriage, food, worship, and the resurrection.[396] In his return letter, Paul deals with these issues and makes plans to spend time with the church when he continues his journey (1 Cor. 16:3). But he also makes a quick voyage to Corinth to address the church in person before returning to Ephesus (2 Cor. 12:14, 13:1). His brief stay is not described, but it did not go well; Paul refers to it as a visit made "in sorrow" (2 Cor. 2:1).[397]

*****

Timothy has rejoined Paul at some point during his stay in Ephesus, and when Paul prepares to resume his journey to Macedonia and Corinth, he sends Timothy and a disciple named Erastus ahead of him (Acts 19:22). While Paul is completing his work in Ephesus, another commotion arises because his teaching is affecting the profits of the silversmiths who make idols. A near riot develops, but the city clerk manages to quiet the crowd and tells them to go before the courts if they have a case against Paul (Acts 19:23–41).

Once the uproar has ceased, Paul is able to gather the Ephesian disciples together and embrace them before taking his leave. He travels to Troas and then on to Macedonia. As he travels through the cities, heading toward Corinth, he is at some point joined by Timothy (2 Cor. 1:1) and then by another trusted disciple named Titus whose presence brings Paul great joy (2 Cor. 2:13, 7:6, 13–14).[398] He is greatly encouraged when Titus tells him that the Corinthian church has repented and has regained its zeal for him. After this good news, Paul writes his second letter to the Corinthians, giving thanks for the Godly sorrow that has led to their renewed obedience (2 Cor. 7:5–16). He also urges them to complete the collection they have begun for the needy disciples in Jerusalem (2 Cor. 9:1–5).

*****

[396] Introduction to 1 Corinthians, Ryrie, *Ryrie Study*, 1726.
[397] Introduction to the Second Epistle to the Corinthians, Sproul, *New Geneva*, 1826.
[398] Titus had been involved in Paul's ministry in Crete (Titus 1:5). Paul will eventually write a letter to Titus outlining the qualifications necessary for elders in the Church (Titus 1:5–9).

Paul stays three months in Greece (Acts 20:2–3) and makes his third visit to Corinth where he apparently spends the winter of AD 57–58 (Rom. 15:25–26, 16:1). It is during this time that Paul writes his letter to the Christians in Rome, telling them that he intends to visit them after he makes his journey to Jerusalem (Rom. 15:22–28). There must have been both Jews and Gentiles in the Roman congregation because Paul addresses the question of Israel and the Church in his letter, an issue that is at the heart of the disputes he has been having with his Jewish antagonists. The Jews know they are God's chosen people; they are heirs of the promises made to Abraham, Isaac, and Jacob, and these promises cannot be broken. They know that Paul, a Pharisee, understands this, and yet his ministry to the Gentiles seems to ignore the Law and the special relationship God has with the nation of Israel. Paul deals with these issues in this epistle, and his teaching will affect the way we understand God's kingdom and the end-times in redemptive history.

Paul's letter to the Romans is the most theological of all his epistles. He first goes into great depth explaining the means of salvation, focusing on the concepts of grace and especially justification through the sacrificial work of Jesus Christ (Rom: 1:1–8:39).[399] This is how God saves His people.

Paul then addresses the question of Israel. He has great sorrow for his Jewish brethren because as a nation, they have rejected the Messiah and will suffer the consequences (Rom. 9:1–5, 10:1–2). But this does not mean the promises to Israel have been revoked or that God has rejected His people (Rom. 9:6, 11:1–2); instead, the promises are being fulfilled in a way that the Jews do not understand. Paul explains that "it is not as though the Word of God has failed. For they are not all Israel who are descended from Israel" (Rom. 9:6). There is an Israel within ethnic Israel which inherits the promises. Paul proves this was already evident in the Old Testament, first by God's election of Isaac rather than Ishmael to be the son of the promise,[400] and then again by His choice of Jacob over his twin brother, Esau (Rom. 9:6–13).

The Israel within Israel are the Jews who have faith in the Messiah, Jesus Christ; Paul says they have been "prepared beforehand for glory," they have been "called" (Rom. 9:23–24).[401] But that is not the complete story for the same is true of the believing Gentiles (Rom. 9:24). Paul declares "there is no

---

[399] See pp. xvii–xviii for a brief summary of "justification."
[400] Genesis 17:17–22.
[401] In Scripture, God's calling is irresistible and irrevocable (Rom. 8:28–30, 11:29).

distinction between Jew and Greek, for the Lord over all is rich to all who call upon Him" (Rom. 10:12). Jews and Gentiles come to God in the same way; they form one people of God to whom the promises belong (Rom. 9:6–8, 9:23–26). Paul had already stated this in Rom. 2:28–29, saying, "For he is not a Jew who is one outwardly, neither is circumcision that which is outward in the flesh; but he is a Jew who is one inwardly; and circumcision is that which is of the heart, by the Spirit, not by the letter; and his praise is not from men, but from God."

And in his letter to the Gentiles in Galatia where he said, "If you belong to Christ, then you are Abraham's seed, and heirs according to the promise" (Gal. 3:29).

The promises to Abraham belong to all who believe in Christ, both Jews and Gentiles; they are the true Israel, the one people of God.

In further explaining the relationship between the Jews and Gentiles, Paul says that it is through Israel's fall that salvation has come to the Gentiles (Rom. 11:11) and then illustrates this with his example of the olive tree. He begins with the root of the olive tree and says if it is holy, then the branches are holy (Rom. 11:16). The root is the beginning of true Israel, the patriarchs who were the elect of God and looked forward to the coming Messiah.[402] The branches are their descendants who also believed in the coming Savior. They, too, were holy, not in uprightness of character but in the basic meaning of the word. They were set apart,[403] chosen to be God's people.

But now the nation as a whole has fallen into unbelief, and most of the Jews have rejected the Messiah. These unbelieving Jews are the branches of the olive tree which have been broken off so that branches from the wild olive tree, the Gentiles, can be grafted into the cultivated olive tree (Rom. 11:17, 24). Paul indicates that there will come a time when the broken and separated branches of Israel are grafted back into their own olive tree "if they do not continue in their unbelief" (Rom. 11:23). He concludes by saying, "And thus all Israel will be saved" (Rom. 11:26).

"All Israel" in this context means all of the believing Jews from Abraham to the second advent of Jesus Christ, the Israel within Israel. It cannot mean the entire Jewish nation because Paul says, "Israel has not obtained what it seeks;

[402] See Robert Haldane, *Commentary on Romans* (Grand Rapids: Kregel, 1996), 542–543; also Charles Hodge, *Romans* (repr., Edinburgh, Scotland: Banner of Truth Trust, 1989), 366.
[403] Holy—to be separate, set apart. Robert Young, *Analytical Concordance to the Bible* (Grand Rapids: Eerdmans, 1964), 487.

but the elect have obtained it, and the rest were blinded" (Rom. 11:7). The Jews who come to faith are being grafted back into their own olive tree along with believing Gentiles (Rom. 11:23–24).

The promises to Israel belong to these believing Jews, but they also belong to believing Gentiles because they are part of the same olive tree, the elect people of God. It is Paul's ministry to call these Gentiles to faith, to graft them in with the believing Jews. There is one olive tree, the true Israel, the one people of God to whom the promises belong.

When Paul writes his letter to the Ephesians, he emphasizes the union between Jews and Gentiles in Christ. He says in Ephesians 2:12–18 that Gentiles in the past were:

> [S]eparate from Christ, excluded from the commonwealth of Israel, and strangers to the covenants of promise, having no hope and without God in the world. But now in Christ Jesus you who formerly were once far off have been brought near by the blood of Christ. For He Himself is our peace, who made both groups into one, and broke down the barrier of dividing wall, by abolishing in His flesh the enmity, which is the Law of commandments contained in ordinances, that in Himself He might make the two into one new man, thus establishing peace, and might reconcile them both in one body to God through the cross, by it having put to death the enmity. And He came and preached peace to you who were far away, and peace to those who were near; for through Him we both have access in one Spirit to the Father.

Just as there is one olive tree, there is "one new man from the two;" Christ has reconciled Jews and Gentiles "in one body through the cross." Believing Jews are now part of the Church and the new covenant, just like the Gentiles, not separate from them.

There was a temporary earthly fulfillment of the promises to Abraham with Solomon and his kingdom. But Solomon's kingdom could not endure; it was only a type of what was to come. The ultimate fulfillment will be to the Jews and Gentiles who make up the true Israel in the new heaven and earth, the heavenly kingdom that Abraham himself had come to expect (Heb. 11:8–16;

Rev. 21:1–4). Through his Seed, Jesus, the promises are fulfilled, and Abraham becomes a blessing to all the nations (Gen. 12:3).

For the present and the future, until Christ returns, the Church is the extension of the olive tree that began with elect Israel, the patriarchs in the Old Testament.[404] The Church is the means by which God continues to call in His kingdom people, "the fullness of the Gentiles" (Rom. 11:25) and "all Israel" (Rom. 11:26). This is the ministry to which Paul has devoted his life.

The length of time required for the Church to complete its work is unknown to human beings; the Apostle John uses figurative language in Revelation 20 and refers to this period as a "thousand years." During this time, Satan, the strong man, is bound within the true Church; his house is being plundered. The elect are being called into the kingdom (Rev. 20:1–3; Mark 3:27).

The spirits of the martyrs and other faithful believers who die during this emblematic thousand years are united with Christ and reign with Him in heaven (Rev. 20:4, 6) while the Church completes its work on earth through the ministry of the Holy Spirit. This spiritual reign with Christ in heaven is called the "first resurrection" (Rev. 20:5) because the second resurrection, the bodily resurrection, will not occur until Christ's second advent. These saints have experienced the first death, physical death, but the second death, eternal judgment, has no power over them (Rev. 20:6). Their bodies are in the grave, but they are spiritually alive with Christ, awaiting the second resurrection, the bodily resurrection.

The rest of the dead, unbelievers, are in torment in Hades during this time (Luke 16:22–26); they do not live again during the thousand years (Rev. 20:5). They remain spiritually dead until the final judgment; there is no second chance for unbelievers after their deaths.[405]

The Dispensational view[406] literalizes the thousand years of Revelation 20, applies it to an earthly reign of Christ over national Israel, and says this will

---

[404] Elect Israel and the true Church form the one people of God, but elect Israel in the Old Testament is not the Church. The Church begins at Pentecost with the outpouring of the Holy Spirit and initiates a dramatic change in the outworking of redemptive history.

[405] For a thorough discussion of Rev. 20:4–6, see James A. Hughes, "Revelation 20:4–6 and the Question of the Millennium," *Westminster Theological Journal*, 35:3 (1973), https://www.galaxie.com/article/wtj35-3-03.

[406] See p. xix, n. 33 for a brief summary of the way Dispensationalists understand the fulfillment of the promises to Israel.

be the fulfillment of the promises to Abraham. But Israel is not mentioned in this chapter,[407] and as we have seen, the promises to Abraham are ultimately fulfilled in the true Israel, believing Jews and Gentiles in the new heaven and earth. And this is what Abraham, who had received the promises, had come to expect.

Scripture does not support a separate destiny for national Israel, and therefore, the entire Dispensational system becomes untenable. When we consider future events in the plan of redemption, we cannot follow the timeline proposed by the Dispensational view.[408]

*****

After considering God's amazing plan for the salvation of both Jews and Gentiles, Paul breaks forth in ecstatic praise in his letter to the Romans:

> Oh, the depth of the riches both of the wisdom and knowledge of God! How unsearchable are His judgments and unfathomable His ways!
> For from Him and through Him and to Him are all things, to Him be glory forever. Amen. (Rom. 11:33, 36)

*****

After writing his letter to the Romans, Paul begins to plan his return journey to Jerusalem. He wants to sail for Syria, but the Jews are plotting against him, and he decides to travel through Macedonia. He is accompanied by several disciples, including Luke who will author the book of Acts (Acts 20:3–5). When they reach Troas, Paul meets with the Christians living there, and they

---

[407] The word *Israel* is used only three times in the book of Revelation (Rev. 2:4, 7:4, 21:12), and those references have nothing to do with a thousand-year reign.

[408] In the most common Dispensational timeline, the first end-time event is the rapture of the Church when it is suddenly taken up to heaven. This is followed by seven years of great tribulation on the earth. After this tribulation, Christ returns to earth to rule over Israel for a thousand years until there is a final rebellion when Satan and his forces are defeated. Then unbelievers are resurrected, followed by the last judgment and the beginning of the eternal state (Grudem, *Systematic*, 1113). If there is no separate destiny for Israel, then this time line is invalid.

break bread on the first day of the week. As he is teaching late into the night in an upper room, a young man sitting in a window falls asleep and tumbles to his death. Paul goes down, embraces him, and to the relief of all, he comes back to life (Acts 20:6–12).

After staying a week in Troas, Paul continues his journey on land while his fellow workers travel by ship and meet him in Assos. From there, they sail together to Miletus where Paul calls for the Ephesian elders to meet with him. The elders make the short journey to Miletus and have an emotional meeting with Paul; he had spent three difficult and dangerous years in ministry with these men. After recounting his time among them, Paul warns them that "savage wolves will come in among you, not sparing the flock" (Acts 20:29). He gives the elders final instructions and then prays with them; they know they will not see him again. After much weeping and embracing, they accompany Paul to the ship for his departure (Acts 20:14–38).

Paul and his companions continue their journey by sea, making stops in Cos, Rhodes, and other ports before arriving at Caesarea where they stay at the house of Phillip, one of the first deacons in the Jerusalem church (Acts 21:8, 6:3–5). After a few days, a prophet named Agabus tells Paul that the Jews in Jerusalem will bind him and deliver him into the hands of the Gentiles. The disciples beg Paul to not go to Jerusalem, but he will not be persuaded, and they eventually say, "The will of the Lord be done!" (Acts 21:14, 1–14).

When Paul, Luke, and the other disciples arrive in Jerusalem, the brethren receive Paul gladly. He meets with James[409] and the elders of the church. They glorify God when they hear about Paul's ministry to the Gentiles, and they tell him about the thousands of Jews who have become believers (Acts 21:15–20). The "fullness of the Gentiles" and "all Israel" are being grafted into the olive tree, the one people of God (Rom. 11:25–27). The Church is growing, and the influence of the kingdom is expanding.

*****

A week passes, and Jews from the cities in Asia where Paul had preached come to Jerusalem and see him in the Temple. These Jews inflame the people and cry out that Paul has brought Greeks into their holy place. The entire city is aroused, and an angry crowd seizes Paul and drags him out of the Temple.

---

[409] James, the Lord's half-brother, has become a leader in the Jerusalem church.

The Levitical guard immediately shuts the Temple doors; they want to prevent any further violation of the Temple, but they also want to prevent Paul from gaining sanctuary on the horns of the altar. The Jews intend to kill Paul, and they begin to beat him. The commander of the Roman cohort hears about the commotion and rushes to the scene with his soldiers. This stops the assault on Paul, and he survives, but the commander puts him in chains so that he can take him to the barracks for questioning.

Paul has to be carried by the soldiers because the mob tries to renew its attack on him. When they reach the stairs of the barracks, Paul tries to talk to the Jews but they shout him down (Acts 21:27–22:24).

The Roman commander intends to interrogate Paul by scourging him but stops when he learns that Paul is a Roman citizen. The next day, he brings Paul before the Sanhedrin. When Paul claims that he is on trial because of the resurrection, a dissension arises between the Pharisees and Sadducees because the Sadducees do not believe in an afterlife. The commander is afraid that Paul is going to be torn apart and orders his troops to take Paul back to the barracks (Acts 22:25–23:10).[410]

When he learns that the Jews are forming a plot to kill Paul,[411] the commander orders two hundred spearmen and seventy horsemen to take Paul to Felix, the Roman governor in Caesarea. Paul arrives safely, and Felix tells him that there will be a hearing when his accusers arrive (Acts 23:23–35).

After five days, Ananias, who is still acting as high priest, comes to Caesarea with other Jewish elders and a lawyer named Tertullus. They go before Felix and lay out their charges against Paul, but the governor delays in ruling on their complaint; he is hoping Paul will offer him money to gain his freedom. Felix puts Paul under house arrest, and he and his wife listen to Paul speak about faith in Christ. Felix becomes frightened when the discussion turns to righteousness and judgment, and he sends Paul away. He keeps Paul confined and continues to talk to him but takes no action to decide his case (Acts 24:1–26).

After two years (Acts 24:27), Felix is succeeded as Judean governor by Porcius Festus who decides to send Paul to the Jews in Jerusalem. Paul, as a Roman citizen, says, "No one can hand me over to them, I appeal to Caesar" (Acts 25:11).

---

[410] This is a generally brutal era of history, but the violence of the Jews is still stunning.
[411] Paul's nephew is the one who tells the commander about the plot (Acts 23:16–22).

When Festus and his council hear Paul's demand, they decide to send him to Rome, but before they can begin his transfer, King Agrippa II and his sister, Bernice,[412] come to Caesarea and visit Festus. Festus tells Agrippa about Paul, and the next day, with great pomp before prominent men, the king gives Paul a chance to defend himself. Paul gives his background, the history of his ministry, and finishes with a testimony to Christ's resurrection (Acts 26:1–23).

Festus exclaims, "Paul, you are out of your mind!" (Acts 26:24).

But Agrippa says, "In a short time, you will persuade me to become a Christian" (Acts 26:28). Both men know that Paul has done nothing worthy of death or imprisonment, but since he has appealed to Caesar, they decide they must send him to Rome.

*****

Paul had told the Romans that he was going to visit them, but he did not know that he would make the trip as a prisoner under Roman guard.[413] Paul is delivered to a centurion named Julius and his contingent of soldiers who are taking other prisoners by ship to Rome. Luke and Aristarchus, a disciple from Thessalonica, board with Paul and the other prisoners; they are going to accompany Paul on the journey to Rome (Acts 27:1–2).

Luke, who is a physician (Col. 4:14), is also interested in ships and sailing and relates details of their different passages in route. After departing from Sidon, they sail under the shelter of Cyprus because of the winds and land at Myra in Lycia. There the centurion puts them on a large grain ship that is bound for Italy.[414] Winter is approaching, and the weather is becoming a concern. They sail south of Crete, and Paul advises the centurion to anchor for the winter at a port called Fair Havens on the south side of the island. But the centurion is convinced by the captain to continue to a port called Phoenix,

---

[412] Agrippa II was seventeen when his father died. He obtained the title of King, but he had no real power over Israel; Roman governors ruled the Jews. Bernice's husband had died, and she was living with Agrippa, apparently in an incestuous relationship. She will eventually become the mistress of Titus, the Roman general who destroys Jerusalem in AD 70. See Pheiffer, Vos, and Rea, *Wycliffe Bible*, Vol. 1, 36, 220; also, Josephus, "Antiquities," 20.7.3.

[413] God's providence, his unseen guiding hand, is the outworking of His divine decrees. Providence often does not match our personal anticipations.

[414] This ship was carrying wheat (Acts 27:38). Luke will eventually tell us that there are 276 men aboard, so it is one of the larger vessels of that era.

further west on Crete because he thinks its harbor gives better protection from the coming harsh weather (Acts 27:3–13).[415]

As they make their way along the southern shore of Crete, a furious storm arises and blows the ship to the west. The gale is so strong that the sailors cannot control the ship's course and can only let it run with the wind. The vessel is thrown about so violently that the crew begins to jettison cargo, and even the ship's tackle, to remain afloat. The wind keeps the ship within the storm and when the men do not see the sun or the stars for many days, they gradually give up hope of surviving.

But an angel of God tells Paul that he must stand before Caesar and that all the men on the ship will be saved. Paul encourages everyone to eat food and tells them that none of them will perish, but they will run aground on an island.

During the fourteenth night of the storm, the sailors begin to sense that they are approaching land; they put out four anchors from the stern and pray for daylight. When some of them try to escape on the ship's lifeboat, Paul tells them they must stay on board to stay alive, and the soldiers cut the ropes holding the skiff and let it fall away.

When daylight comes, the shoreline of a bay can be seen; the sailors cast off the anchors and let the vessel run aground on a reef. When the stern of the ship begins to break up, the soldiers decide to kill the prisoners to keep them from escaping, but the centurion stops them, and all the men swim or ride pieces of the ship toward the land. The storm has driven them halfway across the Mediterranean, and the ship has been destroyed, but the crew and all the passengers struggle to safety on the island of Malta (Acts 27:14–44).

The natives of Malta aid the wet and battered men who wash up on shore and help them build a fire. As Paul is laying an armload of brushwood on the flames, a viper comes out of the bundle, bites him, and stays attached to his hand. Paul shakes the snake off into the fire. When it is evident the venomous bite has not harmed him, the people think he is a god.

The leader of the island, a man named Publius, receives the men from the ship and treats them well. His father is sick, and after Paul prays for him, the man recovers. Other people begin bringing their sick and diseased to Paul, and

---

[415] Pictures of the sheltered harbor at Phoenix can be seen at "Phoenix, Crete," *BiblePlaces.com*, accessed December 1, 2018, www.bibleplaces.com/phoenix-crete.

they too are healed. The grateful inhabitants esteem Paul and the other survivors and supply them with all they need (Acts 28:1–10).

The shipwrecked men remain on the island for three months until the winter has passed and a ship anchoring at Malta can sail for Syracuse in Sicily. From Sicily, they sail along the western coast of Italy until they arrive at Appii Forum where some of the brethren from Rome come to meet Paul. When he sees them, he thanks God and takes courage.[416] They travel the forty miles to Rome on the Appian Way, one of the earliest Roman roads. When Paul arrives in Rome, he is allowed to stay in his own separate quarters with a soldier guarding him (Acts 28:11–16). The journey to Rome has taken almost a year.[417]

After only three days, Paul calls together the leading men of the Jews who tell him that they have had no correspondence from Judea concerning him but have heard of this new "sect" that is spoken against everywhere. Paul solemnly testifies to them about "the kingdom of God"[418] and tries to persuade them concerning Jesus from both the Law of Moses and from the prophets, teaching "from morning until evening" (Acts 28:23).

Some of the Jews are persuaded, but others will not believe. Paul speaks to these doubters and quotes Isaiah, showing that their unbelief, and indeed the unbelief of Israel as a whole, was foreseen over seven hundred years before when God directed the Prophet Isaiah to speak to the nation, saying,

> Go to this people and say, you will keep on hearing, but will not understand; and you will keep on seeing, but will not perceive; For the heart of this people has grown dull, And with their ears they scarcely hear, And they have closed their eyes; Lest they should see with their eyes, and hear with their ears, and understand with their heart

---

[416] Leaders need assistance and encouragement, even a leader as strong as Paul. Luke is apparently still with Paul, but as the one recording the events, he does not interject himself into the account.

[417] Paul's ship arrived in Fair Havens just before winter began, probably late October, so he would have left Caesarea in July or August. He sailed from Malta in early spring and would have arrived in Rome by May or June, so he was en route ten to eleven months. The year is most likely AD 61; see McGee, *Chronology*.

[418] As we continue to see, Paul's kingdom preaching cannot refer to a future millennial kingdom that has not yet been mentioned in Scripture. The kingdom was present then, and it is present now.

and return, and I should heal them. (Acts 28:26–27; Isa. 6:9–10).

Paul concludes by saying, "Let it be known to you, therefore, that this salvation of God has been sent to the Gentiles; they will also listen" (Acts 28:28).

Paul stays in his own rented quarters for two years, waiting for his case to come before Caesar. While confined, he writes his "prison" epistles to the Ephesians (Eph. 3:1; 4:1), Philippians (Phil. 1:7; 4:22), Colossians (Col. 4:18), and Philemon (Philem. 1:1). Peter and Mark are also in Rome during this time, and Mark has been reconciled to Paul (1 Pet. 5:13; Col. 4:10).[419] Luke ends the book of Acts by saying Paul "was welcoming all who came to him, preaching the kingdom of God, and teaching concerning the Lord Jesus Christ with all openness, unhindered" (Acts 28:30–31).

*****

Acts closes with Paul under house arrest in Rome. But we know from his subsequent letters that at some point, he was released and continued his ministry in the areas of Crete (Titus 1:6), Nicopolis (Titus 3:12), Corinth and Miletus (2 Tim. 4:20), and Troas (2 Tim. 4:13). After these missionary travels, which must have lasted at least two years, Paul is arrested again and returned to prison in Rome. He writes his last epistle to Timothy, his beloved "son" (2 Tim. 1:2; 2:1), whom he had met on his second missionary journey over fifteen years before (Acts 16:1–3; p. 241) and who is now ministering in Ephesus (1 Tim. 1:3). Paul seems to know that this time, the Romans will execute him (2 Tim. 4:6), but he asks Timothy to come to him and bring the cloak he had left at Troas. Paul is not under house arrest now; he is in a cold dungeon.

Paul has been deserted by his helpers except for his faithful companion, Luke. He tells Timothy to bring Mark with him because "he is useful to me for ministry" (2 Tim. 4:9–11). This is high praise for the young man who had abandoned Paul on his first missionary journey and whom Paul had then refused to take on his next evangelical mission. Mark is not a prominent figure like the apostles, and he had been weak and had failed at a critical time. But Mark gives us an important lesson—he just keeps showing up, and eventually,

---

[419] Peter writes 1 Peter while in "Babylon" (1 Pet. 5:13), so his first epistle was likely written from Rome during the time of Paul's house imprisonment.

God uses him to write one of the four gospels. None of us are going to be a Paul or a Peter, but we can be like Mark, continue to serve even after we fail, and stay available for God to use us.

Paul instructs Timothy to bring "the scrolls, especially the parchments" (2 Tim. 4:13). These writings are likely Paul's copies of the Old Testament manuscripts. He is going to study Scripture to the end. Paul also tells Timothy to greet his friends Prisca and Aquila, the tentmakers he had lived with during his first trip to Corinth. And he wants Timothy to "make every effort to come before winter"—the prison is cold, and Paul needs the cloak and the parchments to make it through the chilling days ahead. He ends his letter with a prayer for Timothy's spiritual well-being, "The Lord be with your spirit. Grace be with you" (2 Tim. 4:9–22).

*****

Shortly after this, likely in AD 67, Paul is executed during the severe persecution instituted during the reign of Nero. The emperor had falsely accused the Christians of starting the great fire that destroyed much of Rome in AD 64, and he began killing them in horrible ways. According to church tradition, Peter is also executed by crucifixion during this same severe oppression.[420] The two most significant apostles have finished their ministries, and their lives have ended at the cruel hand of Nero. James, the brother of John, has already been executed, and Church tradition indicates that within a few years, all the other apostles will also be martyred, except for John.

*****

During the last days of Peter and Paul in Rome, dramatic events have been taking place in Jerusalem. Festus has been succeeded as governor of Judea by Gessius Florus, a Roman ruler who loves money and hates the Jews.[421] He oppresses the people, and in the year 66, when the revenue from taxation is deemed insufficient, Florus raids the Temple of a vast quantity of silver, leading

---

[420] John Foxe, *Foxe's Book of Martyrs*, prepared by W. Grinton Berry (Grand Rapids: Baker Book House, 1978), 12–13.
[421] Josephus, "Antiquities," 20.11.1.

to a widespread revolt.[422] The Zealots, who had hoped Jesus would lead an insurgency, attack and overwhelm the Roman garrison manning the mountain-top fortress of Masada near the Dead Sea. The insurrection spreads throughout Judea and becomes so fierce in Jerusalem that Florus and the Roman guard are forced to flee the city.[423]

The imperial governor of the entire region, Cestius Gallus, marches from Syria with 20,000 men and besieges Jerusalem, but the Jews kill many of his soldiers, and after six months, he ceases his attack. Nero dispatches Vespasian, a decorated general, with four Roman legions to quell the rebellion.[424] Vespasian defeats the insurgents in Galilee, the Transjordan, and Idumea before encircling Jerusalem. But before he can assault the city, he learns that Nero has committed suicide. An ensuing struggle for the leadership of the empire ends when the eastern armies call for Vespasian to become the next emperor. With Jerusalem surrounded by his imperial army, the general leaves the siege to assume the throne. In one of his first official acts, he directs his son, Titus, to finish the Jewish war.[425]

Titus takes over the siege of Jerusalem, which has now been isolated from the rest of the nation for over half a year. Factions within the city actually fight each other over defensive strategies, and people begin dying from starvation and the plague. The Romans have battering rams and new war machines which hurl boulders against the city walls. The Jews battle during the day and try to repair their fortifications at night. Eventually, the outer and then the inner walls are broken down, and the remaining Jewish fighters make their last stand in the Temple.

Infuriated by this unyielding resistance, the Roman soldiers set fire to the holy building; the last few defenders are overcome by flames or Roman swords. The fire melts the gold and silver adorning the Temple, and the precious met-als flow into the cracks between the stones of the Temple, causing the sol-

---

[422] "Ancient Jewish History: The Great Revolt," accessed December 1, 2018, www.jewishvirtuallibrary.org/the-great-revolt-66-70-ce. Reprinted by permission of the author, Joseph Telushkin, *Jewish Literacy* (NY: William Morrow, 1991).

[423] Richard Gottheil and M. Seligsohn, "Florus, Gessius," *JewishEncyclopedia.com*, accessed December 1, 2018, http://www.jewishencyclopedia.com/articles/6200-florus-gessius.

[424] A Roman legion was a force of approximately 5,000 soldiers.

[425] A. Kenneth Curtis, J. Stephen Lang, and Randy Peterson, *The 100 Most Important Events in Christian History* (Grand Rapids: Revell, 1991), 15–17.

diers to demolish the entire building to reach the molten treasure.[426] Then they loot and plunder the city, abusing the women who remain alive. The Second Temple and the city of Jerusalem are utterly destroyed in AD 70.[427]

The Zealots, who have been joined by some of their family members, defend Masada for almost three more years. When the Romans complete their siege ramp and manage to break through the fortress walls, they find that of the 960 men, women, and children inside the stronghold, only two women and five children are alive. The rest have all committed suicide to avoid being captured by the Roman soldiers.[428]

The nation of Israel has suffered a devastating defeat. Jerusalem and the Temple have been destroyed, and it is likely that over a million Jews have been killed in the rebellion against Rome.[429] Some of the Jews remain in Israel, but Josephus says that "the Jewish nation is widely dispersed over all the habitable earth" with the largest numbers going to Syria, especially the city of Antioch.[430] The judgment on Israel for disregarding the Mosaic covenant and rejecting the Messiah is horrendous and will continue. With no Temple, the Jews are unable to offer sacrifices, and their religious meetings will now center on the synagogues.

Eusebius, the third-century Church historian, says the Christians in Jerusalem had left the city before it was attacked and traveled across the Jordan to a city in Perea called Pella. In his words, they had heeded "a divine revelation," perhaps referring to Jesus's prophecy in Matthew 24.[431] Many of these believers would have been "moderate" Jewish Christians who had confessed faith in Jesus but maintained a traditional Jewish lifestyle. With the destruc-

---

[426] Jesus had told the disciples that the time was coming when not one stone of the Temple would be left on another (Matt. 24:1–2; Luke 19:43–44). Although the Temple was destroyed, the wall that supported its western foundation is still standing and is sometimes referred to as the "Western Wall" or "Wailing Wall."

[427] Lambert Dolphin, "The Destruction of the Second Temple," *The Temple Mount of Jerusalem*, accessed December 1, 2018, www.templemount.org/destruct2.html

[428] Pheiffer, Vos, and Rea, *Wycliffe Bible,* Vol. 2, 1087–1088. It is possible to visit Masada today. I have walked up the Roman siege ramp to the ruins of the fortress.

[429] "The Destruction of Jerusalem in 70 AD," *Bible History Online*, accessed December 1, 2018, https://www.bible-history.com/jerusalem/firstcenturyjerusalem_destruction_of_jerusalem_in_70_a_d_.html.

[430] Flavius Josephus, "The Wars of the Jews," in *The Works of Josephus*, trans. William Whiston (Peabody, MA: Hendrickson, 1987), 7.3.3.

[431] Eusebius, *The Church History*, trans. Paul L. Maier (Grand Rapids: Kregel, 1999), 82.

tion of Jerusalem and the Temple, their form of Christianity will decline as the Church's separation from the practices of Judaism becomes complete. Paul's teaching will become more prominent.

*****

The apostles had also left Jerusalem before the siege to preach the gospel in other parts of the Middle East and eventually more distant countries.[432] According to Church tradition, as the years pass, they all suffer persecution and are martyred, with the exception of John.[433] John writes his gospel and three epistles sometime around AD 90 before he is exiled during the last years of Domitian's reign (AD 81–96) to the small island of Patmos in the Aegean Sea (Rev. 1:9). While on Patmos, he completes the apocalyptic book of Revelation[434] before he is allowed to return to Ephesus where Church tradition says he dies a natural death about AD 100.[435]

*****

With the death of John, the apostolic age comes to an end. The apostles had the exceptional experience of close personal contact with Jesus before His death and after His resurrection.[436] They had received direct teaching from the Son of God and had been the first recipients of the special presence of the Holy Spirit on the day of Pentecost. They were fallible men who had failures and great sufferings, but they had been empowered to do miraculous works to establish the Church and spread the gospel. Now their unique era has ended; they have gone home to be with the Lord, and changes will take place. But the age of the Holy Spirit, working through the Church to establish the kingdom, has begun and will continue until Christ's Second Coming.

* ******

---

[432] Ibid., also see pp. 243–244 in this book.
[433] Walton, *Chronological Charts*, Chart 1.
[434] Carson, Moo, and Morris, *Introduction*, 451, 473.
[435] Walton, *Chronological Charts*, chart 1.
[436] Paul had no personal encounter with Jesus until after His resurrection and ascension.

As the Church loses the apostles, new leaders begin to emerge, mainly men who had direct interactions with the apostles, men who will be called the apostolic fathers. We will next examine the role of these men as we continue to follow the unfolding of redemptive history up to the present day. But we have come to the end of the historical manuscripts found in the New Testament. We must now rely on accounts outside of the Bible until we begin to consider future events when we will return to Scripture and its prophetical writings.

CHAPTER 27

THE POST-APOSTOLIC AGE OF THE CHURCH

We next consider the advancement of the kingdom through an interval of more than 1,900 years of redemptive history from the time of the Apostolic Fathers to the present when immense changes take place in population, technology, and philosophy throughout the world. Despite these enormous changes, along with the wars and disasters of this long period of history,[437] there remain two constants: the true Church continues to proclaim the gospel, and human beings continue to need it. Even though we now write on computers instead of scrolls and travel on airplanes instead of donkeys, we remain fallen people who have sinned against a Holy God and need a Savior.

The Church has grown through the centuries and, in some ways, prospered as it has met the challenges of population growth and advancing technology up to the present time. Pew's Research shows that 2.18 billion people claimed to be Christians in 2010.[438] But there is a question as to the number of true believers. George Barna says that his surveys within the United States indicate that "fewer than 10 percent of all born-again Christians[439] possess a biblical worldview that informs their thinking and behavior."[440] This is a stunning reminder that secular culture and worldly philosophy have always affected

---

[437] The Church always faces new and difficult problems. As this is being written, an infectious coronavirus is killing thousands, disrupting the world economy, and preventing the meetings of churches. The Church is also being confronted with the problem of lifelike robots with artificial intelligence as well as the possibility of human cloning.

[438] See p. 219, n. 346.

[439] Born-again Christians are those who claim to have had a life-changing experience, a spiritual rebirth as described in John 3:3–8.

[440] George Barna, *The Habits of Highly Effective Churches* (Ventura, CA: Regal Books, 1999), 131.

the teaching and conduct of the Church, and therefore, the establishment of God's kingdom on the earth.

As we follow the course of redemptive history through two post-Apostolic millennia, we will focus on how the Church has responded to the three distinct periods of world thought during this time, the premodern, modern, and postmodern eras.[441] We will also examine the historical events that led to these shifts in philosophical thinking, widespread changes which affected the Church and the entire world. The basic tenets and approximate dates for these three philosophical periods are: (1) premodern—belief in a rational world and acceptance of the supernatural (creation to the 1650s); (2) modern—belief in a rational world but rejection of the supernatural (1650s to the 1950s); and (3) postmodern—belief that there is no objective truth and no universal morality; everything is relative (1950s to the present).

We will look at the life of the Church and the advancement of the kingdom in each of these eras of thought, these different philosophical conceptions of reality, beginning with the premodern era.

---

[441] See Erickson, *Theology*, 160–174; also, Andy Kalan, "Analysis of History: The Story of Premodernism, Modernism, and Postmodernism," *Directions on Upward Existence*, July 2, 2012, https://andykalan.wordpress.com/2012/07/02/analysis-of-history-the-story-of--premodernism-modernism-postmodernism-2/; also see, "The Evolution from Premodern to Modern & Postmodern Societies." Study.com, May 18, 2015, https://study.com/academy/lesson/the-evolution-from-premodern-to-modern-postmodern-socities.html.

CHAPTER 28

THE KINGDOM IN THE PREMODERN ERA[442]

The Church has its beginning in the age of premodern thinking. This is a time when there is a general consensus in the world that the supernatural exists and that human beings must deal with a deity or deities greater than themselves. Religious conflicts center on the nature and number of the gods or who is the most powerful god, but the existence of the supernatural is commonly accepted as reality.

Paul confronted this belief in various gods when he preached to the Athenians after observing their many idols, especially the idol to an unknown god (Acts 17:16–34; p. 242). His dispute with the Jews was different; it was not about different deities but rather about the nature of the God of the Bible. The Church does not have to convince the premodern world that the supernatural exists; the task for premodern Christians is to show that the God of Christianity is the one true God among many competing deities.

In order to overcome the rampant errors of polytheism and the resistance of Judaism to the message of the gospel, the apostles had been given miraculous powers to verify their message about the Messiah, the Son of God, who had come to earth to save His kingdom people. But now that the Church is established, the next generation of Church leadership is not given the same kind of miraculous gifts. The gospel will continue to advance through personal testimonies and the teachings of Church leaders, but now the message will be

---

[442] Some of the material on the three eras of thought is adapted from a paper by the author, Dan Westerfield, "Foundations for an Adult Lay Education Program," (submitted for The Master of Arts in Religion Program, Reformed Theological Seminary, Baltimore/Washington, April 15, 2005.)

confirmed by the New Testament writings[443] as illumined by the Holy Spirit, rather than miracles.

*****

After the loss of the Apostles, Christians continue to meet in house churches, and they begin to look to the apostolic fathers for new leadership. Believers need help to refute the Jewish legalists (Gal. 3:1–9) to defend against Gnostic tendencies[444] (1 John 1:1–3) and to identify false teachers (2 Pet. 2:2–3). After their direct interactions with the apostles, we would expect the apostolic fathers to have a doctrinal foundation to help instruct and direct the growing congregations. However, their writings show this is not the case.

The apostolic fathers write simple catechetical texts or apocalyptic works with little discussion about the nature of the Trinity, Christology, or the complexities of soteriology.[445] Clement of Rome (AD 30–100), one of the earliest apostolic fathers, writes an epistle to the Corinthians,[446] but he focuses on pastoral matters and moralism with little emphasis on salvation or theological issues. The letters of Ignatius (d. 117)[447] emphasize works righteousness rather than grace, a common tendency of post-apostolic authors. In the apocalyptic work, *Shepherd of Hermas*, the author speaks of repentance but suggests that there are a limited number of times to repent for sins, possibly only once.[448] The contacts these men had with the apostles did not automatically give them an organized system of truth that could inform and help structure the emerging churches.

In addition to a decline in theological understanding after the deaths of the apostles, the Church still faces persecution and has to defend itself against a variety of charges. The animosity of official Judaism continues, and although Nero's intense persecution in AD 67 begins to subside after his suicide in AD

---

[443] See pp. 239–240.

[444] The Gnostics believed they received direct revelation from God and claimed that although Jesus appeared to be human, He was only a spirit, not really a man.

[445] *Soteriology* is a theological term for summing up the different aspects of salvation.

[446] Clement, "The Epistle of St. Clement," in *Ancient Christian Writers, No. 1*, trans. James A. Kleist (New York: Newman Press, 1946).

[447] Ignatius, "The Epistles of Ignatius," in *Ancient Christian Writers, No. 1*, trans. James A. Kleist (New York: Newman Press, 1946).

[448] Hermas, *Shepherd of Hermas*, trans. Joseph M. F. Marique, in *The Fathers of the Church—The Apostolic Fathers* (Washington, DC: Catholic University of America Press, 1947), 266.

68, Romans often charge Christians with being atheistic (rejecting the pagan gods), cannibalistic (partaking of the body and blood of Christ), and licentious (greeting each other with a holy kiss).[449]

Despite these obstacles, the Church grows rapidly during the time of the apostolic fathers. But there is little progress in doctrinal formulation. Even though the New Testament writings are circulating among the local congregations, it is difficult for church leaders to develop a broad theological foundation because individual assemblies do not have all the texts, and there is still disagreement over the validity of different books. Until there is a generally accepted Canon, there will be slow and uneven advancement in sound Christian teaching.

The apostolic fathers can be criticized for a lack of doctrinal discernment, but they did not lack dedication. They were concerned for the local churches, and they suffered persecution as they attempted to guide the growing assemblies. At least three of them—Clement, Ignatius, and their contemporary, Polycarp—were martyred by Roman rulers for refusing to deny Jesus Christ.[450]

*****

As the years of the apostolic fathers pass by, sporadic persecution of the Church continues, and a new group of Church leaders arises. These men defend the Church and its beliefs before the Roman authorities and a hostile culture; they are eventually called the apologists from the Greek word *apologia,* meaning "a verbal defense." But their efforts lack consistency since they are still struggling with such basic issues as the formation of the Canon and the nature of the Trinity. Teachers like Aristides (early AD 100s), Justin Martyr (AD 100–165), and Tatian (AD 110–172) try to explain the truths of the faith, but there is great pressure to compromise and avoid the antagonism of Roman society.

---

[449] Frank A. James, "History of Christianity 1, Section III A," (class notes, Washington D.C.: Reformed Theological Seminary course, 2000); also see James E. Reed and Ronnie Provost, *A History of Christian Education* (Nashville: Broadman & Holman, 1993), 76.

[450] Walton, *Chronological Charts*, Chart 3. The bravery of the 86 year old Polycarp as he was being burned alive by the Romans amazed the pagans. See "Polycarp," *Christianity Today*, accessed December 11, 2018, https://www.christianitytoday.com/history/people/martyrs/polycarp.html.

Whether because of caution or misinterpretation, the apologists at times downplay the uniqueness of Jesus Christ.[451] But these men are important in sustaining the Church, and they, too, suffer for the faith. Justin Martyr is eventually beheaded in Rome.[452]

*****

During the first two centuries, the Church achieves expansive growth without an established doctrinal foundation (Acts 2:41, 46–47, 5:14).[453] Even brief statements of faith, such as the Apostles Creed and the Nicene Creed, are not finalized until the third century. This raises two questions: first, what caused the Church's rapid growth? And secondly, does this mean that doctrinal education is unimportant for the Church?

In answer to the first question, scholars have suggested different explanations for the swift expansion of the Church, some even suggesting that early believers employed growth strategies similar to those used by some churches today.[454] But there are more fundamental reasons for the Church's initial rapid advance.

First and foremost was the bodily resurrection of Jesus Christ. The gospel writers and Paul list a number of instances where people saw, talked to, ate with, and touched the risen Messiah. Paul writes of one occasion where over five hundred people saw Jesus after he had risen from the dead (1 Cor. 15:6). If these individuals told their account to just one new person each week, after one year, 26,000 people would have talked to someone who had personally seen the risen Christ. This was not a story that went untold, and this outreach is in addition to the evangelism of the apostles and other missionaries. The resurrection not only transformed the apostles but the entire early church.

---

[451] Justin Martyr stressed that Christ had counterparts in pagan mythology. Justin Martyr, "The First Apology," in *The Fathers of the Church—Justin Martyr*, trans. Thomas B. Falls (New York: Christian Heritage, 1948), 57–58.

[452] Walton, *Chronological Charts*, chart 4.

[453] This early growth is revealed by the book of Acts, but there are no secular records to give precise numbers in Palestine. Rodney Stark traces later Church growth in Rome and the rest of the Empire. See Rodney Stark, *The Triumph of Christianity* (New York: HarperCollins, 2011), 153–165.

[454] Wim A. Dreyer, "The Amazing Growth of the Early Church," *HTS Theological Studies* 68(1), art. #1268, accessed December 20, 2018, www.hts.org.za/index.php/HTS/article/view/1268/2546.

The sure knowledge of Jesus's resurrection assured believers of their own resurrections and gave them courage to proclaim their faith. They were able to endure persecution and face deadly dangers, such as the plague, without fear and with compassion for others, while the pagans were consumed with terror. As late as 362, after the Church had spread further into the Roman Empire, the Emperor Julian complained that Christians were doing more to help poor pagans than the pagans themselves. Christians were known for risking their lives to care for the diseased and the rejected. They strongly opposed the legal practice of infanticide which, because of the preference for sons, had resulted in a shortage of women in Roman society.[455]

Secondly, the pouring out of the Holy Spirit at Pentecost had enabled the disciples to speak with clarity and authority in different languages, initiating an early proclamation of the gospel to different cultures. In addition, the miraculous powers given to the apostles, especially Peter and Paul, helped verify their amazing testimonies.

Thirdly, the Jews and the pagans, seeing the bravery, kindness, and fellowship within the local churches were drawn to these assemblies. The Christian community offered something more meaningful than the legalism of the Jews and the permissive polytheism of the Romans.

And, finally, Christianity followed the example of Jesus and treated women with a respect that was not only uncommon but revolutionary for that time (John 4:27, 8:1–11, 19:26–27; Luke 8:1–3, 13:10–13). The Christians took to heart Paul's teaching that, although they were to have different roles in the Church (1 Tim. 2:12), women were equals in salvation through their faith in Jesus Christ (Gal. 3:28). Women were included in the New Covenant through their own confessions of faith—their own volitions—just as men were (Acts 8:12), not through family relations as in the Old Covenant. Many women had supported Jesus before His death and were committed to Him and the Church after His resurrection. During the times of persecution, many of them also paid the ultimate price for their devotion. Faithful women played a significant role in the growth of the early church.

But then for the second question, the importance of doctrinal teaching for the Church, we can turn to the Lord Himself for the answer. Jesus seemed to anticipate this question when He told doubting Thomas that those who

---

[455] Rodney Stark, *The Rise of Christianity* (Princeton, NJ: Princeton University Press, 1996), 82–84, 118–124.

believe without seeing Him are blessed (John 20:29). Not everyone can be an eyewitness or know one. When the two disciples on the road to Emmaus met the resurrected Jesus, He first revealed Himself through the Scriptures and then by sight (Luke 24:13–32). Scripture is the most reliable witness, more trustworthy than our own eyes.

As biblical events recede further into the past, understanding the substance of the recorded accounts becomes more and more important. Without a knowledge of doctrine, people are less likely to grasp that Jesus provides the only way to the one true God (John 14:6; Acts 4:12). The writer of Hebrews tells us that we should move beyond the elementary teachings about the Christ and press on to maturity (Heb. 6:1). This requires a theological understanding of the Old and New Testaments to establish the background for what Jesus has accomplished. A sure knowledge of Scripture and its abiding precepts are essential for a grounded faith.

*****

By the end of the second century, the New Testament books have become widely circulated, enabling teachers and theologians such as Irenaeus (late second century AD) and Tertullian (AD 160–220) to engage in more comprehensive studies. Irenaeus is a strong opponent of Gnosticism, and Tertullian advances the understanding of the Trinity.[456] Origen tries to combine Greek philosophy with Christian thought and mistakenly claims every person will be saved.[457] These early theologians make some progress in doctrinal thinking, but they are often influenced by the religious concepts of the Jews, Greeks, and Romans. Their writings are not part of the Canon and often combine errors with biblical truth. It will take further time and scriptural study to develop a more complete understanding of Christ and His redeeming work, but it becomes difficult for the Church to advance theologically because serious oppression begins again.

In AD 248, Rome is celebrating the thousandth year of its founding, but the populations surrounding the empire, the "barbarians,"[458] are becoming

---

[456] Roger E. Olson, *The Story of Christian Theology* (Downers Grove, IL: InterVarsity Press, 1999), 73, 95.

[457] Ibid., 99–123.

[458] "Barbarian" at first referred to someone speaking an unintelligible language but eventually came to mean someone rough and crude. See Pheiffer, Vos, and Rea, *Wycliffe Bible*, Vol. 1,

more threatening. When compared to its glorious past, Rome is in decline, and its emperors know it. Decius, who reigns from AD 249–251, believes this deterioration is occurring because the Roman gods are not being worshipped properly. The Christians refuse to venerate them and are persuading others to become "irreligious." The emperor issues a decree ordering all Christians to offer sacrifices to the pagan gods. Those who refuse suffer imprisonment, torture, exile, and even death. Decius intends to destroy the Christian "atheists."

The next emperors, Gallus (AD 251–253) and Valerian (AD 253–260) continue the persecutions. Under Valerian, many bishops, presbyters, deacons, and men and women of high social rank are put to death. The brutality of this tyranny is frightful, even to some Romans. When Gallienus (AD 260–268) succeeds Valerian, he rescinds the edicts, and Christianity is unofficially tolerated for almost forty years. The Church has survived a bloody period of persecution, but many Christians have died, and many others have compromised the faith to save their lives.[459]

*****

During these four decades of relative peace, the Church makes some progress in several significant areas including recognition of the Canon and theological studies. Christian basilicas—meeting halls—become numerous in the Roman Empire as congregations become too large to gather in houses.[460] Liturgy is becoming standardized and creeds are being developed for testing orthodoxy. Bishops rule over churches and meet occasionally to settle disputes. The kingdom is advancing rapidly, but then persecution resumes.

*****

In AD 284, Diocletian becomes emperor; like earlier rulers, he is concerned about the decline of Roman civilization and agrees the Christians are to blame. In 295, he orders Christian soldiers to offer sacrifices to the Roman gods. When a military commander resists, he is martyred, and persecutions begin to

---

204.

[459] Ibid., Vol. 2, 1311–1312. Some Christians made the Pagan sacrifices, some pretended to, and some bribed Roman officials to list them as complying.

[460] Olson, *Story*, 135–137. Olson estimates that five percent of the subjects of the empire were Christian at the beginning of the fourth century.

multiply in the army. In 303, Diocletian issues more edicts and the oppression becomes widespread; it becomes known as the Great Persecution because of the large numbers involved. Christians lose their legal rights, their buildings and books are burned, and many are tortured and killed. Even Diocletian's Christian wife and daughter are forced to sacrifice to the gods.[461]

In 305, Diocletian suddenly abdicates his throne to retire in solitude, although he still exercises influence over his successors, Constantius Chlorus in the west and Galerius in the east. When Chlorus dies in 306, Galerius wants to name one of his own allies to replace him, but Chlorus's army proclaims his son, Constantine, as emperor in the west. Constantine follows his father's example and is deliberately lax in enforcing Diocletian's edicts against Christians.[462]

Galerius continues the persecution of the Church in the east until fearfully and grudgingly granting toleration on his deathbed in 311. His demise leaves four principal generals with separate armies and different regions of control in the Empire, Constantine and Maxentius in the west, Licinius and Maximinus Daia in the east.[463]

Not surprisingly, a civil war breaks out. Also not surprisingly, Galerius's deathbed concession to Christianity has little effect; it remains an anxious and dangerous time for the Church.

In the west, General Constantine eventually vanquishes his principal rival, Maxentius, in a brutal confrontation at Milvian Bridge in AD 312. Before the decisive battle, Constantine has a vision in which he believes he sees Christ and is told to put the first two letters of Christ's name (XP in Greek) on the shields of his soldiers. After his triumph the next day, he credits his victory to this symbol and will greatly favor the Church as he begins his reign in the western empire.[464]

Shortly after Constantine's victory, Diocletian dies in seclusion in his palace home; his influence as a ruthless opponent of Christianity has come to an end. In 313, Constantine and Licinius meet in Milan and reach an

---

[461] Pheiffer, Vos, and Rea, *Wycliffe Bible*, Vol. 2, 1312.
[462] Editors, Encyclopaedia, "Constantius I, Roman Emperor," *Encyclopaedia*, accessed December 20, 2018, https://www.britannica.com/biography/Constantius-I.
[463] Editors, Encyclopaedia, "Galerius, Roman Emperor," *Encyclopaedia*, accessed December 20, 2018, https://www.britannica.com/biography/Galerius.
[464] Super Admin, "The Battle of Milvian Bridge and the history of the book," *Libraries University of Missouri*, November 1, 2012, http://library.missouri.edu/news/special-collections/the-battle-of-milvian-bridge-and-the-history-of-the-book

accommodation to maintain peace in the empire. Constantine gives his sister, Constantia, in marriage to Licinius to seal their agreement. The two generals issue a joint declaration called the Edict of Milan which grants religious freedom in the areas under their control. Christians gain official status in the west and in Licinius's territory in the east; they have legal and personal protections, the freedom to worship, and the right to establish churches.

Maximinus, the general who controls Syria and Egypt is a pagan who hates Christians, and he takes no part in the decree.[465] In fact, as the Edict of Milan is being enacted, Maximinus is leading his army from Syria to attack Licinius in order to gain complete control of the eastern empire. But the long march exhausts his soldiers, and he suffers a crushing defeat by Licinius's forces at Campus Serenas. Maximinus is not killed in the battle but dies as he flees.[466]

Two generals have fallen and two are still standing with Constantine ruling in the west and Licinius ruling in the east. The co-emperors maintain an uneasy truce for a few years, but Licinius continues to build up his military and attempts to undermine his western rival through political allies. He also begins to ignore the Edict of Milan and starts persecuting Christians. In 324, Constantine orders his army into the East, defeats Licinius's forces, and imprisons him. After twelve years of turmoil and civil war, Constantine has become the sole ruler of the Roman Empire. The next year, Licinius is accused of trying to instigate a revolt from prison and Constantine, despite his sister's pleas, has him hanged.[467]

Constantine had begun his rule in the west, but with control of the entire Empire, he does not make Rome his capital. Recognizing the strategic location of the ancient city of Byzantium in the East, he builds a great walled metropolis on the site of the old city and renames it Constantinople. His choosing of this

---

[465] Editors, Encyclopaedia, "Licinius, Roman Emperor," *Encyclopaedia*, updated January1, 2019, https://www.britannica.com/biography/Licinius.

[466] Michael DeMaio, Jr., "Maximinus Daia (305–313 AD)," *De Imperatoribus Romanis*, accessed December 20, 2018, www.roman-emperors.org/daia.htm.

[467] Ralph W. Mathisen, "Diocletian (284–305 AD)," *De Imperatoribus Romanis*, accessed December 21, 2018, www.roman-emperors.org/dioclet.htm. Also see Editors, *Encyclopaedia*, "Licinius," *Encyclopaedia*, last updated January 1, 2019, https://www.britannica.com/biography/Licinius.

site, with water on three sides, will have major consequences for the empire and Europe when the Arab Muslims advance from the south centuries later.

*****

Some question whether Constantine ever became a true believer.[468] He never makes Christianity the official religion of the empire, but he supports the Church and under his rule it prospers greatly, at least in membership and finances. Large numbers of Roman citizens, many of them influential, join the Church simply because it is beneficial to be a member. The zeal and dedication of the Church, which was actually strengthened under persecution, becomes seriously diluted with the influx of "hordes of unconverted pagans."[469] Many of these new "converts" are not interested in the doctrines and practices of the faith.

During Constantine's reign, the Church goes from being persecuted to being privileged. With this amazing change in status, its leaders have the time and resources to consider and clarify essential issues of the faith. In 325, Constantine calls for and presides over the first ecumenical council, the Council of Nicaea; he wants to unify the Church to help unify the Empire. The assembly condemns the view of Arias, a Libyan priest, that Jesus was a created being.

With the leadership of Alexander, Bishop of Alexandria, and his deacon assistant, Athanasius, the assembly produces an official orthodox doctrine of the Trinity affirming that Jesus is truly God, eternal, and of one substance with the Father.[470] The Nicene Creed, with a final version written in 381 that further outlines the deity and role of the Holy Spirit, is still the universal statement of faith for most branches of Christianity.[471] Constantine may have been using the council to help advance his political kingdom, but God uses the council to

---

[468] Kuiper, *The Church*, 23–27; also see John Misachi, "Battle of the Milvian Bridge: The Battle That Helped Establish Christianity," *WorldAtlas*, August 1, 2017, https://www.worldatlas.com/articles/battle-of-the-milvian-bridge-the-battle-that-helped-establish-christianity.html.

[469] Olson, *Story*, 139.

[470] Although Arias's view was rejected, he has had followers (Arians) throughout the history of the Church. See "Christian History, Athanasius," *Christianity Today*, accessed December 21, 2018, https://www.christianitytoday.com/history/people/theologians/athanasius.html.

[471] Curtis, Lang, and Peterson, *100 Events*, 32–36. For an English translation of the creed see Editors, Encyclopaedia, "Nicene Creed, Christianity," *Encyclopaedia*, accessed December 21, 2018, https://www.britannica.com/topic/Nicene-Creed.

help clarify critical doctrines of the Church and advance His own kingdom on the earth.

*****

Some of the emperors who succeed Constantine are less favorable to the Church. Julian especially denigrates the faith, but his reign is short (361–363) and Christianity is too well-established for persecution to resume; the Church continues to grow and make progress. In 386, Athanasius sends his Easter letter listing the New Testament manuscripts, and they are the same twenty-seven books that compose the New Testament Canon today.[472] The Church has a finalized Bible, an established doctrine of the Trinity, and a prominent place in the Roman Empire.

With a firm standing in the nation, members of the clergy begin to have influence in the political realm. In 390, the Emperor Theodosius (AD 379–395), a professed Christian, orders his soldiers to brutally crush a rebellion in Thessalonica where Roman officers have been killed. Seven thousand citizens are slain. Ambrose, the powerful and devout Bishop of Milan, calls for Theodosius to repent and bans him from partaking in the rite of the Lord's Supper.

Theodosius resists for months but finally submits to Ambrose's demands. He publicly repents, wears sackcloth and ashes, and then is allowed to return to the Lord's Table. In the first major power struggle between the Church and the state, the Church has won.[473]

*****

In 391, Theodosius closes the pagan temples and bans pagan worship. Paganism, once the official religion of the empire, has been replaced by Christianity. Although the pagans cannot openly practice their religion, they are not violently attacked, and they retain their civil rights.

In less than eighty years after the battle of Milvian Bridge, the Church has seen an incredible change in its circumstances. For better or worse, Theodosius

---

[472] See pp. 240.
[473] Timothy P. Jones, *Christian History Made Easy*, (Torrance, CA: Rose Publishing, 2009), 51.

has established what not even Constantine envisioned, the Christian state.[474] Christianity has moved from being persecuted to being privileged to now being the official religion of the Roman Empire.

*****

We have been following the struggles of the Church as it tries to establish itself in the premodern era. The religious conflicts which take place are among people who believe in the supernatural but who proclaim different deities. Even kings and emperors believe they must answer to a god or gods, and it appears that the Christian God is winning. But the Roman Empire is not the kingdom of God; the Christian state initiated by Theodosius is not the kingdom that Jesus preached.

The Church has survived severe persecutions and grown in numbers and influence. But with its prosperity, it now faces another kind of danger; the Church is becoming secularized and intermixed with the government of the empire. This first began under Constantine when many unbelievers, the "unconverted hordes of pagans," joined the Church to enhance their political and social positions. In reaction, a significant number of believers had begun to retreat from what they saw as a compromised Church. Some of them followed the example of Anthony of Egypt (251–356)[475] who had withdrawn to the desert in 285 to live the ascetic life of a hermit. Anthony's severe physical and spiritual disciplines became widely known and admired and soon were seen as an acceptable alternative to a Church that was becoming a political partner with Roman emperors.

Under Constantine's rule, many Christians had decided to abandon a "worldly" church, and the exodus to the wilderness became a significant movement. Bainton says, "When the masses entered the Church, the monks went to the desert. The desert was chosen because of the belief that the waterless places were the abode of demons and therefore the places where the battle was to be joined."[476]

---

[474] Roland H. Bainton, *Christianity*, (Boston: Houghton Mifflin, 1987), 99–100. Also see, "Theodosius I," *Christianity Today*, accessed December 21, 2018, https://www.christianitytoday.com/history/people/rulers/theodosius-i.html.

[475] Anthony's influence was enhanced by his exceptionally long life, especially lengthy for that era.

[476] Bainton, *Christianity*, 101.

Asceticism, the renouncing of worldly concerns and pleasures, has been an influence in many religions. It has its roots in Greek philosophy which saw the spiritual as good and the material as evil. For Platonism, salvation was the escape of the soul from the body. But this is in contrast to the understanding of Christianity.[477] When God looked at His creation on the sixth day and saw that "it was very good" (Gen. 2:31), He was including the physical as well as the spiritual. Human beings in their earthly lives have always been body-soul unities. Although death temporarily separates the soul from the body, the two will be reunited at the time of the resurrection when Christ returns, and our resurrected bodies will be part of our eternal state (Matt. 26:29; Acts 24:15).

A moderate asceticism was practiced by the early Church when they pooled their resources and lived simple humble lives. But the men who follow Anthony into the desert, perhaps believing they are emulating John the Baptist, take self-denial to a different level. They become known as the Desert Fathers and punish themselves with extreme physical disciplines. They live as hermits and eat and drink only the minimum to survive, often only bread and water. They fast, beat themselves with whips, deny themselves marriage, and reject cleanliness, refusing to bathe or cut their hair or fingernails,[478] even though such asceticism is directly refuted in Scripture (Col. 2:20–23; 1 Tim. 4:1–3). These men fight their battles with sin and the devils isolated from the rest of the Church and civilization. And although less is known about the women who withdraw from society, there are many Desert Mothers such as Amma Syncletica of Alexandria who choose a lonely life in the wilderness.[479]

But human beings are created to be in fellowship, not only with God, but with other human beings. Anthony eventually organizes other hermits to meet for Sunday worship and a shared meal.[480] This marks the beginning of a desert community; soon, monasteries are built where each monk has his own cell, but

---

[477] Ronald Nash, "Was The New Testament Influenced by Pagan Philosophy?," *CRI*, April 6, 2009, www.equip.org/article/was-the-new-testament-influenced-by-pagan-philosophy.

[478] B. K. Kuiper, *The Church in History*, (Grand Rapids: Eerdmans, 1951), 92–93; Editors, Encyclopaedia, "Asceticism," *Encyclopaedia*, accessed December 21, 2018, https://www.britannica.com/topic/asceticism; Jack Zavada, "Asceticism," *ThoughtCo.*, accessed December 21, 2018, https://www.thoughtco.com/what-is-asceticism-700046.

[479] John S. Knox, "The Monastic Movement: Origins & Purposes," *Ancient History Encyclopaedia*, August 23, 2016, www.ancient.eu/article/930/. Also see Laura Swan, *The Forgotten Desert Mothers* (Mahwah, NJ: Paulist Press, 2001).

[480] Editors, Encyclopaedia, "St. Anthony of Egypt," *Encyclopaedia*, accessed December 21, 2018, https://www.britannica.com/biography/Saint-Anthony-of-Egypt

meals, worship, and other activities are shared. The excessive disciplines begin to diminish. In AD 358, Saint Basil codifies the practice of monasticism for the Church in the east; Saint Benedict will do the same in the west a century and a half later.[481]

Once the early extremes subside and the monks begin to live in more reasonable conditions, some take on tasks that are very beneficial to the Church. The monasteries provide places for study, and many monks become serious scholars. Saint Jerome (340–420) translates the Old and New Testaments into literary Latin.[482] John Chrysostom (349–407), who becomes Archbishop of Constantinople, serves his apprenticeship as a hermit-monk.[483] After being converted from a licentious lifestyle, Saint Augustine desires to live a monastic life but circumstances press him into service as Bishop of Hippo in North Africa. However, he still agrees that asceticism is essential to godliness, and he leads an austere life.

Despite his ecclesiastical duties, Augustine becomes a prolific author and one of the greatest theologians of the Church. His dispute with the British monk Pelagius over the nature of man after the fall continues up to the present time,[484] and his numerous books are still valuable resources today.[485]

---

[481] Bainton, *Christianity*, 102.

[482] Jerome soon decides that the desert is not for him. He is eventually supported by a rich widow and other women who build a monastery and a convent in Bethlehem. Editors, Encyclopaedia, "St. Jerome," *Ecyclopaedia*, accessed December 22, 2018, https://www.britannica.com/biography/Saint-Jerome.

[483] Bainton, *Christianity*, 102.

[484] Augustine's belief, that Adam's fall affected the nature of all his descendants so that every person is born innately sinful, was vehemently opposed by the British monk, Pelagius, who believed that every person is born in a state of righteousness and is able to lead a life of perfect obedience. Pelagius's view was condemned by the Church, but as time has progressed, the Roman Catholic Church and most Protestant churches have adopted a semi-Pelagian view saying that the fall affected all mankind, but human beings are still able to do good works and justify themselves before God. The unbiblical view that even after the fall, human beings are born basically good is predominant in many churches today and drastically affects their understanding of God's grace and the outworking of salvation. See R.C. Sproul, "The Pelagian Controversy," *Ligonier Ministries*, accessed December 22, 2018, https://www.ligonier.org/learn/articles/pelagian-controversy/

[485] The preserved works of Saint Augustine comprise some 100 books, 240 letters, and more than 500 sermons. "Chronology of the Life of Saint Augustine, Bishop of Hippo (A.D. 354–430)," *Great Books 202*, accessed December, 22, 2018, http://www-personal.umich.edu/~rdwallin/syl/GreatBooks/202.W99/Augustine/AugustineChron.html.

Despite such accomplishments, the entire monastic movement was contrary to the teaching of Jesus Christ. Instead of instructing His disciples to withdraw from the world, He had told them to "let your light shine before men in such a way that they may see your good works, and glorify your Father who is in heaven" (Matt. 5:16).

When Jesus prayed to the Father for His disciples the night before His crucifixion, He said, "I do not pray that You should take them out of the world, but that You should keep them from the evil one" (John 17:15).

The kingdom of God is not found in isolation in the desert. It is located where Christians are making Christ known through their interactions in the daily activities of the world. Christians are to be in the world without being worldly. Sanctification comes through the Holy Spirit applying God's Word to our hearts, usually in fellowship with other believers.

An unbiblical asceticism coupled with humanly imposed restrictions can lead to the kind of hidden depravity that has recently been exposed in the Roman Catholic priesthood. The extensive sexual abuse of children, especially of young boys, by Roman Catholic priests has been widely chronicled in the news media. The *National Catholic Reporter* says that by 2012, the Vatican had paid at least $2.2 billion to about 100,000 victims in the United States alone and suggests that a similar amount has been paid out in the rest of the global Catholic community.[486]

Donald B. Cozzens PhD, President-Rector and Professor of Pastoral theology at Saint Mary Seminary and Graduate School of Theology in Cleveland, does not condemn homosexuality, but he cites studies which indicate that approximately 50 percent of Roman Catholic priests are now homosexuals.[487] In July 2017, numerous news sources reported the arrest of the secretary of a high-ranking Vatican cardinal for hosting a drug-fueled homosexual orgy in a Vatican apartment next to Saint Peter's Basilica.[488] The *National Catholic*

---

[486] John L. Allen, Jr, "Vatican abuse summit: $2.2 billion and 100,000 victims in US alone" *National Catholic Reporter*, February 8, 2012, https://www.ncronline.org/blogs/ncr-today/vatican-abuse-summit-22-billion-and-100000-victims-us-alone. Stunningly, the subheading of this article says "Experts reject homosexuality as risk factor."

[487] Donald B. Cozzens, *The Changing Face of the Priesthood: A Reflection of the Priest's Crisis of Soul* (Collegeville, MN: Liturgical Press, 2001), 99.

[488] "Vatican police 'break up drug-fueled gay orgy at home of secretary of one of Pope Francis's key advisors,'" *Daily Mail.com*, updated July 5, 2017, http://www.dailymail.co.uk/news/article-4667098/vatican-police-break-gay-orgy-apartment.html.

Register reported that the Vatican had refused to comment on the arrest, which was first reported by the Italian newspaper, *Il Fatto Quotidiano*. The problems for the Roman Catholic Church are just beginning in this area, and a root cause is the ban on married priests, the outgrowth of an unbiblical belief that asceticism equals godliness.

*****

While the state-supported Church is grappling with the monastic movement in the fourth century, the deterioration of the Roman Empire continues. The encroachment of the barbarians from the north and east intensifies. The rugged Germanic tribes believe they can profitably till some of the poorer lands that the Romans have abandoned. They work without the slave labor used by the Romans, and they keep encroaching further into the territory of the empire.

But around AD 370, a new threat suddenly appears that endangers both Rome and the barbarians. The Huns, a tribe of fierce horsemen, come "thundering out of Asia's Central Steppes"[489] into Eastern Europe. They begin to push the resident Germanic tribes, the Vandals and the Visigoths, further west and south. Although the Romans called these German people barbarians, they have a stable government, a form of writing, and a legal system. They have already been introduced to Christianity by a Gothic bishop named Ulfilas, and both the Vandals and Visigoths have embraced the Arian concept of the faith.[490] Now pressed by the Huns, they expand deeper into the Roman empire. As they take over more territory and towns, they begin to battle Roman military forces.[491]

The army of Rome has been the supreme fighting force in the world for a thousand years, but like Roman society as a whole, it is becoming weaker and less disciplined. An eastern division of the army suffers a devastating defeat in

---

[489] "The Fall of Rome," *EyeWitness to History.com*, accessed December 22, 2018, http://www.eyewitnesstohistory.com/fallofrome.htm.

[490] Ulfilas (311–383), a Cappadocian reared among the Goths, is credited with translating the first Germanic version of the Bible and is seen as the evangelist who converted the barbarians, although it was to the heresy of Arianism. Bainton, *Christianity*, 126; also see Editors, Encyclopaedia, "Ulfilas," *Encyclopaedia*, updated January 13, 2019, https://www.britannica.com/biography/Ulfilas.

[491] "Barbarian Breakthrough," *Church History for the Masses*, accessed December 22, 2018, http://www.christianchronicler.com/history1/barbarian_breakthrough.html.

378 to the Visigoths at Adrianople in European Turkey. Historians mark this battle as a pivotal point in the eventual fall of Rome.[492] The victory gives the Visigoths control of most of the Balkans. Meanwhile, the Vandals continue their pressure further west by crossing over the Rhine River.

After their victory at Adrianople, the Visigoths move on to Greece and then Northern Italy. Beginning in AD 401, they make repeated invasions to the south against a weakening Roman army.[493] The empire's boundaries are collapsing toward Rome.

*****

Historians list a number of reasons for the decline of Rome: (1) the barbarian invasion; (2) economic troubles and overreliance on slave labor; (3) overexpansion; (4) government corruption and political instability; (5) a weakening of the Roman legions—the military was unable to recruit enough Roman citizens and came to rely on foreign mercenaries.[494] And although many historians ignore it, it appears that institutionalized and rampant homosexuality was a significant factor.[495]

For the United States, a nation that mirrors many of these problems and that has recently (2015) seen its president and Supreme Court endorse homosexual marriage, these issues should give citizens and politicians serious pause.

The issue of homosexuality is difficult for Christians who must treat homosexuals as fellow human beings deserving respect without condoning

---

[492] Joshua J. Mark, "Roman Empire," *Ancient History Encyclopedia*, March 22, 2018, www.ancient.eu/Roman_Empire/.

[493] Editors, Encyclopaedia, "Visigoth," *Encyclopaedia*, accessed December 22, 2018, https://www.britannica.com/topic/Visigoth.

[494] Evan Andrews, "8 Reasons Why Rome Fell," *History*, January 14, 2014, https://www.history.com/news/8-reasons-why-rome-fell

[495] According to Italy's renowned Professor of History, Roberto De Mattei, homosexuality was the primary reason for the decline of Roman society. When he stated his conclusion in 2011, he was immediately attacked by Italian politicians and academics, but they did not deny that homosexuality had become rampant in the Roman military and government. See Nick Squires, "Fall of Roman Empire Caused by Contagion of Homosexuality," *The Telegraph*, April, 8, 2011, http://www.telegraph.co.uk/news/worldnews/europe/italy/8438210/Fall-of-Roman-Empire-caused-by-contagion-of-homosexuality.html. Also, see Kerby Anderson, "When Nations Die," *Probe Ministries*, accessed February, 21, 2019, https://www.leaderu.com/common/nationsdie.html.

their lifestyles. Both Old and New Testament passages condemn homosexuality as well as other sexual behavior outside of heterosexual marriage.[496] Under the Old Testament laws, which were written for the theocratic government of Israel, such sexual sins warranted the death penalty (Lev. 20:10–16). But Jesus demonstrated mercy when He was confronted with a woman caught in adultery (John 8:1–13), and the Church does not function under the theocratic government of Israel. Under the New Covenant, and the civil laws of the United States, no one is sent to prison or executed for adultery or consensual homosexual activity.

But the moral laws concerning sexual activity are restated in the New Testament, and there is no doubt that homosexual activity is condemned and cannot be sanctioned by the Church. Mainline churches which condone gay marriage such as the Episcopal Church, the Presbyterian Church (USA), and the Evangelical Lutheran Church of America[497] have made worldly opinion and political correctness their primary authority rather than Scripture. As someone has said, "Christians in the past feared the raised sword; today, Christians in the United States fear the raised eyebrow." Such churches cannot advance the kingdom of God.

God revealed his plan for sexuality when he created human beings, male and female, and made that relationship the bedrock of the family and society (Gen. 1:27–28, 2:24). Nations will collapse, as did Rome, without that firm foundation. The Church must mirror Jesus's compassion and mercy toward anyone caught up in sexual sin, but it must also remain true to His parting words to the woman caught in adultery, "From now on, sin no more" (John 8:11).

Some state governments are already attacking Christian businesses for refusing to participate in homosexual weddings. A Christian florist in Richland, Washington, who did not want to participate in such an event, was

---

[496] The Scripture verses concerning homosexuality, beginning with the Old Testament, are as follows: Gen: 2:20–24; Gen. 19:1–11; Lev. 18:22, 20:13; Judg. 19:16–24; 1 Kings 15:12; 2 Kings 23:7; Mark 10:6–9; Rom. 1:26–28; 1 Cor. 6:9–11, 7:2; 1 Tim. 1:8–10; Heb. 13:4; and Jude 7. Some say that Jesus never spoke about homosexuality, but He affirmed Old Testament Laws, saying, "For truly I say to you, until heaven and earth pass away, not the smallest letter or stroke shall pass away from the Law, until all is accomplished" (Matt. 5:18). There is mercy in Christ, but God's principles do not change, and New Testament writers restate the Old Testament condemnations of homosexuality.

[497] Nolan Feeney, "3 Other Christian Denominations That Allow Gay Marriage," *Time*, March 18, 2015, http://time.com/3749253/churches-gay-marriage/

fined $1,001 and "ordered" to serve homosexual ceremonies.[498] A small bakery in Oregon has been fined $135,000 for refusing to bake a cake for a lesbian wedding.[499] The Canadian Supreme Court ruled in 2013 that biblical speech opposing homosexual behavior is a "hate crime."[500] In Sweden, a pastor has been jailed for preaching against homosexuality,[501] and the homosexual lobby is pushing for similar rulings in the United States.[502]

According to Gallup's polling in 2015,[503] the number of people who identify as homosexual, including lesbians, gays, bisexuals, and transgenders (the LGBT[504] community) make up only 3.8 percent of the United States population. Yet because of their dominance in Hollywood and the mainstream media, they are winning the political battle against Christians who try to defend what Scripture teaches. It appears that the persecution of Christians over this issue will only increase.

*****

In 410, the Visigoths under Alaric march into Rome and sack the "Eternal City." So many people are killed that blood runs in the streets; the palace of the

---

[498] "Hundreds support Christian florist fined for refusing to work gay wedding," *Fox News*, November 18, 2016, www.foxnews.com/us/2016/11/18/hundreds-support-christian-florist-fined-for-refusing-to-work-gay-wedding.html.

[499] Todd Starnes, "Christian bakers fined $135,000 for refusing to make wedding cake for lesbians," *Fox News*, July 3, 2013, https://insider.foxnews.com/2015/07/07/bakery-owners-fined-135000-refusing-make-gay-wedding-cake.

[500] Heather Clark, "Canadian Supreme Court Rules Biblical Speech Opposing Homosexual Behavior is a 'Hate Crime'," *Christian News*, February 28, 2013, https://christiannews.net/2013/02/28/canadian-supreme-court-rules-biblical-speech-opposing-homosexual-behavior-is-a-hate-crime/.

[501] Albert Mohler, "Criminalizing Christianity: Sweden's Hate Speech Law," *Christian Headlines.com*, accessed, February 16,2019, https://www.christianheadlines.com/columnists/al-mohler/criminalizing-christianity-swedens-hate-speech-law-1277601.html.

[502] Paige Winfield, "Christian Groups Eye Hate Crime Bill," *Christianity Today*, July 16, 2009, www.christianitytoday.com/news/2009/july/128-42.0.html.

[503] Frank Newport, "Americans Greatly Overestimate Percent Gay, Lesbian in US," *Gallup*, May 21, 2015, https://news.gallup.com/poll/183383/americans-greatly-overestimate-percent-gay-lesbian.aspx.

[504] LGBTQ is becoming a common designation for this community where the Q indicates those who are questioning their sexual identity. Other letters for other sexual categories are already being added.

emperors and the houses of the rich are stripped of their furnishings, jewels, and art. The bishop of Rome does more to protect the citizens than Emperor Honorius, who stays in his palace in Ravenna just north of Rome. But the bishop's efforts to stem the worst excesses of the marauders have little effect. The barbarians terrify and plunder the city for six days before Alaric orders his army to regroup and depart for Spain. The city that had ransacked the world has been pillaged.[505] The weakened Roman forces farther north in Europe had not aided the city, and the Eastern Empire, struggling to defend its own territory from the barbarians, sent very limited aid. Rome had been left virtually defenseless and was ravaged.

This calamity shocks pagans and Christians alike. Honorius is compelled to make peace with the Visigoths. When Alaric leaves, he takes Honorius's young sister, Placidia, with him. The Visigoths continue to southern Gaul and begin to settle there. When Alaric suddenly dies, Placidia marries his successor Atauf. The new Visigoth ruler recognizes the inability of his people to govern the empire, but he wants to establish a major role for his military in an alliance with the Roman government. The potential for such a coalition ends in 415, when Atauf is assassinated by a disgruntled aide in Barcelona.[506]

*****

Jerome, who is writing in his monastery in Bethlehem, is so struck with horror over the sacking of Rome that he believes the Antichrist is at hand; he finds it difficult to continue his work. When the pagans blame the Christians for this disaster, Augustine defends the faith by writing his most significant book, *The City of God*.[507] He says there are two societies, that of the elect (the City of God) and that of the damned (the City of Man). But because so much sin remains within the saints, it is difficult to tell the difference between the two. Augustine perceives history as linear and predestined from creation to Christ's second advent with the two cities intermingled until Christ comes again.[508] He does not want the Church to take up arms, but he insists the generals and

---

[505] Kuiper, *The Church*, 49–50.

[506] Editors, Encyclopaedia, "Ataulphus," *Encyclopaedia*, updated January 1, 2019, https://www. britannica.com/biography/Ataulphus.

[507] Augustine, *The City of God* (London: Penguin Books, 1972).

[508] Editors, Encyclopaedia, "The City of God," *Ecyclopaedia*, accessed December 24, 2018, https://www.britannica.com/topic/The-City-of-God.

the army should defend the empire against the barbarians. Augustine believes Rome's sins have brought her down, not the Christians and their faith.[509]

*****

In 451, Attila the Hun and his army are continuing the Hunnic expansion which has now reached Gaul. They assault towns and villages as they continue their westward movement through the European countries. The Roman army in the northwest and the Visigoths decide to combine their forces, something Atauf had envisioned years earlier. They confront the Hunnic army at Chalons, in present-day France. The Roman soldiers manage to gain control of a critical ridge and, with the advantage of high ground, the combined armies inflict a bloody defeat on the Huns. Attila is forced to retreat, and the loss damages his reputation as an invincible conqueror. Two years later, he mysteriously dies at his own wedding, a serious setback for his military.

In 454, a coalition of Germanic armies, without Roman help, defeats the Huns at the Battle of Nedao, and the Hunnic nation begins to be dismantled. A major threat to Europe and the empire has been vanquished, but the Roman army's assisted triumph at Chalons will be its last major victory in the west.[510] The defeat of the Huns cannot save the Western Empire.

*****

While the battles rage for control of the west, the Church continues to struggle with its own conflicts. At the time of the Battle of Chalons, the Fourth Ecumenical Council is meeting in the eastern city of Chalcedon (modern Kadikoy, Turkey) to try to resolve the disputes dividing the Church over the person and nature of Christ. The view of the Monophysites, that Christ has only a divine nature, is rejected as is the view of the Nestorians that the divine and human natures are completely separated.

The Council then affirms that Jesus is of one substance with the Father in agreement with the Nicene Creed. It further confesses that Jesus Christ is:

---

[509] Bainton, *Christianity*, 120–23.
[510] Kennedy Hickman, "Attila the Hun at the Battle of Chalons," *ThoughtCo.*, February 23, 2018, https://www.thoughtco.com/hunnic-invasions-battle-of-chalons-2360875.

> [T]o be acknowledged in two natures, without confu-
> sion, without change, without division, without separation;
> the distinction of natures being in no way abolished because
> of the union, but rather the characteristic property of each
> nature being preserved and concurring into one person and
> one subsistence (hypostasis), not as if Christ were parted or
> divided into two persons, but one and the same Son and
> only-begotten God, Word, Lord, Jesus Christ.[511]

Although often criticized,[512] the Chalcedonian Definition is still seen as
setting the parameters for discussing the humanity and deity of the Messiah.
In summary, it confesses that Jesus Christ is *one* person who is *both* divine *and*
human."[513] The Personhood of Jesus, the God-Man, is simply beyond complete
comprehension for finite human beings.

Developments have also been taking place in the government of the
Church. The bishops in the larger cities are seen as deserving more prestige and
become known as patriarchs. And although there is resistance from the bishops
of Antioch, Alexandria, and Constantinople, it is gradually accepted that the
Patriarch of Rome has the most authority of these Archbishops. Even after the
sacking of Rome, the ruling order remains in the Holy City and the Roman
Pope is still acknowledged as the leader of the Church.[514] During these years,
popes are appointed by their predecessors or secular rulers. It is not until 1059
that Pope Nicholas II is able to institute the election of popes by senior bishops,
eventually known as the College of Cardinals.

*****

In 455, the Vandals, who now control Spain and North Africa, sail across
the Mediterranean and plunder Rome. The Romans offer no serious resistance,

---

[511] English translation as quoted in, Frances M. Young, *The Making of the Creeds* (Philadelphia: Trinity Press, 1991), 77.

[512] "The Definition of the Council of Chalcedon (451 AD)," *The Puritan Board*, accessed December 24, 2018, http://files.puritanboard.com/confessions/chalcedon.htm.

[513] Paul Kroll, "The Council Of Chalcedon And The 'Two Natures' Controversy, *Grace Communion International*, accessed December 24, 2018, https://www.gci.org/articles/the-council-of-chalcedon-and-the-two-natures-controversy/.

[514] Kuiper, *The Church*, 39–42.

and this second sacking does not result in many deaths. The Vandals spend two weeks stripping the city of its remaining treasure before sailing back across the Mediterranean with their stolen bounty.[515]

Eventually, the barbarians conquer every province of the Western Empire: Italy, Spain, Gaul, the Netherlands, Britain, and North Africa. In 476, Odoacer, a German commander in the Roman army leads his tribesmen in a revolt, deposes and exiles the last Roman Emperor, Romulus Augustus, and declares himself king.[516] The fall of Rome and the Western Empire is complete; the barbarians have brought Ancient History to an end and are ushering in the Middle Ages.[517]

*****

The Western Empire has fallen to the barbarians, but amid the ruins, the Church, although weakened, remains standing. Many Christians have suffered and died during the attacks on the West, but the community is still able to function. With a stable governing structure of bishops, an established body of doctrine, and considerable resources accumulated while it was protected by the state, the Church is still capable of proclaiming Christ to the barbarians who have caused all the devastation. It helps that some of the invaders have an acquaintance with Christianity and have respect for the bishop of Rome, but more than anything else, the Church has millions of believers who still take care of their families and help others, almost unknowingly sustaining the kingdom of God by their acts of faith during these desperate times. Earthly kingdoms come and go, but God's kingdom is forever (Dan. 7:13–14).

But now the Church will be carrying out its mission under drastically different conditions. From its beginning, the Church had ministered under the rule of the Roman empire. Although some of the emperors had severely persecuted the Church, the government had maintained a functioning state. The Apostle Paul and later missionaries could travel on Roman roads and ships,

[515] Joshua J. Mark, "Vandals," *Ancient History Encyclopedia*, November 25, 2014, https://www.ancient.eu/Vandals/ Evan Andrews, "6 Infamous Sacks of Rome," August 24, 2015, www.history.com/news/6-infamous-sacks-of-rome.

[516] Editors, Encyclopaedia, "Odoacer," *Encyclopaedia*, accessed December 24, 2018, https://britannica.com/biography/Odoacer.

[517] The Middle Ages are generally defined as the period from the fall of Rome in 476 to the beginning of the Renaissance in the 13th century.

and the people they were seeking to convert were "civilized;" they could read, write, and converse in theological thought. But now the empire is gone, and in its place is a disarray of new barbaric kingdoms.[518]

A number of these new domains, like the Anglo-Saxons in Britain and the Franks in Gaul, are heathen territories—they refuse to acknowledge the God of the Bible. Other heathen tribes live in lands that are wild, uncultivated, and without roads. All these nations and tribes are "barbarous, ignorant, uneducated, and uncultured."[519] As the Middle Ages begin, the Church has the challenge of not only evangelizing but educating the new rulers and their subjects.

*****

It is still the premodern age and the different barbarian tribes have multiple gods, usually with a chief god—Woden for the Anglo—Saxons, Odin for the Scandinavians, Thor for the northern peoples, etc. As during its early ministry, the Church does not have to convince the barbarians that a god or gods exist. The Church must again proclaim the one true God of the Bible and then educate the barbarians so they can understand Him and His precepts.

The early Middle Ages, from 476 when the last Western emperor was deposed to 800, are sometimes called the Dark Ages. There is frequent warfare as the different tribes, and eventually, emerging countries battle for territory and power. Urban life virtually ceases to exist as the various groups of Goths, Vandals, Huns, Bulgars, Alani, Suebi, and Franks move into what had been the Western Empire; it is the era of the "distribution of peoples."[520]

The term Dark Ages is applied to this period because information is limited about these centuries and what is known seems to indicate a time of intellectual darkness and barbarity.[521]

The Eastern or Byzantium Empire[522] (the Balkan Peninsula, Asia Minor, Syria, Palestine, and Egypt) with its capital at Constantinople has survived. Although there are still some pagans in the Eastern Empire, the emperors and

---

[518] Kuiper, *The Church*, 50–53.

[519] Ibid., 53.

[520] Ibid., 51.

[521] Editors, Encyclopaedia, "Migration period," *Encyclopaedia*, accessed December 24, 2018, https://www.britannica.com/event/Dark-Ages.

[522] The Eastern Empire is often called the Byzantine Empire after the ancient city of Byzantium where Constantine built his eastern capital of Constantinople.

the great majority of the citizens are Christians, at least in name. They are also advanced in the arts and human thought. During these tumultuous times, the east, especially Constantinople, maintains treasures of civilization, works of art, copies of the Scriptures, and other significant books.

In the fallen West, the monks in their monasteries perform a similar service. When the barbarians invaded the Empire, they destroyed many but not all of the books. Educated men who survive continue to write, and they pass on much of the learning of the ancient world. But the printing press has not yet been invented so the only way to duplicate manuscripts, whether old or new, is through hand-copying. The monks, those who can read and write, take on this task and render an invaluable service to civilization.

During this period, for almost three hundred years, few barbarians take an interest in education. But when the new nations are ready for learning, through the patient and persistent work of the monks, there will be books.[523]

The Church begins its ministry to the barbarians in what can only be considered desperate times in the West. But by the year 1,000, some five centuries after the fall of Rome, in an amazing achievement attained only through the mercy and providence of God, the Church has Christianized all the barbaric nations of Europe. One by one, beginning with Ireland, the new countries begin to acknowledge the God of the Bible.[524] God's kingdom continues to advance.

*****

Ireland had begun turning to Christianity before the fall of Rome. In the early fifth century, the Irish had enslaved a young man from Britain who eventually escaped back to his homeland. He joined a monastery for training but was a slow learner and underwent fourteen years of instruction before he returned to Ireland with a papal authorization, the status of a bishop, and a dream to evangelize the people who had enslaved him. The young man's name was Patrick; he became "the Apostle of Ireland" and eventually, Saint Patrick.

By the time of his death in 461, the Church was firmly established in the Emerald Isle. Monasteries were constructed and became famous for their level

---

[523] Kuiper, *The Church*, 54.

[524] The following section on the conversion of the barbarians relies primarily on the more in-depth discussion of this period in Kuiper, *The Church*, 53–58.

of learning and their missionary zeal.[525] Thomas Cahill has written about the important role the Irish monks played in helping to save civilization during the Dark Ages.[526]

*****

The monasteries begin to play a crucial role in propagating the faith not only in Ireland but throughout Europe. Saint Benedict (480–547), after living as a hermit, had established a monastic community in Italy which became the model for western monasticism after the fall of Rome. He devised an order that was ascetic but livable; he encouraged no severe physical disciplines and added the principle of stability to the vows of poverty, chastity, and obedience. The monks were not allowed to be either "hermits or holy vagabonds"[527] but instead lived in community with strict discipline.

The number of monasteries increases, and they become self-sustaining with their own gardens, wells, and coops for poultry and rabbits. In the early days, the monks supply the labor and exist on simple meals of bread, wine, and vegetables with meat being reserved for the sick. Bathing is considered a luxury and is discouraged. In addition to their outdoor work, the monks engage in study, meditation, and the communal chanting of prayers. The life is austere but does not approach the severe asceticism of the hermits who had followed Saint Anthony into the desert.

The purpose of the monasteries had been to provide separation from society to allow full-time pursuit of the religious life, but they soon evolve into a larger role. The barbarians had initially viewed the monks with some disbelief and contempt, but when the monks clear land and become self-sustaining communities in the wilderness territories, the local tribes begin to settle around them as they see the benefits of an orderly society. The monasteries become outposts of civilization spreading Christian influence to the barbarians surrounding them.[528]

*****

---

[525] Bainton, *Christianity*, 128; Kuiper, *The Church*, 55.

[526] Thomas Cahill, *How the Irish Saved Civilization*, (New York: Anchor Books, paperback, 1996).

[527] Bainton, *Christianity*, 129.

[528] Ibid., 129–131.

The Franks in Gaul, under the leadership of King Clovis, are the first Germanic tribe to adopt Christianity after the fall of the Empire.[529] In a story similar to Constantine's conversion, Clovis, desperate in the heat of battle with another barbarian tribe, thinks he sees the sign of the cross in the sky. After the Franks win the battle, Clovis and three thousand of his soldiers are baptized on Christmas day in 496. We should not imagine that these hardened fighters are convicted by a deep sense of sin and fully understand their need for a Savior. They want a God who rules and defends them, but this is an important first step in Christianizing the Franks. Prior to this large-scale conversion, people had been accepting Christianity individually or as families, but now entire tribes will begin to adopt the faith when their kings become Christians.[530]

The other Germanic tribes, like the Goths and the Vandals, who had adopted Christianity a century before the fall of Rome,[531] were essentially heretics, Arians who denied the divinity of Jesus. In an outcome important for the future of the Church, the Franks accept the orthodox understanding of the faith and adopt the Nicene Creed.

*****

About 560, an Irish monk named Columba establishes a monastery on the island of Iona off the west coast of Scotland. He and several companions cross over to the mainland and do missionary work; their efforts are successful and the Church is planted among the Scots. Other Irish monks bring the gospel to the Germans east of the Rhine. Despite the difficult circumstances following the fall of Rome, the gospel and God's kingdom are moving forward.

In 590, Gregory becomes the first monk to become Pope. Seven years later, he sends forty-one monks to England, which was known as Britain before its conquest by the Angles and Saxons in the fifth century when it became *Angleland* or *England*. The Angles and Saxons are fierce heathens who had erased Christianity in their kingdom. It takes more than a hundred years, but Christianity is eventually reestablished, and heathenism is driven out of England.

---

[529] After Clovis establishes his reign, Gaul will be called France.
[530] Kuiper, *The Church*, 54–55; also see Steven Kreis, "The Conversion of Clovis," *The History Guide*, revised February 28, 2006, http://www.historyguide.org/ancient/clovis.html.
[531] See p. 280, n. 490.

Gregory is the first pope to assume broad political powers. He begins to fill the void left by the collapse of the Empire. The Church has properties and resources that were not destroyed by the barbarians as well as ongoing income from tithes and donations. Gregory begins to appoint heads of cities, raise armies, and make peace treaties. The Church assumes the tasks of education, caring for the poor, and maintaining civil order. By assuming these responsibilities, the Church becomes a guiding power in European politics. Gregory, as the bishop of Rome, also strongly asserts his claim of authority over the entire Church. It is possible to criticize Gregory for undertaking roles that do not belong to the Church, but if he had not responded in these dire circumstances, the damage from the fall of the empire would have been much greater. In history, Pope Gregory—initially a humble monk—becomes Gregory the Great.[532]

*****

As the Church is making progress in Christianizing Europe, the Eastern Empire is still fighting for its life. It had managed to repel the Germanic tribes that advanced from the north and had even reconquered parts of Italy and North Africa. But in 627, Emperor Heraclius is waging a desperate war with Persia. He manages to defeat the Persian army in the Battle of Nineveh and reduces the danger from the east, but the security gained is short-lived. There is a greater threat building to the south in Arabia.[533]

The inhabitants of Arabia are descendants of Ishmael, son of Abraham and half-brother of Isaac. God had told Ishmael's mother, Hagar, before he was born that he would be a wild donkey of a man and that his hand would be against everyone and that everyone's hand would be against him (Gen. 16:12; p. 47). When Sarah remained barren, Abraham had asked God to let Ishmael be the son of the promise; God had said no but had promised to make Ishmael a great nation (Gen. 17:19–20; p. 48). Both of those prophecies are now coming to fulfillment with Ishmael's descendants.

The Arabians or Arabs had been polytheists, worshipping idols and many gods, until a man named Mohammad arises. Mohammad (570–632) is an illiterate shepherd and trader who in his commercial travels comes into contact with Jews and Christians and their religious beliefs. At the age of forty,

---

[532] Kuiper, *The Church*, 55–58.
[533] Ibid, 61–62.

he claims that the Angel Gabriel has dictated a book called the Koran to him. Mohammad has several revelations over time, but since he cannot write, it is not clear how or with what accuracy the book came to be transcribed. The Koran introduces Allah as the only god, and Mohammad and his followers establish a new monotheistic religion in Arabia called Islam (surrender or submission in Arabic). The followers of Islam are called Muslims, and they sum up their religion with the saying, "Allah is great, and Mohammad is his prophet."

Mohammad uses force to gain absolute power in Arabia and takes many wives and concubines, one of them a little girl named Aisha who is still playing with her dolls. Islamic records show that Mohammad married Aisha when she was six years old and consummated the marriage when she was nine.[534] Some Islamic countries still allow Muslim men to follow Mohammad's example and take child brides as revealed in CNN's horrifying report from Yemen in 2010.[535]

Muslim fighters of the Islamic State in Syria (ISIS) and Boko Haram in Nigeria captured and sexually enslaved thousands of women and young girls, many of them Yazidis and Christians.[536] Feminists in the United States condemn the concept of male headship in traditional marriages[537] but are silent about the oppression and abuse of women and young girls by Muslim men.[538]

Mohammad dies in 632, but his influence and the religion of Islam continue. Soon after his death, a horde of fierce horsemen sweep out of Arabia and begin to spread their religion by force. By 636, the Muslims control Syria and Palestine, including Jerusalem. They take the city of Alexandria in 642 and Mesopotamia four years later. In 651, they conquer Persia, which had been weakened by its battles with the Eastern Empire, and advance into India. From 674–678, the Arabs besiege Constantinople, but with its strong walls and water

---

[534] Sam Shamoun, "An Examination of Mohammad's Marriage to a Prepubescent Girl And Its Moral Implications," https://www.answering-islam.org/Shamoun/prepubescent.htm

[535] Mohammed Jamjoom, "Yemeni child bride dies of internal bleeding," *CNN*, April 9, 2010, https://edition.cnn.com/2010/WORLD/meast/04/09/yemen.child.bride.death/index.html.

[536] Vladimir Duthiers, Faith Karimi, and Greg Botelho, "Boko Haram: Why Terror Group Kidnaps Schoolgirls, and What Happens Next," *CNN*, May 2, 2014, http://www.cnn.com/2014/04/24/world/africa/nigeria-kidnapping-answers/index.html.

[537] "Feminist Perspectives on Reproduction and the Family," *Stanford Encyclopedia of Philosophy*, November 6, 2004, revised October 21, 2013, https://plato.stanford.edu/entries/feminism-family/.

[538] Pamela Geller, "Lone Feminist Calls Out Islamic Misogyny," *WND*, July 9, 2013, www.wnd.com/2013/07/lone-feminist-calls-out-islamic-misogyny/.

on three sides, the Muslim army and navy meet a resistance that they cannot overcome. Constantine's great walled city turns back the Arabs.

After losing a reported 30,000 men, the Arabs withdraw to their home-land. This is a critical military victory in world history because it keeps the Muslims from sweeping into a fragmented Europe from the east and conquer-ing the continent for Islam. But the Arab marauders continue to advance into Africa, take the city of Carthage in 697, and soon control all of North Africa. The city of Constantinople and its military forces are all that remain of the once-proud Roman empire.[539]

In 711, fourteen years after the fall of Carthage, the Arabian forces that have conquered North Africa use their navy to cross the Strait of Gibraltar and begin advancing north through Spain. As these Muslim forces in the west are solidifying their control of the Iberian Peninsula, the Muslim forces in the east have reorganized and again attack Constantinople. After two years of fighting, in 718, the Arabs are again forced to withdraw after suffering devastating losses to their army and navy. It is estimated that of 210,000 Muslim soldiers and sailors, only 30,000 returned to Arabia. Only five of their 2,000 naval vessels survived.[540]

The Christian forces had developed "Greek fire," a flammable substance that could be propelled onto the Muslims' wooden ships. For the second time in forty years, Constantinople has saved Europe from an Arab invasion from the east which its developing and divided countries could not have countered.

After twenty years of fighting in Spain, the Arabs have solidified their control and cross the Pyrenees Mountain range into France. At the beginning of 732, the Muslims are again poised to invade Europe but this time from the west. They pose a twofold threat, combining religious and military power. Islam overthrows political states and then offers the conquered people (or forces on them) a new religious system.[541]

---

[539] Kuiper, *The Church*, 62–63; also see "The Siege of Constantinople," *Byzantine Military*, Oct. 4, 2011, http://byzantinemilitary.blogspot.com/2011/10/siege-of-constantinople.html.

[540] "Second Arab Siege of Constantinople in 717–718," *Weapons and Warfare*, October 15, 2015, https://weaponsandwarfare.com/2020/06/01/second-arab-siege-of-constantinople-in-717–718/.

[541] Curtis, Lang, and Peterson, *100 Events*, 63.

At this point, the Franks, who two centuries earlier had converted to orthodox Christianity under the rule of Clovis,[542] are the only significant barrier to a Muslim takeover of France and then all of Europe. Their leader, Charles, sends out a call for every man in all the Frankish lands to come to his aid. The people understand the great danger facing them, and even the German tribes across the Rhine respond. When the Muslims advance across the plain of Tours in west-central France, there is a great army of Christian soldiers massed to meet them.

The two armies face each other for seven days before the battle begins. Charles has formed his forces into a large square on wooded, elevated ground that will hinder the Arab cavalry. The Arabs attack and make charge after charge, but they have to ride uphill to reach the Frankish foot soldiers waiting in close ranks with shields, swords, and spears. Both sides suffer losses, but the Franks stand firm; each assault is repulsed, and the attacks end with nightfall. The Arab losses are estimated to be ten thousand casualties to less than a thousand for the Franks.

The next morning, the Muslim forces are not in sight. Fearing a ruse, the Franks send out search parties, but they find only piles of plunder which have been abandoned. The Arabs have retreated back to Spain behind the Pyrenees. Charles's troops have defeated the Arab cavalry, and he becomes known as Charles Martel—Charles the Hammer. The once barbarian Franks have saved Europe for Christianity. But in southeast Spain, it will be hundreds of years before the last Muslims are driven out.[543]

*****

Three times between 678 and 732, a disastrous military takeover of European civilization by Islam was repelled by heroic Christian fighters. Today, it is amazing to watch European politicians assist Muslims in a takeover of European countries through immigration. Europeans and their current leaders seem to have no understanding of history and the religion of Islam, even after suffering many horrendous terrorist attacks. When we reach the study of current postmodern thought, we will see that there is a widespread rejection of

[542] See p. 291.
[543] Kuiper, *The Church*, 64–65; also see William Mclaughjin, "AD 732 Battle of Tours," *War History Online*, February 25, 2018, https://www.warhistoryonline.com/medieval/battle-of-tours-charles-martel.html.

objective truth; as a result, all religions are deemed equally valid, and therefore, Islam must not be discriminated against, no matter what its adherents believe or do. It is political correctness run mad. Postmodern thought can only lead to the demise of those nations who adopt it as a governing philosophy.

Islam is more than just a religion. It is a theocratic structure of government operating through the imposition of Sharia law, a religious legal system which controls all aspects of personal and public life—by force, if necessary. It is not a system that can live at peace within democratic societies because the ultimate goal for Muslims must be the imposition of Sharia law over the nation in which they live; otherwise, they are not being true to Islam.

Paul tells Christians to be subject to their governing authorities (Rom. 13:1). Christians are to obey their rulers as long as these leaders do not compel them to sin. In a democratic republic such as the United States, Christians have a right to influence public policy, but their faith does not require or recommend that they establish a theocratic government. For Muslims, obeying a law other than Sharia can only be a temporary tactic until they have the power to impose their system on everyone. Their religion and their government cannot be separated. This is why Muslims in Europe have not assimilated but remain congregated together while attempting to establish areas under Sharia law.

On March 1, 2018, German Chancellor Angela Merkel admitted that there are "no-go" zones in Germany where outsiders and even police officers are afraid to go. Police Union Chief Rainer Wendt said that mass immigration has made it impossible to enforce German law in these areas and that they could end up being ruled by Sharia law.[544] It remains to be seen if the European people have the courage, religious foundation, or common sense to resist the current invasion. If not, the various countries will gradually commit national suicide.

Many politicians and citizens in the United States have similar postmodern views and demand that there be no restrictions on immigration, even though the leaders of ISIS as well as other Muslim leaders openly proclaim they will infiltrate refugee and immigrant populations with fighters who will cause death and chaos. Biden's open border policy with Mexico has led to an influx of 5 million illegal aliens and a huge increase in dangerous drugs and sex traf-

---

[544] Rebecca Perring, "Angela Merkel admits German NO-GO zones are 'a REALITY'," *Sunday Express*, March 1, 2018, https://www.express.co.uk/news/world/925727/ Angela-Merkel-Germany-latest-news-no-go-zone-reality-refugee-crisis.

ficking. Democrats have said they intend to make voting citizens of these new arrivals as soon as possible because it will give their party permanent political power. National ethics depend on theological convictions, which are now sadly lacking in European countries and the United States.

We are to take the gospel to every tribe and nation and that includes Muslims. We should treat each individual as a potential believer, but we must not close our eyes to the threat that Islam poses to Christianity and Western civilization.

*****

Charles the Hammer, and his army have turned back the Muslims at Tours in 732, but the Christian losses to Islam over the prior century are immense. Many Christians have been killed and many churches destroyed. The provinces of Syria, Palestine, Egypt, and North Africa had been the home of many flourishing Christian churches, but now those churches have been destroyed, and the surviving believers are under the thumb of Islam. The Arabs have raised a Muslim barrier against Christianity and have deprived the Church of mission fields among many heathen nations. Millions in India will become Muslims and Persia will become almost entirely Islamic. "Palestine had been the cradle of the Church,"[545] but now Jerusalem and Bethlehem are under the rule of Arabic Muslims. In North Africa, the Church will be completely wiped out for hundreds of years.

*****

After the Franks' defeat of the Arabs, the Church continues to evangelize in Europe. The English become great missionaries after the nation's conversion, and they cross the channel and labor among the barbarian tribes on the continent. An English monk named Willibrord (658–739) succeeds in evangelizing the Netherlands despite opposition from the Frisians, a hostile Germanic tribe. Boniface (675–754), a Benedictine monk, crosses the Rhine, wins many converts, and helps establish monasteries. His work is so successful that he becomes known as the Apostle of Germany. His missionary work continues for decades until a group of Frisians murders him and fifty-three of his companions during

---

[545] Kuiper, *The Church*, 66.

a baptism. But this vicious attack does not stop the influence of Boniface or the advancement of the gospel among the German tribes.[546]

*****

By the middle of the eighth century, with Europe divided under numerous rulers, the influence and power of the papacy has increased, but neither the pope nor the kings have been able to restore order in a divided and crime-ridden Europe. Murder and robbery are common, and ignorance and rudeness are the order of the day. Christians are in peril from the general lawlessness, and the papacy itself is threatened by the Lombards (Longbeards), a Germanic people who rule Northern Italy and have seized the city of Ravenna and the territories north of Rome. In 753, Pope Stephen II travels over the Alps, the first pope to do so, in an effort to obtain aid from the Frankish king, Pepin III, son of Charles the Hammer. Pope Stephen anoints Pepin and his two sons as king and heirs of the crown, demonstrating his support for the family's reign over France.

Pepin and his army then accompany the pope as he makes his way back to Italy. When they reach the Alps, they are confronted by the Lombard army. In a fierce mountain battle, Pepin's troops rout the Lombards. Their king, Aistuff, flees back to his capital city, Pavia, where he promises to relinquish Ravenna and the adjoining lands; Pepin "donates" this territory to the papacy. In addition to his ecclesiastical office, the pope now becomes a temporal ruler with "States of the Church."[547] The immediate threat to the papacy has been thwarted, but the Lombards remain a dangerous adversary in northern Italy.

*****

When Pepin dies in 768, his two sons, Charles and Carloman, divide the kingdom of the Franks. A possible civil war between the two is averted when Carloman dies in 771. Charles ignores Carloman's heirs and takes control of the entire nation.

---

[546] Kuiper, *The Church*, 56–57; Consuela Aherne, "Saint Boniface," *Encyclopedia*, accessed January 7, 2023 www.britannica.com/biography/Saint-Boniface.

[547] Kuiper, *The Church*, 70–71; Curtis, Lang, and Peterson, *100 Events*, 64–65; Eleanor Shipley Duckett, "Pippin III," *Encyclopaedia Britannica*, updated January 11, 2019, https://www.britannica.com/biography/Pippin-III.

A tall imposing figure physically, Charles has a sharp intellect, a strong will, and spiritual sensibility. By Frankish tradition, he is a warrior king who is expected to lead his followers in wars that produce rewards for his countrymen. Charles lives up to all the expectations; he engages in military campaigns almost his entire life and conquers much of Europe.

Charles begins by defeating the Lombards, ending their kingdom, and then pushes the Muslims in Spain back from the Pyrenees to the Ebro River. He eventually rules the northern half of Italy, the northeast corner of Spain, all of France, Belgium, the Netherlands, and a large part of Germany and Austria. But he is more than a great military leader. Charles makes wise laws and then enforces them, ending the widespread lawlessness and establishing security in his realm.

Although he is barely literate, Charles thinks highly of education, starts a school in his palace, and decrees that each monastery should have a school for instructing anyone who can learn. He has five wives in sequence, several concubines, and eighteen children whose interests he watches over carefully. His favorite reading is Augustine's *The City of God*, and he believes that his empire is the kingdom of God upon the earth.

In the year 800, Charles kneels in Saint Peter's Church in Rome. and Pope Leo III places the imperial crown on his head, making Charles the emperor of Christendom, the Holy Roman Empire. It must seem appropriate to the pope because Charles stands for the law, order, and civilization once represented by the Roman empire. Charles becomes known as Charlemagne, French for Charles the Great. But his crowning by the pope also seems to trouble Charles—if the pope can make him emperor, he can also remove this power. In 813, when Charlemagne crowns his son, Louis, as King of Aquitaine (southwestern France), he presides over the ceremony himself and does not invite the pope.[548]

When Charlemagne dies in 814, there are three great political kingdoms in the world, the Muslim empire, the remains of the weakened Eastern Empire in Constantinople, and Charlemagne's empire, which represents the brightest future for humanity. However, when Louis succeeds his father, the empire begins to fragment, and the popes again gain power in Europe. "But

---

[548] Kuiper, *The Church*, 71–74; Mr. Dowling, "Charlemagne and the Holy Roman Empire," *Browse Through History*, accessed December 24, 2018, www.mrdowling.com/703-charlemagne.html.

Charlemagne had bequeathed the West an alluring vision: a Christian ruler with supreme authority throughout his domain."[549] The stage is set for future struggles between popes and kings who think they should be that Christian ruler.[550]

*****

Charlemagne had done a great deal to reestablish order in Europe and aid the Church. With his rule, the period called the Dark Ages comes to an end. But despite what Charlemagne believed, his empire was not the kingdom of God. The true kingdom of God was within his political kingdom, and that true kingdom will survive and continue to advance and grow, even as popes and kings struggle to establish their own kingdoms over the coming centuries.

*****

Charlemagne's empire, which had begun to decline under the rule of his son, Louis, falls apart under the rule of his three grandsons. They fight over the empire and eventually, in 843, divide their grandfather's realm. But they emerge too weak to protect the people in their territories from the raids of Slav and Hungarian horsemen from the east and the wild Norsemen from Scandinavia who sail south and then up the European rivers on fast ships. The inability to protect against these raiders leads to a new form of government. The kings begin to divide their lands among their leading warriors on the condition that they provide military aid when necessary. These new princes (lords) then divide their estates (manors or fiefs)[551] among lesser vassals (knights) who then grant their land to lesser tenants, on down to the serfs who do the labor, and are bound to the land of their lord who is expected to protect them. This political and economic system is called feudalism and depends on land ownership and personal loyalty to function. This decentralization means that the kings soon become just chief lords among many. Instead of having one strong

---

[549] Curtis, Lang, and Peterson, *100 Events*, 66.

[550] The following section is condensed from Kuiper, *The Church*, 71–74, Curtis, Lang, and Peterson, *100 Events*, 64–66, and Richard E. Sullivan, Charlemagne, *Encyclopaedia Britannica*, updated January 24, 2019, https://www.britannica.com/biography/Charlemagne.

[551] The central administrative location would be the lord's home, a fortified manor house or a castle for security.

central government as under Charlemagne, Europe is split into many smaller principalities under leaders who often fight each other.

The Church had become a significant landowner when it received the Lombard territories from King Pepin. It had obtained other properties through the years when wealthy people donated land to churches and monasteries. This ownership eventually brings the Church into the feudal system, and the more powerful lords begin to see the popes as their vassals.[552]

*****

With Charlemagne's empire devolving into numerous small domains, the next few centuries are unsettled times for Christians in Europe. Since nearly all the lords and their citizens claim to be Christians, in the ongoing battles for territory and supremacy, Christians fight Christians. The Church tries to gain control of this internecine warfare by issuing the Truce of God, which restricts when battles can be fought, and the Peace of God, which limits combatants with nuns, priests, and farmers being protected. When princes disregard these restrictions, the bishops raise armies to punish them. But then the armies of the Church become disorderly and ravage parts of the country, and the kings raise armies to suppress the Church's armies.[553]

As this struggle for power goes on, Pope Nicholas I (858–867) declares that the Church is superior to all earthly governments. Although he cannot fully enforce his claim, he lays the foundation for future popes who will try to exercise temporal power.

Europe has become a region of Christendom, an area where Christianity prevails, but the Christians fight each other, and it is not clear if popes or kings should rule. The local lords have different views about this matter, almost always predicated upon what most advances their own personal wealth and power. It soon becomes apparent that Christendom is not the same as the kingdom of God.

*****

---

[552] Kuiper, *The Church*, 80–82.
[553] Bainton, *Christianity*, 164–165.

The Italian lords continually battle for supremacy and the right to control the election of the pope for their own benefit, sometimes resulting in the appointment of utterly decadent men to the highest office in the Church. Popes are involved in crimes including bribery, murder, and most commonly, gross sexual immorality—Sergius III (904–911), John X (914–928), and John XII (955–964) are three of the worst. From 891 to 955, there are no less than twenty popes. Pope Benedict IX is named pope on three different occasions between 1032 and 1048. He finally sells the office to Gregory VI for one thousand pounds of silver and then refuses to vacate his position. The former bishop of Sabina, Sylvester III, also claims the office during this time, so there are three popes at once. It is a shameful era for the papacy.

The claim of the Roman Catholic Church that there is an unbroken line of popes beginning with Saint Peter and that they are infallible in their official proclamations should have been laid to rest and deeply buried during these centuries.[554] The papacy supposedly reigns over spiritual Christendom, but it does not appear to be part of the kingdom of God.

*****

Historians necessarily focus on the principal figures and decisive events of the past in trying to understand how and why we have reached the circumstances under which we presently live. It is important to realize that while everyone may be affected by the aftermaths, only a small number of people play significant roles in history-changing events.

During feudalism in the Middle Ages, about 90 percent of the people in Western Europe were serfs or peasants. A peasant village would have perhaps ten to sixty families who worked for their lord. About half their time was spent tending the lord's needs—working his fields, cutting timber, hauling water, spinning and weaving clothing, repairing buildings, and waiting on his household. In time of war, the able-bodied men would have to fight in the lord's army.

Peasant houses of wood or wicker daubed with mud were dark and dank with only tiny open windows and a small hole in the roof so smoke could escape from a cooking fire on the earthen floor. Furniture was usually limited

---

[554] Kuiper, *The Church*, 81–85; www.granddesignexposed.com/indexmystery/12chap/papa. html, accessed November 8, 2022.

to a plank table, stools, and perhaps a chest. Beds were made of leaves and straw, and the peasants often slept in their work clothes with animal skins for cover. Although some towns had public baths, bathing for serfs in the winter was often limited to washing from wooden barrels or basins. Toilets were chamber pots often emptied somewhere near the peasant's house. Serf families usually had garden plots, and any domesticated animals were sheltered in the owner's home.

The serfs were required to pay taxes to their lord in money or produce and also had to pay a tithe of their produce to the manor church.[555] Plagues,[556] famines, and warfare were common while doctors and medicines were rare. Although hard data is scarce, it is estimated that 30 percent of peasant children died before the age of five, and only a few adults made it into their sixties.[557]

Peasant children worked; they did not go to school. Among the estimated 5 percent of the people who could read and write in medieval Europe, there were virtually no serfs; usually, only sons from rich families went to school. Serfs taught their children how to do the work of the manor, and peasant craftsmen passed on their skills to their sons. Peasant marriages were usually arranged by parents.

As grim as peasant life was, serfs went to the village church on Sundays and observed many holy days when they did not work. They took part in church festivals, watched jugglers and plays, and engaged in wrestling, cockfights, and dancing.[558] Historians cannot tell us the name of the serf who loved his wife and children, was loyal to his prince, and confessed his sins to the

---

[555] Simon Newman, "Peasant Life in the Middle Ages," *The Finer Times*, accessed May 30,219, www.thefinertimes.com/Ancient-History/the-harsh-life-of-peasants-in-medieval-times. html; "The Middle Ages—Peasants," *Western Reserve Public Media*, accessed December 24, 2018, http://westernreservepublicmedia.org/middleages/feud_peasants.htm.

[556] The plague of the "Black Death," spread through airborne transmission but also from the fleas of infected rats, originated in central Asia and reached Europe aboard trading ships in 1347. Between 1347 and 1351, the disease killed an estimated 20 million people, a third of the population of the continent. See Editors, Encyclopaedia, "Black Death," *Encyclopaedia*, updated January 17, 2019, https://britannica.com/event/Black-death.

[557] Sarah Woodbury, "Life Expectancy in the Middle Ages," *Sarah Woodbury (blog)*, March 11, 2014, www.sarahwoodbury.com/life-expectancy-in-the-middle-ages/.

[558] "Peasants," *International*, http://history-world.org/peasant.htm.

manor priest. But it seems the kingdom of God was more likely to be found in the dank peasant homes than in the palaces of the popes and kings.

*****

Pope Leo IX (1049–1054) sees the need for reform in the Church and begins to make changes. The chief emissaries of the papacy are still Roman descendants and belong to the ruling families who have been corrupting the office of the pope. Leo chooses new legates from various areas of the Church who support his desire to institute reforms. He travels through France and Germany enforcing papal authority. He forbids the priests to practice simony, the buying and selling of their offices.[559] In a misguided attempt to enforce sexual purity, he forbids priests to marry.[560] He insists that church offices should be appointed by the clergy and the people rather than temporal rulers. And, finally, Leo insists that the Eastern churches still existing in southern Italy are under his rule. This provokes an angry reaction from Michael Cerularius, the patriarch of Constantinople—he closes the Latin churches in Constantinople and raises serious dogmatic charges against Leo concerning the rite of Holy Communion. This causes a crisis in an already divided Church.

For many years, the east had been growing apart from the west and the rule of the pope in Rome. What had been a single Church has gradually become two distinct entities.[561] The initial minor disagreements between Rome and Constantinople have grown into significant differences. The east uses Greek as its language whereas the west uses Latin, the language in which its theologians write. The form of worship differs in how the mass is celebrated, down to the bread used in Communion. Clergy in the east can marry and wear beards; in the west, priests are to remain celibate and be clean-shaven. Theologically,

---

[559] The term *simony* is derived from Simon the Sorcerer who tried to purchase the power of the Holy Spirit from the apostles (Acts 8:18–19).

[560] The first impetus for a celibate priesthood seems to have been the emphasis on asceticism in the third century (see pp. 277–278). The Council of Nicaea in 325 had refused to order celibacy for priests, but popes eventually began to enforce the concept, partly because of the problem of children inheriting Church property. Although these early efforts had limited success, after Pope Leo the Church tries to maintain a celibate priesthood. See "A Brief History of Celibacy in the Catholic Church," *Future Church*, accessed December 24, 2018, https://www.futurechurch.org/brief-history-of-celibacy-in-catholic-church.

[561] This section relies primarily on the summary of Curtis, Lang, and Peterson, *100 Events*, 70–71.

the east objects to the change in the Nicene Creed in 381, which added that the Holy Spirit proceeds "from the Son" as well as the Father. The east also never accepts the west's conception of purgatory.[562] A separation already exists between the two branches of the Church, but it is about to become official.

In response to Michael's accusations against him, Pope Leo sends delegates to Constantinople with a letter of excommunication, which they lay on the high altar of Saint Sophia Church. When Michael learns of this, he in turn excommunicates the pope and his emissaries.[563] The pope of Rome and the patriarch of Constantinople have declared each other unfit for fellowship with other Christians.[564] The breach between Rome and Constantinople, now formalized, is called the "Great Schism" and lasts, with only short interruptions, until the present day.

*****

The two distinct branches of the Church will now progress in different ways, affected not only by the above disagreements, but also by their geographic locations and ethnic backgrounds. The Eastern Church, even with the Balkans and Russia included in its realm,[565] remains Middle Eastern in character. However, the Western Church, while still influenced by its Roman heritage in Italy, has become Germanic in the rest of Europe due to the large-scale conversions of the barbarians. The Eastern or Greek Orthodox Church has

---

[562] Purgatory was supposedly an intermediate state after death in which saved sinners made full satisfaction for their sins before entering heaven. This unbiblical invention was used by the papacy to extort money from parishioners who could purchase "indulgences" from Church officials to shorten the time of suffering for friends and relatives in this state of purification. This papal conception denied the full satisfaction supplied for believers through the sufferings and death of Jesus Christ. But purgatory is still an official doctrine of the Roman Catholic Church. See *Catechism of the Catholic Church* (New York: Doubleday, 1995), 291.

[563] Excommunication is the most serious discipline of the Church and excludes the sinner from communion with the faithful.

[564] Michael's censure of Leo probably was not binding since Leo had died before it was issued, but the excommunications remained in place. Walter Ullmann, "Saint Leo IX," *Encyclopaedia Britannica*, accessed December 24, 2018, https://www.britannica.com/biography/Saint-Leo-IX.

[565] In the tenth century, the Russian ruler Prince Vladimir had chosen to embrace the Eastern Church. His envoys were impressed by the beauty of its rituals and the fact that its theology permitted the drinking of alcohol, which was important to the Russians. See "Vladimir the Great," *Wikipedia*, https://en.wikipedia.org/wiki/Vladimir_the_Great.

aged and become stagnant and exhausted after its confrontations with Islam, while the Western Church, with its new and unruly nations, is energetic and tumultuous. It is primarily through the Western Church that the kingdom of God now continues to advance.

*****

After the break between the east and the west, the struggle between the secular rulers and the Church for control of the papacy continues. The powerful lords not only appoint popes but lesser church officials, often based on who offers them the most financial gain. The Church has property, treasure, and ongoing donations; churchmen and secular rulers fight over who gets to control this wealth and power. Who gets to appoint or "invest" church offices is critical and the conflict becomes known as the "Investiture Controversy."

A powerful papal aide by the name of Hildebrand, who is popular with the people and supports Church reform, becomes Pope Gregory VII in 1073. In 1075, Pope Gregory forbids investiture by laymen. The king of Germany, Henry IV, counters by calling for a council of his bishop allies, who demand that Gregory step down from the office of Pope. Gregory responds by excommunicating Henry and adds, "I forbid anyone to obey him as king."[566]

Henry's reign, already in danger because of his oppression of the people, is now seriously imperiled. He decides that his best strategy is to repent, and he travels to the castle of Canossa, where Gregory has taken refuge. When Henry appears in the courtyard as a bareheaded and barefooted penitent, Gregory leaves him standing in the snow for three days before granting him absolution. Henry has lost the battle but saved his kingdom; the Church has won the battle but not the war. In 1084, Henry marches on Rome with his troops and installs Clement III as his pope, or "antipope." Henry is crowned emperor, and Pope Gregory flees to Salerno where he dies in 1085.

*****

While the Church has been struggling with the Investiture Controversy in the west, the Muslim Turks have displaced the weakened Arabs in the east, and now the Turks threaten Constantinople. The emperor of the east, Alexius

---

[566] Kuiper, *The Church*, 111.

I, had requested help from Pope Gregory, promising to end the "Great Schism" if Gregory came to his aid. Although he had wanted to personally lead an army to rescue Constantinople and end the Church's divide, Gregory had been too embroiled with the investiture dispute to organize an expedition to the Middle East. Constantinople had managed to survive, but when Urban II is named Pope in 1088, the Eastern Empire is still under Muslim threat and Christian sites in Syria and Palestine have been under Muslim control for over 450 years.

Upon assuming his office, Urban first tries to bring about reconciliation with Henry IV and Clement, his antipope.[567] Not surprisingly, they are not able to come to an agreement, but Urban continues Gregory's efforts to reform the Church and gains the support of the rulers of Italy, Sicily, and most importantly, France. In 1095, when Emperor Alexius I in Constantinople again calls for aid against the Turks, Urban preaches a fiery sermon at the Council of Clermont. He appeals for unity in the Church, and he denounces the Muslims and makes an impassioned entreaty for the Middle East, saying, "Tear that land from the wicked race and subject it to yourselves."[568]

The people are greatly stirred and begin to cry out *"Deus Vult! Deus Vult!* (God wills it!)."[569] Urban's powerful oratory inspires a military response, the First Crusade, and "God wills it!" becomes the Crusader battle cry.

*****

The passionate response to Urban's emotional plea surprises even him and is not tempered with realism and planning. Before regular armed forces can be gathered from different regions of Europe, a poorly organized band of knights and peasants, known as the "People's Crusade," sets off under the command of a popular preacher known as Peter the Hermit. His estimated 20,000 troops and pilgrims, including women and children, refuse to wait for the conventional armies. After they cross the Bosporus in early August of 1096, the Turks attack them while Peter is away soliciting aid and supplies. The peasant army

---

[567] Clement III reigns as an opposition pope against four "anti-imperial" popes until his death in 1100. The Church considers Clement an "antipope" and eventually Pope Paschal II (1099–1118) has Clement's body exhumed and thrown into the Tiber River. See "Antipope Clement III," *Infogalactic*, accessed December 24, 2018, https://infogalactic.com/info/Antipope_Clement_III.

[568] Curtis, Lang, and Peterson, *100 Events*, 73.

[569] Ibid., 73.

is slaughtered; survivors are given the choice of converting to Islam or dying. Those who convert are enslaved, never to be heard from again. Some of the peasants manage to escape and flee to Constantinople.[570]

Other Crusader forces gather in the Rhineland. As they advance through various towns, they begin to massacre Jews, causing a major crisis in Jewish-Christian relations. Throughout the time of the Crusades, there is zeal without knowledge and an overall lack of spiritual understanding.[571]

After the destruction of the "People's Crusade," four regular armies form in Europe and begin separate marches to the Holy Land. They gather outside Constantinople by early 1097 and meet with Emperor Alexius.[572] He insists that the commanders of the western armies swear allegiance to him and recognize his authority over any land they capture from the Turks. Three of the four generals refuse to comply, but despite these deteriorating relations, the four armies and their Byzantine allies capture Nicaea in 1097 and Antioch in 1098.

They besiege Jerusalem in June 1099 and capture the city by mid-July. When the Crusaders enter the city, they kill thousands of Muslim men, women, and children in a shameful slaughter that still enrages Muslims today. Many Jews who had remained in Jerusalem are also killed. Pope Urban dies shortly before the news reaches Rome that Jerusalem is under Christian control.[573]

Having completed their mission sooner than expected, many of the crusaders depart for home. Those that remain elect Godfrey Buillon as their leader and set up the Latin Kingdom of Jerusalem with the Crusader states of Jerusalem, Edessa, Antioch, and Tripoli. The soldiers move from offense to defense and build Crusader castles for security against the Muslims.[574]

*****

[570] Jones, *Christian History*, 72. Also see Austin Cline, "A Timeline of the First Crusade," *ThoughtCo.*, May 30, 2018, https://www.thoughtco.com/first-crusade-christianity-vs-Islam-4078432.

[571] "Crusades," History.com editors, *History*, June 7, 2010, https://www.history.com/topics/middle-ages/crusades

[572] The total number of troops is estimated to have been 30,000 to 35,000 men. "Four Crusade Armies Leave Europe," *WHP*, accessed December 24, 2018, https://worldhistoryproject.org/1096/8/four-crusade-armies-leave-europe.

[573] "Crusades" *History*, accessed February 2, 2019, www.history.com/topics/middle-ages/crusades.

[574] Curtis, Lang, and Peterson, *100 Events*, 74. A number of Crusader castles are still standing and can be seen online.

Although Pope Urban and the kings were united in supporting the first Crusade, the Investiture Controversy continues until 1122, when the combatants, weary from the constant struggles, reach a compromise known as the *Concordat of Worms*. According to the agreement, the popes will invest the bishops with the symbols of their spiritual office, while the emperors bestow upon them their feudal estates.

With this compromise, the secular rulers still have considerable influence over the operations of the Church. But gradually, as the monks exercise their freedom of election to ensure their monasteries are not taken over by outsiders, the papacy gains more control of the episcopacy. What is not settled is to what extent kings are subject to the authority of the pope or to what extent the pope is subject to the authority of the kings.[575]

*****

The knights and soldiers who return from the First Crusade bring back with them perfumes, silk tapestries, gems, and food items such as rice, spices, dates, and coffee.[576] With Christian control of Syria and Palestine, thousands of Europeans, especially businessmen and traders, begin traveling to Constantinople and other eastern cities. Through social and commercial interactions, these Westerners encounter societies that are more civilized and educated than those in their own emerging European countries. An already growing desire for culture and scholarship in the West is further stimulated, and universities begin to spring up in Italy, Germany, France, and England. Many of the barbarians who had become Christians want to understand not only the rich tradition of Western theology but also the philosophical ideas of the Greeks and the political concepts of the Romans.

The University of Bologna had been established in 1088; the University of Paris will be inaugurated in 1150, with the University of Oxford (1167) and others soon to follow. The renowned teachers of these schools, such as Anselm, Abelard, Peter the Lombard, Duns Scotus, and Thomas Aquinas are called Schoolmen, and their learning is known as Scholasticism, a mixture of theology

---

[575] Uta-Renate Blumenthal, "Investiture Controversy," *Encyclopaedia Britannica*, accessed December 24, 2018, https://www.britannica.com/event/Investiture-Controversy.

[576] Joseph Cummins, "How Did the Crusades Affect Exploration and Trade?" *Classroom*, updated June 25, 2018, https://classroom.synonym.com/did-crusades-affect-exploration-trade-8887.html.

and philosophy. Their concept of joining faith to reason, found much earlier in Augustine (354–430) and also Boethius (470?–524) to achieve "the whole of attainable truth" will later be criticized by philosophers such as Immanuel Kant who reject their logical "proofs" for the existence of God.[577] Luther and other Reformers will also reject Scholasticism, but for a more basic concern. For Luther, Scripture is the ultimate authority, and reason is employed to understand biblically established truths, not to act as an independent judge who verifies them. Divine revelation leads men to God, not autonomous reason.[578]

Schoolmen live in the premodern era and accept that the supernatural exists; for them, the God of the Bible must be considered in scholarly deliberations but they are not able to synthesize faith and reason. There can only be one ultimate authority, and *Sola Scriptura* will eventually become the battle cry of the sixteenth century Reformation. But the new universities and the Scholastic scholars contribute to the intellectual advancement of the western nations. Thomas Aquinas's massive work, *Summa Theologica*, his personal attempt to synthesize classical and Christian thought, is still the basis of Roman Catholic teaching today.[579]

*****

The Crusader states have been in control in Syria and Palestine for over forty years when Muslim forces begin winning battles in their own holy war (jihad) against the Christians. The Muslims capture Edessa, the northernmost Crusader state, alarming Europe and leading to a call for a Second Crusade. In 1147, King Louis VII of France and King Conrad III of Germany lead their armies to the Holy Land, but they are decisively defeated and the Muslims maintain control of Edessa.

In 1187, the Muslim ruler Saladin begins a major campaign against the region of Jerusalem. His forces destroy a Christian army at the battle of Hattin and Saladin takes control of the Holy City. He does not slaughter the inhab-

---

[577] Joseph Pieper, "Scholasticism," *Encyclopaedia Britannica*, accessed December 24, 2018, https://www.britannica.com/topic/Scholasticism.

[578] "Lutheran Scholasticism," *Wikipedia*, February 12, 2018, https://en.wikipedia.org/wiki/Lutheran_scholasticism#initial_rejection.

[579] Kuiper, *The Church*, 131–132. The desire for intellectual advancement and a richer culture also led to the building of many beautiful cathedrals during this time, with the most illustrious in Milan, Rheims, and Cologne.

itants as the first Crusaders had done. Saladin allows the Christians, many of whom are women and children, to purchase their freedom and leave Jerusalem, but those who cannot pay are forced into slavery.[580]

Saladin's conquest of Jerusalem leads to a Third Crusade led by three rulers, Emperor Frederick Barbarossa, King Phillip of France, and Richard I (the Lion-Hearted) of England. Before their forces reach the Holy Land, Barbarossa drowns crossing a river, and King Phillip returns to France. Richard, living up to his name, continues his march to the Middle East and, in September, 1191, defeats Saladin in the Battle of Arsuf and regains partial control of Palestine. He approaches Jerusalem but does not lay siege to the city.

In 1192, Richard and Saladin sign a peace treaty that gives Christian pilgrims the right to visit the Holy Sepulcher, the supposed tomb of Christ, and the Third Crusade comes to an end. Richard and his knights have reestablished the kingdom of Jerusalem but without the city itself.

When Innocent III (1160–1216) becomes pope in 1198, he calls for a Fourth Crusade, and another Christian army is mustered and marches toward Palestine. But because of the power struggle going on between Rome and the east, the Crusaders are diverted to Constantinople. When they arrive in the eastern capital, they topple the reigning Emperor, Alexius III, and place his nephew, Alexius IV, on the throne in 1204. The efforts of Alexius IV to submit the Byzantium Church to Rome are met with strong resistance, and the new emperor is strangled in a palace coup.

For the next three days, the enraged Crusaders ransack Constantinople, killing and brutalizing many eastern Christians including the women of the city. Rather than live under the control of the west, many of the survivors flee across the Bosporus to Nicaea. It will not be until 1261, when Crusader enthusiasm is fading, that a coalition of Byzantine aristocrats regains control of Constantinople and establishes an eastern emperor over the city.[581] For now, Pope Innocent has established his complete authority over the east and the west, and he has also finalized the break between eastern and western Christians.

*****

---

[580] "The Crusades: The Siege of Jerusalem," *ThoughtCo.*, Hickman, Kennedy. Feb. 11, 2020, https://www.thoughtco.com/crusades-siege-of-jerusalem-2360716.

[581] Jones, *Christian History*, 73–74; History.com Editors, "Crusades," *History*, 10. Effects of the Crusades, September 14, 2018, www.history.com/topics/middle-ages/crusades.

Although the Crusades have caused the loss of many lives and have done great harm to the cause of Christ, the popes have increased their power in the west. The Church leaders are given credit for uniting Europe against the Muslims and securing control of Syria and Palestine for Christianity. With kings and commoners responding to their calls for military action, the popes become recognized as the leaders of all Christendom.[582]

The popes still reluctantly admit that kings and emperors are supreme in the political sphere, but they maintain they are supreme in the religious and ethical spheres. They can decide if a ruler's actions are moral, and if not, hold him liable for excommunication, which negates the duty of his people to obey him. This gives popes great power in the European political realm, making them virtual dictators over kings and emperors.

*****

It is while Innocent III reigns as Pope (1198–1216) that the power of the papacy reaches its greatest height. With the Fourth Crusade and the sack of Constantinople, Innocent has become ruler of not only the Western but also the Eastern Church. He has the support of the northern Italian towns which have become prosperous through trade and are willing to support him against the kings, even to the point of armed conflict. Across the middle of the Italian peninsula, he restores the boundaries of the Papal States, which had been shrinking as previous popes made concessions to kings. Innocent III proclaims that he will tolerate no opposition from temporal powers.

In 1208, when John Lackland, King of England, dares to oppose him, Innocent places England under an interdict—no church service can be held in all of England. The next year, the Pope excommunicates King John, essentially depriving him of his throne. The king defies Pope Innocent for four years until, facing a potential war with France, he submits a formal document to the pope's legate, acknowledging that he is a vassal of the pope and pledging to send a percentage of his royal revenue to Rome each year. One after another, the emperor, kings, lords, and princes of Europe acknowledge the pope as their spiritual lord. With the exception of the king of France, they also acknowledge him as their feudal and temporal lord, declaring themselves to be the pope's vassals, holding

---

[582] Kuiper, *The Church*, 125.

their kingdoms as fiefs of the Church.[583] Instead of being held accountable for instigating the tragic Crusades, the popes are empowered by them.

*****

After Innocent III gains control over the secular rulers, he wants to eliminate any spiritual resistance in the church. He calls on the French King and the French lords to take action against the growing cult of the Cathars (Albigenses) in Southern France, who are promoting a dualistic faith and claiming that Jesus was only an angel. A group of barons responds to the pope and leads an army from northern France; they attack the cities of Toulouse and Provence and indiscriminately massacre the inhabitants, both Cathari and Catholic.[584]

Innocent also begins to persecute the Waldenses who seek to follow Christ in simplicity and poverty. Although they reject some of the Catholic sacraments and the concept of purgatory, the Waldenses are not heretics like the Cathars. But their preaching becomes so popular among the common people that the papacy sees them as a threat, and Innocent decides to eliminate them. While the Cathars are largely destroyed, many of the Waldenses escape and flee to the high valleys of the Cottian Alps.[585] Innocent has begun the repression of dissent which will soon lead to the Inquisition Courts.

*****

There will be four more Crusades before the popes are unable to whip up fervor for such misguided military quests. But before Pope Innocent calls for the Fifth Crusade, a twelve-year-old French boy named Stephen, believing that Christ has spoken to him, manages to inspire a large children's crusade beginning in 1212. Thousands of young boys and girls, many with their parents' approval and some with adult accompaniment, gather at various places and begin the long trek to the Middle East. Some of them manage to board ships bound for Palestine. Reports of what happens to them vary, but some of them

---

[583] Ibid., 125–126.

[584] John A. Thomson, *The Western Church in the Middle Ages* (London: Hodder Headline Group, 1998), 131–133; Editors, Encyclopaedia, "Cathari," *Encyclopaedia*, accessed December 25, 2018, https://www.britannica.com/topic/Cathari.

[585] Kuiper, *The Church*, 141–143; Editors, Encyclopaedia, "Waldenses," *Encyclopaedia*, accessed December 25, 2018, https://www.britannica.com/topic/Waldenses.

are shipwrecked and some are kidnapped by slave traders. None ever make it to the Holy Land. Thousands of the other children, many of them under twelve, eventually attempt to return to their homes, but most of them, especially the little girls, never make it. Of all the sad aspects of the Crusades, this is the saddest.[586]

*****

These religious/military campaigns, lasting for two centuries, grew out of a perverted view of Christianity and a misunderstanding of the kingdom of God. The desire of the Crusader popes to control the sites associated with Jesus's earthly life is similar to the Catholic Church's veneration of relics,[587] which still continues today. But the kingdom of God is not made up of relics or particular locations in Palestine. Instead, it consists of the living Lord being manifested in the lives of Christians through His Word and the work of the Holy Spirit in all areas of the world.[588] The Muslim Turks will control Palestine until World War I,[589] but they never control the true kingdom of God.

*****

When Gregory IX becomes Pope in 1227, he continues the policy begun by Innocent III and persecutes those who disagree with official Church doctrine. In 1231, he institutes the Papal Inquisition for the apprehension and trial of heretics. The Inquisition (from the Latin verb *inquiro*—inquire into)

---

[586] S. M. Houghton, *Sketches from Church History* (Carlisle, PA: The Banner of Truth Trust, 1980), 56; Steven Kreis, "The Children's Crusade (1212)," *The History Guide*, February 28, 2006, www.historyguide.org/ancient/children.html; Gary Dickson, "Children's Crusade," *Encyclopaedia*, accessed December 25, 2018, https://www.britannica.com/event/Childrens-Crusade.

[587] Relics are artifacts associated with Jesus and His disciples, such as bones, clothing, or wood from the cross. Saint Augustine had called these venerations "a vile and sordid traffic" and doubted their authenticity, but the practice continues in the Roman Catholic Church today. See Gearoid S. Marley, "The Veneration of Relics," *Banner of Truth*, April 1, 2015, https://banneroftruth.org/us/resources/articles/2015/the-veneration-of-relics/.

[588] It is amazing and moving to walk up the steps of the southern entrance to the Temple Mount and realize that the Son of God walked on those same stones. But having the Church control those steps will not save anyone.

[589] England took control of Palestine through a League of Nations mandate after World War I.

is initially created to combat the Cathars and Waldenses, but its activity is soon extended to include witches, diviners, blasphemers, and other sacrilegious people. A second persecution, the infamous Spanish Inquisition authorized by Pope Sixtus IV in 1478, will become renowned for its brutal tortures and many death sentences.[590] A third version of the Inquisition will be established by Pope Paul III in 1542 to help defeat the spread of Protestantism.

*****

By the thirteenth century, the Church has accumulated enormous wealth through its properties and its ongoing income from tithes and other donations. Many of the clergy see a church office as an easy and pleasant lifestyle, and spiritual conditions are often deplorable among the monks. Despite this general corruption, there are good and sincere Christians during these dark days. Faithful priests and monks continue to minister to their congregations. Theologians such as Anselm of Canterbury (1033–1109) and Peter Abelard (1079–1142) enrich the church with their studies, and the many hymns written during the middle ages testify to a deep spiritual life among some in the clergy. The beautiful hymn, "O Sacred Head, Now Wounded," created during this time by the monk Bernard of Clairvaux, is still sung, and his writings will influence Martin Luther during the Reformation.[591]

Many earnest Christians try to institute change in the Church during this period, and the effort for reform gives rise to a wave of new monastic orders such as the Franciscans and the Dominicans. The number of nuns and monks increases rapidly when the new orders reject the laxity of the old fraternities and instill an attitude of duty and service. The Franciscans and Dominicans stress the dignity of manual labor, the duty of Christians to care for the poor, and the need for reform in the clergy. Both of these orders still exist today.[592]

*****

---

[590] History.Com Editors, "Inquisition," *History*, November 17, 2017, updated August 21, 2018, https://www.history.com/topics/religion/inquisition.

[591] Franz Posset, "Bernard of Clairvaux as Luther's Source," *Concordia Theological Quarterly*, Volume 54: Number 4, Oct. 1990, 281.

[592] Kuiper, *The Church*, 125–130.

In 1291, Acre, the last significant Crusader city, falls to the Muslims. The forces of Islam have taken back all the territories that the Crusaders had conquered. Christian troops will make a few more minor excursions against the Muslims, but the large-scale campaigns begun by Pope Urban in 1095 are over. Although the popes who followed Innocent III were able to maintain his structure of temporal power through most of the thirteenth century, the heightened authority the papacy had gained during the Crusades is beginning to wane. When Pope Boniface VIII assumes the office in 1294, things change rapidly. Boniface has a quarrel with Philip the Fair, King of France, and not surprisingly, it is over money.

When King Philip imposes a tax upon the French clergy, Pope Boniface forbids them to pay it. The king retaliates by forbidding the transfer of any gold, silver, or precious stones from his kingdom, effectively cutting off the revenue the pope has been receiving from France. The pope then issues several *bulls*,[593] official papal declarations, asserting his power over Philip. Boniface, an extremely arrogant man, says, "It is necessary for salvation for every human creature to submit to the Roman Pontiff." He quotes God speaking to Jeremiah, "Behold, I have set thee over nations and kingdoms" (Jer. 1:10), claiming for himself the authority that God had granted to the Old Testament prophet.[594] Boniface next excommunicates Philip, expecting to humble him in the way previous popes had brought kings to heel. But Boniface has not grasped the changes taking place in Europe.

The era of feudalism, when lords and commoners were often inclined to follow the lead of the pope and rebel against their kings, is giving way to a strong sense of nationalism in the European countries. The structure of feudalism is beginning to decay and kings are reasserting their power over the nobles and their territories. When the French people learn of Philip's excommunication, instead of forsaking him, they support their King in his defiance of Pope Boniface. Philip sends soldiers to the city of Anagni, Italy with orders to arrest the Pope in his palace, but the local people defend the sixty-seven-year-old Pontiff. Philip's troops decide not to take Boniface into custody, but they beat and humiliate him. The pope is broken in spirit and dies shortly after returning to Rome in 1303.

---

[593] These documents were called *bulls* because the affixed leaden seals were called "bullas" in Latin.
[594] Kuiper, *The Church*, 135.

No pope had ever claimed such complete power as Boniface, and no pope had ever suffered such a complete and humiliating defeat. Boniface's downfall marks the beginning of the decline of the secular power of the Church. The three estates of the French realm, the nobles, the common people, and the clergy have decided that in civil matters, the pope has no authority and that the king has no superior other than God.[595]

After the death of Boniface, the ongoing drama of the papacy continues. The next pope, Benedict XI, dies within a year of taking office and, in 1305, is succeeded by Clement V, a Frenchman. He appoints French cardinals, which makes him unpopular in Rome, so in 1309, he moves the papal court to Avignon, France. For almost seventy years, the next seven popes will exercise their authority from Avignon where they live luxuriously corrupt lives under the thumbs of the French kings. This is called the "Babylonian Captivity" of the papacy, but the popes are willing captives.[596]

*****

The thirteenth century decline of the feudal system continues into the fourteenth. The initial impetus for establishing the lords and their fiefs in the ninth century had been the inability of weak kings to protect the people from raiders making swift attacks into European territories. But with traders and businessmen prospering from their contacts in the east, largely made during the time of the Crusades, kings are able to raise taxes, hire mercenaries, rebuild their armies, and gain control of the lords. The inventions of gunpowder and cannons undermine the ability of a lord in his castle to defy the king.

Prosperity from trade and commerce also leads to new towns and cities, giving peasants work opportunities away from the fiefs. A serf could become a freeman if he stayed away from his manor for a year. Additionally, the tragic loss of life from the plague of the Black Death[597] resulted in a scarcity of labor, giving serfs bargaining power and hastening the eventual demise of the feudal system.[598]

---

[595] Ibid., 134–136.
[596] Bainton, *Christianity*, 209–210.
[597] See p. 303, n556.
[598] Samir, "Brief Notes on the causes for the Decline of Feudalism," *Preserve Articles*, accessed December 26, 2018, http://www.preservearticles.com/2011090413015/brief-notes-on-the-causes-for-decline-of-feudalism.html.

The newfound wealth of the Italian city states has another impact which initially does not affect the poorer classes. Rich merchants and politicians begin to support the desire for learning and culture which had begun with the Scholastics. Florence, Venice, and Rome lead a rebirth—a "Renaissance"—of interest in ancient Greek literature, art, and rhetoric. But where the Scholastics had tried to incorporate the knowledge of God into their studies, Renaissance scholars focus on the positive actions of human beings; they are "humanists." Thinkers, like the writers Francesco Petrarch (1304–1374) and Giovanni Boccaccio (1313–1375), see medieval life as primitive and backward and look to the ancient Greeks and Romans for inspiration. This focus on the pagan classics contributes to the development of the philosophy of humanism, an emphasis on individual achievement and life in this world above concern for religion and the next world. The Renaissance begins to shift the focus from seeing human beings as fallen creatures to extolling them as capable of great accomplishments.

*****

Although the popes are ruling from Avignon for most of the fourteenth century, the Church continues to persecute dissenters. "Heretics" who do not repent and recant are seen as breaking not only Church law but civil law as well. Conviction by an Inquisition Court results in being handed over to civil authorities for punishment, which can include burning at the stake.

The popes have difficulty overseeing the monastic orders, mainly Franciscans and Dominicans involved in the court trials. Kings and local rulers waver between accepting and resisting the Church's proceedings. A lack of consistent control over inquisition trials leads to widespread abuse of those being accused of heresy and other religious crimes.[599]

Despite the potential consequences, many individuals criticize the doctrine and government of the Roman Church during this time. John Wycliffe (1320–1384), a professor at Oxford, says that wealth and political power have so corrupted the Church that radical reform is necessary. He calls the pope the Antichrist and says the Bible should be the only rule of faith.

---

[599] "Historical Overview Of The Inquisition," *Rice University*, accessed December 26, 2018, http://galileo.rice.edu/lib/student_work/trial96/loftis/overview.html.

In 1377, while Wycliffe is teaching and preaching in England, the Italians have become greatly dissatisfied with the popes residing in France. They assist Pope Gregory XI, and he is able to bring the papacy back to Rome. When Gregory dies in 1378, the cardinals elect Urban VI as the next pope, but he becomes so abusive that there are doubts about his sanity. The cardinals repudiate Urban VI and elect one of their own, Clement VII, to be pope. But he is unable to unseat Urban in Rome and takes up residence in Avignon.

Now there are two popes, one in Italy and one in France. A "Great Schism" has existed between the eastern and western churches; now there is a "Great Schism" between popes. The two pontiffs take turns denouncing, excommunicating, and pronouncing curses on each other.[600]

Urban VI and the Roman clergy eventually turn their attention to Wycliffe and his teaching; they intend to kill him, but some powerful English nobles support Wycliffe and keep him from falling into the hands of the Inquisitors. He spends his last years studying the Scriptures and focuses on doctrine, especially the biblical themes concerning salvation, election, and predestination, which will become important to the Reformers in the sixteenth century. In a critical service to the Church, Wycliffe leads a group of scholars in the translation of the Bible from Latin to English so that his countrymen can read it. Pope Urban is unable to arrest him, and he dies in peace in 1384.

Wycliffe's followers, who are called *Lollards* by the papacy,[601] spread his teaching through much of England. But when the bishops succeed in passing a law against heresy, many of them are burned at the stake. Those who survive go into hiding and continue their ministry in secret until the time of the Reformation.[602]

*****

The teachings of Wycliffe spread to continental Europe and have a great effect on a Bohemian preacher in Prague by the name of John Huss (1369–1415). He begins to preach with boldness against the corruption of the clergy, eliciting a strong response from the common people, some of whom

---

[600] Kuiper, *The Church*, 137.

[601] Lollards was a derogatory term derived in Middle English from *lollen*, to mumble, indicating uneducated speech. "Lollard," *The Free Dictionary*, accessed December 26, 2018, www.thefreedictionary.com/Lollard.

[602] Kuiper, *The Church*, 137–138; 143–144.

are Waldensians, as well as the nobility. Like Wycliffe, Huss teaches many of the biblical concepts which will later become critical doctrines during the Reformation. In 1414, when he speaks out against indulgences,[603] Pope John XXIII excommunicates him.

After Huss is excommunicated, Emperor Sigismund calls for a general council in Constance[604] to try to end the growing divisions in the Church— there are now not two but three bishops claiming to be pope. The emperor invites Huss to attend the council and promises him safe conduct. Relying on the emperor's guarantee, Huss accepts the invitation, but upon his arrival, Pope John imprisons him for heresy. Huss and the Bohemians protest vehemently, but the pope quotes canon law which states heretics have no rights; it is a pious act to deceive and betray them.

Huss languishes in the Constance dungeon for eight months with no chance to defend himself. On the sixth of July 1415, he is brought before the emperor and the bishops in the Constance cathedral where he is cursed and degraded before being led to the edge of the city. There he is tied to a stake and burned to death. Huss recites the litany, "O Christ, thou Son of the living God, have mercy upon me" until the flames consume him. The bishops then throw his ashes into the River Rhine.[605]

After executing Huss, the Council members posthumously condemn Wycliffe as a heretic and direct that his writings be destroyed. They also order that his body be exhumed and burned. In 1428, the Bishop of Lincoln will dig up Wycliffe's bones, burn them, and throw the ashes into the River Swift.[606]

The bishops at Constance continue their deliberations until 1417 when they elect an Italian cardinal, Martin V, as Pope. The other three popes, weary of the continual conflicts, give Martin their support; the Church in Western Europe again has one head and the "Great Schism" is healed, but the wounds to the reputation and authority of the papacy are not. For sincere Christians, the papacy has become a sad but dangerous spectacle.[607]

---

[603] Indulgences are the acts by which the Roman Church claims to forgive the temporal punishment of sins for donations or good deeds. The papacy also claimed that purchasing an indulgence for a loved one would hasten their release from purgatory. These sales became a very profitable business for the Church. See p. 305, n. 562.

[604] Constance is located in what is now Southern Germany.

[605] Houghton, *Sketches*, 70; Bainton, *Christianity,* 217–219.

[606] Houghton, *Sketches*, 68.

[607] Kuiper, *The Church*, 138.

The new pope organizes a military campaign against the followers of Huss, but they manage to fend off the attacks. When the Reformation begins in the sixteenth century, the spirit of reform and opposition to the Roman Church will be strong in Bohemia.[608]

*****

While the Roman Church has been embroiled with papal discord and the persecution of doctrinal dissenters, Constantinople, the last remaining structure of the Old Roman Empire, has been isolated by the conquests of the Ottoman Turks in the east. On May 29, 1453, a 70,000-man Muslim army uses cannons to break down the massive walls that had protected the citizens of Constantinople for a thousand years. The Turks capture the city, kill the last Byzantine Emperor Constantine XI, and massacre so many of the inhabitants that blood flows like "rainwater." A Muslim teacher walks into the Church of Holy Wisdom and intones, "There is no god but Allah, and Muhammad is his prophet."[609]

Hundreds of Eastern scholars manage to survive the fall of Constantinople. They gather their most precious possessions, the ancient manuscripts that the city had protected for so long, and flee to the west. These teachers, and especially their ancient texts, will give added momentum to the Renaissance in Italy.[610]

During the last days of Constantinople, another event is occurring which will have far-reaching effects not only for that city's manuscripts but for publications everywhere. Johann Gutenberg borrows money in Mainz, Germany, and in 1450 is finally able to assemble moveable metal type and incorporate it into a printing press. It is a quantum leap forward over hand-copying and wooden block printing. For the first time, manuscripts can be mass produced

---

[608] Ibid, 143–146; "John Huss," *Christianity Today*, accessed December 26, 2018, www.christianitytoday.com/history/people/martyrs/john-huss.html.

[609] Jones, *Christian History*, 100. This church becomes a mosque and will remain one until the 1930's. Today it is a museum and Constantinople has become Istanbul, Turkey.

[610] Tony Bunting, "Fall of Constantinople," *Encyclopaedia*, accessed December 26, 2018, https://www.britannica.com/event/Fall-of-Constantinople-1453; "The Ottoman Turks Capture Constantinople, Resulting in the Transfer of Invaluable Manuscripts to Venice and the West," *HistoryofInformation.com*, accessed December 26, 2018, www.historyofinformation.com/detail.php?entryid=35.

and made available to people who before could never afford a book. As printing presses multiply, the price of books plummet. Greek and Roman classics, as well as Bibles, begin to pour into the different countries of Europe.[611]

As the years pass, this revolution in book production fosters rapid development in science, art, and religion through the proliferation of texts.[612] It is doubtful that the coming Reformation, one of the most important events in Church history, could have occurred without Gutenberg's invention.[613]

*****

During the time of the Renaissance (approximately 1330–1550), most of the popes support the humanistic philosophy energizing the advancements in art, literature, and science. They not only fund new artists and writers; they embrace the secular emphasis of the movement. During the Renaissance era, very few popes are noted for their spirituality.

Although the Roman bishops support the revival of classical texts, they neglect an increased focus on Scripture. Scholars begin to read the ancient biblical writings in the original Greek and Hebrew and focus on the author's intent; the Renaissance watchword is *Ad Fontes*, meaning "to the fountains" (back to the sources). There is an increased understanding of Scripture in addition to texts being more widely available, but sadly, popes are not interested in parishioners having their own Bibles.

The individualism inherent in Renaissance humanism leads to excesses in society, and the papacy is not immune. Rome is an Italian city-state, and the popes have "all the splendid vices as well as the dazzling endowments of the secular despots in the other cities."[614]

---

[611] Jones, *Christian History*, 100–101.

[612] Mary Bellis, "Johannes Gutenberg and His Revolutionary Printing Press," *ThoughtCo.*, September 9, 2018, https://www.thoughtco.com/johannes-gutenberg-and-the-printing-press -1991865.

[613] Apparently, Gutenberg's lenders were given control of his printing press by the courts, and he never profited from it. See Evan Andrews, "7 Things You May Not Know About the Gutenberg Bible," *HISTORY*, February 23, 2015, https://www.history.com/ news/7-things-you-may-not-know-about-the-gutenberg-bible.

[614] Bainton, *Christianity*, 222.

Pope Sixtus IV (1471–84) builds the Sistine Chapel (1480) and has the artists Perugino and Botticelli decorate the walls with religious frescos.[615] But he also plots to overthrow the rule of the Medici family in Florence for the benefit of his own relatives. One of the Medici brothers, Giuliano, is assassinated by a priest during Mass in the Florence Cathederal. But the family fights back, and a number of the conspirators are hanged, including the Archbishop of Pisa. Pope Sixtus understands that it is best for him to remain quiet.

Alexander VI (1492–1503) is the most scandalous of the Renaissance popes. He has a number of mistresses and does not shrink from using the Vatican for his orgies. Two of his at least four illegitimate children are considered criminals. Pope Leo X (1513–21) spends more on gambling than on artists and prefers his hunting lodge over the Vatican.[616] Leo sums up the view of the Renaissance popes when he reportedly says, "The papacy is ours. Let us enjoy it."[617]

Although the Humanists focus on personal achievement and gratification during this time, they do not directly attack the central doctrines of the Church. The doctrine of the Trinity and the conviction of an afterlife remain strong both in the Church and secular society. It is still the age of premodern thought, and belief in the God of Christianity remains central to European culture. But for many believers, it is becoming clear that reform in the Church is not only necessary but unavoidable.

*****

For three centuries, the Church has been in turmoil in many areas. In the early thirteenth century, the Albigenses and Waldenses were seen as heretics and viciously attacked. The Inquisition courts were initiated, and many people were persecuted for beliefs which were often more biblical than the decrees of

---

[615] Michelangelo will paint the ceiling from 1508–1512. Considered the greatest artist of his lifetime, Michelangelo seems to epitomize the time of the Renaissance. His paintings and sculptures (*Pieta, David, etc.*) of religious themes are awe-inspiring, but he also apparently engaged in homosexual activity. He wrote many love sonnets to Tommaso Cavalieri, a handsome young nobleman. See Creighton E. Gilbert, "Michelangelo," *Encyclopedia*, updated March 2, 2019, https://www.britannica.com/biography/Michelangelo; also "Tommaso dei Cavalieri," *Wikipedia*, edited February 17, 2019, https://en.wikipedia.org/wiki/Tommaso_dei_Cavalieri.

[616] Bainton, *Christianity*, 222–223.

[617] Ibid., 223.

the Church. Pope Boniface VIII was beaten and humiliated by the soldiers of the king of France, and the papacy lost much of its secular power. Boniface's successors were held "captive" in Avignon, France, for almost seventy years leading to the "Great Papal Schism," with popes in Italy as well as France. Wycliffe and Huss were declared heretics; their followers were severely persecuted, and Huss was burned at the stake. And now the Church hierarchy is deeply involved in the dissipations brought about by the humanistic thinking of the Italian Renaissance.

As the sixteenth century approaches, Renaissance scholars, who are examining the Scriptures as well as the writings of the early Church Fathers in the original languages, realize that the changes that have developed regarding doctrine and the functions of the Church go far beyond the minor differences in customs and forms of worship that would naturally occur. Academic researchers begin to realize that doctrines such as purgatory, transubstantiation,[618] and indulgences are not found in the Bible or early Christian writings. Such discoveries, along with the manifest corruption of the papacy, raise concerns among many Christians, especially university men. It is clear that changes need to be made in the Church, but the popes still have great power, and dissenters face the threat of the Inquisition courts.[619]

*****

One of the scholars who sees the need for reform in the Church is Desiderius Erasmus of Rotterdam (1469–1536). Born the second illegitimate son of a priest and his concubine, Erasmus had been placed in a strict religious school by his guardian after the deaths of his parents. He eventually entered a monastery and was ordained a priest. After taking a post as Latin secretary to the influential bishop of Cambrai in northern France, he was sent to study theology at the University of Paris where he was recognized as a brilliant student and lecturer. One of his supporters, Lord Montjoy, established a pension for Erasmus, allowing him to move from city to city as an independent scholar, teaching and lecturing. He also began extensive correspondence with the most

---

[618] Transubstantiation is the claim that the bread and wine actually become the body and blood of Christ when consecrated during the Mass.
[619] Kuiper, *The Church*, 152–153.

eminent thinkers in Europe. In 1499, he visited England, where he became friends with the social philosopher and statesman, Thomas More.

After his time in England, Erasmus continued teaching and traveling and eventually came to be acknowledged as the greatest intellect in Europe. In a great service for the Church, he eventually translates the New Testament from Latin into Greek, an excellent work upon which future scholars will rely.

As the corruption in the papal hierarchy continues and becomes widely apparent, Erasmus begins to use his great learning and sharp pen to criticize the ignorance of the monks and the abuses in the Church.[620] Erasmus wants to see reform, but he is careful not to do anything that threatens his standing with the pope or his reputation as the "Prince of the Humanists."

While Erasmus is pursuing his academic life, a German youth named Martin Luther (1483–546)[621] is completing his master's degree and beginning his law studies at the University of Erfurt. After the sudden and unexplained death of one of his friends, he takes a break from his classes to visit his parents in Mansfield.[622] On the way to his home, he is caught in a violent thunderstorm. Terrified and fearing immediate death from the lightning flashes, he cries out to Saint Anne, the patron saint of miners, that he will become a monk if his life is spared.

Luther survives the storm and makes it to his family's house, but his father, Hans, is very angry when he hears about Martin's vow. For years, he had struggled and saved while working in copper mining so that his gifted son could go to the University of Erfurt and become a lawyer. Hans and Martin's companions try to talk him out of fulfilling his vow, but with a deep fear of God's wrath, he believes he has only one choice.

Although Luther later spoke lovingly of his parents, his childhood discipline had at times been excessive. He had received severe whippings from his parents and had been harshly rodded by his teachers for minor transgressions during classes. With no Bible available in his peasant home, his view of God came from the Mass and the teaching and discipline he received at home and

---

[620] Ibid., 151; also see Biography.com Editors, "Erasmus Biography," *Biography*, April 2, 2014, https://www.biography.com/people/erasmus-21291705.

[621] The details of Luther's early life are drawn primarily from Julius Kostlin's shorter 587-page biography of Luther: Julius Kostlin, *The Life of Martin Luther* (New York: Charles Scribner's Sons, 1883), 10–55.

[622] Luther was born in Eisleben, but his family moved to Mansfield the year after his birth.

school. As a sensitive child with a tender conscience, he grew up seeing God as a harsh taskmaster waiting to mete out punishment.

Now, still troubled by the death of his friend and fearing God's judgment, Luther keeps his vow. He gives his law books to his companions, tells them goodbye, and enters the monastery in Erfurt on July 17, 1505.

*****

In the monastery, Luther studies theology instead of law. He receives a Bible, which will become especially important. After a six-month trial period, he takes the vow to become a monk, and then in 1507, he is ordained a priest. Luther is a brilliant but troubled young cleric. His fear of God as the Holy Judge and his acute sense of sin lead to hours of confessions that exasperate his superiors. In 1508, he is sent to the university in Wittenberg as a tutor and obtains his first degree in theology, that of Bachelor of Bible. After a year, he is transferred back to Erfurt where he teaches and receives his second theological degree, that of *Sententiarius*.[623]

At the age of twenty-six, Luther occupies a prominent position, but his spirit remains troubled as he tries to earn his salvation by strict asceticism[624] and good works.

In 1511, he is sent to Rome as a companion to an older monk who is on an errand for his monastic order. Luther visits all the shrines and is amazed at the splendor and pomp which surround the office of the pope, now occupied by Leo X. But he is shocked by the immorality and outright unbelief of some of the highest dignitaries of the church. He also hears these men speak of the "stupid Germans" and "German beasts" who are not entitled to any notice or respect from Rome.[625]

When he returns to Erfurt, he remains a "good" monk still loyal to the papacy but a monk with a more realistic view of the Church. He is assigned a permanent residence at the University of Wittenberg where he is to teach the Bible. But he continues to be in a state of mental and spiritual turmoil; he cannot rid himself of such sins as anger and envy and falls into deep despair.

---

[623] The title was derived from the *Sentences* of Peter Lombard, the standard textbook of theology at that time. Kuiper, *The Church*, 161.

[624] Luther fasted for days and slept in the cold until he "well-nigh froze himself to death." Roland H. Bainton, *Here I Stand: A Life of Martin Luther* (Nashville: Abington, 1950), 34.

[625] Kostlin, *Life of Luther*, 62.

Luther fears he will never obtain salvation despite all his study and efforts as a priest; he does not see how he can ever be righteous before a Holy God. He finds some comfort from the works of Saint Augustine and from the writings of Bernard of Clairvaux, both of whom had written about the free grace of Christ for salvation. And despite his frame of mind, he continues to intently study Scripture for his class lectures.[626]

Eventually, Luther teaches the Epistle to the Romans. As he pores over the text in his cell at Wittenberg, he begins to focus on Romans 1:17 where Paul quotes Habakkuk, "For in it the righteousness of God is revealed from faith to faith; as it is written, 'But the righteous man shall live by faith'" (Hab. 2:4).

It dawns on Luther that the righteousness he has been desperately seeking through his own works is granted to a person through the means of faith. He later wrote, "There I began to understand that the righteousness of God is…a gift of God, namely by faith…as it is written, 'He who through faith is righteous shall live.' Here I felt that I was altogether born again and had entered paradise through open doors."[627] Luther begins to see God as a merciful heavenly Father who saves by grace rather than as a Taskmaster ready to strike.

With a newfound peace and hope, Luther begins to teach and preach with increasing power. As time passes, he becomes an accomplished theologian and preacher respected by his peers. Luther sees ever more clearly the abuses of the Church and speaks out boldly against them. He has begun to understand the important theological implications associated with salvation by God's grace, doctrines that he will expound in future conflicts with the pope and Erasmus.

*****

In early 1517, Pope Leo authorizes indulgences to help complete the great Cathedral of Saint Peter in Rome, and Johann Tetzel, a Dominican friar, begins to sell them at the village of Juterbok, near Wittenberg. Tetzel claims that people will be purchasing not only forgiveness for the temporal penalty of sins, punishment in this life, but also forgiveness for eternity. Tetzel is in effect claiming that the Church can sell salvation for money.[628]

---

[626] Kuiper, *The Church*, 162.

[627] Lewis William Spitz, *Luther's Works, Volume 34, Career of the Reformer IV*, (St. Louis: Concordia, 1960), 336.

[628] Kostlin, *Life of Luther*, 88–89.

The people are being deceived in a matter which affects their eternal destinies, and it is too much for Luther. He writes a series of propositions for debate, later known as the *Ninety-Five Theses*, and on October 31, 2017, posts them on the door of the Castle Church at Wittenberg. This is the first step in a series of actions which will lead to an upheaval in the Church, an upheaval which will be called the Reformation.[629] Luther and many other Christians are beginning to realize that the Church hierarchy has become corrupt, not only in behavior but in doctrine—the Roman Church has forsaken the gospel.

*****

When Luther posts his *Ninety-Five Theses*, he is not calling for a revolution in the Church; posting propositions on the church door is only an invitation for scholars to debate his ideas—a common practice in that day. But Luther posts his theses on All Saints Day when people come from near and far to view the extensive relic collection of the Castle Church. Many people read Luther's propositions and tell others. Some copy his writings, which are in Latin, translate them into other languages, and reprint them on printing presses. Within four weeks, much to Luther's surprise, his thoughts are being read and discussed, not only in Germany but throughout much of Europe.

The archbishop of Mainz, who was to receive a share of the proceeds from the sale of Tetzel's indulgencies, sends a copy of Luther's theses to Pope Leo. Leo is not overly concerned, but he instructs the head of Luther's monastic order to tell "that monk" in Wittenberg to keep quiet. Tetzel, Mazzolini (a Dominican inquisitor in Rome), and the theological professor, John Eck, all write works attacking Luther. Luther answers in a pamphlet but is disappointed when none of his friends rise to his defense.

Then, in April 1518, at the meeting of the Augustinian Order in Heidelberg, Luther meets stronger opposition than he expects. When he returns to Wittenberg, Luther writes a response called *Resolutions* in which he defends each of his theses, and he addresses it to the pope.

Luther does not yet seem to recognize the danger that his attack on indulgences poses to the papacy. His *Ninety-Five Theses* include a number of different theological contentions, but indulgences are the crucial issue because they help the Church hierarchy keep control of the people. Over the centuries, the

---

[629] Kuiper, *The Church*, 163.

Roman Church had gradually developed a sacramental system of salvation; by the twelfth century, there were seven official sacraments in three categories:

1. Sacraments of initiation (Baptism, Confirmation, Eucharist).
2. Sacraments of healing (Penance, Extreme Unction).
3. Sacraments of commitment (Holy Orders, and Matrimony).[630]

According to Church doctrine, God's grace, and therefore salvation, is dispensed through these sacraments. Only priests are permitted to administer the sacraments, so a person's eternal destiny is controlled by the Church. Without absolution through penance, there is no forgiveness and no salvation. Since indulgences are often the least painful form of penance, they produce huge streams of revenue for the popes, and an attack on this practice is an attack on the entire sacramental system. Luther had only wanted to debate issues and abuses, but he represents a serious threat to the power and the purse of the Roman Church.[631]

When Pope Leo sees that Luther has not been silenced, he issues a summons for Luther to appear before him in Rome. If Luther goes to Rome, he will be killed. But the Elector, Frederick the Wise, who rules Saxony and therefore Wittenberg, uses his political influence to keep the summons from being enforced.

The pope next orders Luther to appear before his legate, Cajetan, at the Diet of Augsburg.[632] Frederick again protects Luther by obtaining a letter of safe-conduct for him from Emperor Maximilian. Luther's close friends try to persuade him to relent and settle things peaceably. But in three contentious meetings with Cajetan in October 1518, Luther refuses to recant and leaves Augsburg secretly at night. At Cajetan's urging, the pope issues a bull condemning Luther's views. Luther can no longer claim that his issues have not been settled by the Church.

The pope, realizing that he cannot arrest Luther without the cooperation of Frederick, sends Frederick's own papal representative, Charles von Miltitz, to consult with Luther. Luther agrees not to speak about indulgences if his

---

[630] "The Sacraments", *Introduction to Roman Catholicism*, accessed December 26, 2018, http://catholicfaith.co.uk/sacraments.
[631] Kuiper, *The Church*, 164–170.
[632] A diet is a formal, deliberative assembly, in this case a meeting of the German princes.

opponents also refrain; the pope is pleased, and it appears the immediate crisis is over.[633]

*****

Emperor Maximilian dies in January 1519, and Pope Leo becomes consumed with persuading the Prince-Electors[634] to choose a new emperor that he can control. For sixteen months, he refrains from further charges against Luther, but the two sides in Germany do not remain silent. Andreas Karlstadt, a fellow professor of Luther's at Wittenberg, comes out with a set of theses against Eck who had been one of the first to attack Luther's writings. Eck counters with an extreme view of the supremacy of the pope. Luther then replies to Eck, saying that the Roman Church's claim to authority over all the other churches rests on weak papal decrees issued over the last four hundred years and that such a claim had not existed before that.

Such an attack on the preeminence of the pope has not been made before, and it causes a sensation. Eck cannot ignore Luther's claim and challenges him to a debate on the role of the pope. During the months leading up to the confrontation, Luther prepares by studying church history and canon law. He learns from reviewing historical works that many of the decretals concerning the papacy are forgeries. The supremacy of the pope, one of the pillars of the Church and one of Luther's earliest beliefs is crumbling before his eyes.

Luther and Eck face each other on the fourth of July 1519 at the palace of the duke in Leipzig. The atmosphere is so tense that armed guards are posted to keep brawls from breaking out between supporters of the pope and those who back Luther. Both men are well-prepared, and neither gains a significant advantage until Eck questions Luther on some of Huss's writings. When Luther defends Huss's concepts, he is aligning himself with a man whom the Church has burned as a heretic. Eck has accomplished his main objective; if Luther supports a heretic, then he is one.

When Eck returns to Rome, he urges Pope Leo to issue a bull excommunicating Luther. The pope is more than willing, but he is still occupied with the politics surrounding the installation of the new emperor, Charles V of Spain,

---

[633] Kuiper, *The Church*, 171–172.

[634] The Prince-Electors were members of the electoral college of the Holy Roman Empire empowered since the thirteenth century to choose the Holy Roman Emperor.

who was elected just before the Leipzig debate. Leo decides to delay taking action against Luther.

The first thing Luther does after leaving Leipzig is to publish an account of the debate; he follows this up with an abundance of pamphlets and letters. Luther has rejected the supremacy of the pope and the infallibility of councils—his break with the Roman hierarchal system is complete. The debate and his writings strengthen his growing support; his followers are even more convinced that his views are correct, and he gains many new adherents, including Martin Bucer who will help lead the Reformation and will influence the thinking of John Calvin.[635]

In Switzerland, the Zurich priest, Huldrich Zwingli, has also begun teaching against indulgences and the abuses of the Roman Church. Zwingli is influenced by Erasmus, whom he knows personally, and like the great humanist, he wants to bring about gradual improvements in the Church. In 1519, he discontinues the lessons assigned by the papacy and begins to teach the Gospel of Matthew chapter by chapter. The response is so strong that the city council considers revising the town's worship services to follow scriptural teaching rather than the dictates of Rome. Zwingli will later move beyond Erasmus's view of reform when Luther's influence begins to cross the Alps.[636]

*****

The period between the Leipzig debate and Luther's appearance at the Diet of Worms in April 1521 is a hectic time for the now widely known German theologian. After the dispute with Eck, Luther publishes a small book called *On Good Works*. He applies his new understanding of salvation to everyday life and says common workers—shoemakers, housekeepers, farmers, etc.—who do their work to the glory of God are more pleasing to Him than monks and nuns. Luther is discarding the distinction between the clergy and the laity; every Christian is a believer-priest. The kingdom of God is something different from and much larger than the realm of Church officials (Exod. 19:6; 1 Pet. 2:5, 9–10).

When someone sends Luther one of Huss's manuscripts, he sees that the Prague "heretic" taught many of the same things which are now central to his

---

[635] Kuiper, *The Church*, 171–174.
[636] Ibid., 187–189.

own doctrinal understandings. Luther begins to say that he is a disciple of the Bohemian. He also reads the writings of the humanist Lorenzo Valla which reinforce his findings that many papal decretals are forgeries. Scripture study, new books, and conversations with friends drive him forward from position to position as his understanding of theology and Church history rapidly advance. Luther begins to think that the pope is the Antichrist.[637]

*****

By the beginning of 1520, Charles V of Spain, with the backing of Pope Leo, has been established as the new emperor of the Holy Roman Empire. Although political turmoil and even threats of war over the election of Charles are concerning Europe, Leo begins to turn his attention to Luther. On June 15, 1520, he signs a papal bull excommunicating him. The bull calls for all faithful people to burn Luther's writings and forbids him to preach. His followers are ordered to recant within sixty days, and if they do not, they are to be treated as heretics. The bull orders the government to imprison Luther and seize anyone who follows him. Towns that shelter Luther are to be placed under an interdict; they can have no church services.

Eck is entrusted with publishing the bull in Germany, but only a few places allow him to distribute it. The students at Erfurt seize as many copies as they can and throw them into the river. Luther reacts by publishing a tract, *Against the Execrable Bull of Antichrist*, in which he declares, "Whether this bull is by Eck or by the pope, it is the sum of all impiety, blasphemy, ignorance, impudence, hypocrisy, lying—in a word, it is Satan and his Antichrist." Luther ends his tract by saying, "And as they excommunicated me for the sacrilege of heresy, so I excommunicate them in the name of the sacred truth of God. Christ will judge whose excommunication will stand. Amen."[638]

In December 1520, Luther, not satisfied with just writing against Rome, burns the bull with a large crowd of students, professors, and citizens assembled

---

[637] Ibid., 174.
[638] Bainton, *Here I Stand*, 126.

outside the walls of Wittenberg. He is now in a life and death battle with the pope.[639]

*****

The new emperor, Charles V (1500–558), was king of Spain and only nineteen years old when he was nominated by the Prince-Electors. He is a devout Roman Catholic who now reigns over more territory than any emperor since Charlemagne, including the parts of America discovered by Columbus only twenty-nine years before. In order to solve the problem of the wild "boar" in his vineyard,[640] Pope Leo appeals to this powerful inexperienced monarch "in an attempt to bring Luther either to obedience or to the stake."[641]

Charles summons Luther to appear at the Diet of Worms, the council of German rulers, scheduled to meet in early 1521. Although he is granted a guarantee of safe passage, Luther believes that, like Huss, he is going to his death; he encourages Philipp Melanchthon, a young university colleague, to continue teaching the truth if he does not return.

Luther leaves for Worms on the second of April. As he makes his way through the German towns, people line the streets to see the man who has dared to defy the pope. They, too, believe that he is going to die.

On April 17, Luther appears before Emperor Charles who is arrayed in all his pomp and splendor. The powerful emperor, descendant of royal lines, and Martin Luther, son of peasants, face each other for the first time. Pointing to a small table holding Luther's books, an official asks him if the books are his and if he still adheres to them. Luther answers the first question in the affirmative but then requests some time to consider the second question. After a short conference, the Diet announces that Luther must give his answer in twenty-four hours.[642]

At dusk the next day, with torches lining the hall, Luther tries to defend himself, knowing that his life hangs in the balance, but the emperor demands a plain answer—will he recant or not? Luther replies that it is impossible for him to recant unless he is proven wrong by Scripture. He concludes his defense

---

[639] Kuiper, *The Church*, 176.
[640] Pope Leo used this analogy in his bull excommunicating Luther. See Kuiper, *The Church*, 174.
[641] Ibid., 177.
[642] Ibid., 179.

by saying, "My conscience is captive to the Word of God. I cannot and I will not recant anything, for to go against conscience is neither right nor safe. God help me. Amen."[643]

The emperor signals that the meeting is over, and he and the other members of the Diet retire to their quarters. Luther is surrounded by a group of German nobles who escort him safely back to his lodgings.

*****

During the next few days, several conferences are held, but there is no possibility of a compromise. The Diet orders Luther to return to Wittenberg and forbids him to preach; they plan to wait until Luther's safe conduct expires and then execute him as a heretic.

In a horse-drawn cart, Luther begins the trip back to Wittenberg. After several days, he is traveling in the forest at night when a small band of masked riders sweep down on him. They lift Luther out of his cart and take him to Wartburg Castle on the wooded heights overlooking the city of Eisenach. The Elector Frederick the Wise has had Luther kidnapped for his own safety.

On May 25, Charles V issues the *Edict of Worms*, declaring Luther a criminal and public outlaw and making it illegal to possess his books. Luther waits in the castle to see if the storm surrounding him will subside. Spending most of his time writing, he completes a rigorous German translation of the entire New Testament. In the Roman Church, only church leaders and scholars study the Bible; Luther's translation will enable the common people to read the Scriptures for themselves.[644]

*****

While Luther is isolated in Wartburg Castle, Christian leaders in Germany and Switzerland continue their efforts to bring about changes in the Church. It has taken a special man like Luther to ignite real reform, but events over the previous centuries have been preparing European Society to confront the power and corruption of the Roman Church.

---

[643] Bainton, *Here I Stand*, 144. Bainton says the words "Here I stand, I cannot do otherwise" were not recorded at the time of the debate but were in the first printed version and therefore are possibly genuine.

[644] Kuiper, *The Church*, 180–181; Bainton, *Christianity*, 250.

The establishment of universities in the twelfth century and the attempts of the scholastics to harmonize faith and knowledge helped set the stage for Renaissance humanism and rapid advances in literature, art, and science. Courageous sailors had extended the boundaries of the known world; Christopher Columbus reached America in 1492, and five years later, Vasco De Gama rounded the southern tip of Africa and established a profitable trade route to India.[645] In 1513, Ponce de Leon explored Florida, and in 1517, Hernando Cortez reached the Aztec capital of Tenochtitlan. The explorers were seeking gold and other treasures, but some of them also wanted to spread Christianity to the new lands.[646]

Because of the printing press, news and information about new discoveries and developments spread throughout Europe. Citizens in the different nations became aware of new possibilities for themselves and their communities. European society is undergoing changes, and many citizens, especially in Germany, want to see changes in the Church.

But the papacy remains very powerful, and the people have long viewed the Church as the repository of religious truth. The model for the dissemination of God's Word has been the same for a thousand years—God speaks through the Scriptures, the pope and priests interpret the texts, and then they develop decrees and rituals for the common people. For most Church members, their Christian education consisted of baptism and the Mass. Luther had not held a Bible until he discovered one at the University of Erfurt when he was twenty years old; he had never heard of some of the books in the Bible.[647]

But now, with copies of the Old and New Testaments becoming available, serious believers are seeing that many official dogmas of the Roman Church, doctrines concerning Mary, the celibacy of priests, the supremacy of the pope, purgatory, indulgencies, and salvation through the sacramental system are not found in the Scriptures. The watchword for Renaissance scholars had been *Ad Fontes* (Back to the Sources). For those trying to reform the Church, the battle

---

[645] The Ottoman Empire in Asia had cut off any possible land routes.

[646] Nate Sullivan, "Spreading Religion in the Age of Exploration," *Study.com*, accessed December 26, 2018,https://study.com/academy/lesson/spreading-religion-in-the-age-of-exploration.html.

[647] John Rae, *Luther, Student, Monk, Reformer* (London: Hodden and Stoughton, 1884), 24.

cry becomes *Sola Scriptura* (Scripture Alone); the Bible is the final authority, not popes and priests and their traditions.

*****

During Luther's absence, Karlstadt and Melanchthon institute changes in the Wittenberg churches. The worship service is simplified, and German is substituted for Latin. Masses for the dead are discontinued, and days of fasting and abstinence are abolished. Melanchthon begins to offer the cup as well as the host to the laity during Communion. A number of monks and nuns leave their monastic communities and get married. Luther is kept informed about the changes and agrees with them until Karlstadt and some of his followers begin tearing down pictures of the saints in the churches; Luther recommends moderation.

When he learns that three laymen from Zwickau have confounded Melanchthon by claiming to be prophets receiving direct revelation from God, Luther decides he must return to Wittenberg. Luther knows that if he leaves the castle, Frederick may not be able to protect him, but he trusts in God and understands that the current political circumstances favor him. Although Emperor Charles is determined to stamp out the Lutheran "heresy," he is confronting a more immediate danger than the Reformer. Francis I, King of France, was displeased when Charles was elected to be the new Emperor and is now threatening military action. Charles cannot afford to alienate any of the German princes who may be supportive of Luther.[648]

Luther arrives in Wittenberg in March 1522 and is able to restrain the Zwickau prophets and restore stability in the local churches. Although Luther desires orderly change, the intensity and scope of the Reformation will inevitably bring about conflicts beyond his control.

*****

Luther and his followers are breaking away from the yoke of the Roman system and reestablishing Christian liberty. Luther discards the sacramental system as the means for salvation and says there are only two sacraments, bap-

---

[648] Justo L. Gonzalez, *The Story of Christianity,* Vol. 2, *The Reformation to the Present Day* (New York: Harper Collins, 1985), 38–39.

tism, and the Eucharist. Prayers to the saints and Mary, the worship of images, the veneration of relics, pilgrimages, monasticism, and the papacy itself are all rejected.

Reformation within the Church also brings political, economic, and social changes in the districts which are beginning to accept Reformed teaching. A Lutheran form of church government is established with a pastor and officers elected by parishioners forming a church council for each congregation. New materials for study and worship are developed and a Lutheran statement of faith, the *Augsburg Confession*, is eventually drawn up. The concept that each Christian is a believer-priest leads individuals to view their vocations and family lives in a more positive way.

Luther and Melanchthon, with the willing aid of Reformed princes, revise and improve the public education system. In contrast to the popes who had banned the reading of the Bible by laity, Luther wants every person to be able to read the Scriptures.

Luther had not set out to disrupt the social order in Germany or separate from the Roman Church; his intention was to reform a corrupted Church. The changes taking place in German society are the outflow of a theology based on Scripture, not an attempt at revolution.[649]

*****

Luther is not a politician, but he appears to be influenced by Augustine's concept of government. He speaks of two kingdoms, spiritual and secular, which seems to parallel Augustine's idea of a city of God and a city of man. The early Reformers believe both the church and secular government are ordained by God and should therefore work in unity as opposed to the concept of a "wall of separation" eventually adopted by most Western democracies. As the Reformation makes progress across Europe, the relationships between the divided Church and the different political rulers become very complicated and unsettled. The Reformers face strong opposition from some of the German princes and other rulers who remain loyal to the Roman Church.

In addition, the movement has unforeseen consequences that result in tragedies. In 1524, the peasants in western and southern Germany invoke Reformation concepts to demand agrarian rights and improved treatment from

---

[649] Kuiper, *The Church*, 182–185.

landlords. Luther and Zwingli are both sympathetic to the peasants' cause, but when they form armies and begin a violent revolution, Luther urges the German rulers to suppress the insurrection. The princes combine their militaries and battle the peasant forces of approximately 300,000 fighters.

The rebellion is crushed in the spring of 1525, and an estimated 100,000 peasants die. The hierarchy of the Roman Church blames Luther, and a great number of peasants believe that he has betrayed them; many of them return to the old faith.[650] Luther's reputation suffers and the progress of the Reformation slows significantly.

As Luther is being impugned for his role in the Peasants War, Erasmus publishes a book attacking him on a crucial theological issue. Luther had affirmed the doctrine of predestination because it was a necessary corollary of justification by faith as a free gift of God. Erasmus, under pressure to choose between Rome and the Reformers, sides with the papacy and attacks Luther on this particular point. He writes a treatise on the freedom of the will, denying predestination by claiming that human beings have an inherent ability to turn to God for salvation.

Luther replies with his most famous book, *The Bondage of the Will*,[651] where, citing Saint Paul and Augustine, he shows that humans are bound by their sinful natures; they are fallen in all their faculties and will not and cannot turn to God of their own volition. Sinners must be born again by the Holy Spirit before they can repent and come to faith. Good works flow from a changed heart. They do not gain salvation; they are the result of salvation. Luther thanks Erasmus for raising this most crucial issue in the theological debates between the Roman Church and the Reformers.[652]

Although Zwingli and other reformers have differences with Luther over some issues like the sacrament of communion, they are uniformly in agreement with him about the bondage of the will. The sovereignty of God is fundamental to Reformed thinking. Human beings enter God's kingdom through His grace and predetermined plan, not freewill choices, which are essentially good works. Luther's debate with Erasmus was similar to Augustine's dispute with Pelagius in the fifth century over the nature of man and the ability of the will, a debate

---

[650] Gonzalez, *The Story*, Vol. 2, 42.
[651] Martin Luther, *The Bondage of the Will*, reproduced in, *Luther and Erasmus: Free Will and Salvation*, eds, E. Gordon and Philip S. Watson (Philadelphia: Westminster Press, 1969).
[652] Ibid., 104, 322, 333; *Gonzalez, The Story*, Vol. 2, 42.

which continues in the Church today.[653] But for many Christians, Luther's book provides a definitive conclusion.

*****

In 1525, an event occurs which will have a dramatic effect on Luther's personal life. After a group of "Reformed" nuns escape from a Cistercian convent and begin new occupations, one of them, Katharina von Bora, states that she might be willing to marry Luther. Luther pursues this possibility because it would "please his father, provoke the pope, and pass on his name."[654] Luther, a former monk, and Katharina, a former nun, are married and move into a former monastery in Wittenberg, a wedding gift from the new elector, John the Steadfast.[655]

Despite his initially unromantic motivations, Luther comes to dearly love his "lord Katie" and greatly enjoys married life. Because money is short, Katie takes in boarders; the monastery becomes a very busy place because additional guests, often scholars and students, come to visit Luther. He continues to preach and teach and also begins to write hymns.

A few years after his marriage, he pens "A Mighty Fortress Is Our God," the battle hymn of the Reformation, which will eventually be translated into more languages than any other religious song. The hymn expresses Luther's heart and helps him overcome his fears.[656]

Martin and Katie eventually have six children, three boys and three girls, and their neighbors get to see the famous theologian hanging diapers on the clothesline. The illnesses and deaths of their first two daughters, Elizabeth at eight months and Magdalena at thirteen years, are crushing for the couple. But

---

[653] In 1618, the Synod of Dort will meet and condemn the teaching of Jacobus Arminius, who claimed that the human will is able to turn to God through its own ability. But Arminius's view has now come to be the dominate theology of most churches in the United States.

[654] Jones, *Christian History,* 109.

[655] Luther's protector, the elector, Frederick the Wise, had died a month before Luther's wedding. Despite their interconnected lives, Frederick and Luther never met face-to-face.

[656] "Hymns by Martin Luther," *Zion Lutheran Church,* accessed December 26, 2018, http://atlanta.clclutheran.org/bibleclass/Hymns%20of%20Martin%20Luther.pdf.

their union survives and they go on to become a model for what a Christian family can be.[657]

*****

During its history, the Roman Church had at times been closely united with secular rulers and at other times at war with them. Luther and the Reformers believe that the Church and secular government are both decreed by God and therefore should cooperate in serving the people. Prince Frederick's protection of Luther, along with the support of the German princes in improving public education, reinforced this view, which was common to both the Swiss and German Reform movements. But mixing the functions of Church and state leads to problems.

With the advancement of the Reformation, regions in Switzerland and Germany have separated into either Reformed or Roman Catholic territories, depending on the allegiances of the ruling princes. Although the population in a Reformed area is comprised of people of both denominations as well as unbelievers, the people as a whole are assumed to be part of the Reformed Church. And because the Reformers had retained the Roman Church's practice of infant baptism, all children are baptized, becoming not only a member of the Reformed Church but a citizen of the Reformed government. The Church and the state have become intertwined; supporting the Reformed Church and infant baptism are civic duties sometimes having little to do with anyone's religious convictions.

Adding to this problem for the Church is an important parallel issue. A misapplication of Luther's doctrine of salvation by grace alone is leading to a lapse in morality among some members of Reformed congregations. These developments are corrupting the faith in many assemblies and set the stage for another tragedy in the progress of the Reformation.

Troubled by these growing threats to the purity of the Church, a group of Reformers led by Conrad Grebel meet in Zurich, Switzerland, to study the Scriptures, where they see a New Testament Church free from the state, composed of only believers, with no mention of infant baptism.[658] In one of their

---

[657] Jones, *Christian History*, 109; Eric W. Gritsch, "Martin Luther," *Christianity Today*, accessed December 26, 2018, https://www.christianitytoday.com/history/people/theologians/martin-luther.html.

[658] See pp. 417–418, for further discussion of infant baptism.

meetings, a man named Blaurock asks to be baptized again; Grebel complies, and a movement within the Reformed community begins. The Anabaptists (from the Greek, *to baptize again*) are not ascetics, but like the early monastics, they believe that the union of Church and state is resulting in a corrupt Church. They want baptism and Church membership reserved for only those who are genuine believers. They see infant baptism as meaningless, so the Anabaptists begin rebaptizing church members who give a credible profession of faith.

With surprising rapidity, groups of Anabaptists spring up in Switzerland, then Austria, Bohemia, Southern Germany, and even into the Netherlands. Some of the congregations espouse communal living and form unions called *Bruderhofs*, "brother estates." The belief that the Church should be separate from the state leads many Anabaptists to be pacifists, something unacceptable to rulers trying to protect their territories and maintain social and political order. The Anabaptists also insist that the Church should be supported by free-will donations, not tithes collected by the government. The movement comes to be seen not only as a serious threat to the Reformed Church but to the foundations of society. At the Diet of Speyer in 1529,[659] both Catholic and Reformed princes agree to subject Anabaptists to the death penalty throughout the Holy Roman Empire. Luther is slow to agree but eventually gives his consent because of his fear of sedition and anarchy. Thousands of Anabaptists are drowned in mock baptisms or burned at the stake.[660]

As the movement's more moderate leaders are executed, extremists emerge and begin to espouse polygamy and the slaughter of the ungodly. Some of them take over the German city of Munster, and Jan Matthys declares himself to be the Prophet Enoch,[661] claiming that Munster is going to be the New Jerusalem. Thousands of Anabaptists stream into the city which is soon besieged by an army of Catholics and Lutherans. The Anabaptists hold out for a year, suffer horribly, and are eventually overrun and slaughtered.

The radicals have discredited the movement, and Anabaptism appears to have been vanquished. But some moderate adherents survive, largely by isolat-

---

[659] It is at the meeting of this diet that the Reformed German princes begin to be called Protestants, a name which will come to be applied to the entire Reformed movement. See Gonzalez, *Story of Christianity,* Vol. 2, 56.

[660] Gonzalez, *Story of Christianity,* Vol. 2, 53–59.

[661] Enoch was taken up by God without experiencing death (Gen. 5:24) as was Elijah (2 Kings 2:11). Some Anabaptists believed that Enoch was to be one of the two witnesses who will prophesy just before Christ's Second Coming (Jude 14; Rev. 11:1–13).

ing themselves, and eventually flourish in the late sixteenth century under the guidance of a Dutch Reformer named Menno Simons. The Mennonites and Amish are the heirs of this revival and today are acknowledged to be peaceful and industrious citizens.[662]

*****

For those of us living in a multicultural society such as the United States with its history of religious tolerance, such brutality between Christian groups takes us aback. Although it is very distressing, we see that even Christian societies react violently when they feel threatened. The Reformers made huge advances in understanding Scripture and applying biblical doctrine, but their understanding of the kingdom of God and its outworking in history were flawed. They saw the kingdom as existing in cooperation with secular governments instead of being an entity apart from but existing within the realms of secular regimes. When the church and state are closely connected, a disagreement over doctrine can become a crime against the state. Both the Roman Catholics and the Reformers were willing to use secular authorities to brutally enforce their understandings of religious truth.

The sixteenth century is a period of great spiritual dynamism, a religious storm that engulfs both Protestants and Roman Catholics from peasants to kings. It is one of the most convulsed times in the history of Christianity, and the Peasants War and the persecution of the Anabaptists are just the beginning of the violent turmoil.

*****

By 1531, the Roman Catholic princes in Switzerland have become so concerned about the spread of the Reformation that five of them form a confederation and send their troops to attack the Reformers in Zurich. A hastily raised Zurich force is defeated, and Zwingli, who had joined the troops as a chaplain, is killed. A peace treaty, signed on November 24, 1531, upholds the Roman Catholic claims in the disputed areas of Switzerland. These events are serious setbacks, but the Reformed movement is too strong to be halted by the

---

[662] Kuiper, *The Church*, 204–209.

loss of one battle or the death of one individual, even a man as important as Zwingli.[663]

Despite Roman Catholic opposition and their internal divisions, the Reformers or Protestants as they have become known, continue to make progress throughout the European countries. When Luther's manuscripts begin to pour into France, alarmed Catholic theologians begin to publish tracts to counter the Reformation movement, and they condemn recent French translations of the New Testament. Despite this opposition, Luther has thousands of followers in Paris and other areas of France, but they are unorganized and lack unified leadership.[664]

Among the Frenchmen who accept Reformed doctrine is a young man named John Calvin. Born in 1509 in Noyon, a small town just north of Paris, Calvin had gained entrance to the University of Paris through the efforts of his father who recognized his son's keen intellect. Calvin drove himself to master his studies in logic, the classical languages, the writings of the Church Fathers, and law. After three years in Paris, he continued his studies in Orleans and Bourges where he met influential friends such as Nicolas Cop and Theodore Beza. Although Calvin does not mention an exact date, it is during this time that he says, "God by a sudden conversion subdued...my heart."[665]

In 1533, Cop, who has become rector of the University of Paris, makes his annual All Saints' Day address. Government officials and Catholic leaders believe that Cop is expressing Luther's ideas and that he has been influenced by Calvin. Cop and Calvin have to flee for their lives; Calvin escapes out of a back window while the bailiffs are at his front door. He is hunted from city to city but manages to teach small groups in secret meetings and eventually makes his way to Basel, Switzerland.

It is in Basel that he formulates the truths of the Bible in a systematic way, and in the spring of 1536, when he is only twenty-six years old, Calvin publishes his *Institutes of the Christian Religion*,[666] a catechism and systematic explanation of the fundamental teachings of the Reformation movement. This work, written in classic Latin and later translated into elegant French, is soon known as the leading statement of Protestant doctrines. Eventually updated

---

[663] Gonzales, *Story of Christianity*, Vol. 2, 122–132.

[664] Kuiper, *The Church*, 211.

[665] Ibid., 190.

[666] John Calvin, *Institutes of the Christian Religion*, ed. John T. McNeill, trans. Ford Lewis Battles (Philadelphia: Westminster Press, 1960), Vols. I and II.

and expanded several times by Calvin, it is still recognized as one of the ablest expositions of the teaching of Scripture.

In late summer of 1536, Calvin, a frail young man, leaves Basel to go to Strasbourg in southwestern Germany where he intends to lead the quiet life of a scholar. On his way, he passes through Geneva, a city in the French-speaking area of Switzerland. When Guillaume Farel, a fiery preacher who has been leading the Protestant movement in the district, learns that the author of the *Institutes* is in Geneva, he confronts a surprised Calvin and demands that he stay and help with the work in the city. Calvin protests that he needs to do more study and that he is not suited for the work that Farel is doing. Farel thunders, "May God curse your studies if now in her time of need you refuse to lend your aid to His Church."[667] Calvin later admits that he was struck with terror, and he consents to stay in Geneva.

*****

As Calvin begins his first residency in Geneva, an English priest named William Tyndale has been imprisoned for heresy in the Netherlands. Tyndale, who spoke seven languages, had fled Britain for Germany when his bishop refused to let him publish his English version of the Greek New Testament. After his excellent translation was published in Worms in 1525,[668] he managed to smuggle copies into England in flour sacks. Tyndale was condemned in England by the Roman Church, King Henry the VIII, and the famous humanist Thomas More. Eventually, their agents captured Tyndale near the city of Brussels. He is convicted of heresy, and on October 6, 1536, he is strangled and then burned. But his English New Testament and his other writings greatly further the cause of the Reformation in England and Scotland.[669]

In 1534, prior to Tyndale's arrest, King Henry had split the English Church away from Rome. Henry's reasons were not theological. He had wanted to end his marriage to his aging wife, Catherine, in order to marry the much younger Anne Boleyn in the hope of having a male heir. When the pope refused to grant

---

[667] Kuiper, *The Church*, 193–194.

[668] In contrast to Wycliff's translation, Tyndale's was from the original Greek, not the Latin Vulgate, and was in contemporary English. See Kuiper, *The Church*, 222.

[669] Ibid, 222; also see John A. R. Dick, "The Pen-and-Ink Wars, or Tyndale vs. More," *Christianity Today*, accessed December 27, 2018, https://www.christianitytoday.com/history/issues/issue-16/pen-and-ink-wars-or-tyndale-vs-more.html.

an annulment, Henry defiantly divorced Catherine and married an already pregnant Anne in 1533. The next year, he declared himself to be the head of the English Church. Those who objected to his assuming the role of the pope were executed, including Thomas More. But Anne failed to bear a son, and in 1536, Henry accuses her of adultery and has her beheaded.[670] He quickly marries Jane Seymour who dies in 1537, giving birth to a son. King Henry has an heir, and England has its own church, but not a Reformed one.

*****

Calvin works with Farel and, after a year, is appointed to be one of the preachers in Geneva, but in 1538, both he and Farel are banished from the city when they refuse to accept the form of worship the city council wants to impose in regard to the Sacrament of the Eucharist. Farel retreats to Neuchatel, just north of Geneva, where he will serve as pastor until his death in 1565. Martin Bucer, who had been won for the Reformation during Luther's Leipzig debate,[671] invites Calvin to join him in his ministry at Strasbourg, Calvin's original destination.

Calvin moves in with Bucer and his wife, Elizabeth, and has the opportunity to become acquainted firsthand with followers of both Luther and Zwingli. Calvin is, in effect, a second-generation leader in the Reformation and is getting to know those who have led the movement before him. He becomes pastor of a refugee church whose members have escaped from the Catholic persecutions in France. He also lectures in theology and, after seeing the happy marriage of the Bucers, begins to consider taking a wife who could aid him in his daily affairs and help him with his fragile health. He eventually marries Idelette de Bure Stordeur, a young widow with two children who becomes his helper and faithful companion.[672]

---

[670] Marilee Hanson, "Anne Boleyn Facts & Biography Of Information," *English History*, February 6, 2015, https://englishhistory.net/tudor/monarchs/anne-boleyn/.

[671] See p. 331.

[672] Idelette and Calvin have three children but all die in infancy. Her health deteriorates and her death after nine years of marriage is an intense grief for Calvin. See "Odd Romance Of John And Idelette Calvin," *Christianity.com*, April 28, 2010, https://www.christianity.com/church/church-history/timeline/1501-1600/odd-romance-of-john-and-idelette-calvin-11629964.html

Calvin never meets Luther, but he becomes friends with Luther's young colleague, Philip Melanchthon. Despite their friendship, the two have doctrinal differences, and Calvin's goal of uniting the Lutheran and Calvinistic movements is eventually frustrated.[673]

Calvin spends a peaceful three years in Strasbourg, although his commitment to assisting the Reformed churches in Europe means more travel than he likes. When men friendly to Calvin regain control of the Geneva council in 1541, they ask him to return to the city. He is reluctant to leave Strasbourg for the turmoil in Geneva, but eventually, the council members persuade him, and he receives an enthusiastic welcome from the citizens of the city. For the next twenty-three years, Calvin will labor for the Reformed cause in Geneva.

One of the first things he does upon his return is to draw up a *Church Order*, a set of rules for governing churches based on the teaching of Scripture. The directives ordain four offices for congregations: pastors, teachers, elders, and deacons. Elders are to be the cornerstone of governance and oversee the purity of doctrine and life in assemblies. The ultimate discipline which elders can enforce is excommunication; any further penalty is to be enacted by the civil magistrate. Calvin's work goes smoothly until he insists that openly immoral members be excluded from the communion table, which reignites the prior Eucharist controversy. His life is threatened, and it appears that he may again be driven from the city.[674]

*****

While Calvin is struggling in Geneva, Luther continues to minister in Wittenberg, despite his deteriorating health. In January 1546, Luther leaves Wittenberg with his three sons to settle a serious dispute in the church at Eisleben. Cold rain and icy roads make the journey difficult, but Luther receives a warm welcome from cheering crowds when he reaches the city of his birth. Although he is quite ill, Luther preaches on Sunday, January 31—it will be his last sermon. After receiving an anxious letter from Katie, he replies on the seventh of February. Luther dies eleven days later at the age of sixty-two in the city where he was born. His three sons accompany Luther's body back to

---

[673] The followers of Calvin differed with the Lutherans somewhat over Church government but primarily over the presence of Christ during the Sacrament of Communion. Luther insisted that Christ was physically present in the elements and would not relent.
[674] Kuiper, *The Church*, 189–198.

Wittenberg where his devoted wife and large crowds gather to pay their final respects.[675]

Luther had been the fiery catalyst that God used to ignite the firestorm of the Reformation. With his death, a new stage of the movement will now advance under the leadership of a man with a very different nature. Calvin is a reserved theologian and preacher, but his systematic explanations of Scripture and Reformation principles will have an effect that goes beyond what even Luther had accomplished.

*****

For centuries, the many scandals and abuses of the Roman Church had been a sore grief to many Christians and had helped provoke the Reformation. Seeing the changes being instituted by Protestants, believers who remain loyal to Catholicism begin to insist on thoroughgoing reform in the Roman Church as well. It is clear to all that the major problems with the Church center on the popes and the papal hierarchy.

There had been attempts to bring about reform within the Church in the years before Luther began voicing his objections. In the latter days of the fifteenth century, a Franciscan monk named Ximenes (1436–1517), with the support of Queen Isabella, had initiated changes for the Spanish clergy. He had enforced strict discipline in the monasteries and high moral standards for the priests. He had also renewed the Inquisition courts for anyone who resisted. Isabella had protected Ximenes from the interference of the popes, but his changes had no effect on the basic structure and doctrines of the Roman Church.

Charles V, after condemning Luther, had tried to bring about reform and sought to reunite the followers of Luther and the papacy, but without success. In 1545, with the Reformation threatening to sweep through all of Europe, Pope Paul III finally summons a council in the northern Italian city of Trent. This council meets, with some interruptions, until 1563 and brings about some major changes in the Roman Church.

Following the lead of the Reformed churches, the Council formulates a creed for Roman Catholicism and adopts a catechism. The seven sacraments

---

[675] Stephen Nichols, "Martin Luther's Death and Legacy," *Ligonier Ministries*, February 17, 2016 www.ligonier.org/blog/martin-luthers-death-and-legacy/

are declared necessary for salvation and the doctrine of salvation by faith alone is denied. The cup is still forbidden for the laity during the mass. Provisions are made for better education of the clergy, and some of the worst abuses of the papacy are corrected.[676] A list of forbidden books called the *Index* is drawn up to prevent Catholics from reading Protestant literature. The writings of Luther and Calvin had circulated freely in Europe, but now the *Index* begins to slow the spread of their theological understandings. These significant changes help strengthen the unity of the Roman Church, but the primary result of Trent is that the supremacy of the pope is more firmly established than ever before. The essential character of Catholicism does not change and the differences with the Reformers become more defined and further hardened. The Council of Trent begins what is called the Counter Reformation and sets the stage for a major struggle between Roman Catholics and Protestants.[677]

*****

During the years the Council of Trent is meeting, Calvin continues his work in Geneva. In 1553, a Spanish physician named Michael Servetus, who had written a book attacking the doctrine of the Trinity, arrives in the city. Servetus had been condemned to death by the Catholic Church in France but had escaped from his Inquisition prison. When he is recognized, the Geneva Council has him arrested. Calvin helps draw up charges against Servetus, but he also pleads with him to repent and renounce his heretical views. Servetus refuses, and the Council, with the concurrence of Calvin, Melanchthon, and the religious leaders of the surrounding cantons, executes Servetus by burning him at the stake, a common penalty in the Catholic Church which had been adopted by some Protestant governments. Both denominations fail to understand the nature of God's kingdom under the new covenant.[678]

Eventually, Calvin's opponents will use this episode to try to discredit him and his theological beliefs. But in Geneva, Servetus's defenders are widely condemned, and Calvin's influence is strengthened; he soon has the undivided

---

[676] See Kenneth Scott Latourette, *A History of Christianity*, Vol. II (Peabody, MA: Prince Press, 1997), 866–871 for a more complete summary of the Council of Trent.

[677] Kuiper, *The Church*, 230–234.

[678] The execution of Servetus, like the persecution of the Anabaptists, highlights the dangers of inter-mixing the Church with civil government. The Church was not meant to function like the failed theocratic nation of Israel.

support of the City Council. In addition, Protestants fleeing from persecution continue to stream into Geneva, and they are strong backers of Calvin and his theology.[679]

With a secure standing in Geneva, Calvin does some of his most important work. He continues his copious writing and eventually pens commentaries on forty-eight books of the Bible.[680] In 1559, he completes his third and final edition of the *Institutes*, which is five times as long as his first version in 1536. In the same year, he establishes the Geneva Academy, the first Protestant university, built and supported by the sacrificial giving of the common people of Geneva. From its very beginning, the academy enjoys the highest reputation, and soon, nine hundred students from all over Europe are enrolled. Theodore Beza becomes the first rector and will eventually take over as pastor of the Geneva Reformed Church after Calvin's death.[681]

The university produces so many pastors and missionaries for Europe that the king of France becomes alarmed and sends an official warning to Geneva to try to stop the Protestant progress in his territory. But the Geneva Academy continues to thrive, and Calvin's influence, through his writings and academy graduates, extends into not only France but also Italy, Hungary, Poland, and Western Germany before the Counter Reformation and the *Index* begin to slow his widespread influence.

*****

With the Council of Trent helping to revive the Roman Church, the clashes with the Protestant movement begin to intensify. Central Europe has become a vast complex of hundreds of semiautonomous political precincts separated by religious loyalties whose ruling princes are willing to call for outside military help to maintain control of their territories. Although Charles V

---

[679] Gonzalez, *The Story*, Vol. 2, 67–68.

[680] The original copies of Calvin's books had to be written by hand in pen and ink. With our technology today, it is much easier to write a manuscript, especially when making changes and revisions. Calvin did not have this great advantage and yet the quality and quantity of his work is astounding, especially considering his frail health and his extensive responsibilities.

[681] Calvin's health will continue to deteriorate and he dies in 1564 at the age of 54. He had first met Beza during his studies in France. See p. 343. Beza could not have imagined the immense influence the frail young man would have in the coming years.

would still like to wipe out the "Lutheran heresy," he also wants to maintain peace in his Holy Roman Empire and, in 1555, calls for a diet at Augsburg, Germany. In the "Peace of Augsburg," Roman Catholic and Lutheran delegates agree that no principality should attack another while efforts are being made to reunite the churches. This treaty helps protect the Lutherans in Germany, but it does not include those Protestants in other areas who are followers of Zwingli or Calvin and consider themselves to be "Reformed" but not Lutheran.[682]

*****

Because of the Peasants War, the Anabaptist Persecution, internal divisions over such issues as the sacrament of communion, and deteriorating moral conditions due to misapplications of the central doctrine of justification by faith alone, the initial rapid advance of the Reformation has slowed. Now a strengthened papacy empowers a new order, the Jesuits, who act as religious enforcers to educate and discipline the Catholic masses.[683] The Inquisition courts, which had been renewed in Spain, are now reestablished by the papacy in the Catholic-controlled areas of Europe. Under Pope Paul IV (1555–1559), the activity of the Inquisition authorities increases to the point of terror. Despite the Peace of Augsburg, the Roman Church is determined to regain what it has lost to the Protestant movement.

The Inquisition courts include a grand inquisitor, local inquisitors, notaries, legal consultants, servants, and jailers. With this large force at its disposal, the Roman Church is able to quickly extinguish the Reformed movement in Spain and Italy. Protestants are jailed, killed, or driven to flight.

In France, battles for control of the government break out between Catholic forces and Reformed Frenchmen called Huguenots. After a peace agreement in 1570, the leading Huguenots are invited to Paris to celebrate a royal wedding, unaware that Catherine de Medici, the regent mother of young Charles IX, is plotting with Catholic extremists.

Early in the morning of August 24, 1572, Saint Bartholomew's Day, the city bells are rung as a signal to Catholics to begin the premeditated attack

---

[682] The Editors of Encyclopaedia, "Peace of Augsburg," *Encyclopaedia*, accessed December 27, 2018, https://www.britannica.com/event/Peace-of-Augsburg.

[683] The Jesuits have been called the "shock troops" of the Counter Reformation. See https://www.nytimes.com/2004/12/12/weekinreview/jesuits-show-strength-even-as-their-numbers-shrink.html.

on the Huguenots. The massacre goes on for three days, and an estimated three thousand Protestants are killed. The attacks extend to other cities, with over ten thousand Huguenots being slain throughout the country. The Saint Bartholomew Massacre comes to be known as one of the foulest crimes recorded in history. But the remaining Huguenots continue to resist, and eventually, in 1598, King Henry IV of France grants them freedom of worship and civil rights in two hundred towns and three thousand castles.[684]

The leaders of the Counter Reformation extend their persecutions to England and Scotland where Protestants are burned at the stake as heretics. But it is the Netherlands, under the rule of Spain, which suffers the most from the Spanish Inquisition.[685] Many men and women, some of them very young, are tortured and executed as the Roman Catholic Church tries to destroy the Protestant movement in Northern Europe.[686] The Catholic hierarchy inflicts a systematic terror on those who dare to disagree with them while claiming to represent true religion.

*****

In 1606, despite the ongoing religious struggles, King James I of England turns his attention to finances and attempts to profit from the natural resources of the huge territories that have been discovered across the Atlantic Ocean. He authorizes the London Company, an English joint stock company, to begin establishing colonial settlements in North America. In 1607, the company's first settlement, Jamestown, is founded on the James River about forty miles upstream from its mouth on the Chesapeake Bay. The colony suffers great hardship—more than half the settlers die from disease and starvation the first winter—but it manages to survive and becomes the first permanent English settlement in North America.[687] The establishment of this colony opens up the

---

[684] Kuiper, *The Church*, 234–239; Gonzalez, *The Story*, Vol. 2, 119.

[685] Kuiper, *The Church*, 240–243.

[686] The number of executions during the Inquisitions is estimated to be in the tens of thousands by some early sources. See Will Durant, *The Reformation* (New York: Simon and Schuster, 1957), 213–216. Rodney Stark claims, on the basis of recent studies, that these numbers are exaggerated, see Stark, *Triumph*, 333–350. He does agree that three thousand people were killed in Paris during the Saint Bartholomew Massacre.

[687] A previous settlement had been attempted at Roanoke, Virginia, in 1587, but the fate of these colonists is unknown. That attempt is now called the "Lost Colony." See Jonathan Hogeback, "The Lost Colony of Roanoke," *Ecyclopaedia*, accessed December 27, 2018,

possibility of a sanctuary for European Christians who want to practice their faith without interference and hostile attacks.

In 1620, a group of Puritan Separatists,[688] who have given up on reforming the Church of England, are provided passage on the ship *Mayflower* by its owners who want to start a colony in North America. The approximately 100 passengers and 30 crewmen, who become known as the Pilgrims, land in Massachusetts and start the Plymouth Colony. During the first winter, most of the women and half the men die of disease and hunger, but by the next fall, they harvest a crop and celebrate a meal with the native people, an occasion which will eventually be commemorated as the first Thanksgiving Holiday.[689]

Nine years later, the Massachusetts Bay Colony, with almost 1,000 Puritans, is established near the present site of Boston. They, too, suffer losses, with approximately 200 settlers dying the first year. But living conditions improve, and over the next decade, more than 20,000 new colonists, most of them Puritans, arrive in "New England." The Puritans are Calvinists and want to establish a society that conforms to the laws of God.[690] Despite all the hardships, the kingdom of God has advanced into North America.

*****

While a few Protestants are attempting to establish new communities across the Atlantic Ocean, the vast majority in Europe continue to defend themselves against the forces of the Roman Church and the Counter Reformation. Although the people of Germany have experienced a tenuous truce because of the Peace of Augsburg, in 1618, a complex combination of religious, eco-

---

https://www.britannica.com/story/the-lost-colony-of-roanoke. Spain had established a settlement at St. Augustine, Florida in 1565, but it was repeatedly attacked by pirates and English forces and not continually maintained. See Peter Feuerherd, "St. Augustine, the Real First European Settlement in America," *JSTOR Daily*, April 15, 2017, https://daily.jstor.org/st-augustine-the-real-first-european-settlement-in-america/.

[688] The Puritans were Christians in England who wanted to reform or "purify" the Church of England. The Separatists were those who had given up on reform and had decided to break away from the state church.

[689] Caleb Johnson, "Mayflower and Plymouth History," *Mayflower History.com*, accessed December 27, 2018, www.mayflowerhistory.com/pilgrim-history/.

[690] "John Calvin & The Puritan Founders of New England," *Chalcedon Presbyterian Church, Resources/Articles*, accessed December 27, 2018, http://chalcedon.org/resources/articles/john-calvin-the-puritan-founders-of-new-england.

nomic, and political quarrels erupt into a series of conflicts with battles fought in central European countries but primarily in Germany. These brutal engagements will last for three decades and become known as the Thirty Years War. The hostilities will rearrange the countries of Europe and change the way kings, statesmen, and the people of Europe view religion.

*****

The war begins in 1618, when Ferdinand II, King of Bohemia, attempts to impose Catholicism throughout his domain. The Protestant districts rebel and appeal for help from Protestants in Great Britain, the Dutch Republic, and Denmark. Ferdinand in turn calls upon the German Catholics, Spain, and the papacy; Ferdinand's allies not only respond with troops but, in 1619, elect him to be the Holy Roman Emperor. The large-scale and ruthless battles, often fought with mercenary forces, continue for over a decade until by 1629, Catholic armies have overrun most of Protestant Germany and much of Denmark.

The Protestant cause is saved by the intervention of Gustavus Adolphus, king of Sweden, who leads his army into Europe and, with the remaining Protestant fighters, drives Ferdinand and his allied forces out of much of Germany. But the fighting continues, and eventually, the major states of France, Spain, and Austria feel compelled to enter the conflict. France, although a Catholic nation, fights on the side of the Protestants because it fears being attacked by Spain and the Holy Roman Empire.

Germany remains the central battleground and is devastated. The mercenary armies often lack supplies and food and their troops ravage towns and farms to sustain themselves, often abusing the inhabitants, especially the women. It is estimated that Germany's overall population was reduced by 30 percent (in the territory of Brandenburg by 50 percent) due to battles, famines, and diseases.[691]

As the middle of the sixteenth century approaches, the European countries are materially depleted and spiritually drained from the continual warfare. There is a widespread desire for peace and an end to the breakdown of gov-

---

[691] New World Encyclopedia contributors, "Thirty Years War," *New World Encyclopedia*, accessed December 28, 2018, http://www.newworldencyclopedia.org/entry/Thirty_Years%E2%80%99 War.

ernment and general lawlessness that has led to the deaths of many civilians. Leaders understand that law and order must be restored, and in 1648, the nations end the long conflict with the Treaty of Westphalia. The Netherlands, whose citizens had suffered so much from the Spanish Inquisition, gains its independence from Spain. Sweden gains control of the Baltics, and France becomes the preeminent Western nation. The power of the Holy Roman Emperor is broken, and the German princes are again able to determine the religion that will be proclaimed in their territories.[692] The papacy's dream of a reunited Church under the rule of Rome is gone for good.

*****

Thousands of individual Englishmen had volunteered to fight in the Protestant armies during the Thirty Years War, but the nation had avoided sending its armed forces into the battles while it dealt with its own serious internal problems. The Puritans, who had been under persecution from the Church of England, gained control of Parliament in 1640 and executed two of their chief oppressors. But the Puritans continued to have disputes with King Charles, and in 1642, he decided to use military force against Parliament. The Puritans fought back, plunging the nation into civil war. Even while the outcome of the conflict was in doubt, the Puritans took on the task of defining the doctrines of the Church. They called for an assembly at Westminster where 121 clergymen and 40 laymen completed a *Directory of Worship* and *The Westminster Confession of Faith* in 1646. *The Westminster Confession* is the last of the great Protestant creeds to come out of the Reformation and is a strong presentation of Reformed beliefs.

After seven years of fighting, the Parliament forces are victorious and King Charles surrenders. He is tried as a "tyrant, traitor, murderer, and public enemy" and is executed in January 1649 as the Treaty of Westphalia is being

---

[692] Latourette, *History,* Vol. II, 885–889; Bainton, *Christianity,* 288–292; New World Encyclopedia contributors, "Thirty Years;" The Editors of Encyclopaedia Britannica, "Thirty Years War," *Encyclopaedia Britannica,* accessed December 30, 2018, https://www.britannica.com/event/Thirty-Years-War; Wallbank, "The Thirty Years War," *History World International,* 2002, https://www.history.com/topics/reformation/thirty-years-war.

implemented in Germany.[693] Peace and a semblance of order are beginning to return to England and Continental Europe.

*****

The Thirty Years War marks the end of major religious wars in Europe, ending large-scale sectarian bloodshed. National leaders and the common people are not only exhausted from all the fighting and death; they are fatigued with religion. Many Europeans are no longer willing to follow religious leaders, whether Catholic or Protestant, because they seem to lead to death and destruction. Organizers of the evolving nations begin to form secular governments with little or no connection to religious authorities. The divided Church has lost its moral and intellectual standing as the ultimate authority for disseminating truth and structuring society.[694] Statesmen and philosophers want to establish administrations apart from the influence of religion, which will eventually mean apart from the influence of God.

Religious leaders, both Catholic and Protestant, had attempted to establish their views of the kingdom of God by employing the forces of secular governments. National leaders and the religious citizens of the different nations have come to recognize this as a worldly and deadly ambition, but it is not clear if Church leaders have reached the same conclusion.

*****

The Reformation movement has recovered and clarified great biblical truths about salvation and advanced the mission of the Church in very significant ways. But the Reformation and the response of the Roman Catholic Church have also contributed to tragedies such as the Peasants War, the persecution of the Anabaptists, and the Thirty Years War. These unforeseen consequences, partly if not largely due to misunderstandings about the kingdom of God, are heartrending but not surprising. The people of God are saved sinners struggling in a fallen world, not perfect people. These sinner saints are laboring through earthly turmoil on the way to the consummation of the kingdom.

---

[693] Kuiper, *The Church*, 251–255; for a complete copy of the Confession see "The Westminster Confession of Faith," *CRTA*, accessed December 30, 2018, www.reformed.org/documents/wcf_with_proofs/.

[694] Bruce L. Shelley, *Church History in Plain Language* (Dallas: Word, 1995), 313.

Like David and Solomon, their sins and misguided efforts often damage the kingdom rather than advance it. We should remember that when God ratified His covenant with Abraham, He alone passed between the split animals.[695] And Jesus has told us that *He* will build His Church (Matt. 16:18). We are to strive to advance the kingdom of God, but we must remember that it is accomplished through His concepts and power, not our own. We must not decide, like Adam and Eve, to try to build a kingdom based on our own moral conceptions.

Surveying the progress of the kingdom during the era of premodern thought, we have seen struggles and wars between people and nations who were fighting for their particular beliefs concerning gods or God. As the Church moves into the last of the seventeenth century, the Treaty of Westphalia marks the point in time when the premodern era begins to give way to the age of modern thought. A different way of thinking will challenge the foundations of Western Christianity as men begin to question first the authority, and then the very existence of God.[696] The leaders of the Church, especially Roman Catholics but also Protestants, have helped discredit the one in whom they profess to believe.

---

[695] See p. 46–47.
[696] Shelley, *Church History*, 311–312.

CHAPTER 29

THE KINGDOM AND MODERNITY

As the people of Europe struggle to recover from three decades of war and the nations begin to adjust to the new political realities, statesmen and philosophers begin to reflect on the years of destruction that began when a Roman Catholic king decided to drive Protestant Christians out of his country. Although religion was not the only cause of the war, it was the major factor and the reason for the first attacks. With militant Christians leaders initiating such a long and disastrous catastrophe, secular officials and intellectuals throughout Europe begin to consider how to diminish or completely negate religious influence on the new political orders emerging in Europe. Christian fanaticism and prejudice are seen as a greater danger than atheism.[697] The movement toward secular governments begins and will soon be followed by the development of secular societies.

The intellectual and spiritual authority of the Roman Church had been challenged even before the end of the Thirty Years War. After greatly improving the recent invention of the telescope, the Italian astronomer and mathematician, Galileo Galilei (1564–1642), had confirmed the claim of Copernicus (1473–1543) that the earth rotated around the sun, not vice-versa, contradicting the teaching of the Roman Church.[698] Called before an inquisition court in 1633, Galileo was forced to disavow his findings and was sentenced to spend the rest of his life under house arrest. But he continued his technical investigations by employing a new technique called the scientific method, which used observation and experiments to confirm theories about natural phenomena.

---

[697] This section relies on Shelley, *Church History*, 314–319.

[698] The Roman Church leaders believed the sun rotated around the earth and claimed Galileo was contradicting scriptural teaching such as Josh 10:12–15. They ignored that the biblical writers at times used common language; today, we still speak of a beautiful sunset, not a beautiful earth rotation.

A French mathematician and philosopher named Rene Descartes was alarmed when he learned of Galileo's condemnation, and he refrained from publishing his own book on cosmology in which he agreed with Galileo. Instead, in 1641, he published a philosophical work entitled *Meditations on First Philosophy in Which Is Proved the Existence of God and the Immortality of the Soul.* Using a system called methodic doubt, Descartes doubted everything except his own doubting. His starting point was basically, "I think; therefore I am." From this initial self-reference, he attempted to prove the existence of God and the soul. It may not have been Descartes's initial goal, but his method established human reason as an autonomous judge that has the ability to decide if God exists. Often credited with being the "Father of Modern Philosophy," Descartes helped to introduce the age when man's reason would become the ultimate authority for truth, even before the end of the Thirty Years War.[699]

Another decisive step in elevating man's reason occurs after Europe has begun to make progress in establishing secular governments. In 1687, Isaac Newton publishes his momentous work, *Mathematical Principles of Natural Philosophy*, in which the laws of motion, in the heavens and on the earth, are harmonized in a master principle for the universe, the law of gravitation. Intellectuals and the reading public of Europe are captivated by the wonder of Newton's "world machine."[700] This new understanding of the universe has great scientific consequences, but it also has a significant philosophical impact because it seems to open up the secrets of cosmic existence if mankind just thinks clearly. The idea that human beings have the ability to find ultimate truth through observation and reason continues to advance. The intellectual world is beginning to move into the era of modern thought, the "Age of Reason."[701]

The Church cannot escape this growing philosophical revolution. For over sixteen hundred years, the Church has been teaching that man is a fallen sinner who can only be saved by God's grace. Now, intellectuals are suggesting that the mysteries and problems of the world can be solved through reason and an understanding of the universe rather than through God's mercy.

---

[699] Richard A. Watson, "Rene Descartes," *Encyclopaedia*, updated December 20, February 7, 2019, https://www.britannica.com/biography/Rene-Descartes; also "Rene Descartes," *Internet Encyclopedia of Philosophy*, accessed December 31, 2018, https://www.iep.utm.edu/descarte/.

[700] Shelley, *Church History*, 313.

[701] Ibid., 314.

At first, some academics try to harmonize reason and faith. An English philosopher named John Locke (1632–1704) writes that a rational creature who observes creation "cannot miss the discovery of a Deity."[702] But Locke abandons much of what Scripture teaches about God; his God is the God of rational proof, and he dismisses much of traditional theology as irrelevant. Eventually, he develops political theories stressing rule by the consent of the governed and religious tolerance, which will eventually influence the founding documents of the United States.[703]

Newton and Locke are forerunners of deism, the concept that God created the universe and lets it run according to natural laws. Deists come to see God as the great "watchmaker" who does not interfere in the actions that occur in the world. Miracles and special revelation through Scripture are rejected. This evolving religious belief is a transitional step in the movement toward a complete denial of the existence of God.[704]

As the deists gain influence, the most celebrated is a French philosopher, Francois-Marie Arouet, who is known as Voltaire (1694–1778). A fierce critic of both Protestant and Catholic Churches, he authors a prodigious number of histories, plays, essays, and novels advancing the cult of reason. Voltaire personifies the thinking of this period, which becomes known as the "Enlightenment" because of the advances in science and changes in philosophical thought.

Enlightenment ideals spread throughout Europe and Paris becomes the major center of this new cosmopolitan culture. A group of intellectuals known as the *philosophes* herald the supremacy of science, tolerance, and the merits of deism. One of these philosophers, Denis Diderot, edits the famous *Encyclopedia,* seventeen volumes proclaiming the preeminence of these new values and beliefs. A militant attitude toward Christianity develops in Europe, especially in France, that dismisses the "myths and miracles" found in the Bible.

---

[702] John Locke, "An Essay Concerning Human Understanding" in *From Plato to Nietzsche, Second Edition,* ed. Forrest E. Baird (Upper Saddle River, New Jersey: Prentice Hall, 1997), 574.

[703] Shelley, *Church History,* 315; History.com Editors, "John Locke," *History,* November 9, 2009, https://www.history.com/topics/british-history/john-locke.

[704] Leading English Deists of the seventeenth and eighteenth centuries were: John Roland (1670–1722), Anthony Collins (1676–1729), Matthew Tindal (1655–1733), and Thomas Woolston (1669–1733). Men such as William Law (1686–1761), Joseph Butler (1692–1752), and William Paley (1743–1805) offered rebuttals to deistic theology. See Walton, *Chronological Charts,* chart 45.

These attacks on the foundations of Christianity require a strong response; however, it is sadly lacking from Roman Catholicism whose Church leaders try to stop this rising tide of heresy by demanding that deist books be banned, rather than addressing the issues being raised. But a Church of England bishop, Joseph Butler (1692–1752), along with several other Englishmen, write effectively against deism. Butler shows that there are many mysteries in the universe that reason cannot explain. The rationality of finite man is limited and is not sufficient to give meaning to our lives.[705]

Reason, with a small r, is a tool that God gives us so that we can think His thoughts after Him. But in the "Age of Reason," men succumb to the same temptation that brought down Adam, wanting to determine good and evil, ultimate reality, by their own supreme reckonings—"Reason" with a capital R.

For many thoughtful people, Butler's writings are decisive in discrediting deism, but its ultimate demise will be caused by its own inherent weaknesses. Deists assume that moral choices in daily life can be as simple and unchanging as the laws of nature. They have no solution for the evils and disasters of life. The idea of a creator god who has no ongoing concern for his creation, especially the people of his creation, is eventually rejected by the broader public.

However, the collapse of deism will not restore Christianity to its central place in Western culture; the negative effects of the Age of Reason endure. By the beginning of the eighteenth century, modern culture—its art, education, and politics—is largely free from formal Christian influence. The continent-wide organized attempt to create a religiously neutral civilization means that faith must "be confined to the home and the heart."[706] The attitude that Christianity must be banned from the public square becomes the predominate view in Europe and will eventually become the prevailing view in the United States.

*****

Although the English have begun Protestant settlements in North America, it is the Roman Catholics who lead in introducing Christianity to the lands being discovered in the seventeenth and eighteenth centuries. The

---

[705] Joseph Butler, *The Analogy of Religion*, reprint (Chestnut Hill, MA: Adamant Media, 2005); Shelley, *Church History*, 318.

[706] Ibid., 319.

Catholic nations of Portugal and Spain provide most of the exploratory voyages and establish the largest colonial empires. Spain soon rules the West Indies, the southern coasts of North America, most of Central America, the north, south, and western coasts of South America, and the Philippines. Portugal holds Brazil and establishes posts along the shores of Africa as well as in India, the Malay Peninsula, the East Indies, and China. The Portuguese begin transporting African slaves and will dominate this terrible trade until the eighteenth century when England becomes the major transgressor.

Roman Catholic France stakes out a claim to the heart of North America—the Great Lakes and the Mississippi River Valley. The new and invigorated orders arising from the Counter Reformation provide the monastic manpower for establishing Catholicism in the newfound territories. These missionary priests have traditions and resources, which the Protestants have only begun to develop, for reaching people in the new lands.[707] Despite these widespread endeavors, two large populaces remain virtually sealed off from Christianity—the Chinese and Japanese.[708]

During this time, the majority of Protestants are in Germany, Scandinavia, and Switzerland, countries that have little to do with the European expansion to new regions. Great Britain and Holland become active explorers, but their territorial possessions are small compared to the Roman Catholic powers.[709] God's kingdom is spreading throughout the world, but it will often struggle under the Roman Catholic doctrines reaffirmed at the Council of Trent.

In the developing colonies in North America, the colonists who have church affiliations are mostly Protestants from the British Isles with only Maryland being established by Roman Catholics. But these Catholics are

---

[707] Laourette, *History*, Vol. II, 925–926.

[708] Even today, only about one percent of Japanese are Christians. Michelle A. Vu says it is because the Japanese value harmony more than truth. See Michelle A. Vu, "Mission Leader: Why So Few Christians in Japan," *The Christian Post*, May 18, 2010, https://www.christianpost.com/news/mission-leaderwhy-so-few-christians-in-japan-45217/. In China, where people are more committed to truth, in 2010, there were more than 58 million Christians among the 1.3 billion citizens and the Church continues to see extensive growth. See Tom Phillips, "China on course to become world's most Christian nation within 15 years," *The Telegraph*, April 19, 2014, https://www.telegraph.co.uk/news/worldnews/asia/china/10776023/China-on-course-to-become-worlds-most-Christian-nation-within-15-years.html.

[709] Latourette, *History*, Vol. II, 924–926.

English, and within a generation, the Church of England becomes the state religion of Maryland.

A large majority of the new settlers in America are from the poorer classes in Europe who have migrated for social or economic reasons and have no official church affiliation. Although the churched population is generally made up of Protestants, it is very diverse and becomes more so as immigrants from various denominations continue to flow into the new territories. Most of the Christians are of the Reformed tradition, Puritans, Presbyterians, Independents, Separatists, Baptists, and Quakers, but there are also German and Swedish Lutherans and a small number of Roman Catholics.[710] No denomination is dominant enough to become a "state" church. As these groups participate in governing their colonies, they soon realize that the only way to have freedom of religion for themselves is to grant it to everyone else.[711]

It seems that the many different denominations would have a fracturing effect on the developing colonies, but the mutual need for tolerance has a unifying effect; there is a developing "national consciousness." The Christians in America begin to step out from under the protectorate of the established European churches and assert control, not only over their religious identities but over a shared national future.[712]

*****

In Europe, where the Reformers had proclaimed a strong and active doctrine of justifying faith, the elevation of the intellect during the Age of Reason is beginning to transform Protestant Christianity into a mental exercise, leading to a period called Protestant Scholasticism or Confessionalism. The essential marks of a good Christian become faithful attendance at the state church and a formal assent to the doctrines set forth by scholars and pastors, rather than an abiding faith in Jesus Christ for salvation and sanctification.

German Christians known as Pietists, initially led by such men as Philip Jacob Spener (1635–1705) and August Franke (1663–1727), react against what they see as a dead orthodoxy and stress the importance of personal faith.

---

[710] Large-scale Roman Catholic immigration begins with the devastating Irish potato famines in in the mid-1840s.

[711] Shelley, *Church History*, 342–343; Latourette, *History*, Vol. II, 954.

[712] "Significance Of The Great Awakening: Roots Of Revolution," *Great-Awakening.com*, accessed December 31, 2018, www.great-awakening.com/roots-of-revolution/.

They believe that Christianity begins with regeneration, a spiritual rebirth, so they witness to members of established churches as well as pagans. The Pietists want to shift the center of Christian life from official state churches to fellowships that have a living faith in God.

In the Age of Reason, the Pietists emphasize preaching and the care of souls, and they have a great effect not only in Germany but eventually in worldwide Christianity. This emerging development is referred to as the Evangelical Awakening in Europe; it will continue in Great Britain through the preaching of the Methodists and in the American Colonies during the time of the Great Awakening in North America.[713]

*****

The Awakening in England is led primarily by three men, two sons of an Anglican cleric, John (1703–1791) and Charles (1707–1788) Wesley, and George Whitefield (1714–1770), the son of an innkeeper. The brothers become acquainted with Whitefield when he arrives at the University of Oxford in 1732; he joins them in leading Bible studies and encouraging others to lead virtuous lives. Although many students mock their group by calling it the "Holy Club," their meetings become the forerunner of the Methodist denomination. In 1735, when John and Charles are invited to minister in the colony of Georgia in North America, Whitefield stays behind and soon becomes well known for his stirring sermons in Bristol.

During the brothers' voyage to North America, their ship is caught in a fierce storm, and John especially fears for his life. He is amazed at the faith of the Moravian Christians onboard,[714] whole families, men, women, and children who calmly sing hymns at the height of the storm. The ship survives, and the brothers arrive in Georgia and begin their ministry. But they make no progress in converting the natives and soon become involved in controversies in the colony, including an incident concerning John's failed love for a young woman who elopes with a rival suitor. John bars her from communion and is sued by her husband for defamation.

Then Charles becomes ill and returns to England in 1736. He survives and eventually becomes a prolific writer of hymns, many of which are still sung

---

[713] Shelley, *Church History*, 324–330.
[714] The Moravians were German Pietists whose Protestant roots were in Bohemia and Moravia.

today. John leaves Georgia the next year in failure and despair. Neither brother will ever again return to America.[715]

*****

A few months after returning to Great Britain in a distressed spiritual state, John undergoes a transforming experience at a meeting in Aldersgate while Luther's preface to *The Commentary on Romans* is being read. He writes of his heart being strangely warmed and knowing that he did trust in Christ alone for salvation. He soon makes a trip to Germany to confer with Moravian leaders where he adopts some of their methods. After his return, he and Charles continue to preach in many churches in England, but their formal sermons focus on holiness and becoming acceptable to God, and they often stir opposition.

In contrast, Whitefield's sermons are arousing great excitement. He has a powerful voice and begins to preach open-air sermons to the miners of Bristol. They are deeply moved, and Whitefield sees channels of tears on thousands of begrimed faces. He invites John Wesley to join him, but John is reluctant to preach outside of a church. He eventually relents, preaches in the open, is surprised at the enthusiastic reception, and embraces the practice.

Charles joins his brother and also begins to preach outdoors. The Wesleys and Whitefield attract large audiences, people mainly from the lower and middle classes in England. Many Church dignitaries deplore the emotional outbursts that often occur in the large crowds during the meetings. But the Wesleys continue their ministry and lead the Evangelical Awakening throughout England, and although the brothers do not return to North America, their adherents will eventually make Methodism one of the largest denominations on the new continent.[716]

Whitefield, however, makes prolonged visits to America. In 1739, his strong preaching in the colonies strengthens the Great Awakening that had begun in 1734 under the preaching of men like Jonathan Edwards, Theodore J. Frelinghuysen, and William Tennent. Edwards later wrote about the revival in Northampton, Massachusetts, saying that a concern for eternal things swept through the town, and "souls did, as it were, come by flocks to Jesus Christ."[717]

---

[715] Shelley, *Church History*, 331–335.
[716] Ibid., 335–340.
[717] Ibid., 346.

Just as in England, emotional enthusiasms accompanied the revival and divisions developed in the churches. Congregations split and new denominations were formed. As we have seen, the advancement of the kingdom is never without turmoil, never without resistance from Satan and confusion among human beings. But the widespread conversions continued, and even Benjamin Franklin, a confirmed deist, was impressed when he attended one of Whitefield's sermons. He also saw the changes the revival was creating throughout the colonies and said that it appeared "all the world were growing religious."[718]

Whitefield and the Wesleys continue their different ministries and maintain their friendship, but a deep divide develops as Whitefield continues to study the Scriptures and becomes more Calvinistic in his beliefs. He is dismayed when John Wesley begins to openly preach against him and the doctrines of election and predestination. In 1740, he writes an open letter to Wesley defending his Reformed views.[719] The two will continue to express affection for each other, but their doctrinal divide will endure for the rest of their lives.[720]

*****

In the 1760s, Enlightenment thinking and the Christian awakenings are at crosscurrents with each other, but they are both part of the intellectual developments in Europe and North America that are sweeping away old orders. In country after country, from small states like Geneva to large nations like England, radical politicians are challenging the established order. And everywhere, the demands are similar: the right to participate in politics, the right to vote, and the right to freedom of expression.[721] The desire for greater freedom begins to affect kings and their ability to rule their territories. The first significant revolution occurs when the American colonies rebel against King George III of England.

The circumstances that ignite the rebellion are not complex, and as usual, financial concerns are a central issue. The British had defeated France in the

---

[718] "Benjamin Franklin On Rev. George Whitefield 1739," *National Humanities Center Resource Toolbox,* accessed February 22, 2019, www.ushistory.org/franklin/autobiography/page49.htm.

[719] For the complete letter, see "George Whitefield To The Rev, Mr. John Wesley," *Five Solas.com,* accessed December 31, 2018, https://www.fivesolas.com/gw2jw.htm.

[720] Shelley, *Church History,* 329–338.

[721] Ibid., 356.

French-Indian War (1754–1763) and gained control over the Great Lakes and the Mississippi River Valley.[722] The colonies had provided troops, including Major George Washington,[723] to supplement the Regular British Army. The war had lasted nine years, and the cost to the British Crown was immense. Now that the war has ended, King George decides to replenish his treasury by levying oppressive taxes on the colonies. He also orders the colonists to quarter British troops in their private homes, which becomes intolerable when residents begin to have confrontations with British soldiers. The colonies do not have their own representatives in the British Parliament, and they rally around the refrain, "no taxation without representation."

Although these disputes are at the forefront of the complaints against the Crown, the underlying defiance arises from two more basic sources. The colonies have many Enlightenment men, such as Jefferson, Franklin, and Madison who believe that free individual consent is the basis of government for "reasonable" men; they are opposed to being ruled by a king. Although these men are deists, they are not outwardly hostile to Christianity, and they find common ground with the different denominations that have arisen from the Great Awakening who also prize independence. The resistance to autocratic rule in religion begins to manifest itself in other areas of colonial life.[724]

Clergymen, who had largely been loyal to England, begin to denounce King George, and they sanction resistance when he implements his program of taxation. This leads the British statesman William Knox to comment, "Every man thus being allowed to be his own Pope, he becomes disposed to wish to become his own King."[725] John Adams will credit the Great Awakening with being the source of motivation behind the American Revolution. In some parts of England, the War for Independence will be called the "Presbyterian Rebellion."[726] The colonists have come to greatly value religious liberty, and now they intend to have political liberty.

The thirteen colonies declare their independence on July 4, 1776, and the Declaration is sent to parish ministers to be read to their congregations

---

[722] The British Navy decided the conflict when it cut off the French supply lines from Europe.

[723] Washington was in the Colony of Virginia Militia and gained valuable military and political experience during the French-Indian war, which he will eventually use against the British in the War for Independence.

[724] See p. 362, n. 712, "/roots-of-revolution/."

[725] Ibid.

[726] Ibid.

after church services. General George Washington manages to muster, hold together, and lead a militia military through great hardships and five years of conflict. On October 17, 1781, British General Charles Cornwallis surrenders to Washington at Yorktown, Virginia, effectively ending the war. Washington congratulates his troops and recommends that those off duty the next day attend divine services and give thanks to God.[727] On September 3, 1783, the Treaty of Paris is signed, formally recognizing the United States as a free and independent nation.

It takes almost six years after the signing of the Treaty of Paris to complete and begin the implementation of the Constitution of the United States. All the colonies were concerned about maintaining their rights and some had been reluctant to form a central government, but the Constitution is finally put into effect on March 4, 1789, along with ten amendments known as the Bill of Rights. The first amendment bars Congress from making any law "respecting an establishment of religion or prohibiting the free exercise thereof." The colonies have become an independent country with the fundamental right of freedom of religion. Not everyone in the new union is a Christian, but the kingdom of God has spread throughout the colonies and will have a significant effect in the new nation.

*****

While the political revolution has been underway in North America, the philosophical revolution has continued in Europe. Scientists and intellectuals have brought about a change in the general perception of what philosophers call ontology, the study of being or existence, the basis of what is real. For many Europeans, belief in the biblical God who is active in His world had been replaced by the deistic idea of a creator God who lets the world run according to natural laws. Now this concept is giving way to the view that the world is just a vast machine where humans and their minds are supreme. This change in the conception of reality necessarily affects the other two major concerns of

---

[727] Cassandra Niemczyk, "Christianity and the American Revolution: Did You Know?" *Christianity Today*, accessed December 31, 2018, http://www.christianitytoday.com/history/issues/issue-50/christianity-and-american-revolution-did-you-know.html.

philosophy, epistemology (how do we know what we know) and ethics ("how should we then live").[728]

Prior to the late eighteenth century, there had been two primary views of epistemology, two basic theories of knowledge. Empiricists claimed that sensory experience was the source of all human concepts and knowledge. Rationalists maintained that there were significant ways in which we gain knowledge beyond our senses and that reason was the chief source and test of what we know. It appeared that this debate would go on indefinitely until, in 1781, a German philosopher named Immanuel Kant publishes a book called *Critique of Pure Reason.*[729]

Kant, a pietistic Lutheran, sees that Enlightenment thinking is discrediting the Christian faith. The goal of his book is to show the limits of reason in determining ultimate truth and thereby leave room for faith. He says, "I have therefore found it necessary to deny knowledge, in order to make room for faith."[730]

In demonstrating the limits of reason, Kant shows that the formal proofs for God's existence proposed by Scholastics like Aquinas are logically flawed.[731] Although Kant is showing the inability of reason to determine the existence or nonexistence of God, his dismantling of Theistic proofs alarms many Christians. But this should not be disturbing for believers; it is beyond the ability of finite man to prove or disprove the existence of an infinite God. Christians live by faith buttressed by an abundance of evidence, both without and within (Ps. 19:1–6; Rom. 1:19–20), but there are no formal arguments that can logically coerce anyone to accept the existence of the one true God.[732]

---

[728] "How Should We Then Live" is the title of a helpful book written by Francis Schaeffer (1912–1984) concerning the rise and fall of Western thought and culture. A weeklong seminar by Schaeffer played a significant role in my own conversion. See Francis A. Schaeffer, *How Should We Then Live* (Old Tappan, NJ: Revell, 1976).

[729] Immanuel Kant, *Critique of Pure Reason*, trans. Norman Kemp Smith (New York: St. Martin's, 1965).

[730] Ibid., 29.

[731] Ibid., 495–525.

[732] Theologians who approach apologetics through the use of evidence to try to prove that God exists are called Traditional Apologists. Their starting point, much like Descartes, is the ability of human reason. Pre-suppositional Apologists begin with the presupposition that God exists, and then reason from that starting point. The latter seems to be the correct approach since Scripture says every person knows that God exists but suppresses that knowledge in unrighteousness (Rom. 1:18–23). Scripture assumes not just the existence

Faith comes through the supernatural work of the Holy Spirit (John 3:5–8) which allows a person to see the logical consistency between God's Word and the natural world.[733]

Kant's biggest impact arises from his epistemology; in effect, he synthesizes empiricism and rationalism. Kant says that we receive data through our senses from phenomena, those physical things that surround us, and that our minds are hardwired to interpret this data. If every person is different, no one can be sure that they are interpreting the world just the same as someone else. According to Kant's model, each person's mind is constructing its own reality. Spiritual entities like the soul and God, which Kant calls noumena, cannot affect our senses and therefore are unknowable to us—God has no input in the different realities that human minds construct.[734] Kant wants to leave open the possibility that God exists, but with his epistemology, if God does exist, He cannot communicate with us.[735] Kant will eventually argue that the sense of morality in human beings implies God's existence. But for secular philosophers, Kant has moved beyond the deists and their god who does not care to a god who may not exist and, even if he does, cannot make himself known to us.

Kant cannot tell us how our minds became "hardwired," but Scripture does; God made us in his own image (Gen. 1:26–27, 2:7). Scripture also tells us that God *is* communicating to us though our consciences (Rom. 2:14–16), through nature (Ps. 19:1–6), and through supernaturally inspired writings (2 Tim. 3:16–17). And, finally, He has made Himself known to us through His Son who entered the physical world and was heard, seen, and touched by His disciples (Heb. 1:1–2; 1 John 1:1–2; John 20:19–20, 27). We are able to think God's thoughts after Him and perceive, within finite human limits, the reality that God reveals. Contrary to Kant's epistemology, the God of the Bible communicates with human beings in the world that He has created. That world, and God's complete knowledge of it, are ultimate reality whether human beings acknowledge it or not (Rom. 1:18–23). And eventually, every person

---

of a God, but a particular God, the one true God, and then reveals His attributes and His works.

[733] Calvin, *Institutes*, Vol. I, 68.

[734] Kant, *Critique*, 257–275. The concept that each person creates his own reality will become even more pervasive when modernity is replaced by the thinking of postmodernity. See pp. 397–406.

[735] Ibid., 645–652.

will acknowledge it—on the Last Day, every knee will bow to Jesus Christ and confess that He is Lord (Phil. 2:9–11).

For Enlightenment intellectuals, reason is the supreme authority. For Christians, the biblical God, who speaks in Scripture and through His Son, is the Supreme Authority. Sinful human beings who come to believe the words of Scripture and then live their lives accordingly are abundant evidence that God is active and communicating in His world. But Kant's thinking has enormous influence on the philosophers and theologians of his day, and it continues to the present time. He has given secular thinkers an epistemology that frees them from having to consider God as they develop their worldviews. With the changing views in ontology and the influence of Kant's epistemology, it naturally follows that there will be a change in ethics, a change in the view of how human beings should live.

*****

The nations in Europe have been closely watching the results of the revolution in North America, especially France, who had aided the colonies against England, most notably with its navy. But France's costly support and the extravagant spending of King Louis XVI (1754–1793) has left the nation in a perilous position with its royal coffers depleted. Compounding the nation's problems are two decades of poor grain harvests, drought, cattle disease, and skyrocketing bread prices that have created rising unrest among peasants and the urban poor.

For the first time since 1614, King Louis calls for an Estates-General in Paris, an assembly representing France's clergy, nobility, and middle class. As the delegates are meeting on July 14, 1789, rioters capture the Bastille fortress and free the few prisoners being held there.[736] A wave of revolutionary fever and widespread hysteria begin to sweep into the countryside. Revolting against years of exploitation, peasants loot and burn the homes of tax collectors, landlords, and nobles. This triggers the "Great Fear" and hastens the exodus of many in the upper classes to neighboring countries—many of the refugees resettle in Britain, Germany, and Austria. On August 4, 1789, the National Assembly

---

[736] Bastille Day is still an important holiday in France.

abolishes the feudal system and adopts the *Declaration of the Rights of Man and Citizen*, grounded on the philosophical ideas of Enlightenment thinkers.[737]

A new Legislative Assembly is elected, and in April 1792, the members declare war on Austria and Prussia, where they fear counterrevolutionary forces are forming. The Assembly intends to use warfare to spread its radical ideals across Europe. In Paris on August 10, 1792, a group of the more extreme insurgents attack the royal residence and arrest King Louis. The next month, they massacre hundreds of accused resistors in Paris, and the Legislative Assembly is replaced by the National Convention, which proclaims the abolition of the monarchy and the establishment of the French Republic. King Louis is condemned of treason and crimes against the state and, on January 21, 1793, is sent to the guillotine; nine months later, his wife, Marie-Antoinette, suffers the same fate.

The differences between the American Revolution and the French Revolution soon become starkly evident. Paris had been the center of Enlightenment intellectualism and now the deification of reason progresses to its logical conclusion. The radicals controlling the government begin to take extreme measures. They reject Christianity, create their own religion called the "Cult of Reason," and turn churches into temples for their new god. Rites are prescribed for weddings, the dedication of children to Freedom, and funerals. Young girls decked out as Reason or Liberty lead processions through towns to altars erected to the new religion. Catholic priests who refuse to swear before the altar of Freedom are subject to the guillotine; over two thousand are executed as well as dozens of nuns and countless laypeople in what is called the "reign of terror."[738] As Dostoevsky eventually suggests, without God, everything is permitted.[739]

The killing begins to abate by 1795, but the government still officially opposes Christianity. A new five-member directorate is appointed by the parliament, and they maintain power through military force until Napoleon Bonaparte stages a coup in 1799 and appoints himself France's "first consul."[740] Napoleon seeks reconciliation with the pope and also grants religious freedom

---

[737] History.com Editors, "French Revolution," *History*, November 9, 2009, https://www.history.com/topics/france/french-revolution.

[738] Shelley, *Church History*, 357–358; Gonzales, *Story of Christianity*, 262–266.

[739] Fyodor Dostoevsky, *The Brothers Karamazov*, trans. Richard Pevear and Larissa Volokhonsky (San Francisco: North Point, 1990), 589.

[740] In 1804, Napoleon will appoint himself emperor.

for Protestants,[741] ending the fevered tyranny of the French Revolution and beginning the Napoleonic era in which France will come to dominate much of continental Europe.

With the French Revolution, we see the ethical consequences of deifying human reason. If the human mind is the measure of all things, then humans determine ultimate right and wrong, which is what Adam had wanted to do in the Garden. But since humans will differ in their aspirations, ethics in a world without God are ultimately determined by who has the most power, whether it is through armaments, money, or votes.

We have seen how Enlightenment thinking has changed the concepts of ontology and epistemology, and now the French revolution has terrifyingly shown us the ethics that eventually result. Without Christians and the restraining work of the Holy Spirit in the world (John 16:7–11), humanity would be careening into a worldwide French Revolution or what Scripture refers to as the Great Tribulation, which will eventually come (see pp. 430–431 and Dan. 12:1; Matt. 24:21–22, 29; Rev. 7:14).

*****

In 1803, to raise money for his wars in Europe, Napoleon sells France's Louisiana Territory in North America to the United States for 15 million dollars. He successfully overthrows the reigning governments of Spain, Portugal, Italy, the Low Countries, and Scandinavia but eventually suffers a final defeat to British and Prussian forces at the Battle of Waterloo in 1815. He is eventually exiled to the island of Saint Helena where he dies of natural causes in 1821.

*****

The national powers that had opposed Napoleon—Britain, Austria, Prussia, and Russia—determine the new shape of Europe's political map and, with the exception of the Crimean War (1854–1856) and the Franco-Prussian war (1870–1871), are able to establish a time of relative peace for the rest of the century. This allows for the rapid progress of a widespread technological and commercial expansion, which will eventually be called the Industrial Revolution.

---

[741] P. 371, n. 737, "french-revolution."

Since the beginning of the nineteenth century, most of Europe and some areas of the New World had already been advancing in industrial output. Now, in a time of peace, the harnessing of steam leads to rapid growth in manufacturing and transportation. The telegraph and the telephone drastically increase the speed of communication, and electricity lights homes and businesses. Advances in medicine help control diseases and prolong lifespans. Large cities begin to spring up as people move from agricultural work to jobs in industrial centers. A general prosperity, led by Great Britain, reinforces the Enlightenment concept that reason and science can provide answers to the problems of mankind.[742] For Enlightenment philosophers and theologians who do not accept that human beings are innately sinful, a potential earthly utopia is on the horizon. But the changes being brought about in family life are an early indication that this is an overly optimistic hope.

Traditional extended families—parents, grandparents, uncles, aunts, cousins, and lifelong friends—that existed on farms and in villages begin to disintegrate in the movement to urban life. Fathers no longer work in the fields with their children and are away from their homes while they labor as "cogs" in the ever-expanding factories, increasing the pressure on mothers trying to rear children. Families become more isolated and must bear the responsibility of passing on values and traditions without the support of community relationships; an increasing number of people see their lives as their own private concern. Individualism and preoccupation with the "I" begin to replace a broader sense of self previously founded on family and natural affiliations.[743]

*****

In this world of increasing isolation and mechanization, Christians like the Pietists continue to focus on preaching and the care of souls in their efforts to revitalize and spread their faith. But as the nineteenth century progresses, many Church leaders and theologians begin making accommodations to Enlightenment thinking. Instead of the Church affecting society, it is affected by society.

Theologians begin to investigate the Scriptures in a different way. They study the secular history and context surrounding the development of different

---

[742] Latourette, *History*, Vol. II, 1064.
[743] Gonzales, *Story of Christianity*, 282.

biblical writings, especially the New Testament books. This comes to be called higher criticism[744] and can aid in understanding some passages of Scripture. But some of these men approach the Bible with skepticism and develop their own criteria for authenticating the Scriptures.

The basic assumption for these academics is that the Jesus revealed in the Bible is not the real or "historical" Jesus, and they intend to discover Him. They succumb to the spirit of the age and want a Christianity that is not offensive to human reason—Christianity without the supernatural, without such "myths" as the virgin birth, and the resurrection. If they find such a Jesus, it will not be a Jesus who can save. But these critics are not looking for a savior because they believe that humanity can save itself through its own, continually advancing powers.

These proponents of higher criticism are dismissive of orthodox Christianity, although some of them believe they are saving religion by changing it and making it more acceptable to Enlightenment society. Herman Samuel Reimarus (1694–1768) writes that Jesus conceived of the kingdom simply in political terms and therefore was a failure; he commends a natural religion of reason. H. E. G. Paulus (1761–1851) emphasizes the ethical personality of Jesus and explains the miracle stories as staged events or pure fables. He introduces the "swoon" theory, saying Jesus was not actually dead when He was placed in the tomb.

George Wilhelm Friedrich Hegel (1770–1831) believes that the religious representations of Christianity were helpful in an earlier stage of man's development but now must be outgrown, and he introduces the concept of the Weltgeist or ever-developing world process in the place of the biblical God. Ludwig Feuerbach (1804–1872), in his book, *The Essence of Christianity*, develops the idea that God is merely the outward projection of man's inward nature. His thinking will influence Karl Marx and Friedrich Engels, the writers of the *Communist Manifesto*. Friedrich Schleiermacher (1768–1834) defines religion as simply a feeling of dependence upon the absolute.[745] None of these men

---

[744] In contrast to higher criticism, lower criticism is the study of the oldest manuscripts in an effort to develop the most accurate translations, a benefit to all Christians.

[745] See Robert B. Strimple, *The Modern Search for the Real Jesus* (Phillipsburg, NJ: P&R Publishing, 1995), 9–29 for more details on the beliefs of these men; also see Editors, Encyclopaedia, "Ludwig Feuerbach," *Encyclopaedia*, accessed January 2, 2019, https://www.britannica.com/biography/Ludwig-Feuerbach.

seem to have a sense of personal sin or see a need for the Savior presented in the Bible.

*****

In this philosophical environment, it is not surprising when someone offers an alternative to the concept of a Creator God. In 1859, an English naturalist, Charles Darwin (1809–1882), publishes his book, *On the Origin of Species*.[746] Darwin's theory is straightforward—all living things have a common ancestry and have evolved from the simple cell through a process of natural selection, "numerous successive, slight, favourable, variations"[747] where the fittest survive and progress into ever higher forms, eventually into plants and animals. In what seems to be a crucial omission, Darwin does not speculate on how the first cell came to life. He writes a second book, *Descent of Man*,[748] in 1871 in which he suggests that the ancestors of human beings were monkeylike animals.

As mentioned previously,[749] under Darwin's system, there would have to be trillions upon trillions of intermediate forms for a simple cell to evolve into human beings, elephants, whales, etc. Darwin knew that these "intermediate varieties" were missing in the fossil record and that this was a huge problem for his theory.[750] One hundred and sixty years later, it still is. Occasionally, an evolutionist will discover the unusual or malformed skeleton of an animal and claim it is the "missing link" that proves evolution, but if Darwin's theory is correct, there should be billions of these missing links in the fossil record as different species gradually changed into new species.

As someone has said, if dogs evolved into horses, then we should find many discernible stages of "dorses."[751] Such Darwinian progressions have not been found among the billions of fossils discovered since Darwin wrote his book, but there have been many fraudulent attempts to display missing links, ranging from transitional drawings in many textbooks to the falsification of

---

[746] Charles Darwin, *Origin of Species* (London: Arcturus Publishing Limited, 2017).

[747] Ibid, 435.

[748] Charles Darwin, *Descent of Man* (New York: D. Appleton, originally pub. 1871).

[749] P. 20, n. 65.

[750] Darwin, *Origin*, 319–320.

[751] Eric Blievernicht, "Transitional Fossils," *Revolution Against Evolution*, accessed February 26, 2019, https://www.rae.org/essay-links-/faq01

skulls like the Piltdown man, the Nebraska man, and the Java man.[752] No fossil sequences have been found to indicate the change of even one species into another species.

But there is an even more fundamental problem for Darwin's theory. The tremendous advances in biology, biochemistry, and genetics over the past few decades have shown that there are thousands of individual irreducibly complex systems in the "simple" cell. An example of an irreducibly complex system would be a watch. The different inner workings of the watch must be prefabricated, come together at the same time, and then be assembled in a particular way. The individual parts have no reason to exist except that someone, the designer, wants them to be part of a preplanned watch. If any one part of the mechanism is missing, the watch will not be a functioning entity—it is irreducibly complex.

The thousands of irreducibly complex systems in a single living cell are analogous to a watch but immensely more complicated.[753] Darwin's concept of incremental beneficial change cannot explain how or why these thousands of systems would evolve individually and simultaneously prior to functioning together as a cell, much less how time and chance could assemble them all. The cell, like the watch, is irreducibly complex. All of its independent parts must come together at the same time and in a certain order to be functional.

Intelligent design is necessary. If time and chance cannot produce the "simple" cell, they cannot be the means for eventually producing a vastly more complex plant or animal.

In 2008, Antony Flew, the most influential atheist of the twentieth century, renounced his atheism and published his book, *There Is a God: How the*

---

[752] Henry M. Morris, *What Is Creation Science*, rev. by Gary E. Parker (Green Forrest, AR: Master Books, 1982), 151–163; also see Peter Hastie, "Evolution frauds," *Evolution isn't science*, copyright 1996, https://evolutionisntscience.wordpress.com/evolution-frauds/. Two examples of books meant to indoctrinate children into evolution with unsupported illustrations are: Dorothy Hinshaw Patent, *Evolution Goes on Every Day*—drawings by Matthew Kalmenoff (New York: Holiday House, 1977), and Steve Jenkins, *Life on Earth— The Story of Evolution* (Boston: Houghton Mifflin, 2002).

[753] Some of the parts of the cell are: cytoplasm, cytoskeleton, endoplasmic reticulum, golgi apparatus, lysosomes and peroxisomes, mitochondria, nucleus, plasma membrane, and ribosomes, see "What is a cell?," *US National Library of Medicine*, accessed January 2, 2019, https://ghr.nlm.nih.gov/primer/basics/cell.

World's Most Notorious Atheist Changed His Mind.[754] The scientific evidence for intelligent design in the universe had become too great for him to maintain his atheistic faith based on evolution.

Molecular Biologist Michael Denton, who rejects the God of the Bible, nonetheless stresses the impossibility of Darwin's theory and says, "Although the tiniest bacterial cells are incredibly small, weighing less than 10^{-12} grams, each is in effect a veritable micro-miniaturized factory containing thousands of exquisitely designed pieces of intricate molecular machinery, made up altogether of one hundred thousand million atoms, far more complicated than any machinery built by man and absolutely without parallel in the nonliving world."[755]

He goes on to say that "The complexity of the simplest known type of cell is so great that it is impossible to accept that such an object could have been thrown together by some kind of freakish, vastly improbable, event. Such an occurrence would be indistinguishable from a miracle." Irreducibly complex systems in the cell rule out evolution of species by random change, either incrementally or catastrophically.

Evolutionists berate Denton and accuse him of being a theist, but they cannot deny the validity of his objections.[756] He has published a new book, *Evolution: Still a Theory in Crisis,*[757] in which he argues for structuralism, inherent configurations in species which prevent them from evolving into another species. Although he still denies biblical creationism, Denton is in effect agreeing with the Genesis passages which tell us that God created plants and animals "after their kind" (Gen. 1:12, 21).[758]

We do not need a microscope to observe irreducible complexity; the eye, the ear, and the heart are obvious examples. Even Darwin admitted he could discern no possible evolutionary progression for the development of the eye

---

[754] Anthony Flew, *There Is a God: How the World's Most Notorious Atheist Changed His Mind* (New York: Harper Collins, 2008, paperback).

[755] Michael Denton, *Evolution: A Theory in Crisis* (Chevy Chase, MD: Adler & Adler, 1986), 250. Also Stephen C. Meyer makes a similar argument based on the functions of DNA and RNA in the simple cell, see Stephen C. Meyer, *Signature in the Cell: DNA and the Evidence for Intelligent Design* (New York: Harper Collins, 2009).

[756] "Michael Denton," *Rational Wiki*, accessed January 2, 2019, https://rationalwiki.org/wiki/Michael_Denton.

[757] Michael Denton, *Evolution: Still a Theory in Crisis* (Seattle: Discovery Institute, 2016)

[758] There is obviously micro-evolution, different breeds of horses, dogs, birds, etc., but these changes are within the same species, within the same "kind."

when he said, "To suppose that the eye with all its inimitable contrivance for adjusting the focus to different distances, for admitting different amounts of light, and for the correction of spherical and chromatic aberration could have been formed by natural selection seems, I freely confess, absurd in the highest degree."[759] But he goes on to argue that we should just accept that transitional states of the eye have occurred, although we have no evidence, and he cannot suggest an evolutionary pathway.[760]

This is not science; this is belief in the face of contrary evidence—"leap of faith" atheism. It is similar to the thinking of present-day evolutionists who want us to accept that there were transitional animal forms, even though there is no support in the fossil record.

Very briefly, critics raise three other crucial problems for Darwin's theory:

(1) There is serious doubt about the validity of the assumptions concerning the evolutionary geologic column found in so many textbooks. The rock layers in many deep canyons do not support the dating or conclusions presented for the column.[761]

(2) In the geological rock layers, there is an "explosion" of fully developed life forms in the Cambrian layer, which lies above a granite layer, with no indication of evolutionary development between the two. These new forms burst into being, fully formed, without any indication of a long period of gradual development.[762]

(3) The second law of thermodynamics, entropy, says that everything left to natural processes deteriorates into disorder, not greater more complex order.[763]

To sum up this brief overview, it takes great leaps of faith to believe Darwin's theory. Recent evolutionists such as Stephen Jay Gould (1941–2002)

---

[759] Darwin, *Origin*, 181.

[760] Ibid., 183.

[761] Sean D. Pitman, "The Geologic Column," *Detectingdesign.com*, updated March, 2010, http://www.detectingdesign.com/geologiccolumn.html.

[762] Raul Esperante, "The Cambrian Explosion," *Geoscience Research Institute*, May 11, 2015, https://grisda.wordpress.com/2015/05/11/the-cambrian-explosion/.

[763] Danny R. Faulkner, "Does the Second Law of Thermodynamics Favor Evolution?," *Answers in Genesis*, November 3, 2015, https://answersingenesis.org/physics/second-law-of-thermodynamics.

and Niles Eldredge (b. 1943) understood this and have offered modifications to Darwin's theory. They propose what they call "punctuated equilibrium," rapid bursts of change which result in many new species that leave few fossils behind.[764] They not only deny Darwin's foundational assumption of gradual incremental change; their theory conveniently eliminates the need for fossil evidence to justify their own adaptation of evolution.[765] The title of Denton's new book is an appropriate evaluation of their new premise—*Evolution: Still a Theory in Crisis.*

*****

During Darwin's day, many Enlightenment intellectuals had been looking for a replacement for biblical creation, and he had given them what they wanted, an alternative that excluded the God of the Bible. Despite the public enthusiasm for his book, Darwin had serious doubts about his own theory; he knew that the lack of a fossil record, marvels such as the human eye, and the Cambrian explosion of fully developed life-forms all seemed to refute his hypothesis. His mental health problems have been well-documented,[766] and his wife, as well as others, believed his psychological difficulties stemmed from guilt over his effort to refute the argument for God based on design in the world.[767] In the last ten years of his life, Darwin shifts away from evolution and focuses on studying plants and earthworms in his garden.[768]

If Darwin lived today, with the continuing lack of fossil evidence and the increasing knowledge of the vast complexity of the simple cell, it seems likely that he would have rejected the theory of incremental evolution as have Gould and Eldridge. But amazingly, his theory is now generally accepted as fact. Academia, news media, and some politicians ridicule anyone who ques-

---

[764] Editors, Encyclopaedia, "Stephen Jay Gould," *Encyclopaedia*, updated January 11, 2019, https://www.britannica.com/biography/Stephen-Jay-Gould.

[765] "Punctuated Equilibrium," evolution library, *PBS*, accessed January 3, 2019, www.pbs.org/wgbh/evolution/library/03/5/l_035_01.html.

[766] For a list of books that discuss Darwin's mental illnesses, see Jerry Bergman, "Was Charles Darwin Psychotic? A Study of His Mental Health," *Institute for Creation Research*, January 1, 2004, http://www.icr.org/article/was-charles-darwin-psychotic-study-his-mental-heal/.

[767] W. B. Bean, 1978, "The Illness of Charles Darwin" *The American Journal of Medicine* 65 (4), 572–574.

[768] "Charles Darwin Summary—Brief Overview," *sparknotes*, accessed January 3, 2019, https://www.sparknotes.com/biography/darwin/summary/.

tions Darwin's theory;[769] many people in the United States still unthinkingly accept what should be a discredited concept. Those who deny the God of creation need an alternative for origins, and with no substitute for Darwinism in sight, they must cling to this unworkable hypothesis.

*****

As Darwin's *On the Origin of Species* is being hailed in Europe, tensions between the northern and southern states in North America are reaching a breaking point. At the heart of the long simmering economic and States' rights issues dividing the industrial North and the agrarian South is the practice of slavery.

The Portuguese and English had begun the African slave-trade, and it was the English who brought most of the slaves to America. The unrelenting efforts of William Wilberforce had led to the abolishment of the slave trade in the British Empire in 1807, but the practice had continued in the United States, especially in the agricultural South. When Abraham Lincoln is elected president in 1861, the Southern states believe the industrial powers of the North will use the abolition movement to destabilize the South and gain control of its agricultural and natural resources. Fearing for their way of life, they begin to secede from the Union. To stop the secession, the North invades the South; once again, Christians battle their fellow Christians. After four years of devastating battles and huge losses of life,[770] the Northern States are victorious. The North and the South remain one country, and the terrible practice of slavery is ended in the United States.

Today, although over 150 years have passed, the repercussions from the time of slavery are still felt throughout American society. The primary role of the Church is to preach the Gospel to all the nations and to every people, but it also must take a leadership role in addressing and healing the issues that still linger from the evil of slavery.

*****

---

[769] "The Crafty Attacks on Evolution," *The New York Times*, Archives, January 23, 2005, https://www.nytimes.com/2005/01/23/opinion/the-crafty-attacks-on-evolution.html.

[770] There were an estimated 620,000 military deaths. See "Civil War Casualties," *American Battlefield Trust*, accessed January, 3, 2019, https://www.civilwar.org/learn/articles/civil-war-casualties.

While America begins to deal with the aftermath of its civil war, in Europe, the embrace of Darwin's theory continues the progression of modern thinking that had begun on the Continent during the Thirty Years War. Descartes had introduced the idea that man's mind is the judge of God's existence. After the Treaty of Westphalia, intellectuals and statesmen had tried to eliminate the influence of religion in their governments, leading to increasingly secular societies. The Deists had then introduced the concept of the "watchmaker god," a god who is not concerned for his creation and just lets the world proceed through natural laws.

With his epistemology, Kant next asserted that even if God exists, He cannot communicate with human beings. Following Kant's lead, theologians developed a system of "higher criticism" by which they judged the Bible to be unreliable and guilty of presenting a false Jesus. During the French Revolution, Enlightenment radicals deified the human intellect, making man's reason the measure of all things. Darwin then presented a "scientific" alternative to creationism making God unnecessary. Enlightenment religion had progressed from a god who does not care to a god who cannot communicate to a god who is unnecessary. In 1885, the evolving suppositions of the modern era reach their logical conclusion when the famous philosopher, Friedrich Nietzsche (1844–1900), has the main character in his book, *Thus Spoke Zarathustra*, declare that God is dead.[771]

Nietzsche,[772] who hated the idea of an all-powerful and all-knowing God, did not mean that God had been alive and has now died; what has died is man's reliance upon the "concept" of God for establishing ethical behavior. It is time for the superman to arise, who in his freedom creates and enforces his own rules. For the superman, God is dead. The perpetuation of Adam's fundamental sin is once again brought forth with stunning clarity.[773]

*****

With Nietzsche's expression of an already widely accepted worldview, it becomes clear that modern thinking has replaced the long-held assumptions of

---

[771] Friedrich Nietzsche, *Thus Spoke Zarathustra* (in part) in *From Plato to Nietzsche (Second Edition)*, ed. Forrest E. Baird (Upper Saddle River, NJ: Prentice Hall, 1994), 1137.

[772] Nietzsche was a friend of the composer Richard Wagner (1813–1883), an anti-Semite and proponent of Aryan superiority whose operas eventually became favorites of Adolf Hitler.

[773] See pp. 10–11 for a summary of Adam's sin.

premodernism. The prevailing philosophical worldview is that the supernatural does not exist. Human beings no longer have to answer to God or gods, only to themselves. This should be frightening, but there is an optimism in most nations because human beings have developed an overly inflated confidence in two things—their own self-righteousness and their abilities to manage their own destinies. There is still an orderly world that can be understood and controlled. Throughout the globe, new inventions and discoveries continue to enhance the lives of many millions of people. The gasoline engine is being improved and adapted for use in automobiles and the first "aeroplanes," opening up new and exciting possibilities for business and travel. According to modern thinking, education, advances in science and technology, and the unity of human beings will lead to a utopian existence on earth.

With this climate of disbelief in the biblical God, it seems that the Christian Church would be declining and the kingdom diminishing. But this is not entirely the case; not everyone has succumbed to Enlightenment thinking. The expansion of European people throughout the world has given Christianity a wider influence than at any previous time. During the nineteenth century, missionaries translate the Bible into hundreds of new languages. Orphanages and hospitals are built in new lands, saving thousands of lives. Famine relief and improvements in agriculture rescue even more people from starvation. All this is largely accomplished through a thinly spread body of missionaries which probably number less than 250,000 at any one time.[774]

In Europe and the Americas, Christians help bring about prison reforms, better care for the mentally ill, and protections for laborers, especially women and children. New programs for educating the masses are introduced, and hundreds of colleges and universities are founded. Christian writers such as the Russians Gogol and Dostoevsky, the German Goethe, the Englishmen Tennyson and Browning, and the Americans Hawthorne, Longfellow, and Lowell help stem the influence of Enlightenment thinking. This collective resistance is no more important than the continuing conversions of millions of people who are lifted from despair and moral defeat to enduring hope and eternal life.[775]

Although Roman Catholic missionaries had been the dominant force in the early evangelization of new lands, this nineteenth century movement is

---

[774] Latourette, *History*, Vol. II, 1335.
[775] Ibid., 1337.

fueled by Protestantism. Even during the era of Enlightenment thinking, there is a remnant; there is always a remnant (Ezek. 6:8; Zech. 8:12; Rom. 11:3–5). As the twentieth century begins, the Church is still fulfilling its charge, and the kingdom is advancing toward its preordained consummation.

*****

World War I, which begins in July 1914, is a setback for the optimism of modern thinking and the utopian idea that human beings naturally love each other and can live in harmony.

The war begins when Austria-Hungary declares war on Serbia. Because of treaty agreements, other European nations are soon drawn into the war; the Allies, primarily France, Great Britain, Italy, Russia, and eventually the United States join Serbia in opposing the Central Powers, Austria-Hungary, Germany, and the Ottoman Empire (Turkey). The great factories of the Industrial Revolution, which had produced beneficial machines and prosperity for many, are now used to mass-produce the weapons of war: tanks, battleships, airplanes, submarines, and guns. As Latourette says, "Never before had mankind massed such large armies or produced weapons which worked wholesale destruction on so gigantic a scale."[776] Never before has so much of the human race been simultaneously engaged in war.

After the initial deployments of troops and strategic engagements, the war devolves into brutal trench warfare with the use of bombs, machine guns, and poisonous gas, a hellish war of attrition that lasts for more than three years. In 1917, after German U-boats begin sinking US merchant ships, the United States enters the war, assuring an Allied victory. Germany signs an armistice on November 11, 1918. More than 16 million soldiers and civilians have died in the war. With the Treaty of Versailles in 1919, the Allies impose harsh punishments which diminish Germany financially, militarily, and territorily. This sparks an intense resentment among the German people, a factor in the initi-

---

[776] Ibid., 1351.

ation of an even greater conflict two decades later.[777] Contrary to the claims of modern statesmen, this will not be the "war to end all wars."

*****

The political disruptions surrounding the war contribute to the demise of the three European dynasties on the losing side—Germany, Austria-Hungary, and Turkey. But tragically for Christianity, the Russian government, which had been fighting on the winning side, also falls. Vladimir Lenin and the Bolsheviks had begun their revolution in 1917 while the war was still in progress, causing the Russians to withdraw their troops from the hostilities. But this does not save the crumbling empire, and the Bolsheviks gain control of the government in October 1917. They kill Tsar Nicholas II and his family and establish the first Marxist state in the world.

After Lenin's death in 1924, Joseph Stalin becomes the leader of Soviet communism. He sets up concentration camps and kills millions of people as he centralizes government power and becomes the ruthless dictator of Russia and its satellites, the Union of Soviet Socialist Republics (USSR).

The Russian Orthodox Church had enjoyed official status in the autocratic state of Tsar Nicholas, but under Lenin and Stalin, the USSR becomes the first state to have an official ideology of banishing religion and establishing state atheism. Stalin has most of the clergy of the Russian Orthodox Church shot or taken to labor camps. Within a few years, only 500 of 50,000 Russian churches remain open, and atheism is taught in the public schools.[778] Christians who try to maintain their faith are persecuted, and millions are sent to concentration camps. Todd M. Johnson of Gordon-Conwell Seminary estimates that 20 million Christians died in Soviet prison camps from 1921–1980 in addition to the 3.9 million executed by Stalin from 1925–1937.[779]

*****

---

[777] History.com Editors, "World War II," *A&E Television Networks*, October 29, 2009, https://www.history.com/topics/world-war-ii/world-war-ii-history

[778] "Revelations from the Russian Archives—Anti-Religious Campaigns," *Library of Congress*, August 31, 2016, https://www.loc.gov/exhibits/archives/anti.html.

[779] Todd M. Johnson, "Christian Martyrdom: A Global Demographic Assessment," *Notre Dame*, November 2012,

After the end of the fighting in World War I, the relocation of troops and the movement of people help facilitate the spread of a deadly influenza virus called the Spanish flu. Between 20 and 40 million people die worldwide, a death toll that exceeds the casualties from the war. There are over 675,000 flu deaths in the United States, ten times the number of American combat casualties. The year 1918 goes down as a year of military peace but with an incredible amount of suffering and death from the influenza[780] and with just the beginning of the suffering and death that will occur under godless communism in Russia.

*****

Despite the devastation of the First World War, the forces of modernity have not abandoned hope for the progressive advancement of mankind. Enlightenment thinking has crossed the Atlantic and is becoming the prevailing philosophy in the United States. Darwin's theory is being taught in public schools, although not without some resistance, especially in the South. "Fundamental Christians," many of whom prefer to be called "conservatives" or "evangelicals," decry modernism and seek to preserve their view of the inerrancy of the Bible and their fundamental beliefs in the deity of Christ, His virgin birth, His substitutionary death, His bodily resurrection, the work of the Holy Spirit in conversion, and the reality of heaven and hell.[781]

Beginning in 1921, twenty state legislatures, including Tennessee, introduce antievolutionary bills. When the Tennessee bill becomes law, it leads to a confrontation with John Scopes, a young biology teacher in the small town of Dayton who is teaching evolution. In 1925, Scopes is brought to trial.

Businessmen, reporters, and the American Civil Liberties Union (ACLU) turn the proceedings and the small Tennessee town into a nationwide circus during the summer of 1925. William Jennings Bryan, a three-time candidate for the presidency and a flamboyant Christian who has publicly denounced Darwin's theory, becomes the prosecuting attorney while a famous Chicago lawyer, Clarence Darrow, serves as the defense lawyer for Scopes. Darrow

---

https://mcgrath.nd.edu/assets/84231/the_demographics_of_christian_martyrdom_todd_johnson.pdf.

[780] Molly Billings, "The Influenza Pandemic of 1918," *stanford.edu*, June, 1997, https://virus.stanford.edu/uda/

[781] Latourette, *History*, Vol. II, 1421.

argues that intellectual freedom is on trial and makes the aging Bryan the real defendant, turning the fumbling prosecutor into a caricature of "fundamentalist" stupidity.

Journalists, critics, cartoonists, and newspapers attack Bryan from every angle, and for the first time, radio broadcasts a trial. Scopes loses in court and is fined a token sum, but for reporters and the rest of the country, the real loser is conservative Christianity. Five days after the trial, Bryan dies in his sleep. Most of the antievolutionary legislation of the other states is never implemented.

Facing increasing national ridicule, many fundamentalists withdraw from public expressions of their faith. Social Darwinism is affecting every area of national life. If human beings are continually evolving to a higher plane and an ultimate utopia, there is no place for the concept of sin and no need for a Savior. Conservative churches become more isolated, and most refrain from getting involved in political issues. The major denominations have been downplaying the doctrines of sin and damnation for some time and continue to offer a less offensive "social" gospel focusing on civic deeds and ethical behavior while dismissing the supernatural events of the Bible. Modernity and the Scopes trial have damaged the evangelical hope for a Christian America.[782]

*****

Soon after the Scopes trial, most of the Western world begins to fall into a financial downturn which progresses into a great economic depression in America. On October 24, 1929, panic grips the New York Stock Exchange; prices crash and continue to decline until the middle of 1930. One-fourth of the labor force in the United States is unemployed. Britain and some other European nations have social security systems and unemployment insurance, but the fear of socialism had prevented such programs in the United States. The unemployed are on their own and must turn to relatives, friends, or churches. Soup kitchens and breadlines are common sights in major cities and small towns. Bankruptcies and foreclosures reach record highs by the time Herbert Hoover and his cabinet members intervene in an effort to prevent further closures in industry and commerce. The optimism of modernism takes another blow, and socialism begins to gain influence in American politics.

---

[782] Shelley, *Church History*, 435–437; also see "Fundamentalism" *United States History*, accessed January 3, 2019, https://www.u-s-history.com/pages/h3806.html.

When Franklin D. Roosevelt becomes president in 1933, he rapidly enacts a number of national programs in an effort to stabilize the economy and provide jobs. Over the next eight years, the federal government initiates a series of experimental plans and projects called the "New Deal" to try to restore some measure of prosperity. These socialistic endeavors had been demanded by many Church leaders, and some of them help the poor, but they fail to bring the economy back to life. Some of the New Deal programs such as Social Security, unemployment insurance, and agricultural subsidies are still with us today.[783] Roosevelt forever changes the relationship between the US government and its people; federal authority will become an ever-increasing force in the lives of Americans.

*****

During this time, theologians such as J. Gresham Machen (1881–1937) and the Niebuhr brothers, Reinhold (1892–1970) and H. Richard (1894–1962), come to the foreground with strong criticisms of the established churches for promoting a social gospel and forsaking the doctrines of Scripture. In *The Social Sources of Denominationalism* published in 1929, H. Richard declares that "a Christianity which surrenders its leadership to the social forces of national and economic life, offers no hope to the divided world,"[784] an apt criticism of the direction of the faith in the United States and a prophetical insight into the rise of Adolf Hitler and the approaching rule of the Nazis in Germany.[785]

In his 1937 book, *The Kingdom of God in America*, H. Richard sums up the theology of the "liberal" gospel in one sentence, "A God without wrath brought men without sin into a kingdom without judgment through the ministrations of a Christ without a cross."[786] Men like the Niebuhrs and Machen[787] know

---

[783] Gonzales, *Story of Christianity,* Vol. 2, 376–377.

[784] H. Richard Niebuhr, *The Social Sources of Denominationalism* (New York: New American Library, 1959 reprint), 275.

[785] Gonzales, *Story of Christianity,* Vol. 2, 377.

[786] H. Richard Niebuhr, *The Kingdom of God in America* (New York: Harper & Brothers, 1973), 193.

[787] Machen had written a book in 1923 contrasting the views of orthodox Christianity and Liberalism; J. Gresham Machen, *Christianity & Liberalism* (Grand Rapids: Eerdmans, reprint 1996).

that this liberal gospel is taking over many, if not most, pulpits in the United States. Despite strong resistance from some orthodox believers, the mainline churches continue to move away from the essential doctrines of the faith as they accept the concepts of modernity and its optimistic view of mankind despite the lessons of World War I and the Great Depression. They agree that human beings are basically good, perhaps in need of some guidance, but they are not condemned sinners in desperate need of a Savior. As in Europe, instead of changing society, the Church in America is being changed by society.[788]

*****

Having been convinced by the sages of modernism that the prosperity arising from the industrial revolution would inevitably continue, most people in the United States are ill-prepared for hard times. Many churches help provide material sustenance to those in need, but the social gospel that had painted a rosy future by ignoring the fallen nature of humanity is of little spiritual comfort in the Great Depression.[789] With Hitler beginning to take control in Germany, the whole world is soon going to see the potential evil residing within the hearts of human beings.

*****

After the end of World War I, the European nations had set up an organization called the League of Nations for the purpose of averting future conflicts, but the League cannot prevent the rise of fascist[790] governments. The first fascist power to emerge is Italy under the leadership of Benito Mussolini. Mussolini had become prime minister in 1922 and soon centralized control, turning the nation into a totalitarian military machine. In Germany, political and economic instability and the lingering resentment over the harsh terms of the Versailles Treaty fuel the rise of Adolf Hitler and the Nazis who take power in 1936. In violation of the Versailles Treaty, Hitler begins to secretly use German industry to rearm his military.

---

[788] Gonzales, *Story of Christianity,* Vol. 2, 360.
[789] "Religion 1931–1939," Encyclopedia.com, accessed May 5, 2021, https://encyclopedia.com/education/news-and-education-magazines/religion-1931–1939.
[790] Fascism involves not only a centralized government and oppression of opposition, but a nationalistic militarism.

By this time, fascism also has a measure of power in Japan, Poland, Austria, Hungary, Greece, Romania, and Bulgaria. The fascist movements all oppose democracy, but they have differing views toward Christianity. In predominately Catholic Italy, Mussolini's attitude varies with circumstances. In Japan, the small number of resident Christians are viewed with suspicion, and some are eventually forced to work in munition plants while British and American missionaries are confined. Although Hitler sees Christian teachings as antithetical to his goals of nationalism and conquest, he is able to manipulate and gain the support of many church officials.[791]

German theologians had been leaders in Enlightenment theology in Europe and had contributed to the erosion of Orthodox Christianity. Many German Christians welcome Hitler's Nazi party and offer little resistance when Hitler begins to persecute the Jews.

In 1938, Hitler sends troops to occupy Austria, and the following year, he annexes Czechoslovakia. With the United States and Russia focused on internal politics and France and Britain fearful of another war, Hitler's aggression goes unchecked. In 1939, Germany, Italy, and Japan form a coalition called the Pact of Steel, an alignment of fascist powers which becomes known as the "Axis." All three nations are inflamed by a desire for military expansion. Without delay, Hitler next completes a treaty with Soviet leader Joseph Stalin to assure Russia's neutrality toward the Axis powers. After only a month, on September 1, 1939, Hitler invades Poland from the west; two days later, France and Britain declare war on Germany, and Europe is again at war.

Hitler quickly responds and attacks France through Belgium with air raids and swiftly advancing Panzer tank divisions that bypass the French fortifications facing the German border, the ineffective Maginot Line in which the French military had placed its trust. Britain sends troops to reinforce France, but the nation is overwhelmed by the rapid German advance, and the French surrender on June 22, 1940. In an event critical to the eventual outcome of the war, the British manage to evacuate 338,000 of their soldiers from Dunkirk back to Britain on ships and hundreds of small boats. By 1941, most of Western Europe is in the hands of the fascists; at the same time, Japan is invading China and expanding its holdings in the Orient.

As the German military is taking control of Europe, Hitler's "Schutzstaffel" (Protective Echelon) troops, usually called the SS or Brownshirts, are brutally

---

[791] Latourette, *History,* Vol. II, 1449; Gonzales, *Story of Christianity,* Vol. 2, 333–334.

persecuting the Jews who have fallen under Nazi control. Concentration camps are set up in occupied Poland, and soon, Hitler's "final solution" is initiated with approximately six million Jews from all over Europe being either shot to death or killed in gas chambers in Poland. Pastors, such as Martin Niemoller and Dietrich Bonhoeffer,[792] lead resistance against Hitler, but they have little effect against the nationalistic zeal raging through Germany. Niemoller and hundreds of other pastors are imprisoned, and Bonhoeffer is eventually hanged. The Christian opposition to Hitler's regime has little effect.

Stalin had taken advantage of his treaty with Germany to invade and take over the Baltic States, but on June 22, 1941, Hitler ignores the accord and attacks Russia. The Soviet Union joins the war against Germany and will experience the most casualties of all the nations in the conflict.

A strong isolationist sentiment keeps the United States out of the war until December 7, 1941, when Japan uses carrier-based bombers to launch a surprise attack on the US fleet anchored at Pearl Harbor, Hawaii, virtually destroying the naval power of the United States in the Pacific. On December 8, 1941, the United States declares war on Japan, followed by a declaration of war on Germany and Italy on December 11, three days later. Before the fighting is over, fifty-seven nations will have declared war on each other in what is truly a worldwide conflict.

World War II takes far more lives than any other conflict in history. The war was incredibly brutal; the killing machines had become much more effective after World War I. Total fatalities are estimated to be between 70–85 million with approximately 25 million military deaths and 55 million civilian deaths.[793] The swift movements of tanks and mechanized vehicles which engulfed both troops and civilians, the carpet-bombing of cities, the indiscriminant killing of civilians by the Axis powers, the systematic killing of the Jews, and disease and famine lead to an overwhelming amount of carnage.

The Allied armies, with the British and Americans advancing through Italy and France and the Russians attacking from the east, eventually crush the Italian and then the German forces. On May 8, 1945, a week after Hitler has

---

[792] Bonhoeffer had written a book called *The Cost of Discipleship* in 1937 which is still read by many Christians. Dietrich Bonhoeffer, *The Cost of Discipleship* (New York: Touchstone, paperback, 1995). The Nazis eventually arrest him for trying to aid the Jews, and he is hanged on April 9, 1945, one month before the Germans surrender.

[793] "World War II Casualties" *Wikipedia*, ed. February 21, 2019, https://en.wikipedia.org/wiki/World_War_II_casualties.

committed suicide in his Berlin bunker, the Germans surrender. Japan continues the war until the United States drops the first atomic bomb on Hiroshima on August 6, 1945, and then the second on Nagasaki on August 9. On August 15, Japanese Emperor Hirohito makes a radio address to the nation announcing that Japan is going to surrender. The formal signing ceremony takes place on September 2, 1945, aboard the battleship *USS Missouri* in Tokyo Bay, ending World War II throughout the rest of the world.

Although the League of Nations had been a failure in preventing the Second World War, the international community forms a similar association called the United Nations (UN) in October 1945 in the hope of settling international disputes before warfare begins again.

*****

In the face of such devastation with supposedly Christian nations on both sides of the war, we must ask, "Where were the Church and the kingdom of God?"

The Vatican under Pope Pius XII had remained neutral in Italy, and its city was never occupied during the war. The pope did try to organize humanitarian aid, but after the war, he was criticized for not reacting more forcefully against the persecution of the Jews of which he was well aware. Individual Catholics and Protestants in Italy and throughout Europe developed clandestine networks to help Jews escape from Germany, France, and other Eastern European countries, but they were not aided by the Vatican.[794] Pius did denounce Nazi atrocities against Catholics in Poland, but his main concern was to continue "the basic mood of the papacy since the Council of Trent: to protect the church at all costs, seeking for it as much freedom and power as possible, and to subordinate all other issues to this overriding concern."[795]

In Germany, large numbers of both Roman Catholics and Protestants supported the Nazi rise to power. A movement called the "German Christians" claimed three thousand Protestant pastors who wanted closer relations with Hitler and vowed to dismiss anyone of Jewish origin from church offices. They were countered by Niemoller's group, known as the Confessing Church,

---

[794] Gonzales, *Story of Christianity*, Vol. 2, 348–349.
[795] Ibid., 348.

but even before the war began, Hitler had arrested seven hundred of these Confessional ministers, and their opposition was severely limited.

The orthodox churches in Germany had already been weakened by the "higher criticism" of German theologians. Pastors had become almost exclusively concerned with individualistic personal belief; they had abandoned the broader context of Christian faith, the kingdom of God in the here and now. In addition, a traditional submission to the state going all the way back to Luther, and an outlook that saw the Nazis as the only alternative to a Soviet-style communism, affected many Church leaders. With these strong influences and the support of many lay people, Hitler was able to keep enough pressure on the churches to eliminate the possibility of any significant Christian resistance.

In Russia, Stalin took a much different approach. Realizing that churches could make a valuable contribution to public morale during the war, he had allowed them to set up their organizations again. They were permitted to collect funds and even provide some private instruction to children. By 1945, the Orthodox Church, although closely supervised, had gained legal status and was permitted to own property; the war had brought the Church in Russia to its most favorable position since the 1917 Revolution.[796]

The mainland United States had escaped the devastation visited on Continental Europe, Great Britain, and the Far East during the war. American churches supported the war effort but with a realistic perspective after seeing the lack of a lasting peace following World War I, the "war to end all wars." Many pastors served as chaplains for the armed forces, and Church leaders declared their abhorrence for the crimes of Nazism. Many believers volunteered for the military, but most pastors and their congregations tried to avoid combining faith and national pride. Some Americans had friends and relatives who were living under and sometimes fighting for the Axis Powers. These ties, the deaths of many US soldiers, and the knowledge of the great sufferings in other parts of the world had a sobering effect on Christians in the United States.

Christians struggled and died with their fellow citizens on both sides during the war; some were heroes and some betrayed the faith, even to the point of supporting Hitler. But most Christians, especially those bearing the brunt of the war in Europe, simply tried to take care of their families and survive while they prayed for the war to be over.[797] Even before the fighting ended,

---

[796] Shelley, *Church History*, 422–427.
[797] Ibid., 427.

Christians on both sides were seeking to build bridges to fellow believers in other nations, efforts which become manifest in the ecumenical movement after the war. The first assembly of the World Council of Churches will meet in 1948, representing 147 denominations from 44 countries[798] with an appropriate theme, "Man's Disorder and God's Design."[799] God's kingdom people were able to look forward with hope, even in a time of worldwide death and destruction.

*****

There is great relief and large celebrations in the United States at the end of the Second World War. The United States emerges as the least damaged major world power and with the Marshall Plan, named after Secretary of State George Marshall, assists in Western Europe's recovery. General Douglas MacArthur leads a smaller but similar effort in rebuilding Japan. The US invests billions of dollars to help restore war-torn regions, remove trade barriers, modernize industry, and prevent the spread of Communism. Because of his fear of US economic domination and his unwillingness to open his secret society, Stalin rejects any aid from the Marshall Plan for Russia and its Eastern European satellites.[800]

*****

One of the notable outcomes of World War II is the reestablishment of Israel as a sovereign nation in the land of Palestine after almost two thousand years without a Jewish homeland. After World War I, the League of Nations had given Great Britain a mandate for governing the territory of Palestine as part of a plan to administer parts of the defunct Ottoman Empire until the

---

[798] Ibid., 445–446. Over the years, the World Council of Churches begins to focus on issues such as racism, poverty, women's liberation, and homosexual rights as it evolves into a social, political organization. See M. H. Reynolds, "The Truth about the World Council of Churches," *FEA News & Views*, accessed January 8, 2019, www.cnview.com/on_line_resources/world_council_of_churches.htm.

[799] "Assembly," World Council of Churches," accessed January 8, 2019, https://www.ministrymagazine.org/archive/1948/08/world-council-of-churches-amsterdam-1948.

[800] "Marshall Plan," *Office of The Historian*, accessed January 8, 2019, https://history.state.gov/milestones/1945-1952/marshall-plan.

countries could rule themselves. Britain had issued a declaration formalizing their intent to establish a Jewish homeland in Palestine. Jews began to immigrate to the area, but because of Arab opposition to the establishment of a Jewish state, the British government continued its rule. By 1929, Jews and Arabs had begun to fight openly in Palestine.

At the end of World War II, the United States takes up the cause for a Jewish state. Britain, unable to find a solution to the problem of Jewish and Arab hostilities, refers the issue to the newly formed United Nations, which in 1947 votes to partition Palestine. Although the Arab forces in Palestine fight to prevent it, the Jewish military secures Israel's allocated share of Palestine while also capturing some Arab territory. When the British mandate ends on May 14, 1948, the British Army withdraws, and on the same day, the State of Israel is proclaimed. To the joy of the Jews, the United States immediately recognizes Israel as a sovereign country.

The next day, Egypt, Transjordan, Syria, Lebanon, and Iraq invade the new State of Israel. Although less well-equipped, the Israelis manage to fight off the military forces from these nations and even gain key areas such as Galilee and the Palestinian coast. A United Nations brokered ceasefire in 1949 leaves Israel in control of this additional territory. The Jews, as a nation, are back in Palestine.[801]

For Christians everywhere, this is a significant historical event. For many Dispensationalists, who believe that Christ is going to reign over national Israel on the earth for a thousand years, this is an important step in the fulfillment of their eschatological view and raises their expectation of the imminent return of Jesus Christ. But as we have seen in Paul's teaching, there is one people of God made up of both Jews and Gentiles, and there is no separate destiny for Jewish believers.[802] Presently, about 2 percent of the citizens of Israel are Christians, and these believers are almost entirely Arabic.[803] We should be supportive of Israel because it is a democracy with Judeo-Christian values in an area of the world where most nations are led by Muslim dictators, not because we think

[801] History.com Editors, "State of Israel proclaimed," *HISTORY*, February 9, 2010, https://www.history.com/this-day-in-history/state-of-israel-proclaimed.
[802] See pp. 247–251.
[803] Daniel K. Eisenbud, "The State Of Christianity In Israel," *The Jerusalem Post*, July 22, 2013, https://www.jpost.com/National-News/The-state-of-Christianity-in-Israel-320670.

Christ is soon going to reign there for a thousand years. The state of Israel is not and will not become the kingdom of God.

*****

In June 1950, the countries making up the United Nations face a major challenge; North Korea, supplied and advised by the Soviet Union, invades and controls much of South Korea. The UN intervenes on behalf of South Korea with the United States providing most of the military forces. Although China reinforces North Korea with hundreds of thousands of soldiers, United States troops eventually retake the southern part of the peninsula. An armistice is declared in 1953, and the Thirty-Eighth Parallel is established as the boundary between the two Koreas, but no peace treaty is signed. The US had suffered over 405,000 combat deaths in WWII and loses over 36,000 soldiers in the Korean conflict. The fighting stops, but the North Korean government remains belligerent, and the US leaves a large military force in the South as a deterrent to another invasion from the North. The western influence in the South leads to a growing Christian population; the Pew Research Center reported in 2014 that Christianity, largely Presbyterian, is the largest religion in the country.[804]

Despite the tragedy of this limited but brutal war, God is calling in his sheep, and the kingdom is moving forward.

*****

Another effect of World War II is the return to prominence of evangelical Christianity in the United States. The frightful carnage of the Second World War had taken a toll on the utopian optimism of modern thinking. Three wars in less than forty years along with the concentration camps and mass executions ordered by Hitler and Stalin have resulted in over 120 million deaths world-

---

[804] Phillip Conner, "6 facts about South Korea's growing Christian population," *Pew Research Center*, August 12, 2014, www.pewresearch.org/fact-tank/2014/08/12/6-facts-about-christianity-in-south-korea/. The two Koreas present a stark comparison between Democracy and Communism. The South has become a prosperous, modern nation while the North has failed to even provide adequate food for its people. The North has spent most of its limited resources on its military, has developed nuclear weapons, and has threatened to strike the US mainland.

wide.[805] The self-assurance of Enlightenment thinking is rapidly diminishing; human beings cannot be trusted to live in peace, and their great achievements in science and technology have been used to make weapons that have wreaked unimaginable havoc on soldiers and civilians alike. Gratitude for victory in World War II and the overpowering evidence of human evil in the world leads to increased Church attendance throughout America. In 1940, 47 percent of US citizens belonged to a church; by 1950, that number had increased to 57 percent, a large increase in overall numbers.[806] Many people have learned that the atheistic philosophy of modernism provides no comfort in the crucible times of life.

In the 1950s, Billy Graham begins a decades-long evangelical ministry, which eventually reaches an estimated 200 million people in 185 countries through rallies at major stadiums and radio and TV broadcasts.[807] His preaching can be criticized for its lack of theological depth and ultimate effectiveness—the vast majority of those "converted" at his meetings never join a church[808]—but millions are introduced to Jesus Christ as the Savior of the world at a time when people are beginning to understand how badly one is needed. At the very least, the huge audiences for Billy Graham's crusades show that people everywhere are realizing that human reason and technology are not going to lead to a heaven on earth. The humanistic optimism of the modern age is approaching its end.

---

[805] There were approximately 16 million total deaths in WWI, 80 million in WWII, 3 million in the Korean War, 6 million in German concentration camps, and 23 million in Russian concentration camps, an almost unbelievable loss of human life in such a short time.

[806] Latourette, *History*, Vol. II, 1410.

[807] "Billy Graham," *Theopedia*, accessed January 8, 2019, https://www.theopedia.com/billy-graham.

[808] Thomas Williamson, "Case Studies in Easy-Believism," *The Biblical Examiner*, accessed January 8, 2019, http://www.rogershermansociety.org/easy-believism.htm.

CHAPTER 30

THE KINGDOM AND POSTMODERN TIMES

In the seventeenth century, the tragic effects of the Thirty Years War in Europe had begun the philosophical shift from the era of premodern thought to the era of modern thinking. Philosophers, statesmen, and much of the general public had blamed Catholic and Protestant leaders for the hostilities that led to three decades of destructive warfare. The militant dogmatism of Church leaders was seen as a greater threat to peace than atheism, and the public influence of religion was greatly curtailed, leading to the growth of secular governments and soon to secular societies. Advances in science and changes in philosophical thought continued to erode trust in the teachings of the Church, eventually resulting in the modern era of thought when there was a general rejection of Christianity. Human reason was elevated and an optimism developed that autonomous human beings could find a unifying absolute that would lead to peace and prosperity in the world. Despite the overall rejection of the supernatural during the modern era, God's kingdom people not only survived but made great progress in spreading the gospel to newly discovered areas of the world. But with the end of World War II, the Church soon faces a new threat from a different form of secular thinking that begins to have worldwide effects.

The destruction and suffering of the Second World War lead to another major philosophical change, first in Europe and then in the United States. Now it is the concepts of modernity which are being rejected, especially among younger people. The faith that citizens had placed in secular governments, science, and education for human progress has been eroded by world wars and mass killings that have led to immense suffering and the deaths of over 120 million people in four decades. Fallen human beings have used increasing technological advances to gain power and destroy other people, not benevolently aid them.

Mankind's inherent evil has been graphically and tragically displayed. The modern belief that humanity can progress to a utopian paradise through its own efforts has turned out to be a cruel illusion. The fundamental concept of modernity that there is a rational world that can be understood and beneficially controlled on the basis of autonomous human reason is being rejected.

It seems as though this rejection might lead to a renewed interest in Christianity, but except for the short-term revival in the United States, this is not the case. Instead, a new way of thinking begins to develop in Europe which will progress to the United States, a movement that will be called postmodernism.

*****

Postmodern thinking begins to emerge in the 1960s in France and is a mixture of bewildering art and perplexing philosophical theories, but its cornerstone is the rejection of objective truth and unifying human values. It draws on experimental and surrealistic art and on atheistic philosophers such as Nietzsche and Heidegger. In this new way of thinking, there is no ultimate reality that unites human beings; truth is individual and relative. As Nietzsche put it, "You have your way. I have my way. As for the right way, the correct way, and the only way, it does not exist."[809] Or as Christians often hear when they try to evangelize today, "That may be true for you, but it is not true for me."

Kant's epistemology looms in the background of postmodern thinking. First, we have seen that according to Kant's theory of knowledge, *if* God is there, he cannot communicate with us to inform us about reality.[810] Secondly, if individual minds are hardwired to receive and process data from phenomena and no two human beings are the same, then knowledge and reality are always individual constructs, and no one can claim to know ultimate truth. As we have previously noted, Kant cannot explain how we became hardwired, so his concepts lack a rational foundation. But for the relativism of postmodernists, a logical basis is not necessary for forming what are often contradictory beliefs. Emotions and feelings determine reality for the postmodernist; each person has their own unique "truth." In a real sense, each postmodernist is recreating Adam's sin for himself.

---

[809] "Friedrich Nietzsche > Quotes," *goodreads*, accessed January 8, 2019, https://www.goodreads.com/author/quotes/1938.friedrich_Nietzsche.
[810] See p. 369.

Martin Heidegger (1889–1976) also has a strong influence on postmodern thought. He writes about the "throwness" of man; "he is 'just there,' projected into nothing."[811] According to Heidegger, human beings live in a constant state of *Angst*, a nameless dread as they face coming death and nothingness.[812] The sexless shrieking figure in *The Scream*, painted in 1893 by Edvard Munch (1863–1944), had already captured this *Angst*, the horror and despair of human beings in a postmodern world before Heidegger describes it.[813] For those living in *Angst* with no belief in God, seeking personal security and pleasure is the only possible response. And no one has a right to disagree or interfere by claiming that there are objective truths or universal ethical norms.

The rejection of objective truth appears to be liberating for many people who are feeling betrayed by their governments and the rational philosophy of modernism that has resulted in so much death and destruction. The postmodernists reject establishment principles and the progressive goals of modernity. In the 1960s and 1970s in the United States, this is summed up by the axiom, "If it feels good, do it," an attitude which leads to sexual liberation, the use of mind-altering drugs, and rebellion against any kind of authority.

College students and other young people protest violently against the US government's decision to engage in the Vietnam War, especially against being drafted into the military. In a world without ultimate truth, no form of government is superior to another and all governmental policies are just means for coercion. For postmodernists, there is no national cause that can justify the risking of their lives.

There is a great divide between the anti-war demonstrators and those who feel an obligation to serve their country. Some protesters vilify returning veterans; they do not know these men personally but the soldiers represent a concept of right and wrong that justifies the use of force, and the postmodernists vehemently oppose it.[814] They do not articulate it, but the protestors are attacking modernity and its belief in a rational world, and they are determined

---

[811] Martin Heidegger, *Being and Time*, trans. John Macquarrie and Edward Robinson (New York: Harper & Row, 1962), 13.

[812] See Strimple, *The Modern Search*, 118.

[813] The painting can be seen at "The Scream, 1893 by Edvard Munch," *Edvard Munch Paintings, Biography, and Quotes*, accessed January 11, 2019, www.edvardmunch.org/the-scream.jsp. The pastel on board version of the painting, one of four originals, was sold at auction by Sotheby's for a record $120 million on May 2, 2012.

[814] I was in the military during the Vietnam War.

to replace it with a system where each person is allowed to create his or her own reality. But they are inconsistent; they do not believe the soldiers should be allowed to live out their own views of life. As we have seen, rational consistency is not essential for postmodern thinking.

*****

Relativism is a central principle for postmodernists. We see a religious fervor in their rallies for homosexual and abortion rights. They display an obvious hatred and disdain toward those who disagree with them. Their anger erupts not just because someone opposes their beliefs but because someone dares to assert a transcendent moral value, a right and wrong that applies to everyone. For postmodernists, such a claim is bigotry and an intolerant judgment that no one is allowed to make. Although postmodernists demand tolerance for their own beliefs, they are selective in offering it to others. This is especially apparent on college campuses where conservative speakers are shouted down and violently protested, usually with the acquiescence of school administrators.[815]

Postmodernists believe they have attained what Adam wanted: the right for each individual to determine right and wrong without having to consider any external norms, including absolutes from God. And now, this has progressed to the point where some are claiming the right to decide their own gender by their personal feelings, a rejection of physical reality, and a protest against the God who has made them. At the present time, United States federal guidelines require that schools have transgender bathrooms. And the Biden administration has instituted a policy allowing transgender men to participate in women's college sports if they receive hormone treatments.[816]

---

[815] John Leo, "Free Inquiry? Not on Campus," *City Journal*, winter 2007, www.uvm. edu/~dguber/POLS21/articles/leo.htm; also see Natalie Johnson, "Campus Protesters Try to Silence Conservative Speaker, Demand President's Resignation," *The Daily Signal*, February 26, 2016, https://www.dailysignal.com/2016/02/26/campus-protesters-try-to-silence-conservative-speaker-demand-college-presidents-resignation/.

[816] In 2016, the Obama Education Department established sex integration of restrooms in schools through a guidance letter threatening legal action. The Trump Administration initially rescinded the guidelines, but the Office of Civil Rights has for now reinstated them. See Thomas Ascik, "Trump Education Department Will Enforce Transgenderism In Schools," *The Daily Caller*, August 23, 2017, https://dailycaller.com/2017/08/23/trump-education-department-will-enforce-transgenderism-in-schools/.

Just as modernism affected the theology of the Church, postmodernism is now having its own effect. But where modernity denied the supernatural, postmodernism is open to personal spirituality as long as no one makes universal truth claims. Since Christianity does, it is not only rejected, it is seen as bigoted and therefore evil. For Kantian-influenced postmodernists, *if* God is there, each individual can determine their own approach to Him, and each approach is equally valid because no one knows ultimate truth. This leads to a swirling moral chaos, a world without ethical or intellectual equilibrium.

Evangelical theologians influenced by postmodern thinking have begun to present new and different views of God. In 1994, Clark Pinnock and four other theologians wrote a book called *The Openness of God* in which they claim that God does not know the future and is flexible in how He reacts to what human beings do.[817] These men believe the actions of human beings are determinative, and God can only respond. Two years later, the theologian, John Hick, once an evangelical, stated that he now opts "for the pluralistic view that the God-figures of the great theistic religions are different human awarenesses of the Ultimate."[818]

This trend has continued, and many seminaries, pastors, and local churches have been significantly affected by the changing views arising from the influences of postmodernism. A George Barna survey in 2001 found that only 44 percent of born-again Christians were certain that moral truth is absolute; for Christians who do not claim to be born again, it was just 17 percent.[819] Christians are absorbing the views of society rather than the teaching of Scripture.[820] These survey results would likely be much worse today.

Gene Edward Veith Jr., in his helpful book, *Postmodern Times*,[821] sums up some of the effects of postmodernism on the Church. He says that with the rejection of objective truth, many Christians are not interested in linear thinking or theological studies. Subjective experiences and emotions become the criteria for evaluating doctrine.[822]

---

[817] Clark Pinnock, et al., *The Openness of God* (Downers Grove, IL: InterVarsity, 1994).

[818] John Hick, "Normative Pluralism," in *Four Views on Salvation in a Pluralistic World*, eds. Dennis L. Okholm and Timothy R. Phillips (Grand Rapids: Zondervan, 1996), 39.

[819] George Barna and Mark Hatch, *Boiling Point* (Ventura, CA: Regal Books, 2001), 80.

[820] B. A. Robinson, "Does Absolute Moral Truth Exist," *Religious Tolerance*, December 16, 2001, updated November 29, 2015, www.religioustolerance.org/chr_poll5.htm.

[821] Gene Edward Veith, Jr., *Postmodern Times* (Wheaton, IL: Crossway, 1994).

[822] Ibid., 211.

A well-known example of this thinking is the story of Carlton Pearson, a one-time star Pentecostal preacher who, after seeing the suffering of African children on TV, has begun preaching that earthly anguish is the only kind of hell that people will experience. He no longer accepts the teaching of Scripture about judgment and says it has been invented to control people. Pearson has started a church that is open to any type of religion and teaches that everyone will go to heaven, regardless of their beliefs or actions on earth.[823] This, of course, eliminates the concept of sin and the need for a Savior. A recently completed movie of Pearson's life will appeal to those who believe harmony is more important than truth in a pluralistic environment.

Another recent very public manifestation of the effects of postmodernism in the United States is the reaction of the Democratic Party and their constituents to President Trump's nomination of a conservative, Brett Kavanaugh, to fill a Supreme Court vacancy. The Democrats brought forth three women who claimed to have been sexually abused by Kavanaugh over thirty-five years ago. Although the FBI found no corroborating evidence to substantiate any of their claims, and witnesses actually refuted each story, Democratic lawmakers insisted the accusers had to be believed because they were victims and women; their own personal "truths" had to be accepted. Most Republicans were afraid to even express doubts about the claims of these women.

Despite the efforts of Democrats, Kavanaugh was confirmed by a narrow 50–48 vote, which reflects the increasing influence of postmodern thinking in the United States.

In the postmodern world, each person gets to determine his or her own reality, and no one is allowed to question it. The rule of law cannot survive if this kind of thinking prevails. Without a presumption of innocence and a requirement for actual evidence, a charge alone establishes guilt, and courts and the media can be used to destroy anyone. Postmodern thinking leads to anarchy, which we saw previewed in the virulent protests during Kavanaugh's Supreme Court confirmation process.

As disturbing as the Kavanaugh episode was, several even more impactful events have followed that are having ongoing devastating consequences while further exposing the concepts of postmodern thinking. The most major is a worldwide pandemic that originated in Wuhan, China. A highly contagious

---

[823] "The fall and rise of Carlton Pearson," *Religion News Blog*, accessed January 9, 2019, https://www.religionnewsblog.com/13829/the-fall-and-rise-of-carlton-pearson.

and deadly virus, eventually designated COVID-19, began affecting residents of Wuhan in late 2019. As the world learned later, the Communist Chinese leaders quickly began taking drastic measures in the city, locking people in their apartments and shutting down travel to destinations within China. But they continued to allow international travel from Wuhan, including many flights to the United States and Italy, revealing their malicious intent to have other countries suffer from this disease, not just China. As of November 8, 2022, the virus had spread worldwide with a global total of 638,287,396 infections and 6,607,556 deaths. On the same date, the United States reported a total of 99,685,828 infections with 1,098,422 deaths due to COVID.

The national and international ramifications of this pandemic are beyond the scope of this book. But one aspect of postmodern thinking stands out. When President Trump called the virus the Wuhan or Chinese virus, he was vilified for being hateful and xenophobic by much of the mainstream media. In the postmodern world, criticism of any nation suggests universal norms and, therefore, bigotry. Even facts become racist and prejudicial and must be reworded or eliminated.

During this time, two protest groups, Black Lives Matter (BLM) and a group that claims to be anti-fascist, Antifa, began violently attacking police headquarters and federal buildings in the northwest cities of Portland and Seattle, seriously injuring policemen and federal officers.[824] The mayors of these cities sympathized with these rioters and refused to let the police take the actions necessary to end the violent destruction, which continued for months. Many peaceful residents had to abandon their homes and businesses. For these postmodern mayors, the right to demonstrate and destroy took precedence over law and order. Like many of the rioters, they had become idealistic tools for rich billionaires who want the United States to be part of a worldwide socialist/communist hegemony.

Another episode was the horrific death of a Black man named George Floyd while in the custody of four Minneapolis policemen. The actions of the police were recorded on cell phones, and although the officers were universally condemned and quickly arrested, violent and lengthy protests erupted in numerous cities with serious injuries to more policemen and the burning

---

[824] Kiro 7 News Staff, *Kiro 7*, July 25, 2020, https://www.kiro7.com/news/local/thousands-gather-capitol-hill-solidarity-with-demonstrations-portland/STVDEK5XUJHWLL2HQZT2NWDYVY/.

of many city blocks. The rioters and their supporters in the news media claim that the United States is an inherently racist nation that has to be fundamentally changed. The BLM organization helped instigate the riots and have been calling for the killing of policemen.[825]

Many companies paid millions of dollars to this group, apparently to avoid being attacked physically or socially as racists. Liberal politicians have denounced and defunded the police in large cities, leading to looting and anarchy. White celebrities have publicly confessed their "white guilt" and have stated their support for Black Lives Matter. But the Marxist organizer of BLM is not living out her rhetoric. She has recently purchased four expensive homes—one of them a 1.4 million dollar mansion in a 98 percent white neighborhood—while proclaiming the evil of white people. She has now decided to step down from her leadership position to enjoy the riches she has accumulated from intimidating American companies.[826] Other Black lives no longer seem to matter very much.

Christians must stand against racism wherever it is found, and they must help heal the racial divides in our country. But they must also stand against the hypocrisy of those who incite racial strife to promote and enrich themselves—especially politicians and celebrities. Their emotional provocations must be refuted with a determined commitment to objective truth and racial equality under the law.

*****

Although postmodernists claim there is no absolute truth, they seem to be embracing three concepts which every person must accept to be "woke" (aware of and accepting of the current postmodern view of reality): (1) every white person is inherently racist and must confess his or her guilt; (2) homosexual rights, especially homosexual marriage, must be upheld and never spoken against; (3) abortion is a positive good that must never be denied or condemned. Social and mainstream media, especially TV anchors, now play the

---

[825] Kim Kapria, *Snopes*, July 18, 2016, https://www.snopes.com/fact-check/black-lives-matter-protesters-chant-for-dead-cops-now-in-baton-rouge/.

[826] Rebecca Downs, "BLM Founder with Massive Wealth and Four Homes to Step Down," *Townhall*, May 27, 2021, https://townhall.com/tipsheet/rebeccadowns/2021/05/27/blm-with-massive-wealth-and-four-homes-to-step-down-n2590130.

role of modern-day inquisitors who enforce these sacrosanct beliefs through social shaming that is destroying careers and lives.

In citing a profound effect of postmodern thinking, Veith mentions a young man who said that he believed in the inerrancy of Scripture, Reformed theology, and reincarnation, apparently unconcerned that the last concept is logically incompatible with the teaching of the first two.[827] The fact that many high school and college graduates in the United States do not come to conclusions through rational thinking is a great victory for Satan. God communicates to us through logical propositions in His Word, and He intends for us to think His thoughts after Him (Isa. 1:18–20). The inability to do this is an overwhelming loss.

The above examples illustrate the basic difference between postmodernism and Christianity. For the postmodernist, individual feelings and emotions determine truth; for the Christian, it is God's rational precepts revealed in Scripture. For postmodernists, the biblical claim to absolute truth is an expression of bigotry and a desire to oppress.

Christians who believe God has spoken the truth to human beings in the Bible find it difficult to engage with people whose most central tenet is relativism. In conversations with postmodernists, it is helpful to remember that each person is created in God's image and knows not only that God exists but that they have an obligation to Him. Every human being has a conscience—a sense of right and wrong—even though after the fall, it is suppressed in unrighteousness (Rom. 1:18–19). God's invisible attributes are understood by the things that He has made; His eternal power and Godhead are manifest so that anyone who denies Him is without excuse (Rom. 1:20–23). The anger and rebellion of many postmodernists arise from their sense of isolation and guilt without any hope of resolution. Even though it is difficult, Christians should be patient and kind when discussing ultimate truth with them.

*****

In the United States, Christians presently live in a culture that is a mixture of modernism and postmodernism. Although postmodernism is a rejection of modernism, the two philosophies agree that Christianity must be rejected. The modernist rejects the existence of God; the postmodernist accepts the possi-

---

[827] Veith, *Postmodern*, 211.

bility of the supernatural but rejects a God that asserts universal truths. Both reject Jesus Christ when he makes the exclusive claim, "I am the way, the truth, and the life. No one comes to the Father except through me" (John 14:6).

The various expressions of modernism and postmodernism can be confusing and troubling, but basic realities remain the same; the God of the Bible is there, every person has sinned against Him, every person needs a Savior, and that Savior is Jesus Christ. God's kingdom people need to focus on these universal unchanging truths until Christ returns for the consummation of His kingdom.

The postmodern view may seem new, but the writer of Hebrews had described the hopeless state of mankind in the face of approaching death almost two thousand years ago (Heb. 2:14–15). Human beings have no hope without the God of the Bible. Munch and Heidegger understood the "thrownness," the fear and anxiety, of isolated human existence, but they have no solution for *angst*. Scripture does—eternal life through faith in the saving work of Jesus Christ, which gives life meaning, purpose, and a destination—a firm foundation[828] (Rom. 8:12–17; Heb. 1:10–14).

*****

With the onset of the postmodern era, we have reached the present time in the progress of God's kingdom on the earth. We will next consider kingdom life in our own time—what the kingdom means for Christians in the here and now.

---

[828] A wonderful hymn, "How Firm a Foundation," begins with the words, "How firm a foundation, ye saints of the Lord, is laid for your faith in His excellent Word."

CHAPTER 31

THE KINGDOM AT THE PRESENT TIME

We have traced the progress of redemptive history up to the present time through the repetitions of the kingdom paradigm. Before considering present-day life in the kingdom, it will be helpful to briefly review the problems previously noted with the Dispensational and Covenantal views which make them inadequate for understanding and summarizing God's plan of redemption, not only for the past but for the present and the future.

*****

Dispensationalism has become the predominant view of redemptive history in the United States. Its foundational concept is the belief in separate destinies for ethnic Israel and the Church. In this view, the kingdom is Christ's thousand-year earthly reign over the nation of Israel and will not be established until His Second Coming.[829] But as we have seen from Jesus's teaching in the kingdom parables and His explanations about the nature of the kingdom, it was present when He was instructing His disciples. The kingdom began with His first advent.[830]

Secondly, the Apostle Paul's teaching contradicts the concept of separate futures for Israel and the Church. Paul tells us that in Jesus Christ, God has broken down the dividing wall between Jew and Gentile, making one new man. There is one olive tree, one people of God. There is no separate future for Israel. Jews and Gentiles are saved in the same way and together become

---

[829] A few Dispensationalists have come to believe that Jesus is ruling over believing Jews in the present and will eventually rule over national Israel in the millennial kingdom. See Craig A. Blaising and Darrell L. Bock, *Progressive Dispensationalism* (Wheaton, IL: BridgePoint, 1993).

[830] See pp. 180–185.

God's kingdom people.[831] Abraham's ultimate blessing is the same for Jews and Gentiles. If there is no separate destiny for Israel, Dispensationalism as a coherent system collapses. This view of redemptive history is flawed for understanding present circumstances and future events.

*****

We have also seen that there are problems with the Covenantal approach of summarizing redemptive history through three theological covenants. In contrast to six other covenants definitively stated in Scripture, these theological covenants are not directly proposed by God but are seen as "implied," which raises an initial concern.

The first suggested covenant, the covenant to redeem, is supposedly made within the Triune Godhead in eternity past before time and creation. But as O. Palmer Robertson says, to propose such a covenant "extends the bounds of scriptural evidence beyond propriety."[832] In addition to Robertson's concern, the use of the word *covenant* suggests the forming of an agreement, something unnecessary within the eternally omniscient and harmonious Trinity. If we are going to speak of such things, the terminology of an eternal "decree" to redeem would be more fitting. The concept of this initial "covenant" is invalid.

The second implied covenant, the covenant of works, says that God was testing Adam and Eve while withholding the tree of life, eternal life, until they had been faithful for some indeterminate time. But God was not withholding this tree; it was available to them from the beginning (Gen. 2:9). To suggest that God was withholding the tree of life distorts the conditions under which Adam and Eve were living in the Garden. Adam and Eve could have confirmed their status as sinless human beings and lived in paradise forever by eating of this tree at any time. But they did not, and this is the background when they are tempted by the serpent, and Adam decides to become his own god. The second implied covenant is at least a flawed conception of the circumstances in the Garden.

The third suggested covenant of this system, the covenant of grace, is based on God's revelation in Genesis 3:15 concerning the coming of the one who will crush the head of the serpent, Satan. God does not call this a cove-

---

[831] See pp. 247–251.
[832] See p. ix, n. 9.

nant, and it seems more correct to see it as a promise of the coming Savior. It is true that humanity does live in a period of grace after the fall until the time of the final judgment, a time when sinners can repent and be saved by faith in the one who crushes the serpent's head. But summing up the entire plan of salvation after the fall through such a broad theological "covenant" does little to help us understand and cherish our roles in redemptive history as the kingdom advances to its glorious consummation. These three implied covenants appear to be a system imposed on the text.

Both Covenantal and Dispensational views are inadequate for outlining God's overall salvation plan. The history of redemption is a living story, and neither of these systems seems to summarize or describe its amazing progression.

*****

In contrast to these established understandings, we have followed the course of redemptive history from the Garden of Eden to the present time through the progress of the kingdom paradigm. After Adam, Noah, and Israel failed to establish God's kingdom, He sent His only Son to earth and Jesus came preaching, saying, "The time is fulfilled, and the kingdom of God is at hand. Repent and believe in the gospel" (Mark 1:15). Although it was not the political reign Israel was looking for, Jesus began establishing the kingdom of God even before founding the Church, and we have traced the kingdom's progress through two thousand years of history. Despite the many wars, technological changes, and shifts in human philosophy, the kingdom has continued to advance as God's people look forward to the return of Christ and the consummation of the kingdom. But Christians, since they do not know the timing of Christ's return (Matt. 24:36), must focus on kingdom life in the present while looking forward to its fulfillment in the new heaven and earth.

We have noted the problems with the implied covenants of Covenantal Theology, but present-day kingdom life *is* lived out through a covenant—the final scriptural covenant, the new covenant prophesied by Jeremiah and initiated by Jesus the night before His death. But before looking at this final covenant and present life in the kingdom, we should briefly review the five previous covenants instituted by God that lead up to the new covenant.

*****

The first covenant that God established was with Noah. God initiates this covenant by telling Noah to build the Ark and then expands it after the deluge ends by saying that he will never again destroy the earth with a flood. This final addition is an unconditional covenant; it does not depend on the actions of human beings and extends through all the kingdom paradigms. It is also universal in that it applies to all the nations. God places His bow in the sky as a sign that He is not going to destroy the human race. He is going to have a righteous people for Himself (Gen. 6:18–19, 9:11–17).

The second covenant is with Abram who becomes Abraham. God calls Abram out of Ur of the Chaldeans and promises that He is going to make him a great nation; he will have many descendants and a land, and he will be a blessing to all the nations. It is through Abraham's descendants that God is going to establish His kingdom (Gen. 12:1–3, 17:1–8). This also is an unconditional covenant; it does not depend on Abraham's efforts, and God confirms this by unilaterally performing a Suzerain Treaty ritual. But it is not universal; God has narrowed the scope of his salvation plan to the descendants of Abraham. Eventually, Scripture reveals that the true children of Abraham are those who have faith in the Messiah, Jesus Christ, and they come from every tribe and nation (Gal. 3:26–29).

The third covenant is made at Mt. Sinai after Abraham's descendants have been rescued from captivity in Egypt through Moses's leadership and great miracles. Moses organizes the tribes of Jacob into a nation as they camp before Mt. Sinai where God gives them His Law, the Mosaic Covenant (Exod. 20:1–27:21). God is telling his covenant people how they are to live in His kingdom; they must be righteous or He will cast them out of the promised Land. This is a conditional covenant with its continued existence depending on the obedience of the children of Israel. If they are not righteous, God will judge them. This is not a universal covenant; its moral, civil, and ceremonial laws are given to the nation of Israel. However, the moral laws do have universal application because they are essentially what each person knows through his or her conscience (Rom. 2:14–16); thus, they have meaning for every human being after the fall. The people of Israel fail to keep the Mosaic Covenant, and God eventually judges them and sends His chosen nation into Babylonian captivity. Jesus Christ perfectly fulfills this covenant, and although the moral law continues to be a universal guide, this covenant, the old covenant, fades away because the Messiah to whom it pointed has come (2 Cor. 3:11; Heb. 8:13). Jesus Christ is the end of the law for righteousness to everyone who believes

(Rom. 10:1–10), and He initiates a new covenant the night before His crucifixion (Luke 22:19–20).

The fourth scriptural covenant is the Land Covenant, which God tells Moses to make with the second wilderness generation just before the nation enters Canaan (Deut. 29:1–28). This is a renewal of the conditional Mosaic covenant, and God warns the people not to worship idols in the land or they will be cast out. He goes on to reveal that Israel will not keep the covenant and will be sent into captivity. But He adds a promise that they will return and that He will circumcise their hearts and they will greatly prosper. The prophecy added to this covenant looks ahead to the time of the final covenant, the New Covenant, which Jeremiah will prophesy and which Jesus will initiate.

The fifth covenant is the Davidic Covenant in which God promises to raise up a seed of King David, who will build a house for God's name and whose kingdom will be forever (2 Sam. 7:12–17; Luke 30–33). This is again an unconditional covenant; it is not annulled by David's and Solomon's sins and the destruction of the nation of Israel. God's promise is ultimately fulfilled in David's descendant, Jesus Christ, and His rule over His kingdom people through eternity. This is not a universal covenant; it is fulfilled through the everlasting King and His kingdom people.

The sixth and final scriptural covenant is the new covenant revealed to Jeremiah when Nebuchadnezzar destroyed Jerusalem and took the nation of Israel into captivity (Jer. 31:31–34). Israel's failure to keep the Mosaic Covenant and be a righteous people for God had led to the nation's destruction. But even as Jeremiah wept for Israel, God told him that there was going to be a new covenant where God's law is not written on tablets of stone but on the hearts of His people. He will be their God and He will remember their sins no more, pointing to the work of the Suffering Messiah, already prophesied by Isaiah, who with His stripes heals His people (Isa. 53). Jesus institutes this everlasting covenant, the covenant which will never be broken (Jer. 31:36–40), the night before His crucifixion and says it is a covenant in His blood for the remission of sins (Matt. 26:27–28).

The New Covenant supersedes the Mosaic Covenant and reveals the final outworking of the Abrahamic and Davidic Covenants. Jesus is the ultimate Son of David, and through Him, Abraham becomes a blessing to all the nations.

All the previous covenants fall within the repetitions of the kingdom paradigm as redemptive history advances to the consummation of the kingdom. The conditional Mosaic Covenant and its renewal in the Land Covenant are

superseded—they vanish away (2 Cor. 3:4–11; Heb. 8:13) while the unconditional Noahic, Abrahamic, and Davidic covenants are fulfilled in the New
Covenant. After Jesus's death and resurrection, we are now living in the time of
this new covenant, and we need to understand what that means for present-day
kingdom life.

*****

Adam and Noah failed to establish the kingdom, and although they were
part of God's people, they never lived life in the kingdom. The same was true
of Abraham. When he died, he only possessed the cave in which he was buried. But he had come to understand that the kingdom he had been promised
was not going to occur in his lifetime and that ultimately, it would be a heavenly kingdom (Heb. 11:13–16). David and Solomon, Abraham's descendants,
had impressive reigns over Israel, but because of Solomon's sins, God judged
the nation; it was divided, and eventually, the north and the south were both
destroyed. The reigns of David and Solomon were only brief failed previews of
the coming kingdom.

It is only when Jesus begins his earthly ministry that God's people begin
to experience life in the kingdom; with His first advent, it is "at hand" (Matt.
4:17). But it is not the political kingdom which the Jews had come to expect.
Jesus has to explain the nature of the kingdom, and as we have seen, he uses
parables and many other examples.[833] Jesus's first advent is about salvation and
the inauguration of the kingdom, not judgment and the consummation of the
kingdom. The gospel is preached to the poor, the blind see, and the lame walk.
At its beginning, the kingdom is small, but it grows like the tiny mustard seed
which becomes a tree where birds can nest (Matt. 13:31–32). The kingdom
continues to advance and becomes a blessing to all the nations as God's people
look forward to the return of Christ and the kingdom's consummation.

Jesus goes into great detail about kingdom life when he preaches the
Sermon on the Mount (Matt. 5:1–7:28). He had been "proclaiming the gospel
of the kingdom" in Galilee (Matt. 4:23) and had healed a multitude of people
of many different diseases and torments, including those who were demon-possessed. Jesus is establishing His rule, and Satan's minions are being cast out.
Great multitudes follow Him from Galilee, Decapolis, Jerusalem, Judea, and

---

[833] pp. 180–185.

beyond the Jordan, huge crowds of Jews and Gentiles—different nations are already being blessed (Matt. 4:23–25).

After demonstrating His authority, His rule, Jesus goes up the mountain and preaches to the people about life in His kingdom.

> Blessed are the poor in spirit, For theirs is the kingdom of heaven. Blessed are those who mourn, For they shall be comforted. Blessed are the meek, For they shall inherit the earth. Blessed are those who hunger and thirst for righteousness, For they shall be filled. Blessed are the merciful, For they shall obtain mercy. Blessed are the pure in heart, For they shall see God. Blessed are the peacemakers, For they shall be called sons of God. Blessed are those who are persecuted for righteousness' sake. For theirs is the kingdom of heaven. (Matt. 5:3–10)

Jesus goes on to explain that sins such as murder and adultery begin in the heart, that marriage is sacred and binding, that we should love our enemies, we should not judge, etc., etc. (Matt. 5:11–7:29). Jesus is describing kingdom life lived out under the new covenant, which He will initiate the night before His crucifixion (Matt. 26:27–29). The members of this final covenant have the law written on their hearts (Jer. 31:31–34), or as Jesus says, their sins are forgiven (Matt. 26:28). He is bringing about reconciliation, fellowship with God Most High, through the shedding of His blood, which He will signify with bread and wine when he inaugurates the new covenant, the first celebration of the Lord's Supper.[834] Reconciliation with God makes it possible for human beings to be reconciled with each other, and the Sermon on the Mount is describing this blessed condition in the kingdom, even before its consummation.

Jesus is initiating the time when Abraham is a blessing to all the nations. After Christ's death and resurrection, redemptive history will no longer be worked out through Israel, a single theocratic nation, but through the Church, a subculture in all the nations. The new covenant community will be based on

---

[834] This had been foreshadowed over two thousand years prior when the preincarnate Christ, in the person of Melchizedek, had brought Abraham into fellowship with God Most High, symbolized with bread and wine. See pp. 43–45.

a spiritual reality instead of the national physical identity of Israel under the old covenant—the law will be written on hearts instead of tablets of stone.

*****

Today, Christians of every tribe and nation are living under the new covenant as history progresses toward the return of Jesus Christ and the consummation of the kingdom. He has paid for the sins of His people, and His righteousness is imputed to them. There is no further condemnation for those in Christ Jesus; Christians are no longer under God's judgment and the threat of eternal punishment (Rom. 8:1). Despite all the difficulties and distractions of modern living, this abiding truth should lead to a sense of celebration and joy in the meetings of the Church and the daily lives of Christians. If we forget the damnation from which we have been rescued and our future glorification (Rom. 8:30), it is easy for dissatisfaction to creep into our often troubled lives. But gratitude for what God has done for us leads to obedience and a peace that passes understanding, even in trying times (Phil. 4:6–7).

*****

If, under the new covenant, the law is written on our hearts, does that mean we are still under law? No, it means that we have been changed so that we want to keep the law and please our heavenly Father in the way little children want to please a loving earthly father. Since the outpouring on the day of Pentecost, every Christian has the permanent indwelling of the Holy Spirit; God is working within us "both to will and to work for His good pleasure" (Phil. 2:13).

"For we are His workmanship, created in Christ Jesus for good works, which God prepared beforehand that we should walk in them" (Eph. 2:10).

Although we still fall into sin, Christ is the end of the law for both salvation and sanctification (Rom. 10:4–13; Phil 2:13). There is a great sense of freedom in this; we want to please God, but we are not trying to gain His favor by meeting standards. God is already pleased with us because Christ's righteousness has been imputed to us. True freedom is wanting to do what God says we should do.

But some church leaders feel they have to place their parishioners back under law to sanctify them, to make them good Christians. I recently visited a congregation that had a church covenant, a list of at least a dozen requirements to which you had to agree, in writing, before you could join the church, including tithing, mandatory church attendance, regular home Bible study, submission to the elders, etc. Since these are legitimate Christian activities, the church leaders had decided to turn them into signed obligations—in effect, laws—for church members. But laws, especially humanly initiated church laws, cannot save us or sanctify us.

If a church member is not living like a Christian, then perhaps he is not one. A church covenant will not change that. Church members who believe they are meeting the terms of a church covenant will invariably become self-satisfied or proud. Those who know they are not keeping such legalistic requirements will become frustrated when they cannot keep church laws, much less God's laws.[835]

Paul warned the Galatians about putting themselves back under law to try to become acceptable to God (Gal. 3:1–14). Those who have faith in Jesus Christ have become acceptable through Christ's work of salvation; we have been adopted into God's family, and we should be living out that joyful reality (Rom. 8:15; Eph. 1:5). This can be difficult in a fallen world, but when we join like-minded Christians in worship, Bible studies, fellowship, and community activities, we experience a sense of union with Christ and fellow believers. We have a foretaste of the joys we will have in the consummation of the kingdom.

But these communal blessings should also affect our interactions beyond the Church. Someone has said that we each go through life like a glass full of water. When circumstances and people bump, jostle, and sometimes slam us, what spills out depends on what is within us. If we are full of the joy of new covenant life, "rivers of living water" will pour out (John 7:38), and the influence of the kingdom will be expanded.

*****

What role does the law then have in a Christian's life? Because we are still sinners, we will be struggling with the remnants of the old man within

---

[835] Discipline is sometimes needed in churches and Jesus has given us instructions for dealing with Christians who become openly sinful (Matt. 18:15–17), but they do not include church covenants. In today's world, churches may need founding documents to help protect them from being sued for refusing to perform same-sex marriages or hire people that are engaged in public sins.

us throughout our lives. The law reveals our sins, which continually drives us back to Christ and teaches us how to better please our merciful heavenly Father. Through this process, the law is continually clarified within our hearts. Or as the Psalmist says, "How sweet are Your words to my taste, Sweeter than honey to my mouth! Through Your precepts I get understanding; Therefore I hate every false way. Your word is a lamp to my feet And a light to my path" (Ps. 119:103–105).

Sanctification has no end in this life because it leads to an increasing awareness of our own sinfulness; even the Apostle Paul writes that he is the "foremost" of all sinners (1 Tim. 1:15). But as the knowledge of our sins grows larger, the cross grows larger, and it is always adequate for covering the sins of those who trust in Christ.

This understanding of living under the new covenant should affect the lives of local churches; if the Son has set us free, then we are free indeed (John 8:36), and it should be manifest in church life. God's people are no longer living under the Mosaic Covenant; Christ has fulfilled it for us in every way. But as noted above, many denominations have not completely abandoned the old covenant for the new.

Church covenants or requirements such as tithing and mandatory church attendance put us back under law. Under the new covenant, some people may want to tithe, others may need to first pay their bills, and some can give much more than a tithe. Elders can offer some guidance in such matters, but it is up to believing households to determine how they can best serve God. God loves cheerful givers (2 Cor. 9:7).

As for church attendance, if a church is presenting the gospel in a meaningful way, believers will want to be there each Sunday; it will not require a church mandate. These are just two simple examples of not understanding new covenant life where Christians are living out the law written on their hearts, not on tablets of stone. Preaching and teaching that extols the greatness of God and what He has done for us leads to gratitude, and gratitude leads to loving obedience, something the law, and especially church laws, can never achieve. Attendance at many mainline churches has declined in the last few decades, and many have closed; they were not living out the gospel under the new covenant and were no longer of use to the kingdom. They had changed the joy of serving God into an obligation.

*****

Another example of how many denominations have not moved on from the old covenant is the dispute over infant baptism, often called "paedobaptism," derived from the Greek word *pais*, meaning "child." Many books have been written on this issue, but baptism is simply the sign of inclusion in the new covenant in the same way that circumcision was the sign of inclusion in the old covenant. These signs belong to those who are actually included in the covenants. Under the old covenant, if you were a male and part of Israel, whether by birth, proselytization, or slavery, you were part of the covenant and therefore received the sign of the covenant; you had to be circumcised. Women were included in the covenant through family relations. A confession of faith was not a requirement and could not be for male infants who were circumcised on the eighth day.

Circumcision was the sign that someone *physically* belonged to the nation of Israel. When Israel failed to keep the old covenant and was destroyed, Jeremiah was given the revelation of a new covenant where the covenant people are not identified through a physical relationship but through a *spiritual* reality—by the Law written on their hearts (Jer. 31:34), by their sins being forgiven though faith in Jesus Christ (Matt. 26: 27–28). Since the sign belongs to those who are actually part of the covenant, the sign of baptism should only be given to those who give credible professions of faith signifying that they are included in the covenant. The sign should not be given to infants or others who may never become part of the covenant. The possibility that someone might give a false profession of faith does not somehow justify infant baptism. Church leaders have the responsibility of applying baptism to those who are actually part of the covenant as best as they can determine in a fallen world.

It is understandable that parents want to do everything possible to ensure their children's salvation, and some denominations, primarily Roman Catholics and Lutherans, believe in baptismal regeneration. But that is not taught in Scripture, and many of these baptized infants prove they are not saved as they grow older. Other church groups—Presbyterians, Methodists, etc.—deny baptismal regeneration but claim that infants should still be baptized, even though some of these children also never come to faith and therefore are never part of the new covenant. These unbelieving children have been given the sign of inclusion in the covenant without belonging to it.

We cannot implement God's electing grace through rites wrongly administered. Parents can become tools of God's redeeming mercy by raising their children in such a way that they have every opportunity to come to faith.

Parents who affirm believer baptism desire salvation for their children as much as paedobaptists, but understand that their children are not part of the new covenant until they come to faith, and then they receive the sign.[836] This fits the pattern that we see in Acts 8:12 where men, and now also women, are baptized after they believe.

In the early Church, baptism could lead to a death sentence, so it was a dramatic event. Such a risk is not present in the United States today, but baptism is still a momentous occasion and a faith-affirming celebration of God's salvation under the new covenant.

*****

Present kingdom life means living each day knowing that we are no longer under condemnation because Christ has paid for our sins and fulfilled the law on our behalf. As born-again people, we want to keep God's law out of love and gratitude. It is written on our hearts; it is who we are. Paul describes the fruit of the Spirit in the life of believers "love, joy, peace, longsuffering, kindness, goodness, faithfulness, gentleness, self-control" (Gal. 5:22–23). As Psalm 105:43 says, God brings forth "His chosen ones with a joyful shout."

"So that they might keep His statutes And observe His laws. Praise the Lord!" (Ps. 105:45).

We should be living out this new covenant reality as we look forward to the return of Jesus Christ and the consummation of the kingdom.

---

[836] Some paedobaptists say there is complete continuity between the old and new covenants and that baptism must be administered in the same way as circumcision, but this denies the newness of the New Covenant and the different and essential characteristic of membership in the New Covenant. Others claim that the household baptisms in Acts prove that infants were baptized by the apostles, but this is not the case. No infants are mentioned in these texts, and there is evidence of belief in all these accounts. See Appendix A, p. 437.

CHAPTER 32

THE KINGDOM AND THE FUTURE

As Christians live in the final kingdom paradigm and look forward to Christ's return, questions arise about what we should expect in the future. There are many different views concerning end-time events, but most Christians agree that when Christ returns. there will be a judgment of unbelievers and that believers will enter everlasting life with Christ in the new heaven and earth (Matt. 25:31–44). The disagreements relate to the events that surround these basic expectations. Although some aspects of the last days seem clear, many Old and New Testament texts concerning the future are rich in symbolic and figurative language, making it difficult to decisively interpret some of these passages. However, we should be able to discern the basic outline of future redemptive history.

We have already seen that Dispensational and Covenantal theologians have very different understandings about what will occur at Christ's second advent.[837] There are a number of variations within both systems, but nearly all Dispensationalists see a literal thousand-year reign of Christ over ethnic Israel after His Second Coming. But we have seen that there is no separate destiny for the nation of Israel; Jewish and Gentile believers are all part of the same olive tree, the one people of God.[838]

This means we should not expect to see a separate earthly reign of Christ over the nation of Israel nor a separate secret rapture of the Church. As we look at end-time events, we would expect them to center around a single universally

---

[837] See p. xix, n. 33.
[838] See pp. 247–251.

observed return of Christ that initiates the eternal state for both believers and unbelievers (Matt. 24:30–31; 1 Thess. 4:16–17; Rev. 1:7).

*****

At the present time, we know that Jesus is seated at the right hand of God the Father as He reigns from heaven and intercedes for the saints, a great comfort as we struggle with faith and sin in our daily lives (Luke 22:69; Rom. 8:34). Through the ministry of the Holy Spirit and the Scriptures, Christ is present with His kingdom people until the end of the age, just as He promised at His Ascension (Matt. 28:20). Although the end-times should not be the primary concern for Christians, Scripture reveals much about the future, and we should try to understand the events associated with Christ's return.

Some passages suggest that Christ could return at any time and encourage us to be ever-vigilant. Jesus told his disciples, "Be on the alert then, for you do not know the day nor the hour" (Matt. 25:13). "You too, be ready; for the Son of man is coming at an hour that you do not expect" (Luke 12:40; also see Matt. 24:42–44, 50; Mark 13:32–33; 1 Thess. 5:2). These verses seem to express the imminence of Christ's return, but they do not give us a time reference and the focus seems to be on our spiritual readiness.

Other verses say there are a number of signs that precede Christ's return:[839]

1. False prophets working signs and wonders (Mark 13:22; Matt. 24:23–24).
2. A calling in of Jewish people—being grafted back into the olive tree (Rom. 11:11–29).
3. The coming of the man of lawlessness, the Antichrist (1 John 2:18; 2 Thess. 2:1–10; Rev. 13).
4. The Great Tribulation (Mark 13:14–27; Matt. 24:15–22; Luke 21:20–28).
5. The preaching of the gospel to all the nations (Mark 13:10; Matt. 24:14).
6. Signs in the heavens (Mark 13:24–25; Matt. 24:29–30; Luke 21:25–27).

---

[839] Grudem, *Systematic*, 1097–1098.

An initial question is how to harmonize the imminence of Christ's Second Coming with these major events that must occur. "Preterism," meaning past fulfillment,[840] sees all these events as having already occurred, centered around the fall of Jerusalem in AD 70.[841] "Historicism," the view of most of the Reformers, sees the prophecies as being fulfilled in ongoing history; many of these men believed the papacy, or the pope himself, was the Antichrist. "Futurists" say that the ultimate fulfillment of these signs will occur in the future.

At least some aspects of these signs, with the possible exception of signs in the heavens, have already occurred: the gospel has gone out into much of the world, false prophets have continually vexed the Church, Antiochus IV, Hitler, and Stalin were at least types of the Antichrist. Christians have always been persecuted and have recently undergone great tribulation at the hands of Muslim terrorists in the Middle East. But it appears that even more dramatic fulfillments are likely to come. We should be vigilant, without being obsessed, in discerning signs of Christ's return while living in such a way that we are ready for His appearance.

*****

One of the major issues for Christians concerning the last days is the Great Tribulation that exceeds the previous great oppressions endured by God's people (Matt. 24:20–22). The recent persecutions of Christians in territories held by the Islamic State of Iraq and Syria (ISIS) from the Middle East to Africa were brutal and deadly and seem to be a terrible harbinger of that coming time. Such severe repression is not occurring in the United States, but governmental power *is* being used to force Christians to not only accept but support such issues as abortion and homosexual marriage. Over five hundred million dollars in taxpayer money goes to support Planned Parenthood, the nation's largest abortion provider.[842]

---

[840] Preterism is taken from the Latin root for "past."

[841] *The Parousia*, written by J. S. Russell in 1878, is a foundational text for Preterism and was highly regarded by scholars such as R. C. Sproul and Charles H. Spurgeon. See "What is the Preterist View," *International Preterist Association*, accessed January 9, 2019, www.preterist.org/about-us/what-is-preterist-view/. But this view depends on dating the book of Revelation before AD 70, before the destruction of Jerusalem, which seems unlikely. See Carson, Moo, and Morris, *Introduction,* 473–476; also Kim Riddlebarger, *The Man of Sin* (Grand Rapids: Baker Books, 2006), 179–191.

[842] "Planned Parenthood receives record amount of taxpayer support," *Fox News*, January 8, 2013, updated December 20, 2015, www.foxnews.com/politics/2013/01/08/planned-

The Obama administration sued nuns who refused to accept contraception, including abortive methods in their health plans for employees.[843] In 2018, the Democratic National Committee Chairman, Tom Perez, "closed the door" on supporting any candidate who does not back abortion on demand.[844] The New York State Senate on January 23, 2019, legalized abortion up to the baby's delivery date. When the vote was announced, the delegates erupted in a "feverish" standing ovation.[845] They voted for infanticide, "murder for convenience," and then applauded themselves—a frightening thing to have on your resume when you meet the Living God.

A week later, the Virginia governor discussed proposed legislation that would allow ending the life of an unwanted baby after the child was born— legal infanticide.[846] Forty-six years after *Roe v. Wade*, abortion became the leading cause of death in the world.[847]

---

parenthood-receives-record-amount-taxpayer-support.html. Although Planned Parenthood is a 501(c) tax exempt organization and is not supposed to endorse candidates, it spent $33.9 million from 2012 to 2016 to elect Democrats. Planned Parenthood takes taxpayer money and gives it to politicians who will vote to give them more money, essentially money laundering government grants for these politicians. For the abortionists and the politicians, money is the main concern, but they also seem to want to force each American, each taxpayer, to somehow participate in, and therefore justify this terrible evil (Rom. 1:28–32). Planned Parenthood does nothing to help women who have physical or spiritual problems after having abortions. Christians can help these women in many ways but mainly by assuring them that there is forgiveness in Jesus Christ. See Leah Jessen, "Planned Parenthood Entities Spend Over $38 Million to Elect Democrats," *The Daily Signal*, November 3, 2016, https://www.dailysignal.com/2016/11/03/planned-parenthood-arms-spend-over-38-million-to-elect-democrats/.

[843] John Garvey, "ObamaCare vs. Little Sisters of the Poor," *The Wall Street Journal*, March 20, 2016, https://www.dailysignal.com/2016/05/16/little-sisters-of-the-poor-win-big-in-obamacare-case/.

[844] Laura Bassett, "Democratic Party Draws a Line in the Sand on Abortion Rights," *HUFFPOST*, April 21, 2017,
https://www.huffingtonpost.com/entry/democrats-tom-perez-abortion-rights_us_58fa5fade4b018a9ce5b351d.

[845] Will Maule, "New York Senate Erupts in Applause After Passing Late-Term Abortion Bill," *FAITHWIRE*, January 23, 2019, https://www.faithwire.com/2019/01/23/new-york-senate-erupts-in-applause-after-passing-horrific-late-term-abortion-bill/.

[846] Ryan Saavedra, "WATCH: Virginia Governor Doubles Down on Infanticide, Suggests He's the Victim," *The Daily Wire*, January 31, 2019, https://www.dailywire.com/news/watch-virginia-governor-doubles-down-infanticide-ryan-saavedra.

[847] Ronnie Floyd, "46 Years After Roe v. Wade, Abortion Is Now the Leading Cause of Death in the World," January 22, 2019, https://www.faithwire.com/2019/01/22/46-years-after-roe-v-wade-abortion-is-now-the-leading-cause-of-death-in-the-world/.

In July 2018, a Supreme Court vacancy led to mass demonstrations organized by the Democratic Party to insist that the new justice support abortion rights. It is a sobering time when, for a large percentage of the women in the United States, the most important political concern is the right to terminate the life of their own unborn child.

This same political party removed the word *God* from their platform at its 2012 convention. When party leaders decided they needed to reinstate it for political reasons, many delegates began a long and loud protest. This demonstration against even mentioning God's name was recorded and is disturbing to watch.[848] And as previously discussed, states have tried to force small businesses to participate in homosexual marriage ceremonies (see p. 282–283). Politicians in the Republican Party are not as openly anti-God, but most of them never follow through on their promises to oppose abortion and defund Planned Parenthood, and they are afraid to resist the homosexual lobby because the media will brand them as bigots.

Mainstream media and most of the entertainment industry ridicule anyone who believes in creationism or traditional Christian values. The disdain and hostility exhibited toward believers who dare to uphold Christian morality is widespread and increasing. Barack Obama scorned small-town people who "cling to their guns and religion."[849] The media and big tech communication companies are now cooperating to censor anyone who speaks out against the Biden administration's attempts to advance a socialist/Marxist agenda. Conservative speakers are routinely shouted down and prevented from speaking on college campuses.[850] Former Vice President Pence's Christian faith was recently characterized as a mental illness on a popular TV show.[851] Catholic Church leaders barely criticized New York's Governor Cuomo, a Roman Catholic in good standing, when he publicly cheered the infanticide bill. President Biden says he is personally opposed to abortion, but he supports

---

[848] Jake Tapper and Amy Bingham, "Dems Quickly Switch to Include 'God,' 'Jerusalem,'" September 5, 2012, https://abcnews.go.com/politics/OTUS/democrats-rapidly-revise-platform-include-god/story?id=17164108.

[849] Ed Pilkington, "Obama Angers Midwest Voters with Guns and Religion Remark," *The Guardian*, April 14, 2008, https://www.theguardian.com/world/2008/apr/14/barackobama.uselections2008.

[850] See p. 400, n. 815.

[851] Washington Free Beacon Staff, "'The View' Hosts Call Pence's Christian Faith 'Dangerous,' Form of 'Mental Illness,'" *The Washington Free Beacon*, February 13, 2018, https://freebeacon.com/politics/the-view-hosts-call-pences-christian-faith-dangerous-form-of-mental-illness/.

laws that permit abortion up to the day of delivery and is endeavoring to make taxpayers finance this evil.[852] Catholic Church bishops are "discussing" whether the president should be banned from taking communion.

The "cancel police" who operate online and through other media are destroying the careers and lives of many people whom they deem to be insufficiently "woke." The right to free speech is under attack in many ways, and many people are afraid to reveal their opinions for fear of being attacked verbally or even physically and losing their jobs. Christians are expected to express their faith only in their homes and churches, not in the public square.

Although most believers in the United States are still unaffected in their daily lives, the trends are becoming ominous. Christians in the United States should use their votes and influence to maintain the freedom of religion guaranteed in the United States Constitution,[853] but at some point, possibly in our own lives, there will be a Great Tribulation that will include not only wars and natural disasters but severe religious persecution as the end of the age approaches (Matt. 24:4–12).

As we have seen, we should not expect a rapture of the Church that spares Christians from the suffering that is to come. The night before His crucifixion, when Jesus prayed for His disciples, He did not pray that the Father would take them out of the world but that He would keep them from evil (John 17:15). Christ will be with us and is sufficient for us as we go through tribulation, even if it is the Great Tribulation. He says, "But the one who endures to the end, he shall be saved" (Matt. 24:13).

*****

In considering the end of the age, many scholars focus on the prophetical passages in Daniel and Revelation, but it is Jesus Himself who gives us the series of events that surround His Second Coming (Matt. 24:1–31, 25:31–46; Mark 13:1–27; Luke 21:5–28). The apocalyptic passages of the Old and New Testament writers are important and deserve our study, but their symbolism

---

[852] Sarah Maccammon, NPR, May 31,2021, https://www.npr.org/2019/06/06/730515910/biden-reverses-position-rejects-hyde-amendment-cites-attacks-on-abortion-access.

[853] This does not mean Christians should try to establish a theocratic government in the United States. The United States is not the kingdom of God. The expansion of Christ's kingdom within any country can help bring about a more righteous and just civil government.

and fierce imagery are often unfamiliar to us today and have led to many different interpretations. These prophetical visions expand on the information that Jesus gives the apostles about the end-times, but they must fit within the succession of events that He reveals.

Two days before His arrest at the hands of the Jewish leaders, Jesus is leaving the Temple with His disciples when they comment on the magnificent structure that Herod the Great had built. Jesus tells them that a time is coming when, "Truly I say to you, not one stone here shall be left upon another, which will not be torn down" (Matt. 24:2). Jesus is prophesying the coming destruction of the Temple, and this confuses and greatly concerns the apostles. Peter, James, John, and Andrew follow Jesus to the Mount of Olives and begin to ask Him questions about the future (Mark 13:3). Jesus responds with a discourse on the end of the age, a passage that has come to be called the Olivet Discourse.

*****

It is important to note that it is Christ's prophecy of the destruction of the Temple that initiates His discussion of the end-times. In just two days, at the Passover meal the night before His crucifixion, Jesus will initiate the new covenant that replaces the Mosaic Covenant, which Israel had failed to keep and is now going to fade away (2 Cor. 3:5–11). His coming death will be the ultimate consummating sacrifice to which the thousands and thousands of Temple sacrifices have been pointing; there will be no further need for the old covenant sacrifices and, therefore, no further need for the Jewish Temple. The Old Testament types are going to be replaced by New Testament realities. After His resurrection, Jesus will begin building a new Temple, the Church, made of living stones, believer-priests who will minister within His kingdom as it progresses to its fulfillment. As Peter will eventually proclaim to the scattered Christians who had been persecuted because of their faith, "you also as living stones, are being built up as a spiritual house for a holy priesthood, to offer up spiritual sacrifices acceptable to God though Jesus Christ" (1 Pet. 2:5).

The animal sacrifices by the priests in the Temple are going to be replaced by the service and sacrifices of Christians in the Church. Paul, in his admonishment to Jews and Gentiles in his letter to the Romans, will say (Rom. 12:1), I urge you therefore, brethren, by the mercies of God, to present your bodies a living and holy sacrifice, acceptable to God, which is your spiritual service of worship."[854]

It is Christians themselves who will be living sacrifices in the new covenant. Although the Temple will not be destroyed until AD 70, its role in the progress of salvation will end with Christ's death and resurrection; the Sacrifice to which all the other sacrifices pointed has come. The role of the Temple has ended. Future redemptive history will be worked out through the Church and the new covenant (Heb. 8:7–12). The writer of Hebrews tells us, "When He said, 'A new covenant,' He has made the first obsolete. But whatever is becoming obsolete and growing old is ready to disappear" (Heb. 8:13).

Because Israel did not accept that the Messiah had come, the priests continue to offer animal sacrifices until the Roman army destroys the Temple in AD 70. The continuation of the sacrifices is a public demonstration of Israel's rejection of the Messiah. Titus, the Roman general who will lead the final assault on Jerusalem, tries to save the Temple, but his soldiers, in a battle rage, burn and entirely dismantle the building in order to loot its treasures.[855] The horrific destruction of Jerusalem and the Temple, ending the sacrifices, is a judgment on Israel and will finish the transition from the old covenant to the new covenant. The writer of Hebrews, before the fall of Jerusalem, had given a severe warning to the Jews who had a knowledge of the truth but rejected the Messiah, who made the consummating sacrifice (Heb. 10:1–16, 26–31), "How much severer punishment do you think he will deserve who has trampled underfoot the Son of God, and has regarded as unclean the blood of the covenant by which he was sanctified, and has insulted the Spirit of grace? For we know Him Who said, *'Vengeance is Mine, I will repay.'* And again, *'The LORD will judge His people'*" (Deut. 32:35, 36).

"It is a terrifying thing to fall into the hands of the Living God." (Heb. 10:29–31).

Since Jesus's death will end the need for further sacrifices, Ezekiel's prophecy of a new Temple with renewed sacrifices is a symbol of the Church and its perfection in the new heaven and earth (Ezek. 40:1–43:27), not a new Temple built during a future millennial reign of Israel. The resumption of sacrificial rites

---

[854] Jesus tells us to take up our crosses and follow Him (Matt. 16:24; Mark 8:34; Luke 9:23).
[855] Josephus, *The Wars*, 6.4.7.

would disregard the efficacy of Christ's sacrifice and would be similar to what the Temple priests had done that brought them such devastation in AD 70.[856]

*****

Jesus's prophecy of the destruction of the Temple is a disturbing revelation to His Jewish disciples because of its national and religious implications. The sacrificial system, carried out first in the Tabernacle and then in the Temple, was at the heart of the formation of Israel. Now the central role of the nation in redemptive history is going to come to an end. When Jesus initiates the new covenant, the old covenant is going to vanish away. This imminent and dramatic transformation, not yet fully understood by the disciples, provides the backdrop for Christ's discourse on the future.

*****

Jesus had already told his disciples about His coming death and resurrection and that after ascending to His Father, He would come again "in the glory of His Father with His angels" (Matt. 16:21, 27; Mark 8:31, 38; Luke 9:21, 26). Now with His prophecy of the destruction of the Temple—in effect, the destruction of the traditional Jewish world—the apostles are concerned and want to know when these things will be—what will be the sign of Christ's return and the end of the age (Matt. 24:3)?

Jesus tells them that prior to His Second Coming, there will be false Christs, wars and rumors of wars, famines, pestilences, and earthquakes (Matt. 24:5–7), but these are just the beginning of "birth pangs" (Matt. 24:8). Although they may increase in intensity, these are the tragedies that the fallen world has always endured. But as the end-time approaches, the persecution of

---

[856] Ezekiel's temple and the resumption of sacrifices are a great problem for Dispensationalists with their insistence on a literal interpretation of Scripture. Some admit the sacrifices cannot be resumed; others insist on maintaining a literal interpretation and say sacrifices will resume but will be only memorial in nature; others who say the Temple is symbolic are accused by other Dispensationalists of "spiritualizing" Scripture. See Paul Henebury, "Ezekiel's Temple: Premillennial Achilles' Heel?," 2005, at http://www.spiritandtruth.org/teaching/documents/articles/88/88.htm?x=x. The basic error causing these contradictions is the belief that Jesus Christ is going to reign over an earthly millennial kingdom of ethnic Israel.

Jesus's disciples will increase. They will be killed and hated by all the nations, false prophets and lawlessness will abound, and the love of many will grow cold (Matt. 24:9–12); however, even these events do not signal His immediate return. Jesus goes on to tell the apostles that "this gospel of the kingdom shall be preached in the whole world for a witness to all the nations, and then the end shall come" (Matt. 24:14). Christ will not return until all His sheep have heard His voice and followed Him (John 10:27). When the gospel has gone out to the uttermost parts of the earth, the end of the age will begin.

Jesus then begins speaking of the end-time events and tells the apostles, "When you see the *Abomination of Desolation*, which was spoken of through Daniel the prophet (Dan. 9:27, 11:31, 12:11), standing in the holy place (let the reader understand), then let those who are in Judea flee to the mountains" (Matt. 24:15–16). Daniel in his prophecy says the Abomination of Desolation will desecrate the Temple and "will turn to godlessness those who act wickedly toward the covenant" (Dan. 11:31–32). With the destruction of the Jerusalem Temple and the initiation of the new covenant, this end-time desecration can only take place in the new temple of living stones, pointing to a future rejection of Christ and the gospel within the Church.

The *Abomination of Desolation* seems to be the same person as the Apostle Paul's "man of lawlessness" who, after a time of apostasy in the Church, "exalts himself above every so-called god or object of worship, so that he takes his seat in the temple of God, displaying himself as being God" (2 Thess. 2:3–4). John the Apostle apparently refers to this same person as the "Antichrist" who arises after there have been many lesser antichrists and denies that Jesus is the Christ (1 John 2:18, 22).[857] There is going to be a time of apostasy, and then the Antichrist will appear and work desecration in the Church.

Preterists say Daniel's prophecy was fulfilled when the Seleucid ruler, Antiochus IV, set up an idol to Zeus in the Jerusalem Temple and sacrificed pigs to it in 167 BC, after which the Jews revolted, regained control of the Temple, and cleansed it. But this two-thousand-year-old blasphemy of Antiochus does

---

[857] There have been different views of the Antichrist. Luther and many of the Reformers in the sixteenth century believed the pope or the papacy in its entirety was the Antichrist. See Steve Wholberg, "The Antichrist and the Protestant Reformation," *White Horse Media*, February 11, 2014, https://www.whitehorsemedia.com/the-antichrist-and-the-protestant-reformation. George Eldon Ladd sees the antichrist as various states and governments which will persecute God's people. George Eldon Ladd, *The Last Things* (Grand Rapids: Eerdmans, 1982), 58–72.

not seem to have been an end-time event. Antiochus seems to be a type of the coming antichrist who will enter the Church and defile it by misleading many through false teaching and self-deification. Antiochus is an example of the double fulfillment of prophecy, the occurrence of a near-time event which points to a greater fulfillment in the future, a type and then the antitype.[858]

Jesus has said that there will be many false Christs (Matt. 24:5), but now by citing the *Abomination of Desolation*, He appears to be indicating a particular person whose appearance will lead to the Great Tribulation (Matt. 24:15–22). Although there is a spirit of Antichrist that will prevail in the latter days (1 John 4:3; Rom. 1:26–32), there seems to be a final person, the ultimate Antichrist, to whom all the others have been pointing.

The Apostle John says that this Antichrist will deny that Jesus is the Christ (1 John 2:22; 4:3) as many have done. But Daniel and Paul indicate that he will go much further than this; he will take his seat in the "Temple," within the Church, and exalt himself above every god, "displaying himself as being God" (2 Thess. 2:4–5; Dan. 11:36–37). The antichrist will not only overwhelm the Church but also all other religions and set up his own worldwide adulation.

It is not surprising that apostasy and the appearance of the *Abomination of desolation* lead to the Great Tribulation. Paul tells us that the man of lawlessness, the son of destruction, will not be revealed until "he who now restrains… is taken out of the way" (2 Thess. 2:7–8). After the Holy Spirit has completed His work of calling in God's kingdom people, His influence in convicting "the world concerning sin, and of righteousness, and judgment" (John 16:8) is going to end.[859] Although the Spirit's presence will always remain with the true Church, His influence is going to be withdrawn from the rest of the world.[860] This leads to the rise of the Antichrist and the beginning of the Great Tribulation.

---

[858] Some theologians object to the concept of a double fulfillment of prophecy saying that a text can only have one meaning, but it seems a text can have a double reference or more than one application. See David Jeremiah, "The Principal of Double Fulfillment," *Grace Journal*, accessed January 10, 2019, https://biblicalstudies.org.uk/pdf/grace-journal/13-2_13.pdf for further discussion.

[859] Some theologians see the restraining power to be civil government, but the one who restrains is a person, which indicates the Holy Spirit. See Ryrie, *Ryrie Study*, n. on 2 Thess. 2:7, 1813.

[860] "14.4.2. Who is the Restrainer," *Bible Study Tools*, accessed January 14, 2019, https://www.biblestudytools.com/commentaries/revelation/related-topics/who-is-the-restrainer.html.

Paul also says that the coming of the "lawless one...is in accord with the activity of Satan, with all power, and signs, and false wonders, and with all the deception of wickedness for those who perish" (2 Thess. 2:8–10). The Antichrist, empowered by Satan, will work within the Church and deceive many who "did not receive the love of the truth so as to be saved" (2 Thess. 2:10). Satan will continue the deception he began in the Garden to the very end. Those "professed" Christians who accept the false doctrine of the Antichrist will perish, along with all the other unbelievers, for their unrighteousness. They were never part of the true Church (1 John 2:19).

We have seen in the past and now see in the present many churches rejecting the teaching of the Bible to accommodate the lies of worldly culture.

The Antichrist will accept no restraint on his power, so we understand the urgency in Christ's warning to those "in Judea to flee to the mountains" (Matt. 24:16). There is no time to hesitate, no time to get possessions or different clothes, and it is going to be very difficult for those who are pregnant or nursing babies (Matt. 24:17–19). This again appears to be a double fulfillment of prophecy with the suffering during the destruction of Jerusalem pointing to the final Great Tribulation, a tribulation the likes of which the world has never seen and will not see again. If the days of the final tribulation were not shortened, no one would survive, but for the sake of the elect, they will be shortened (Matt. 24:15–21).

During the Great Tribulation, Christ's people will be desperately hoping for His return, but He warns them to not be confused by false Christs and false prophets. When He returns, it will be like lightning flashing across the sky; it will be evident to everyone (Matt. 24:23–27). Jesus says nothing about a secret appearance for the rapture of the Church. Dispensationalists who rely on 1 Thessalonians 4:17 to say there will be a secret return of Christ for the rapture of the church seem to ignore the previous verse, 4:16, which says He will come "with a shout, with the voice of the archangel, and with the trumpet of God." It does not sound like Christ's return will be a secret. And there is no indication of Christ returning to heaven with the church after this heralded return.

He then describes His return:

> Immediately after the tribulation of those days the sun
> will be darkened, and the moon will not give its light, and
> the stars will fall from the sky, and the powers of the heav-
> ens will be shaken. and then the sign of the Son of Man will

appear in the sky, and then all the tribes of the earth will mourn, and they will see the Son of Man coming on the clouds of the sky with power and great glory. And He will send forth His angels with a great trumpet, and they will gather together His elect from the four winds, from one end of the sky to the other. (Matt. 24:29–31)

Since Jesus uses apocalyptic language in verse 29, some commentators see the references to heavenly disturbances in this verse as metaphors referring to earthly individuals or events.[861] But the next verse describes the Lord's literal return on the clouds of the sky, so it seems there will be actual signs in the heavens that immediately precede His return. Isaiah and Joel describe the same kind of celestial disruptions when the Lord comes in judgment (Isa. 13:9–10; Joel 2:31, 3:14–15). These cosmic events will have the world focusing on the heavens when the Son of Man appears on "the clouds of the sky with power and great glory."

Verse 31 tells us that Jesus will assemble His kingdom people "from the four winds" when He returns. Paul says in 1 Thessalonians 4:16–17 that when the Lord Himself descends "from heaven with a shout, with the voice of the archangel, and with the trumpet of God," the dead in Christ will rise first, and then those who are alive shall be caught up with them to meet the Lord in the air. Paul does not say what happens next, but apparently, Christ and His people descend to the earth together for the Great White Throne Judgment (Matt. 25:31; Rev. 20:11–15).

Jesus goes on to warn the disciples to be continually ready for his Second Coming, "Be on the alert then, for you do not know the day nor the hour" (Matt. 25:13).

But the Lord is not only returning to gather His people, He is going to judge the nations. Jesus tells the disciples:

But when the Son of man comes in His glory, and all the angels with Him, then He will sit on His glorious throne. And all the nations will be gathered before Him, and He will separate them from one another, as the shep-

---

[861] See Comment, "Matthew 24:29," *BibleHub*, accessed January 10, 2019, https://biblehub.com/commentaries/.

herd separates the sheep from the goats; and He will put the sheep on His right, and the goats on the left. Then the King will say to those on His right, "Come, you who are blessed of My Father, inherit the kingdom prepared for you from the foundation of the world." (Matt. 25:31–34).

Jesus's return as Judge and King initiates the consummation of the kingdom in the new heaven and earth. God's plan of establishing a righteous people for Himself will then be complete. The struggles and sufferings of His saints will be at an end and their joyful, everlasting rule with Christ will begin. Jesus tells the disciples what He will say to those on His right hand, "For I was hungry, and you gave Me something to eat; I was thirsty, and you gave Me drink; I was a stranger and you invited me in; naked and you clothed Me; I was sick and you visited Me; I was in prison and you came to Me" (Matt. 25:35–36).

The righteous will ask Jesus when they did all these things for Him. "And the King will answer and say to them, 'Truly I say to you, to the extent that you did it to one of these brothers of Mine, even the least of them, you did it to Me'" (Matt. 25:40).

We are saved by grace through faith, not through good works, but our works reveal whether or not our faith is real. If we are part of God's kingdom people, it will be evident in our lives (James 2:18).

> Then He will also say to those on His left, "Depart from me, accursed ones, into the eternal fire which has been prepared for the devil and his angels; for I was hungry, and you gave Me nothing to eat; I was thirsty and you gave Me nothing to drink; I was a stranger and you did not invite Me in, naked and you did not clothe Me, sick and in prison and you did not visit Me." (Matt. 25:41–43)

Those on the left hand will also speak, and they will ask when they failed to do these things. Then Jesus will answer them, saying, "Truly, I say to you, to the extent that you did not do it to one of the least of these, you did not do it to Me. And these will go away into eternal punishment, but the righteous into eternal life" (Matt. 25:45–46).

*****

Jesus has told us about His future glorious return when the unrighteous will be judged, and His righteous people will inherit the kingdom prepared for them from "the foundation of the world." This is the fulfillment of the promises to Abraham; Christ's everlasting kingdom is the land, the heavenly country that God had promised to Abraham and which he had come to expect (Heb. 11:10, 16). The people that enter Christ's kingdom will come from every tribe and nation. Abraham has become a blessing to them all through his descendant Jesus Christ, David's Son, the Messiah, who has crushed the head of the serpent.

*****

John records a final vison of the consummated kingdom in Revelation 21:

> And I saw a new heaven and a new earth; for the first heaven and the first earth passed away, and there is no longer any sea. And I saw the holy city, new Jerusalem, coming down out of heaven from God, made ready as a bride adorned for her husband. And I heard a loud voice from the throne, saying, "Behold, the tabernacle of God is among men, and He shall dwell among them, and they shall be His people, and God Himself shall be among them, and He shall wipe away every tear from their eyes; and there shall no longer be any death; there shall no longer be any mourning, or crying, or pain; the first things have passed away." (Rev. 21:1–4).

Christians today still live in the time of the painful first things, but we have the sure hope of the coming glorious consummation of the kingdom. Jesus ends his revelation to John by saying, "Yes, I am coming quickly."

And we can respond with John, "Amen. Come, Lord Jesus!" (Rev. 22:20).

SUMMARY

We have followed the progress of redemptive history from the Garden of Eden to the New heaven and earth through the repetitions of the paradigm of the kingdom of God. We have seen that Adam, Noah, and the nation of Israel failed to fulfill God's mandate to establish His righteous rule on the earth and fell under His judgment.

Throughout the history of these eras, there were people who believed in the one true God, but their sinfulness prevented them from establishing a righteous kingdom. God's mandate could not be accomplished by a sinless couple, a redeemed family, or a chosen nation. We have traced these failures through the Old Testament, which ends with Israel in a defeated and diminished state. But with at least some of its people still clinging to the hope of the promised Messiah, who would restore the glory of David and inaugurate God's kingdom on the earth.

The New Testament tells us that God, in the fullness of time, sent the Messiah, His only begotten Son, to earth to take on human flesh and accomplish what men had shown they could never do. Jesus, as a sinless man, had a right to rule, and He began to establish His kingdom of faithful followers, but it was not the political kingdom that had become the hope of the people of Israel. Through his sacrificial ministry, Jesus obtains a righteous people from all the nations, a people fit for His kingdom because He has paid for their sins on the cross and His own righteousness is imputed to them. They are justified by grace through faith,[862] and they will live for eternity with Christ in the consummation of the kingdom.

Those who believe in Christ can now, amazingly, approach the throne of a Holy God without fear (Heb. 4:16). The veil of the Temple has been torn apart from the top to the bottom by God Himself (Mark 15:38). Through the work of Christ, we have access to the Holy of Holies. For His justified people, God is

---

[862] This includes Old Testament saints who looked forward to the advent of the Messiah and who will dwell in the eternal kingdom with New Testament believers. It will be amazing to talk to Abraham or David or Jeremiah.

no longer their righteous Judge; He is their loving Heavenly Father. And their response is gratitude and loving obedience.

God's people do not inhabit a particular political nation; they inhabit the Church, a subculture in all the nations. God's kingdom exists wherever Christians are living out His precepts for His glory. Believers have widely different roles in the kingdom from businessmen and women to laborers, to pastors, to housewives, and mothers with newborn babies, but all are important for its advancement. Understanding that we each play a vital role in God's kingdom helps us to lead lives of joyful purpose despite the difficulties we often face in a fallen world.

James says we should count it all joy when we encounter trials because the testing of our faith brings steadfastness, which perfects us and makes us complete (James 1:2–4). Paul tells us "that all things work together for good to those who love God" (Rom. 8:28).

As individual Christians are progressing in the faith, the kingdom as a whole is moving forward; it cannot be stopped. Although Satan is still a dangerous adversary, he has been defeated at the cross, and his house is being plundered. The kingdom is advancing to its glorious consummation when Christ returns, and we begin everlasting life with Him in the new heaven and earth. We can look forward with a sure hope and pray with the disciples:

> Our Father Who art in heaven, Hallowed be Thy name, Thy kingdom come Thy will be done On earth, as it is in Heaven. (Matt. 6:9–10)

> For Thine is the kingdom, and the power, and the glory, forever. Amen. (Matt. 6:13; 1 Chron. 29:11)

APPENDIX A

INFANTS AND HOUSEHOLD BAPTISMS IN ACTS.

1. Cornelius—Acts 10:44–48—Those who were baptized were those whom "the Holy Spirit fell upon," as evidenced by their "speaking with tongues and exalting God," which would seem to exclude infants.
2. The Philippian Jailer—Acts 16:30–34—Verse 34 concludes with "he… rejoiced greatly, having believed in God with his whole household." It appears that the jailer's entire household believed; they gave evidence of faith, which would exclude infants. For those who argue that only the jailer believed, then the adults in his family were baptized on the basis of the jailer's faith, an act found nowhere else in the New Testament.
3. Crispus—Acts 18:8—"Crispus…believed in the Lord with all his household." Again, there is evidence that the entire household believed and no mention of infants.
4. Stephanas—1 Cor.1:16, 16:15—Those baptized by Paul "devoted themselves for ministry to the saints"—evidence of faith and sufficient maturity to be involved in ministry.
5. Lydia—Acts 16:13–15—Verse 14 says that the Lord opened Lydia's heart to respond to the things spoken by Paul, an indication of belief. She and her household are baptized but there is no mention of infants.

These baptisms support the pattern of believer's baptism described in Acts 8:12, "But when they believed Philip as he preached the things concerning the kingdom of God and the name of Jesus Christ, both men and women were baptized." The sign of the covenant is now given to both men and women, and it is on the basis of faith.

BIBLIOGRAPHY

Bainton, Roland H. *Christianity*. Boston: Houghton Mifflin, 2000.

Bainton, Roland H. *Here I Stand: A Life of Martin Luther*. Nashville: Abingdon, 1950.

Barna, George, and Mark Hatch. *Boiling Point: It Only Takes One Degree*. Ventura, CA: Regal Books, 2001.

Barna, George. *The Habits of Highly Effective Churches*. Ventura, CA: Regal Books, 1999.

Bean, William B. "The Illness of Charles Darwin." *The American Journal of Medicine* 65, no. 4 (1978): 572-74. doi:10.1016/0002-9343(78)90843-4.

Blaising, Craig A., and Darrell L. Bock. *Progressive Dispensationalism*. Wheaton, IL: BridgePoint, 1993.

Bonhoeffer, Dietrich. *The Cost of Discipleship*. New York: Touchstone, 1995.

Bright, John. *The Kingdom of God: Scriptural Studies in the Kingdom of God*. Nashville: Abingdon, 1978.

Butler, Joseph. *The Analogy of Religion*. Chestnut Hill: MA, Adamant Media, 2005.

Bruce, F. F. "Christanity under Claudius." *Bulletin of the John Rylands Library* 44, no. 2 (March 1962): 309-26. doi:10.7227/bjrl.44.2.3.

Burrows, Millar. *The Dead Sea Scrolls*. New York: Gramercy, 1986.

Cahill, Thomas. *How the Irish Saved Civilization*. New York: Anchor Books, 1996.

Calvin, John. *Genesis*. Carlisle, PA: Banner of Truth Trust, 1992.

Calvin, John. *Institutes of the Christian Religion*. Edited by John T. McNeill. Translated by Ford Lewis Battles. Vol. 1 and 2. Philadelphia: Westminster, 1960.

Camping, Harold. *1994?* New York: Vantage, 1992.

Carson, D. A., Douglas J. Moo, and Leon Morris. *An Introduction to the New Testament*. Grand Rapids: Zondervan, 1992.

Catechism of the Catholic Church. New York: Doubleday, 1995.

Cozzens, Donald B. *The Changing Face of the Priesthood: A Reflection on the Priest's Crisis of Soul*. Collegeville, MN: Liturgical Press, 2001.

Crabb, Larry. *The Silence of Adam*. Grand Rapids: Zondervan, 1995.

Currid, John D. *Ancient Egypt and the Old Testamant*. Grand Rapids: Baker Books, 1997.

Curtis, A. Kenneth, Randy Petersen, and J. Stephen Lang. *The 100 Most Important Events in Christian History*. Grand Rapids: Revell, 1991.

Darwin, Charles. *Descent of Man*. New York, 1871.

Darby, John Nelson, *Synopsis of the Books of the Bible, 5 vols*. Sunbury, PA: Believers Bookshelf, 1992

Darwin, Charles. *Origin of Species*. Danbury, CT: Grolier Enterprises, 1981.

Deane, Herbert A. *The Political and Social Ideas of Saint Augustine*. New York: Columbia University Press, 1963.

Denton, Michael. *Evolution: A Theory in Crisis*. Chevy Chase, MD: Adler & Adler, 1986.

Denton, Michael. *Evolution: Still a Theory in Crisis*. Seattle: Discovery Institute, 2016.

Dostoevsky, Fyodor. *The Brothers Karamazov*. Translated by Richard Pevear and Larissa Volokhonsky. San Francisco: North Point Press, 1990.

Douthat, Ross. "Liberated and Unhappy." Editorial. *The New York Times*, May 25, 2009.

Durant, Will. *The Reformation*. New York: Simon & Schuster, 1957.

Erickson, Millard J. *Christian Theology*. 2nd ed. Grand Rapids: Baker Books, 1983.

Falls, Thomas B., DD, PhD, trans. "Justin Martyr." In *The Fathers of the Church*. New York: Christian Heritage, 1948.

Flew, Antony. *There Is a God: How the World's Most Notorious Atheist Changed His Mind*. New York: HarperCollins, 2008.

Foxe, John. *Foxe's Book of Martyrs*. Grand Rapids: Baker Book House, 1978. Prepared by W. Grinton Berry.

Fuller, Daniel P. *The Unity of the Bible: Unfolding God's Plan for Humanity*. Grand Rapids: Zondervan, 1992.

Gentry, Peter J., and Stephen J. Wellum. *Kingdom Through Covenant*. Wheaton, IL: Crossway Books, 2012.

Gerstner, John H. *Wrongly Dividing the Word of Truth: A Critique of Dispensationalism*. Brentwood, TN: Wolgemuth & Hyatt, 1991.

Gonzalez, Justo L. *The Story of Christianity*. Vol. 2. New York: HarperCollins, 1985.

Grudem, Wayne. *Systematic Theology*. Grand Rapids: Zondervan, 1994.

Haldane, Robert. *Commentary on Romans*. Grand Rapids: Kregel, 1996.

Heidegger, Martin. *Being and Time*. Translated by John Macquarrie and Edward Robinson. New York: Harper & Row, 1962.

Hick, John. "Normative Pluralism." In *Four Views on Salvation in a Pluralistic World*, edited by Dennis Okholm and Timothy Phillips. Grand Rapids: Zondervan, 1996.

Hodge, Charles. *Romans*. Edinburgh, Scotland: Banner of Truth Trust, 1989. Reprinted 1989.

Houghton, S. M. *Sketches from Church History*. Carlisle, PA: Banner of Truth Trust, 1980.

Hughes, James A. "Revelation 20:4–6 and the Question of the Millenium." *Westminster Theological Journal* 35 (1973).

Hunnex, Milton D. *Chronological and Thematic Charts of Philosophies and Philosophers*. Grand Rapids: Zondervan, 1961.

James, Frank A. History of Christianity 1, Section 3A. 2000. Class notes. Reformed Theological Seminary, Washington, DC.

Jenkins, Steve. *Life on Earth: The Story of Evolution*. Boston: Houghton Mifflin, 2002.

Jones, Timothy P. *Christian History Made Easy*. Torrance, CA: Rose, 2009.

Kant, Immanuel. *Critique of Pure Reason*. Translated by Norman Kemp Smith. New York: St. Martin's Press, 1965.

Kleist, James A., trans. "The Epistle of St. Clement." In *Ancient Christian Writers*, by St. Clement. New York: Newman Press, 1946.

Kline, Meredith G. "Covenant Theology Under Attack." *New Horizons*, February 1994.

Kline, Meredith G. "Suzerain Treaties and the Covenant Documents of the Bible." Lecture, Westminster Theological Seminary, Philadelphia.

Kline, Meredith. "Suzerain Treaties and the Covenant Documents of the Bible." Lecture, Westminster Theological Seminary, Philadelphia, PA. www.fivesolas.com/suzerain.htm.

Köstlin, Julius. *The Life of Martin Luther*. Translated from the German. New York, 1883.

Kuiper, B. K., *The Church in History*. Grand Rapids: Eerdmans, 1951.

Ladd, George Eldon. *The Gospel of the Kingdom: Scriptural Studies in the Kingdom of God*. Grand Rapids: Eerdmans, 1959.

Ladd, George Eldon. *The Last Things*. Grand Rapids: Eerdmans, 1982.

Latourette, Kenneth Scott. *A History of Christianity*. Vol. 1 and 2. Peabody, MA: Prince, 1997.

Locke, John. "An Essay Concerning Human Understanding." In *From Plato to Nietzsche*, edited by Forrest Baird, 574. 2nd ed. Upper Saddle River, NJ: Prentice Hall, 1997.

Machen, J. Gresham. *Christianity and Liberalism*. Grand Rapids: Eerdmans, 1996.

Marique, Joseph M. F., SJ, PhD, trans. "Shepherd of Hermas." In *The Fathers of the Church: The Apostolic Fathers*. Washington, D.C.: Catholic University of America Press, 1947.

Morris, Henry M., and Gary E. Parker. *What Is Creation Science*. Green Forrest, AR: Master Books, 1982.

Murray, John. *Principles of Conduct*. Grand Rapids: Eerdmans, 1957.

Nettelhorst, R. P. "The Geneology of Jesus." *Journal of the Evangelical Theological Society*, June 1988, 169–72.

New Geneva Study Bible: Bringing the Light of the Reformation to Scripture. Nashville: Thomas Nelson, 1995.

Niebuhr, H. Richard. *The Kingdom of God in America*. New York: Harper & Brothers, 1973.

Niebuhr, H. Richard. *The Social Sources of Denominationalism*. New York: New American Library, 1959.

Nietzsche, Friedrich. "Thus Spoke Zarathustra." In *From Plato to Nietzsche*, edited by Forrest E. Baird. Upper Saddle River, NJ: Prentice Hall, 1994.

Olson, Roger E. *The Story of Christian Theology: Twenty Centuries of Tradition and Reform*. Downers Grove, IL: InterVarsity Press, 1999.

Patent, Dorothy Hinshaw. *Evolution Goes on Every Day*. New York: Holiday House, 1977.

With drawings by Matthew Kalmenoff

Pentecost, J. Dwight. *Thy Kingdom Come*. Wheaton, IL: Victor Books, 1990.

Petersen, Randy, J. Stephen Lang, and A. Kenneth Curtis. *The 100 Most Important Events in Christian History*. Grand Rapids: Revell, 1991.

Pfeiffer, Charles F., Howard Frederic Vos, and John Rea, eds. *The Wycliffe Bible Encyclopedia*. Vol. 1 and 2. Chicago: Moody Press, 1976.

Posset, Franz. "Bernard of Clairvaux as Luther's Source." *Concordia Theological Quarterly* 54, no. 4 (1990): 281.

Radmacher, Earl D., Ronald B. Allen, and Wayne House. "Note on Exod. 2:22–25." In *Nelson's NKJV Study Bible*. Nashville: Thomas Nelson, 1997.

Rae, John. *Martin Luther: Student, Monk, Reformer*. London, 1883.

Reed, James E., and Ronnie Prevost. *A History of Christian Education*. Nashville: Broadman & Holman, 1993.

Rice, Richard, John Sanders, William Hasker, David Basinger, and Clark Pinnock. *The Openness of God*. Downers Grove, IL: InterVarsity Press, 1994.

Ridderbos, Herman. *The Coming of the Kingdom*. Translated by H. De Jongste. Philadelphia: Presbyterian & Reformed, 1962.

Riddlebarger, Kim. *The Man of Sin: Uncovering the Truth about the Antichrist.* Grand Rapids: Baker Books, 2006.

Robertson, O. Palmer. *The Christ of the Covenants.* Phillipsburg, N.J: Presbyterian & Reformed, 1980.

Rupp, E. Gordon, and Philip S. Watson, eds. *Luther and Erasmus: Free Will and Salvation.* Philadelphia: Westminster, 1969.

The Ryrie Study Bible. Chicago: Moody, 1978. edited by Charles Caldwell Ryrie, ThD, PhD.

Schaeffer, Francis. *How Should We Then Live?* Old Tappan, NJ: Revell, 1976.

Seay, Frank. "Genesis 6—Sons of God/Daughters of Men." Lecture, Foundations: Genesis and Jesus, Park Cities Presbyterian Church, Dallas, May 16, 1999.

Shapiro, Rami M., Rabbi. *Amazing Chesed: Living a Grace-Filled Judaism.* Woodstock, VT: Jewish Lights, 2013.

Shelley, Bruce L. *Church History in Plain Language.* Dallas: Word, 1995.

Spitz, Lewis W. *Luther's Works: Career of the Reformer IV.* Vol. 34. St. Louis: Concordia, 1960.

St. Augustine. *The City of God.* New York: Penguin Books, 1972.

St. Ignatius. "The Epistles of Ignatius." In *Ancient Christian Writers*, translated by James A. Kleist, SJ, PhD. New York: Newman Press, 1946.

Stark, Rodney. *The Rise of Christianity.* Princeton: Princeton University Press, 1996.

Stark, Rodney. *The Triumph of Christianity.* New York: HarperCollins, 2011.

Stevenson, Betsey, and Justin Wolfers. "The Paradox of Declining Female Happiness." *American Economic Journal: Economic Policy, American Economic Association* 1(2) (August 2009): 190–225. doi:10.3386/w14969.

Strimple, Robert B. *The Modern Search for the Real Jesus: An Introductory Survey of the Historical Roots of Gospels Criticism.* Phillipsburg, NJ: P&R, 1995.

Swan Laura. *The Forgotten Desert Mothers.* Mahwah, NJ: Paulist Press, 2001.

Thomson, John A. *The Western Church in the Middle Ages.* London: Hodder Headline Group, 1998.

Van Til, Cornelius. *A Christian Theory of Knowledge.* Grand Rapids: Baker Book House, 1969.

Veith, Gene Edward, Jr. *Postmodern Times: A Christian Guide to Contemporary Thought and Culture.* Wheaton, IL: Crossway Books, 1994.

Walton, Robert C. "Chart 1." In *Chronological and Background Charts of Church History.* Grand Rapids, MI: Zondervan Publishing House, 1986.

Westerfield, Dan. *Foundations for an Adult Lay Education Program*, Master of Arts in Religion Program, Reformed Theological Seminary, Baltimore/Washington, 2005.

Whiston, William, trans. "The Antiquities of the Jews." In *The Works of Josephus*, 231. Peabody, MA: Hendrickson, 1987.

Young, Frances. *The Making of the Creeds*. Philadelphia: Trinity, 1991.

Young, Robert. *Analytical Concordance to the Bible*. Grand Rapids: Eerdmans, 1964.

Zens, John. "An Examination of the Presuppositions of Covenant and Dispensational Theology." In *Studies in Theology and Ethics*. Malin, OR: Brem, 1981.

Zodhiates, Spiros. *The Hebrew-Greek Key Word Study Bible: New American Standard*. Chattanooga, TN: AMG Publishers, 1984.

INTERNET BIBLIOGRAPHY

"The 1918 Influenza Pandemic." Brief Ebola General History. Accessed June 14, 2018. https://virus.stanford.edu/uda/.

"The 1918 Influenza Pandemic." Brief Ebola General History. Accessed May 03, 2018. http://virus.stanford.edu/uda/.

"Ages of Muhammad's Wives at Marriage." Muslim Statistics (Terrorism)—WikiIslam. Accessed May 16, 2018. http://wikiislam.net/wiki/Ages_of_Muhammads_Wives_at_Marriage.

"Ancient Jewish History: The Great Revolt." Claus Von Stauffenberg. Accessed May 15, 2018. http://www.jewishvirtuallibrary.org/the-great-revolt-66-70-ce.s

Andrews, Evan. "6 Infamous Sacks of Rome." History.com. August 24, 2015. Accessed May 16, 2018. http://www.history.com/news/6-infamous-sacks-of-rome.

Andrews, Evan. "7 Things You May Not Know About the Gutenberg Bible." History.com. February 23, 2015. Accessed May 17, 2018. https://www.history.com/news/7-things-you-may-not-know-about-the-gutenberg-bible.

Andrews, Evan. "8 Reasons Why Rome Fell." History.com. January 14, 2014. Accessed May 16, 2018. https://www.history.com/news/history-lists/8-reasons-why-rome-fell.

Andy Kalan. "Analysis of History: The Story of Premodernism, Modernism, and Postmodernism." Directions on Upward Existence. June 08, 2013. Accessed May 15, 2018. https://andykalan.wordpress.com/2012/07/02/analysis-of-history-the-story-of-premodernism-modernism-postmodernism-2/.

"Anne Boleyn The Tudors Facts and Biography of Information." English History. February 08, 2017. Accessed May 18, 2018. https://englishhistory.net/tudor/monarchs/anne-boleyn/.

"Anti-Religious Campaigns." Apple Computers: This Month in Business History (Business Reference Services, Library of Congress). Accessed June 14, 2018. https://www.loc.gov/exhibits/archives/anti.html.

"Anti-Religious Campaigns." Apple Computers: This Month in Business History (Business Reference Services, Library of Congress). Accessed May 03, 2018. http://www.loc.gov/exhibits/archives/anti.html.

BARBARIAN BREAKTHROUGH. Accessed May 16, 2018. http://christianchronicler.com/history1/barbarian_breakthrough.html.

Bellis, Mary. "Johannes Gutenberg and His Revolutionary Printing Press." ThoughtCo. Accessed May 17, 2018. https://www.thoughtco.com/johannes-gutenberg-and-the-printing-press-1991865.

Bergman, Jerry. "Was Charles Darwin Psychotic? A Study of His Mental Health." The Institute for Creation Research. Accessed June 14, 2018. http://www.icr.org/article/was-charles-darwin-psychotic-study-his-mental-heal/.

Bergman, Jerry. "Was Charles Darwin Psychotic? A Study of His Mental Health." The Institute for Creation Research. Accessed May 03, 2018. http://www.icr.org/article/112/.

"Billy Graham." Theopedia.com. Accessed June 18, 2018. https://www.theopedia.com/billy-graham.

"Brief Notes on the Causes for the Decline of Feudalism." Accessed May 17, 2018. http://www.preservearticles.com/2011090413015/brief-notes-on-the-causes-for-decline-of-feudalism.html.

Britannica, The Editors of Encyclopaedia. "Asceticism." Encyclopaedia Britannica. June 20, 2013. Accessed May 15, 2018. https://www.britannica.com/topic/asceticism.

Britannica, The Editors of Encyclopaedia. "Ataulphus." Encyclopaedia Britannica. March 01, 2018. Accessed May 16, 2018. https://www.britannica.com/biography/Ataulphus.

Britannica, The Editors of Encyclopaedia. "Black Death." Encyclopaedia Britannica. January 05, 2018. Accessed May 16, 2018. https://www.britannica.com/event/Black-Death.

Britannica, The Editors of Encyclopaedia. "Cathari." Encyclopaedia Britannica. August 09, 2007. Accessed May 17, 2018. https://www.britannica.com/topic/Cathari.

Britannica, The Editors of Encyclopaedia. "The City of God." Encyclopaedia Britannica. November 21, 2011. Accessed May 16, 2018. https://www.britannica.com/topic/The-City-of-God.

Britannica, The Editors of Encyclopaedia. "Constantius I." Encyclopaedia Britannica. May 04, 2018. Accessed May 15, 2018. https://www.britannica.com/biography/Constantius-I.

Britannica, The Editors of Encyclopaedia. "Galerius." Encyclopaedia Britannica. July 27, 2007. Accessed May 15, 2018. https://www.britannica.com/biography/Galerius.

Britannica, The Editors of Encyclopaedia. "Licinius." Encyclopaedia Britannica. July 24, 2013. Accessed May 15, 2018. https://www.britannica.com/biography/Licinius.

Britannica, The Editors of Encyclopaedia. "Ludwig Feuerbach." Encyclopaedia Britannica. July 31, 2014. Accessed June 14, 2018. https://www.britannica.com/biography/Ludwig-Feuerbach.

Britannica, The Editors of Encyclopaedia. "Migration Period." Encyclopaedia Britannica. March 23, 2018. Accessed May 16, 2018. https://www.britannica.com/event/Dark-Ages.

Britannica, The Editors of Encyclopaedia. "Odoacer." Encyclopaedia Britannica. March 08, 2018. Accessed May 16, 2018. https://www.britannica.com/biography/Odoacer.

Britannica, The Editors of Encyclopaedia. "Peace of Augsburg." Encyclopaedia Britannica. February 03, 2016. Accessed May 18, 2018. https://www.britannica.com/event/Peace-of-Augsburg.

Britannica, The Editors of Encyclopaedia. "Saint Willibrord." Encyclopaedia Britannica. November 12, 2014. Accessed May 16, 2018. http://www.britannica.com/biography/Saint-Willibrord.

Britannica, The Editors of Encyclopaedia. "Stephen Jay Gould." Encyclopaedia Britannica. May 17, 2018. Accessed June 14, 2018. https://www.britannica.com/biography/Stephen-Jay-Gould.

Britannica, The Editors of Encyclopaedia. "Thirty Years' War." Encyclopaedia Britannica. November 22, 2017. Accessed June 14, 2018. https://www.britannica.com/event/Thirty-Years-War.

Britannica, The Editors of Encyclopaedia. "Ulfilas." Encyclopaedia Britannica. July 06, 2012. Accessed May 16, 2018. https://www.britannica.com/biography/Ulfilas.

Britannica, The Editors of Encyclopaedia. "Visigoth." Encyclopaedia Britannica. April 13, 2017. Accessed May 16, 2018. https://www.britannica.com/topic/Visigoth.

Britannica, The Editors of Encyclopaedia. "Waldenses." Encyclopaedia Britannica. December 29, 2017. Accessed May 17, 2018. https://www.britannica.com/topic/Waldenses.

Bunting, Tony. "Battle of Tours." Encyclopaedia Britannica. March 28, 2017. Accessed May 16, 2018. https://www.britannica.com/event/Battle-of-Tours-732.

Bunting, Tony. "Fall of Constantinople." Encyclopaedia Britannica. September 05, 2017. Accessed May 17, 2018. http://www.britannica.com/event/Fall-of-Constantinople-1453.

"The Cambrian Explosion." Geoscience News. May 11, 2015. Accessed June 14, 2018. https://grisda.wordpress.com/2015/05/11/the-cambrian-explosion/.

Case Studies in Easy-Believism. Accessed June 18, 2018. http://www.rogershermansociety.org/easy-believism.htm.

Case Studies in Easy-Believism. Accessed May 03, 2018. http://www.rogershermansociety.org/easy-believism.htm.

"Charlemagne and the Holy Roman Empire—The Middle Ages." Browse through Ancient History. Accessed May 16, 2018. http://www.mrdowling.com/703-charlemagne.html.

"Charles Darwin." SparkNotes. Accessed June 14, 2018. http://www.sparknotes.com/biography/darwin/summary/.

"Charles Darwin." SparkNotes. Accessed May 03, 2018. http://www.sparknotes.com/biography/darwin/summary.

"The Children's Crusades (1212)." Historyguide.org. Accessed May 17, 2018. http://historyguide.org/ancient/children.html.

"Christian Bakers Fined $135,000 for Refusing to Make Wedding Cake for Lesbians." Fox News. Accessed May 16, 2018. http://www.foxnews.com/opinion/2015/07/03/christian-bakers-fined-135000-for-refusing-to-make-wedding-cake-for-lesbians.html.

"Christianity in Russia." Christian Assemblies International Banner. Accessed May 17, 2018. http://www.cai.org/bible-studies/christianity-russia.

"A Chronological Sequence of the Resurrection Events." Community in Mission. June 10, 2015. Accessed May 15, 2018. http://blog.adw.org/2011/04/a-chronological-sequence-of-the-resurrection-events/.

"A Chronological Study of Paul's Ministry." Men, Women and Gender Roles in Marriage | Xenos Christian Fellowship. Accessed May 15, 2018. http://www.xenos.org/essays/chronological-study-pauls-ministry.

Chronology of Apostle Paul's Journeys and Epistles. Accessed May 15, 2018. http://matthewmcgee.org/paultime.html.

"Civil War Casualties | American Battlefield Trust." Civil War Trust. Accessed June 14, 2018. https://www.civilwar.org/learn/articles/civil-war-casualties.

"Civil War Casualties." Civil War Trust. Accessed May 03, 2018. https://www.civilwar.org/learn/articles/civil-war-casualties.

Clark, Heather. "Canadian Supreme Court Rules Biblical Speech Opposing Homosexual Behavior Is a 'Hate Crime.'" Christian News Network. March 30, 2013. Accessed May 16, 2018. https://christiannews.net/2013/02/28/

canadian-supreme-court-rules-biblical-speech-opposing-homosexual-behavior-is-a-hate-crime/.

Cline, Austin. "A Timeline of the First Crusade, 1095–1100." ThoughtCo. Accessed May 17, 2018. https://www.thoughtco.com/first-crusade-christianity-vs-Islam-4078432.

"Columnists." ChristianHeadlines.com. Accessed May 16, 2018. http://www.christianheadlines.com/columnists/al-mohler/criminializing-christianity-swedens-hate-speech-law-1277601.html.

Connor, Phillip. "6 Facts about South Korea's Growing Christian Population." Pew Research Center. August 12, 2014. Accessed June 18, 2018. http://www.pewresearch.org/fact-tank/2014/08/12/6-facts-about-christianity-in-south-korea/.

Connor, Phillip. "6 Facts about South Korea's Growing Christian Population." Pew Research Center. August 12, 2014. http://www.pewresearch.org/fact-tank/2014/08/12/6-facts-about-christianity-in-south-korea/.

Cummins, Joseph. "How Did the Crusades Affect Exploration and Trade?" Synonym. May 10, 2018. Accessed May 17, 2018. https://classroom.synonym.com/did-crusades-affect-exploration-trade-8887.html.

"THE DEFINITION OF THE COUNCIL OF CHALCEDON (451 AD)." The Definition of Chalcedon—The PuritanBoard. Accessed May 16, 2018. http://files.puritanboard.com/confessions/chalcedon.htm.

"The Destruction of Jerusalem in 70 AD." https://www.bible-history.com/jerusalem/firstcenturyjerusalem_destruction_of_jerusalem_in_70_a_d_.html.

"The Destruction of the Second Temple." Solomon's Temple. Accessed May 15, 2018. http://www.templemount.org/destruct2.html.

"The Development of the Canon of the New Testament." The Development of the Canon of the New Testament—Justin Martyr. Accessed May 15, 2018. http://www.ntcanon.org/Athanasius.shtml.

Dickson, Gary. "Children's Crusade." Encyclopaedia Britannica. March 18, 2018. Accessed May 17, 2018. https://www.britannica.com/event/Childrens-Crusade.

Dreyer, Wim A. "The Amazing Growth of the Early Church." HTS Teologiese Studies / Theological Studies. Accessed May 15, 2018. https://hts.org.za/index.php/HTS/article/view/1268.

Duckett, Eleanor Shipley. "Pippin III." Encyclopaedia Britannica. May 25, 2010. Accessed May 16, 2018. https://www.britannica.com/biography/Pippin-III.

Duthiers, Vladimir. "Boko Haram: Why Terror Group Kidnaps Schoolgirls, and What Happens." CNN. May 02, 2014. Accessed May 16, 2018. https://www.cnn.com/2014/04/24/world/africa/nigeria-kidnapping-answers/index.html.

"Evolution Frauds." Evolution Is Not Science. June 02, 2009. Accessed June 14, 2018. https://evolutionisntscience.wordpress.com/evolution-frauds/.

"The Fall of Rome." The Death of President Lincoln, 1865. Accessed May 16, 2018. http://www.eyewitnesstohistory.com/fallofrome.htm.

Faulkner, Danny R. "Does the Second Law of Thermodynamics Favor Evolution?" Answers in Genesis. November 03, 2015. Accessed June 14, 2018. https://answersingenesis.org/physics/second-law-of-thermodynamics.

Feeney, Nolan. "3 Other Christian Denominations That Allow Gay Marriage." Time. March 18, 2015. Accessed May 16, 2018. http://time.com/3749253/churches-gay-marriage/.

"FutureChurch." Questions and Answers about Women's Ordination | FutureChurch. Accessed May 16, 2018. http://www.futurechurch.org/brief-history-of-celibacy-in-catholic-church.

"Galileo Unmasked at Last!" Emperor Nero's Perverted Same-Sex Marriage! Accessed June 13, 2018. http://reformation.org/galileo-unmasked.html.

Gallup, Inc. "Americans Greatly Overestimate Percent Gay, Lesbian in US" Gallup.com. May 21, 2015. Accessed May 16, 2018. http://www.gallup.com/poll/183383/americans-greatly-overestimate-percent-gay-lesbian.aspx.

Geller, Pamela, and American Freedom Defense Initiative. "Lone Feminist Calls out Islamic Misogyny." WND. Accessed May 16, 2018. http://www.wnd.com/2013/07/lone-feminist-calls-out-islamic-misogyny/.

"Grace Communion International." Four Major Worldviews | Grace Communion International. Accessed May 16, 2018. https://www.gci.org/history/chalcedon.

Hickman, Kennedy. "Hunnic Invasions: The Battle of Chalons." ThoughtCo. Accessed May 16, 2018. https://www.thoughtco.com/hunnic-invasions-battle-of-chalons-2360875.

"Historical Overview of the Inquisition." The Galileo Project | Science | Sector. Accessed May 17, 2018. http://galileo.rice.edu/lib/student_work/trial96/loftis/overview.html.

History.com. Accessed June 14, 2018. http://www.history.com/topics/french-revolution/print.

History.com Staff. "Crusades." History.com. 2010. Accessed May 17, 2018. http://www.history.com/topics/crusades.

History.com Staff. "French Revolution." History.com. 2009. Accessed June 14, 2018. http://www.history.com/topics/french-revolution.

History.com Staff. "John Locke." History.com. 2009. Accessed June 14, 2018. http://www.history.com/topics/john-locke.

History.com Staff. "World War I." History.com. 2009. Accessed June 14, 2018. http://www.history.com/topics/world-war-i-history.

History.com Staff. "World War I." History.com. 2009. Accessed May 03, 2018. http://www.history.com/topics/world-war-i-history.

Historyguide.org. Accessed May 16, 2018. http://www.historyguide.org/ancient/clovis.html.

"Homosexuality and the World Council of Churches." Home Page of the ReligiousTolerance.org Web Site. Accessed June 14, 2018. http://www.religioustolerance.org/hom_wcc.htm.

"Homosexuality and the World Council of Churches." Home Page of the ReligiousTolerance.org Web Site. Accessed May 03, 2018. http://www.religioustolerance.org/hom_wcc.htm.

"Hundreds Support Christian Florist Fined for Refusing to Work Gay Wedding." Fox News. Accessed May 16, 2018. http://www.foxnews.com/us/2016/11/18/hundreds-support-christian-florist-fined-for-refusing-to-work-gay-wedding.html.

"Intermediate Fossils in the Fossil Record." Evosecrets.com Evolution Secrets. Accessed June 14, 2018. http://evosecrets.com/intermediate-fossils-in-the-fossil-record/.

Jamjoom, Mohammed, and Hakim Almasmari. "Yemen Minister on Child Marriage: Enough Is Enough." CNN. September 16, 2013. Accessed May 16, 2018. https://www.cnn.com/2013/09/15/world/meast/yemen-child-bride/index.html.

"JewishEncyclopedia.com." AMON, KING OF JUDAH—JewishEncyclopedia.com. Accessed May 15, 2018. http://www.jewishencyclopedia.com/articles/6200-florus-gessius.

"John Calvin: Theologian and Pastor." The Master's Seminary. February 03, 2018. Accessed May 18, 2018. https://www.tms.edu/preachersandpreaching/john-calvin-theologian-pastor/.

"John Huss." Christian History | Learn the History of Christianity and the Church. Accessed May 17, 2018. http://www.christianitytoday.com/history/people/martyrs/john-huss.html.

Kern, Soeren. "Europe: "You Are Entering a Sharia Controlled Zone"." Gatestone Institute. Accessed May 16, 2018. https://www.gatestoneinstitute.org/2530/denmark-sharia-hezbollah.

Kerrigan, Michael. "Battle of Milvian Bridge." Encyclopædia Britannica. March 23, 2017. Accessed May 15, 2018. https://www.britannica.com/topic/Battle-of-the-Milvian-Bridge.

Knox, John S. "The Monastic Movement: Origins and Purposes." Ancient History Encyclopedia. May 15, 2018. Accessed May 15, 2018. https://www.ancient.eu/article/930/the-monastic-movement-origins--purposes/.

"Life Expectancy in the Middle Ages." Sarah Woodbury. August 30, 2016. Accessed May 16, 2018. http://www.sarahwoodbury.com/life-expectancy-in-the-middle-ages.

THE LIFE OF THE ARTIST MICHELANGELO. Accessed May 17, 2018. http://cecelia.physics.indiana.edu/life/art/michelangelo.html.

Liu, Joseph. "Global Christianity—A Report on the Size and Distribution of the World's Christian Population." Pew Research Center's Religion and Public Life Project. December 19, 2011. Accessed May 15, 2018. http://www.pewforum.org/2011/12/19/global-christianity-exec/.

"Lollard." The Free Dictionary. Accessed May 17, 2018. http://www.thefreedictionary.com/Lollard.

Mark, Joshua J. "Roman Empire." Ancient History Encyclopedia. May 15, 2018. Accessed May 16, 2018. http://www.ancient.eu/Roman_Empire.

Mark, Joshua J. "Vandals." Ancient History Encyclopedia. May 15, 2018. Accessed May 16, 2018. http://www.ancient.eu/Vandals/.

"Marshall Plan, 1948." US Department of State. Accessed June 14, 2018. https://history.state.gov/milestones/1945-1952/marshall-plan.

"Martin Luther's Death and Legacy." Ligonier Ministries. Accessed May 18, 2018. http://www.ligonier.org/blog/martin-luthers-death-and-legacy/.

"Media Significance—Influence of Scopes Trial of 1925." Google Sites. Accessed June 14, 2018. https://sites.google.com/site/influenceofscopestrialof1925/change-the-banner.

"Media Significance—Influence of Scopes Trial of 1925." Google Sites. Accessed May 03, 2018. https://sites.google.com/site/influenceofscopestrialof1925/change-the-banner.

"Michael Denton." Pseudoscience—RationalWiki. Accessed June 14, 2018. https://rationalwiki.org/wiki/Michael_Denton.

"The Middle Ages | Feudalism." Western Reserve Public Media. Accessed May 16, 2018. https://westernreservepublicmedia.org/middleages/feud_peasants.htm.

"Middle Ages, Peasant's Life." Greece, A History of Ancient Greece, Mythology. Accessed May 16, 2018. http://history-world.org/peasant.htm.

"The New Testament First Popularized the Codex in 100AD and Was the First Book Ever Produced from the Printing Press in 1500AD." Why Are There Different Versions of the Bible? Accessed May 15, 2018. http://www.bible.ca/b-canon-codex-printing-press.htm.

Nicholson, Helen. "Women and the Crusades." Academia.edu. Accessed May 17, 2018. http://www.academia.edu/7608599/women_and_the_Crusades.

"Odd Romance of John and Idelette Calvin." Christianity.com. Accessed May 18, 2018. https://www.christianity.com/church/church-history/timeline/1501-1600/odd-romance-of-john-and-idelette-calvin-11629964.html.

"The Ottoman Turks Capture Constantinople, Resulting in the Transfer of Invaluable Manuscripts to Venice and the West (May 29–June 1453)." About HistoryofInformation.com. Accessed May 17, 2018. http://www.historyofinformation.com/expanded.php?id=35.

"Papal Immorality!" Keith Hunt—The Wit of Winston Churchill—Page Seven. Accessed May 16, 2018. http://www.keithhunt.com/Midages9.html.

PaulBenedict. "Relativism, Rome, Homosexuality, and the Fall of the West." War of Words by Paul Benedict. August 19, 2015. Accessed May 16, 2018. http://theminutemenmedia.com/2015/01/194/.

Perring, Rebecca. "Angela Merkel Admits German No-Go Zones Are 'a REALITY'." Express.co.uk. March 01, 2018. Accessed May 16, 2018. https://www.express.co.uk/news/world/925727/Angela-Merkel-Germany-latest-news-no-go-zone-reality-refugee-crisis.

"Phoenix, Crete (BiblePlaces.com)." BiblePlaces.com. Accessed May 15, 2018. https://www.bibleplaces.com/phoenix-crete/.

Pieper, Josef. "Scholasticism." Encyclopædia Britannica. June 23, 2015. Accessed May 17, 2018. https://www.britannica.com/topic/Scholasticism.

"Pilgrim History." MayflowerHistory.com. Accessed June 13, 2018. http://mayflowerhistory.com/pilgrim-history/.

Pitman, Sean. "An Alternative Explanation." J Harlen Bretz—And the Great Scabland Debate. Accessed June 14, 2018. http://detectingdesign.com/geologiccolumn.html.

"Premodernism, Modernism, and Postmodernism: An Overview." Postmodern Psychology. March 14, 2017. Accessed May 15, 2018. http://postmodernpsychology.com/premodernism-modernism-postmodernism-an-overview/.

"Punctuated Equilibrium." PBS. Accessed June 14, 2018. http://www.pbs.org/wgbh/evolution/library/03/5/l_035_01.html.

"Punctuated Equilibrium." PBS. Accessed May 03, 2018. http://www.pbs.org/wgbh/evolution/library/03/5/l_035_01.html.

"A Reformation Timeline." Lutheran Reformation. Accessed May 17, 2018. https://lutheranreformation.org/history/reformation-timeline/.

"René Descartes." Internet Encyclopedia of Philosophy. Accessed June 14, 2018. http://www.iep.utm.edu/descarte/.

Robinson, Julian. "Vatican Police 'Break Up Drug-fuelled Gay Orgy at Home of Secretary of One of Pope Francis's Key Advisers.'" Daily Mail Online. July 05, 2017. Accessed May 15, 2018. http://www.dailymail.co.uk/news/article-4667098/vatican-police-break-gay-orgy-apartment.htl.

"Roman Emperors—DIR Diocletian." Roman Emperors—DIR Livia (Wife of Augustus). Accessed May 15, 2018. http://www.roman-emperors.sites.luc.edu/dioclet.htm.

"Roman Emperors DIR Maximinus Daia." Roman Emperors—DIR Diocletian. Accessed May 15, 2018. http://www.roman-emperors.org/daia.htm.

Ryan, Edward A. "Spanish Inquisition." Encyclopaedia Britannica. December 18, 2017. Accessed May 17, 2018. https://www.britannica.com/topic/Spanish-Inquisition.

"The Sacraments." Introduction to Roman Catholicism. Accessed May 17, 2018. http://catholicfaith.co.uk/sacraments.

Satz, Debra. "Feminist Perspectives on Reproduction and the Family." Stanford Encyclopedia of Philosophy. October 21, 2013. Accessed May 16, 2018. https://plato.stanford.edu/entries/feminism-family/.

Sdootson. "POSTMODERNISM: The Good Stuff." 2012. January 01, 1970. http://postmodernismthegoodstuff.blogspot.com/2012/.

"Second Arab Siege of Constantinople in 717–718." Weapons and Warfare. November 24, 2015. Accessed May 16, 2018. https://weaponsandwarfare.com/2015/10/15/second-arab-siege-of-constantinople-in-717–718/.

"Sharing StoriesInspiring Change." Jewish Women's Archive. Accessed May 15, 2018. https://jwa.org/encyclopedia/article/berenice.

"The Siege of Constantinople." The Roman and Byzantine Senate. January 01, 1970. Accessed May 16, 2018. http://byzantinemilitary.blogspot.com/2011/10/siege-of-constantinople.html.

"Significance of the Great Awakening: Roots of Revolution." Great-Awakening.com. Accessed June 14, 2018. http://www.great-awakening.com/roots-of-revolution/.

Sproul, R.C. "The Pelagian Controversy." Ligonier Ministries. Accessed May 15, 2018. https://www.ligonier.org/learn/articles/pelagian-controversy/.

Squires, Nick. "Fall of Roman Empire Caused by 'contagion of Homosexuality.'" The Telegraph. April 08, 2011. Accessed May 16, 2018. http://www.telegraph.co.uk/news/worldnews/europe/italy/8438210/Fall-of-Roman-Empire-caused-by-contagion-of homosexuality.html.

"State of Israel Proclaimed." History.com. Accessed June 18, 2018. https://www.history.com/this-day-in-history/state-of-israel-proclaimed.

"State of Israel Proclaimed." History.com. Accessed May 03, 2018. http://www.history.com/this-day-in-history/state-of-israel-proclaimed.

Sullivan, Richard E. "Charlemagne." Encyclopædia Britannica. December 27, 2017. Accessed May 16, 2018. https://www.britannica.com/biography/Charlemagne.

Tamborrino, Kelsey, Jeff Greenfield, Jack Shafer, Rich Lowry, and Brianna Ehley. "Evolution's Just a 'Theory,' Pruitt Says in 2005." About Us. March 02, 2018. https://www.politico.com/newsletters/morning-energy/2018/03/02/evolutions-just-a-theory-pruitt-says-in-2005-121202.

Taylor Marshall. "Eusebius on the Flight from Jerusalem in AD 64." Taylor Marshall. August 28, 2008. Accessed May 15, 2018. http://taylormarshall.com/2008/08/eusebius-on-flight-from-jerusalem-in-ad.html.

"Theodosius I." Christian History | Learn the History of Christianity and the Church. Accessed May 15, 2018. https://www.christianitytoday.com/history/people/rulers/theodosius-i.html.

Theopedia.com. Accessed May 03, 2018. https://www.theopedia.com/billy-graham.

Thiede, Carsten Peter, and Patrick Henry Reardon. "Athanasius." Christian History | Learn the History of Christianity and the Church. Accessed May 15, 2018. https://www.christianitytoday.com/history/people/theologians/athanasius.html.

Thigpen, Paul. "Martin Luther's Later Years: A Gallery—Family Album." Christian History | Learn the History of Christianity and the Church. Accessed May 18, 2018. https://www.christianitytoday.com/history/issues/issue-39/martin-luthers-later-years-gallery--family-album.html.

"Thirty Years' War." Jama Masjid, Delhi—New World Encyclopedia. Accessed June 13, 2018. http://www.newworldencyclopedia.org/entry/Thirty_Years'_War.

"Timeline—World Council of Churches." African Methodist Episcopal Church—World Council of Churches. April 22, 2014. Accessed June 14, 2018. https://www.oikoumene.org/en/about-us/organizational-structure/assembly/since-1948.

"Timeline—World Council of Churches." African Methodist Episcopal Church—World Council of Churches. April 22, 2014. http://www.oikoumene.org/en/about-us/organizational-structure/assembly/since-1948.

Timmons, Greg. "Erasmus." Biography.com. November 08, 2016. Accessed May 17, 2018. https://www.biography.com/people/erasmus-21291705?_escaped_fragment=.

Ullmann, Walter. "Saint Leo IX." Encyclopaedia Britannica. April 12, 2018. Accessed May 16, 2018. https://www.britannica.com/biography/Saint-Leo-IX.

US Department of State. Accessed May 03, 2018. https://history.state.gov/milestones/1945-1952/marshall-plan.

"Vatican Abuse Summit: $2.2 Billion and 100,000 Victims in US Alone." National Catholic Reporter. February 08, 2012. Accessed May 15, 2018. https://www.ncronline.org/blogs/ncr-today/vatican-abuse-summit-22-billion-and-100000-victims-us-alone.

"Vatican Cardinal's Secretary Arrested for Hosting 'Cocaine Fueled' Homosexual Orgy Near St. Peter's." CNS News. July 12, 2017. Accessed May 15, 2018. https://www.cnsnews.com/blog/theresa-smith/vatican-cardinals-secretary-ar-rested-hosting-cocaine-fueled-homosexual-orgy-near.

"The Veneration of Relics." Banner of Truth USA. April 01, 2015. Accessed May 17, 2018. https://banneroftruth.org/us/resources/articles/2015/the-veneration-of-relics/.

"Was The New Testament Influenced by Pagan Philosophy?" Christian Research Institute. Accessed May 15, 2018. http://www.equip.org/article/was-the-new-testament-influenced-by-pagan-philosophy.

Watson, Richard A. "René Descartes." Encyclopaedia Britannica. April 06, 2018. Accessed June 14, 2018. https://www.britannica.com/biography/Rene-Descartes.

"Westminster Confession of Faith." Antithesis at Reformed.org. Accessed June 14, 2018. http://www.reformed.org/documents/wcf_with_proofs/.

"When Did the Church Abandon Animal Sacrifice? Archive of Comments and Discussions—Questions and Answers From All-Creatures.org." When Did the Church Abandon Animal Sacrifice?: Comments and Discussions—Questions and Answers. Accessed May 15, 2018. http://all-creatures.org/discuss/when-didthe.html.

White, J. Gene. "The Resurrection of Jesus Christ." Accessed May 15, 2018. https://theologue.files.wordpress.com/2014/05/harmony-resurrectionofchrist.

Winfield, Paige, Vishal Arora, Kate Shellnutt, Caleb Lindgren, and Mark Galli. "Christian Groups Eye Hate Crimes Bill." Christian History | Learn the History of Christianity and the Church. Accessed May 16, 2018. http://www.christianitytoday.com/news/2009/july/128-42.0.html.

"World War 2 Casualties." World War 2 Facts. May 20, 2017. Accessed June 14, 2018. http://www.worldwar2facts.org/world-war-2-casualties.html.

"World War 2 Casualties." World War 2 Facts. May 20, 2017. http://www.worldwar2facts.org/world-war-2-casualties.html.

www.edvardmunch.org/the-scream.jsp.

Zavada, Jack. "Picture the Life of Asceticism." ThoughtCo. Accessed May 15, 2018. https://www.thoughtco.com/what-is-asceticism-700046.

SCRIPTURAL INDEX

Mark

Romans

SUBJECT INDEX

Aaron
    meets Moses at Mt. Sinai 92
    will speak for Moses 90
    makes the golden calf 104
    appointed as High Priest 106
    complains with Miriam about Moses 108
    stands with Moses against a rebellion 110
    dies at Mt. Hor 112
Abel
    God has regard for his offering 19
    killed by Cain 19
Abiathar 139, 140
Abimelech
    takes Sarah 50
    has covenant with Abraham 50
    contends with Isaac 61
Abinadad 124, 132
Abner
    supports David over Ishbosheth 129
    killed by Joab, mourned by David 130
Abominations 118, 148
Abortion
    argument against 165
    present conflicts 400
Abram/Abraham
    life summary 58
    God's covenant with 37
    battle of kings and Melchizedek 42
    Sarai's plan and the birth of Ishmael 47
    name change and circumcision initiated 47
    destruction of Sodom and Gomorrah 49
    birth of Isaac and the great testing 51–53
    Sarah's death and a burial plot 54–55
    a bride for Isaac 55–57
    dies satisfied with life 57
Absalom
    Amnon violates his sister, Tamar 135
    his men kill Amnon 136
    reconciles with, then plots against David 136
    leads rebellion and is killed 137
Achan
    steals from the spoils of Jericho 118
    he and his family stoned 118
Adam
    the beginning of the paradigm 3
    his creation in the Garden of Eden 3
    temptation, fall, and judgment 9–16
    first promise of a Savior 14
    cast out of Eden and has sons 19
    dies, as God has said 21
Adonijah
    attempts to succeed David 139
    executed by Solomon 140
Adultery
    David's sin with Bathsheba 133–134
    example of a woman caught in 282
Advent
    nature of kingdom during first 178

ABOUT THE AUTHOR

Dan Westerfield grew up on a farm in central Texas, attended Texas A&M on a football scholarship, graduated with an engineering degree, and flew as a pilot with the USAF during the Viet Nam War. He had left the Air Force and was flying for an airline when he became a Christian after attending a Francis Schaeffer seminar.

Dan attended several different churches, and eventually became an elder at Alexandria Presbyterian Church in Virginia, where he taught a systematic theology course and made missionary trips to Eritrea. He received a master of arts in religion degree from Reformed Theological Seminary, Baltimore/Washington, in 2005. After his airline declared bankruptcy, he worked for ten years in the offshore oil business in Louisiana where he began writing this book. He moved to Churchton, MD, in 2019 and is an elder at South County Community Church.